TRAVEL

NORTH

CAROLINA

Published by John F. Blair, Publisher

UNLESS OTHERWISE NOTED, ALL PHOTOGRAPHS ARE
COURTESY OF NORTH CAROLINA DIVISION OF TOURISM,
FILM AND SPORTS DEVELOPMENT

Library of Congress Cataloging-in-Publication Data
Travel North Carolina : going native in the Old North State / by Carolyn
Sakowski . . . [et al.].—3rd ed.
p.   cm.
Includes index.
ISBN-13: 978-0-89587-337-8 (alk. paper)
ISBN-10: 0-89587-337-0 (alk. paper)
1. North Carolina—Guidebooks. I. Sakowski, Carolyn, 1948–
F252.3.T73 2007
917.56'0444—dc22
2006034248

Design by Debra Long Hampton
Maps by The Roberts Group

TRAVEL
NORTH
CAROLINA

Going Native in the Old North State

BY THE STAFF OF JOHN F. BLAIR, PUBLISHER

JOHN F.
BLAIR   WINSTON-SALEM, NORTH CAROLINA

Contents

Acknowledgments   ix
Introduction   xii

THE COAST

The Outer Banks   3
   Northern Banks and Beaches   7
   Roanoke Island   30
   Bodie Island   49
   Hatteras Island   53
   Ocracoke Island   68

The Coastal Plain   83
   Albemarle Region   85
      Elizabeth City   86
      Edenton   100
      Bath   114
   Neuse River Region   122
      New Bern   123
      Morehead City   140
      Beaufort   146
      Bogue Banks   157
   Cape Fear Coast   165
      Topsail Island   167
      Wilmington   174
      Wrightsville Beach   191
      Pleasure Island   197
      Southport and the Brunswick Islands   204

THE PIEDMONT

The Triangle   217
    Raleigh   220
    Durham   242
    Chapel Hill and Carrboro   260
    Research Triangle Park   280
    Triangle Nearby   283

The Sandhills   289
    Fayetteville   290
    Pinehurst and Southern Pines   304

The Triad   319
    Winston-Salem   321
    Greensboro   344
    High Point   365
    Triad Nearby   375

Charlotte   385

THE MOUNTAINS

The Blue Ridge Parkway   419

The High Country   429
    Alleghany County   433
    Ashe County   438
    Boone   448
    Blowing Rock   458
    Banner Elk, Beech Mountain, and Linville   466
    Spruce Pine and Burnsville   479

Asheville   487

The Southern Mountains   509
    Hendersonville   511
    Brevard   521
    Highlands   529
    Franklin   536

The Great Smoky Mountains   543
    Great Smoky Mountains National Park 545
    Cherokee   550
    Maggie Valley   558
    Waynesville   562

Appendix   567
Index   580

Acknowledgments

Sue Clark would like to thank Marissa Jamison of the Asheville Convention and Visitors Bureau; Guy and Hylah Smalley of Mountain Creek Bed-and-Breakfast in Waynesville; Richard Hazen of Cool Beans Café in Waynesville; Mary Sidney of Skyline Lodge in Highlands; Carl Caudle of the Pine Crest Inn in Tryon; Susie Zimmerman of Richmond Hill Inn in Asheville; Karen Baker of Henderson County Travel and Tourism; Angela Beattie of the Crowne Plaza Resort in Asheville; Jackie Whitman, my mom and traveling guru; and Chris, Chad, and Ben Clark, the world's best traveling companions—I'd go anywhere with you guys!

Angela Harwood would like to thank Anne Waters for being so thorough the first time around; Connie Nelson of the Cape Fear Coast Convention and Visitors Bureau for all her help (and a very fine dinner); the employees at the Craven County Convention and Visitors Bureau, the Carteret County Tourism Bureau, the Harkers Island Visitor Center, the Southport-Oak Island Chamber of Commerce, and the South Brunswick Islands Chamber of Commerce; John F. Blair summer interns Will Singletary and Lauren Dupuis for their helpful fact-checking; the staff at the North Carolina Division of Tourism, Film and Sports Development; Ken Loerzel for his help with Emerald Isle; Kim Byerly and Carolyn Sakowski for feeding and entertaining my dogs while I traveled; and most of all, my husband, Jeff, who accompanied me and made my research trips feel like vacations.

Sunny Smith Nelson would like to thank the kind and gracious folks with the Outer Banks Visitors Bureau, the Whalehead Club, the National Park Service, Roanoke Island Festival Park, the North Carolina Aquarium at Roanoke Island, Elizabethan Gardens, the Ocracoke Island Visitor Center, the Frisco Native American Museum and Natural History Center, the Dismal Swamp Canal Welcome Center, the Greater Hyde County Chamber of Commerce, the Museum of the Albemarle, the Albemarle Economic Development Commission, the Elizabeth City-Pasquotank County Tourism Board, the Elizabeth City Area Chamber of Commerce, the Chowan County Tourism Development Authority, Historic Edenton State Historic Site, Historic Bath State Historic Site, Somerset Place State Historic Site, the North Carolina Estuarium, the North Carolina Division of Tourism, Film and Sports Development, and Loeffler Ketchum Mountjoy. Love and gratitude go to Marc Nelson, Linda and Dewey Smith, Mason and LaRae Smith, and Joshua Smith and Nikki Wildman. I'm looking forward to many more beach trips with you guys.

Carolyn Sakowski would like to thank the following people for their assistance: Bob and Mary Choate; Judy Donaghy of North Carolina High Country Host; and the staffs of North Carolina High Country Host, the Ashe County Chamber of Commerce, the Avery-Banner Elk Chamber of Commerce, the Beech Mountain Chamber of Commerce, the Greensboro Area Convention and Visitors Bureau, the Yancey County Chamber of Commerce, and the Mitchell County Chamber of Commerce. She would especially like to thank her summer intern, Will Singletary, for all his help in checking facts throughout the book.

John Tarleton would like to thank Sheryl Monks for her diligent work on the previous edition of this book; Carolyn Sakowski and Steve Kirk for their expertise; Wendy Livingston at the Nasher Museum of Art; Charlene Harless at Gallery C; Gloria and Phil Teber at the Arrowhead Inn; Jim Bickelhaupt of InnAssist for his kind help; Sasha Travers at the Siena Hotel; Brian K. Fletcher, Stacy Herring, and Shelly Green at the Durham Convention and Visitors Bureau; Patrick Tremblay at the Airborne and Special Operations Museum in Fayetteville; Melody Foote at the Fayetteville Area Convention and Visitors Bureau; Patricia Griffin at the Chapel Hill-Orange County Visitors Bureau; Martin Armes and Mark Worrell at the Greater Raleigh Convention and Visitors Bureau; and Mary Kim Koppenhofer at the Pinehurst, Southern Pines, Aberdeen Area Convention and Visitors Bureau. He would also like to thank Greg DeMarchi, Lizz Torgovnick, Jim Tarleton, Judi Livernois, Jeanette Mayo, and Matt Tarleton for their help and encouragement.

Anne Holcomb Waters would like to thank Ed Southern for his excellent work on the first two editions of this book. Much of his original writing about Charlotte and Winston-Salem remains because he is both a darn good writer and an ardent advocate for these two cities. I am also grateful to Bobbie Baker and Amy Rogers for their restaurant recommendations; I only wish space had permitted more entries. Finally, thank you to my husband, Andrew, and son, Elias, two great travel companions.

Introduction

Who better to publish a travel guide to North Carolina than the staff of a North Carolina publisher? As the staff of John F. Blair, Publisher, planned its future projects, we asked ourselves that very question. We looked around and realized that, collectively, we were in a better position to write about our state than some guy from New York City who popped in for one weekend and recorded his snap judgments.

When we decided to undertake this project, we also decided that we wanted the guide to reflect our individual personalities. That's why you may notice distinct styles for each section.

Here's a brief look at who we are:

Sue Clark is a native of Detroit. In March of her senior year at Oakland University in Rochester, Michigan, her father sent her pictures of dogwood trees in bloom. That was enough to entice her to move south. She's been here over 25 years and considers herself one of North Carolina's biggest fans. Sue has a B.A. in history with a minor in English from Oakland University. She is currently enrolled at Salem College, where she is working on a Master of Arts in teaching. She worked for John F. Blair, Publisher, for 14 years before becoming a middle-school teacher. Sue is married and has two sons. The Clark family loves to travel and especially enjoys camping in the mountains. Sue's hobbies include cooking, needlework, and singing. Yankee by birth, Southern by choice, Sue plans to call North Carolina home for the rest of her life.

Angela Harwood revised the sections for the Neuse River region and the Cape Fear coast. A navy brat, she spent most of her school years moving from one coastal city to another from Maine to Florida and as far west as Louisiana, so she is no stranger to the sea. Her family eventually settled in Olive Branch, Mississippi, practically a suburb of Memphis. She pursued a degree in landscape architecture at Mississippi State University for three years before changing her major to English. She received her B.A. in English with a minor in history from the University of Mississippi at Oxford. Angela moved to North Carolina in 2004 to work for John F. Blair, Publisher, after meeting Carolyn Sakowski, the president of Blair, at the Denver Publishing Institute. Now the special-projects director, she enjoys traveling the state with her husband, Jeff, and their two dogs, Buff and Uma.

Sunny Smith Nelson is the author of the sections on the Outer Banks and the Albemarle region. She was born and raised in Winston-Salem, where her family has resided for over 200 years as members of the Moravian Church. She earned her degree in international studies from the University of North Carolina at Chapel Hill. After a brief stint in Savannah, Georgia, she returned to "the southern part of heaven," where she can almost hear the UNC bell tower chime. When she's not driving down N.C. 12 looking for her next beach adventure, she serves as the director of public information for the North Carolina State Energy Office.

Carolyn Sakowski wrote the sections for Greensboro, High Point, and the High Country. She was born in North Carolina and has lived in the state for almost 50 years. She grew up in Morganton, graduated from Queens University in Charlotte with a B.A. in history, and got an M.A. in history from Appalachian State University in Boone. She and her husband have an Avery County farm, which he inherited from his grandfather. That's where they escape to mow the fields most weekends in the summer and fall. She is also the author of *Touring the Western North Carolina Backroads* and *Touring the East Tennessee Backroads*.

John Tarleton grew up in Raleigh and Durham before earning a B.A. in English and Romance languages from the University of North Carolina at Greensboro. After college, he interned at Blair and decided against moving to New York or Los Angeles with his friends. Now, he designs ads, maintains the Blair Web site, troubleshoots computers, and is an assistant to Blair's marketing and production departments. He hangs all of those hats (and one more) in Greensboro. He loves to travel, cook, and entertain and is thankful that in North Carolina he can afford to do so.

Anne Holcomb Waters is an Arkansas native who has lived and worked in North Carolina since 1996. She is the former vice president of sales and marketing for John F. Blair and a graduate of Randolph-Macon Woman's College. She is a master gardener, an avid yoga practitioner, and co-owner of Two Bad Dogs Folk Art. She and her husband, Andrew, live in Salisbury with their son, Elias, and their three cats and two dogs.

When discussing a format for the book, we decided that we didn't want an inclusive listing of every accommodation in each city. If you want that kind of list, we've provided contact information for local convention and visitor bureaus. What we tried to do was avoid the chains, unless there was something unique about a particular chain hotel or motel. We looked for locally owned, one-of-a-kind places that visitors might be unaware of. We did the same thing when choosing restaurants. We tried to find the places that the locals would put on their list if you asked them for the best places to eat. We couldn't include them all, but we tried to offer a variety of cuisines and price ranges. We didn't charge any establishment a fee to be included in this book. We wanted to approach these places just like regular visitors would.

Because prices for both food and lodging fluctuate, we've simply categorized each establishment as Deluxe, Expensive, Moderate, or Inexpensive, based on the scales below.

For accommodations, the breakdown is

Deluxe—Over $125 for a double room
Expensive—$95 to $125
Moderate—$60 to $95
Inexpensive—Under $60 (There aren't many of these left!)

Prices often vary according to the season. For example, you might find some good bargains on the coast if you decide to vacation there in the late fall or winter. In the mountains, the bargains come after the summer and the fall foliage seasons but before ski season.

For restaurants, the breakdown is

Expensive—Over $18 for most entrées
Moderate—$10 to $18
Inexpensive—Under $10

Although each of us came to our section with some previous knowledge of the area we were writing about, we all learned even more about our state. Each of us is proud to live in North Carolina, and we're glad we can share our enthusiasm with you.

Carolyn Sakowski
President, John F. Blair, Publisher

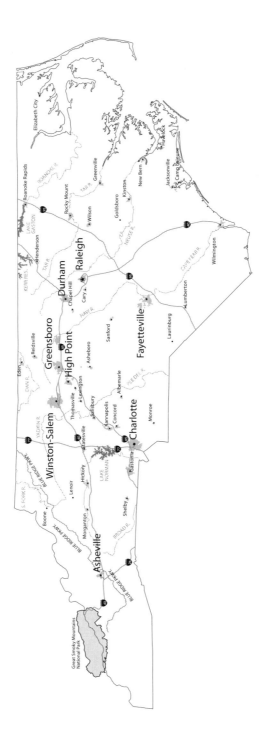

THE COAST

The Outer Banks

Northern Banks and Beaches

Roanoke Island

Bodie Island

Hatteras Island

Ocracoke Island

By Sunny Smith Nelson

A lifelong resident of North Carolina, I was in my mid-20s and on my honeymoon before I ever visited the Outer Banks. I never visited as a child because, I suspect, my parents thought there wasn't much there that would interest someone my age. Their image of the Outer Banks was that of a string of small, thin islands offering nothing but sand, surf, and wind, reached by a grueling six-hour drive from where we lived. My then-fiancé (now husband), a transplant from New York who had visited the Banks many times since attending the University of North Carolina at Chapel Hill, told me stories about the long, sandy beaches where one could sit in silence and hear nothing but nature, about the oyster- and steam-bar restaurants where you could go in to get a bite to eat and end up making friends with the bartender and the person sitting next to you, and about sand dunes as big as houses, where hang gliders with colorful wings would take flight and hover over the waves. We decided to take our honeymoon there because of the things he had told me about—the peace, the friendliness, and the beauty of the Banks. Since then, we have made the Outer Banks a regular destination.

Our times at the Banks are usually a whirlwind. We climb lighthouses, attend outdoor dramas, kayak in Shallowbag Bay, listen to afternoon jazz concerts, walk where the first English child born in the New World probably took her first steps, climb sand dunes to visit the memorial to the first men in flight, hike the trails of wildlife refuges, stroll the docks of marinas, and stop by many a restaurant to make friends with other diners and the staffs. There is much to see and do on the Outer Banks, and we always look forward to discovering new adventures with each visit. We've learned over time that the Outer Banks can be whatever you want them to be—the quiet, wind-swept dunes of my parents' imaginations or the friendly, outgoing, and active vacation spot I love more and more with each subsequent visit.

JUST THE FACTS

There are two main roads on the Outer Banks, U.S. 158 (also known as the Croatan Highway) and N.C. 12 (also known as Virginia Dare Trail or the Beach Road). The two parallel one another in the northern section of the Outer Banks. Note that local directions from these roads are customarily given by milepost, rather than by street number. Milepost 1 is in Kitty Hawk and Milepost 16 in Nags Head.

To reach the Banks from the north, follow either U.S. 17 or Va. 168 to U.S. 158. Take U.S. 158 East across the Wright Brothers Memorial Bridge over Currituck Sound. To reach the northern communities of Duck, Sanderling, and Corolla, turn left on N.C. 12. To go south toward Kitty Hawk, Kill Devil Hills, and Nags Head, turn right on either of the two main roads.

From the south, you can take either a land or a water route. Via land, take U.S. 264 East to U.S. 64 East, which will lead you through Roanoke Island to Bodie Island. For a scenic trip, the ferry system is the way to go. The Swan Quarter ferry and the Cedar Island ferry both take travelers to Ocracoke Island, the southernmost island in the Outer Banks. Either ferry ride takes about two and a half hours. Reservations are required in the summer and are advisable year-round. To contact the Swan Quarter ferry office, call 800-773-1094; to contact the Cedar Island ferry office, call 800-856-0343. From Ocracoke, travelers can take a free 40-minute ferry ride to Hatteras Island to gain access to the rest of the Outer Banks; no reservations are required for the Hatteras ferry. The toll-free number for the Hatteras ferry is 800-368-1665. The Ocracoke office can be reached at 800-345-1665. For complete information on ferry schedules, fees, and crossing times, call 800-BY-FERRY or visit www.ncferry.org.

From central North Carolina, U.S. 64 leads directly across Roanoke Island to Nags Head. From there, travelers can turn left on either U.S. 158 or N.C. 12 to head up the coast toward Kill Devil Hills and points north or turn right on N.C. 12 to head south toward Hatteras Island.

The Dare County Regional Airport is located on Airport Road in Manteo. Its two runways are 3,290 feet and 4,300 feet in length. Fuel, services, restrooms and an area for pilots to sleep are offered. For information, call 252-475-5570 or visit www.fly2mqi.com. Air charters are available to and from the airport via Sea Air from just about anywhere east of the Mississippi River. Call 252-453-3656 or visit www.flyseaair.com for more information. A few local shuttle services and car and limousine rentals are available at the airport as well. Additional paved runways are located at Kill Devil Hills, Hatteras Island, and Ocracoke Island, but no support services are available at those locations.

One of the best sources of information about the area is the Outer Banks Visitors Bureau, at One Visitors Center Circle off U.S. 64/U.S. 264 in Manteo. For more information about the history, culture, and folklore of the area, call 877-629-4386 or 252-473-2138 or visit www.outerbanks.org. Those interested in learning more about Ocracoke Island should contact the Greater Hyde County Chamber of Commerce at 888-493-3826 or 252-926-9171 or www.hydecounty.org.

Currituck Beach Lighthouse
PHOTO BY BILL RUSS, COURTESY OF NORTH CAROLINA DIVISION OF TOURISM, FILM AND SPORTS DEVELOPMENT

NORTHERN BANKS AND BEACHES

*D*epending on your perspective, N.C. 12, the main artery on the Outer Banks, either gets its start or meets its end in the northern Banks and beaches. This makes it a great jumping-off point or a good destination as it traverses sand dunes, sea grass, and ocean inlets cut by hurricanes to take you over a peninsula, across two islands, and through more than 400 years of history. This northern frontier stretches from Corolla to Nags Head. Here, you'll discover the northernmost lighthouse on the Banks, the tallest sand dune on the East Coast, and the spot where man first took flight. Or you can just relax in your lounge chair and watch the day pass by. The northern Banks and beaches offer some of both the least-developed and most-developed seashore on the Outer Banks. Visitors thus have the opportunity to be alone or in the middle of everything.

Things to Do

HISTORIC PLACES, GARDENS, AND TOURS

■ **Currituck Beach Lighthouse**, located off of N.C. 12 in Corolla, is the northernmost lighthouse on the Outer Banks. This was the last major brick lighthouse built on the Outer Banks. Its approximately 1 million bricks were left unpainted to distinguish it from its famous counterparts. Begun in 1873 and completed two years later, it served the 40-mile area of dark coastline between Cape Henry Lighthouse to the north in Virginia and Bodie Island Lighthouse to the south. The 162-foot Currituck Beach Lighthouse had a light visible at 18 nautical miles. Before the advent of electricity, it was powered by a mineral-oil lamp that consisted of five concentric wicks, the largest of which was four inches in diameter. The lighthouse keeper was required to physically move the huge lens every two and a half hours to keep the light flashing. Cranking by hand the weights that were suspended from a line beneath the lantern, he moved the light much in the way a grandfather clock's gears turn to make the hour chime. The beam flooded the night sky for three seconds before fading to black for 17 seconds. This not only warned passing ships of the treacherous coastline but allowed them to decipher where they were on their journey as well.

The lighthouse is still a navigational tool for sailors today, emitting its beam from dusk until dawn, though the keeper doesn't have to crank the lens nowadays. Visitors are invited to climb the 214 steps to the top, weather permitting. An interpretive guide is on hand to share facts about the lighthouse.

Also on the grounds is the lighthouse keepers' home. Shipped by barge to the Banks already precut and labeled for easy assembly, the Victorian Stick-style dwelling was completed in 1876. Two keepers and their families moved in to share the duplex. Visitors are not allowed to tour the home, as it is undergoing restoration by Outer Banks Conservationists, Inc.

Other structures on the property include cisterns for catching rainwater for household use, an outhouse, a chapel, and a schoolhouse. A museum shop is located in a second lighthouse keeper's home, built in 1870 at Long Point Lighthouse Station on Currituck Sound and shipped to its current location in 1920.

No keepers have lived here since the light was automated in 1939.

Currituck Beach Lighthouse and the museum shop are open daily from 10 A.M. to 6 P.M. from Easter to Thanksgiving. An admission fee is charged. Children must be at least four years old to climb the lighthouse. For information, call 252-453-4939 or 252-453-8152 or visit www.currituckbeachlight.com.

■ The **Whalehead Club** is located within walking distance of Currituck Beach Lighthouse. Completed in 1925 after three years and $383,000 in construction costs, it was for a time a private residence called Corolla Island, the first home on the Outer Banks to have a basement, an elevator, and a swimming pool.

The local legend surrounding that stunning home reads like a romance novel. Edward Collings Knight, Jr., a wealthy executive with the Pennsylvania Railroad and the American Sugar Refinery, married a beautiful, talented French huntress by the name of Marie Louise LeBel. Marie loved vacationing in what was one of the best duck- and waterfowl-hunting spots in the world (Currituck is Indian for "Land of the Wild Goose"), but when she tried to join a local hunt club, she was turned down due to her gender. So Marie convinced Edward to build her a home that would eclipse any hunt club on the Outer Banks.

Visitors to their dinner parties found numbered and signed Tiffany

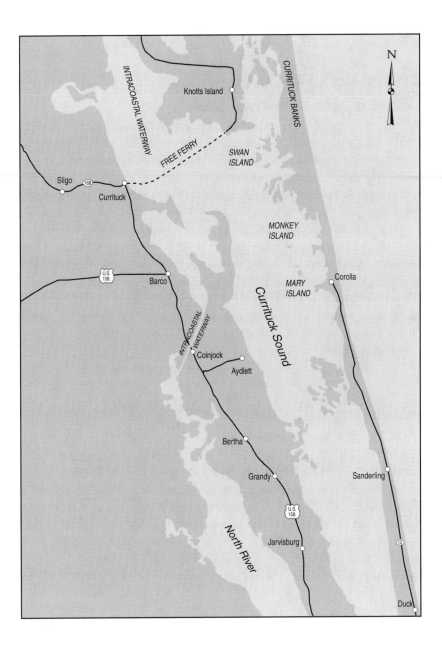

N

Knotts Island

INTRACOASTAL WATERWAY

CURRITUCK BANKS

FREE FERRY

SWAN ISLAND

Sligo

168

Currituck

MONKEY ISLAND

U.S. 158.

Barco

MARY ISLAND

Corolla

Currituck Sound

INTRACOASTAL WATERWAY

Coinjock

Aydlett

Bertha

Grandy

Sanderling

U.S. 158.

North River

Jarvisburg

12

Duck

Whalehead Club

lighting fixtures, a custom-made dining-room table and chairs with a signature water lily design carved into the wood, and door handles and hinges molded to look like water lily buds. Five chimneys, a large library, cork floors, corduroy walls, copper shingles, and pink tiles on the walls of the kitchen were other features of the lavish Art Nouveau-style home.

The Whalehead Club began to fall into disrepair after the Knights' tenure. It was used for purposes ranging from a boys' school to a facility for testing solid rocket fuel for the nation's space program. The club was bought by Currituck County in 1992 and has been restored to its original grandeur as part of the 39-acre Currituck Heritage Park. The main house, the original boathouse, and the pedestrian footbridge are listed on the National Register of Historic Places. The grounds are open from dawn until dusk.

A variety of tours are offered. Regular tours of the club's first two floors and gallery are given daily from 10 A.M. to 5 P.M. during daylight saving time and from 10 A.M. to 6 P.M. otherwise. The "Behind the Scenes" tour reveals the home's third floor, servants' quarters, attic, curator's office, and boathouse; it is offered Monday through Friday at 11 A.M. and 3 P.M. For those with children ages six to 12, the "Children's Tour and Treasure Hunt" features lessons in history, art, and environmental awareness Monday through Friday at 10 A.M. and 4 P.M. Ghost tours are offered Monday through Friday at 2 P.M. and 5 P.M. Reservations are required for all tours except the regular tour. An admission fee is charged for each tour, though children eight and younger are admitted free with an adult on the regular tour. For information, call 252-453-9040 or visit www.whaleheadclub.com.

■ While in Currituck Heritage Park, you may spot one of the **wild ponies of Corolla**. These ponies are said to be descendants of mustangs that survived the wreck of a Spanish galleon and swam ashore on the Outer Banks. Efforts are under way to protect them, as their numbers have

Outer Banks Wild Ponies

dwindled because of local development. Visit www.visitcurrituck.com/corolla-wild-horses.cfm to learn more.

■ *Wright Brothers National Memorial*, at Milepost 8 on U.S. 158 in Kill Devil Hills, honors a moment that changed history.

Orville and Wilbur Wright, bicycle shop owners from Dayton, Ohio, had dreams of flying while they worked on their spokes and gears. They began pursuing their dream in earnest in 1899, when Wilbur wrote to the Smithsonian Institution asking for information on flight. Then the brothers set about finding out for themselves how to fly. For three years, they tested various gliders in and around Kitty Hawk and Kill Devil Hills. They also built a wind tunnel back in Ohio to learn the aerodynamics that would enable them to get off the ground. As Wilbur once said, "It is possible to fly without motors, but not without knowledge and skill."

It was December 14, 1903, when the brothers were ready to test a powered machine. They flipped a coin to see who would fly first; Wilbur won. He eased himself into the plane and took off from the launching rail, but the plane climbed too steeply and stalled. For three days, they repaired the plane. On the morning of December 17, they once again took their 40-foot, 605-pound *Flyer* into the sand. Amid 27-mile-per-hour wind gusts, Orville took flight for the first time, staying aloft for 12 seconds and 120 feet. The brothers took turns flying after that. The fourth and final flight—by Wilbur—was the most successful, lasting 59 seconds and covering 852

Wright Brothers National Memorial
PHOTO BY BILL RUSS, COURTESY OF NORTH CAROLINA DIVISION
OF TOURISM, FILM AND SPORTS DEVELOPMENT

feet. After that, a gust of wind overturned the plane and damaged it beyond repair.

The visitor center, administered by the National Park Service, is the first stop at Wright Brothers National Memorial. It contains full-scale reproductions of one of the brothers' gliders and the famous *Flyer* that made the first flight. Interpretive talks are given in the center. The gift shop on the premises offers books and memorabilia.

Guests can see how the brothers lived and worked by visiting the reconstructed camp buildings on the grounds. Near the camp buildings are markers commemorating the takeoff and landing points of the first four flights.

The centerpiece of the memorial, however, is the 60-foot granite monument atop the 90-foot Kill Devil Hill, from which the brothers launched hundreds of glider flights before they ever built their first powered machine. Visitors can walk to the top of the hill and gaze down upon the entire site. There are bronze busts of the Wrights on one side of the monument.

The memorial is open daily except Christmas. An admission fee is charged for visitors 17 and older. For information, call 252-441-7430 or visit www.nps.gov/wrbr.

■ *Colington Island*, just south of Wright Brothers National Memorial, is the site of the first permanent settlement on the Outer Banks. Accessible by Colington Road off U.S. 158, the island features several seafood shops and campgrounds and offers visitors a nice photographic opportunity in a relatively undeveloped area of the Banks.

MUSEUMS AND SCIENCE CENTERS

■ Located on the grounds of Currituck Heritage Park in Corolla is the *Outer Banks Center for Wildlife Education*. The spacious 22,000-square-foot center features a waterfowl decoy gallery, an exhibit hall, and an auditorium with informational videos on the area's unique history, traditions, and natural resources. Group programs and special events such as workshops on coastal wildlife and outdoor skills are offered seasonally. The center is open daily from 8 A.M. to 5 P.M. Call 252-453-0221 or visit www.ncwildlife.org for more information.

■ The *United States Army Corps of Engineers Field Research Facility*, located on the beach in Duck off N.C. 12, is the home of the Waterways Experiment Station. Waves, winds, currents, and tides are monitored and recorded at this site. Walking tours are given Monday through Friday at 10 A.M. from mid-June to August only; those who arrive after 10 A.M. will not be permitted within the facility due to security reasons. There is no admission fee. For information, call 252-261-6840 or visit www.frf.usace.army.mil.

SPECIAL SHOPPING

North Carolina has seen a boom in wineries in the past decade, and the Banks claim two of their own on Knotts Island, located northwest of Corolla in Currituck Sound.

■ *Martin Vineyards*, at 213 Martin Farm Lane off N.C. 615, was started by the Martin family in 1977 as a peach and scuppernong grape farm. Today, it boasts a variety of wines from muscadine to Merlot. Wine tastings are given year-round; the fee is waived with the purchase of a bottle of wine. Visitors can pick their own fruit seasonally. From April through December, Martin Vineyards is open daily except Wednesday from noon to 5 P.M. From January through April, it is open weekdays except Wednesdays from noon to 3 P.M. and weekends from noon to 5 P.M. For more information, call 252-429-3542 or visit www.martinvineyards.com. *Moonrise Bay Vineyard*, at 134 Moonrise Bay Landing off N.C. 615 and Woodleigh Road, is named after the stunning moonrises owner Richard "Oakie" Morris and his wife, Kate, enjoy nightly over the quiet and starry sound. They created the winery as a hobby in 1997 and made it into a family business in 1999. Since then, the vineyard has grown to offer more than a dozen award-winning wines. Moonrise Bay Vineyard is open for tours and tastings daily from noon to 5 P.M. and by appointment. Special-event dinners are also available by reservation. Call 866-888-9463 or 252-429-9463 or visit www.moonrisebaywine.com for more information.

The northern Banks and beaches are also home to an ever-growing arts community. More than 20 galleries are located between Duck and Nags Head alone. Gallery Row in Nags Head features some of the best outlets in the state. Be sure to check out the Dare County Arts Council's Web site at www.darearts.org for a complete listing of the area's art events.

■ Perhaps one of the best-known galleries is *Glenn Eure's Ghost Fleet Gallery*, at Milepost 10.5 in Nags Head. Eure is a noted character in these parts, having created everything from the artwork on display to the building housing the gallery. Offerings here range from gallery showings to poetry readings and guest lectures. For more information, call 252-441-6584.

Seaside Art Gallery is located at Milepost 11 on N.C. 12 in Nags Head. In addition to the work of local artists, visitors can view and purchase original pieces by the likes of Picasso, Whistler, Dali, and Renoir. Kids will enjoy the artwork by Warner Brothers Studios and Hanna Barbera Animation. For more information, call 252-441-5418 or visit www.seasideart.com.

You should also plan to visit *Lighthouse Gallery and Gifts*, at 301 East Driftwood Street in Nags Head. This gallery offers original works of art, memorabilia, and books pertaining to lighthouses. Call 800-579-2827 or visit www.seabeacons.com.

■ I'd be remiss if I didn't mention the *Tanger Outlet Mall*, at Milepost 16.5 on U.S. 158. This is a good place to spend a rainy day or to hide out if you've had too much sun. Shoppers can find bargains from clothing retailers like Polo by Ralph Lauren and Gap and shoe manufacturers like Bass and Nine West. Call 252-441-5634 or visit www.tangeroutlet.com for more information.

RECREATION

Swimming, fishing, kayaking, windsurfing, parasailing, surfing, water-skiing—the northern Banks and beaches are the place for some great recreation. Watersports are the pastime of choice here. Thanks to the bounty of water, there are countless ways to keep wet. But please note that not all the beaches here have lifeguards. And since the area's currents and tides have sunk over 1,500 ships and given it the infamous nickname "Graveyard of the Atlantic," be sure to keep your wits about you while enjoying all the amusements the sea has to offer.

■ **Kitty Hawk Sports** touts itself as the watersports headquarters of the Outer Banks. Everything from swimwear to surfboards to kayaking gear is offered at its various stores in Corolla (252-453-4999 or 252-453-6900), Duck (252-261-8770), Kitty Hawk (252-261-0145), and Nags Head (252-441-6800 or 252-441-2756). Windsurfing and kayaking lessons are available, as is sailing, windsurfing, and kayaking rental equipment. For more information, visit www.kittyhawksports.com.

■ If fishing is your sport of choice, you'll be pleased to see the piers and marinas dotting the Banks. Indeed, the area is known as "the Billfish Capital of the World."

River Kayaking
PHOTO BY BILL RUSS, COURTESY OF NORTH CAROLINA DIVISION OF TOURISM, FILM AND SPORTS DEVELOPMENT

Surf fishing on the Outer Banks
PHOTO BY BILL RUSS, COURTESY OF NORTH CAROLINA DIVISION OF TOURISM,
FILM AND SPORTS DEVELOPMENT

Avalon Fishing Pier in Kill Devil Hills (252-441-7494; www.avalonpier.com) is open spring, summer, and fall. Its Web site features a live Web cam, daily fishing reports, and a chat room. *Nags Head Fishing Pier* (252-441-5141; www.nagsheadpier.com) is open year-round; it offers a tackle shop and a restaurant that will cook your catch for you. Fishing Unlimited, a local business, operates the 600-foot *Outer Banks Fishing Pier* (252-441-5740; http://fishingunlimited.net/OuterBanksPier.html), the pier located closest to Oregon Inlet. It includes a tackle shop, a grill, and an arcade. The granddaddy of Outer Banks fishing piers, though, is *Jennette's Fishing Pier* (252-441-6421) in Nags Head. Built in 1939, it has withstood time and hurricanes to join the 21st century. In partnership with the North Carolina Aquarium at Roanoke Island, it offers a large ocean classroom. Jennette's also features one of the largest trophy-fish collections along the Banks.

Fees are charged at each of the piers to fish or just to watch others reel in their catch; weekly and seasonal passes are available.

If you're feeling waterlogged, you'll be happy to note that there are plenty of recreational opportunities to be had on land, too.

■ The *Pine Island Audubon Sanctuary* is a 6,000-acre wildlife sanctuary that stretches from Currituck Sound to the Atlantic Ocean. It can be accessed just north of Duck off N.C. 12 near The Sanderling. Visitors to this natural oasis can take a free self-guided hike along a 2.5-mile trail through sand dunes, sea oats, live oaks, and maritime marshes to discover what the northern Banks looked like a century ago, before development took over. Two observation platforms are stationed along the trail for resting and picture taking. For over a decade now, the Audubon Society has overseen the sanctuary and its more than 350 species of plants and 159 species of birds in an effort to conserve the state's natural habitats. For information, call 252-453-2838 or visit www.ncaudubon.org/ Sanctuaries_PineIsland.html.

■ The **Nags Head Woods Ecological Preserve**, a 1,092-acre maritime forest managed by the Nature Conservancy, is located on the western shore of Nags Head on Ocean Acre Drive, off U.S. 158. The preserve, designated a national natural landmark by Congress in 1974, is home to over 50 bird species and an array of aquatic life, including the rare water violet. Visitors may be surprised to learn that the Outer Banks is the northern limit of the American alligator's habitat; the gators here are a bit smaller than their Florida counterparts. The preserve offers walking trails and a visitor center, where you can pick up maps and learn more about the research conducted on the grounds. It is open Monday through Friday from 10 A.M. to 3 P.M.; Saturday hours are offered during the summer. Admission is free. For information, call 252-441-2525 or visit http:/ /nature.org/wherewework/northamerica/states/northcarolina/preserves/ art5618.html.

■ **Jockey's Ridge State Park**, near Milepost 12 off U.S. 158 in Nags Head, is a 414-acre park that features the tallest sand-dune system on the East Coast; its tallest dune stands around 140 feet high, depending on the prevailing winds. Used as a horse-racing track at the beginning of the 20th century, this land is now most famous for its kite-flying and hang-gliding opportunities. It was on dunes like these that the Wright brothers learned to fly; on a clear day, you can even see the granite monument at Wright Brothers National Memorial. The trails leading up the sand dunes offer a view of the entire width of Nags Head all the way from Roanoke Sound to the Atlantic Ocean. It's this unbeatable panorama that draws so many people to the "Sunset on the Ridge" program that park rangers present around 8 P.M. nearly every evening during the summer. Visitors can bring a picnic dinner and enjoy the sunset as they learn how the dunes were formed and the complete story behind the ridge's name. The park offers a variety of educational programs, hiking trails, picnic facilities, restrooms, and a visitor center. The hours vary according to the season, so be sure to call

Jockey's Ridge in Nags Head, the East Coast's tallest sand dune
PHOTO BY BILL RUSS, COURTESY OF NORTH CAROLINA DIVISION OF TOURISM, FILM AND SPORTS DEVELOPMENT

before you visit. Admission is free. For information, call 252-441-7132 or visit www.jockeysridgestatepark.com.

■ Across the street from Jockey's Ridge State Park is the largest of more than a dozen *Kitty Hawk Kites* stores dotting the Outer Banks. The Nags Head location is home to the world's largest hang-gliding school. Here, instructors certified by the United States Hang Gliding Association teach an average of 10,000 students per year in beginning, intermediate, and advanced foot-launch and tandem hang gliding. Kitty Hawk Kites also offers guided outdoor activities including kayak ecotours and jet-boat tours. For more information, call 877-359-8447 or visit www.kittyhawkkites.com.

■ Getting out of the sand and onto the greens is also possible on the Banks. There are some very impressive golf courses in the area. Corolla features *The Currituck Club* (252-453-9400; www.thecurrituckclub.com/golf.htm), a Rees Jones-designed championship course located on N.C. 12. Southern Shores offers the *Duck Woods Country Club* (252-261-2609; www.duckwoodscc.com), a venerable 18-hole course that has welcomed golfers since the late 1960s. Kitty Hawk boasts a number of courses, including *Sea Scape Golf Links* (252-261-2158;

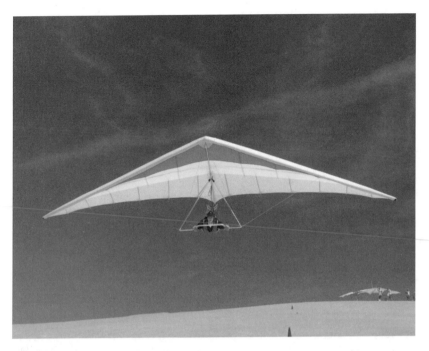

Hang gliding on the Outer Banks
PHOTO BY BILL RUSS, COURTESY OF NORTH CAROLINA DIVISION OF TOURISM, FILM AND SPORTS DEVELOPMENT

Golf on the Outer Banks
PHOTO BY BILL RUSS, COURTESY OF NORTH CAROLINA DIVISION OF TOURISM, FILM AND SPORTS DEVELOPMENT

www.seascapegolf.com), located on U.S. 158 at the edge of the area's maritime forest. The course offers a nice view of the ocean from several holes. **Nags Head Golf Links** (252-441-8073; www.nagsheadgolflinks.com), an 18-hole championship course designed by Bob Moore, is just down the road at Milepost 15. Be sure to call for reservations at these courses.

SEASONAL EVENTS

The Outer Banks prides itself on its good-time atmosphere, so the abundance of festivals and celebrations throughout the year should come as no surprise. As you may guess, many center around the area's greatest assets—the wind and water. From seafood feasts to sailing regattas, the Outer Banks knows how to throw a good party.

- The nation's oldest hang-gliding competition occurs in Nags Head in mid-May. The **Annual Hang Gliding Spectacular and Air Games**, held at Jockey's Ridge State Park, offer an impressive and multicolored array of flyers. For more information, call 877-359-8447 or 252-441-4124 or visit www.kittyhawkkites.com.

- The **Annual Nags Head Surf Fishing Club Invitational Tourna-**

Sand and surf on the Outer Banks
PHOTO BY BILL RUSS, COURTESY OF NORTH CAROLINA DIVISION OF TOURISM, FILM AND SPORTS DEVELOPMENT

ment is held in early October. It has hosted many of the area's best competition fishermen for over 50 years. For information, call 252-441-5464.

■ Jockey's Ridge State Park, arguably the best kite-flying spot on earth, and Kitty Hawk Kites offer the ***Annual Outer Banks Stunt-Kite Competition*** in October. The competition, sanctioned by the American Kiting Association, features workshops, demonstrations, and kite-flying ballets. For information, call 877-359-8447 or 252-441-4124 or visit www.kittyhawkkites.com. The good folks at Kitty Hawk Kites can tell you about the many other kite-flying competitions in the area the rest of the year, too.

Places to Stay

The northern Banks and beaches offer a wide range of places to stay, from charming bed-and-breakfasts to steadfast, reliable chains. Families, honeymooners, and salty old fishermen alike will be able to find the place that fits them best. You'll discover that Corolla, Duck, Sanderling, Southern Shores, and Kitty Hawk have much to offer in the way of cottages and bed-and-breakfasts. Kill Devil Hills and Nags Head are where you'll find the majority of hotels and motels.

There are two very pronounced seasons on the Banks; lodgings are very crowded in the summer and nearly uninhabited in the winter. Rates for the same accommodations can differ by as much as $500 between the peak season and the off-season. Minimum stays may be required at some places. Be sure to call well in advance to book your perfect spot. Two good resources to check before booking are the Web sites of the Outer Banks Visitors Bureau (www.outerbanks.org) and the Outer Banks Chamber of Commerce (www.outerbankschamber.com).

RESORTS, HOTELS, AND MOTELS

■ ***The Sanderling***. Deluxe. 1461 Duck Road in Duck (866-369-0764 or 252-261-4111; www.thesanderling.com). Comprised of three inns, a spa, and a conference center, The Sanderling is one of the most lovely—and most expensive—places to stay on the Outer Banks. Featuring luxuriously appointed guest rooms and five three- and four-bedroom villas, the resort sits on 12 acres that span the peninsula from Currituck Sound to the Atlantic Ocean. Many guests come to this resort to enjoy the quiet, natural beauty of the area, though I've heard several folks say the full-service spa is the real draw. Guests are also pampered by the pool, the health club, the tennis courts, the sun deck, and the private beach. If you decide to stay here, you should definitely look into the adjoining Life-saving Station Restaurant.

■ *Hampton Inn & Suites Outer Banks/Corolla*. Deluxe/Expensive. 333 Audubon Drive in Corolla (252-453-6565; www.hamptoninn.hilton.com). This beachfront hotel, located close to Currituck Heritage Park, features 123 standard rooms and studio suites with complimentary high-speed Internet access for those who must check their e-mail while on vacation. Other amenities include an indoor pool, an outdoor pool, and a "lazy river" water ride that's great for cooling off. A guest laundromat is on the premises, as are exercise and game rooms. During the week, free On the Run™ breakfast bags are offered for those who can't wait to get out and explore. A daily complimentary continental breakfast is served in the dining room for those who prefer a more leisurely pace.

■ *Comfort Inn North Oceanfront*. Expensive/Moderate. 401 North Virginia Dare Trail in Kill Devil Hills (800-854-5286 or 252-480-2600; www.comfortinn.com/hotel/nc130). This clean, friendly hotel has three floors with 119 guest rooms and an oceanfront pool. The rooms include refrigerators, microwaves, and coffee makers. A complimentary breakfast is offered each morning. This is among the more affordable options for visiting families. According to hotel policy, an adult 21 or older must be booked for each room.

■ *Days Inn Mariner*. Expensive/Moderate. 1801 North Virginia Dare Trail in Kill Devil Hills (800-325-2525 or 252-441-2021; www.outer-banks.com/days-mariner). Another of the many reliable chain lodgings along the northern Banks, this oceanfront hotel located one mile from Wright Brothers National Memorial offers standard, double, and king rooms and ocean-view suites featuring a kitchen, a living room, and two bedrooms. Kids will enjoy the outdoor pool, and those looking to get in some exercise can use the hotel's complimentary YMCA passes. Oregon Inlet Fishing Center parties receive a discount. Complimentary continental breakfast is served daily.

Inns and Bed-and-Breakfasts

- **Advice 5¢**. Deluxe. Scarborough Lane in Duck (800-238-4235 or 252-255-1050; www.advice5.com). This intimate and friendly inn is close to area shops and restaurants, making an evening stroll for ice cream a pleasure. Featuring four guest rooms and one suite, all with private baths and decks, the inn gives visitors a home-away-from-home feeling. A swimming pool, tennis courts, and a private walkway to the beach are available. Tea, coffee, and yummy home-baked goods are provided for breakfast, and a lovely afternoon tea offers a nice respite from the sun. The inn hosts an annual 5K race around Thanksgiving, an event that's eagerly anticipated all over the Banks.

- **Cypress Moon Inn**. Deluxe. 1206 Harbor Court in Kitty Hawk (877-905-5060 or 252-261-5060; www.cypressmooninn.com). The proprietors of this inn have lived on the Outer Banks for more than a quarter-century, and they know how to make their guests feel at home. The inn's three guest rooms feature comfy queen-sized beds, private bathrooms, refrigerators, satellite television and radio, and, most importantly, gorgeous views of Kitty Hawk Sound. Guests can also enjoy the view from the inn's double-decker wraparound porches, from the hammocks stationed around the property, and from the kayaks furnished by the innkeepers. A full breakfast with vegetarian options is provided daily.

- **Bald View Bed-and-Breakfast**. Deluxe/Expensive. 3805 Elijah Baum Road in Kitty Hawk (252-255-2829; www.baldview.com). Bordering 11 acres of Kitty Hawk Sound and a maritime forest, this bed-and-breakfast offers a breather from the busy pace of the northern Banks. You'll feel like you're in a secluded retreat when you stay in one of the four guest rooms, each of which has a private bath and a television. The shared public rooms feature antiques, and the many family portraits hanging throughout the home have lots of stories behind them. The best feature, though, is the spectacular view of the sound. The ocean is only five minutes away, too. Breakfast is served every morning.

- **First Colony Inn**. Deluxe/Expensive. 6720 South Virginia Dare Trail in Nags Head (800-368-9390 or 252-441-2343; www.firstcolonyinn.com). One of the largest inns in Nags Head, First Colony Inn opened its doors in 1932 and is now listed on the National Register of Historic Places. Its 27 guest rooms have been given a Four Diamond rating by AAA. Each unique room is appointed with English antiques. Some feature a wet bar, a kitchenette, a whirlpool tub, a sitting room, or a private screened porch. Guests are invited to enjoy a few quiet moments reading in the library or taking in the salty air and the beautiful sunset from the inn's gazebo on the dunes. A hot continental breakfast buffet is served daily in the breakfast room.

■ **The Inn at Corolla Light.** Deluxe/Expensive. 1066 Ocean Trail off N.C. 12 in Corolla (800-215-0772 or 252-453-3340; www.corolla-inn.com). If you want to be away from the hustle and bustle of the Banks, this is the place to come. Located two miles from the end of N.C. 12, the inn offers 43 spacious rooms, each with its own bathroom and many with a whirlpool tub, a gas fireplace, and a kitchen and lounge area. The ocean, the sound, and Currituck Beach Lighthouse are all within walking distance, but guests can use the inn's bicycles or the local trolley service to get there. A sports complex featuring an Olympic-sized swimming pool and clay tennis courts is only two blocks away, for those who want to work off their complimentary continental breakfast. The innkeepers' son, Bob, runs a wild horse tour that explores the uninhabited beaches and the wildlife north of Corolla.

Places to Eat

The restaurants along the northern Banks offer far more than the normal beach fare of fried seafood. You'll find an eclectic blend of Caribbean, Italian, French, Southwestern, and vegetarian cuisines. Everything from elegant wine dinners to burgers and fries is available. Since most restaurants recognize that you're on vacation, casual, neat beach attire is the accepted form of dress. During the busy summer season, you can expect a wait for dinner almost anyplace you go. Reservations may be required at some restaurants and not accepted at others, so call ahead just to be sure. Most importantly, though, remember to relax and savor a good meal as you people-watch and enjoy the smells coming from the kitchen.

■ **The Blue Point.** Expensive. The Waterfront Shops in Duck (252-261-8090; www.goodfoodgoodwine.com). This restaurant, formerly known as The Blue Point Bar and Grill, quickly became a local favorite when it opened in 1989. There's no doubt as to why when you try its delicious Southern coastal cuisine, described by the classically trained chef as "cutting edge with a comfort factor." Dishes such as the prosciutto and melon and the jumbo lump crab cakes with seasonal vegetables rely on locally grown—and often organic—products. Reservations are accepted up to one month in advance; you should probably take advantage of this time window if you want to enjoy The Blue Point during the summer.

■ *Elizabeth's Café and Winery.* Expensive. Scarborough Faire Shopping Village in Duck (252-261-6145; www.elizabethscafe.com). Voted one of the top 100 restaurants of the 20th century by the International Restaurant and Hospitality Rating Bureau, Elizabeth's serves up haute cuisine without the attitude or the price. Guests can order international cuisine from a prix fixe menu that changes nightly or an à la carte menu. A wine dinner is also available, allowing guests to enjoy Elizabeth's special wines, given an Award of Excellence by *Wine Spectator* magazine. In fact, there are generally around 1,600 wines on hand at any given time. Dinner is served daily during summer and Tuesday through Saturday the rest of the year.

■ *Lifesaving Station Restaurant.* Expensive/Moderate. On the grounds of The Sanderling in Duck (252-261-4111; www.thesanderling.com/dining.aspx). This casual restaurant features traditional and coastal Southern cuisine prepared with the finest and freshest ingredients available. The menu changes regularly to take advantage of what the season has to offer. Housed in what used to be the Caffey's Inlet Lifesaving Station and decorated with memorabilia from times gone by, it gives a sense of what the area was like before it became a tourist destination. An outdoor pavilion open on weekdays offers a casual dining experience. From the pavilion, guests can watch the sun set over the sound and take in the cool ocean breeze. Dinner reservations are recommended. Breakfast, lunch, and dinner are served daily; a three-course Sunday brunch is available as well.

■ *Meridian 42.* Expensive/Moderate. Southern Shores Crossing Shopping Center in Southern Shores (252-261-0420; www.meridian42.com). Once inside this airy, Mediterranean-inspired restaurant, you'll know you're about to experience a special meal. The dishes served here, some of the best along the Banks, take their inspiration from Spain, France, and Italy—all countries located along the 42nd meridian, or latitude line. You'll definitely notice the emphasis on fresh local ingredients, including seafood caught from the Atlantic just that morning. All tapas (Spanish-style appetizers), pastas, and baked goods are made on the premises to complement the large wine selection, for which Meridian 42 was named a *Wine Spectator* Award of Excellence recipient. Dinner is served nightly; reservations are accepted up to two weeks in advance.

■ ***Port O' Call Restaurant and Gaslight Saloon***. Expensive/Moderate. Milepost 8.5 in Kill Devil Hills (252-441-7484; www.outerbanksportocall.com). Feeding locals and tourists alike for over 20 years, this restaurant is an Outer Banks landmark. The plush Victorian atmosphere is unique, to say the least; velvet settees, Tiffany lamps, and copious artwork adorn the restaurant. The menu brags that it's the most extensive on the beach, featuring seafood seven ways, from baked to blackened to broiled to grilled to sautéed to steamed to fried. Angus beef, chicken, pasta, soups, and salads round out the menu. You can await your table in the Gaslight Saloon or retreat there after dinner for a nightcap and some live entertainment. The gift shop in the restaurant offers jewelry, nautical items, collector dolls, local and national artists' work, and Tiffany and Victorian lamps. Dinner is served daily March through December. A Sunday brunch buffet is also offered.

■ ***Black Pelican Oceanfront Café***. Moderate. Milepost 4 in Kitty Hawk (877-890-6049 or 252-261-3171; www.blackpelican.com/main.cfm). The Black Pelican is housed in the 120-plus-year-old former lifesaving station and telegraph office where Orville and Wilbur Wright sent out the news of their first flight to the world. Diners can enjoy wood-oven pizzas and fresh local seafood. An on-site gift shop offers Wright brothers memorabilia. Lunch and dinner are served daily year-round.

■ ***Outer Banks Brewing Station***. Moderate. Milepost 8.5 in Kill Devil Hills (252-449-2739; www.obbrewing.com). Besides brewing tasty seasonal beers with interesting names like "Muddy Waters" and "Sledgehammer," this restaurant serves delicious homemade pasta, grilled duck and steak, and fresh seafood. It also offers burgers and fries, if you're looking for more homey fare. Live entertainment is offered most nights in the bar. Dinner is served daily.

■ ***The Rundown Café***. Moderate. Milepost 1 in Kitty Hawk (252-255-0026). Housed in a structure made to look like a Caribbean beach house, The Rundown Café offers a menu heavy on fresh ingredients and local seafood with an island flair. The entrées range from Jerk chicken to fish tacos to seasoned shrimp. Vegetarian dishes include deliciously spicy Thai noodles. Among the desserts are chocolate peanut butter pie and—what else?—Key lime pie. A children's menu is available here, a feature you won't find at all Banks restaurants. Lunch and dinner are served daily from February through November.

■ **RV's Restaurant.** Moderate. Milepost 16.5 in Nags Head (252-441-4963). Located on the sound at the end of the bypass connecting Manteo and Nags Head, RV's features a great view of the water separating Roanoke Island from the northern Banks. It's been a local favorite for over two decades. Steaks and seafood are the specialties here. A lounge and a full bar serve up a variety of appetizers while you're waiting on your table. RV's is open from March through November for lunch and dinner.

■ **Awful Arthur's Oyster Bar.** Moderate/Inexpensive. Milepost 6 in Kill Devil Hills (252-441-5955). Awful Arthur's is a casual hangout where you can get a dozen oysters at the steam bar or an entire meal in the adjoining restaurant. The local seafood, steaks, chicken, and pasta served here can be washed down with an assortment of beers. Awful Arthur's T-shirts, a favorite of locals and frat guys, are sold in the neighboring gift shop. Lunch and dinner are offered daily year-round.

■ **Sam and Omie's.** Moderate/Inexpensive. Milepost 16.5 in Nags Head (252-441-7366; http://sam-n-omies.com/home2005.htm). Breakfast is the specialty here, as evidenced by the special "Omie-lettes" on the menu. This is also a nice place to select a quick yet satisfying lunch from among the restaurant's "Samiches." You can't go wrong with one of the salads, the she-crab soup, the steamed local seafood, or the homemade desserts either. Sam and Omie's is open daily from March through November for breakfast, lunch, and dinner.

Windswept Outer Banks Seashore
PHOTO BY BILL RUSS, COURTESY OF NORTH CAROLINA DIVISION OF TOURISM, FILM AND SPORTS DEVELOPMENT

A RIBBON OF SAND

Excerpted from *Duck: An Outer Banks Village*
by Judith D. Mercier

They call it a "ribbon of sand." They consider it one of the
most fascinating land formations on earth. Dozens of geologists
. . . have spent years studying this narrow string of low-lying
islands off the North Carolina coast. The interest isn't recent,
this area having been a source of scientific curiosity for nearly a
century. To the theorizing geologist, the Outer Banks are as
much mystery as beauty.

Decades of research have precipitated some heated debates.
Scientists still argue about how this line of barrier islands came
to be, how it got so far from the mainland, how it will or won't
survive. On one point, geologists seem to agree: the entire length
of the Outer Banks, all 175 miles, is comprised of nothing but
sand, layer upon layer of it sculpted and styled by the mighty
hands of nature, wind, and water.

It is on this Outer Banks sand that Duck's centuries-old
genesis came about, its evolution a complex series of temperature shifts and a quirky combination of winds, currents, and

storm waves that started almost eighty thousand years ago. During the Ice Age, the sea diminished, its waters drawn away and frozen into glaciers. Within thirty thousand years, the Atlantic sank to a low point, almost four hundred feet below current levels. More land was exposed. The North Carolina coast extended almost twenty miles east of Cape Hatteras, forty miles east of Cape Lookout. One by one, sand ridges ruptured the ocean's shrinking membrane like chicks grown too big for their shells.

Eventually, the world warmed. Glaciers began to loosen twelve thousand years ago, and higher waters gradually returned. The sea kept climbing, and with it, the Outer Banks began to grow, their fledgling bulk nourished by the sand, gravel, and rock flour that great rivers carried across the shrinking coastal plain. At first, the Banks were only spits. In time, they grew into islands, steadily building as the water rose. By 1500 B.C., geologists speculate, the Outer Banks were approximately the size and shape they are today. . . .

Before scientists arrived here, nineteenth-century Bankers already understood that the sand spits they lived on were constantly shifting and changing. What latter-day geologists have proven is that this ribbon of sand continually travels toward the mainland. They refer to it as "landward retreat" or "shoreface recession," explaining that most of the movement results from the ever-rising sea.

Industrialization, increased population, and the human tendency to use without putting back have created a greenhouse effect. The earth is heating up again, and the polar icecaps are still melting. Over the last two hundred years, the ocean has risen fourteen inches, most of that occurring since 1890. Geologists estimate that global warming is causing the sea to rise at a rate of three inches per decade, and they expect that rate to accelerate.

With these rapidly climbing waters comes the westward migration of the barrier islands. Duck—like all of the Outer Banks north of Cape Hatteras—is advancing five feet closer to the mainland every year. As the beachfront constantly recedes and erodes, geologists issue their warning: what now rests on top of the sand will eventually lie beneath the Atlantic.

Roanoke Marshes Lighthouse in Manteo

ROANOKE ISLAND

*S*urrounded by the waters of Roanoke Sound and Croatan Sound, Roanoke Island claims the honor of being the birthplace of English America. More than 400 years ago, intrepid explorers discovered this "goodliest land under the cope of heaven" and convinced Queen Elizabeth I to send settlers here to claim the land for England. Several attempts to settle the area were made—including one that saw the birth of the first English child on American soil—but none succeeded. Roanoke Island owes its heritage to this group of brave souls who gave up everything to seek out new opportunities and a new life in a strange land.

Manteo, named for one of the friendly Indians who helped the colonists, is the largest town on Roanoke Island. It prides itself on being a "walkable" community. It is here that you will find the majority of shopping and dining opportunities on the island. Plan on spending a morning exploring the many shops on the waterfront, taking breakfast at one of the coffee shops, browsing the history section of the local bookstore, checking out the kayaking and windsurfing gear at the outdoor shops, and feeding the sociable sea gulls that fly over Shallowbag Bay. You'll have chances to explore local history at Roanoke Island Festival Park and *The Lost Colony* outdoor drama as well.

Wanchese, to the south, is the other town on the island. It is much sleepier than Manteo. Also named for one of the Native Americans who assisted the colonists, Wanchese is a fishing village. More than 20 million pounds of fish are caught here every year, making this a fun place to watch boats and fishermen depart or later return with their catch. Wanchese is worth the drive just to see what the Outer Banks without the crowds is like.

Roanoke Island is considered by many to be the heart of Outer Banks art and culture. You won't find any major beaches here. Instead, it's the plays, museums, living-history exhibits, gardens, concerts, and ballets that keep people coming to this small island between the mainland and the barrier islands.

JUST THE FACTS

From the north or the northern Banks, take U.S. 64/U.S. 264 West over the Washington Baum Bridge. From the mainland, take U.S. 64/U.S. 264 East over the William B. Umstead Memorial Bridge.

The Dare County Regional Airport is on Airport Road in Manteo. Its two runways are 3,290 feet and 4,300 feet in length. Fuel, services, restrooms, and an area for pilots to sleep are offered. For information, call 252-475-5570 or visit www.fly2mqi.com. Air charters via Sea Air are available to and from the airport from just about anywhere east of the Mississippi River. Call 252-453-3656 or visit www.flyseaair.com for more information. A few local shuttle services and car and limousine rentals are available at the airport as well. Additional paved runways are located at Kill Devil Hills, Hatteras Island, and Ocracoke Island, though no support services are available at those locations.

Many different services offer information about the Outer Banks. One of the best is the Outer Banks Visitors Bureau (877-629-4386 or 252-473-2138; www.outerbanks.org), at One Visitors Center Circle off U.S. 64/U.S. 264 in Manteo. A useful page on the bureau's Web site lists the rates and availability of rental units in the area. The town of Manteo has its own Web site at www.townofmanteo.com.

Things to Do

Visitors who want to see and do it all but still maintain their budgets may be interested in the free Outer Banks Getaway Card, which offers discounts on accommodations, shopping, dining, and recreational activities at participating area businesses during the off-season. The cards, a joint venture between the Outer Banks Visitors Bureau and Dare County businesses, are available by e-mailing the bureau at information@outerbanks.org or by filling out an online form at www.outerbanks.org/seasonal_savings/getaway_card.

Historic Places, Gardens, and Tours

■ *Fort Raleigh National Historic Site*, located off U.S. 64/U.S. 264 at the northern end of the island, allows visitors to step back in time to see how the area looked over 400 years ago to the newly arrived English colonists. You can walk in the footsteps of those who attempted to tame this wild island and disappeared without a trace. A visitor center administered by the National Park Service tells the story of the first colonists on Roanoke Island.

The English tried to settle the area many times, beginning in 1585 under the direction of Richard Grenville, a cousin of Sir Walter Raleigh, who was a leader in the move to explore the New World. Grenville led 600 men to found the first colony. He left a group of them under the direction of Ralph Lane to build fortifications while he returned to England. Relations with the natives soon turned sour, however, and when Sir Francis Drake and his men visited the colony on their way home from Florida, the first colonists took advantage of the opportunity and returned to England.

Undeterred, Grenville came back a short time later with two years' worth of supplies and a smaller, more reliable group of settlers. Before returning to England, he gave the settlers strict instructions about establishing fortifications. It was this group of men who built what is now known as Fort Raleigh.

The appointed governor of the area, John White, came by boat in 1587 with a number of other colonists to assume his duties and further build the colony. He was undoubtedly shocked to find all of the men

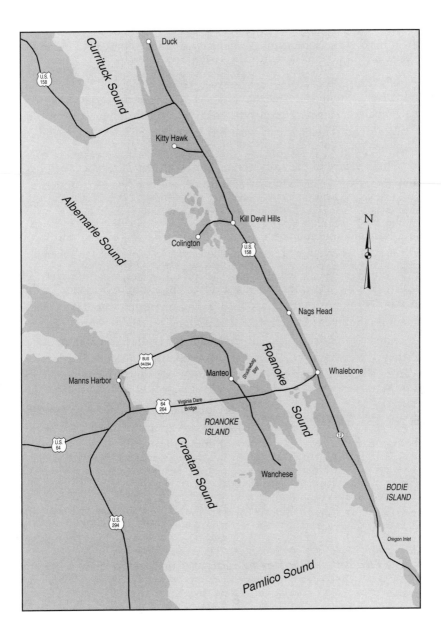

Duck

U.S.
158

Currituck Sound

Kitty Hawk

Albemarle Sound

Colington

Kill Devil Hills

U.S.
158

N

Nags Head

BUS
64/294

Roanoke Sound

Manns Harbor

Manteo

Croatan Bay

Whalebone

64
264

Virginia Dare
Bridge

ROANOKE
ISLAND

U.S.
64

12

Croatan Sound

Wanchese

BODIE
ISLAND

U.S.
294

Oregon Inlet

Pamlico Sound

missing and only one skeleton inhabiting the fort.

Thousands of miles of ocean between him and Mother England and many travel-weary wards in his care, the governor set about reestablishing the colony. White's colonists were families who had a vested interest in making the settlement permanent, in order to provide a better life for their loved ones. Included was White's own daughter, pregnant at the time with the now-famous Virginia Dare, the first English child born in the New World. Unfortunately, the colonists soon discovered that they were unable to live off the land, which was much different from their native ground. The governor was thus forced to sail back to England for more provisions.

The mystery of the story enters here. War was raging between England and Spain when White arrived home, and the Spanish Armada ensured that it wasn't until 1590 that he was able to return to the colony. Sailing back into the familiar bay, he was once again shocked to find Fort Raleigh uninhabited. At the entrance, he discovered the word *CROATOAN* carved on a post, but there was no cross with it—the colonists' agreed-upon signal of danger. Before he was able to search the nearby islands, Governor White was forced to return to England. To this day, no one knows what happened to the colonists of Roanoke Island. Theories abound as to their fate, but nothing has ever been proved.

The earth embankments at Fort Raleigh, restored in 1950, are much as they were when the colonists lived on Roanoke Island. The Lindsay Warren Visitor Center exhibits relics from the era of Governor White and Virginia Dare and offers maps of the area, books on the Lost Colony, and a 17-minute film on the history of Roanoke Island. The Waterside Theatre, located on the grounds of Fort Raleigh National Historic Site, is the home of *The Lost Colony* outdoor drama during the summer. The site is open daily from 9 A.M. to 6 P.M. from June to the end of August; the hours during the rest of the year are 9 A.M. to 5 P.M. The park is closed Christmas Day. Admission to the site is free, though a fee is charged to see *The Lost Colony*. For information, call 252-473-5772 or visit www.nps.gov/fora.

■ The **Elizabethan Gardens** are adjacent to the Waterside Theatre in the heart of Fort Raleigh National Historic Site. Created in 1951 by the Garden Club of North Carolina, the 10.5-acre gardens are a memorial to America's first English colonists. Designed by M. Umberto Innocenti and Richard Webel to bloom year-round, the gardens feature plants native to the Outer Banks. Visitors enjoy an array of flowering shrubs, trees, plants, and herbs along the property's winding paths. Among the several gardens

Elizabethan Gardens

here are the formal Queen's Rose Garden (which features the "Lost Colony Rose"), the Shakespearean Herb Garden, and the Great Lawn.

The centerpiece may well be the 15th-century Italian fountain, pool, and balustrade in the Sunken Garden, given by John Hay Whitney, a former ambassador to Great Britain. Visitors can stop here to smell the flowers and listen to the gurgling fountain.

Situated next to Roanoke Sound is a 16th-century gazebo made of daub siding and thatched roofing. This area is said to be where the English flag was first raised in the New World.

The gardens are open daily year-round except for Thanksgiving, Christmas Eve, Christmas Day, and New Year's. Extended hours are offered during the summer. Admission is charged for adults and children ages six to 17. For information, call 252-473-3234 or visit www.elizabethangardens.org.

■ Like Fort Raleigh National Historic Site, **Roanoke Island Festival Park** is dedicated to re-creating the history of the early colonists. This living-history theme park is located on the 25-acre Ice Plant Island in Shallowbag Bay across from downtown Manteo.

Your first stop upon entering the visitor center will be the 8,500-

Elizabeth II
PHOTO BY BILL RUSS, COURTESY OF NORTH CAROLINA DIVISION OF
TOURISM, FILM AND SPORTS DEVELOPMENT

square-foot **Roanoke Adventure Museum**, which features paintings, artifacts, relics, and interactive exhibits on the important figures and events in Roanoke Island's history. One of the best exhibits is the Civil War cannon found underwater off the island; it was so well packed with firing material that the gunpowder was still dry, meaning that the cannon was still ready for action. A Native American village, a Civil War encampment, a pirate ship, a duck blind, and a 1950s general store are among the other exhibits. Children love the area where they can dress up in swashbuckling buccaneer and dainty m'lady costumes. Actors in period costumes trained in Elizabethan dialect are spread throughout the park to share stories of pioneering on Roanoke Island. Inquisitive children and adults can find out what it was like to survive in the hot, swampy, buggy conditions without any of the conveniences we depend upon today. The Native Americans' story is shared as well. A 50-minute film titled *The Legend of Two-Path* tells what the people already settled on Roanoke Island thought of the new "settlers" who appeared in 1585. Outside the museum are several trails leading to different exhibits, including a settlement site featuring historically costumed soldiers who share what the settlers did for shelter, food, and protection.

The most impressive feature of Roanoke Island Festival Park is perhaps the 69-foot **Elizabeth II**. An authentic representation of the 16th-century *Elizabeth*, one of seven merchant ships used to sail to the new colony, the *Elizabeth II* was built to commemorate the New World's quadricentennial. Interpretive guides on the three-mast, "50-tunne" Elizabethan ship share stories of what it was like to cross the Atlantic and try to settle the New World.

During the summer, the famed North Carolina School of the Arts offers special dance, theater, and musical performances and film in the park by some of the art world's up-and-coming stars. Past performances have included *A Midsummer Night's Dream*, *Cinderella*, and the musical *She Loves Me*. Three performances are generally given each day. The morning offering includes puppet shows and fairy and folk tales as part of the Children's Series. The afternoon performance is often a concert of chamber or jazz music in the park's art gallery. The evening performances—dance, musical concerts, and dramas presented in the outdoor pavilion—are perhaps the highlight of the series. Admission to performances is free with admission to the park, though making a donation is a good way to ensure performances for the next year.

Roanoke Island Festival Park is open mid-February through December with the exception of Thanksgiving and Christmas. Hours vary seasonally. Admission is charged for adults and students; children age five and under are admitted free. For information, call 252-475-1500 or visit www.roanokeisland.com.

MUSEUMS AND SCIENCE CENTERS

■ The *North Carolina Aquarium at Roanoke Island*, tucked away down the long and winding Airport Road off U.S. 64, offers 68,000 square feet of freshwater and saltwater galleries. Creatures from North Carolina's rivers, marshes, sounds, and reefs are all highlighted.

The first stop inside the aquarium is the open-air natural-habitat atrium. Lined with real trees and topped with a huge skylight, the habitat gives a sense of the North Carolina wetlands. Wood ducks, river otters, and alligators all inhabit this area. Mists spray throughout the atrium periodically to keep the "wetlands" wet.

The centerpiece of the aquarium is undoubtedly the 285,000-gallon "Graveyard of the Atlantic" ocean tank, the largest in the state. Inside it

North Carolina Aquarium at Roanoke Island

are the skeletal remains of a 53-foot re-created USS *Monitor* shipwreck, a one-third-scale replica of the famed Civil War ship now lying off Cape Hatteras. Created by a team of movie-set designers in Wilmington, the replica is covered with fiberglass orange, pink, and yellow corals, sponges, and sea fans. The fish swimming inside the tank sometimes confuse the replica with the real thing and try to take a nip out of it. The sharks gliding stealthily by the 35-foot-long, five-and-a-half-inch-thick viewing window steal the show. Custom-made in Japan and set into place with a crane, the window wraps overhead, so viewers gets a sense of actually being in the water with the ship, the sharks, and other ocean creatures.

The aquarium's Discovery Gallery gives kids a chance to touch skates, rays, sea stars, crabs, urchins, and other invertebrates. Charts and graphics on the walls tell about the evolution and characteristics of each animal.

A theater, a gift shop, a shoreline boardwalk, and nature trails are also on the premises.

The aquarium is open daily year-round except for Thanksgiving, Christmas, and New Year's. A modest fee is charged for adults; children five and under and Aquarium Society members are admitted free. For information, call 252-473-3493 or 866-332-3475 or visit www.ncaquariums.com.

■ The **North Carolina Maritime Museum on Roanoke Island**, located on the Manteo waterfront, is a repository of information on the long seafaring history and natural resources of the Outer Banks. During the summer, the museum offers educational programs on sailing and boat safety for children and adults. Visitors can also witness the art of boat restoration and construction at the George Washington Creef Boathouse, home to a working boat shop that relies on traditional boat-building and repair techniques.

Nearby, you'll find the **Roanoke Marshes Lighthouse**, the Banks' newest lighthouse, opened in 2004. It's a replica of a screw pile lighthouse built in 1877 to light the way for boats in Croatan Sound. The lighthouse served as both a guiding light for sailors and a residence for the keeper, thus explaining why it looks more like a cottage built over the water than a traditional lighthouse. Sailors in the sound now rely on the lighthouse's fourth-order Fresnel lens to light the night.

The museum and lighthouse operate on seasonal hours, so call ahead. Admission is free. For information on the museum, call 252-475-1750; for information on the lighthouse, call 252-475-1500. You can visit www.obxmaritime.org to learn more about both attractions.

SPECIAL SHOPPING

Downtown Manteo offers an array of browsing choices, from shops selling outdoor gear or local artwork to a unique independently owned bookstore. It's easy to spend a few leisurely hours wandering the shops and soaking up the culture. One of the best times to do this is during the town's "First Friday" events—held, as the name implies, on the first Friday of every month. Visitors also can listen to live music and enjoy a candlelight walking tour on these Fridays.

RECREATION

- The **Downeast Rover**, a reproduction of a 19th-century topsail schooner, is berthed on the Manteo waterfront adjacent to Roanoke Island Festival Park. The *Rover* offers daytime and sunset cruises that can accommodate up to 29 guests. Sailors aboard the 55-foot boat can see Roanoke Island from a completely different perspective and get a close look at the local wildlife, including dolphins, ospreys, and herons. Below decks are accommodations for up to six adult passengers, for those who choose to charter the *Rover* for longer trips. Be sure to check availability, prices, and departure time for the date you're interested in. Reservations are recommended. For more information, call 252-473-4866 or visit www.downeastrover.com.

- *Alligator River National Wildlife Refuge*, located on U.S. 64/U.S. 264 on the Dare County mainland, is comprised of more than 150,000 acres of

Alligator River National Wildlife Refuge
COURTESY OF NORTH CAROLINA DIVISION OF TOURISM, FILM AND SPORTS DEVELOPMENT

wild wetland separating the mainland from the Outer Banks. The Alligator River—actually a small sound—is part of the larger Albemarle Sound, one of the most important waterways in the state. Snaking from Alligator Lake in the Dismal Swamp to Albemarle Sound, the Alligator River is said to have received its name from the area's first settlers, who encountered quite a few of those stealthy, beady-eyed creatures. Little did those pioneers know that they were lucky—or unlucky, as the case may be—to have stumbled into the northernmost habitat of the American alligator. Wildlife specialists say the alligators in the Alligator River are smaller than their counterparts in Florida and Georgia, but that fact probably wouldn't have provided much comfort to the first men and women crossing these waters.

Besides alligators, visitors to the refuge will find black bears, bobcats, bald eagles, white-tailed deer, and red wolves. The red wolf faced extinction as recently as 1996, but thanks to a reintroduction project, the numbers are growing today. All along the highway in the refuge, you'll see red wolf crossing signs, so take care to share the road with these shy creatures.

Admission to the refuge is free. Visitors can take advantage of the hiking and wildlife trails, the observation platforms, and the fishing areas. Kayaking and canoeing are permitted; a guided canoe tour is available for a fee. There's also a wildlife drive where cars and bikes are permitted. For more information, call 252-473-1131 or visit http://alligatorriver.fws.gov.

■ **Kitty Hawk Sports** offers kayak ecotours led by trained guides. One of the best tours starts in Manteo and heads through Shallowbag Bay into the maritime forest. Kayakers learn useful information about local flora and fauna—like how to distinguish between bug-repellent plants and poison ivy. Call 252-441-6800 or visit www.kittyhawksports.com for more information.

■ For those looking to do a little fishing while the family is exploring the nearby shops and museums, Fishing Unlimited, a local business, operates the 300-foot-long **Roanoke Sound Pier**. Located along the Manteo causeway, the pier is known as a hot spot for crabbing and catching speckled trout, striped bass, and flounder. For more information, call 252-441-5740 or visit http://fishingunlimited.net/SoundPier.html.

- Marinas line the Outer Banks. Those along Roanoke Island include *Manteo Waterfront Marina*, also known as Dough's Creek (252-473-3320), *Pirate's Cove Marina* (252-473-3906), *Ray Hollowell Marina* (252-473-3324), *Salty Dawg Marina* (252-473-3405), and *Shallowbag Bay Marina* (252-473-4946) in Manteo and *Thicket Lump Marina* (252-473-4500) and *Broad Creek Fishing Center & Marina* (252-473-9991) in Wanchese.

SEASONAL EVENTS

- First performed in 1937, **The Lost Colony** is the oldest outdoor drama in the United States. Over 4 million theatergoers have witnessed the passion and mystery surrounding the British colonists lost to the wilderness of Roanoke Island. Performed on the grounds of Fort Raleigh National Historic Site at the Waterside Theatre overlooking Roanoke Sound, *The Lost Colony* tells the story of Governor John White; his daughter, Eleanor Dare; her daughter, Virginia Dare, the first English child born in America; and the native Algonquin Indians. The production includes dance, song, fights, and fireworks. Guests witness how Sir Walter Raleigh convinced Queen Elizabeth I to support a settlement in the New World, yet how he was denied the chance to participate in building the colony; how the colonists became friends with the natives yet later lost their allegiance; and how they came to the conclusion that they could no longer survive at Fort Raleigh. Of course, you'll have to attend a performance to see what Pulitzer Prize-winning playwright Paul Green imagined to be the fate of the colonists.

    If you're planning an evening at the Waterside Theatre, you'll be well advised to buy your tickets in advance and to bring a healthy supply of bug repellent. If you come prepared, you'll be justly rewarded with a tale of love, loss, and heroic courage.

    The Lost Colony is performed Monday through Saturday at 8:30 P.M. from early June to late August. Children 11 and under are admitted for half price on Friday and Saturday. Refunds are not given except in case of bad weather, and performances are never canceled before 9 P.M. For more information or to order advance tickets, call the box office at 866-468-7630 or 252-473-3414 or visit www.thelostcolony.org.

- **Elizabeth R**, a one-woman show about the thoughts, aspirations, loves, and fears of Queen Elizabeth I, is performed at Meeting Hall on the grounds of the Elizabethan Gardens on Tuesday afternoons during the summer. To

The Lost Colony *outdoor drama*

reserve tickets, call 252-473-3234; tickets can be purchased at the gardens as well. For additional information, visit www.elizabethangardens.org/special_programs.aspx.

Elizabeth R and Company Productions also produces **Bloody Mary and the Virgin Queen**, a musical comedy that intersperses the complex relations between Queen Elizabeth I and her half-sister, Mary Tudor, with contemporary American politics and culture. Performances are held on Wednesdays in May and June in the film theater at Roanoke Island Festival Park. Admission is free with the purchase of a ticket to the park. For more information, call 252-473-1061 or visit www.roanokeisland.com.

■ The several seasonal festivals on Roanoke Island are not to be missed if you're in town.

The ***Dare Day Festival*** is held annually the first Saturday in June in downtown Manteo. It honors the memory of Virginia Dare and the other Lost Colonists of Roanoke Island. The festival features all-day entertainment, arts and crafts, food, dance, and live music. Call 252-475-5629 for more information.

The ***Herbert Hoover Birthday Celebration***, held on August 10 and sponsored by Manteo Booksellers, honors the birthday of our nation's

31st president. This is a quirky way to enjoy a day of book signings, live music, trivia, and birthday cake. Call 866-473-1222 or 252-473-1221 or visit www.manteobooksellers.com for more information.

The **Weeping Radish Oktoberfest**, held in September at the Weeping Radish Brewery and Bavarian Restaurant on U.S. 64/U.S. 264, features traditional German dishes, Oktoberfest beer, an oompah band, and dancing. For information, call 800-896-5403 or 252-473-1157 or visit www.weepingradish.com.

Places to Stay

Roanoke Island is noted for its unique inns and bed-and-breakfasts. If you're looking for the tried-and-true chains, you may need to try up the road in Nags Head or Kitty Hawk. Rates vary seasonally.

RESORTS, HOTELS, AND MOTELS

■ **Elizabethan Inn**. Expensive/Moderate/Inexpensive. 814 U.S. 64 in Manteo (800-346-2466 or 252-473-2101; www.elizabethaninn.com). This 78-room, two-efficiency Tudor-style motel, located close to all of Roanoke Island's cultural offerings, boasts a wide range of amenities. Guests can enjoy an indoor heated pool, an outdoor pool, a whirlpool, a sauna, and a well-equipped gym. Complimentary bicycles are available for trips to the Manteo waterfront, Roanoke Island Festival Park, the North Carolina Aquarium, and Fort Raleigh National Historic Site. Breakfast is offered at the inn's Virginia Dare Restaurant. Pets are welcome in some of the rooms.

■ **Duke of Dare Motor Lodge**. Moderate/Inexpensive. 100 U.S. 64/U.S. 264 in Manteo (252-473-2175; www.ego.net/us/nc/ob/duke/index.htm). This no-frills 57-room motel offers the basics for a reasonable price. The Duke of Dare has been owned and operated by the same family for over 25 years. It features televisions, phones, and an outdoor pool.

INNS AND BED-AND-BREAKFASTS

- **The Cameron House Inn.** Deluxe. 300 Budleigh Street in Manteo (800-279-8178 or 252-473-6596; www.cameronhouseinn.com). This restored 1919 Arts and Crafts-style bungalow features seven guest rooms with plush bedding, Oriental carpets, and individual bathrooms. One room is actually located in a separate condo about a block from the inn; it features a full kitchen and a gorgeous view of the nearby bay. The main inn's wraparound porch is the perfect place to read a book, take in the breeze off the water, and enjoy a quiet afternoon lazing in the restored 50-year-old porch swing. During the winter, guests can enjoy rocking by the back porch's outdoor fireplace.

- **The White Doe Inn Bed-and-Breakfast.** Deluxe. 319 Sir Walter Raleigh Street in Manteo (800-473-6091 or 252-473-9851; www.whitedoeinn.com). Built in 1898 as the Theodore Meekins House and listed on the National Register of Historic Places in 1982, The White Doe is now a Three Diamond, three-story, eight-room Queen Anne-style inn. Each of the rooms is individually decorated with antiques and features amenities ranging from four-poster beds to private whirlpools to stained-glass windows to chandeliers. A four-course gourmet breakfast, afternoon tea, and bicycles are some of the extras provided for guests. No stay would be complete without partaking of the inn's luxurious spa services, provided in the privacy of your own room.

- **Roanoke Island Inn.** Deluxe/Expensive. 305 Fernando Street in Manteo (877-473-5511 or 252-473-5511; www.roanokeislandinn.com). Built in the 1860s for the current innkeeper's great-great-grandmother, the Roanoke Island Inn grew steadily throughout the 20th century to accommodate the growing family and the guests who stayed here. This waterfront inn offers eight guest rooms and a bungalow, most of which have a view of the nearby bay. Continental breakfast and access to the innkeeper's pantry ensure that you will be well fed. The inn is generally open from April to late October, though the owners charmingly advertise their season as ranging from "Easter 'til we're tired." If you're looking for a more secluded hideaway, ask the innkeepers about their Island Camp, a lovely house situated alone on an island south of the causeway. Guests must provide their own transportation by boat; a number of restaurants are located within boating distance.

- **Tranquil House Inn**. Deluxe/Expensive. 405 Queen Elizabeth Street in Manteo (800-458-7069 or 252-473-1404; www.tranquilinn.com). Guests staying here enjoy being in the middle of everything. The Tranquil House is located on the Shallowbag Bay waterfront in downtown Manteo. The majority of its 25 individually decorated rooms feature a view of the water. This turn-of-the-20th-century reproduction offers suites with sitting rooms, an upstairs porch with rocking chairs, evening wine and cheese, and complimentary continental breakfast. One of the best restaurants on the Outer Banks, 1587, sits conveniently next door.

- **Island House of Wanchese**. Expensive/Moderate. 104 Old Wharf Road in Wanchese (252-473-5619; www.islandhouse-bb.com). Located away from the hustle and bustle of Manteo in the quiet fishing village of Wanchese, this is the place to truly get away from it all. The three rooms and one suite have private baths, antique furnishings, Oriental rugs, televisions, and radios. Guests enjoy the turn-down service at night and are welcomed in the morning with a home-cooked, Southern-style buffet breakfast. A screened porch, beach chairs, beach towels, beach showers, bicycles, and a freezer for your catch all make this seem like a home away from home. The inn is open year-round.

- **Scarborough House Inn**. Moderate/Inexpensive. 323 Fernando Street in Manteo (252-473-3849; www.scarboroughhouseinn.com). The keepers of this inn are as local as they come. The Scarboroughs boast lineages on both sides extending as far back as pre-Revolutionary War times. The photos of ancestors that decorate the walls of the five rooms and the two-story guest house chronicle the story of Roanoke Island and the Outer Banks for close to a century. The rooms include antique beds covered with handmade spreads, gleaming pine floors, and modern amenities like refrigerators, microwaves, coffee makers, and televisions. Continental breakfast is included in the price of your stay.

Places to Eat

Though there are not as many restaurants on Roanoke Island as on the northern Banks, you'll find good variety and tasty food. As you might expect, seafood is available at just about every restaurant and is as fresh as it comes. Those who don't care for seafood will be able to find plenty to satisfy them as well.

- **1587**. Expensive. Queen Elizabeth Street at the Tranquil House Inn in Manteo (252-473-1587; www.1587.com). Named for the year the Lost Colonists arrived on Roanoke Island, this restaurant is one of the most sophisticated on the Banks. The cuisine at 1587 changes seasonally to reflect the local bounty. The chefs blend herbs grown in the restaurant's own garden with free-range chicken, certified Angus beef, and seafood from the Atlantic to create their unique dishes. Guests can enjoy the breeze off Shallowbag Bay and listen to the water lapping against the docks as they enjoy their evening meal. Dinner is served nightly year-round.

- ***Queen Anne's Revenge***. Expensive/Moderate. Old Wharf Road in Wanchese (252-473-5466). Queen Anne's is a nice place to get away from the crowds of the northern beaches and downtown Manteo to enjoy a fine meal. Its location in the fishing village of Wanchese is to the restaurant's advantage when it comes to seafood dishes. Queen Anne's is also renowned for its homemade bouillabaisse and handmade fettuccine. Desserts prepared on-site by the chefs round out a menu that is high on fresh Outer Banks ingredients. Dinner is served nightly.

- ***The Waterfront Trellis***. Expensive/Moderate. Queen Elizabeth Street in Manteo (252-473-1727). This restaurant affords a lovely view of the Manteo waterfront, a casual atmosphere, and a large menu. Diners will find the tried-and-true fried seafood they expect at the beach, along with healthier choices such as a full steam bar and vegetarian options. This is a great place to catch lunch while trekking through downtown Manteo. Recommended dishes include the crab rolls and the stuffed shrimp. Lunch and dinner are served daily; brunch is offered on Sunday.

- ***Full Moon Café***. Moderate. Queen Elizabeth Street in Manteo (252-473-6666; www.thefullmooncafe.com). Full Moon Café, located in a brick building under Manteo's clock tower, offers standard fare—delicious homemade salads, wraps, burgers, and seafood—in addition to an eclectic blend of world cuisines ranging from baked Brie to eggplant Napoleon. This is a terrific place to fill up without breaking the bank. Lunch and dinner are served daily.

- ***Hurricane Mo's Restaurant and Raw Bar***. Moderate. At Pirate's Cove

Marina on the Manteo-Nags Head Causeway (252-473-2266). Located at the point where Roanoke Island and Nags Head meet, this casual restaurant is a wonderful place to get a plate of oysters on the half shell and a cold beer and watch the boats come in. Fishermen and families alike are welcome here, and the service is gracious and helpful. Among the favorites are the very generous seafood platters and the "Chicken Marsala Florentine" with spinach, sun-dried tomatoes, and mushrooms. Lunch and dinner are served daily during the peak season.

- **Weeping Radish Brewery and Bavarian Restaurant.** Moderate/Inexpensive. U.S. 64/U.S. 264 in Manteo (800-896-5403 or 252-473-1157; www.weepingradish.com). For a unique dining experience on the Outer Banks, the Weeping Radish is the place to go. It is named after the radish typically served alongside beer in Bavaria. The radish is spiral-cut, salted, and folded back together; the salt draws the water out of the radish and gives it the appearance of weeping. At this restaurant, you'll find dishes you'd expect in Germany—sausages, cabbage, potato cakes, and even pretzels. Beer is the Weeping Radish's claim to fame, though. It is one of just a few breweries in the country using the 1516 German Reinheitsgebot, or purity law. Only four ingredients—water, hops, malt, and yeast—go into the beer, which is left unfiltered to give it a stout, authentic taste. Lunch and dinner are served daily from February to December.

Bodie Island Lighthouse
PHOTO BY BILL RUSS, COURTESY OF NORTH CAROLINA DIVISION OF TOURISM, FILM AND SPORTS DEVELOPMENT

BODIE ISLAND

*B*odie Island provides a glimpse into what the Outer Banks looked like long before tourists arrived, when the only people inhabiting the area were the lighthouse keepers. It is a unique, peaceful place.

Bodie Island is really just the southern tip of the northern Banks and not an island at all. The pronunciation of the name is also a little quirky. I've heard many lifelong North Carolinians pronounce it "Bo-dee," although the correct way of saying the name is "Body." As with every place on the Outer Banks, there are several explanations of how the island came to be named. Some say the name honors the vast number of bodies that washed ashore from ships wrecked in the Graveyard of the Atlantic. Others a little less melodramatic claim it comes from the island's being a body of land. Still others say Bodie Island was named after a now-unknown person who helped build the lighthouse or was stationed there.

Established in 1953, Cape Hatteras National Seashore was the first national seashore in the country. It begins on Bodie Island and extends 75 miles through Hatteras and Ocracoke islands, covering over 30,000 acres. Some of the country's best fishing and surfing are found in the national seashore.

JUST THE FACTS

Driving south from the northern Banks, take either U.S. 158 (Virginia Dare Trail) or N.C. 12 (the Beach Road). From Roanoke Island, take U.S. 64/U.S. 264 East until you reach Whalebone Junction, then head south down N.C. 12.

Bodie Island has no airport. Charters into the area will need to land at the Dare Country Regional Airport on Roanoke Island.

Your best bet for gathering information is the Outer Banks Visitors Bureau (877-629-4386 or 252-473-2138; www.outerbanks.org), located at One Visitors Center Circle off U.S. 64/U.S. 264 in Manteo.

Things to Do

HISTORIC PLACES, GARDENS, AND TOURS

■ Encircled by its one-of-a-kind horizontal black and white bands, the **Bodie Island Lighthouse** has protected its small section of the coast since 1847. History has not always been kind to the lighthouse, though. Only 12 years after its creation, it was torn down and rebuilt because of improper construction. Three years later, in 1862, Confederate troops blew up the lighthouse so the Union wouldn't be able to use it. The lighthouse was rebuilt for the second (and so far last) time in 1871 at the staggering cost to Reconstruction North Carolina of $140,000. Shortly after it was reactivated, the lighthouse proved it was still on a bad-luck streak when a flock of wild geese flew into the lantern and damaged the lens.

Now long repaired, the 156-foot Bodie Island Lighthouse still flashes its 160,000-candlepower beacon 19 miles into the dark night over the Atlantic Ocean. The lighthouse is not open for climbing, but the keeper's quarters have been restored and now serve as a museum, gift shop, and visitor center for Cape Hatteras National Seashore. A nature trail winds through the marsh surrounding the lighthouse.

No admission fee is charged. The lighthouse grounds are open year-round with the exception of Christmas; hours are seasonal, so be sure to phone ahead. For more information, call 252-441-5711 or visit www.nps.gov/caha/bodielh.htm.

RECREATION

■ Almost directly across N.C. 12 from the entrance to the Bodie Island Lighthouse is one of the best beaches on the Outer Banks, **Coquina Beach**. Named for the tiny white shells you'll find scattered all over, Coquina offers good swimming and surf fishing. Do take note that there is no lifeguard on duty, so use common sense while visiting here.

Coquina Beach is rich in history. The **Laura A. Barnes**, built in 1918, was one of the last schooners constructed in the United States. It lies not far from where it grounded after a nor'easter blew it ashore in 1921. The crew survived thanks to the heroic actions of the men at the nearby lifesaving station. In 1973, the National Park Service moved the remains of the ship to their present location.

During World War II, this area came to be known as Torpedo Junction because the United States suffered such heavy losses to German submarines here. America also made one of its greatest comebacks at this place, though, when it sank a German U-boat for the first time. The remains of that submarine now lie 15 miles offshore.

■ *Oregon Inlet Fishing Center and Full-Service Marina*, located just down N.C. 12 at the north end of the Herbert C. Bonner Bridge, is home to the largest and most modern fishing fleet on the East Coast. Serious fishermen from around the world come to this marina to charter boats for Gulf Stream fishing. Facilities include a general store, boat ramps and docks, and areas to clean your catch. If you're driving past here in the late afternoon, be sure to stop to see the boats come in with their daily catch of sea bass, mullet, bluefish, billfish, and even shark. The National Park Service administers a boat-launch facility adjacent to the marina that offers ample free parking. For more information, call 800-272-5199 or 252-441-6301 or visit www.oregon-inlet.com.

■ The National Park Service also operates the only place to stay on Bodie Island, the **Oregon Inlet Campground**. Here, you'll find 120 sites serving tents, trailers, and motor homes with only the basics—cold showers, toilets, picnic tables, potable water, and grills. No utility connections are offered, but the reasonable price makes up for the no-frills accommodations. The campground is open from mid-April to mid-October. Availability is on a first-come, first-served basis, though you can make reservations for groups of seven or more by calling 252-441-7425, extension 230. The National Park Service recommends that campers using tents bring longer-than-normal tent stakes, due to the shifting sands and winds of the area. Insect netting and bug spray are a good idea, too. For more information, call 252-473-2111 or visit www.nps.gov/caha/pphtml/camping.html.

Cape Hatteras Lighthouse

Hatteras Island

*T*he largest island of the Outer Banks, Hatteras has a heritage rich in maritime history and lore. Even the trip between Bodie Island and Hatteras Island is a history lesson. Going from one island to the next, you'll cross Oregon Inlet, a body of water that came into existence in 1846 after a large storm blew a channel open. The *Oregon*, the first ship to sail through this passageway, gave the inlet its name. Oregon Inlet is now the main entrance to Pamlico Sound. The three-mile Herbert C. Bonner Bridge connects the two islands. The inlet requires constant dredging, as sand is perpetually deposited along the stone pillars of the bridge.

Once on Hatteras Island, you'll find several small towns connected by N.C. 12: Rodanthe, Waves, Salvo, Avon, Buxton, Frisco, and Hatteras. Each has a story and flavor all its own.

The most recognized symbol of the island is the Cape Hatteras Lighthouse. Threatened by the same winds and tides that created

Oregon Inlet, the lighthouse underwent a monumental move in 1999 to preserve it from the forces of nature.

While hazardous to lighthouses, the waves are a boon to surfers. Hatteras Island is one of the best spots on the East Coast to catch a wave.

JUST THE FACTS

Driving south from the northern Banks, take either U.S. 158 (Virginia Dare Trail) or N.C. 12 (the Beach Road). From Roanoke Island, take U.S. 64/U.S. 264 East to Whalebone Junction, then go south on N.C. 12.

Hatteras Island has no airport, so charters will need to land at the Dare Country Regional Airport on Roanoke Island.

The best place to turn for information is the Outer Banks Visitors Bureau (877-629-4386 or 252-473-2138; www.outerbanks.org), located at One Visitors Center Circle off U.S. 64/U.S. 264 in Manteo.

Things to Do

HISTORIC PLACES, GARDENS, AND TOURS

■ In 1873, the United States Life Saving Service was established by Congress to assist poor souls caught in storms or grounded by sand bars and reefs. The treacherous Graveyard of the Atlantic was one of the areas most in need of such service. **Chicamacomico Life Saving Station**, located in Rodanthe, was one of the stations constructed at seven-mile intervals along this portion of the North Carolina coast. Crews patrolled the beaches by foot or on horseback. They used Lyle guns to fire rescue lines to sinking ships or rowed out to rescue endangered crews. A bigger, improved Chicamacomico station was built in 1911.

The most famous rescue by the men at Chicamacomico occurred in 1918, when the English tanker *Mirlo* was torpedoed by a German U-boat. Captain John Allen Midgett, Jr., and his crew of five braved the surf and flames to save 47 of the 57 men aboard the ship. They were awarded medals by the British government in 1921 and were later recognized by the United States government.

Chicamacomico Life Saving Station now serves as a museum. Visitors enjoy the shipwreck exhibit with actual artifacts from, and pieces of, the ships themselves. Lifesaving equipment is also on display. The station is open Tuesday through Saturday from 9 A.M. to 5 P.M. Easter to Thanksgiving. The grounds are open year-round. Admission is free. For more information, call 252-987-1552 or visit www.cr.nps.gov/maritime/park/chiclss.htm.

■ *Little Kinnakeet Life Saving Station*, off N.C. 12 in Avon, was another of the lifesaving stations scattered along the North Carolina coast. The original building, commissioned in 1874, was condemned and modified twice before it was finally moved to its current location to rescue it from the encroaching tides. Like the Chicamacomico station, Little Kinnakeet was decommissioned in 1954 and turned over from the Coast Guard to the National Park Service. It is undergoing repairs and is closed to visitors, though the grounds are open for exploring. Admission is free. Visit www.cr.nps.gov/maritime/park/kinnlss.htm for more information.

■ The tallest and perhaps most famous lighthouse in the United States is the 208-foot *Cape Hatteras Lighthouse*, located off N.C. 12 at Cape Point near Buxton. Over the years, it has come to be the unofficial emblem of the Outer Banks.

Like the other lighthouses along the Banks, the Cape Hatteras Lighthouse has a long and complicated history. Built in 1803 over a mile from the shoreline, the first version of the lighthouse was poorly constructed and gave out only a weak signal to passing ships. The lighthouse was damaged by Union naval shells in 1861. Shortly thereafter, the Confederate army removed its lamp altogether.

The lighthouse was rebuilt in 1870 more than 1,000 yards from the sea. It rested on a floating foundation this time, meaning that it sat on yellow pine timbers in fresh water on compacted sand with a brick-and-granite foundation on top. As long as the sands held steady and no salt water seeped into the foundation, the lighthouse was safe. What the engineers did not account for, though, was that Hatteras Island itself was moving westward. The federal government abandoned the lighthouse in

1935 due to the constant erosion. The following year, it set up a temporary skeletal steel light tower. Once the 1870 lighthouse was abandoned, vandals damaged its lens.

It wasn't until 1950 that the light was moved back to the 1870 lighthouse, after extensive repairs. But beach erosion continued. In 1980, a storm washed away the foundation of the original 1803 lighthouse, which until then had stood more than 600 feet from the shore. That storm reinforced the idea that something had to be done to save the existing lighthouse. In 1989, after much debate, the National Park Service decided to move the aged structure.

It was nearly a decade later that the move was approved by Congress. The 1870 lighthouse closed its doors on November 22, 1998, as the National Park Service readied for the move. Engineers lifted the lighthouse from its foundation, sunk eight feet deep into the sand. They moved it 2,900 feet and reanchored it in a safer spot, leaving it about the same distance from the sea as back in 1870. After being closed for 550 days, the lighthouse reopened for visitors on May 26, 2000. The beam again lights up the night sky to a distance of 20 miles offshore.

Also on the grounds are the double keepers' quarters, which house a museum and visitor center, the principal keeper's quarters, and the

Cape Hatteras Lighthouse
Photo by Bill Russ, Courtesy of
North Carolina Division of Tourism,
Film and Sports Development

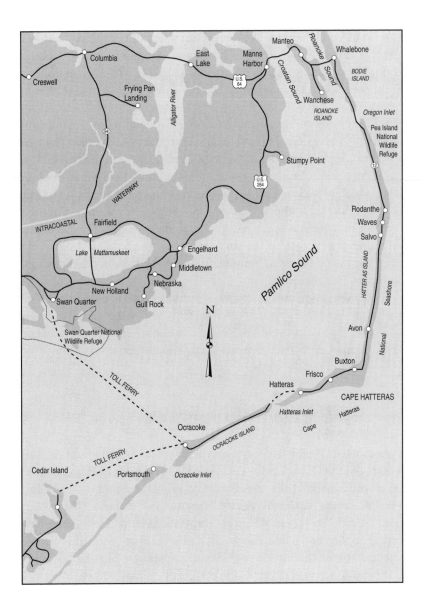

Hatteras Island Visitor Center. Admission to the grounds is free, though a fee is charged to climb the lighthouse. The grounds are traditionally open year-round from 9 A.M. to 5 P.M. except for Christmas; hours are extended in the summer. The lighthouse is open for climbing from Easter weekend to Columbus Day weekend, weather permitting. Just keep in mind that the climb is equivalent to trekking up a 12-story building—without air conditioning. For information, call 252-473-2111 or 252-995-4474 or visit www.nps.gov/caha.

■ Off Cape Hatteras is the **USS Monitor** *National Marine Sanctuary*. The *Monitor* and its Confederate counterpart, the CSS *Virginia* (formerly the *Merrimack*), inaugurated a new age in naval warfare during their famous fight in 1862. Only nine months after battling the *Virginia*, the *Monitor* met a watery end in a ferocious storm while en route to Beaufort. It wasn't until 1974 that the *Monitor* was discovered. A year later, the site of the wreck became America's first national marine sanctuary. Archaeologists and engineers believe the ship cannot be recovered without further damage, so the *Monitor* will continue to rest in the same spot where it met its end over 140 years ago.

The Coast Guard strictly enforces restrictions on activity in the sanctuary to preserve the wreck. The closest history buffs can get is the reduced-scale reproduction at the North Carolina Aquarium on Roanoke Island and the interactive Web site http://monitor.nos.noaa.gov.

MUSEUMS AND SCIENCE CENTERS

■ Museums and exhibits where you can learn about the life of the early colonists dot the Outer Banks. But there are few places to learn about the people who inhabited the area hundreds of years before the English arrived. The **Frisco Native American Museum and Natural History Center**, off N.C. 12 in Frisco, sheds light on this often-overlooked group of people. Founded and operated by Carl and Joyce Bornfriend, this is a non-profit educational foundation that displays collections of authentic Native American artifacts and explores the origins of different tribes, their tools, their religions, and their ways of surviving. Also on the grounds are nature trails, a pavilion, a gift shop, and a bookstore. The annual Inter-Tribal PowWow, held in the spring, features dancers and drummers from all over the country. The museum is open year-round Tuesday through Sunday from 11 A.M. to 5 P.M. and Monday by appointment. A nominal admission fee is charged. Call 252-995-4440 or visit www.nativeamericanmuseum.org.

■ *Graveyard of the Atlantic Museum*, at 59158 Coast Guard Road off N.C. 12 in Hatteras village, is dedicated to the preservation and presentation of maritime history and the shipwrecks of the Outer Banks from the mid-1500s to today. More than 1,500 ships, including Civil War blockade runners and German U-boats, have sunk off the treacherous North Carolina coast since settlement efforts began over 400 years ago. The museum chronicles the stories of these ill-fated ships— and those like Blackbeard's *Adventure* that safely navigated the area's infamous sand bars and shoals— through artifacts, models, and exhibits. The museum offers regular author appearances and book signings during the summer as part of its heritage series, which is free and open to the public. Museum hours are subject to change, so call ahead. A nominal admission fee is charged. For more information, call 252-986-2996 or visit www.graveyardoftheatlantic.com.

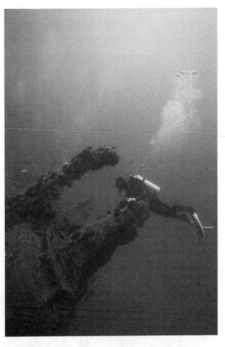

Diving in the Graveyard of the Atlantic
PHOTO BY BILL RUSS, COURTESY OF NORTH CAROLINA DIVISION OF TOURISM, FILM AND SPORTS DEVELOPMENT

RECREATION

The sportfishing and surfing are legendary here. But visitors should use common sense while exploring the waters of the island, as the weather can change at a moment's notice. Riptides and strong currents can surprise even the hardiest swimmer.

■ For fishermen, the places to go include **Hatteras Island Fishing Pier** (252-987-2323; www.hatterasislandresort.com) in Rodanthe, **Avon Golf and Fishing Pier** (252-995-5480; www.avonpier.com/avonpierwebsite/ap.asp) in Avon, and **Cape Hatteras Fishing Pier** (252-986-2533) in Frisco.

All offer about the same features, including bait, tackle, ice, and snacks. They are open seasonally. You can also check out www.hatterashi.com/HatterasIslandBeachAccess.html to learn more about these piers and what's biting at each.

For those interested in Gulf Stream fishing, several marinas in Hatteras offer charter boats. These include **Hatteras Landing Marina** (800-551-8478 or 252-986-2077; www.hatteraslanding.com), **Hatteras Harbor Marina** (800-676-4939 or 252-986-2166; www.hatterasharbor.com), **Oden's Dock** (888-544-8115 or 252-986-2555; www.odensdock.com), and **Teach's Lair Marina** (888-868-2460 or 252-986-2460; www.teachslair.com).

■ Surfers, windsurfers, and kiteboarders can turn to **Hatteras Island Sail Shop** (252-987-2292; www.hiss-waves.com) in Waves, **Fox Watersports** (252-995-4372) in Buxton, and **Carolina Outdoors** (252-986-1446) in Hatteras. **Canadian Hole** in Pamlico Sound has been called "the Windsurfing Capital of the East Coast," thanks to its calm waters and steady breezes.

■ Golfers shouldn't despair about being on a long, thin scrap of land surrounded by hundreds of miles of sound and ocean. They can get their fix at **Ocean Edge Golf Course** (252-995-4100), located off N.C. 12 in Frisco.

Windsurfing on the Outer Banks
PHOTO BY BILL RUSS, COURTESY OF NORTH CAROLINA DIVISION OF TOURISM, FILM AND SPORTS DEVELOPMENT

This nine-hole, par-30 course is open year-round. More than 50 golfers have scored holes in one since the course opened a little more than a decade ago. Ocean Edge is a fun way to get in some tee time while enjoying unparalleled views.

■ **Pea Island National Wildlife Refuge**, at the northern tip of Hatteras Island, is known as a birder's paradise, as it is the feeding and resting area for more than 365 species of migratory birds. Established in 1937 by an act of Congress, the refuge covers 5,834 acres of Hatteras Island and 25,700 acres of Pamlico Sound. No migratory waterfowl hunting is allowed here, but visitors may canoe, kayak, surf, fish, meander the beaches, and participate in an interpretive program.

The name comes from the acres of "dune peas" that cover the refuge. These beans, packed with protein, are a good source of energy for the birds on their long flights. Birds spotted here include piping plovers, peregrine falcons, Canada and snow geese, tundra swans, herons, egrets, ibises, bald eagles, and over 25 species of ducks. Observation decks and nature trails enable visitors to view all the different winged visitors. Pea Island is also home to river otters, muskrats, rabbits, and raccoons. In addition, loggerhead turtles use the refuge as their northernmost nesting ground. The temperature at which the eggs incubate determines the sex of loggerheads; this northern nesting ground produces many members of the male loggerhead population.

The refuge's visitor center offers wildlife exhibits and a gift store; it is open daily from 9 A.M. to 5 P.M. in the summer and from 9 A.M. to 4 P.M. the rest of the year. The refuge is administered by Alligator River National Wildlife Refuge. Admission is free. For more information, call 252-473-1131 or visit http://peaisland.fws.gov.

■ **Buxton Woods Reserve** is a 1,725-acre maritime forest, the largest in North Carolina. It features interdune ponds, live oak and red cedar forests, and freshwater marshes that are home to a variety of water-loving plants, including ferns, saw grass, cattails, and wild rice. Over 135 species of migratory birds make this a stopping place on their long annual journeys. Visitors can enjoy a day of hiking, birding, and picnicking. For more information, call 252-995-4474 or visit http://nature.org/wherewework/northamerica/states/northcarolina/preserves/art5593.html.

Places to Stay

It used to be that the majority of hostelries on Hatteras Island were no-frills hotels and motels that catered to fishermen and those on a budget. Those places are still there, but as the area's popularity has surged, so have the options in accommodations. Now, road-weary travelers can choose from several bed-and-breakfasts and even a resort. Everyone visiting Hatteras Island should be able to find a place to suit his or her needs and tastes.

RESORTS, HOTELS, AND MOTELS

There's a dearth of chain hotels on Hatteras Island, which is pretty refreshing to discover anywhere along the coast. The only one you'll find is the **Comfort Inn—Hatteras Island** (800-432-1441 or 252-995-6100; www.comfortinn.com) in Buxton.

■ **Hatteras Landing**. Deluxe/Expensive. N.C. 12 next to the ferry landing in Hatteras (800-551-8478 or 252-986-2077; www.hatteraslanding.com). This resort offers 10 rooftop residences ranging in size from 1,400 to 2,200 square feet, ample room for a family to spread out. Guests will feel like they're staying in a home, thanks to the granite countertops, maple cabinets, and state-of-the-art appliances. The residences sit atop shops and restaurants. When not downstairs shopping or visiting the local bakery, guests can enjoy the large decks with nearly 360-degree views of the ocean and sound. The resort will assist with reservations for charter boats, scooters, bikes, and beach equipment.

■ **Avon Motel**. Moderate. N.C. 12 in Avon (252-995-5774; www.avonmotel.com). This ocean-side motel has been family owned and operated since 1954. Its 45 units include the basics, like air conditioning, phones, and televisions; some have fully equipped kitchens. A guest laundry and a lighted fish-cleaning station are available. The motel is open from March to December.

■ **Cape Hatteras Motel**. Moderate. N.C. 12 in Buxton (800-995-0711 or 252-995-5611; www.capehatterasmotel.com). Offering 11 rooms, two efficiencies, and 21 apartments, this motel has much to choose from. All rooms have a television, a microwave, a small refrigerator, and a coffee maker. Fully equipped kitchens and linens are provided in the efficiencies and apartments. All guests have access to a pool, a Jacuzzi, and a freezer for the day's catch. This motel is one of the closest accommodations to Canadian Hole and is only a 20-minute walk from the lighthouse. It is open year-round.

- **Hatteras Harbor Marina & Efficiencies**. Moderate. N.C. 12 at Hatteras Harbor Marina in Hatteras (800-676-4939 or 252-986-2565; www.hatterasharbor.com/efficiencies.html). This motel's five one-bedroom efficiencies are located on the second floor of the marina building, making this the perfect place for sincere fishermen. Some rooms can accommodate up to six people and offer full kitchens with linens and dishes. Each room has a balcony, from which guests can enjoy watching the boats come in and the sunset over the sound.

- **Lighthouse View Motel and Cottages**. Moderate. N.C. 12 in Buxton (800-225-7651 or 252-995-5680; www.lighthouseview.com). Guests here are located almost at the foot of the lighthouse. This large complex offers over 75 units ranging from single rooms to cottages and villas. The amenities include cable television, private porches and decks, washers and dryers, a pool, and a hot tub.

- **Sea Gull Motel**. Moderate. N.C. 12 in Hatteras (252-986-2550; www.seagullhatteras.com). This motel, located within a mile of Hatteras Fishing Center, offers 45 oceanfront apartments and efficiencies, all with televisions and phones and many with refrigerators and microwaves. A fish-cleaning area and outdoor showers are provided for fishermen. Kids love the outdoor pool and the private beach. The motel is open March through November.

INNS AND BED-AND-BREAKFASTS

- **The Inn on Pamlico Sound**. Deluxe/Expensive. N.C. 12 in Buxton (866-995-7030 or 252-995-7030; www.innonpamlicosound.com). The dozen suites in this lovely inn offer stunning views of the sound and the innkeepers' well-tended garden; many of the rooms are in fact named after the flowers found there. All suites offers king- or queen-sized beds, private baths, phones, TVs, and high-speed Internet connections. Many have whirlpool tubs as well. The innkeepers pride themselves on the sumptuous homemade three-course breakfasts served here, which include selections such as blueberry bread pudding and raspberry-stuffed French toast.

- **Cape Hatteras Bed-and-Breakfast.** Expensive/Moderate. Old Lighthouse Road in Buxton (800-252-3316 or 252-995-6004). The street address for this bed-and-breakfast lets you in on how close it is to the lighthouse. It is only 500 feet from the ocean as well. Its seven rooms and two suites include basic amenities like private baths and cable television. Guests can also take advantage of the inn's sun deck, surfboard and sailboard storage, bicycles, beach chairs, coolers, and beach bags. A hearty breakfast is served each morning. The inn is open from April to December.

Places to Eat

You'll discover a surprising number of restaurants on Hatteras Island. Most are located on the sound side and offer nice view of the water. You'll find everything here, from gourmet fare to a quick bite on the run. Most people are also surprised and pleased at the lack of chain eateries.

- **Austin Creek Grill.** Expensive/Moderate. N.C. 12 at Hatteras Landing (252-986-1511; www.hatteraslanding.com/austincreekgrill/index.cfm). This casual waterfront bistro, under the leadership of Ed Daggers, a Culinary Institute of America-trained chef, has quickly gained a reputation among locals and visitors for some of the best seafood, steaks, and pasta on Hatteras Island. Seasonal dishes include the delicious Parmesan-crusted Ocracoke flounder and scallops. Reservations are highly recommended. Afterward, be sure to check out the Austin Creek Baking Company next door for its to-die-for desserts and pastries. Dinner is served nightly.

- **The Breakwater Restaurant.** Expensive/Moderate. N.C. 12 at Oden's Dock in Hatteras (252-986-2733; www.thebreakwater.us). The second-story dining room, deck, and bar of this restaurant overlook Pamlico Sound and afford great views of the sunset and of boats on their way to dock for the evening. The specialties include seafood, prime rib, veal, and pasta. Just try not to fill up on the freshly baked bread and appetizers like Carolina shrimp with Cajun remoulade before the meal! Dinner is served Thursday through Saturday from March to December.

■ **The Dolphin Den**. Moderate. N.C. 12 in Avon (252-995-7717). If you're looking for good North Carolina seafood, this is an excellent place to try. From traditional fried seafood platters to soft-shell crab sandwiches, The Dolphin Den revels in its prime location by the ocean. Angus steaks, pasta, and burgers are offered as well. Lunch and dinner are served daily.

■ **The Froggy Dog Restaurant and Pub**. Moderate. N.C. 12 in Avon (252-995-5550; www.froggydog.com). This ultracasual restaurant is a good place to bring the kids for a relaxed meal. While the adults enjoy the restaurant's famous wings and peel-and-eat shrimp from the steamer menu, the kids can enjoy the toys and games at "Tadpole Corner." Breakfast, lunch and dinner are served daily.

■ **Harbor Seafood Deli**. Moderate. N.C. 12 in Hatteras (252-986-2552; www.hatterasharbor.com/deli.html). Located adjacent to Hatteras Harbor Marina, this eatery offers a menu heavy on seafood. Try the scallop burger or the shrimp pasta salad. The porch is a nice place to go in the afternoon to enjoy hand-dipped ice cream and to watch the boats come in. If you're a fisherman, you'll appreciate the deli's prepacked breakfasts and lunches for those all-day trips; call a day ahead to request what you want. Breakfast and lunch are served daily year-round.

A WELL-WEATHERED PAST

Excerpted from *Hatteras Journal* by Jan DeBlieu

Theodore Stockton Midgett was the son of a commercial fisherman. His wife, Ersie, a short, red-haired, and jovial woman, was the daughter of Efrica and Jethro Anderson Midgett, who ran a business delivering food and dry goods that they brought to the island by sailboat. At the time Stockton and Ersie built the white house, Hatteras Island was still little more than a sparsely vegetated bar of sand. There were no paved roads, no running water, no electricity, no dunes. Construction on the Oregon Inlet bridge was forty years away. With no reliable weather forecasting system, the island's residents stayed continually prepared for major blows. . . .

. . . When the Civilian Conservation Corps set up a base camp in Rodanthe to headquarter their dune-building project, Stockton realized the crews of men needed a source of food and supplies. In 1936 he built a general store just west of the white house. At first he intended to turn the store's operation over to his sons, Harold, Anderson, and Stockton, Jr. But the boys soon tired of staying inside to clerk and put up stock. Within two years the storekeeping had been delegated to Ersie, who was quick at figuring prices and balancing books.

Stockton had other plans for his sons. In the fall of 1938 he went to Baltimore and came back with a franchise for the island's first transportation system, a bus line from Hatteras village to Manteo. . . .

. . . Harold and Anderson were determined to start running their new business as soon as they could. To help drive their first "bus"—a brand-new Ford station wagon—they recruited their young brother, Stocky. Once a day the station wagon made its way from Hatteras village to a ferry at Oregon Inlet, then on to Manteo and back. "We called the route one-O-one—a hundred and one different ways," Stocky recalled. "At low tide we drove the beach. At high tide we drove the bank—the top of the beach, where the dunes are now—or the inside road, which consisted of several different tracks. There were always more people than we had room for; most of the time we'd put 'em on the running boards and in each other's laps, and sometimes on the hood. If we got stuck, which we often did, everybody got out and pushed."

The modern world had begun to discover Hatteras Island. In addition to the debut of public transportation, 1938 brought electricity to Hatteras village with the formation of a municipal cooperative. Electricity meant running water, indoor toilets, refrigeration. Slowly residents began to enjoy more luxuries and to have more contact with the outside world. Occasionally a hurricane or a strong wind blow would disrupt the island's development, but storms were accepted as sporadic, shortlived dangers, like tornados in the Midwest. In 1944 a major hurricane pushed eight feet of water through Rodanthe. As Ersie, Joyce, and Anderson sat in the wood-frame house, a sudden blast of wind twisted the structure and sent it sliding twelve feet off its foundation. When the eye passed overhead, the family rushed to the home of a relative—only to have that house picked up beneath them by a surge and floated fifty yards, tossing and lurching in the waves. The receding tide left the relative's house perched on top of Anderson's brand-new Ford.

And still the pace of progress quickened. In 1948 the electric cooperative extended its service to the north section of Hatteras Island, and the state paved the first portion of Highway 12, a twenty-mile stretch between Hatteras village and Avon. In 1952 the surfaced road reached the length of the island. Although easier to drive than the beach, it was frequently overwashed or covered with sand, and the Midgett brothers' vehicles continued to get stuck. One evening

as Stocky was driving back from Manteo in a school bus loaded with people, he suddenly found himself driving through water. "The sea had backed up right behind the dunes, and one of the dunes broke through," he says. "Water came rushing through like a funnel. I had on a pair of leather boots, so I climbed around on the fenders trying to get the hood up without getting my feet wet. By the time I dried off the engine, the front wheels of the bus had settled down through the highway. And before we could do anything else, the rear wheels fell through. The bus started settling down just like you'd put a casket in a grave."

Passengers piled out of the vehicle and climbed a dune while Stockton started north, walking and swimming toward the nearest Coast Guard station. An hour later when he returned with help, the bus had disappeared. "When the tide fell, the highest point of the bus was the left front corner. It was about eighteen inches above the surface of the road. I called my brother to tell him I'd lost the bus. He wanted to know if I'd been off drinking someplace."

Ocracoke Island Lighthouse
PHOTO BY BILL RUSS, COURTESY OF NORTH CAROLINA DIVISION OF
TOURISM, FILM AND SPORTS DEVELOPMENT

OCRACOKE ISLAND

The last of the barrier islands that make up the thin, long, wind-swept Outer Banks, Ocracoke has always been known for its seclusion. Over the centuries, it has been the haunt of wild ponies, pirates, and German U-boats. Tourism didn't develop on the island until after World War II; it was only then that electricity, telephone lines, and paved roads were installed here. Even today, the 16-mile-long island is accessible only by ferry or plane. This seclusion and the slow pace of life attract people looking to get away. Regulars have made Ocracoke their destination for vacations and retreats for generations.

Ocracoke village, the only town on the island, wraps around the beautiful Silver Lake. The island has only one major road; walking and biking are the ways most people get around.

You definitely don't want to miss a thing Ocracoke has to offer.

JUST THE FACTS

Ocracoke is accessible by water or air. A free ferry crosses from Hatteras Island to Ocracoke about every half-hour in the summer. No reservations are accepted; passengers cross on a first-come, first-served basis. Two ferries operate between Ocracoke and mainland North Carolina, one to the west from Swan Quarter in Hyde County and the other to the south from Cedar Island in Carteret County. Reservations are accepted for these ferries, and a fee is charged. For information on ferry schedules, fees, and crossing times, call 800-BY-FERRY or visit www.ncferry.org. For information on the Hatteras ferry, call 800-368-8949; for information on the Cedar Island ferry, call 800-856-0343; for information on the Swan Quarter ferry, call 800-773-1094. The toll-free number for the Ocracoke terminal is 800-345-1665.

The Greater Hyde County Chamber of Commerce on the mainland in Swan Quarter is a good source for information about Ocracoke; call 888-493-3826 or 252-926-9171 or visit www.hydecounty.org.

North Carolina ferry
PHOTO BY BILL RUSS, COURTESY OF NORTH CAROLINA DIVISION OF TOURISM, FILM AND SPORTS DEVELOPMENT

HISTORIC PLACES, GARDENS, AND TOURS

■ When many people think of Ocracoke, the **Ocracoke Lighthouse** comes to mind. Built in 1823, this lighthouse is the oldest in operation in North Carolina and the second-oldest in the United States. It's the shortest on the North Carolina coast, too, standing only 75 feet in height. Its beam penetrates 14 miles out to sea. The lighthouse was first given its distinctive whitewash in 1868; the wash was a brew of unslaked lime, a peck of salt, a half-pound of powdered Spanish whiting, three pounds of ground rice, a pound of glue, and enough boiling water to hold it all together. The builders of the lighthouse had the good sense to situate it on the highest point on the island, so it has been spared from flooding several times. When a hurricane in 1944 flooded many of the island's homes with as much as two and a half feet of water, the waves merely lapped at the

Ocracoke Lighthouse
PHOTO BY BILL RUSS, COURTESY OF
NORTH CAROLINA DIVISION OF
TOURISM, FILM AND SPORTS
DEVELOPMENT

lighthouse's doorstep. The lighthouse is now fully automated and is administered by the United States Coast Guard. Guests can tour the grounds, but the lighthouse is not open for climbing. For more information, visit www.nps.gov/caha/ocracokelh.htm.

■ Some people strolling Ocracoke are surprised to find a British flag flying here. The **British Cemetery**, located not far from Silver Lake, is a memorial to the men of the HMS *Bedfordshire*, a British antisubmarine ship that was torpedoed and sunk off Cape Lookout by a German U-boat in May 1942. All aboard perished. Four bodies washed ashore on Ocracoke and were given a burial befitting men serving their country and helping to protect the United States. The graveyard, surrounded by a white picket fence and maintained by the Coast Guard, contains concrete crosses with bronze plaques. One features the words of Rupert Brooke: "If I should die, think only this of me; / That there's some corner of a foreign field / That is for ever England."

■ Another British legacy on the island may be the **wild ponies of Ocracoke**. Legend has it that on at least one of Sir Walter Raleigh's expeditions to the New World, his colonists left ponies on Roanoke Island. The ponies spread throughout the Outer Banks, as the islands used to be connected by land bridges until various hurricanes and nor'easters shifted the sands and created channels. A second theory postulates that the ponies may be descended from mustangs that swam ashore from Spanish galleons that met their watery end in the Atlantic. In either case, hundreds of wild ponies roamed the Banks until the advent of development and tourism after World War II. In 1959, those on Ocracoke were corralled into a 180-acre pasture near the northern end of the island. The Boy Scouts took over the care of the ponies around that time, becoming the nation's only mounted troop. The National Park Service stepped in to care for the ponies in the early 1960s and continues in that role to this day. While viewing the ponies, you can conjecture for yourself whether they are descended from shipwreck survivors or Raleigh's brood. Visit www.nps.gov/caha/oc_ponies.htm for more information.

MUSEUMS AND SCIENCE CENTERS

■ Though Ocracoke isn't large, it is steeped in history and legend. The Native Americans of the area called the island Wokokon. Legend has it that the infamous Edward Teach, better known as the pirate Blackbeard, renamed the island on his final night. Anxious to do battle against the British who were trying to capture him, he cried out, "O Crow Cock!" during the night, beckoning the morning to appear. You can find out the complete history of the island at the **Ocracoke Visitor Center**, located in Ocracoke village by Silver Lake. The entire village was placed on the National Register of Historic Places in July 1990. The visitor center offers exhibits detailing the important events in the island's history. The National Park Service administers the site. Rangers are on hand to answer questions and to guide you to good books in the book shop. The center is open year-round from 9 A.M. to 5 P.M. except Christmas Day; longer hours are offered in the summer. To contact the visitor center for information on Ocracoke, including docking fees, call 252-928-4531 or visit www.nps.gov/caha/pphtml/facilities.html.

■ Another excellent resource for information on the island's history is the **Ocracoke Preservation Society Museum**, located near the ferry docks off N.C. 12. The society is dedicated to honoring Ocracoke's unique cultural, environmental, and architectural history. It was instrumental in getting many of the area's homes and businesses recognized by the National Register of Historic Places. The society opened its museum in 1992 in the circa-1900 Captain David Williams House, home to the island's first Coast Guard station chief. During the summer, the society hosts art shows and museum porch talks on the village's history. Admission is free. For more information, call 252-928-7375 or visit www.ocracokemuseum.org.

SPECIAL SHOPPING

Ocracoke offers a number of distinctive shops where visitors can find anything from the basic necessities to memorabilia and souvenirs to commemorate their trip.

■ **Deepwater Pottery**, at the corner of N.C. 12 and School Road, offers pottery, hand-blown glass, candles, and jewelry, much of it either by local artisans or certified by the Fair Trade Federation. It is housed in a historic home set amid a grove of live oaks and cedars, so the exterior is as charming as what you'll find inside. For information, call 888-625-7556 or visit www.deepwaterpottery.com.

- Next door to Deepwater Pottery is **Books to be Red**, an excellent bookstore offering new and used books ranging from local history to the latest fiction. Call 252-928-3936 for more information.

- The **Ocracoke Variety Store**, on N.C. 12, offers exactly what its name implies—a variety of everything. You'll find grocery items, T-shirts, tools, postcards, and just about anything in between. Call 252-928-4911.

- Not to be missed is **Teach's Hole**, on Back Road. This is a self-proclaimed "Blackbeard Exhibit and Pirate Specialty Shop." A short film tells shoppers about Blackbeard's connection to the island, his supposed haunts, and how he met his bloody end. History buffs will enjoy the displays of weapons, bottles, maps, coins, and flags of Blackbeard's day. There are over 1,000 pirate-related items visitors can take home, including books, maps, music, and even pirate party supplies. Call 252-928-1718 or visit www.teachshole.com.

RECREATION

- One of the best ways to take in the natural bounty of Ocracoke is through the kayak ecotours offered by **Ride the Wind Surf & Kayak**. Several tours are available, including a sunrise tour, a sunset tour, and a full-moon tour. Be sure to bring bug spray so the pests won't enjoy the tour more than you do. Surf camps for kids are offered as well. Call 252-928-6311 or visit www.surfocracoke.com for more information.

- Fishermen will want to make **Anchorage Marina** one of their first stops. Only 18 miles from the Gulf Stream, this marina is one of the closest jumping-off places for those in search of yellowfin tuna, wahoo, amberjack, and bluefish. The marina offers charter boats, dockage, gas and diesel, water and power hookups, showers, and even bikes for touring the island. A café on the premises sells drinks, lunches, and fishing supplies. Call 252-928-6661 or visit www.theanchorageinn.com/marina.htm for more information.

SEASONAL EVENTS

- The annual **Ocrafolk Music and Storytelling Festival**, held in early

June along School Road, features a variety of local artists and performers sharing their talents and wares. The festival includes a cookoff, a parade, a fund-raising auction, and boat-building demonstrations. Admission is free. For more information, visit www.ocrafolkfestival.org.

■ Those who can't make it to town for the festival should visit **Deepwater Theater**, located on School Road off N.C. 12. During the summer, the theater is home to Molasses Creek (a local bluegrass band of national acclaim), the Ocrafolk Opry, and several other performing artists. General-admission tickets are sold 30 minutes prior to show time; show times vary, so call ahead. For information, call 252-928-4280 or visit www.molassescreek.com.

Places to Stay

Many Ocracoke regulars have a certain hotel or bed-and-breakfast that they come back to time and again. You're sure to find your favorite spot, too. Be sure to book early, since lots of new "regulars" discover Ocracoke each season.

RESORTS, HOTELS, AND MOTELS

■ *Captain's Landing*. Deluxe/Expensive. N.C. 12 (252-928-1999; www.thecaptainslanding.com). This luxury hotel was named to honor the many captains in the proprietors' families, including hometown hero Horatio Williams, a noted sailor who evaded the Yankees during the Civil War. The hotel's comfortable waterfront suites overlook Silver Lake and feature queen beds, full kitchens, and private decks. The top-of-the-line penthouse offers a master suite, a guest room, a gourmet kitchen, and a laundry room. And if neither of these options suits you, you can go for the Captain's Cottage for the ultimate in private, spacious relaxation—two bedrooms with private bathrooms, a full kitchen, a living room, a dining room, and a private patio.

■ **Blackbeard's Lodge.** Expensive/Moderate. 111 Back Road (800-892-5314 or 252-928-3421; www.blackbeardslodge.com). The family of a friend of mine has made Blackbeard's Lodge its regular place to stay. It could be the friendly staff, the second-story sun deck, or the front desk made of a ship's prow. The lodge, which has been around since 1936 and touts itself as the island's oldest hotel, offers 38 rooms and apartments. Guests may choose from a variety of rooms, some of which have full kitchens and whirlpool tubs. Kids can enjoy the heated pool and the game room. The hotel is open January through November.

■ **Anchorage Inn.** Moderate. N.C. 12 (252-928-1101; www.theanchorageinn.com/inn.htm). The Anchorage Inn has five floors with 35 rooms and suites, many offering excellent views of the ocean and sound. The suites have full kitchens and private decks. A café, a pool, and grills are among the popular features here. Because of its proximity to the marina, guests can charter boats from the inn.

INNS AND BED-AND-BREAKFASTS

■ **Ocracoke Harbor Inn.** Deluxe. 144 Silver Lake Road (888-456-1998 or 252-928-5731; www.ocracokeharborinn.com). Overlooking Silver Lake, the

Ocracoke Island
COURTESY OF NORTH CAROLINA DIVISION OF TOURISM, FILM AND SPORTS DEVELOPMENT

Ocracoke Harbor Inn offers 16 rooms and seven suites, most of which feature a private porch that provides a stunning view of the village and the harbor. All rooms and suites have televisions, telephones with modem ports, coffee makers, and refrigerators; the suites include kitchenettes and Jacuzzis. Guests can enjoy the luxury of strolling to dinner or biking to nearby shops. The inn is open year-round.

■ **Castle Bed-and-Breakfast and Courtyard Villas**. Deluxe/Expensive. On Silver Lake (800-471-8848 or 252-928-3505; www.thecastlebb.com). This bed-and-breakfast offers two types of accommodations. Those looking for traditional lodging will like the 11 guest rooms, which have paneled walls, big, comfy beds, and private baths. Those looking for more spacious digs can enjoy one of the 22 studio suites, which offer fully equipped kitchens and washers and dryers. Treats for all guests include a masseuse, a heated pool, and a sauna. Outdoor lovers will appreciate the on-site marina and the complimentary bicycles.

■ **The Cove Bed-and-Breakfast**. Deluxe/Expensive. 21 Loop Road (252-928-4192; www.thecovebb.com). Nestled near the foot of the lighthouse, this charming establishment features four guest rooms and two suites, each with queen-sized beds and private baths and balconies. The great views of the sound will surely inspire guests to lounge on the wraparound porch after breakfast or to borrow one of the inn's bicycles. Continental breakfast and an evening wine reception are offered. The Cove is open year-round.

■ **Pelican Lodge**. Expensive/Moderate. 1021 Irvin Garrish Highway (888-7-PELICAN or 252-928-1661; www.bbonline.com/nc/pelican). This rustic-looking lodge, split into Pelican Lodge East and Pelican Lodge West, prides itself on its attention to guests' special needs and desires. A registered dietitian supervises the lodge's breakfast. A car-rental service and the lodge's own air service, Pelican Airways, provide transportation; aerial sightseeing tours are available. The five guest rooms have private baths and cable television. Complimentary bicycles are available if you'd like to explore the island. The lodge is open year-round.

■ **Thurston House Inn**. Expensive/Moderate. N.C. 12 (252-928-6037; www.thurstonhouseinn.com). The Thurston House Inn was built in the 1920s by Captain Tony Thurston Gaskill and is now operated by his granddaughter. It offers six guest rooms and a cottage, all with private baths and televisions; some rooms have private decks and entrances. An expanded continental breakfast greets guests before the day's activities, all of which are easily accessible from the inn's large, breezy front porch. The inn is open March through mid-December.

Places to Eat

You really can't go wrong with any of the eateries on Ocracoke Island, so be adventurous and try a new one each opportunity you get. The variety—fresh-off-the-boat seafood, good old meat and potatoes, Italian, gourmet, casual—is enough to satisfy any palate. As with every place on the Outer Banks, hours are seasonal, so it's best to call ahead to make sure your restaurant of choice is serving.

■ *The Back Porch*. Moderate. 110 Back Road (252-928-6401). This restaurant prides itself on being out of the way on the already out-of-the-way Ocracoke. Secluded from N.C. 12 by trees and cacti, The Back Porch does indeed feature a lovely back porch where you can enjoy your dinner. Or you can select the indoor dining room. You can taste from the first bite that all the sauces, condiments, and breads are made on-site. Freshly ground coffee and homemade desserts round out the evening. If you'd like to try your hand at any of The Back Porch's unique dishes, a cookbook is available at the hostesses' station. Dinner is served seven nights a week in season.

■ *Creekside Café*. Moderate. N.C. 12 (252-928-3606; www.ocracokeisland.com/creekside_cafe.htm). Creekside Café, overlooking Silver Lake, is a nice place to take a rest from your island explorations and get a cool drink and a bite to eat. Light fare like soups, salads, and sandwiches is offered. The truly hungry can choose from the seafood and burger selections. Try to get a seat on the porch to enjoy the breeze and the great view. Lunch and dinner are served daily.

■ *Howard's Pub and Raw Bar*. Moderate. N.C. 12 (252-928-4441; www.howardspub.com). Open 365 days a year, this is a popular hangout for locals and visitors alike. The only raw bar on the island, Howard's features more than 200 imported, domestic, and microbrew beers. So it follows that it's famous for things like the spicy "Ocracoke Oyster Shooter."

The dishes most in demand include steaks, barbecued ribs, blackened tuna, and marinated mahi-mahi. The hand-shaped half-pound burgers, the hand-cut fries, the homemade salsa, the chili, the chowder, and the desserts are popular, too. The screened-in porch invites you to sit back and relax—and to see if you can spot Portsmouth Island from your lounge chair.

- **Island Inn Restaurant.** Moderate. At the Island Inn on Lighthouse Road (877-456-3466 or 252-928-4351; www.ocracokeislandinn.com/dining.htm). You don't have to be a guest of the Island Inn to enjoy this appealing restaurant; you just have to be hungry for a great meal. One of the oldest restaurants on Ocracoke, it serves meals on china like you'd find at Grandma's house. The cooking here, though, is definitely not Grandma's, unless she serves shrimp and oysters in the morning. And you won't be disappointed by the homemade fish cakes or the paella. Guests who would like to take a part of their dining experience home with them can purchase Chardonnay bottled specially for the restaurant. Breakfast and dinner are served daily.

Nearby

- **Lake Mattamuskeet**, located on the Hyde County mainland, is accessible from Ocracoke via the Swan Quarter ferry. This is the largest natural lake in North Carolina, covering more than 40,000 acres and stretching for 18 miles at a width of five to six miles. But the water is surprisingly shallow, averaging a depth of only two feet. The massive lake is a bird watcher's paradise; thousands of tundra swans winter here every year.

It comes as a surprise to some that Lake Mattamuskeet has not always been here. *Mattamuskeet* is, in fact, Algonquian for "dry dust." Some conjecture that the lake came into existence only when wildfires burned deep into the peat soil, transforming the flat, dry land into a lake bed.

A group of investors tried to drain the lake in 1914. They renamed the area New Holland, after similar drainage projects in Holland. A network of canals, a model community, and the largest pumping station in the world—capable of pumping 1.2 million gallons of water a minute—were built. When investors discovered that the project was too expensive, however, they abandoned New Holland.

The United States government bought the lake in 1934 and established

Mattamuskeet National Wildlife Refuge. The pumping station was converted into a lodge, and the nearby smokestack was transformed into a 100-foot-tall observation tower. The lodge closed in 1974 and was added to the National Register of Historic Places in 1980.

Today's visitors to Lake Mattamuskeet and Mattamuskeet National Wildlife Refuge enjoy crabbing, fishing, bird-watching, and hunting. The refuge is open during daylight hours year-round with the exception of federal holidays. For more information, call 252-926-4021 or visit http://mattamuskeet.fws.gov.

■ A significant wildlife sanctuary located just south of Lake Mattamuskeet is the **Swan Quarter National Wildlife Refuge**. Those taking the toll ferry between Ocracoke Island and Swan Quarter will travel through the refuge and get a unique view of the area's natural beauty. The refuge, created in 1932, covers more than 8,800 acres of salt-marsh islands and forested wetlands. Like Lake Mattamuskeet, it is a vital wintering and breeding ground for many waterfowl, including ospreys and canvasback and black ducks. Many visitors come to the refuge to fish from the 1,000-foot-long Bell Island Pier. Boating, hunting, and hiking are permitted as well. The refuge is open year-round during daylight hours with the exception of federal holidays. Call 252-926-4021 or visit www.fws.gov/swanquarter for more information.

THE BATTLE OF OCRACOKE INLET

Excerpted from *Blackbeard the Pirate:
A Reappraisal of His Life and Times* by Robert E. Lee

Lieutenant Maynard, during the early gray light before sunrise on Friday, November 22 [1718], ordered the anchors weighed and headed for what in later years became known as "Teach's Hole." Off the tip of Ocracoke Island, and before passing into the sound waters, men in a rowboat were lowered with instructions to proceed ahead of the sloops and take soundings. Maynard did not care to run the risk of being grounded on a shoal, so the men in the rowboat signaled the course to be followed. Upon coming into firing range of the *Adventure*, the men in the rowboat were greeted with a round of shot and immediately "scurried back to the protection of the sloops". . .

Blackbeard roared rudely across the water: "Damn you for villains, who are you? And from whence come you?"

"You may see by our colors

we are no pirates," answered Maynard.

"Send your boat on board so that I might see who you are," demanded Blackbeard.

"I cannot spare my boat, but I will come aboard you as soon as I can with my sloop," replied Maynard.

Seeing that they intended to board by storm, Blackbeard took up a bowl of liquor; and calling out to the officers of the other sloops, drank to them with these words: "Damnation seize my soul if I give you quarter or take any from you."

In reply to this, Maynard yelled back, "I expect no quarter from you, nor shall I give any."

For the moment, the fortunes of war were in Blackbeard's favor. The two royal sloops had crunched the sands of the submerged bar and their crews set to working feverishly to dislodge them. The rising tide would shortly set them afloat again. Blackbeard acted with dispatch, ordering Philip Morton, his gunner, to train the eight cannons of the *Adventure* towards the attackers in a general broadside. . . .

. . . With a single broadside from his eight cannons, Blackbeard had reduced the attacking force to half its original size. . . .

At this juncture Maynard came up with a typical trick of sea warfare. He ordered all his men below deck, their pistols and swords ready for close fighting, to remain in the hold until he gave

the signal. . . . Maynard's strategy was to ensnare the pirates into doing the fighting aboard his own ship. Maynard himself went into the cabin, ordering the midshipman at the helm and William Butler, the pilot, to inform him of anything that happened.

Blackbeard, seeing Maynard's sloop approaching, alerted his men to prepare to board, with grappling irons and weapons ready for instant use. In addition, he had a lethal surprise which he intended to introduce to His Majesty's Royal Navy—hand grenades: in this case, bottles filled with powder, small shot, and pieces of iron and lead and ignited by fuses worked into the center of the bottle. Captain Teach's own invention, it had served him well during numerous pirate attacks, the resulting explosion invariably creating pandemonium on deck.

Most of the light grenades landed on the deck of Maynard's sloop, exploding resoundingly and rendering the sloop almost invisible in the enveloping smoke. Since most of the men were below deck, the grenades this time failed to achieve their effect. The royal sloop continued to drift forward. Seeing through the smoke only a few or no hands aboard, Blackbeard jubilantly shouted to his crew: "They were all knocked on the head but three or four. Blast you—board her and cut them to pieces!"

Maynard's sloop bumped against the side of Blackbeard's sloop. . . . Teach was the first aboard. . . . According to Maynard's version, ten pirates followed their leader and scrambled aboard, howling and firing at anything that moved. Maynard's men in the hold burst out, shouting and shooting.

The effect of the men pouring out of the hold was as shocking as Maynard had calculated. Everything was in confusion. The pirates were taken aback. Blackbeard instantly saw what was happening. Like the leader he was, he paused to rally and inspire his men.

The blood of the twenty British seamen wounded or killed by the terrific broadside had slickened the deck. The bodies of the dead were still there. Additional blood was to flow from the butchery and the savage melee that was to follow—the bloodiest battle ever fought on the deck of a small craft. . . .

Blackbeard waded into the melee, swinging his great cutlass. It was a wild windmill attack that no one in front of him could repel with a blade. He had to be stopped by a pistol shot or by someone from the rear. Both methods were tried. Blackbeard from time to time supplemented his blade swinging with a pistol snatched from the bandolier of pistols across his chest. These were single-shot pistols, thrown aside after being used.

An heroic touch was given to the battle by the ferocious confrontation of Maynard and Blackbeard—the champion of law and order and the champion of piracy—face to face. In this epic struggle, one or the other had to be annihilated. . . .

In the heat of combat they engaged each other with swords. A powerful blow of Blackbeard's cutlass snapped off Maynard's sword blade near its hilt. A blow of such terrific force would ordinarily have knocked the sword flying, but apparently Maynard was holding it with a frenzied grasp. Hurling the hilt at his adversary, Maynard stepped back to cock his pistol, and at the same instant Blackbeard moved in for the finishing blow with his cutlass. But at the moment in which he swung his cutlass aloft, a British seaman approached Blackbeard from the rear and "gave him a terrific wound in the neck and throat." The cutlass, raised for the finishing blow, swerved as it came down, merely grazing the knuckles of Maynard, cutting them slightly.

The blood spurted from Blackbeard's gashed neck. He staggered, but fought on. Shouting defiance, he continued to swing the heavy cutlass about him. The bullet and sword wounds which he had sustained were, however, weakening him. Others saw that he was approaching his end. The British seamen, who had kept clear of him until now, closed in for the kill. They ducked in behind him to stab him with their swords. "At length, as he was cocking another pistol, having fired several before, he fell down dead." Edward Teach died a violent death, but was in the heat of battle, as he would have wished, still fighting as he fell with the insensate rage of a mortally wounded lion.

Lieutenant Maynard afterwards conducted an informal autopsy, to discover that his opponent had fallen with five pistol shots in him and no less than twenty severe cuts in various parts of his body. Maynard unquestionably recognized Blackbeard as a man superior to others in talent, in courage, and, moreover, in physical strength. . . .

Maynard ordered Blackbeard's head severed from his body and suspended from the bowsprit of Maynard's sloop. The rest of Blackbeard's corpse was thrown overboard. According to legend, when the headless body hit the cold water it defiantly swam around the sloop several times before it sank.

Ocracoke at sunset
PHOTO BY BILL RUSS, COURTESY OF NORTH CAROLINA DIVISION OF TOURISM, FILM AND SPORTS DEVELOPMENT

The Coastal Plain

Albemarle Region

Elizabeth City
Edenton
Bath

Neuse River Region

New Bern
Morehead City
Beaufort
Bogue Banks

Cape Fear Coast

Topsail Island
Wilmington
Wrightsville Beach
Pleasure Island
Southport and the Brunswick Islands

By Sunny Smith Nelson and Angela Harwood

S preading out across the eastern third of the state is North Carolina's vast coastal plain.

Inland are small river towns known for their manufacturing—and, more importantly, their barbecue—and countless farming communities that produce the majority of the state's agricultural products, as well as a politician or two. Much like the Mississippi Delta, the flat landscape can be monotonous, but a closer look reveals lush, fertile fields that yield such crops as tobacco, corn, and peanuts.

Along the coast, a series of seven sounds gives North Carolina one of the longest shorelines in the United States. Dotting it are what are quite possibly the state's most beautiful, historic, and fascinating destinations.

In the north, the region surrounding Albemarle Sound is home to the state's oldest towns, Edenton and Bath, as well as one of the area's most vibrant communities, Elizabeth City. Also here is the Great Dismal Swamp, the continent's only live peat bog.

In the coastal plain's midsection, the Neuse River region encompasses some of the state's premier beaches, collectively called the Crystal Coast, as well as picturesque fishing and sailing villages such as Beaufort and Oriental. Pirates were fond of the protected coves within the enormous Pamlico Sound, and legends of their antics abound. At the North Carolina Maritime Museum in Beaufort, artifacts from Blackbeard's ship, the *Queen Anne's Revenge*, are on display. Upriver, along the banks of the Neuse River, historic New Bern and its impeccably reconstructed governor's mansion, Tryon Palace, should not be missed.

Farther south, the Cape Fear River region and its crown jewel, Wilmington, are among the state's fastest-growing areas. Among those drawn to this fair metropolis are filmmakers, who since the 1980s have given the city the distinction of being "the Hollywood of the East." A visit to the area is not complete without a stop at the sparkling sands of Topsail Island, Pleasure Island, and the legendary Wrightsville Beach. South of Wilmington, the hamlet of Southport and the pristine Brunswick County beaches round out the lower Cape Fear region. As the midway point along the bustling Intracoastal Waterway, Southport is a port of call for all manner of pleasure boats. If golf is your game, you'll be pleased to learn that there are over 35 public courses in the vicinity. Or if your idea of a vacation is lounging on an uncrowded beach all day, then enjoy a sumptuous meal of fresh Calabash-style seafood and head for Oak Island, Holden Beach, or Sunset Beach.

Elizabeth City's historic downtown waterfront
PHOTO BY BILL RUSS, COURTESY OF NORTH CAROLINA DIVISION OF TOURISM, FILM AND SPORTS DEVELOPMENT

ALBEMARLE REGION

By Sunny Smith Nelson

While attending the University of North Carolina at Chapel Hill, I met people from all over the state. I found that some of the students most proud of where they came from were those from the Albemarle region. From them, I learned that Albemarle Sound is the largest freshwater sound in the United States; that Washington, North Carolina, is the "original" Washington; and that the state's oldest communities, including North Carolina's very first town, are located here. In the Albemarle region, you'll find historic sites maintained by the Colonial Dames of America. Unlike other Southerners, when these ladies speak of "the war," they're referring to the Revolutionary War, not the Civil War. History and heritage are a large part of the culture of the Albemarle region, and the extraordinarily gracious people of the area are happy to share them with you.

Another thing I associate with the area is wild naturalness. When I was a child, my father would look forward to the crisp fall days when he and a group of his buddies would go to their patch of swampy woodland outside Windsor in Bertie County to hunt. He would come back and tell my brothers and me about the clear, cold nights sitting alone in his tree stand, where stars covering the skies were his only companions and the silence was so great he could almost hear them twinkling. Once I visited the area on my own, I saw what he was talking about. Passing along tar-patched, winding country roads by gum-tree swamps, old tobacco barns falling in on themselves, and fields of corn that went on forever showed me that there are still parts of the world that "progress" hasn't visited, and that leaving land as untamed as your great-grandfather knew it is far better than putting a mini-mart at every crossroads. The people of the Albemarle know that the beauty of the woods and swamps is easily superior to anything we could replace it with.

If you visit the Albemarle region, remember to soak up the stories and family histories you're sure to hear from the proud residents. And be sure to enjoy the trip to your destination as much as you expect to love the final stop.

ELIZABETH CITY

A self-proclaimed "Main Street Waterfront Community," Elizabeth City sits on the banks of the Pasquotank River, whose Indian name means "Where the Current of the Stream Divides." Water played a major role in the development of Elizabeth City. The area was first explored and navigated in the late 1500s. Settlements started appearing along the river the following century, and Elizabeth City was settled in the 1650s. The Dismal Swamp Canal, the oldest canal still in operation in the United States, brought the likes of George Washington and Patrick Henry to Pasquotank County in the 18th century to survey for rich farmland and good hunting and fishing. Planters used the port to trade with the East Indies. During the Civil War, the Union army captured Elizabeth City and used it as a port.

Though not the important trading center it used to be, Elizabeth City is now home to the largest Coast Guard command complex in the lower 48 states. The Pasquotank River serves as an alternate route to the Intracoastal Waterway between Chesapeake Bay and Albemarle Sound. Elizabeth City takes great pride in this nautical heritage. Most of its cultural activities are centered around the river. Here, you'll find Southern hospitality in its highest form. For example, boats are given free dockage for two days at Mariners' Wharf; members of a volunteer group, the Rose Buddies, greet each disembarking newcomer with a rose and an invitation to a wine-and-cheese party. The town boasts museums, galleries, parks, and six historic districts listed on the National Register. It's no wonder that Elizabeth City was named in Norm Crampton's *The 100 Best Small Towns in America*.

JUST THE FACTS

Elizabeth City is accessible by land, water, and air.

U.S. 17 leads into town from the north and south. U.S. 158 leads into town from the west.

The Intracoastal Waterway and the Pasquotank River give access to the city's docks, which offer free dockage for 48 hours.

The nearest large commercial airport is 50 miles to the north in Norfolk, Virginia. The Elizabeth City-Pasquotank County Regional Airport, at 1028 Consolidated Road, shares runways with the Coast Guard, so it can accommodate aircraft as large as private jets and Boeing 747s, should you happen to have one. For information, call 252-335-5634 or visit www.ecgairport.com.

The Trailways bus station is at 118 Hughes Boulevard. Call 252-335-0887 or visit www.trailways.com for information.

The Elizabeth City Area Convention and Visitors Bureau, at 400 South Water Street, is a great resource for learning about the area. For information, call 252-335-5330 or visit www.discoverec.org. You also can learn more about the businesses in the area through the Elizabeth City Chamber of Commerce, at 502 East Ehringhaus Street. Call 252-335-4356 or visit www.elizabethcitychamber.org.

Things to Do

HISTORIC PLACES, GARDENS, AND TOURS

The best way to begin your sightseeing is to stop by the Elizabeth City Area Convention and Visitors Bureau to pick up a self-guided tour brochure.

■ One of the most popular tours covers the **Elizabeth City commercial district** on Main Street. The commercial district sites let you see what eastern North Carolina downtowns looked liked before the Civil War. This area includes the largest number of brick antebellum commercial buildings in the state. Restaurants, antique shops, galleries, and boutiques perfect for browsing occupy the storefronts today. Elizabeth City is also home to six historic districts on the National Register, so you can spend an enjoyable hour or two casually wandering the charming downtown neighborhoods admiring the architecture and lovely gardens. You'll likely notice many songbirds along the way, since the city is a recognized bird sanctuary.

■ Listed on the National Register of Historic Places are the **Episcopal Cemetery** and **Christ Episcopal Church**, at 200 South McMorrine Street. The graves in the Episcopal Cemetery date back to 1724. Many of eastern North Carolina's most prominent citizens have been laid to rest here, including John C. B. Ehringhaus, governor of North Carolina from 1933 to 1937. In the southeastern corner of the cemetery is a plot containing the remains of at least four unknown Confederate soldiers. The church was completed in 1857, during the ministry of the Reverend Edward M. Forbes, a well-known local Civil War hero. According to legend, he met the invading troops on the bank of the river and asked them to spare the town. Since he was a man of God, his request was honored. The church's 18 large stained-glass windows, added in 1947, depict the life of Christ. In addition to visiting the cemetery, which is open year-round during daylight hours, be sure to visit the lovely memorial garden located between the church and the parish house. Admission is free for both the cemetery and the church, though donations are accepted. Call 252-338-3020 or visit www.christchurch-ecity.org for more information.

Museums and Science Centers

- The *Museum of the Albemarle*, at 501 South Water Street, is a regional branch of the North Carolina Museum of History. The 50,000-square-foot museum explores the history of the Albemarle region through exhibits chronicling the work, culture, and folklore of the area over the past 400 years. Included are Native American artifacts, antique duck decoys, hand-carved boats, lumber-camp supplies, and early-20th-century farm equipment. The museum is open Tuesday through Saturday from 9 A.M. to 5 P.M. and Sunday from 2 P.M. to 5 P.M.; it is closed state holidays. Admission is free. For more information, call 252-335-1453 or visit www.museumofthealbemarle.com.

- The *Elizabeth City State University Planetarium*, at the Jenkins Science Building off Hoffler Street, is open Monday through Friday from 8 A.M. to 5 P.M. year-round for those who wish to learn about space exploration and astronomy. Admission is free, though advance reservations are required. Call 252-335-3759 or visit www.ecsuplanetarium.org for more information. One of the 16 campuses in the University of North Carolina system, Elizabeth City State was established in 1891 as a two-year institution serving African-American students. By 1937, the school had grown into a four-year teachers' college. It still concentrates on turning out some of the state's best teachers.

Special Shopping

- The *Pasquotank Arts Council Gallery*, at 609 East Main Street, provides opportunities to view and purchase local artwork from more than 175 artists. The gallery is open Monday through Saturday from 10 A.M. to 5 P.M. with extended hours on Thursdays. Admission is free. For more information, call 252-338-6445 or visit www.pasquotankarts.org.

Recreation

Elizabeth City boasts an impressive list of activities and recreational opportunities. The town's parks are a nice place to spend a lazy afternoon.

Elizabeth City's downtown waterfront
PHOTO BY BILL RUSS, COURTESY OF NORTH CAROLINA DIVISION OF TOURISM,
FILM AND SPORTS DEVELOPMENT

■ ***Fun Junktion***, at 983 Simpson Ditch Road, is a 133-acre park built on land that was originally slated for landfill expansion. Once the county leaders decided to use it for purposes other than garbage, they came up with plans for an area that would bring people together and provide them with opportunities for relaxation and—as the name says—fun. Visitors to the park will find a handicapped-accessible playground, basketball courts, picnic areas, walking and biking trails, a skateboard park, and an 18-hole golf course. If being in the water is more your idea of fun, there are several lakes, including a catch-and-release fishing pond, a man-made swimming lake, and a 20-acre competition skiing lake. Canoe and paddleboat rentals are available. Admission is free. Call 252-337-6600 or visit www.co.pasquotank.nc.us/departments/park/funjunktion1.htm for more information.

■ The parks of Elizabeth City, including ***Waterfront Park, Moth Boat Park***, and ***Dog Corner Park***, provide visitors with great views of the Pasquotank River and chances to fish, boat, grill, play volleyball, or just fall asleep while reading a good book. Admission is free to all parks. For more information, call 252-335-1424.

SEASONAL EVENTS

Just as you'd expect, the festivals and celebrations in Elizabeth City center around the river.

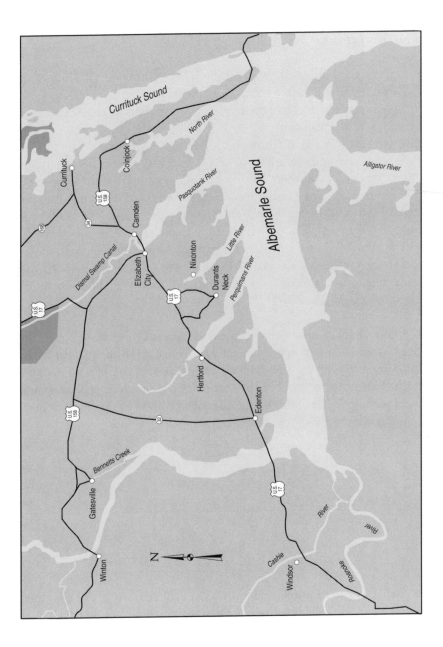

Currituck Sound

North River

Pasquotank River

Alligator River

Little River

Albemarle Sound

Currituck

Coinjock

U.S. 158

168

34

Camden

Dismal Swamp Canal

Nixonton

Perquimans River

Durants Neck

Elizabeth City

U.S. 17

U.S. 17

Hertford

Edenton

U.S. 158

32

Bennetts Creek

Gatesville

U.S. 17

River

River

Winton

N

Cashie

Windsor

Roanoke

■ *Elizabeth City Harbor Nights*, held on the waterfront the first Fridays in June, July, and August, feature live music, children's activities, and vendors selling homemade crafts and foods. The Harbor Nights are sponsored by the Pasquotank Arts Council. Call 252-338-6455 or visit www.pasquotankarts.org/Harbornights.html for more information.

■ Perhaps the biggest draw in Elizabeth City is the annual *Moth Boat Regatta*, sponsored by the Museum of the Albemarle the third weekend in September. The regatta honors the tiny moth boat, a one-person sailboat created in Pasquotank County in 1929. As the story goes, Captain Joel Van Sant stopped in Elizabeth City on his way from Atlantic City to Florida to have some work done on his yacht, the *Siesta*. He met with Ernest Sanders of Elizabeth City to design a boat that could be raced on rivers and lakes. They came up with the moth boat, named because it looks like a quick-winged moth floating over the water. The moth boat quickly caught on because of its great speed and relative inexpensiveness. The regatta celebrates this heritage of boat racing and Elizabeth City's role in the creation of the boat. Visitors to the festival can enjoy harbor tours, live music, an arts festival, and lots of food and crafts. For more information, call 252-335-1453.

■ In late October, near Halloween, the Elizabeth City Historic Neighborhood Association sponsors the annual *Elizabeth City Historic Ghost Walk*. In addition to enjoying an insider's tour of several beautiful homes, you'll learn some of the colorful history behind the ghoulish figures who can't quite seem to let go of this town. All proceeds go to further historic preservation efforts. For more information, call 888-936-7387.

Places to Stay

RESORTS, HOTELS, AND MOTELS

■ The majority of hotels and motels in Elizabeth City are of the chain variety and are located either on Halstead Boulevard or South Hughes Boulevard. They include *Hampton Inn* (800-HAMPTON or 252-333-1800; www.hamptoninn.com), *Quality Inn* (252-338-3951;

www.qualityinn.com), *Holiday Inn Express* (252-338-8900; www.hixpress.com), and *Days Inn* (252-335-4316; www.daysinn.com).

INNS AND BED-AND-BREAKFASTS

■ *Pond House Inn*. Deluxe/Expensive. 915 Rivershore Road (888-335-9834 or 252-335-9834; www.thepondhouseinn.com). As this inn's name suggests, it is surrounded by water, with the Pasquotank River and Waters Pond gently lapping along its six acres. The bucolic environment is a fitting backdrop to the stunning 1941 manor house, which features a winding staircase, a cozy library, and a sunroom. The inn offers three rooms and a suite with king- or queen-sized beds, private bathrooms, plush robes, and all the usual high-tech conveniences like televisions, phones, and high-speed Internet access. A full breakfast and afternoon tea and wine are offered.

■ *The Culpepper Inn*. Expensive/Moderate. 609 West Main Street (252-335-9235; www.culpepperinn.com). This1930s Colonial Revival-style inn, located within the heart of one of the city's historic districts, offers 10 guest rooms individually decorated with antiques. Each room features a king- or queen-sized bed with high-thread-count linens, a claw-foot bathtub, cable television, a phone, and high-speed Internet access. Some have gas fireplaces, and one is handicapped-accessible. A full breakfast is offered every morning, and an evening social gives guests the opportunity to mix and mingle. A meeting room is available. Government and corporate rates are offered.

■ *Elizabeth City Bed-and-Breakfast*. Expensive/Moderate. 108 East Fearing Street (877-324-8922 or 252-338-2177; www.elizabethcitybb.com). This homey establishment offers guest rooms swathed in relaxing colors, comfortable linens, and soft lights. Each room has a private bathroom. You'll feel like you're staying in an old friend's home, particularly when you smell the delightful scents of breakfast. Many guests choose to take their morning repast in the flower-filled courtyard, which is only a few blocks from downtown and the water. Several guest packages are available.

■ *Church Street Bed-and-Breakfast*. Moderate. 1108 West Church Street (252-335-1441; www.innsite.com/inns/A005319.html). Church Street Bed-

and-Breakfast is only six blocks from the water, making it a nice place to retreat after exploring the waterfront. Intimacy is the word here, as only two guest rooms are offered. The rooms are decorated in mauve, gold, and green, reflecting a Victorian mood. A game room and a reading room are available to guests. The bar is a nice place to spend a moment in the evening with a good friend and a drink. A full breakfast is served each morning. Evening refreshments are a nice extra to enjoy on the deck.

Places to Eat

Though there are many chain restaurants in Elizabeth City, you'll also find a good number of independently owned eateries downtown and near the waterfront. Choices range from light fare to casual gourmet to down-home Southern cooking.

■ *Cypress Creek Grill.* Expensive/Moderate. 113 South Water Street (252-334-9915). Located in downtown Elizabeth City, this restaurant serves an inclusive American menu—seafood, chicken, steaks, pasta, sandwiches, and vegetarian dishes. The atmosphere is relaxed yet upscale, exactly the kind of place the locals will recommend you try. And speaking of trying new things, check out the grill's famous "SOBs," which come with the seafood combination platter. Locals swear by these shrimp and oyster appetizers, which are wrapped in bacon and lightly fried. Lunch and dinner are served Monday through Saturday year-round.

■ *Grouper's Waterfront Seafood Grille.* Expensive/Moderate. 400 South Water Street (252-331-2431). Located on the Pasquotank River, this is an excellent place to enjoy an outdoor table while watching the boats sail by. The fare includes chicken, beef, veal, lamb, and pasta, though everyone knows the real reason to come here is the delicious seafood. The portions are generous; try to save at least a little room for dessert. Lunch and dinner are served daily.

■ *West End Station.* Expensive/Moderate. 109 South Hughes Boulevard (252-335-2006). Patrons here are in for a gastronomic treat, especially if they are wine connoisseurs. In addition to serving hand-cut steaks, fresh local seafood, and a variety of homemade tarts topped with mashed potatoes and Parmesan, West End offers the area's largest selection of wines. Lunch and dinner are served daily, and brunch is offered on Sunday.

- **Carolina Theatre and Grille**. Moderate. 109 Poindexter Street (252-337-7600). Dinner and a movie are the specialties of the house here, where patrons can enjoy burgers, sandwiches, salads, and even steaks while catching the latest Hollywood flick. This is a fun way to spend a relaxing evening without having to worry if your waiter is going to get you out of the restaurant in time to catch your movie. Lunch is offered Monday through Friday and dinner Monday through Saturday.

- **City Wine Seller Bakery and Deli**. Moderate/Inexpensive. 102 North Water Street (252-335-1163). Just try to walk by this little shop without getting drawn in by the homemade breads, pastries, and cookies. Breakfast and gourmet sandwiches, salads, and soups are offered as well. For those so inclined, wine and cigars are to be had. Breakfast, lunch, and an early dinner are offered Monday through Friday.

Nearby

The Albemarle region was the cradle of colonial society in North Carolina. Today, it abounds with small towns that, like Elizabeth City, boast rich histories and interesting attractions. Any one of the following would make a wonderful day trip.

- Historic **Halifax**, the legal and administrative seat of Halifax County, is located near N.C. 125 and U.S. 301 about an hour and a half west of Elizabeth City. This is where North Carolina's Fourth Provincial Congress met to declare independence from England, making it one of the first states to do so. The county also has provided the state with more governors, congressional representatives, attorneys general, and brigadier generals than any other county in North Carolina. A visitor center and a guided tour of several downtown historic structures are offered. **Lake Gaston**, located slightly northwest of Halifax, offers more than 20,000 acres of water bordered by 350 miles of shoreline in North Carolina and Virginia. Boating and fishing are permitted with the appropriate licenses. For more information, call 800-522-4282 or 252-583-7197 or visit www.visithalifax.com.

■ Historic **Jackson** in Northampton County is about an hour west of Elizabeth City near N.C. 305 and U.S. 158. It is home to several historic structures, including antebellum homes that are open for viewing on a walking tour. The **Northampton County Museum** offers interesting exhibits on local Native American and African-American history, and the Meherrin and Roanoke rivers are close by. Visit www.northamptonchamber.org for more information.

■ Historic **Murfreesboro**, about a 45-minute drive from Elizabeth City on U.S. 158 West, features a 12-block national historic district containing homes from the 18th and 19th centuries. A guided tour is available from the **Roberts-Vaughan Village Center**. The **Brady C. Jefcoat Museum of Americana** is home to the largest collection of washing machines, irons, and dairy items in the United States. Those interested in the decorative arts will enjoy the **Wheeler House**, a lovely two-story brick mansion constructed in 1810. The home features a classic white portico and columns and is authentically furnished with several original pieces from the period. For information, call 252-398-5922 or visit www.murfreesboronc.com.

■ Located south of Elizabeth City almost halfway to Edenton is the small town of **Hertford** in Perquimans County. Recently declared a North Carolina "Main Street" community, Hertford was settled by Pennsylvania Quakers in the late 17th century and owes much of its history to that group. Here, you'll find a downtown occupied by antique shops, cafés, and Queen Anne and Colonial Revival homes. Hertford was home to one of baseball's most storied players, Jim "Catfish" Hunter, who won the Cy Young Award in 1974 while with the Kansas City Athletics and later led the New York Yankees to three pennants in the late 1970s. Call 252-426-5657 or visit www.visitperquimans.com to learn more.

The **Newbold-White House**, located off U.S. 17 Bypass on the Perquimans River in Hertford, was built in 1730 by Quakers Abraham and Judith Sanders. It is the oldest brick home in the state. Period pieces on display in the house show what life was like during North Carolina's pioneer days. A nominal admission fee is charged for a 45-minute tour of the house, which is open Tuesday through Saturday from 10 A.M. to 4 P.M. and Sunday from 2 P.M. to 5 P.M. from March to Thanksgiving. Also located on the six-acre grounds are a museum shop, an herb garden, and a picnic area. The **Periauger**, a double-masted 30-foot replica of the most common style of colonial workboat in the area, is docked in the river nearby. Call 252-426-7567 or visit www.newboldwhitehouse.com for more information.

■ The **Great Dismal Swamp** begins just north of Elizabeth City and covers almost 600 square miles of North Carolina and Virginia. The only live peat bog on the continent, it contains some of the wildest and most untamed land on the East Coast. Colonel William Byrd II gave the area its name in 1728, when he stated that the place was so dismal that no one could or would want to inhabit it.

President George Washington and Virginia governor Patrick Henry thought differently, however, seeing the economic potential that canals connecting Chesapeake Bay and Albemarle Sound could have on the nation. Canal construction began in 1793. By 1810, both the 22-mile Dismal Swamp Canal and the Jericho Canal were ready for boats. With this ease of transportation, though, came greater deforestation during the 19th and early 20th centuries. Fortunately, the swamp recovered. Most of it is now covered by thick bogs, murky waters, and dense forests. As part of today's Intracoastal Waterway, the Dismal Swamp Canal remains a vital transportation route for folks boating between Chesapeake Bay and points south, making it the oldest continuously operating man-made canal in the United States. It is listed on the National Register of Historic Places.

In 1973, the Union Camp Corporation donated 49,100 acres of the swamp to the Nature Conservancy, which in turn handed the land over to the federal government. That tract has since grown to over 111,000 acres, including the 3,100-acre Lake Drummond. It is operated as the Great Dismal Swamp National Wildlife Refuge. For more information, call 757-986-3705 or visit www.fws.gov/northeast/greatdismalswamp.

The Dismal Swamp Canal Welcome Center, located a few miles north of Elizabeth City on U.S. 17, offers film and slide programs, information on the history and wildlife of the swamp, hiking and biking trails, fishing, and boating. Among the wildlife you may be able to spot in the swamp are 209 species of birds, 21 varieties of reptiles, skinks, bears, bobcats, minks, otters, muskrats, foxes, and deer. From Memorial Day to the end of October, the center is open daily from 9 A.M. to 5 P.M.; from November to Memorial Day, it operates Tuesday to Saturday from 9 A.M. to 5 P.M. For more information, call 877-771-8333 or visit www.dismalswamp.com.

■ *Merchants Millpond State Park*, about 30 miles northwest of Elizabeth City off U.S. 158 near Gatesville, is one of North Carolina's ecological treasures. The 3,252-acre park is home to a mingling of coastal-pond and swamp-forest habitats, one of the most diverse ecosystems on the East Coast. Over 160 species of birds have been spotted here, along with a wide variety of reptiles, amphibians, and mammals such as otters, beavers, minks, deer, and bears. The 760-acre millpond is home to 800-year-old bald cypresses and forests of tupelo gums draped with Spanish moss and resurrection ferns. The tupelo gums' trunks have been twisted into wild shapes by the creeping mistletoe, giving rise to a forest that is a sight to behold. Pine and hardwood forests stand nearby as well.

Because there is so much to see and explore at Merchants Millpond State Park, many people choose to camp here. The park offers both primitive campgrounds and family campsites for tents and trailers. No water or electrical hookups are available. Canoe rentals are offered. Fees are charged for camping and canoe rentals. The park is open daily year-round with the exception of Christmas Day. For more information, call 252-357-1191 or visit www.ils.unc.edu/parkproject/visit/memi/home.html.

ALL GOOD THINGS

Excerpted from *A Historian's Coast: Adventures into the Tidewater Past* by David Cecelski

Even our wildest swamps have a natural history—sometimes gradual, other times cataclysmic—that has been influenced by settlement, exploitation, and other human practices. Most of this past has never been written down and is often not apparent, but you can find traces of it in the land itself if you spend the time and look closely. . . .

. . . A tar pit or rosin mound indicates a site where naval stores were produced, hence where a longleaf pine forest once stood. A tangle of narrow-gauge railroad track reveals that the swamp forest was timbered, most likely between 1880 and 1920, when Northern lumber companies moved into the old-growth forests of the South. Coils of copper wire and rusted barrels are of course evidence of the moonshine liquor industry that thrived on the Carolina coast during Prohibition. The East Lake and "CCC" (Craven County Corn) brands of homemade whiskey were famous in speakeasies from Norfolk to Boston. And when we stumble upon a sunken shad boat on a creek off the Alligator River or a hand-hewn bow net hidden along the White Oak River, we know that we have discovered traces of the springtime fishery that was the largest in the state in the late nineteenth century.

Other times, when we run up against cypress pilings on the waterfronts of tiny river communities like Rockyhock and Colerain, we are reminded of the great herring fisheries that flourished in the Albemarle Sound vicinity before the Civil War. Using seines that were often a mile and a half in length, thousands of slaves and free black fishermen caught the herring as they migrated out of the Atlantic to spawn in tidewater rivers. The pilings mark the old sheds where the laborers headed and salted the herring by the millions.

The canals that pass through coastal swamps also reveal a great deal about the past. Sometimes, all you notice is a narrow, all-too-straight line of visibility through a cypress swamp, but you can bet that it is an old canal once used to float white oak timbers, cypress shingles, and cedar staves to a mill. Along intertidal marshes, I have inadvertently paddled into a labyrinth of intersecting, narrow canals, a sign of rice cultivation in the slavery era, when large gangs of men and women in bondage cultivated the "golden grain" along the Lower Cape Fear. In places like Lake Phelps and Lake Mattamuskeet, I have followed other, larger canals that date to the late eighteenth and early nineteenth centuries, when slaves dug canals to drain swampland for agriculture and to raft crops and lumber to market.

In my travels, I have floated down even larger passages, known as "ships' canals," that bring to life the golden age of canal building between the American Revolution and the Civil War. During that period, many political leaders believed that ships' canals held the greatest promise for overcoming the navigational hazards of North Carolina's shallow sounds and dangerous, shifting inlets. Between 1794 and 1805, for example, slaves dug the twenty-two-mile-long Dismal Swamp Canal to serve as a shipping route between Albemarle Sound and Chesapeake Bay and to skirt the dangerous swash and bar at Ocracoke Inlet.

Though it was antiquated by the opening of the Albemarle and Chesapeake Canal in 1859, the Dismal Swamp Canal had lasting consequences that had nothing to do with shipping. The canal blocked the Great Dismal Swamp's natural water flow from west to east, which eventually dried up the vast wetlands east of the canal and opened them for agriculture. The canal also lowered water levels throughout the moister parts of the Great Dismal, drying out the highly combustible upper layers of peat during summer droughts. Even as early as 1860, unprecedentedly hot peat fires burned much of the old-growth forests of cypress, juniper, and gum in the Great Dismal.

Millponds also have a story to tell. Quite often, [my brother] Richard and I stumble upon old millponds along remote blackwater creeks. We frequently discover relics of the mills' dams and foundations. When on a millpond, I find it easy to imagine what much of our coastal landscape looked like from the Revolutionary War well into the twentieth century, when millponds could be found in practically every tidewater community. Local people dammed creeks and harnessed the water's flow to power sawmills and gristmills. . . .

Millponds, like all wetlands, are an example of what ecologists refer to as an ecotone, a transitional zone between two diverse ecological communities. Ecotones support life native to each of the two communities (woods and river, for instance), as well as plants and animals endemic to only the ecotone. The heightened diversity and density of life in these transitional zones—a phenomenon known as the "edge effect"—is what makes millponds so remarkably rich in life. . . .

Sometimes when I am staying overnight in a coastal swamp, I get a glimpse of an even more distant past. It is often not easy to find a dry campsite in a swamp forest. A few times, I have had to paddle well into the night before finding a place to rest my head. More than once on waking the next morning, I have discovered clusters of arrowheads and shards of pottery around my camp, letting me know that I was hardly the first person who found shelter on that knoll or hammock. The coastal Algonquians—or their ancestors—used these same places for fishing camps long before European contact in the sixteenth century. . . .

Above all, I am haunted by the fragility of these freshwater wetlands—our most endangered and underappreciated coastal habitats. Everybody admires the beauty of ocean beaches and salt marshes, and I think most people understand their importance for tourism and the seafood industry. But far fewer people have had the chance to fall in love with the natural beauty and ecological uniqueness of these coastal wetlands—the cypress swamps, blackwater creeks, river bottom lands, pine savannas, pocosins, and Carolina bays.

EDENTON

One of the oldest communities in the state, Edenton proudly proclaims itself "the South's prettiest small town." Some say it's the profusion of well-maintained colonial and antebellum homes that justifies that claim. The long, tree-lined streets boast 18th- and 19th-century homes that once belonged to governors, aristocrats, and shipping magnates. South King Street is dotted with homes that predate the Civil War, with the exception of two "newcomers" built shortly thereafter. Others attribute Edenton's charm to the perfectly manicured lawns and the abundance of flowers and trees—roses, tulips, lilies, magnolias, and crape myrtles—along the blue waters of Edenton Bay and Albemarle Sound. Still others say Edenton is so beautiful because of the warm people living and working here. Edenton's fiercely proud residents will stop whatever they're doing to give you a history lesson and welcome you to their small piece of paradise.

When it was incorporated in 1715 as "the Towne on Queen Anne's Creek," this area became the first permanent settlement in North Carolina. A few years and a few name changes later, it came to be called Edenton in honor of the Royal governor who made his home here, Charles Eden. The town was designated the first capital of the colony. But good feelings toward Britain did not last. By August 1774, the citizens of Edenton decided that they had suffered enough of Britain's infamous taxation without representation. Daniel Earle, the rector of St. Paul's Church, rallied citizens by the courthouse and publicly denounced the Boston Port Act, signifying support of the revolutionaries in Massachusetts. That October, the ladies of Edenton decided to do their part to support the cause. Vowing not to purchase or drink any more tea or to wear clothes or fabrics from England until the unfair taxation was stopped, the ladies disrupted trade with Britain and proved themselves a force in the battle for independence. A colonial teapot now standing atop one of the Revolutionary War cannons on the courthouse green celebrates the ladies' contribution.

Among Edenton's notable citizens were a pair of signers of the two most important documents in the establishment of our country. Joseph Hewes, a ship owner and merchant, signed the Declaration of Independence, while Hugh Williamson, surgeon general of the state's colonial

Edenton's historic waterfront
PHOTO BY BILL RUSS, COURTESY OF NORTH CAROLINA DIVISION OF TOURISM, FILM AND SPORTS DEVELOPMENT

troops, signed the Constitution in 1787. Both assisted the cause by donating and outfitting ships for the burgeoning United States Navy. Samuel Johnston, another patriot from Edenton, was the first United States senator from North Carolina. Johnston's brother-in-law, James Iredell, was appointed to the United States Supreme Court by President George Washington.

Thanks to its many influential and powerful residents and its favorable location as an inland port, Edenton developed into an important commercial center around the time of the Revolution. But following the construction of various canals in the area at the beginning of the 19th century, it fell out of favor as a trading post. Ever since then, the citizens have worked to maintain Edenton's heritage as the home of the revolutionary spirit of North Carolina.

JUST THE FACTS

Edenton is located on Albemarle Sound at the mouth of the Chowan River. You can reach the town from the east or west via U.S. 17 and from the north or south via N.C. 32.

Edenton Marina, at 607 West Queen Street, offers full-service dockage for boaters passing by on Albemarle Sound. Visit www.edentonmarina.com or call 252-482-7421 for information.

The nearest large commercial airport is in Norfolk, Virginia. Northeastern Regional Airport, at 113 Airport Drive in Edenton, accepts small charter flights; call 252-482-4664 for more information.

Edenton's bus station is located at 810 Broad Street; call 252-482-2424.

Historic Edenton State Historic Site, at 108 North Broad Street, offers written information, guided walking tours, and trolley tours. Visit www.edenton.nchistoricshites.org or call 252-4823-2637. The Edenton-Chowan Chamber of Commerce and the Chowan County Tourism Development Authority, at 116 East King Street, offer a great deal of written information on the area. Call 800-775-0111 or 252-482-3400 or visit www.edenton.com.

HISTORIC PLACES, GARDENS, AND TOURS

The draw for most people coming to Edenton is the state's largest collection of 18th-century homes. Most are listed on the National Register of Historic Places, and a few are national historic landmarks. You can wander the streets on your own, soaking up the Georgian, Federal, Jacobean, Greek Revival, and Victorian architecture, or you can take a guided tour on foot or by trolley.

■ Regardless of which way you choose to see the town, your first stop should be ***Historic Edenton State Historic Site***, also known as the Historic Edenton Visitors Center, at 108 North Broad Street. Here, you can pick up maps and pamphlets detailing the architecture and history of each building for exploration on your own, or you can sign up for a guided tour that includes many of the historic sites listed below. Tours are given daily year-round, though hours are seasonal. A fee is charged; students and school groups receive discounted rates. Trolley tours are offered Tuesday through Saturday in the morning and afternoon. A fee is charged; children under five are free. The historic site is open daily year-round except for major winter holidays; extended hours are in effect during the summer. For more

Edenton
PHOTO BY BILL RUSS, COURTESY OF NORTH CAROLINA DIVISION OF TOURISM, FILM AND SPORTS DEVELOPMENT

information, call 252-482-2637 or visit www.edenton.nchistoricsites.org.

- One must-see stop in Edenton is **St. Paul's Episcopal Church**, at Church and Broad across the street from Historic Edenton State Historic Site. St. Paul's Parish was formed in 1701 on Hayes Plantation. Construction on St. Paul's Church—sometimes called "the Westminster Abbey of North Carolina"—started in 1736. It was here, at the second-oldest church in North Carolina, that Edenton's Revolutionary War effort had its beginnings. The membership log at St. Paul's is a who's who of the state's most important colonial leaders. An active congregation still worships here.

- South down Broad Street from St. Paul's is the **Cupola House**. This Jacobean-style home, built in 1758 by Francis Corbin, a land agent of Lord Granville, is the oldest house still standing in Edenton. Its formal gardens include an herb garden, parterres, an orchard, and an arbor with plants believed to have grown in the original gardens. Tours are coordinated by the Historic Edenton Visitors Center. Visit www.cupolahouse.org for more information.

- The **Barker-Moore House**, located near Edenton Bay farther down Broad Street, was the home of Penelope Barker, who initiated the Edenton Tea Party in 1774. Her husband, Thomas, was the London agent for the colony. Dating to 1782, the Barker-Moore House features a bookstore full of books on the history of the area. Admission is free, and visitors are welcome year-round. Call 252-482-7800 for more information.

- At the water's edge is the 1767 **Chowan County Courthouse**, where you'll see cannons and the famous teapot commemorating the bold actions of the town's ladies during the Edenton Tea Party. A national historic landmark, this is the oldest courthouse in North Carolina and one of the best examples of Georgian architecture in the nation. Check out www.edenton.com/history/court.htm for more information.

- The **Chowan County Jail**, the oldest working jail in the nation, is located next to the courthouse.

- Also of interest is the **Iredell House**, located on East Church Street. Built in 1773, this was the home of James Iredell, United States Supreme Court appointee of President George Washington. Tours are coordinated by the Historic Edenton Visitors Center. For more information, visit www.edenton.nchistoricsites.org.

Cupola House
PHOTO BY BILL RUSS, COURTESY OF NORTH CAROLINA DIVISION OF
TOURISM, FILM AND SPORTS DEVELOPMENT

Barker-Moore House
COURTESY OF CHOWAN COUNTY TOURISM DEVELOPMENT AUTHORITY

MUSEUMS AND SCIENCE CENTERS

■ *Edenton National Fish Hatchery*, at 1102 West Queen Street, is one of 69 federal fish hatcheries spread throughout the United States. Established in 1898, this is one of the oldest. In its time, it has bred a wide assortment of warm-water fish, including largemouth bass, striped bass, channel catfish, bluegill, redear sunfish, shad, and herring. The hatchery currently produces striped bass, Cape Fear shiners, and American shad. The nearly 5 million fish hatched here every year are used to stock the sounds, lakes, and coastal rivers of North Carolina, South Carolina, and Virginia. Visitors are welcome to take self-guided tours of the hatchery's aquarium and grounds. You can also call ahead to arrange for a staff member to show you the facility. Admission is free. The hatchery is open weekdays from 7 A.M. to 3:30 P.M. It is also open weekends and holidays from August through November. For more information, call 252-482-4118 or visit http://edenton.fws.gov.

CULTURAL OFFERINGS

■ The *Chowan Arts Council Gallery and Gallery Shop*, at 200 East Church Street, features the work of local and national artists. The eclectic mix here ranges from commissioned portraits to folk art. A permanent exhibit titled "A Century of Chowan through Photographs" traces life in the county from 1850 to 1954; it includes portraits of many of the area's most important figures and chronicles events significant in the county's history. You might consider this look at post-Revolutionary War Chowan County as an extension of your colonial tour of Edenton homes. The Gallery Shop sells original art and reproductions of some of the works displayed throughout the facility. Admission is free. The gallery and shop are open Monday through Saturday from 10 A.M. to 4 P.M. year-round. Call 252-482-8005 or visit http://chowanarts.org for more information.

RECREATION

■ If walking around Edenton and viewing all the lush lawns gets you in the mood for some golf, try the semi-private *Chowan Golf and Country Club*, at 1101 West Sound Shore Drive. Driving and putting greens are available in addition to the 18-hole course. Those not interested in golf can enjoy the pool or one of the club's tennis courts. Call 252-482-3606 or visit www.chowangolfandcountryclub.com for additional information.

SEASONAL EVENTS

■ The *Biennial Pilgrimage Tour of Homes and Countryside in Edenton and Chowan County* takes place on a Friday and Saturday in mid-April every two years. A number of buildings of historic merit, including private homes usually not open to the public, are made available to visitors wanting to satisfy their curiosity as to exactly what lies behind those doors. A single ticket is good for the entire weekend. All proceeds go to the preservation and promotion of historic sites in the area. For more information or to buy advance tickets, contact the Edenton-Chowan Chamber of Commerce at 800-775-0111 or 252-482-7800.

■ The *Annual Peanut Festival* occurs at the beginning of October and honors one of American's favorite snacks with a parade, a band competition, arts and crafts, and a variety of foods, many of which contain the star of the day. Call 252-482-8426 or visit www.visitedenton.com for more information.

■ Edenton is especially lovely when the historic homes and sites are decorated for the holiday season.

The Iredell House Groaning Board
PHOTO BY BILL RUSS, COURTESY OF NORTH CAROLINA DIVISION OF TOURISM, FILM AND SPORTS DEVELOPMENT

The **Candlelight Christmas Tour**, sponsored by the Edenton Historical Commission, features many free town-wide festivities during the second weekend in December. This is a must-see if you are in town.

The **Iredell House Groaning Board**, a dessert showcase that is fabled to make the table boards "groan" from overabundance, is held at the 1773 home of former United States Supreme Court justice James Iredell. Guests can listen to the wafting notes of harpsichord music and admire the 18th-century-style Christmas decorations while enjoying their desserts.

Just down the street is the **Cupola House Wassail Bowl**, where you can enjoy a cup of wassail, a traditional holiday drink.

You can partake of more holiday refreshments and a bit of art at the Chowan Arts Council's **Candlelight Confection Perfection**. Call 800-775-0111 for more information.

Places to Stay

INNS AND BED-AND-BREAKFASTS

A couple of motels are located outside Edenton's historic district, but since you're here to see the beautiful buildings downtown, the best places to stay are the inns and bed-and-breakfasts. The rates are so reasonable at many of these establishments that you'll pay no more than what a room at a hotel would cost you. And the inns offer much more personal attention, better locations, and prettier surroundings.

■ **The Lords Proprietors' Inn**. Deluxe. 300 North Broad Street (888-394-6622 or 252-482-3641; www.edentoninn.com). A member of the Historic Hotels of America and the Distinguished Inns of North America associations, this inn is comprised of three historic homes covering two acres. It offers 16 rooms and two luxury suites. All rooms have private baths, televisions, and high-speed Internet access and are sumptuously decorated with antiques and reproductions crafted by a local cabinetmaker and woodworker. A full gourmet breakfast is included. A four-course gourmet dinner prepared by the inn's chef can be reserved for an additional fee Tuesday through Saturday.

■ **Granville Queen Inn**. Expensive. 108 South Granville Street (866-482-

8534 or 252-482-5296; www.granvillequeen.com). Guests will have a hard time choosing which of the seven bedrooms they'd like to try in this lovely 1907 mansion with a double-decker wraparound porch. Each room has its own style, ranging from Renaissance Revival to Art Deco. Nearly all of the rooms have a fireplace and a private balcony, and all have a private bathroom, cable television, and a phone. Guests are treated each morning to a large gourmet breakfast.

- **Trestle House Inn at Willow Tree Farm**. Expensive. 632 Soundside Road (800-645-8466 or 252-482-2282; www.trestlehouseinn.com). This bed-and-breakfast, nestled on a private five-acre lot five miles outside town, is named after the Southern Railway trestles used as exposed support beams in the ceiling. Its five guest rooms, named after birds known to frequent this part of the country, feature private baths, ceiling fans, and central air. Guests can canoe from the pond behind the inn to Albemarle Sound and into Edenton. Both canoes and bikes are available for rent. A homemade breakfast is served daily.

- **Captain's Quarters Inn**. Expensive/Moderate. 202 West Queen Street (800-482-8945 or 252-482-8945; www.captainsquartersinn.com). Located in a 1907 Colonial Revival home, the Captain's Quarters offers eight individually decorated and nautically themed guest rooms, each with a private bath, a sitting room, a telephone, cable television, and Internet access. The 65-foot wraparound porch puts you within walking distance of Edenton's major attractions and the waterfront. A full breakfast, morning coffee service, and afternoon refreshments are included in the price of your stay. Sailing, golf, mystery weekends, and wine-and-dine packages featuring gourmet dinners are available.

Places to Eat

For a small Southern town, Edenton has an excellent selection of local, independently owned restaurants that serve tasty, creative meals. You might have to make a second trip to try all the culinary delights the community has to offer.

- **Waterman's Grille**. Expensive/Moderate. 427 South Broad Street (252-

482-7733). Located in a historic building one block from Edenton Bay and within walking distance of all the town's major sites, this restaurant specializes in good, fresh seafood and thick, juicy steaks. Wine connoisseurs and beer lovers will appreciate the wine shop and bar. Dinner is served Monday through Saturday.

■ *Nixon Family Restaurant*. Moderate. 327 River Road (252-221-2244). Don't let the casual atmosphere at this restaurant fool you into thinking that food is taken lightly around here. The big draws are the oyster bar and the large variety of just-off-the-boat seafood. The generous buffet is also popular, particularly at lunchtime. Breakfast, lunch, and dinner are served daily.

■ *Chero's Market Café and Catering*. Moderate/Inexpensive. 112 West Water Street (252-482-5525). This charming restaurant, located in a large brick building that overlooks Albemarle Sound, offers gourmet fare that is both delicious and affordable. Fresh daily specials are offered, including many sandwiches with imported cheeses and tender meats. Vegetarians will find selections to please their palates as well. Lunch is offered Tuesday through Sunday and dinner Wednesday through Saturday.

■ *That Fancy Café*. Moderate/Inexpensive. 701 North Broad Street (252-482-1909). Visitors to this establishment can satisfy two hungers—for food and shopping—at once. The café features good, homemade down-home foods like cornbread, casseroles, and scalloped potatoes that will stick to your ribs. After catching a bite of lunch, head over to Fancy That Antiques & Interiors to satisfy your craving for beautiful things. Lunch is served daily and dinner Tuesday through Saturday.

■ *Acoustic Coffee*. Inexpensive. 302 South Broad Street (252-482-7465; www.acoustic-coffee.com). For those looking for an exceptional cup of joe and some delightful, freshly baked brownies, muffins, and pastries, Acoustic Coffee is the perfect spot. Many regulars attend the live Friday-night sessions featuring talented local musicians playing everything from bluegrass to gospel. The music starts around 6:30 P.M., and the shop fills up pretty quickly. Patrons can also take advantage of the free Internet service. The coffee shop is open Monday through Saturday for breakfast and lunch, with extended hours on Friday for the music.

■ About 45 minutes south of Edenton is the small town of Creswell, home of **Somerset Place State Historic Site**. Located down the oak- and cypress-lined Lake Shore Drive near Lake Phelps, Somerset Place was one of the four largest plantations in North Carolina. Home to several generations of the Josiah Collins family beginning in 1785, the plantation once encompassed 100,000 acres. More than 200 slaves worked the plantation at any given time, digging irrigation and transport canals, building sawmills, gristmills, and other structures, and cultivating rice, wheat, and corn. When the Civil War ended, the Collinses were unable to maintain Somerset Place without their source of unpaid labor, and the plantation ceased operation.

Archaeological research has been under way since the early 1950s to uncover facts about Somerset Place's many residents. Today, visitors can see what life was like for both the Collinses and their slaves through educational programs and tours of the mansion, the detached kitchen, the smokehouse, the dairy, and the Colony House, which was the Collinses' home before the completion of the current plantation house. The historic site is open Monday through Saturday from 9 A.M. to 5 P.M. and Sunday from 1 P.M. to 5 P.M. from April through October. From November through March, it is open Tuesday through Saturday from 10 A.M. to 4 P.M. and Sunday from 1 P.M. to 4 P.M. Admission is free. For more information, call 252-797-4560 or visit www.ah.dcr.state.nc.us/sections/hs/somerset/Main.htm.

■ Somerset Place State Historic Site is part of the larger **Pettigrew State Park**, whose crowning jewel is the 16,600-acre Lake Phelps. The second-largest natural lake in the state, Lake Phelps is remarkably shallow, averaging only four and a half feet deep. Its waters are clear, too, making it an anomaly among the area's brackish bodies of water. Visitors can fish or boat on the lake. While motorboats are welcome, the lake is really a canoeist's paradise. Those looking for dry recreation can camp, picnic, hike, and bird-watch on the park's 1,200 acres of land. Park rangers offer educational programs on the area's history, including the rich Native American legacy of eastern North Carolina. Humans are known to have frequented the region as early as 8000 B.C. Artifacts more than 4,000 years old—including arrowheads, pottery, and dugout canoes—have been found. Admission is free, though a fee is charged for camping. The park is open daily with the exception of Christmas; extended hours are offered in the summer. Call 252-797-4475 or visit http://ils.unc.edu/parkproject/visit/pett/home.html for more information.

- **Pocosin Lakes National Wildlife Refuge**, located off N.C. 94 to the east and N.C. 45 to the west, shares Lake Phelps with Pettigrew State Park. The 113,000-acre refuge was established in 1990, when it absorbed Alligator Lake and the 12,000-acre Pungo National Wildlife Refuge, home of Pungo Lake. It's named after the distinctive pocosin shrub bogs native to the area, which are comprised of fire-tolerant, dense broadleaf evergreen shrubs and pond pines. The refuge now serves as a wetland- and wildlife-restoration site for species such as the Atlantic white cedar and the endangered red wolf, which nearly went extinct in the 20th century. Visitors to the refuge occasionally see one or two of these shy creatures, in addition to black bears, red-cockaded woodpeckers, hooded merganser ducks, wood ducks, snow geese, tundra swans, and raptors. Fishing and hunting are allowed in the refuge with proper permits. The Scuppernong River Interpretive Boardwalk, listed as a national recreation trail by the National Park Service, is located behind the Walter B. Jones, Sr., Center for the Sounds. It offers a great way to see the area's natural beauty. The boardwalk connects to the downtown area of nearby Columbia. The refuge is open year-round except for federal holidays. Admission is free. For more information, call 252-796-3004 or visit www.fws.gov/pocosinlakes.

- Approximately 20 miles west of Edenton and four miles outside the town of Windsor on N.C. 308 is **Historic Hope Plantation**, the former home of North Carolina governor David Stone. The 1803 buff-colored, two-story Georgian- and Federal-style plantation house is authentically furnished with period antiques. Also on the grounds is the 1763 **King-Bazemore House**, one of only two remaining gambrel-roofed homes built with handmade brick end walls. The house is also significant because it is representative of the classic mid-18th-century "hall and parlor" design. Originally situated five miles away, the King-Bazemore House was constructed by William King, a successful planter and cooper. In 1840, it was purchased by Stephen Bazemore. In 1974, the Bazemore family donated the house to the Historic Hope Foundation. Both homes are listed on the National Register of Historic Places.

Hope Plantation is open Monday through Saturday from 10 A.M. to 5 P.M. and Sunday from 2 P.M. to 5 P.M. November through March. Afternoon hours are extended by an hour on weekdays the rest of the year. The plantation is closed Thanksgiving and the last two weeks of December. An admission fee is charged. Call 252-794-3140 or visit www.hopeplantation.org for more information.

■ Historic **Windsor**, near N.C. 308 and U.S. 17 about 20 minutes west of Edenton, was established in 1768 when William Gray offered 100 acres for a town. That original land is now recognized as a national historic district. Call the chamber of commerce at 252-794-4277 or visit www.albemarle-nc.com/windsor for more information.

While you're in Windsor, be sure to check out the **Sans Souci Ferry**, which crosses the Cashie River. It's a rustic, diesel-powered, one- to two-car ferry not affiliated with the state's ferry system. Instead, this independently run ferry represents the important lifeline that local ferrymen provided to rural farmers, doctors, and other residents who needed to cross the river to get to town. Located off S.R. 1500, the ferry cuts the driving distance from riverbank to riverbank by nearly 20 miles. The system is quite informal. When you arrive, honk your horn; the ferry captain will chug across the river to pick you up for the 10-minute ride.

■ The **Roanoke River National Wildlife Refuge** is located a little less than an hour southwest of Edenton in Bertie County. It covers more than 17,000 acres scattered along 70 miles of the Roanoke River. Two large satellite tracts encompass nearly 200 acres; one is located near the town of Hamilton and the other near the mouth of the Roanoke, which flows into the western portion of Albemarle Sound. Hunting, fishing, boating, and hiking are permitted in the refuge. Bird watchers may see dozens of species, including bald eagles, at any given time. The refuge, in fact, is the largest inland heron rookery in the state. It is open year-round with the exception of federal holidays. Admission is free. For more information, call 252-794-5326 or visit www.fws.gov/roanokeriver.

■ Historic **Williamston** is 45 minutes west of Edenton near U.S. 64 and U.S. 17. Its two national historic districts feature homes and buildings from the 19th and early 20th centuries. Railroad and tobacco money helped build the town, including the outstanding former county courthouse, constructed in the Italianate style in 1885. Annual events of interest in Williamston include the **North Carolina Country Stampede** in late September, which is run in conjunction with the Colgate Country Showdown, a national country-music talent contest akin to *American Idol*. The **Roanoke Arts and Crafts Guild Holiday Fair**, held in November, is also a big draw. For more information, call 252-792-5142 or visit www.townofwilliamston.com.

■ Historic *Plymouth*, south of Edenton near N.C. 32 and U.S. 64, is one of the top Civil War destinations in North Carolina. During three days in 1864, Union and Confederate soldiers fought the state's second-largest Civil War battle at the mouth of the Roanoke River, one of Robert E. Lee's supply lines for the Confederate army in Virginia. Visitors can relive that heated fight—the last Confederate victory of the war—at the *Port 'O Plymouth Civil War Museum*. Call 252-793-1377 or visit www.livinghistoryweekend.com/port_o.htm for more information. To learn more about the town, try www.visitplymouthnc.com.

BATH

Established in 1705, Bath is North Carolina's oldest town. As such, it is home to many of the state's "firsts," including the first church, the first public library, the first port of entry, and the first shipyard, among others. Thanks to its advantageous location near Pamlico Sound, Bath became a major port for naval stores, tobacco, and furs only a few years after French Protestants founded the town. The area was home to such notable personages as John Lawson, the surveyor general of the colony and the author of the first history of Carolina, published in 1709, and Edward Teach, better known as the pirate Blackbeard, who is rumored to have taken a wife here for a short time in 1716. Stories still circulate that some of Blackbeard's treasure is buried around Bath, though none has ever been found.

Problems started to beleaguer the town early on. Despite Bath's status as the first town in the state, it failed to grow. In 1711, Cary's Rebellion, a struggle over religion and politics in the area, turned violent. That same year, the town was ravaged by a drought and an outbreak of yellow fever. The Tuscarora War further debilitated Bath. When neighboring towns like Edenton and Washington were founded, many people moved from Bath to pursue other economic and political opportunities.

Today, Bath is a small community measuring only a few blocks. The original town limits survive as the boundaries for a national historic district; the district includes four buildings that connect Bath to its once-prosperous past. Visitors can enjoy an afternoon exploring the town on foot and learning about the old homes and church.

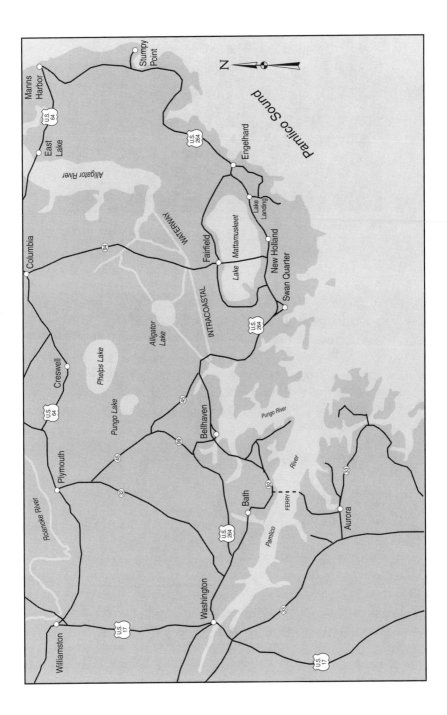

The harbor in historic Bath
PHOTO BY BILL RUSS, COURTESY OF NORTH CAROLINA DIVISION OF TOURISM, FILM AND
SPORTS DEVELOPMENT

JUST THE FACTS

Bath is in Beaufort County on the Pamlico River about 15 minutes east of Washington, North Carolina. It can be reached via N.C. 92 or via a free ferry that crosses the Pamlico from N.C. 306 north of Aurora.

Historic Bath State Historic Site, located on Carteret Street (N.C. 92), is the best source of information on the town. Call 252-923-3971 or visit www.ah.dcr.state.nc.us/sections/hs/bath/bath.htm.

Things to Do

HISTORIC PLACES, GARDENS, AND TOURS

■ Four historic buildings that date to colonial and antebellum times are open for visitors. In order to learn about these landmarks, stop by the visitor center at **Historic Bath State Historic Site**. Here, you can view a short film and pick up maps and pamphlets on the history of the town. From April through October, the visitor center is open Monday through Saturday from 9 A.M. to 5 P.M. and Sunday from 1 P.M. to 5 P.M. From November to March, it is closed Mondays and shuts its doors one hour earlier on the other days. Call 252-923-3971 or visit www.ah.dcr.state.nc.us/sections/hs/bath/bath.htm for more information.

■ The visitor center offers guided tours of two homes in the national historic district—the Bonner House and the Palmer-Marsh House. A modest admission fee is charged. You should plan on spending about an hour and a half going through these houses.

The **Bonner House**, a two-story white frame house built on the water in 1830, is representative of what daily life was like for a prosperous eastern North Carolina family between the Revolutionary War and the Civil War. It was home to Joseph Bonner, a local businessman who operated an expansive farm, a steam sawmill, and a turpentine distillery. Its most interesting features include blown-glass windowpanes, hand-carved mantels, and decorative paint treatments such as wood graining on interior doors and marbleized baseboards, which were considered extravagant at the time.

The 1751 **Palmer-Marsh House** is the oldest home in Bath. It served as the home of Robert Palmer, a wealthy and influential colonial customs collector and general-assembly member, and his troubled son, William, who could not decide between loyalty to his father's homeland (England) or his native Carolina. His indecision and resulting drinking problem drove the Palmers deep into debt. The family's estate was seized by the new revolutionary government. The home eventually came into the hands of brother merchants Jonathan and Daniel Marsh, whose descendants kept it in the Marsh family for more than 120 years. The home's significant features include an imposing double chimney and many 18th- and 19th-

Bonner House
COURTESY OF HISTORIC BATH STATE
HISTORIC SITE

Van der Veer House

century antiques and reproductions representative of the house's style when important visitors such as Royal Governor William Tryon and the Marquis de Lafayette called.

The 1790 **Van der Veer House**, located just down the street, was purchased in 1824 by Jacob Van der Veer, a partner with Joseph Bonner in his sawmill and one of the founders of the nearby Bank of Washington. The house features a gambrel room and double-shouldered Flemish bond chimneys. It now operates as a museum and is open the same hours as the visitor center. Admission is free.

St. Thomas Episcopal Church, on Craven Street near the visitor center, rounds out Bath's roster of historic structures open for visitation. This is the oldest church in North Carolina. It houses the state's first public library, which was donated to St. Thomas Parish in 1701, four years before Bath was incorporated. No admission fee is charged, though donations are accepted. Tours here are self-guided.

St. Thomas Episcopal Church

Aurora Fossil Museum
PHOTO BY BILL RUSS, COURTESY OF NORTH
CAROLINA DIVISION OF TOURISM, FILM AND SPORTS
DEVELOPMENT

Nearby

■ The ***Aurora Fossil Museum***, at 400 Main Street in Aurora, is a free
ferry ride over the Pamlico River from Bath. The museum, which grew
out of discoveries made by the PCS Phosphate Company during mining
operations in the 1950s and 1960s, uses fossil research and an 18-minute
video presentation to explain the formation of the coastal plain. The area
around Aurora and much of the rest of eastern North Carolina once lay
under the ocean. As time passed, calcium phosphate collected on the sea-
bed and preserved the remains of many of the creatures that had lived in
the water. After millions of year, the sea finally receded, leaving a thick
layer of phosphate buried underneath layers of sand and clay. It was in
this fashion that coastal animals from eons ago were preserved.

Visitors to the museum learn about the history of these sea creatures through exhibits that show what ocean life was like millions of
years ago and through displays of fossilized bones, teeth, shells, and
coral. Kids love the small phosphate yard near the museum, where
they can search for their own fossils. The museum is open Monday
through Saturday from 9 A.M. to 4:30 P.M. Admission is free, though
donations are accepted. For more information, call 252-322-4238 or
visit www.aurorafossilmuseum.com.

- **Bennett Vineyards**, located half an hour south of Bath and three miles from the Aurora ferry at 6832 Old Sandhill Road in the community of Edward, is the largest muscadine and scuppernong vineyard in the Carolinas. It is situated between the Pamlico and Neuse rivers on a 138-acre parcel of colonial land-grant soil. The grapes this winery uses are indigenous to only the Southeast and are what the colonists used for their wines. Tours are given daily by appointment. Call 877-762-9463 or 252-322-7154 or visit www.ncwines.com for more information.

- **Belhaven Memorial Museum**, located in the old Belhaven Town Hall on East Main Street, is within easy driving distance of Bath on N.C. 99. Started as a collection of buttons by Mary Eva Blount Way, the holdings quickly grew to include all kinds of antiques and artifacts of life in Beaufort County, eastern North Carolina, and the South in general. "Miss Eva" decided to open her home to visitors in 1940 in order to share her collection—which by then included over 10,000 items—in an effort to aid the American Red Cross. After her death in 1962, a group of citizens purchased the collection in order to keep Miss Eva's memory and work alive. They reopened the museum in the town hall three years later. Today, visitors will find interesting testimonials to the culture and people of the area dating all the way back to the beginning of the 19th century—war memorabilia, toys, household utensils, clothing, tools, and much more. The museum is open Thursday through Tuesday from 1 P.M. to 5 P.M. Admission is free, but donations are accepted. For more information, call 252-943-6817 or visit www.beaufort-county.com/BelhavenMuseum.

  Visitors to Belhaven have a choice of noteworthy inns. **River Forest Manor**, a Victorian mansion built in 1899 by John Aaron Wilkinson, has hosted the likes of James Cagney, Tallulah Bankhead, Twiggy, and Walter Cronkite over the years. It has a marina, a shipyard, and a restaurant. For information, call 800-346-2151 or 252-943-2151 or visit www.riverforestmanor.com. The charming **Thistle Dew Inn Bed-and-Breakfast**, built a century ago for the first mayor of Belhaven, offers three guest rooms in a Queen Anne home near the Pungo River. Call 888-822-4409 or 252-943-6900 or visit www.bbonline.com/nc/thistledew for more information.

- Six miles west of Bath off N.C. 92 is **Goose Creek State Park**. This park is well known for its many recreational offerings, including a swim beach, hiking and canoeing trails, and camping and picnicking sites. Sailing and windsurfing are also popular activities here. Interpretive and educational programs on the area's natural resources and wildlife are offered by the park's rangers at the Environmental Education and Visitor Center. The park is open year-round during daylight hours with the exception of Christmas. Admission is free, though a small fee is charged for camping. For more information, call 252-923-2191 or visit http://ils.unc.edu/parkproject/visit/gocr/home.html.

■ Historic **Washington**, the self-proclaimed "heart of the Inner Banks," is located about 15 minutes from Bath near U.S. 17 and U.S. 264. Founded in 1775, it was the first town in the United States to be named for George Washington. It quickly became a major port on the Pamlico River. When the Beaufort County seat was moved from Bath to Washington in 1785, Washington started to eclipse Bath in importance. Though the War for Independence was a major factor in the development of Washington, the War Between the States proved devastating. Union troops captured the city in 1864 and pillaged and burned it before their departure. The town was rebuilt, but fire destroyed much of the downtown area again in 1900, when a faulty stove flue caught a building on fire. Washington was rebuilt a second time. Today, the town's national historic district includes about 11 blocks of 19th- and early-20th-century buildings, including many Gothic churches. Call 800-546-0162 or visit www.visitwashingtonnc.com for more information.

Overnight visitors to Washington might consider staying at the **Carolina House Bed-and-Breakfast**, an 1880 home only two blocks from the Pamlico River. It is listed on the National Register. For information, call 252-975-1382 or visit www.carolinahousebnb.com. Another good option is **The Moss House**, a 1902 Victorian home in the downtown historic district that was recently awarded a Three Diamond rating by AAA. Call 252-975-3967 or visit www.themosshouse.com for more information.

The **North Carolina Estuarium**, at 223 East Water Street on the Pamlico River in downtown Washington, is the only estuarium in the state. It is dedicated to educating visitors about the Albemarle-Pamlico estuarine system, the second-largest in the nation. Estuaries, which are aquatic areas made up of both fresh and salt water, line the state's shoreline and are a vital part of the area's ecology. Visitors to the estuarium will find a guided river tour, an aquarium, artifacts from local estuaries including boats and fishing equipment, and an audiovisual presentation concerning humans' effects on the estuarine system and the system's effects on man. A gift shop is on the premises. The estuarium is open Tuesday through Saturday from 10 A.M. to 4 P.M. A modest admission fee is charged. For more information, call 252-948-0000 or visit www.partnershipforthesounds.org/nce_home.htm.

Sailing at New Bern
Courtesy of Crystal Coast Tourism Authority

NEUSE RIVER REGION

By Angela Harwood

*T*he Neuse River region encompasses some of North Carolina's most fascinating historical and natural sites. The towns and villages that populate the Neuse River region—named for the Neusiok Indians, who once inhabited the river's shores—date primarily to the 18th century.

Among these is New Bern, the state's colonial capital. Overlooking the point where the Neuse and Trent rivers converge, New Bern is home to the magnificent Tryon Palace, which has secured the town a premier spot on the state's heritage trail. This year-round destination is not only for those interested in Revolutionary War history, however. Over the course of time, New Bern's downtown has undergone a renaissance, as more and more interesting shops and excellent restaurants have opened to serve the tourist trade. One of the town's most recent additions is a convention center on the bank of the Neuse.

Forty-five minutes east of New Bern is Morehead City, where world-class fishing tournaments attract fishermen from far and wide. Be sure to plan a meal here, as the town's bustling waterfront restaurants serve up some of the area's best seafood. Morehead City is also the jumping-off point for the stunning sands of Bogue Banks.

Historic Beaufort is nothing less than idyllic. Overlooking Taylor Creek, this former pirates' hideout now quietly greets sailors of a different ilk. The first-class North Carolina Maritime Museum is headquartered here amid the picturesque inns and bed-and-breakfasts. Some of the area's most innovative and best restaurants are located here as well.

Situated on the Intracoastal Waterway is another quaint fishing hamlet, Oriental. Regarded by many as the East Coast's premier yachting destination, Oriental offers a sailing school that serves both beginners and experienced sailors wishing to hone their skills.

For outdoor enthusiasts, Croatan National Forest is an oasis for birdwatching, hiking, camping, and boating. Hunting and fishing are also permitted for visitors holding the proper permits. Indigenous insect-eating plants thrive here, including the pitcher plant, sundew, and Venus flytrap. This vast 159,000-acre park is surrounded by water and has several lakes within its borders.

And of course, there are the beaches. Atlantic Beach, Pine Knoll Shores, and Emerald Isle—all on Bogue Banks—are among the state's most popular seaside resorts. Fort Macon State Park at Atlantic Beach offers a history lesson and a day at the beach all in one. Or if you'd rather escape the masses, you can ferry over to the incomparable Cape Lookout National Seashore, where a diamond-painted lighthouse continues in service 150 years after it was built. Another ferry ride away is pristine Hammocks Beach State Park, perhaps the land of buried treasure.

Whether you intend to tour the historic sites, to fish or boat, or to hang out on the beach, the Neuse River region is sure to please.

NEW BERN

New Bern is located 35 miles from the Atlantic Ocean at the confluence of the Neuse and Trent rivers. North Carolina's second-oldest town, it was named by its Swiss founder, Christophe von Graffenried, in honor of his home capital, Berne. Throughout the city, you will see New Bern's symbol, the black bear, which it shares with its European mother city.

In 1710—the same year that North and South Carolina were divided—von Graffenried and two partners purchased an 18,750-acre parcel for a

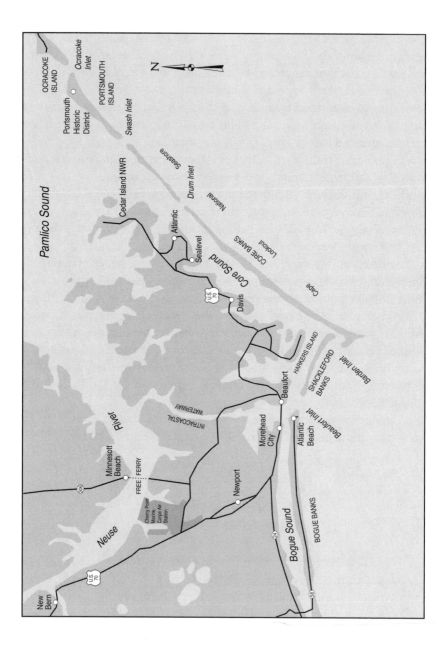

colony of German and Swiss emigrants. The purchase was inspired by colonial surveyor general John Lawson, who had returned to London extolling the virtues of the New World in his book, *A New Voyage to Carolina*. Subsequently dispatched by von Graffenried to select a site for the colony, Lawson laid out a town plan in the form of a crucifix, which served the dual purposes of religious expression and defense against Indians.

The newcomers also had to defend themselves outside the town boundaries, however. Although King Taylor of the Tuscaroras had been paid for the land where New Bern was settled, the influx of immigrants proved too much for him to stand. In September 1711, Lawson and von Graffenried embarked on a canoe trip up the Neuse River. A few days into the journey, they were captured by the Tuscaroras. Von Graffenried managed to save himself by persuading the Tuscaroras that his connections to the English Crown would serve them well should he live. Lawson wasn't so fortunate. The Tuscaroras supposedly pierced him with splinters of wood, then lit him afire and burned him to death.

The three years of fighting that followed drove von Graffenried back to Europe, which left New Bern in the hands of Colonel Thomas Pollock. With the help of some of the Tuscaroras' traditional enemies, the colonists eventually vanquished the tribe. The Indians who survived migrated north, where they gave their new land the name of their Carolina home—Chattawka, now Chautauqua, New York.

Once the Indian threat was removed, white settlers flocked to New Bern, which prospered as a port for shipping tar, pitch, and turpentine. In 1723, it was incorporated and made the seat of Craven County, which it remains today. By the time the colonial assembly convened here in 1737, New Bern was well established as the most vital city between Virginia and Charleston, South Carolina.

In 1776, North Carolina's first governor, Richard Caswell, was heralded into office in New Bern, the state's first capital. When the capital was moved to Raleigh in 1794, New Bern's political role diminished, but the city continued to thrive as a shipping center. It was during this period that many of its lovely homes and buildings were constructed.

In 1862, New Bern was captured by Union forces under General Ambrose Burnside. The city remained a Union outpost for the rest of the Civil War.

During Reconstruction, lumber mills and the seafood industry kept the city going. After World War II, manufacturing and the military were at the heart of New Bern's development. Nearby Cherry Point remains the nation's largest Marine Air Corps station.

Since the reconstruction of Tryon Palace in the 1950s, New Bern has seen a steady increase in tourism. Today, the city boasts a collection of National Register buildings second in number only to Charleston. In and around the historic district, dozens of antique and specialty shops, art galleries, and restaurants have sprouted up, making a trip to New Bern a delight.

JUST THE FACTS

New Bern is accessible by land, water, or air.

Car travelers can take either U.S. 70, U.S. 17, or N.C. 55 to reach town. Those planning to take the bus should contact the Trailways station, located at 504 Guion Street; the number is 252-633-3100.

Portions of the Neuse River double as the Intracoastal Waterway. Those arriving by water can stay at any of the private marinas along the river.

For those flying into New Bern, US Airways offers seven commuter flights daily into Craven County Regional Airport. Fuel and maintenance are available here. Call 252-638-8591 or visit www.newbernairport.com for more information.

The Craven County Convention and Visitors Bureau, located at the new convention center at 203 South Front Street, offers an abundance of information on the area. For information, call 800-437-5767 or 252-637-9400 or visit www.visitnewbern.com.

The *New Bern Sun Journal* is the local daily newspaper.

Things to Do

HISTORIC PLACES, GARDENS, AND TOURS

■ For a self-guided tour of New Bern, pick up a free **Heritage Tour** guide at the Craven County Convention and Visitors Bureau. You can also pick up maps to New Bern's numerous African-American heritage sites, Civil War sites, and historic homes, churches, and cemeteries, all of which are within walking distance of downtown. If you prefer to ride, check out the trolley tour offered by **New Bern Tours**; call 800-849-7316 or 252-637-7316 or visit www.newberntours.com. You can also tour historic New Bern the old-fashioned way—by horse-drawn carriage. For information, call **Springbrook Farms, Inc.**, at 910-251-8889, e-mail horsedrawntours@bellsouth.net, or visit www.horsedrawntours.com/.

■ *Tryon Palace Historic Sites and Gardens* is the cornerstone of historic New Bern. It is located at 610 Pollock Street, one block south of U.S. 17 and U.S. 70 Business. The complex consists of Tryon Palace, its surrounding 14 acres of gardens and grounds, and four other historic landmarks—the John Wright Stanly House, the Dixon-Stevenson House, the Robert Hay House, and the New Bern Academy Museum.

Tryon Palace is a reconstruction of the state's first Capitol, built before the population shifted west and before Raleigh became the capital city in 1794.

In 1765, Royal Governor William Tryon commissioned English architect John Hawkes to design and supervise the construction of Tryon Palace, an elegant Georgian mansion containing public rooms for government functions on the ground floor and family living quarters upstairs. Cooking and laundry facilities were in a wing on the left, while livery stables were in a wing to the right. In 1770, just 13 months after moving his family into the home, Tryon was appointed governor of New York. His successor, Josiah Martin, subsequently moved into Tryon Palace with much fanfare. Martin commissioned Hawkes to add a poultry house, a

Tryon Palace
Courtesy of North Carolina Division of Tourism, Film and Sports Development

smokehouse, and a pigeon house. Martin spent four years lavishly furnishing his abode, impervious to the growing resentment around him. In 1775, patriots forced Martin to flee the house. He left all his possessions behind.

In 1777, the first North Carolina General Assembly convened at Tryon Palace, the newly designated Capitol of North Carolina. By 1798, however, when fire destroyed the main building, Raleigh had been made the state capital, and the role of New Bern and Tryon Palace was greatly diminished. Through the years, portions of the grounds were sold. Tryon Palace languished, only the west wing remaining intact. Recovery began in 1939, when the original architectural plans were discovered in New York. A restoration trust fund was established by Mrs. Maude Moore Latham, a New Bern native whose dedication to the project and philanthropy were largely responsible for its success. Noted architect William G. Perry of the Boston firm that restored Colonial Williamsburg began his work in New Bern in 1951. Mrs. Latham died that same year but passed along her legacy to her daughter, Mrs. John A. Kellerman, who headed the state commission in charge of the project. On April 8, 1959, Tryon Palace opened its doors to the public.

Tours of Tryon Place begin in the visitor center, located across Pollock Street from the northern side of the building. Following a 20-minute orientation film, you'll make your way along the Entrance Allée, which is being redesigned based on newly discovered historical documents; don't be surprised if you are cheerfully met along the way by one of the many historical interpreters, busy with his or her chores. A costumed guide will greet you at the door and lead you into the marble entrance hall, through the public rooms downstairs, and up the pegged mahogany staircase to the private rooms. Thanks to an inventory of William Tryon's original furnishings, the palace contains some 7,000 pieces of art and 18th- and 19th-century American and English antiques that reflect the opulent world of Governor Tryon. Among his personal possessions that remain at Tryon Palace is a library of 400 books.

After your tour of Tryon Palace, take time to stroll the formal **Colonial Revival Gardens**, designed by Morley Jeffers Williams, an expert in 18th-century landscaping. The Latham Garden is designed in the style of cutwork parterre. Hedges define the beds, creating ornate patterns. Nearby is the private Green Garden, designed to be viewed from the palace. The Kellenberger Garden illustrates how ornamentals were grown for their decorative qualities. The wonderful Kitchen Garden produces heirloom varieties of herbs and vegetables grown for cooking, fragrance, and medicinal purposes.

Latham Garden at Tryon Palace
PHOTOGRAPH BY ANGELA HARWOOD

The *John Wright Stanly House*, an elegant 1779 Georgian home at 307 George Street, is one of the properties that is part of Tryon Palace Historic Sites and Gardens. On his Southern tour in 1791, President George Washington dined and danced at Tryon Palace, but he laid his head to rest at the John Wright Stanly House, which he described as "exceedingly good lodgings." The house is named for a powerful New Bern citizen who aided the American cause by raiding British vessels. Ironically, John Wright Stanly traced his lineage to King Edward I of England. The home served as General Ambrose Burnside's headquarters while Union forces occupied the city. The house's interior is noted for its intricate woodwork, especially its Chippendale staircase.

Built between 1826 and 1833, the *Dixon-Stevenson House*, at 609 Pollock Street, is a fine example of Neoclassical architecture. Constructed on a lot that was originally part of Tryon Palace's gardens, it was the home of George W. Dixon, a merchant, tailor, and one-time mayor of New Bern. During the Union occupation, the house was used as a regimental hospital. Inside, you'll find hand-carved woodwork and antiques of the Federal and Empire periods.

The *Robert Hay House*, on Eden Street next to the Tryon Palace Museum Shop, was home to a Scottish wagon maker and a founding member of First Presbyterian Church in New Bern.

The *New Bern Academy Museum* is located four blocks from Tryon Palace at the corner of New and Hancock streets. Completed in 1809, it was the first chartered school in North Carolina. The museum contains four rooms, each focusing on an aspect of local history: the founding and early history of New Bern, the architecture of the city, the Civil War and Reconstruction, and education in New Bern. This is a great place to get a broad overview of the city. Thanks to its dedicated staff of volunteers, the museum is open daily from 1 P.M. to 4:30 P.M. Admission is included with your ticket to the Tryon Palace complex or can be purchased separately.

Tryon Palace Historic Sites and Gardens is open Monday through Saturday from 9 A.M. to 5 P.M. and Sunday from 1 P.M. to 5 P.M. It is closed Thanksgiving, December 24, 25, and 26, and New Year's. An admission fee is charged. Special events include garden tours in April and October and Christmas tours in December. Its two gift shops—the Tryon Palace Museum Shop and the Crafts and Garden Shop—are open daily. For more information, call 800-767-1560 or 252-514-4900 or visit www.tryonpalace.org.

■ The *Attmore-Oliver House*, at 512 Pollock Street, is another museum house well worth visiting. Now home to the New Bern Historical Society, the house was constructed in 1790 and enlarged in 1834. It is furnished with 18th- and 19th-century antiques and features Civil War artifacts and a doll collection. The home is open Thursday through Saturday from 1 P.M. to 4 P.M. from early May to late October or by appointment. An admission fee is charged. For information, call 252-638-8558 or visit www.newbernhistorical.org/attmore.html.

■ The *North Carolina History Education Center* plans to open in 2010, in time to celebrate New Bern's 300th anniversary. The 48,000-square-foot learning center is being built on the Trent River. Visitors will be able to experience the past by utilizing hand-held and other digital devices of the 21st century. Adults and children will have a variety of interactive options such as becoming a crew member trying to sail a ship along the treacherous North Carolina coast. The history center is still in the fundraising stage; over $8 million has been raised so far. To invest in the center, call the Making History Office at 252-514-4956 or visit www.tryonpalace.org.

MUSEUMS AND SCIENCE CENTERS

■ *Firemen's Museum*, at 408 Hancock Street, honors New Bern's firefighting outfits through the years. It houses an array of 19th-century

Fireman's Museum
BILL RUSS, COURTESY OF NORTH
CAROLINA DIVISION OF TOURISM,
FILM AND SPORTS DEVELOPMENT

man- and horse-drawn fire engines, 20th-century steam and motorized fire engines, sundry firefighting equipment, and Civil War relics. Children enjoy learning about Fred the fire horse, whose mounted head hangs near equipment he once pulled. Fred joined the Atlantic Company in 1908 and valiantly served until his death in 1925, long after motorized fire engines came into use. The museum and gift shop are open Monday through Saturday from 10 A.M. to 4 P.M.; winter hours may vary. The museum is closed Thanksgiving, Christmas, and New Year's. An admission fee is charged. For more information, call 252-636-4087 or visit www.newbernmuseums.com.

CULTURAL OFFERINGS

■ *Bank of the Arts*, home of the Craven County Arts Council and Gallery, is located at 317 Middle Street in a 1913 granite Neoclassical Revival building that was once the Peoples Bank. This gallery displays an array of pottery, sculpture, paintings, photography, and fiber art by southeastern artists. It is open Tuesday through Saturday from 10 A.M. to 6 P.M. Admission is free. For information, call 252-638-2577 or visit www.cravenarts.org.

■ The *New Bern Civic Theatre*, at 412 Pollock Street, features professional and local actors performing a pleasing variety of dramas, comedies, musicals, and even sign-language productions. Call 800-346-2770 or 252-633-0567 or visit www.newberncivictheatre.org for information.

■ *A Day at the Farm* is located 15 miles west of New Bern at 183 Woodrow McCoy Road. This historic dairy farm provides a nice outing for the young at heart. It features old dairy barns, milking equipment, and period antiques, as well as farm animals, hayrides, a seasonal pumpkin patch and corn maze, a walking trail, and a picnic area. For an appointment, call 252-514-9494 or visit www.adayatthefarm.com.

SPECIAL SHOPPING

- The **Farmers' Market**, at 421 South Front Street, offers fresh produce, homemade jams and jellies, and local artwork. From March through December, it is open every Saturday from 7 A.M. to 1 P.M.; it is also open Tuesday afternoons in season. Call 252-633-0043 for information.

- Visitors to New Bern can cool off with an ice-cold glass of "Brad's Drink" at the **Birthplace of Pepsi-Cola**, a souvenir shop at the corner of Middle and Pollock streets. It was here that pharmacist Caleb "Doc" Bradham formulated his famous soft drink behind his soda fountain in the 1890s. Unfortunately, Bradham was forced into bankruptcy by the collapse of the sugar market following World War I, and the rights to the drink were purchased by a New York company. Bradham died in 1934, never realizing any of the profits his drink produced. Bradham's old pharmacy is open Monday through Saturday from 10 A.M. to 6 P.M. A film, *The History of Pepsi-Cola*, is shown daily at 11 A.M., 1 P.M., 3 P.M., and 5 P.M. For information, call 252-636-5898 or visit www.pepsistore.com.

- **Carolina Creations**, at 317 Pollock Street, sells an array of wonderful handcrafted pottery, sculpture, jewelry, cards, and prints by local and nationally known artists. For information, call 252-633-4369 or visit carolinacreationsnewbern.com.

- **Mitchell Hardware**, at 215 Craven Street, is an authentic turn-of-the-20th-century hardware store complete with enamelware, crockery, pottery, and more. For information, call 252-638-4261.

- **Weavers Web Gallery**, at 602 Pollock Street, sells hand-woven textiles, skeins of beautiful yarn, and all manner of patterns for cross-stitch, weaving, and needlepoint. For information, call 252-514-2681.

- Middle Street is peppered with antique shops. Check out **A Shopping Guide to the Governor's Walk**, available at the Craven County Convention and Visitors Bureau, for a list of these and other shops.

RECREATION

■ One of four national forests in North Carolina, **Croatan National Forest** is the only true coastal forest east of the Mississippi. Spreading over 159,000 acres south from New Bern to Bogue Sound, the forest encompasses ecosystems ranging from upland hardwoods to pocosins (swamps on a hill). It provides habitat for a variety of flora and fauna, including such endangered species as Venus flytraps, alligators, and red-cockaded woodpeckers. The forest offers numerous boating access areas and hiking trails, including the 21-mile Neusiok Trail, which stretches from the Neuse River to the Newport River. Primitive camping is permitted except in developed day-use areas and actively managed sites. Other outdoor recreational opportunities include bird-watching, camping, and picnicking. Fishing, hunting, and trapping are regulated by the North Carolina Wildlife Resources Commission; information is available where licenses are sold. The ranger's office, located at 141 East Fisher Avenue in New Bern, is open Monday through Friday from 8 A.M. to 4:30 P.M.; an information kiosk is outside. For information, call 252-638-5628 or visit www.cs.unca.edu/nfsnc/recreation/croatan.pdf.

SEASONAL EVENTS

■ The **Spring Historic Homes and Gardens Tour** is held every April, when the azaleas and dogwoods are in full bloom. Cosponsored by the New Bern Historical Society and the New Bern Preservation Foundation, the tour includes many private houses usually closed to the public, as well as churches and other historically significant buildings. A fee is charged. For information, contact Spring Historic Homes and Gardens Tour, P.O. Box 207, New Bern, NC 28563 (252-633-6448 or 252-638-8558).

■ The annual **Mumfest** street festival is held downtown in mid-October. Food, entertainment, and an antiques-and-crafts show are offered. For information, call 252-638-5781 or visit www.mumfest.com.

■ The New Bern Historical Society organizes a **New Bern Ghostwalk** around Halloween to benefit preservation and education programs. A candlelight tour of a cemetery, a presentation about ghosts from the Gilded Age, and a vaudeville show at the Masonic Theatre are just a few of the ticketed events. For more information, contact the New Bern Historical

Society (252-638-8558; www.newbernhistorical.org) or the Craven County Convention and Visitors Bureau (800-437-5767; www.visitnewbern.com).

Places to Stay

Not surprisingly, a number of bed-and-breakfasts operate in New Bern's elegant historic houses. At the other end of the spectrum are newly constructed, well-known chains situated on the waterfront; most of these have marinas.

RESORTS, HOTELS, AND MOTELS

- **Sheraton Grand New Bern.** Expensive. 100 Middle Street (800-326-3745 or 252-638-3585). At least half the rooms here offer a view of the Trent and Neuse rivers. The hotel has 156 boat slips for mariners. Its restaurant overlooks the marina and pool. Senior-citizen discounts are offered.

- **BridgePointe Hotel and Marina.** Expensive/Moderate. 101 Howell Road, at the junction of U.S. 70 and U.S. 70E Bypass (877-283-7713 or 252-636-3637; www.bridgepointehotel.com). All of the newly renovated rooms here have river views. Amenities include in-room coffee makers, cable television, a swimming pool, and a marina. Nikola's Restaurant, a Morehead City favorite, has a location here. Senior-citizen, military, and business rates are offered.

- **Comfort Suites Riverfront Park.** Moderate. 218 East Front Street (800-228-5150 or 252-636-0022). Comfort Suites is situated next to Union Point Park along the bank of the Neuse. Some suites have waterfront balconies and whirlpool baths. A fitness room and an outdoor swimming pool are available to guests. Complimentary continental breakfast is offered.

INNS AND BED-AND-BREAKFASTS

■ **Harmony House Inn.** Expensive/Moderate. 215 Pollock Street (800-636-3113 or 252-636-3810; www.harmonyhouseinn.com). Housed in a handsome 1850s Greek Revival structure with a broad front porch, this friendly inn offers seven spacious guest rooms and three suites decorated with antiques and locally crafted reproductions. All have private baths. A full breakfast is served.

■ **The Aerie.** Moderate. 509 Pollock Street (800-849-5553 or 252-636-5553; www.aerieinn.com). Located one block from Tryon Palace, this charming 1880s bed-and-breakfast features a player piano. Each of its seven individually appointed guest rooms has a private bath, cable television, high-speed Internet access, and a telephone. A full breakfast with a choice of three entrées is served daily in the dining room.

■ **Howard House.** Moderate. 207 Pollock Street (800-705-5261 or 252-514-6709; www.howardhousebnb.com). This lovely Victorian bed-and-breakfast features period antiques in its four guest rooms. Each has a private bath. Complimentary bicycles, terry-cloth robes, chocolates, and fresh flowers add to the experience. The full gourmet breakfast served each morning in the formal dining room may include orange French toast, "Bacon Omelet Baskets," or apple-pecan pancakes.

■ **The Meadows Inn.** Moderate. 212 Pollock Street (877-551-1776 or 252-634-1776; www.meadowsinn-nc.com). Built in 1847, this antebellum home turned inn is located in the heart of the downtown historic district. It offers a two-room suite and six guest rooms with fireplaces and private baths. Breakfast and a morning newspaper are brought to guests' rooms.

■ **Hanna House.** Moderate/Inexpensive. 218 Pollock Street (866-830-4371 or 252-635-3209; www.hannahousenc.net). The Rudolph Ulrich House was built in 1896 and served as the home of one of New Bern's grocery suppliers. Now revived as the Hanna House, it offers two rooms and a luxury suite, each with a private bath. Homemade breads, muffins, and unique breakfast entrées are served each morning in the formal dining room. Refreshments and snacks are served during the afternoon in the dining room and on the front porch.

BAYARD WOOTTEN, PICTORIAL PHOTOGRAPHER

By Anne Holcomb Waters

Mary Bayard Morgan was born in her grandparents' antebellum home on East Front Street in New Bern on December 17, 1875. The elder of two children of Mary Devereaux Clarke and Rufus Morgan was to become one of North Carolina's most illustrious photographers and a woman with an indomitable spirit of adventure.

Bayard Wootten
NORTH CAROLINA COLLECTION,
UNIVERSITY OF NORTH CAROLINA
LIBRARY AT CHAPEL HILL

Like her well-bred mother before her, Bayard (pronounced By-ard) studied drawing and painting as a child. It was a number of years before the camera became her chosen art form. A devotee of the pictorial style of photography, she would be well served by her classical training.

When Bayard was 17, she left New Bern to study at the North Carolina State Normal and Industrial School in Greensboro, now the University of North Carolina at Greensboro. In a letter to the school's president, she wrote, "I am determined to make my own living, and if I cannot do it by teaching I shall have to do it by sewing, and therefore am very anxious for an education."

Bayard left the school after a year and a half to teach art at the Arkansas Deaf-Mute Institute in Little Rock. From there, she went on to teach at the state school for the deaf in Cave City, Georgia, where she met and married Charles Thomas Wootten. The marriage failed following an unhappy incident involving a hot rent check. Barred from entering their apartment by the landlord while her husband was out of town on business, Bayard and son Charles traveled to New Bern on borrowed money. Nine months later, her second son, Rufus, was born.

Since she had children to provide for, Bayard worked with her mother decorating small items such as fans for the tourist trade. According to her son Charles, the first patented label for Pepsi-Cola was Bayard's handiwork.

In 1904, she began to explore camera work at Garrett Gerock's photography studio. He allowed her free reign of his darkroom until he began to see her emerging talent as a threat to his business. Having decided to go into photography, Bayard took a trip to Asheville to study with Ignatius "Nace" Brock, her friend and would-be mentor.

Early in her career, Bayard made her living doing routine trade photography. Beginning in 1898, the United States Post Office Department permitted privately made postcards to go through the mail at a one-cent rate. These penny postcards became enormously popular and gave Bayard her first taste of success as a photographer. From there, she insinuated her way into the North Carolina National Guard, becoming its first woman member. She was named chief of publicity.

Following a failed attempt at opening a studio in New York, Bayard found solid itinerant work at North Carolina's college and university campuses. In 1928, she moved to Chapel Hill, where she and her half-brother, George Moulton, opened a studio to accommodate their newfound business. It was during this period that she hit her artistic stride and created the timeless portraits for which she is famous.

A trip to the Penland School in the North Carolina mountains in 1927 to shoot photographs for the school's catalog was a catalyst for change in Bayard's career. With her boys raised and well educated at the United States Naval Academy and Harvard, and with her business rock-solid under the guidance of George Moulton, she finally had the freedom to pursue her artistic vision with vigor. Often traveling with young men from the Chapel Hill studio, Bayard hit the road with her eight-by-10-inch camera.

Cabins in the Laurel was the first of Bayard's six books to be published. She was well established in the South Carolina Low Country by the time her favorite book—*Charleston: Azaleas and Old Bricks*—was released. The last of the books she illustrated, *From My Highest Hill: Carolina Mountain Folks*, was published in 1941. In her 60s, she was undaunted by the journey for her work on that book, though she needed a team of oxen to extricate her auto from the mire on four separate occasions. Her return to the mountains brought her much acclaim but also ushered in the twilight years of her career.

In 1947, Bayard suffered a hemorrhage in her eye, which effectively ended her serious camera work. In 1954, she sold the Chapel Hill studio and moved back to her grandparents' home on East Front Street with 2,000 of her favorite negatives. She died there on April 6, 1959.

"I have always been chasing something," she wrote her friend Nace Brock, "but one of the surprises that life has held for me is that I am happier as an old woman than I ever was as a young one. Perhaps the reason for this is that I realize now it does not matter whether we arrive. The joy is in the going."

Places to Eat

- **Henderson House.** Expensive. 216 Pollock Street (252-637-4784). Housed in a lovely Federal-style brick home listed on the National Register of Historic Places, Henderson House offers gourmet fare served in an Old World atmosphere. The specialties include steak and seafood entrées. Dinner is served Tuesday through Saturday. Henderson House is available for private parties.

- **The Harvey Mansion Historic Inn & Restaurant.** Expensive/Moderate. 221 South Front Street (252-638-3232). The Harvey Mansion has six formal dining rooms, where it serves award-winning duck, veal, and seafood. The cellar pub offers an equally delicious but more casual menu. The mansion overlooks the Trent River and is listed on the National Register. It is open for dinner Tuesday through Sunday.

- **The Chelsea.** Moderate. 335 Middle Street (252-637-5469; www.thechelsea.com). This restaurant and "publick house" serves up a smorgasbord of cuisines: French, German, Italian, Cajun, and American. The Chelsea is housed in the second drugstore operated by Caleb Bradham, the inventor of Pepsi-Cola. Lunch and dinner are served Monday through Saturday.

- **Morgan's Tavern & Grill.** Moderate/Inexpensive. 235 Craven Street (252-636-2430). This convenient restaurant serves a wide range of salads, soups, entrées, pasta, and sandwiches that will suit any palate. The wine list includes selections from over seven countries. Lunch and dinner are served Monday through Saturday.

- **Amy's Coffee and Confections.** Inexpensive. 1706 U.S. 70E (252-635-2697). This non-downtown coffee shop offers coffee, pastries, and desserts from 6:30 A.M. to 4:30 P.M. Monday through Saturday.

- **Captain Ratty's.** Inexpensive. 202 Middle Street (252-633-2088). This restaurant is housed in a handsome space with wood floors and a pressed-tin ceiling. Although there's a bar, this is nonetheless a good option for families with children. The menu is child-friendly, too. Be sure to try the tasty crab cake sandwich. Lunch and dinner are served daily.

- *Cow Café*. Inexpensive. 319 Middle Street (252-672-9269). This whimsical spot is owned by Maola Dairy employees. The kids can enjoy a "Moonilla" ice-cream cone while you relax over a "Cowpuccino." You can browse the café's "Bovine Bazaar," which has more than 300 cow gift items, or visit "The Farm" if there are "calves in your herd." Lunch and dinner are served Monday through Saturday.

- *The Gallery Café*. Inexpensive. 210 Craven Street (252-633-6407). This is a delightfully funky addition to New Bern's restaurant scene. Original art by owner Charles Hines and timeless photographs by Bayard Wootten are available for purchase. The art-themed sandwiches include "The Duffy," which includes Brie, chicken breast, and mango chutney on a croissant. Live music is offered on the weekends. Breakfast, lunch, and dinner are served Monday through Saturday.

Nearby

- Settled in the 1700s at the gateway to Pamlico Sound, **Oriental** is the sailing capital of North Carolina. Its name was inspired by a Union Civil War ship that sank off the Outer Banks in 1862. This quaint fishing village beckons sailors of all skills, from yachtsmen on the nearby Intracoastal Waterway to novices who want to learn the skills at one of Oriental's sailing schools. Hunting, kayaking, canoeing, birding, cycling, and horseback riding are just a few recreational activities the town has to offer. To reach Oriental, take U.S. 17 North from New Bern, then follow N.C. 55; it's about a 25-mile drive.

  If you are interested in sailing lessons, contact **Oriental School of Sailing** (252-249-0960) or **Carolina Sailing Unlimited** (252-249-0850).

  The **Circle 10 Art Gallery**, at 708 Broad Street, is an artists' cooperative with local artwork for sale. Call 252-249-0298 for hours of operation.

  If you decide to stay in Oriental, you're sure to find a welcome at the **Cartwright House** (252-249-1337), **The Inn at Oriental** (252-249-1078), or **Oriental Marina Motel** (252-249-1818), all of which are within easy walking distance of the harbor.

- **CSS Neuse State Historic Site** and the **Richard Caswell Memorial** are located north of New Bern on U.S. 70 just within the city limits of

Kinston. An audiovisual program and a statue at the Richard Caswell Memorial honor North Carolina's first governor. Under a shelter outside lie the remains of the last ironclad built by the Confederacy, the CSS *Neuse*. In 1865, its crew sank the vessel to keep it from enemy hands. It remained embedded in mud for nearly 100 years before it was extracted and put on display. The sites are open Monday through Saturday from 9 A.M. to 5 P.M. and Sunday from 1 P.M. to 5 P.M. from April to October. From November to March, they are open Tuesday through Saturday from 10 A.M. to 4 P.M. and Sunday from 1 P.M. to 4 P.M. Admission is free. For information, call 252-522-2091 or visit www.ah.dcr.state.nc.us/sections/hs/neuse/neuse.htm.

■ *Minnesott Beach* is located a free 20-minute ferry ride across the Neuse. Take the Cherry Branch ferry to U.S. 306; you can check the ferry schedule by visiting www.pamlico-nc.com/ferry.

■ *Neuse River Recreation Area* is located approximately 11 miles southeast of New Bern on U.S. 70. Camping, hiking, fishing, and swimming are the main activities here. Call 252-638-5628 for information. The ranger station is located at 141 East Fisher Avenue in New Bern.

MOREHEAD CITY

Morehead City is for fishermen what Oriental is for sailors: a mecca. Morehead City is also the gateway to two alluring destinations—charming Beaufort to the east and lively Atlantic Beach to the south. But don't make the mistake of visiting the area without taking a look around Morehead City. At the very least, make the trip to its picturesque waterfront to gaze at its fleet of charter boats, to eat at its famous boat-to-shore seafood restaurants, and to shop at its fish markets and gift and antique shops.

Morehead City is the product of the ambitions of John Motley Morehead, governor of North Carolina from 1841 to 1845. Together with an associate, Silas Webb, Morehead purchased a 600-acre tract in 1853. He dreamed of developing it into a deepwater port that would eventually be linked by rail to the Piedmont and to cities on the Ohio and Mississippi rivers. That town, Carolina City, met an early demise when Morehead decided to subdivide his holdings. He subsequently planned a new town just to the east of the original, sketching out 50-by-100-foot lots that he put up for sale in November 1857. Two months later, excursion trains were bringing regular crowds from Goldsboro. By May 1858, every new lot in town had sold, earning Morehead $1 million. A post office was established here on February 28, 1859.

Morehead City was occupied during the Civil War. It rebounded at the turn of the 20th century to become a fashionable summer resort. Meanwhile, the fishing industry continued to grow. In 1952, a deepwater port was established at Morehead City, fulfilling John Motley Morehead's dream. The town has since become known as a port for shipping bulk cargo, particularly coal and phosphate.

Today, Morehead City is renowned for its fishing waters, fed by the Gulf Stream. Fishermen come to test their skills against marlin, amberjack, mackerel, tarpon, and bluefish. The town is also becoming known as an excellent diving destination among those in search of shipwrecks and buried treasure.

JUST THE FACTS

Morehead City is on U.S. 70. It is accessible from the north via N.C. 101, from the west via N.C. 24, and from the south via N.C. 58.

Three airports serve the area. Craven County Regional Airport in New Bern offers US Airways express and charter flights; call 252-638-8591 for information. To the west in Jacksonville, Albert J. Ellis Airport offers US Airways commuter flights; call 910-324-1100. Michael J. Smith Airport, located in Beaufort, offers private and charter services; call 252-728-2323.

The bus station is located at 105 North 13th Street; call 252-726-3029.

The best source for information on the area is the Carteret County Tourism Bureau, at 3409 Arendell Street; call 800-786-6962 or 252-726-8148 or visit www.crystalcoastnc.org.

The *Carteret County News Times* is the local newspaper.

The shipping port at Morehead City
COURTESY OF NORTH CAROLINA DIVISION OF TOURISM, FILM AND SPORTS DEVELOPMENT

Things to Do

MUSEUMS AND SCIENCE CENTERS

■ The **History Place**, at 1008 Arendell Street, is a 12,000-square-foot facility that houses the Rodney B. Kemp Museum Gallery, the Jack Spencer
Goodwin Research Library, the Les A. Ewen Auditorium, and the Museum Store. It is also the new home of the Carteret County Historical
Society. The History Place contains an interesting collection of artifacts
and memorabilia reflecting the county's Native American, military, and
maritime past. Visitors can literally walk through exhibits such as an old
general store, an early school room, and a Victorian parlor. The History
Place is open Tuesday through Saturday from 10 A.M. to 4 P.M. year-round
except on major holidays. The museum is run by volunteer docents. Admission is free. For more information, call 252-247-7533 or visit
www.thehistoryplace.com.

The **Museum Store** features gifts reflecting the past and present of
Carteret County. It offers a selection of publications, many published by
the Carteret County Historical Society, as well as nautical ornaments, paintings, jewelry, locally crafted carved birds, and other souvenirs.

Scuba diving at Morehead City
COURTESY OF OLYMPUS DIVE
CENTER, MOREHEAD CITY

The *Jack Spencer Goodwin Research Library* houses more than 6,000 publications and an extensive picture file documenting the history of Carteret County. Especially notable are the genealogy materials and the Civil War history collection.

RECREATION

■ Fishing is the reason most people visit Morehead City. Opportunities to test your skills abound. Onshore and offshore fishing trips are available, as are charter rigs. Or you can bring your own boat or rent one at the waterfront. A list of charters and head boats is available from the Carteret County Tourism Bureau.

■ Scuba-diving adventures can be booked through a number of outfits. You might try **Olympus Dive Center**, on the waterfront at 713 Shepard Street. Call 252-726-9432 or visit www.olympusdiving.com.

SEASONAL EVENTS

■ The **Big Rock Marlin Tournament**, held the second week in June, is part of the World Billfish Series. Blue marlin fishermen come from near and far to compete for cash prizes totaling over $1 million; the winner takes home nearly $500,000. For information, call 252-247-3575. For a list of all area fishing tournaments and for information on obtaining tournament licenses, call the North Carolina Division of Marine Fisheries at 252-726-7021 or visit www.ncdmf.net.

THE COASTAL PLAIN *143*

- The **North Carolina Seafood Festival** is held the first weekend in October on the Morehead City waterfront. Thousands flock to the festival to enjoy the music, to admire the arts and crafts, and, of course, to sample the delicious seafood. For information, call 252-726-6273 or visit www.ncseafoodfestival.org.

- The **Bald Is Beautiful Convention and Contest** originally sought to gather at Bald Head Island, off the Cape Fear coast. But Morehead City, which has a sense of humor about its name, is glad the convention opted to meet here instead. On the second Saturday in September, the bald and the proud compete for such titles as "Most Kissable" and "Shiniest Head." For information, call 252-726-1855 or visit www.members.aol.com/baldusa.

Places to Stay

RESORTS, HOTELS, AND MOTELS

Accommodations in Morehead City tend to be a little less expensive than in Beaufort and Atlantic Beach, especially in the high season. Chain hotels and motels have secured the market here.

- **Hampton Inn on Bogue Sound**. Expensive/Moderate. 4035 Arendell Street (800-538-6338 or 252-240-2300; www.vacations.net/atlantic_beach/hampton_inn_16052.htm). This hotel overlooks Bogue Sound. It offers a complimentary continental breakfast, free in-room movies, an exercise room, and an outdoor pool. Its suites have living rooms, microwaves, refrigerators, and wet bars.

- **Best Western Buccaneer Motor Inn**. Moderate. 2806 Arendell Street (800-682-4982 or 252-726-3115). The Best Western offers a complimentary breakfast and newspaper, cable television, a pool, and golf and fishing packages. Rooms with king-sized beds and Jacuzzis are available.

- **Comfort Inn**. Moderate. 3100 Arendell Street (800-422-5404 or 252-247-3434). This motel offers comfortable rooms, free cable television, complimentary continental breakfast, a newspaper delivered to your door, a pool, a fitness room, and golf packages.

- ***Econo Lodge***. Moderate. 3410 Bridges Street (800-533-7556 or 252-247-2940). A motor inn with a colonial theme, the Econo Lodge offers free continental breakfast, cable television, a pool, and golf and fishing packages.

Places to Eat

- ***Key West Seafood Company***. Expensive/Moderate. 506 Evans Street (252-726-6835). Owner Dan Hatch recently returned to his native state from Key West, where he was co-owner of the popular restaurant Blue Heaven. His new place serves island-influenced fare like Jerk chicken and barbecued shrimp. Several vegetarian items are on the menu. Save room for the "Banana Heaven"—banana bread and bananas flambéed with spiced rum and homemade vanilla ice cream. Lunch and dinner are served daily.

- ***Trateotu***. Expensive/Moderate. 506 Arendell Street (252-240-3380). Trateotu specializes in Caribbean-style cuisine with an emphasis on seafood. Its menu changes frequently. When you visit, the entrées may include panko shrimp and scallops with wasabi aioli and chicken breast stuffed with prosciutto and Havarti. Dinner is served Tuesday through Saturday.

- ***William's***. Expensive/Moderate. 4051 Arendell Street (252-240-1755). William's is a fairly new addition to the restaurant scene in Morehead City, and a very good one at that. The hoisin-glazed sea scallops are a great starter, as are the fried oysters. The pan-seared grouper and the grilled tuna are also delicious. Dinner is served Tuesday through Sunday.

- ***Windansea***. Expensive/Moderate. 708 Evans Street (252-247-3000). This bright restaurant on the waterfront offers a nice mixture of entrées, including seafood, lamb, and wood-oven pizzas. Dinner is served Tuesday through Sunday.

- ***Mrs. Willis' Restaurant***. Moderate. 3114 Bridges Street, behind Morehead Plaza (252-726-3741). Mrs. Willis began cooking barbecue, chicken, and pies in 1949. Her family carries on the tradition today. Lunch is served Sunday, Tuesday, Wednesday, Thursday, and Friday; dinner is served daily.

■ **Sanitary Fish Market.** Moderate. 501 Evans Street (252-247-3111; www.sanitaryfishmarket.com). A Tar Heel institution, the Sanitary Fish Market has been serving fresh seafood on the Morehead City waterfront since 1938. This vast, 600-seat restaurant offers broiled and fried seafood, steaks, lobster, homemade soup, chowder, and hush puppies. It is open daily for lunch and dinner from February through November.

■ **Bistro by the Sea.** Moderate/Inexpensive. 4031 Arendell Street (252-247-2777; www.bistro-by-the-sea.com). The specialty here is seafood, but the other entrées, including the "Bistro Burger," are also very tasty. Start with a cup of shrimp bisque before moving on to the almond-encrusted chicken breast with hazelnut cream sauce. The piano-and-cigar bar offers specialty martinis. Dinner is served Tuesday through Saturday; the restaurant is closed during January.

■ **Raps Grill and Bar.** Moderate/Inexpensive. 715 Arendell Street (252-240-1213; www.rapsgrillandbar.com). Housed in a lovingly renovated 19th-century structure that boasts a 35-foot oak bar, Raps offers seafood, pasta, chicken, burritos, burgers, and Maryland-style crab. Lunch is served Monday through Saturday; dinner is offered daily.

BEAUFORT

Beaufort is a lovely old fishing village that has the distinction of being North Carolina's third-oldest town. At the time of the American Revolution, it was the third-largest port in the state. Today, it boasts a 12-block national historic district on the original "Plan of Beaufort Towne," platted by Henry Somerset in 1713.

When French Huguenots and immigrants from Germany, Sweden, England, Scotland, and Ireland arrived here around 1708, the place was known to the Indians as Wareiock, or "Fish Town." It was renamed Beaufort for the duke of Beaufort, one of the Lords Proprietors.

Beaufort was an important military port during the War of 1812,

Beaufort Waterfront
COURTESY OF NORTH CAROLINA DIVISION OF TOURISM, FILM AND SPORTS DEVELOPMENT

when much privateering occurred here. One of the most famous and successful privateers was Otway Burns, captain of the *Snap Dragon*, who between 1812 and 1814 captured cargoes worth millions of dollars. After the war, he stayed in Beaufort and became a successful shipbuilder, merchant, and politician.

In the 19th century, Beaufort continued to prosper as a port and as an agricultural, commercial, and governmental center. Wealthy planters and their families sought its pleasant and healthful environment.

Early in the Civil War, Beaufort was again called to military duty, this time aiding blockade runners bringing supplies to the Confederacy. On March 25, 1862, the town was occupied by Union forces. It was from Beaufort that the Federals launched the formidable fleet that helped conquer the South.

After the war, Beaufort was a seasonal resort town, its economic importance diminished. Fishing became its major industry. The harvesting and processing of menhaden—used for fish meal and industrial oils—proved particularly important.

By the 1970s, Beaufort's waterfront was in serious decline. Residents embarked upon a mission to save their old village. The result of their efforts is one of the most attractive and appealing destinations in the entire state.

JUST THE FACTS

From the north or south, drivers can take U.S. 17 to U.S. 70 to reach Beaufort.

Craven County Regional Airport in New Bern offers express and charter flights via US Airways and Midway Airlines; call 252-638-8591 for information. Michael J. Smith Airport, named in honor of the Beaufort son who perished in the *Challenger* space shuttle accident, offers private and charter service; call 252-728-1777 or 252-728-2323.

The nearest bus station is located at 206 North 15th Street in Morehead City; call 252-726-3029.

Boaters can stop at the Beaufort Municipal Docks (252-728-2503) or Town Creek Marina (252-728-6111; www.towncreekmarina.com).

A good source for information on the area is the Carteret County Tourism Bureau, located at 3409 Arendell Street in Morehead City; call 800-786-6962 or 252-726-8148 or visit www.crystalcoastnc.org. For information on Beaufort, visit www.historicbeaufort.com.

Things to Do

HISTORIC PLACES, GARDENS, AND TOURS

■ *Beaufort Historic Site*, located at 130 Turner Street, includes three restored homes built between 1767 and 1825; the Carteret County Courthouse, constructed in 1796; the Carteret County Jail, built in 1829; and the Apothecary Shop and Doctor's Office, erected in 1859. From March through November, it is open from 9:30 A.M. to 5 P.M. From December through February, it is open 10 A.M. to 4 P.M. For more information, call 800-575-7483 or 252-728-5225 or visit www.beauforthistoricsite.org.

While you're at the site, be sure to browse the books, hand-carved decoys, dolls, fine porcelain, and silver in *The Old Beaufort Shop*, the museum store in the Safrit Historical Center, where tickets for various tours may be purchased. You'll also want to check out the **Mattie King Davis Art Gallery**, which features the works of over 100 local and regional artists. The gallery, located in the historic Rustell House on the grounds of the historic site, is open 10 A.M. to 4 P.M. Monday through Saturday.

The **Old Burying Ground**, on Ann Street, is the site of graves from the Revolutionary War and Civil War eras. The cemetery, administered by the historic site, is listed on the National Register of Historic Places. Shaded by majestic live oaks entwined within ancient wisteria vines, it has many tales to tell. Among those interred here are Otway Burns, privateer hero of the War of 1812, and a 13-year-old girl buried in a rum barrel.

Guided tours of the historic site are offered daily at 10 A.M., 11:30 A.M., 1 P.M., and 3 P.M. Tours of the cemetery are conducted June through October on Tuesday, Wednesday, and Thursday at 10 A.M. and 2:30 P.M. The site also offers English double-decker bus tours, operated by the Beaufort Historical Association (http://historicbeaufort.com/bhaindex.htm). These entertaining tours, available April through October, run about 45 minutes; they are offered Monday, Wednesday, and Friday at 11 A.M. and 1:30 P.M. and Saturday at 11 A.M. A fee is charged for all three tours.

MUSEUMS AND SCIENCE CENTERS

■ A visit to the **North Carolina Maritime Museum**, at 315 Front Street, is a wonderful way to learn about coastal and maritime history. This bus-

tling museum offers exhibits on the United States Life Saving Service and its historic lighthouses, coastal and marine life, watercraft, decoys, and artifacts recently recovered from an 18th-century shipwreck thought to be Blackbeard's flagship, the *Queen Anne's Revenge*. Highlights include a miniature submarine-like "life car," an "observation bell" reminiscent of *20,000 Leagues under the Sea*, and an amazingly primitive, basket-like boat called a "bamboo coracle." Beyond its

North Carolina Maritime Museum
COURTESY OF NORTH CAROLINA DIVISION OF TOURISM, FILM AND SPORTS DEVELOPMENT

fascinating exhibits, the museum offers a broad range of educational programs for children and adults. These programs range from boat-building and sailing classes to environmental studies at the museum's Cape Lookout facility. Quarterly calendars are available.

To watch boatbuilders in action, visit the **Harvey W. Smith Watercraft Center**, located across the street from the museum. The center also houses the **John S. MacCormack Model Shop**, where scale models of watercraft are constructed.

The museum's gift shop stocks a great selection of books on maritime and natural history. Its library is available for research. The North Carolina Maritime Museum is open Monday through Friday from 9 A.M. to 5 P.M., Saturday from 10 A.M. to 5 P.M., and Sunday from 1 P.M. to 5 P.M. Admission is free, though donations are welcome. Call 252-728-7317 or visit www.ah.dcr.state.nc/us/sections/maritime/ or www.ncmm-friends.org.

RECREATION

■ **Island Ferry Adventures**, at 610 Front Street, is a convenient water-taxi service that provides transportation and scenic tours to Cape Lookout, Shackleford Banks, and the Rachel Carson Estuarine Research Reserve. For information, call 252-728-7555 or visit www.islandferryadventures.com.

■ **Lookout Cruises** sails to Cape Lookout twice daily. You can also try a morning dolphin watch or a sunset or moonlight cruise aboard the company's 42-passenger catamaran. Call 252-504-SAIL or visit www.lookoutcruises.com for information.

■ If you want to go snorkeling or diving in search of shipwrecks, you might try **Discovery Diving**. If you're an experienced diver and would like to join up with others, Discovery can help out, too. Call 252-728-2265 or visit www.discoverydiving.com for information.

■ For information on ecology tours, contact the North Carolina Maritime Museum's **Cape Lookout Studies Program** (252-504-2452; www.capelookoutstudies.org) or **Coastal Ecology Sails** (252-241-6866 or 252-247-3860; www.goodfortunesails.com).

Seasonal Events

■ Sponsored by the Beaufort Historical Society, the **Beaufort Old Homes and Gardens Tour** and the **Antiques Show and Sale** are held the last full weekend in June. Visitors enjoy tours of historic homes, churches, gardens, and the Old Burying Ground. Antiques are shown at the Morehead City Civic Center. Double-decker bus tours are conducted throughout the weekend, and entertainment is provided. For more information, call 800-575-7483 or 252-728-5225.

■ Beaufort Historic Site celebrates the holidays with two annual events. Visitors can enjoy Thanksgiving dinner served on the grounds of the historic site at the **Community Thanksgiving Feast**, hosted the Sunday before Thanksgiving. The **Coastal Carolina Christmas Walk**, held the second weekend in December, is a festive open house and self-guided walking tour of the historic site and Beaufort's bed-and-breakfasts, all decorated for the holiday season.

Places to Stay

Inns and Bed-and-Breakfasts

■ **Beaufort Inn**. Expensive. 101 Ann Street (800-726-0321 or 252-728-2600; www.beaufort-inn.com). Beaufort Inn offers 44 well-appointed waterfront rooms overlooking Taylor Creek. It provides boat slips, an exercise room, an outdoor hot tub, and bicycles upon request.

■ **The Cedars Inn**. Expensive. 305 Front Street (252-728-7036; www.cedarsinn.com). Located in the heart of the historic district, The Cedars is comprised of two elegant historic houses, one of them a former shipwright's 1768 home. All 11 guest rooms have private baths. The inn offers a full breakfast, a wine bar, a deck, and bicycles.

■ **Inlet Inn**. Expensive. 601 Front Street (800-554-5466 or 252-728-3600; www.inlet-inn.com). The harbor-front rooms here have a seating area, a refrigerator, a bar, and cable television. Many have private porches with rocking chairs, while others have fireplaces or window seats with a view of Cape Lookout. Continental breakfast is provided. Boat slips are available.

- **Captain's Quarters**. Expensive/Moderate. 315 Ann Street (800-659-7111 or 252-728-7711; www.captainsquarters.com). Captain's Quarters, a charming Victorian inn with a wraparound porch, is located one block from the waterfront. Its three guest rooms have private baths. Continental breakfast is provided. Children under 12 are not allowed.

- **Delamar Inn**. Expensive/Moderate. 217 Turner Street (800-349-5823 or 252-728-4300; www.bbonline.com/nc/delamarinn). This 1866 inn offers three guest rooms furnished with antiques. Each room has a private bath. The gracious hosts will provide beach chairs and bicycles if asked. Refreshments are served in the afternoon. The inn is closed from December to February.

- **Langdon House Bed-and-Breakfast**. Expensive/Moderate. 135 Craven Street (252-728-5499; www.langdonhouse.com). This hospitable inn has three guest rooms, each with a private bath. The rooms are decorated in a simple 18th-century style. A full breakfast is included.

- **Pecan Tree Inn**. Expensive/Moderate. 116 Queen Street (252-728-6733; www.pecantree.com). This inn has seven guest rooms and three suites, all with private baths. Two of the suites have king-sized canopy beds and Jacuzzis, while the third consists of two adjoining rooms. Pecan Tree also has a lovely flower and herb garden. Continental breakfast is provided.

- **Elizabeth Inn**. Moderate/Inexpensive. 307 Front Street (252-728-3861). Staying at the Elizabeth is akin to visiting your grandmother's house. Its three rooms are casually comfortable and its location next to the North Carolina Maritime Museum unbeatable. No breakfast is served.

Places to Eat

- **Beaufort Grocery**. Expensive/Moderate. 117 Queen Street (252-728-3899; www.beaufortgrocery.com). Charles and Wendy Park, executive chef and pastry chef, respectively, have been serving delicious homemade soups, breads, desserts, and Mediterranean-style specialties at this popular deli-by-day, bistro-by-night since 1991. It is open daily for lunch and dinner. Sunday brunch is also served. And they'll gladly pack you a picnic. Reservations are recommended for dinner.

- **Blue Moon Bistro**. Expensive/Moderate. 119 Queen Street (252-728-5800; www.bluemoonbistro.biz). "The Moon" is a welcome addition to the fine-dining establishments of Beaufort. Creative appetizers include a shrimp-and-grits "martini" served in—you guessed it—a martini glass. Ribeye steak, roast chicken, and other entrées come with deliciously fresh vegetables. Dinner is served Tuesday through Sunday. Reservations are recommended.

- **Front Street Grill at Stillwater**. Expensive/Moderate. 300 Front Street (252-728-4956; www.frontstreetgrillatstillwater.com). With its spacious deck and tasteful dining room overlooking Taylor Creek, Front Street Grill is hard to beat for watching the sunset while enjoying appetizers and a glass of wine. Try the tasty coconut fried shrimp or grilled portabello mushroom and asparagus appetizers, but be sure to leave room for dinner. Lunch and dinner are served Tuesday through Sunday; Sunday brunch is also offered. Reservations are accepted.

- **The Net House**. Expensive/Moderate. 133 Turner Street (252-728-2002). The steamed and lightly battered seafood served here has earned The Net House bragging rights for years. The nightly specials and the creamy seafood bisque are favorites, too. Dinner is served nightly.

- **The Spouter Inn**. Expensive/Moderate. 218 Front Street (252-728-5190; www.thespouterinn.com). For over 20 years, The Spouter Inn has served up fresh seafood in a relaxed setting overlooking Taylor Creek. Lunch features a variety of sandwich-and-soup combos, while much of the dinner menu celebrates the fruits of the sea. Lunch and dinner are served daily.

- **The Royal James Café**. Inexpensive. 117 Turner Street (252-728-4573). This local landmark is the oldest continuously operating business in Beaufort. Visitors can enjoy the signature burgers and secret sauce before a game of pool on one of the nearly 50-year-old tables. Lunch is served daily and dinner Monday through Saturday.

- Directly across Taylor Creek from the Beaufort waterfront is the **Rachel Carson Estuarine Research Reserve**, a series of small islands. A half-mile interpretive trail winds through the islands' mud flats, uplands, and salt marshes, illustrating the various environments found in estuarine systems. A small herd of feral horses roams the islands, and over 200 bird species have been recorded here. Access is by boat only, but the islands' proximity to Beaufort makes this a good destination for beginning kayakers to enjoy a day of shelling and swimming. There are restricted areas in the reserve, including nesting areas and freshwater sources for the horses. A trail guide is available over the Internet or from the North Carolina Maritime Museum or the sanctuary office, located at 135 Duke Marine Lab Road. For information, call 252-728-2170 or visit www.ncnerr.org, then go to the Rachel Carson link.

- **Cape Lookout National Seashore** is comprised of 56 miles of pristine barrier islands that include North Core Banks, punctuated by historic Portsmouth village at its northern tip; South Core Banks and its famed Cape Lookout Lighthouse; and Shackleford Banks, home of a herd of wild horses. The seashore's visitor center is located at Shell Point on Harkers Island, a sound island lying behind the string of barrier islands.

  This is truly a national treasure that should not be missed. Cape Lookout is home to myriad bird life and is a protected breeding ground for endangered loggerhead turtles and other marine turtles. A visit can be enjoyed as a day trip to the lighthouse or a week-long vacation for hardy souls desiring rustic accommodations and solitude. With the exception of two cabin-rental agencies, there is no garbage pickup on the islands; visitors are expected to take their trash away with them. Likewise, there are no concessions, so plan to take water, snacks, sunscreen, and insect repellent with you. Cape Lookout's two fishing camps are **Morris Marina Kabin Kamps and Ferry Service** (252-225-4261) and **Great Island Cabins & Ferry Service** (252-729-2791).

  From Beaufort, take U.S. 70 East to Otway and follow the signs for the **Harkers Island Visitor Center**, at 131 Charles Street (252-728-2250; www.nps.gov/calo). The visitor center is a good place to gather information about the seashore's attractions, and it's one of several locations where parking and camping permits can be obtained.

  The seashore is accessible only by water. Private and toll ferries depart from the following towns, ranging from north to south: Ocracoke, Atlantic, Davis, Harkers Island, Beaufort, and Morehead City. Only the ferries from Atlantic and Davis accommodate vehicles, and only four-wheel-drive vehicles are appropriate. The visitor center offers a list of ferry services. *Calico Jacks Inn & Marina* provides ferry service to Cape Lookout and Shackleford Banks, as well as a truck service to Cape Lookout Village and to Cape Point for shelling; for more information, call 252-728-3575. And while it is possible to paddle to the islands, it is not recommended for novices. Experienced paddlers can file their float plans at the visitor center. Private watercraft can also be used to reach the seashore.

Portsmouth village was established in 1753 to encourage development of a port at Ocracoke Inlet. In 1842, more than 500 people lived in Portsmouth, at that time the state's premier port. Successive hurricanes beginning in 1846 drove inhabitants away, however. The surviving structures reflect a sleepy 1930s fishing village, not a lively 19th-century seaport. You can reach Portsmouth village by making private ferry arrangements on Ocracoke Island.

The current *Cape Lookout Lighthouse* was built in 1859 to replace a previous structure erected in 1812 that was deemed too short. Its distinctive black and white diamond "daymarks" give directions to sailors; the black diamonds are oriented east-west and the white diamonds

Cape Lookout Lighthouse
COURTESY OF NORTH CAROLINA
DIVISION OF TOURISM, FILM AND SPORTS
DEVELOPMENT

north-south. In June 2003, the lighthouse was transferred from the Coast Guard to the National Park Service, which currently opens it to the public only on special occasions. The **Innkeepers House**, located adjacent to the lighthouse, operates as a small museum and information center.

Many of the ferry services offer shuttle access to **Cape Point** and **Cape Lookout Village Historic District**. The opportunity for gathering seashells at Cape Point is unsurpassed. Among the several interesting buildings in the historic village is a former Coast Guard station, where the North Carolina Maritime Museum conducts educational tours. You can reach this portion of the island from Harkers Island or Beaufort.

On the ride to the lighthouse, one sight you're likely to see is the famous **wild horses of Shackleford Banks**. If Shackleford is your destination, you can embark from Harkers Island, Beaufort, or Morehead City. If you visit Shackleford, use caution when approaching the horses, as they are wild animals.

■ The **Core Sound Waterfowl Museum** is located at 1785 Island Road on Harkers Island. Like the decoys that inspired its creation, the museum has been a labor of love since its inception in 1987. Located adjacent to Cape Lookout's headquarters, the museum's beautiful new facility houses a large collection of antique and contemporary decoys and pays homage to the area's hunting and fishing traditions. The educational portion of the building opened in 2003. Fund-raising is ongoing to complete the galleries, a research library, and a tower. Situated on 16 acres of maritime forest, the facility includes a four-acre freshwater waterfowl habitat, hiking trails, and viewing platforms. The museum is open from 10 A.M. to 5 P.M. Monday through Saturday and from 2 P.M. to 5 P.M. on Sunday. Admission is free. For more information, call 252-728-1500 or visit www.coresound.com.

■ About 24 miles from Beaufort on U.S. 70 is **Cedar Island National Wildlife Refuge**, which was authorized by the Migratory Bird Act of 1964. Over 270 species of birds can be spotted here, the peak months being December and January. Since approximately 11,000 of the refuge's 14,480 acres are under shallow water, kayaks and canoes are the best way to explore the area. A boat ramp is provided at the end of Lola Road.

Kayaking on the coast
COURTESY OF NORTH CAROLINA DIVISION OF TOURISM, FILM AND SPORTS DEVELOPMENT

BOGUE BANKS

Bogue Banks is a 29-mile-long barrier island that stretches from Beaufort Inlet on the east to Bogue Inlet on the west. Until the 1950s, Bogue Banks was virtually undeveloped. But once people came to recognize it as one of the state's longest, most accessible barrier islands, its beautiful, expansive white beach became one of the most popular vacation destinations on the coast. After several decades of development, much of the native landscape has been supplanted by condominiums, beach houses, hotels, and resorts. However, Bogue Banks still boasts one of the prettiest beaches in the state.

The eastern end of the island is dominated by Atlantic Beach, the oldest town on Bogue Banks. Its bustling commercial area includes shops, restaurants, and entertainment parks; children and teenagers love it. Adjacent to Atlantic Beach is Fort Macon State Park, the most-visited state park in North Carolina, attracting 1.24 million guests a year.

Midway down the island, at Salter Path and Pine Knoll Shores, beach cottages are the norm. Pine Knoll Shores was developed by Theodore Roosevelt's children, who were heirs of his distant cousin Alice Hoffman, the owner of most of the island from 1918 until 1953. The Roosevelt family donated 322 acres of local land, including 2,700 feet of beachfront, to the state. Pine Knoll Shores was incorporated in 1973. It is now home to Theodore Roosevelt State Natural Area.

Past Indian Beach at the island's western end is the town of Emerald Isle. Things are slower and quieter here. Few of the local buildings reach over two stories.

JUST THE FACTS

Bogue Banks is a barrier island sandwiched between Bogue Sound and the Atlantic Ocean. N.C. 58 runs almost the entire length of the island. Visitors coming from the north can connect to N.C. 58 from U.S. 70. Those coming from the south can take U.S. 17 to N.C. 24 in Jacksonville or connect directly to N.C. 58 from U.S. 17 near Croatan National Forest.

Air access is via Craven County Regional Airport (252-638-8591) in New Bern, Albert J. Ellis Airport (910-324-1100) in Jacksonville, or Michael J. Smith Airport (252-728-1777 or 252-728-2323) in Beaufort.

The best source for information on the area is the Carteret County Tourism Bureau, at 3409 Arendell Street in Morehead City; call 800-786-6962 or 252-726-8148 or visit www.crystalcoastnc.com.

Things to Do

HISTORIC PLACES, GARDENS, AND TOURS

■ The top historical draw on Bogue Banks is without a doubt **Fort Macon State Park**, located east of Atlantic Beach at the tip of the island. The War of 1812 demonstrated the coastline's vulnerability to enemy attack. By 1865, some 38 permanent forts had been built from Maine to the Gulf Coast and in California.

For over 150 years, Fort Macon has stood guard over Beaufort Inlet.

The pentagon-shaped fortress, completed in 1834, was named to honor Nathaniel Macon, a former speaker of the House of Representatives and United States senator. Not long after it was garrisoned, Fort Macon began to give way to erosion and storms, so the United States Army sent one of its young West Point engineers, Robert E. Lee, to rectify the problem. The stone jetties designed by Captain Lee are still in use today. During the Civil War, the 500 Confederate troops at Fort Macon were forced to surrender to Union general Ambrose Burnside following an 11-hour bombardment. The fort was garrisoned again during the Spanish-American War and World War II. Between conflicts, it was often occupied by a single caretaker.

A self-guided tour with audiovisual displays provides historical background on the fort for visitors of all ages. From mid-April through mid-October, fort tours are offered daily on the hour from 10 A.M. to 3 P.M. The museum on the premises exhibits tools, weapons, and artifacts and offers a slide presentation. The bookstore has a variety of historical material.

The 385-acre park is a favorite spot for bird-watching, sportfishing, and shelling. In the summer, the lifeguard-protected swimming area, the bathhouses, and the picnic areas are popular with visitors. From June through August, concerts are offered at the fort on Friday nights from 7 P.M. to 8 P.M. Other events include Civil War reenactments, musket-firing and cannon-firing demonstrations, and nature tours and talks. You can pick up a schedule of events at the Carteret County Tourism Bureau or visit www.clis.com/friends/ for more information.

Fort Macon State Park is open from 9 A.M. to 5:30 P.M. daily except Christmas. Admission is free. For information, call 252-726-3775 or visit www.ncparks.net/foma.html.

MUSEUMS AND SCIENCE CENTERS

■ The **North Carolina Aquarium at Pine Knoll Shores** is one of the island's most popular attractions. Its 16-tank viewing gallery, exhibits, touch tank, and two nature trails are designed to educate visitors about North Carolina's fragile and fascinating marine life. Included are the 200-gallon Precious Waters exhibit, a salt-marsh tank, and a riverbank display featuring live alligators. The Loggerhead Odyssey exhibit includes a nursery for injured turtles. The aquarium is located five miles west of Atlantic Beach near Milepost 7 on N.C. 58. It is open from 9 A.M. to 5 P.M. daily year-round; the hours are extended to 9 P.M. on Thursdays in July. An admission fee is charged. Call 866-294-3477 or visit www.ncaquariums.com for information.

RECREATION

■ ***Theodore Roosevelt State Natural Area***, a 250-acre nature preserve at Pine Knoll Shores, is the perfect place to observe local wildlife and get a glimpse of the island in its native state. Few facilities are offered here. Call 252-247-4003 for information.

■ There are two fishing piers on Bogue Banks, both of which charge a fee. ***Oceanana Fishing Pier*** is located at 700 East Fort Macon Road in Atlantic Beach; call 252-726-4111 or visit www.oceanana.com. The town of Emerald Isle was trying to keep the Bogue Inlet Pier open at the time of this writing.

■ ***Outer Banks Sail and Kayak***, at 612 Morehead City-Atlantic Beach Causeway, offers sunset cruises and sailboat and kayak rentals. It is open Monday through Saturday from 9 A.M. to 6 P.M. and Sunday from 1 P.M. to 6 P.M. Call ahead for reservations. For more information, call 252-247-6300 or visit www.obsk.com.

SEASONAL EVENTS

■ **Worthy Is the Lamb** is an inspirational musical drama of the last days of Christ. It is performed in the Crystal Coast Amphitheatre, located three miles north of the bridge to Emerald Isle. The nation's only fully orchestrated passion play, it is performed Thursday through Saturday at 8:30 P.M. from June through September. An admission fee is charged. For tickets, call 252-393-8373. For more information, call the Emerald Isle Business Association at 252-393-3100.

■ The ***Atlantic Beach King Mackerel Tournament***, the largest all-cash king mackerel contest in the country, is held each September. Call 252-247-2334 or visit www.abkmt.com for information.

Places to Stay

RESORTS, HOTELS, AND MOTELS

■ ***Sheraton Atlantic Beach.*** Expensive. 2717 West Fort Macon Road in Atlantic Beach (800-624-8875 or 252-240-1155; www.sheratonatlanticbeach.com). The Sheraton offers 200 ocean-view rooms and suites. Among its amenities are indoor and outdoor pools, a game room, an exercise room, a spa, a restaurant, and a 600-foot fishing pier.

■ ***Best Western Crystal Coast Resort.*** Expensive/Moderate. 109 Salter Path Road in Atlantic Beach (800-733-7888 or 252-726-2544). The Best Western has 114 tropically decorated rooms, each with a private balcony. Some rooms have an ocean view. Children sleep free in their parents' rooms here. The resort has a pool and a wading pool.

■ ***Clamdigger Ramada Inn.*** Expensive/Moderate. Salter Path Road in Atlantic Beach (800-338-1533 or 252-247-4155; www.clamdiggerinn.com). Each room here has a private balcony overlooking the beach, a microwave, a mini refrigerator, a coffee maker, an iron, an ironing board, and cable television. A pool, a restaurant, and a lounge round out the amenities.

■ ***Atlantis Lodge.*** Moderate. Milepost 5 on N.C. 58 in Pine Knoll Shores (252-726-5168; www.atlantislodge.com). The Atlantis is a golden oldie nestled amid the maritime woods. Most of its rooms are suites, complete with kitchens and dining areas. All rooms have a patio or a deck facing the ocean. Pets are allowed in some rooms. Kids will adore the swimming pool.

■ ***Oceanana.*** Moderate. Fort Macon Road in Atlantic Beach (252-726-4111; www.oceanana.com). Located near Fort Macon, Oceanana is an old-fashioned beach place for the whole family. It offers a pool, a playground, a pier, and a lifeguard on the beach during the summer.

■ ***The Seahawk Motor Lodge and Villas.*** Moderate. Milepost 4¾ on N.C. 58 in Pine Knoll Shores (800-682-6898 or 252-726-4146; www.ncbeach-motel.com). This charming motor lodge has been pleasing visitors for generations. Its friendly atmosphere is fostered by seaside hammocks and swings. All of its 38 oceanfront rooms have a balcony or patio.

Bikes, fishing rods, and grills are yours for the asking. A pool is on the premises.

- **Caribbe Inn**. Moderate/Inexpensive. 309 East Fort Macon Road in Atlantic Beach (252-726-0051; www.caribbe-inn.com). Located two and a half blocks from the ocean, this fanciful little motel offers 12 rooms, each with a refrigerator and a microwave. It is pet-friendly, too.

Places to Eat

- **Kathryn's Bistro & Martini Bar**. Expensive/Moderate. 8002 Emerald Drive in Emerald Isle (252-354-6200; www.kathrynsbistro.com). This recent upscale addition to Emerald Isle was highly needed. It features seafood, steak, and chicken entrées prepared on a wood-fired grill. The pastas and the "She Crab & Corn Soup" are also among the favorites. But the real specialty here is the massive variety of martinis. Visitors can try a "Black Martini," a "Chocolate Kiss," and many more. A designated driver is recommended! Kathryn's is open daily for dinner.

- **Amos Mosquito's Restaurant and Bar**. Moderate. 703 East Fort Macon Road in Atlantic Beach (252-247-6222). Recently transplanted from Morehead City, this café offers an array of fresh salads, sandwiches, pastas, and seafood entrées, some bearing Asian and southwestern influences. Dockside dining is available. Guests love the table-side hibachis, where they can make their own s'mores. Breakfast and dinner are served daily.

- **Channel Marker**. Moderate. On the Morehead City-Atlantic Beach Causeway (252-247-2344). Channel Marker offers outdoor dining overlooking Bogue Sound. Dinner specialties include fresh seafood, served steamed or grilled, and Angus beef. Ample boat dockage is available. Call for serving hours.

- **The Crab's Claw Restaurant and Oyster Bar**. Moderate. 201 West Atlantic Beach Boulevard in Atlantic Beach (252-726-8222; www.crabsclaw.com). Fresh from the sea is what The Crab's Claw is all about. Situated on the boardwalk in the thick of things, it serves a variety of steamer pots and a terrific roasted corn and clam chowder. Members of the under-12 crowd can enjoy "Chicken Dinosaur" or a PBJ, if they prefer. Lunch and dinner are served Thursday through Monday; call for days and hours during the winter.

- **Tortugas.** Moderate. 140 Fairview Drive in Emerald Isle (252-354-9397; www.tortugas.net). Opened in 2000, Tortugas has quickly risen to the top of Emerald Isle's restaurant list. Try the baked "Crème de Crab" appetizer or the Costa Rican pork tenderloin marinated in ginger and hoisin sauce. The restaurant also offers gourmet pizzas and pastas. Dinner is served daily during the summer; call for winter hours.

- **South Banks Grill.** Inexpensive. 301 Mangrove Drive in Emerald Isle (252-354-9700). This fresh addition to island dining is unassumingly tucked away in the K & V Shopping Center. Order your conch and corn chowder, yucca fritters, or cornmeal-encrusted oyster burger at the counter and the staff will bring it to your table. Beer and wine are available. Lunch and dinner are served daily during the summer.

Nearby

- **Swansboro** is a pretty, historic fishing village on the White Oak River, just over the Emerald Isle bridge on N.C. 24. This "Friendly City by the Sea," as locals like to refer to it, has been greeting visitors for over 250 years. Among its historic structures are the **William Pugh Ferrand Store**, erected in 1839, and the **Jonathan Green, Jr., House**, built in the mid-18th century and thought to be the town's oldest home. Swansboro offers a picture-perfect look at coastal North Carolina life in days gone by. It is a great place to browse antique and craft shops.

  If you're looking for a bite to eat while you're in town, you're sure to enjoy the waterfront dining at **The Gourmet Café**, at 99 Church Street. The appetizers here include fried pepper jack cheese and spicy black bean chili dip. Two of the house specialties are rack of lamb and flounder almandine. The café is open for lunch and dinner from Tuesday to Sunday year-round; call 910-326-7114. And you can't miss **Yana's Ye Olde Drugstore and Restaurant**, located at 9 Front Street. Yana's is popular, so be prepared to wait. The "Bradburger," a hamburger with egg, cheese, bacon, lettuce, and tomato, will make it worth your while. Yana's serves traditional breakfasts daily at 7 A.M. and a variety of sandwiches and fried fruit pies for lunch until 3 P.M.; call 910-326-5501.

Barrier Island Kayaks, at 160 Cedar Point Boulevard, offers rentals and tours to area destinations including Bear Island and Hammocks Beach. Call 252-393-6457 or visit www.barrierislandkayaks.com.

■ *Hammocks Beach State Park* is one of the most beautiful and unspoiled beaches on the Atlantic coast. Ironically, our nation's ugly segregationist past is largely the reason. In 1914, Dr. William Sharpe, a pioneer in brain surgery, bought the island. Shortly thereafter, he named a black couple, John and Gertrude Hurst, as caretakers. When Sharpe began to receive unsigned letters stating that a black man was unfit to manage the property, he bought an ad in the local paper offering $5,000 for information leading to the arrest and conviction of anyone damaging the island or its occupants. The threats ended.

In the 1940s, when he was an old man, Sharpe decided to leave the island to the Hursts. Mrs. Hurst persuaded him to instead leave it to the North Carolina Teachers Association, a black teachers' alliance. His beloved Hammocks Beach thus fulfilled Sharpe's dream of being a "refuge and a place for enjoyment for some of the people whom America treated so badly."

On May 3, 1961, at the dawn of the civil-rights movement, the property was presented to the state. Visitors to Hammocks Beach today enjoy swimming, primitive camping, picnicking, shelling, surf fishing, and nature programs.

To get to Hammocks Beach State Park, catch the ferry at the park's visitor center on Hammocks Beach Road (S.R. 1511), located off N.C. 24. A nominal fee is charged. For information, call 910-326-4881 or visit www.ils.unc.edu/parkproject/visit/habe/home.html.

Wilmington waterfront
COURTESY OF NORTH CAROLINA DIVISION OF TOURISM, FILM AND SPORTS DEVELOPMENT

CAPE FEAR COAST

By Angela Harwood

*T*he name will probably draw you in, just as it did Hollywood. Since the 1980s, the Cape Fear coast has been the location of such feature films as *Billy Bathgate, The Hudsucker Proxy*, and *Blue Velvet*. It was the film location of the popular television series *Dawson's Creek* and is now the location for the WB's *One Tree Hill*. Wilmington, the area's thriving city, has become known as "the Hollywood of the East." It ranks third to only Los Angeles and New York in cinematic productivity.

But this is much more than a pretty, inexpensive place to make movies. The southernmost promontory of North Carolina's coast gets its name from the deadly shoals at the mouth of its like-named river, the Cape Fear. At the northern edge of the region is Topsail Island, whose name honors its legacy of crafty pirates. Next comes the exclusive Figure Eight Island, where former vice president Al Gore and family have been among those seeking its isolated beauty. Wilmington, the largest deepwater port in the Southeast, is situated on the bank of the Cape Fear River, as is the quaint port town of Southport, a popular stopover for boaters cruising the Intracoastal Waterway. Along the Atlantic coast east and south of Wilmington are some of the state's premier beaches, including Kure Beach, Carolina Beach, and the fabled Wrightsville Beach. Off Southport is the

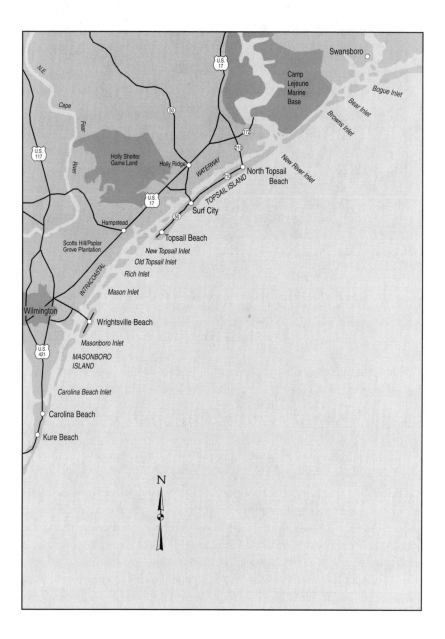

selectively developed Bald Head Island, accessible only by boat. Stretching from Southport to the South Carolina line are the lovely, uncrowded beaches of Brunswick County.

While summer is certainly the most popular time to visit the Cape Fear coast, the area's mild climate makes it an inviting destination any time of year. In the spring, Wilmington is at its showiest during the annual Azalea Festival. In the fall, when the king mackerel are running, fishing tournaments abound. And in winter, Wilmington's vibrant cultural scene heats up the chilly nights. Whenever you choose to visit, the area's abundant recreational opportunities and cultural diversions will make it an ideal destination.

TOPSAIL ISLAND

Midway between Cape Lookout and Cape Fear is the 26-mile barrier island known as Topsail. Although the name sounds like the product of 21st-century resort marketing, legend has it that it dates back to the golden age of piracy, when marauding pirates would moor their vessels in the sound behind the island, waiting to spring on unsuspecting ships. It wasn't long before word spread among ship pilots to keep an eye out for the pirate ships' topsails over the dunes—hence the name. Chances are the infamous pirates Blackbeard and Stede Bonnet roamed these shores. Treasure hunters still flock here with their metal detectors and scuba gear to search for loot.

Written records describing Topsail date from the 1500s, when early European explorers ventured into its protected inland waterways. Artifacts from the Tuscaroras and other Native Americans reveal that the island was a favorite hunting and fishing spot long before white settlers came along.

Interestingly, Topsail Island played an important role in both the Civil War and World War II. During the Civil War, it was the site of a Confederate saltworks. In World War II, Camp Davis, an enormous antiaircraft training center, was constructed on Topsail. Following the war, Camp Davis was deactivated. The island was subsequently selected as a testing ground for missiles, and Operation Bumblebee was thus born. The 200 missiles that were launched here paved the way for the development of the ramjet engine, which enabled aircraft to break the sound barrier. Concrete observation towers from that era still dot the landscape.

When the military left in 1948, civilians moved in. The island has grown steadily as a resort destination since then. The town of Surf City was incorporated in 1949, followed by Topsail Beach in 1963 and North Topsail Beach in 1990. In 1954, Hurricane Hazel leveled nearly all the buildings on the island. Two more hurricanes, Donna and Diane, later wreaked more havoc. The most recent catastrophic weather came in 1998, but the tenacious islanders rebuilt and are once again ready to welcome visitors to their lovely stretch of sand and surf.

JUST THE FACTS

The island can be reached from U.S. 17 via bridges at North Topsail Beach and Surf City.

The nearest airports are at Wilmington, to the southwest, and Jacksonville, to the north. There is also a public airstrip in nearby Holly Ridge.

The Greater Topsail Island Chamber of Commerce is located at Treasure Coast Landing on N.C. 50 in Surf City. For information, call 800-626-2780 or 910-329-4446 or visit www.topsailcoc.com.

Things to Do

MUSEUMS AND SCIENCE CENTERS

■ **Topsail Island Museum: Missiles and More**, at 720 Channel Boulevard in Topsail Beach, offers Indian artifacts and displays on pirate activity and World War II operations. From April to October, it is open from 2 P.M. to 4 P.M. on Monday, Tuesday, Thursday, Friday, and Saturday. Admission is free, though donations are accepted. Call 800-626-2780 or 910-329-4446 or visit www.topsailmissilesmuseum.org for information.

■ The **Karen Beasley Sea Turtle Rescue and Rehabilitation Center** is located at 822 Carolina Boulevard in Topsail Beach. Topsail and the other barrier islands along the North Carolina coast are the breeding ground for several different marine turtles, including the endangered loggerhead. The dedicated volunteers at the turtle hospital rescue and rehabilitate scores of injured animals annually. The center is open for tours from 2 P.M. to 4 P.M. on Monday, Tuesday, Thursday, Friday, and Saturday; it is closed during the winter. For information, call 910-328-3377 or visit www.seaturtlehospital.org.

RECREATION

■ There are three fishing piers on the island. Located in the heart of Surf City, **Surf City Pier** is open 24 hours a day, seven days a week; call 910-328-3521. **Jolly Roger Pier** is located at 803 Ocean Boulevard in North Topsail Beach; call 910-328-4616. **Topsail Island Pier Market and Marina** is in Topsail Beach; call 910-328-3641.

■ Visitors can rent kayaks from **Herrings Outdoor Sports**. Call 910-328-3291 or visit www.herringsoutdoorsports.com.

■ Five public golf courses are located within 15 miles of Topsail Island. Call the chamber of commerce at 800-626-2780 or 910-329-4446 for a list.

Places to Stay

Though cottage and condominium rentals dominate Topsail Island's accommodations, there are a few other options as well.

RESORTS, HOTELS, AND MOTELS

■ **Breezeway Motel**. Moderate. At the corner of Channel and Davis streets in Topsail Beach (800-548-4694 or 910-328-7751;

www.breezewaymotel.com). Located on Topsail Sound, the Breeze-way offers spacious rooms, a pool, balconies, boat docks, a fishing pier, and a waterfront restaurant.

- **Sea Vista Motel.** Moderate/Inexpensive. 1521 Ocean Boulevard in Topsail Beach (800-SEA-VISTA or 910-328-2171; www.seavistamotel.com). Located on the ocean at the southern end of N.C. 50, Sea Vista offers 33 oceanfront rooms, efficiencies, and mini-efficiencies. Pets are allowed for a surcharge.

Inns and Bed-and-Breakfasts

- **The Pink Palace Bed-and-Breakfast.** Expensive/Moderate. 1222 South Shore Road in Surf City (910-328-5114). This is the only oceanfront bed-and-breakfast on Topsail Island. Each suite has access to a screened porch and three open-air decks. The Pink Palace offers all the amenities, including a hot tub.

Places to Eat

- **Indigo Marsh.** Expensive. 602-B Roland Avenue in Surf City (910-328-2580; www.indigomarsh.com). Guests here enjoy chophouse-style steaks and creatively prepared fresh local seafood while dining inside or taking in the view of the Intracoastal Waterway from the back deck. Homemade breads and pastries are also available. Lunch is served Wednesday through Friday, dinner Wednesday through Sunday, and brunch Saturday and Sunday. Reservations are recommended.

- **Latitude 34 Restaurant.** Expensive/Moderate. 1522 Carolina Avenue in Topsail Beach (910-328-3272). The recently renovated, award-winning Latitude 34 overlooks Topsail Sound. It offers nightly specials in addition to its regular menu, which features seafood, chicken, beef, and pork dishes. The appetizers include scrumptious prosciutto-wrapped scallops. A children's menu is available. Reservations are recommended. Dinner is served Tuesday through Sunday.

Sand dunes
COURTESY OF NORTH CAROLINA DIVISION OF TOURISM, FILM AND SPORTS DEVELOPMENT

■ ***The Breezeway Restaurant.*** Moderate. 636 Channel Boulevard in Topsail Beach (910-328-4302). The Breezeway enjoys a solid reputation for its fresh seafood and steaks. In business since 1949, it offers waterfront dining. Dinner is served daily.

■ ***Mollie's Restaurant.*** Moderate/Inexpensive. 107 North Shore Drive in Surf City (910-328-0505; www.molliesrestaurant.com). This friendly restaurant serves breakfast, lunch, and dinner daily. Off-season hours may vary. Its specialties include seafood, steaks, pasta, salads, and sandwiches.

Nearby

■ ***Sneads Ferry*** is a busy fishing community located on the New River near the northern tip of Topsail Island on N.C. 172. Every August since 1971, the ***Sneads Ferry Shrimp Festival*** has attracted seafood lovers from all over. Proceeds from the festival have enabled the town to construct the Shrimp Festival Community Building and acquire a 14-acre park. For information, call 910-327-4911 or visit www.sneadsferrynorthcarolina.com.

If you're looking for a bite to eat in Sneads Ferry, try the ***Riverview Café***, located at Fulcher's Landing. The Riverview has been offering fresh local seafood since 1946. For information, call 910-327-2011.

MAYBERRY BY THE SEA

Excerpted from
Topsail Island: Mayberry by the Sea by Ray McAllister

Topsail Island is a small barrier island off the North Carolina coast south of the Outer Banks and north of Wilmington and Wrightsville Beach. The map shows Topsail—pronounced "TOP-sul" by those who have been here more than once—to be pencil thin. Indeed, it is not much more. There are only 15 square miles on this 26-mile-long strip of sand. The width is rarely much more than a half-mile and sometimes only 200 yards, providing a splendor of almost incomprehensible logistics: morning sunrises over water followed, nearby, by evening sunsets over water. Did the Great Island Creator make a mistake? Was Topsail supposed to get both?

The map also shows Topsail divided among three towns: Topsail Beach at the south, Surf City in the middle, and the newcomer, North Topsail Beach, above them. The relative few residents who live on the island year-round will tell you the three are very much distinctive, that sometimes the towns are at odds politically, one town snubbing another that seeks cooperation, though the snubs seem to be lessening, and that—here their voices drop almost to a whisper—somehow folks who live in the other two towns are, well,

different. It is true, they insist, but they say it with a smile, as if describing a slightly daft aunt or a cousin you just can't help loving anyway.

Visitors do not see the distinctions among the towns—not at first, anyway—nor do they necessarily care. The island is intoxicating. So what does it matter? Everyone is friendly.

Small shop owners—and there are no other kind on Topsail—are supposed to be friendly. But why the requirement that the man you meet walking the other way will not only say hello but will stop to say it? Who has decreed that the woman in the grocery store, whether one of the tiny mom-and-pops on the island or a supermarket just off, will ask how you're doing as if she cares how you are doing?

Who does that anymore?

People search for a way to describe the allure of Topsail. Allan Libby, director of the island's chamber of commerce, calls it simply "The Magic." The Magic, he says, is whatever draws a person to the island. The Magic is different things to different people.

Doug Medlin, who moved with his family to Surf City in 1952, when the number of island families could be counted on one hand, or surely on two, has a ready answer. "I think the quaint family atmosphere," he says. "When you think of Myrtle Beach, you think of all the shows, the rides. This is just a great family atmosphere."

Family is a part of it, to be sure. Quaintness is a part of it, too.

But isn't it odd that so many describe what Topsail has by enumerating what it doesn't have?

The island is always spoken about in those terms. It has a family atmosphere, someone will tell you. Even teenagers like the island, they will say—and then immediately launch into a laundry list of the things a teen would want that the island does *not* have. There is no shopping mall, of course, or anything like it. The nearest movie theater, well, that's the better part of an hour away. And so forth.

What sort of place is this?

"It's like you're back in time, this island is," says Jeffrey Stewart Price, who moved to Topsail Beach to take over the Beach Shop and Grill before the summer of 2002. "It's not a Myrtle Beach. It's not commercialized. People like that. It's for families." Even at the height of the season, the island is not what any new arrivals would call crowded.

The island does seem caught in a time warp, not yet overtaken by the commercial development of Virginia Beach, Nags Head, Wrightsville Beach, or Myrtle Beach. Nor is it likely to be. Topsail now is what those resorts were decades ago, even a half-century

ago, or perhaps what we only thought they once were. Call it "the Little Island That Time Forgot." Many do. The moniker is intended as more endearing than demeaning. Topsail has a small-town feel of beach shops and cafés, a slow pace, and residents who know one another, as their parents and grandparents knew one another. Throw in the sea breezes, dunes, sea oats, and sea gulls and you have a Mayberry by the Sea. More than one smitten visitor has called it that. You can't help feeling that the residents of the fictional North Carolina town in *The Andy Griffith Show* would recognize these islanders. Is it coincidence that Griffith himself has spent much of his life on the North Carolina coast, even keeping a home on Figure Eight Island, just south of Topsail?

Even the Topsail Island police departments, rarely troubled by serious crime, specialize in community relations, just as in the fictional town of . . . well, you know.

That step back in time is part of The Magic. So, too, is the ocean setting. The surf, the breeze, the mist. And the fishing. The surfing. The diving and even nearby parasailing, for those inclined. And no doubt the isolation factors in. You can't get here from there, they say. Sometimes, it seems you can't get here from anywhere, so maybe the difficulty of the journey is part of what makes the destination more rewarding.

But who is in a hurry?

No one, at least not for very long.

The main road down the narrow island—in places, there is room for only one road—rarely carries a speed limit of more than 45 miles an hour; often it is 35 and sometimes 25. And yet the speed limit seems too high. Most drivers go 10 miles an hour under the limit. Who goes 10 miles an hour *under* anymore? "Slow Down," reads one island bumper sticker. "This Ain't the Mainland." Indeed. Vacationers invariably find themselves riding the bumpers of the cars in front when they arrive. By the end of the week, they are the ones slowing down the next week's arrivals.

WILMINGTON

Until the turn of the 20th century, Wilmington was North Carolina's largest city. Today, it remains one of its most vibrant and interesting.

Thanks to the city's preservation efforts, a large section of downtown spreading out from the bank of the Cape Fear River is recorded on the National Register of Historic Places. Down along the river's edge are Riverfront Park and Riverwalk, a lovely pedestrian path that runs alongside Water Street, a mostly brick-and-cobblestone lane lined with antique lamps. Also along the water are cozy specialty shops and restaurants at Chandler's Wharf and the Cotton Exchange. Many of the city's tour operators are based at the foot of Water Street.

Wilmington's historic and cultural attractions include an array of stunning colonial- and antebellum-era homes, such as the Burgwin-Wright House and Bellamy Mansion, as well as splendid museums like the Louise Wells Cameron Museum of Art and the Cape Fear Museum. Boasting more than 200 houses of worship, Wilmington is a showcase of church architecture.

Wilmington's charm has not been lost to popular culture. Over the past two decades, the city has evolved into the third-busiest movie mill in the country. What began in 1983 when Dino DeLaurentiis built a $1.5 million studio has evolved into a multimillion-dollar industry. Star spotting is a favorite pastime here. Some Wilmingtonians have caught the acting bug, appearing as extras in the 400-plus films and television shows that have been shot in and around the city.

Much of Wilmington's appeal lies in its long and illustrious history.

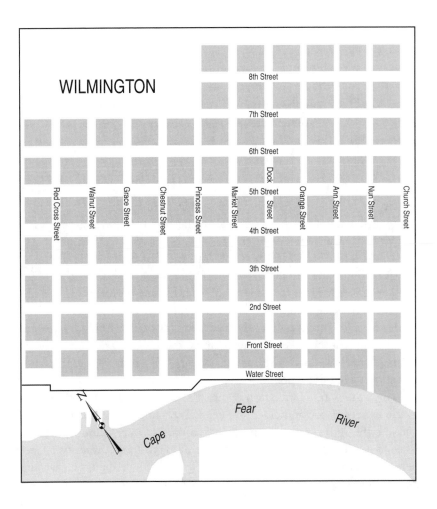

White settlement in the area came in 1725 at Brunswick Town, south of the city. Founded in 1732, the city was originally called New Liverpool and subsequently New Carthage and Newton before it was finally named for Spencer Compton, earl of Wilmington. Wilmington proved to be more strategically located than Brunswick Town, which was ultimately abandoned.

From 1720 to 1870, North Carolina led the world in the production of naval stores—tar, pitch, and turpentine—and Wilmington was the primary export center. Its protected position upriver from the turbulent storms and marauding pirates of the Atlantic would prove the city's salvation again and again.

During the Revolutionary War, the area was spared major bloodshed save for the battle at Moores Creek Bridge, 20 miles north. There,

1,060 clever patriots outwitted 1,600 loyalists by tricking them into attacking their evacuated camps by leaving the fires burning. When the Tories attempted to cross the bridge in pursuit, they discovered that only two logs remained—two logs slathered with grease. On April 12, 1781, Lord Cornwallis and company occupied the city following their costly victory at Guilford Courthouse near Greensboro. The troops reconnoitered here for two weeks before their fateful march to Yorktown, Virginia.

Wilmington grew slowly for the next 50 years, until the Wilmington and Weldon Railroad arrived in 1840. By 1850, Wilmington was the largest city in the state. Over the decade that followed, many of its most impressive buildings—including Thalian Hall, the Zebulon Latimer House, and Bellamy Mansion—were constructed.

In the latter stages of the Civil War, the city became the lifeline of the Confederacy before the fall of Fort Fisher, which overlooks the mouth of the Cape Fear River to the south. Under the fort's protection, stealthy and daring blockade runners played cat and mouse with the formidable Union navy to provide much-needed supplies to the Confederates and to maintain the city's economy. It took the largest war fleet ever assembled to bring down the fort on January 15, 1865. Six months later, Lee surrendered at Appomattox.

After the war, Wilmington endured a brief period of depression until the export of cotton helped the economy rebound. Expansion continued into the 20th century. During the two World Wars, Wilmington flourished as a shipbuilder. In 1952, the North Carolina Ports Authority opened here. Economic decline followed in 1960 when the Atlantic Coast Line Railroad, the area's chief employer, moved its corporate headquarters. About the same time, recognition of the city's treasure trove of historic architecture spurred a preservation movement. In 1974, much of Wilmington's downtown was recorded on the National Register.

Today, the population of Wilmington is 75,000 and growing. Also growing more numerous are the golf and other resort communities that lure thousands of retirees to the area to bask in its temperate climate and enjoy the dynamic cultural scene. Those who come to stay and visitors here for the historic sites can testify that another heyday has arrived in Wilmington.

JUST THE FACTS

Wilmington can be reached via Interstate 40 and U.S. 421 from the northwest, U.S. 74/U.S. 76 from the west, and U.S. 17 from the south.

Wilmington International Airport is served by US Airways, United Express, and A.S.A. Atlantic Southeast, the Delta connection. Call 910-341-4333 for information.

The Trailways bus station is at 201 Harnett Street; call 910-762-6073. The Wilmington Transit Authority provides local bus service; call 910-343-0106.

The Cape Fear Coast Convention and Visitors Bureau is located in the 19th-century courthouse at 24 North Third Street; for information, call 800-222-4757 or 910-341-4030 or visit www.gocapefearcoast.com. The Riverfront Information Booth, at the foot of Market and Water streets, also provides information; its hours vary on a seasonal basis.

The local newspaper is the *Wilmington Star-News*, the state's oldest daily. The *Star*'s entertainment guide, *Currents*, and the free weekly newspaper *Encore* provide up-to-date event listings.

Things to Do

HISTORIC PLACES, GARDENS, AND TOURS

Sightseeing in Wilmington is a treat, especially in the spring and autumn. Although its historic district is one of the largest in the country—over 200 blocks—many of the most interesting sites are concentrated near the Cape Fear River and can easily be seen on foot. However, if you'd prefer a nostalgic ride aboard a horse-drawn carriage, a trolley, or a riverboat, opportunities abound.

■ For a self-guided walking tour, pick up a **Cape Fear Coast Attractions Guide Map** from the Cape Fear Coast Convention and Visitors Bureau.

Another option is a self-guided driving tour that takes about two hours, including the ferry ride from Fort Fisher to Southport. Optional sites along the way include the Battleship *North Carolina*, Orton Plantation, Brunswick Town, Southport, Fort Fisher, and the North Carolina Aquarium at Fort Fisher.

■ Engaging guides lead **Wilmington Adventure Walking Tours** from the Cape Fear River at the corner of Market and Water streets. Tours are offered daily April through October from 10 A.M. to 2 P.M. A fee is charged. Call 910-763-1785.

■ **Horse-Drawn Carriage and Trolley Tours**, based at Market and Water streets, offers narrated tours between 10 A.M. and 10 P.M. Monday through Saturday and between 11 A.M. and 4 P.M. on Sunday from April to October; off-season times vary. A fee is charged. Call 910-251-8889 or visit www.horsedrawntours.com.

■ **Wilmington Trolley Company**, based at Dock and Water streets, offers an eight-mile, 45-minute open-air narrated trolley tour daily from April to October. The tour includes mansions, homes, museums, historic sites, movie locations, and more. A fee is charged. For information, call 800-676-0162 or 910-763-4483 or visit www.wilmingtontrolley.com.

■ **Cape Fear River Boats** conducts sightseeing and dinner-dance cruises and offers water-taxi service to the Battleship *North Carolina*. A fee is charged. Call 800-676-0162 or 910-343-1611 or visit www.cfrboats.com.

■ The 67 acres of **Airlie Gardens**, at 300 Airlie Road, are what remain of a vast estate that dates back to 1886, when Pembroke and Sarah Jones bought the property and commissioned German landscape architect Rudolph Topel to reshape Airlie House, the 155 acres along Airlie Road, and the lodge at Pembroke Park, with its 1,300-acre hunting preserve. The Joneses' parties were legendary, as they were the toast of New York and the Newport society set.

The gardens and lakes date back to 1902. Over a half-million azaleas and 5,000 camellias were added in the 1920s. Visitors can set their own pace in the self-guided walking tour, stand in the shade of the 450-year-old Airlie live oak, and enjoy the natural maritime forest of live oaks, pines, cedars, hollies, wax myrtles, and unusual hardy tropicals. Golf-cart tours are available for those who have difficulty walking. This unique environment is one of the last major undeveloped tracts of land along the Bradley Creek watershed.

The 450-year-old Airlie Oak at Airlie Gardens
PHOTO BY ANGELA HARWOOD

Bottle House, a tribute to artist Minnie Evans at Airlie Gardens
PHOTO BY ANGELA HARWOOD

Airlie Gardens is also an important African-American heritage site. Be sure to visit the Minnie Evans Sculpture Garden and Bottle House, a tribute to Mrs. Evans's "outsider" art. Local artists and area schoolchildren have paid homage to Minnie Evans by interpreting her work through metal sculptures, mosaics, and ceramics.

The gardens are open Tuesday through Sunday from 9 A.M. to 5 P.M. year-round; extended hours are offered during peak azalea season and special events. An admission fee is charged. For more information, call 910-798-7700 or visit www.airliegardens.org.

■ *New Hanover County Arboretum*, located at 6206 Oleander Drive, is a fairly new addition to Wilmington's outdoor attractions. Visitors can explore the arboretum's seven acres and over 4,000 species of native plants. A children's cottage, a Japanese teahouse, a gazebo, the Ability Garden, and various changing displays are open for touring seven days a week from sunup to sundown. Admission is free. For more information, call 910-452-6393 or visit www.arboretumhc.org.

■ *Thalian Hall*, at 310 Chestnut Street, is a historic 1858 Italianate theater designed by John M. Trimble, whose credits include the New York Opera House.

In 1788, the Thalian Association, the oldest amateur theatrical group in the United States, was formed in Wilmington. At the beginning of the 19th century, the group used an auditorium where Thalian Hall now stands. By the time the city acquired that land and announced plans for a new city hall, the Thalians were so entrenched in the cultural scene that citizens demanded the new building also house a theater for the players. Among the luminaries who performed or lectured here were Oscar Wilde, Marian Anderson, Charles Dickens, and William Jennings Bryan.

Today, Thalian Hall is a multiuse facility that houses city hall and Thalian Hall Center for the Performing Arts, Inc. Self-guided tours are available for a fee Monday through Friday from noon to 6 P.M. and Saturday from 2 P.M. to 5 P.M. Guided tours are offered by appointment; call 910-343-3660 or visit www.thalianhall.com.

■ The *Burgwin-Wright Museum House and Gardens* is located at 224 Market Street. The home was built in 1770 upon a foundation of stone from an old jail. The lovely Georgian-style structure features 18th- and early-19th-century furnishings and is surrounded by three gardens and an

Burgwin-Wright Museum House
COURTESY OF CAPE FEAR COAST CONVENTION AND VISITORS BUREAU

orchard. Visitors can take a peek into the 18th-century dungeon. Behind the house is a freestanding building that houses the kitchen and a craft room. Open-hearth cooking demonstrations are presented the second Saturday of each month. The house is open for tours Tuesday through Saturday from 10 A.M. to 4 P.M. An admission fee is charged. For information, call 910-762-0570 or visit www.geocities.com/picketfence/garden/4354.

■ The **Latimer House Museum**, at 126 South Third Street, was built in 1852 for a prosperous merchant who had migrated to Wilmington from Connecticut in the 1830s. An elegant four-story Italianate house, it is a wonderful example of the ornate style so popular in the city at that time. It serves as the headquarters of the Lower Cape Fear Historical Society, which purchased the house and its furnishings from the Latimer family in 1963. Family portraits still adorn the walls. Be sure to view the archives, the library, the Victorian garden, and the servants' quarters. The house is open Monday through Friday from 10 A.M. to 3:30 P.M. and Saturday from noon to 5 P.M. Two-hour "Walk and Talk" tours are given Wednesday and Saturday at 10 A.M. An admission fee is charged. For more information, call 910-762-0492 or visit www.latimerhouse.org.

■ **Bellamy Mansion**, at 503 Market Street, is a magnificent antebellum home constructed in 1859 by free black and slave artisans. Designed by James F. Post, it was the residence of Dr. John D. Bellamy and family, who moved in on the eve of the Civil War. Fear of the Union army and a yellow-fever epidemic forced the Bellamys to flee until after the war. The house remained in the family until 1946, when the last surviving daughter, Ellen Bellamy, died. Since then, it has been under the stewardship of Preservation North Carolina. The restored mansion and Victorian gardens are open for tours. The carriage house serves as the visitor center. Plans are under way for restoration of the slave quarters. The home is open Tuesday through Saturday from 10 A.M. to 5 P.M. and Sunday from 1 P.M. to 5 P.M. Admission is charged. For more information, call 910-251-3700 or visit www.bellamymansion.org.

■ The **Battleship North Carolina**, moored across the Cape Fear River at Eagles Island, was the mightiest sea fighter in World War II. In 1941, as the ship was undergoing sea trials, it passed in and out of New York Harbor so frequently that journalist Walter Winchell dubbed it "the Show Boat," a tribute to the Edna Ferber novel and subsequent musical. During the war, it earned 15 battle stars and participated in every major offensive in the Pacific. Decommissioned in 1960, the battleship was relegated

Battleship North Carolina
COURTESY OF CAPE FEAR COAST CONVENTION AND VISITORS BUREAU

to the mothball fleet until North Carolina's citizens—most notably its schoolchildren—raised the necessary money to bring it to the state.

The battleship's visitor center offers exhibits and an orientation film that illustrate the boat's history. The self-guided tour of the ship takes about two hours. The visitor center has bathrooms, a snack bar, and a picnic area. The site is open daily from 8 A.M. to 8 P.M. Admission is charged. To reach the ship, drive over the Cape Fear Memorial Bridge from Wilmington or take a water taxi from the bottom of Market Street. For more information, call 910-251-5797 or visit www.battleshipnc.com.

■ *Oakdale Cemetery* is a very special place often overlooked by visitors. Canopied by tremendous live oak trees, it is a garden oasis whose stone monuments chronicle the lives of Wilmington's citizenry. It is located on 15th Street off Market Street.

MUSEUMS AND SCIENCE CENTERS

■ The *Cape Fear Museum*, at 814 Market Street, features exhibits and photographs tracing Wilmington's history, science, and culture. It includes a model of 1863 Wilmington, a diorama of the Battle of Fort Fisher, and the Michael Jordan Discovery Gallery, an interactive natural-history exhibit designed for children. Kids will also marvel at the reproduction of a giant ground sloth skeleton. The museum is open Monday through Saturday from 9 A.M. to 5 P.M. and Sunday from 1 P.M. to 5 P.M. from Memorial

Day through Labor Day; it is closed on Monday the rest of the year. Admission is charged. Call 910-341-4350 or visit www.capefearmuseum.com.

- The **Cape Fear Serpentarium**, at 20 Orange Street, boasts the largest collection of venomous snakes in the world. From March to November, it is open weekdays from 11 A.M. to 5 P.M. and weekends from 11 A.M. to 6 P.M. Winter hours vary. Admission is charged. Call 910-762-1669 or visit www.bushmastersonline.com for information.

- The **Louise Wells Cameron Art Museum**, at 3201 South 17th Street, occupies an impressive 42,000-square-foot structure designed by noted architect Charles Gwathmey. It has a fine collection of North Carolina and American art from the 18th century to the present. African-American artists Minnie Evans and Romare Bearden are represented, and there is a gallery dedicated to the work of Claude Howell. Visitors also enjoy the color prints by Mary Cassatt, the glass cases filled with historic and contemporary North Carolina pottery, and the Bruce B. Cameron Decoy Collection. Civil War enthusiasts will be interested in the recently restored Confederate defense mounds from the Battle of Forks Road, which are located on the museum's 10-acre campus.

The museum's café serves fresh salads, sandwiches, and light entrées such as crab cakes. The gift shop sells upscale collectibles and other art-related items. The museum is open Tuesday through Saturday from 10 A.M. to 5 P.M. and Sunday from noon to 4 P.M. Admission is charged except on the first Sunday of each month. For more information, call 910-395-5999 or visit www.CameronArtMuseum.com.

- The **Wilmington Railroad Museum** is located at the corner of Water and Red Cross streets in downtown Wilmington. In 1840, the Wilmington and Weldon Railroad was the longest continuous rail line in the world, measuring 161 miles. Several years later, it merged with other railroads to form the Atlantic Coast Line Railroad, one of the city's largest employers until its move to Jacksonville, Florida, in 1960. The museum is dedicated to preserving the railroad history of the Southeast, the Atlantic Coast Line in particular. Its gift shop stocks T-shirts, books, and railroad memorabilia. The museum is open Monday to Saturday from 10 A.M. to 5 P.M. and Sunday from 1 P.M. to 5 P.M. from March 15 to October 14; the rest of the year, it is open Monday to Saturday from 10 A.M. to 4 P.M. Admission is charged. Call 910-763-2634 or visit www.wilmingtonrailroadmuseum.org.

- The **Children's Museum of Wilmington**, at the corner of Second and Orange streets downtown, is a place where kids can learn about geography, discover the properties of sand, build bridges made of Legos, and create their own puppet shows. Admission is charged. From June through August, the museum is open Monday to Saturday from 9 A.M. to 5 P.M. and Sunday from 1 P.M. to 5 P.M. The rest of the year, it is open Tuesday to Saturday from 9 A.M. to 5 P.M. and Sunday from 1 P.M. to 5 P.M. For more information, call 910-254-3534 or visit www.playwilmington.org.

CULTURAL OFFERINGS

- **Opera House Theatre Company**, at 2011 Carolina Beach Road, is a nonprofit organization that presents professional productions featuring guest artists. Call 910-762-4234.

- **Thalian Hall Center for the Performing Arts** hosts a film series and excellent local theater productions. For box office information, call 800-523-2820 or 910-343-3664 or visit www.thalianhall.com.

- Students and locals give outstanding performances at **Kenan Auditorium** on the campus of the University of North Carolina at Wilmington. For information, call 800-732-3643 or 910-962-3500 or visit www.uncwil.edu/kenan.

SPECIAL SHOPPING

- Because of its long history and continuing appeal to artistic spirits, Wilmington has antique shops and art galleries galore. You can pick up copies of **A Guide to Greater Wilmington Antique Shops** and **Gallery Guide** at the Riverfront Information Booth.

- To meet artists and craftspeople, go to the **Old Wilmington City Market** on South Water Street, where you'll find handwoven baskets, handmade soaps, eclectic gift shops, and even a masseuse.

- The **Cotton Exchange**, located in the 300 block of Front Street, houses a variety of specialty shops and restaurants in several turn-of-the-20th-century buildings, many of which were cotton warehouses. Most of the shops are open Monday through Saturday from 10 A.M. to 5:30 P.M.

■ *Chandler's Wharf* is located on the waterfront at the corner of Water and Ann streets. Its boutiques and restaurants offer a wide range of choices.

RECREATION

■ *Greenfield Park & Gardens*, located on Burnett Boulevard off South Third Street, features a 150-acre cypress-studded lake, paddleboats, and a playground. A path for walking or biking winds around the park, whose 20 acres of gardens are often a showplace during the Azalea Festival. A five-mile scenic drive surrounds the 250-acre city park. Tours are offered on Saturday and Sunday at 11 A.M. and 1 P.M. from May through August. Reservations are required for tours, and a fee is charged. In summer, the amphitheater is filled with music. Call 800-380-3485 or 910-762-5606 or visit www.wilmington.gov/cityparks/tabid/239/default.aspx.

■ Some 39 golf clubs dot the Cape Fear coast, and that number is growing annually. Contact the Cape Fear Convention and Visitors Bureau to ask for a free **Area Golf Guide**. Some notable course designers who have worked in the area include George Cobb, Willard Byrd, Tom Fazio, and Dan Maples.

SEASONAL EVENTS

■ The *North Carolina Azalea Festival* lures thousands of visitors to Wilmington each April, just when the city is looking its best. Guests enjoy the annual coronation of Queen Azalea, a variety show, a parade, a street fair, a circus, and a concert. The main attraction, of course, is the gardens bursting with dogwood trees and the South's signature azaleas. Tickets for the Azalea Garden Tour and the Azalea Home Tour can be purchased in advance or at the garden sites. Call 910-794-4650 or visit www.ncazaleafestival.org.

■ The *Cape Fear Blues Festival* is a three-day draw for blues lovers each July. Call 910-350-8822 or visit www.CapeFearBlues.com.

- **Riverfest** is held each October in Riverfront Park. Boat races, a raft regatta, music, dancing, and booths offering arts, crafts, and deep-fried foods attract visitors and locals alike to the bank of the Cape Fear River. Call 910-452-6862.

Places to Stay

RESORTS, HOTELS, AND MOTELS

- **Best Western Coastline Inn**. Expensive/Moderate. 503 Nutt Street (800-617-7732 or 910-763-2800; www.coastlineinn.com). Though this is a standard Best Western hotel, its downtown location makes it worthy of note. All 53 rooms overlook the river. In-room coffee service, phones with data ports, and fax and copier service are offered. A complimentary continental breakfast is served at your door.

- **Hilton Wilmington Riverside**. Expensive/Moderate. 301 North Water Street (910-763-5900; www.wilmingtonhilton.com). Also located downtown, the Hilton has a commanding view of the river. It offers an outdoor pool, an outdoor whirlpool, exercise facilities, two ballrooms, a gift shop, a restaurant and lounge, and a boat dock for those arriving by water. Children stay free with their parents.

INNS AND BED-AND-BREAKFASTS

- **The Graystone Inn**. Deluxe. 100 South Third Street (888-763-4773 or 910-763-2000; www.graystoneinn.com). The elegant Graystone Inn has appeared in several films and has also played host to many talented actors and actresses who came here to make them. Originally the Bridgers Mansion, completed for Elizabeth Haywood Bridgers in 1906, the inn has been returned to its turn-of-the-20th-century grandeur. The Graystone features a spacious parlor, a baby grand piano, an elegantly set dining room, and a lovely mahogany-paneled library. Many of its rooms have fireplaces and claw-foot tubs.

■ *The River Inn*. Deluxe. 314 South Front Street (910-763-4891; www.theriverinnwilmington.com). Thespian proprietress Jenny Wright serves a divine quiche and homemade breads for breakfast at her lovely 1899 Queen Anne home overlooking the Cape Fear River. Original paintings by Jenny and other area artists adorn the walls. Each of the three guest rooms is handsomely decorated; two open onto a balcony that affords an incomparable view of the river.

■ *The Verandas*. Deluxe. 202 Nun Street (910-251-2212; www.verandas.com). Built in 1853, The Verandas was devastated by a fire in 1992. In 1995, current owners Dennis Madsen and Charles Pennington completely refurbished the home, returning it to its Italianate elegance. Each of the eight large corner guest rooms has it own luxurious bath, equipped with Caswell-Massey toiletries. Guest can venture up the spiral staircase to the cupola for a panoramic view of the city.

■ *The Front Street Inn*. Deluxe/Expensive. 215 South Front Street (800-336-8184 or 910-762-6442; www.frontstreetinn.com). Built in 1923 and once home to the Salvation Army of the Carolinas, this great little inn has airy rooms with patios and balconies and names like the Molly Brown Suite. The place is vibrantly decorated with American art gathered from galleries, fairs, auctions, and attics. You can enjoy a glass of champagne in the Sol y Sombra Bar and Breakfast Room when you arrive or have a tasty breakfast there the next morning.

■ *Blue Heaven Bed-and-Breakfast*. Expensive/Moderate. 517 Orange Street (910-772-9929; www.bbonline.com/nc/blueheaven). This lovely 1897 Victorian retains many of its original features, including seven fireplaces with mantels and some lovely stained-glass windows. All the rooms have private baths, fireplaces, phones, cable television, VCRs, and air conditioning.

■ *The Worth House*. Expensive/Moderate. 412 South Third Street (800-340-8559 or 910-762-8562; www.worthhouse.com). This turreted 1893 Queen Anne-style home is located a short stroll from the river. Antiques and period art grace its seven guest rooms, some of which have fireplaces. Complimentary breakfast is served.

The restaurant scene in Wilmington is vibrant and eclectic. Many of the hot spots are located downtown within easy walking distance of the river.

- **Deluxe Café**. Expensive. 114 Market Street (910-251-0333; www.deluxenc.com). The Deluxe serves delicious local seafood, premium all-natural meats, and locally grown organic produce. Try the "Lemon Sage Roasted Grouper," served with a savory onion-Parmesan bread pudding. The café is open for dinner nightly and for brunch on Sunday.

- **Caprice Bistro**. Expensive/Moderate. 10 Market Street (910-815-0810; www.capricebistro.com). This traditional French bistro with a mirrored wall and white tablecloths offers outstanding food at reasonable prices. Dinner is served nightly; a three-course prix fixe menu is offered from Sunday to Thursday. Upstairs is a sofa bar where you can enjoy a nightcap or a specialty martini.

- **Circa 1922**. Expensive/Moderate. 8 North Front Street (910-762-1922). This is a fun tapas bar that serves Asian-style treats in addition to continental European items. It also has an extensive wine list. Dinner is served nightly.

- **Elijah's Restaurant**. Expensive/Moderate. 1 Ann Street in Chandler's Wharf (910-343-1448). Located on the bank of the Cape Fear River, this grill serves delicious local seafood. Guests enjoy dining al fresco here and at Elijah's parent restaurant, the Pilot House. Lunch and dinner are served daily.

- **Pilot House Restaurant**. Expensive/Moderate. Water Street in Chandler's Wharf (910-343-0200). The venerable Pilot House has been serving fresh seafood for many years. It overlooks the river and offers outdoor dining. Lunch and dinner are served daily.

- **Caffé Phoenix**. Moderate. 9 South Front Street (910-343-1395). Caffé Phoenix offers a variety of Mediterranean-influenced dishes like chicken Marsala and tuna niçoise salad. This has been a downtown favorite for several years. Al fresco dining is available. Lunch and dinner are served

Monday through Friday; brunch is served on Sunday.

- **Genki**. Moderate. 4724 New Centre Drive (910-796-8687). This Japanese restaurant and sushi bar features Maki sushi, sashimi, beef curry, vegetarian entrées, and homemade sauces. Its sushi was voted the best in the city by *Encore* magazine in 2002 and 2003. It is open nightly for dinner.

- **Kiva Grill**. Moderate. 8211 Market Street (910-686-8211; www.k38baja.com). The flavors of the Southwest and the Pacific Rim are captured in the "Baja Fresh" cuisine at Kiva. Try the delicious "Takoshimi" or the shrimp and goat cheese quesadilla. In fact, try anything on the menu—you can't go wrong. Lunch and dinner are served daily.

- **Le Catalan**. Moderate. 224 South Water Street (910-815-0200; www.lecatalan.com). This French café, wine bar, and shop is located right on the Riverwalk in downtown Wilmington. Wine is available by the glass or by the bottle, to be enjoyed as you view the Cape Fear River from the Riverwalk. The atmosphere is noteworthy for its custom woodwork and French café decor. Lunch and dinner are served Tuesday to Sunday from May through August and Tuesday to Saturday the rest of the year.

- **Flaming Amy's Burrito Barn**. Inexpensive. 4002 Oleander Drive (910-799-2919; www.flamingamysburritobarn.com). This is not your Old El Paso kind of place. Although Amy's signature burrito is pretty standard, some of the other wraps—like the "Thai Me Up," the "Wok on the Beach," and the "Big Jerk"—let you know what you're in for. Lunch and dinner are served daily.

- **Nikki's Fresh Gourmet**. Inexpensive. 16 South Front Street (910-772-9151). Vegetarians will delight at the variety of vegetable wraps and tasty tofu offerings at Nikki's, which serves great sushi spring rolls, too. The choices for carnivores include the spicy Asian chicken salad and even a Philly cheese steak. Lunch is served Monday through Saturday and dinner Thursday through Saturday.

Nearby

- **Poplar Grove Historic Plantation** is located nine miles north of

Orton Plantation
PHOTO BY ANGELA HARWOOD

Wilmington on U.S. 17 at Scotts Hill. The estate was purchased from Joseph Mumford by James Foy, Jr., in 1795. Its 628-acre farm produced peas, corn, and beans and held some 64 slaves. In 1849, the manor house was destroyed by fire. It was rebuilt on its present site in 1850. Relying on peanuts as its staple crop, Poplar Grove remained a focal point of the community under the ownership of the Foy family until its sale in 1971. Renovated and opened to the public in 1980, the estate now serves as a museum complex consisting of the house, its outbuildings, and 16 acres of grounds. A host of craftspeople demonstrate traditional skills such as weaving, spinning, basket making, and blacksmithing. The plantation is open Monday through Saturday from 9 A.M. to 5 P.M. and Sunday from noon to 5 P.M. A fee is charged. For more information, call 910-686-9518 or visit www.poplargrove.com.

■ **Orton Plantation Gardens** is located at 9149 Orton Road off U.S. 133, on the Cape Fear River 18 miles south of Wilmington. Orton was the rice-field plantation home of Roger Moore, who came in 1725 from South Carolina and was a founder of the town of Brunswick. Roger Moore's son, George Moore, was one of the leaders of the first armed resistance to British rule in the colonies. The tombs of Roger Moore and members of his family are located in the gardens. After the fall of Confederate Fort Fisher in 1865, Orton was occupied by Union troops and used as a hospital, sparing it the fate of many homes in the South. The beautiful gardens were the inspiration of Luola Murchison Sprunt and her husband, James, who in 1910 inherited the property and began constructing terraces overlooking the river and planting avenues of live oak trees. In 1916, Dr. Sprunt erected the quaint Luola's Chapel as a memorial to his wife. The gardens were greatly expanded by the Sprunts' son and daughter-in-law under the supervision of landscape architect Robert Swann Sturtevant. The impressive house is not open for tours.

A tour of the gardens takes about an hour, but many choose to stretch a visit into a full morning or afternoon. The gardens are open daily from 8 A.M. to 6 P.M. from March to August and from 10 A.M. to 5 P.M. from September to November. Admission is charged. For more information, call 910-371-6851 or visit www.ortongardens.com.

■ *Duplin Winery* is located at 505 North Sycamore Street (U.S. 117) in Rose Hill, 40 miles north of Wilmington. The oldest winery in North Carolina, it follows traditional recipes and methods passed down from the Swiss and German immigrants who settled this part of North Carolina in the 1700s.

Free tours and tastings of Duplin's award-winning scuppernong and muscadine wines are offered. Production tours are also offered. Custom tours are available for a fee. The winery is open from 9 A.M. to 6 P.M. Monday through Saturday. It is closed on major holidays. *The Bistro Restaurant*, located on the grounds, is open for lunch from Monday through Saturday and for dinner on Friday. Dinner comes with a show. The winery also has a gift shop and museum. For more information, call 800-774-9634 or visit www.duplinwinery.com.

WRIGHTSVILLE BEACH

Wrightsville Beach consists of two islands: the inland Harbor Island, connected to the mainland by a drawbridge, and outlying Wrightsville Beach, a four-mile barrier island located across Banks Channel. In the past several years, resort and golf communities here have become permanent homes for retirees and others drawn to Wrightsville Beach's beauty and climate. Year-round residents number about 3,200, but when summer rolls around, the number explodes to approximately 25,000. Although Wrightsville Beach is heavily developed, it is still an exquisite destination. If you don't mind the crowds, head here in the summer. If you do, wait until the off-season, when you can share this bit of coastal paradise with the few who call it home.

Wrightsville Beach is one of the oldest resorts in North Carolina. "The

Wrightsville Beach
Courtesy of Cape Fear Convention
and Visitors Bureau

Banks," as it was originally known, was developed in 1853 by a group of enterprising businessmen who erected a clubhouse they called the Carolina Yacht Club. The club remains one of the oldest of its kind in the country. In 1888, the Wilmington Sea Coast Railway accessed Harbor Island. Shortly thereafter, two bathhouses and a restaurant were built, establishing the island as a resort. After the place was advertised as Ocean View for a time, Wrightsville Beach became the official name in 1900.

In 1905, electric trolleys began to bring passengers to Wrightsville Beach, ushering in its most romantic period. Hoping to entice Wilmingtonians and others to ride the trolleys out to the island, the Tidewater Power Company built several attractions, the foremost of which was the now-legendary Lumina Pavilion, so called for the thousands of incandescent lights that made it sparkle. In the daytime, the Lumina provided bathers with amusement options that included bowling alleys, snack bars, and slot machines. In the evening, it shone so brightly that it served as an aid to mariners. Wilmingtonians and visitors from all over the South danced the nights away to the music of Tommy Dorsey, Guy Lombardo, Cab Calloway, and Louis Armstrong in the Lumina's grand ballroom. Outside, silent pictures projected on a large movie screen entertained people on the beach. Sadly, the Lumina fell to the wrecking ball in 1973. But its legend lives on in memory and lore.

Like Pleasure Island and the Brunswick County beaches, Wrightsville

Beach was practically demolished by the furious Hurricane Hazel in 1954. Few buildings that stood before Hazel remain today. Luckily, one of them is the 1907 Myers Cottage, which houses Wrightsville Beach's small but alluring museum. Other attractions here include world-class fishing, great shopping, fine dining, and, of course, the seashore and all its pleasures.

JUST THE FACTS

Wrightsville Beach is about 10 miles east of Wilmington on U.S. 74/U.S. 76. A small drawbridge separates the island from the mainland.

Air service is available through Wilmington International Airport; call 910-341-4333.

A good source of information about the area is the Cape Fear Coast Convention and Visitors Bureau, at 24 North Third Street in Wilmington; call 800-222-4757 or 910-341-4030 or visit www.gocapefearcoast.com. To contact the Wrightsville Beach Chamber of Commerce, call 800-232-2469 or visit www.wrightsville.com.

The local newspaper is the *Wilmington Star-News*. The *Star*'s entertainment guide, *Currents*, and the free weekly newspaper *Encore* provide event listings.

Things to Do

MUSEUMS AND SCIENCE CENTERS

■ The **Wrightsville Beach Museum of History** is housed in the island's second-oldest cottage, Myers Cottage, which dates to about 1910. In addition to a collection of artifacts and archival photographs, the museum has a scale model of Wrightsville Beach as it looked around that same year. The museum also hosts traveling exhibits. Located at 303 West Salisbury Street, it is open from 10 A.M. to 4 P.M. Tuesday through Friday, from noon to 5 P.M. on Saturday, and from 1 P.M. to 5 P.M. on Sunday. A

modest admission fee is charged. For information, call 910-256-2569 or visit www.WBMuseum.com.

SPECIAL SHOPPING

■ *Roberts Market*, at 32 North Lumina Avenue, has been providing beach residents and visitors with the necessities since 1919. Call 910-256-2641.

RECREATION

This area has one of the largest recreational fishing fleets north of Florida. Numerous charter boats and head boats are available for hire. For information, call 800-232-2469 or visit www.wrightsville.com.

■ The landmark *Johnny Mercer's Pier* is back in business. Devastated by Hurricanes Bertha and Fran in 1996, the pier has been completely rebuilt and is the only all-concrete, steel-reinforced fishing pier in North Carolina. Open 24 hours a day, it offers a snack bar, a game area, and bathrooms. A small fee is charged to walk on the pier and a larger one to fish. Rods are available for rent. Call 910-256-2743.

■ *Wrightsville Beach Park* has 13 acres of tennis courts, basketball courts, softball fields, football fields, soccer fields, sand volleyball courts, playground equipment, and fitness trails. It is located in the middle of Harbor Island.

- **The Loop** is a popular 2.5-mile path that runs from downtown to Wrightsville Beach Park. If you're tired of running on the sand, this is an ideal morning outing, as long as you don't mind sharing the path with others walking, jogging, biking, and skating.

SEASONAL EVENTS

- King mackerel is indeed king around here. The **Wrightsville Beach King Mackerel Tournament** is held in September. For information, call the North Carolina Marine Fisheries Department at 910-395-3900 or visit www.wbkmt.com.

Places to Stay

RESORTS, HOTELS, AND MOTELS

- **Blockade Runner Resort Hotel**. Expensive. 275 Waynick Boulevard (800-541-1161 or 910-256-2251; www.blockade-runner.com). The Blockade Runner offers an excellent stay at the beach. Celebrating more than 30 years in business, this well-managed establishment has one of the prettiest, best-maintained stretches of sand on the island. Amenities include an outdoor pool, a beach-side bar, a spa, and outdoor patio dining. A two-night minimum stay on weekends is required in the summer. Children under 12 stay free with their parents.

- **Carolina Temple Apartments**. Expensive/Moderate. 550 Waynick Boulevard (910-256-2773; www.carolinatempleislandinn.com). This historic inn consists of two large Plantation-style buildings—the oceanfront Carolina Cottage and the sound-front Temple Cottage. Each two-story structure contains eight efficiency apartments. The apartments rent by the week in the summer; a two-night minimum stay is in effect otherwise. They are closed in the winter.

- **Silver Gull Oceanfront Resort Motel.** Expensive/Moderate. U.S. 74 at the ocean end of Salisbury Street (800-842-8894 or 910-256-3728). This motel was completely refurbished in 1994. Every room has a kitchenette and a private balcony with an ocean view. A lifeguard is on duty during the summer.

Places to Eat

- **Oceanic Restaurant.** Expensive/Moderate. 703 South Lumina Avenue (910-256-5551; www.oceanicrestaurant.com). Oceanic's local awards include Best Water View, Best Grilled Seafood, and Best Restaurant. In addition to seafood, it offers superb steaks and fresh pasta dishes. Outdoor dining is available on the pier. Lunch and dinner are served daily.

- **Southbeach Grill.** Moderate. 100 South Lumina Avenue (910-256-4646; www.southbeachgrillwb.com). This grill offers outdoor dining overlooking Banks Channel. Its creative beach cuisine centers around fresh seafood and innovative seasonal entrées. Lunch and dinner are served daily.

- **The Sandwich Pail Seaside Grill.** Moderate/Inexpensive. 1 Stone Street (910-256-8225). This sandwich shop offers hand-pattied Cuban burgers, fresh homemade salads, and more. Kids can order their lunch in a pail and keep the pail! Free beach delivery is available Monday through Friday with a $20 minimum. The grill is open daily from 10 A.M. to 8 P.M. during the summer; call for winter hours.

Nearby

- **Masonboro Island** is the largest undisturbed barrier island along southern North Carolina's coast. The island's nature trails offer the possibility of spotting endangered loggerhead sea turtles and shorebirds. Located off the southern tip of Wrightsville Beach, Masonboro is accessible only by boat. *Cape Fear Kayaks* (910-798-9922), ***Carolina Coastal Adventures*** (910-458-9111), and ***Island Style Adventure Company*** (910-509-9726) are just a few of the companies that offer excursions to the island. For more information, visit www.ncaudubon.org/IBAs/coast/masonboro_island.htm.

PLEASURE ISLAND

Carolina Beach, Kure Beach, and Fort Fisher make up Pleasure Island. This area prides itself on its clean, uncrowded beaches, reasonably priced accommodations, and friendly atmosphere. Don't be discouraged by the commercial nature of the drive in on U.S. 421. The beaches on the other side of all the buildings are well worth the visit.

Carolina Beach occupies the northern end of the island, while Kure is located at its southern end, next to Fort Fisher. Both beaches are characterized by cottages, family-owned motels and restaurants, and a small-town air. Carolina Beach is the livelier and more developed of the two.

Carolina Beach dates to the late 19th century, when Joseph L. Winner, a Wilmington merchant, purchased 108 acres to develop into a resort town. Although his town, which he called St. Joseph, never took off, other developers followed his lead. By 1915, Carolina Beach had both electricity and a paved road leading to Wilmington. In 1954, Hurricane Hazel devastated the town, leveling some 362 cottages and other buildings and damaging that many again.

Today, Carolina Beach takes pride in its post-Hazel renaissance. With its boardwalk, piers, Ferris wheel, merry-go-round, gazebo, and arcade, it is a slice of coastal Americana. And of course, it wouldn't be "the beach" without the requisite water slides and miniature golf courses. Fishing is also a major activity here; anglers can test their skills on the piers, in the surf, and on deep-sea charters. Carolina Beach State Park invites hikers, picnickers, and campers to explore the area's vegetation.

As you drive across the island to Kure Beach, you'll no doubt notice the devices along the road that look like solar panels. For decades, the federal government has been conducting an experiment here to determine the corrosive effects of salty sea air on various types of metals.

Kure Beach is a small, family-oriented community dominated by vacation cottages that by law cannot exceed 30 feet in height. It is named for its founder, Hans Kure, who acquired land here in 1891. In the 1930s, Kure Beach was the site of the world's first facility designed to extract bromine from seawater. (Years ago, ethylene dibromide was the ingredient that made leaded gasoline safe—or so it was thought.) Among other riches discovered while testing the seawater were gold, silver, copper, and aluminum. During World War II, a German U-boat fired—actually, misfired—on the plant, despite heavy security. Shortly after the war, the laboratory closed.

Popular pastimes here today include fishing, strolling the 711-foot-long Kure Beach Fishing Pier, picnicking at nearby Fort Fisher, and enjoying the sand and surf.

JUST THE FACTS

Pleasure Island is about 12 miles south of Wilmington on U.S. 421. It can also be reached via the Southport-Fort Fisher toll ferry.

Air travelers will need to make arrangements through Wilmington International Airport; call 910-341-4333.

The main source for information on the area is the Pleasure Island Chamber of Commerce, at 1121 North Lake Park Boulevard in Carolina Beach; call 910-458-8434 or visit www.pleasureislandchamber.org.

The weekly newspapers of Pleasure Island are the *Island Gazette* and the *Weekly News*.

Things to Do

HISTORIC PLACES, GARDENS, AND TOURS

■ *Fort Fisher State Historic Site* is located on U.S. 421 south of Kure Beach. Named for Colonel Charles Fisher, a North Carolina hero who died at First Manassas, Fort Fisher was the Civil War's largest earthen fortress, built to protect the port of Wilmington. In January 1865, some 10,000 Fed-

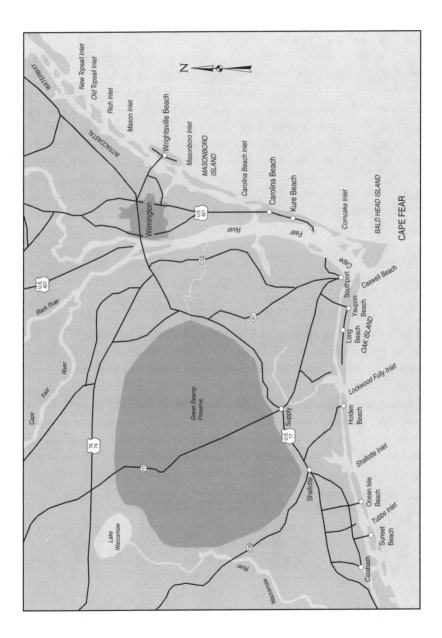

eral troops and history's heaviest naval bombardment to that date finally brought down the fort, signaling the end of the Civil War. What remains of the fort today is slowly being eroded, despite efforts to protect it. The state has seeded the mounds that survive; a trail leads around them and offer views of the Cape Fear River.

A trip to the visitor center will give you an idea of the fort's role in protecting Wilmington and the daring blockade runners that smuggled supplies for the Confederacy. Visitors can enjoy a slide show, dioramas, artifacts, and a complete model of Fort Fisher that was studied in classrooms at West Point following the Civil War. The grounds include a picnic area. From April to October, the site is open Monday through Saturday from 9 A.M. to 5 P.M. and Sunday from 1 P.M. to 5 P.M. From November to March, it is open Tuesday to Saturday from 10 A.M. to 4 P.M. and Sunday from 1 P.M. to 4 P.M. It is closed Christmas and New Year's. Admission is free. Call 910-458-5538 or visit http://www.ah.dcr.state.nc.us/sections/hs/ fisher/fisher.htm.

MUSEUMS AND SCIENCE CENTERS

■ The **North Carolina Aquarium at Fort Fisher**, located off U.S. 421 across the road from Fort Fisher State Historic Site, reopened in a fantastic new facility in 2002. In the Cape Fear Freshwater Conservatory, you'll meander along a path past plant life and tanks filled with freshwater fish. The alligator and turtle tank is filled with small alligators floating limply with only their heads breaking the water. One of the main attractions is the magnificent two-story aquarium filled with sharks, stingrays, and other creatures. Also mesmerizing is the black-lit jellyfish tank. For more information, call 910-458-8257 or visit www.ncaquariums.com.

North Carolina Aquarium at Fort Fisher
COURTESY OF CAPE FEAR CONVENTION AND VISITORS BUREAU

RECREATION

■ *Carolina Beach State Park*, 10 miles south of Wilmington on U.S. 421, has one of the few public campgrounds on this part of the coast. Located inland on the Intracoastal Waterway, it boasts 1,773 acres that encompass a variety of ecosystems, including dune ridges of longleaf pine and turkey oak, longleaf and evergreen savannas, pocosins, and brackish tidal marshes. It is home to the indigenous carnivorous Venus flytrap, red sundew, and pitcher plant. The park offers five hiking trails and a full-service marina with two boat ramps. The campground has shower facilities and 82 drive-up spots available on a first-come, first-served basis. All are shaded, so the heat probably won't bother you. The insects might, though, so pack your bug balm. During the summer, nature programs are offered in the park's amphitheater. For more information, call 910-458-8206 or visit www.ncparks.net.

■ At *Fort Fisher State Recreation Area*, located near Fort Fisher State Historic Site, visitors can picnic in the shade of lovely live oak trees after enjoying a morning on the four-mile stretch of undeveloped beach. Restrooms, showers, and a snack bar are provided. Call 910-458-8206.

■ *Kayak Carolina*, located at 1337 Bridge Barrier Road, offers a two-hour introduction to the sport, as well as an interpretive nature tour. For information, call 910-458-9111 or visit www.kayakcarolina.com.

■ The convergence of the Cape Fear River, the Intracoastal Waterway, and the Atlantic Ocean makes Pleasure Island one of the premier bottom-, pier-, and surf-fishing destinations on the East Coast. The *Carolina Beach yacht basin* is a center for boating activities. A number of charter boats (limited to six passengers) and head boats (up to 150 passengers) are based there.

Reenactors on the mounds at Fort Fisher State Historic Site
Courtesy of Cape Fear Convention and Visitors Bureau

Seasonal Events

- Pleasure Island hosts two fishing tournaments a year—the **East Coast Classic King Mackerel Tournament** in July and the **Carolina Beach Surf-Fishing Tournament** in October. Call the chamber of commerce at 910-458-8434 for information.

- The second weekend of October ushers in the annual **Pleasure Island Seafood, Blues, and Jazz Festival**. The event takes place overlooking the Cape Fear River at the Fort Fisher Air Force Base Recreation Area. Call 910-458-8434 for information.

Places to Stay

Pleasure Island is thick with accommodations; the following list is by no means inclusive. Be mindful that rates vary greatly according to the season. Many places have a two-day minimum, particularly on weekends. In summer, some even have a week's minimum. The chamber of commerce can provide you with a list of rental cottages and condominiums; call 910-458-8434.

Resorts, Hotels, and Motels

- **Sand Dunes Motel**. Expensive/Moderate. 133 Fort Fisher Boulevard in Kure Beach (800-535-4984 or 910-458-5470; www.thesanddunes.com). Sand Dunes has 39 rooms and efficiencies, 27 of which overlook the ocean. A lifeguard is on duty during the summer. The motel offers beach-side Adirondack chairs for relaxing.

- **Savannah Inn**. Expensive/Moderate. 316 Carolina Beach Avenue North in Carolina Beach (800-334-8533 or 910-458-6555; www.thesavannahinn.com). This inn offers clean oceanfront rooms and efficiencies individually decorated with a beach theme. A three-night minimum is required during the summer.

■ *Golden Sands*. Moderate. 1211 South Lake Park Boulevard in Carolina Beach (888-458-8334 or 910-458-8334; www.goldensandscarolinabeach.com). This place has 88 rooms and efficiencies, two swimming pools, and a private pier. Complimentary coffee is served in the lobby.

■ *Admiral's Quarters Motel*. Moderate/Inexpensive. U.S. 421 in Kure Beach (800-743-0556 or 910-458-5050; www.admiralsquartersmotel.com). Admiral's Quarters has 37 rooms, all but three of which overlook the ocean. All have private porches or balconies with rocking chairs. The motel offers two pools, a gazebo, and a sandy playground for the kids.

Places to Eat

■ *Barnacles*. Moderate. 300 North Lake Park Boulevard in Carolina Beach (910-458-6001). For seafood lovers, Barnacles offers fresh fish, lobster, and a raw bar. For the rest, it has plenty of chicken and steak entrées. Lunch and dinner are served daily.

■ *The Cottage Restaurant*. Moderate. 1 North Lake Park Boulevard in Carolina Beach (910-458-4383). The Cottage is, in fact, housed in a renovated 1916 beach cottage. It serves terrific seafood dishes, such as a lobster-and-shrimp torte appetizer, as well as an array of fresh alternatives like a chicken salad wrap and a grilled portabello sandwich. The pasta is great, too. You may dine indoors or outside on the covered deck. Lunch and dinner are served Monday through Saturday year-round.

■ *Deck House*. Moderate. 205 Charlotte Avenue in Carolina Beach (910-458-1026). Housed in a former church, the Deck House specializes in seafood but also offers lots of chicken, pasta, and steak options. All are served with a choice of salad, grouper chowder, or Manhattan clam chowder and—unless the entrée is served over pasta—a choice of baked potato, house potato, rice pilaf, fries, or mixed vegetables. Dinner is served nightly in season; the restaurant is closed on Mondays in the winter.

■ *Michael's Seafood Restaurant and Catering*. Moderate. 1206 North Lake Park Boulevard in Carolina Beach (910-458-7761; www.mikescfood.com). This restaurant is celebrated for its seafood chowder, which it ships around the country. At Michael's, you can have your seafood grilled, broiled, or sautéed, but you can't have it fried. You can dine inside with the 700-gallon fish tank or outside on the deck. Lunch and dinner are served daily.

SOUTHPORT AND THE BRUNSWICK ISLANDS

Located midway between New York and Miami along the Intracoastal Waterway is the quiet town of Southport, which caters to boaters sailing north and south. Southport is listed on the National Register of Historic Places. Originally named Smithville for Benjamin Smith, a Continental Army general who later became governor, Southport was renamed in 1887 to reflect its geography. In recent years, it has become an appealing destination for non-seafaring travelers drawn to its antique shops, historic homes, restaurants, art galleries, and live-oak-shaded parks. Since the town is surrounded by water, it is not surprising that the most popular spot in Southport is Waterfront Park. From there, you can watch ocean ships pass on their way up the Cape Fear River to Wilmington, a remarkable photographic opportunity. Southport itself is so photogenic that a number of motion pictures and television films have been made here.

A good place to begin is Southport's visitor center, on West Moore Street. Here, you can pick up maps, brochures, and information about Southport and the Brunswick County beaches. Just around the corner is the North Carolina Maritime Museum at Southport. Take time to enjoy the town's historic business district, especially the many antique shops along Howe and Moore streets. Also, be sure to stroll the Southport Riverwalk and to visit the shops around the yacht basin and near the marina. Finally, take time to enjoy some local seafood.

Wind-swept live oak and yaupon trees grace Oak Island, a 10-mile stretch of beach with quiet surf and moderate tides. This family-oriented community offers water activities for all ages. Its three piers, marina, and public launch facilities make it popular with fishermen, especially those looking for king mackerel. Oak Island grew from a few prewar cottages to a community of over 300 homes after World War II. In 1954, Hurricane Hazel destroyed all but five houses here. Incorporated in July 1999, the town of

Oak Island consists of the communities once known as Long Beach and Yaupon Beach.

Named after historic Fort Caswell, located at the top of the island, Caswell Beach is home to the brightest lighthouse in the United States. It also boasts a Coast Guard station reminiscent of the old lifesaving stations. Deep dunes and sprawling beach cottages line the ocean. On the marsh side, cottages on pilings overlook the Cape Fear River's shipping channel. The only souvenirs available at Caswell Beach are the shells waiting to be collected on quiet low-tide walks along the beautiful shore.

Holden Beach is an 11-mile-long south-facing island. It, too, was devastated by Hurricane Hazel in 1954, but developers lost no time in rebuilding ample rental space for its numerous visitors. The western end of Holden overlooks Shallotte Inlet, a shrimp-boat harbor said to possess water with curative powers. At Windy Point, the story goes, people have been mysteriously cured of infections. The most plausible reason is a type of reed that grows here but nowhere else. Although the water's curative power is unsubstantiated by scientists, people have come here from as far away as Canada to put it to the test.

Ocean Isle Beach and Sunset Beach round out the Brunswick County beaches. A new and exciting addition to Ocean Isle is the Silver Coast Winery. Ocean Isle also boasts the terrific Museum of Coastal Carolina. Sunset Beach is considered by many to be the most beautiful of North Carolina's southern islands.

Brunswick Town State Historic Site
COURTESY OF CAPE FEAR CONVENTION AND VISITORS BUREAU

JUST THE FACTS

Things to Do

HISTORIC PLACES, GARDENS, AND TOURS

■ **Southport Trail** is a self-guided tour map available from the Southport 2000 Visitors Center or the Southport Historical Society (800-388-9635). This one-mile walk through town visits many interesting historical sites. A few are described below.

The **Adkins-Ruark House** is where author and journalist Robert Ruark spent his childhood summers. His book *The Old Man and the Boy* is an account of his time in Southport.

Keziah Memorial Park, on Moore Street, is the home of the 800-year-old Indian Trail Tree. This live oak was deliberately bent by Native Americans to create a landmark to guide them.

"Gentleman pirate" Stede Bonnet was making repairs to his ship, *The Revenge*, when Colonel William Rhett caught up with him at what is now called **Bonnet's Creek**. A one-time wealthy planter, Bonnet is said to have taken to piracy for a bit of adventure and to get away from his shrewish wife.

MUSEUMS AND SCIENCE CENTERS

■ The **North Carolina Maritime Museum at Southport**, at 116 North Howe Street, houses materials pertaining to the nautical history of the lower Cape Fear. A self-guided tour leads among 12 exhibits linked to each other through a story line. Shipwrecks, navigational aids, and fishing are covered, as is the history of Southport. The museum is open Tuesday through Saturday from 9 A.M. to 5 P.M. An admission fee is charged for visitors over age 16. For more information, call 910-457-0003 or visit http:/ /www.ah.dcr.state.nc.us/sections/maritime/branches/ southport_default.htm.

■ The **Museum of Coastal Carolina**, at 21 East Second Street in Ocean Isle Beach, is a handsome 7,500-square-foot building constructed in 1991. A hands-on interactive museum, it explores the natural history and heritage of the area and has a touch tank with live sea animals. During the high season, it is open Monday and Thursday from 10 A.M. to 8 P.M.; Tuesday, Wednesday, Friday, and Saturday from 10 A.M. to 5 P.M.; and Sunday from 1 P.M. to 5 P.M. Call for hours the rest of the year. Admission is charged. Call 910-579-1016 or visit www.museumofcc.org.

CULTURAL OFFERINGS

■ Housed in a 1904 schoolhouse that subsequently became Southport's city hall, then its library, the **Franklin Square Art Gallery** features the products of local artists working in a variety of media. Legend has it that if you drink from the hand pump in Franklin Square Park, you're sure to return to the town. The gallery is located on West Street behind the park. From March until December, it is open Monday through Saturday from 10 A.M. to 4 P.M. From June through August, it is also open on Sunday from 1 P.M. to 4 P.M. For more information, call 910-457-5450 or visit www.franklinsquaregallery.org.

Special Shopping

Southport has a reputation for its antique shops. More than 15 shops and 75 dealers trade here. Head for Howe and Moore streets to visit a concentration of them.

■ **Olde Southport Village**, at 1102 North Howe Street, is a growing assemblage of painted cottages that are being salvaged and collected by Phil Hemphill. Gift and craft outlets dominate, but a seamstress and a beautician also tend shop here. Most of the shops are open Tuesday through Saturday from 10 A.M. to 5 P.M. For more information, call 910-448-1088.

■ **Silver Coast Winery**, at 6680 Barbecue Road in Ocean Isle Beach, is one of the many fine new wineries that have cropped up in the state in recent years. Located in a lovely wooded setting, this is an ideal place to share a peaceful picnic with friends. In addition to its tasty Barbera and Chardonnay wines, it offers an art gallery, a gift shop, and a monthly wine festival. For more information, call 910-287-2800 or visit www.silvercoastwinery.com.

Recreation

■ **Oak Island Nature Center & Park** is located at the end of 52nd Street in Oak Island. Overlooking the Intracoastal Waterway and the marsh, the facility offers a wide range of activities for adults and children. There are various mineral, rock, and animal exhibits, including a large touch tank. Adjacent to the nature center is a park with trails, a picnic shelter, bathrooms, and opportunities for fishing. **Talking Trees Walking Trail** is an interactive trail where dogwoods, red cedars, Southern magnolias, black gums, and other trees talk to you as you walk. Admission is free. The hours are seasonal; call 910-278-5518.

■ **Scuba South Diving Company** is located at 222 South River Drive in Southport. Owner and skipper Wayne Strickland leads shipwreck scuba tours amid Frying Pan Shoals. For more information, call 910-457-7925 or 910-457-5201 or visit www.scubasouthdiving.com.

SEASONAL EVENTS

■ Southport hosts the official **North Carolina Fourth of July Festival**. The town has been observing Independence Day since 1795. Call 910-457-6964 or visit www.nc4thofjuly.com for information.

■ Two annual fishing tournaments—the **U.S. Open King Mackerel Tournament**, based at Southport Marina, and the **South Brunswick Islands King Mackerel Classic**, based at Holden Beach Marina—offer $100,000 in prizes each. Call 800-426-6644 for details.

■ The **North Carolina Oyster Festival** is held in nearby Shallotte in mid-October. What began as a tiny oyster roast in 1979 has grown into the official North Carolina oyster celebration. The highlight is an oyster-shucking championship. Call 910-754-6644 for information.

Places to Stay

RESORTS, HOTELS, AND MOTELS

■ **The Winds Inn and Suites**. Expensive/Moderate. 310 East First Street in Ocean Isle Beach (800-334-3581 or 910-579-6275; www.TheWinds.com). The Winds offers a complimentary breakfast buffet, three pools, a garden bar and restaurant, and golf packages.

■ **Blue Water Point Motel and Marina**. Moderate. 5710 West Beach Place on Oak Island (www.bluewaterpointmotel.com; 888-634-9005 or 910-278-1230). This motel offers rooms with a view of the water, cable television, mini refrigerators, coffee pots, a restaurant, and free sunset cruises during the summer.

THE BLOCKADE TAKES THE LIFE OF A REBEL SPY

Excerpted from *Gray Phantoms of the Cape Fear* by Dawson Carr

Rose O'Neal Greenhow's brief career as a Southern spy had already exposed her to danger. Her husband, Dr. Robert Greenhow, had been a native Virginian whose position in the State Department had brought him to Washington. There, Rose quickly endeared herself to members of government and the city's elite. After her husband's death, she continued to reside in Washington, although her heart was in the South.

When the war broke out, she resolved to do all in her power to help the Rebels. Upon learning details of the North's plan to attack at Manassas in July 1861, she passed the word to Confederate general P. G. T. Beauregard. Some say this information allowed the Rebels to make advance preparations that led to a major triumph.

Greenhow was later held under arrest in Washington and nearly thrown in prison for passing information to Southern military leaders. At her trial, she was given the option of swearing allegiance to the United States, but she haughtily declined. Uncertain what to do with such a woman, the Union eventually agreed to pardon her if she would at least swear to leave the North and never return. To this, she agreed.

But that did not mean she would abandon the cause. Greenhow understood the impor-tance of good relations between England and the South. She decided to try her hand at being a Confederate agent in Europe. . . .

Her trip to Europe proved more successful than even she had hoped. Honored by high officials in both England and France, Greenhow also won popularity among the residents of those two nations, especially the British. While in England, she published her memoirs, entitled *My Imprisonment and the First Year of Abolition Rule at Washington*. The book was well received all over England, helping further her goal of influencing public opinion in favor of the Confederacy. Copies were snatched up eagerly by people anxious to read a firsthand account of the war across the Atlantic—and especially to hear the story of such an attractive and popular spy.

Now, as she prepared to travel back to Wilmington, Greenhow carried several thousand dollars in gold coins, her share of the profits from the book's sales. Of all the Southern patriots who came across the sea to win over the English, it's unlikely that any was as well liked as she, and it was with some regret that she was leaving. Yet she missed her friends back across the Atlantic and wanted to see them again in spite of the dangers of the forthcoming voyage. Also, it was rumored that she carried secret dispatches for President Jefferson Davis.

She stepped aboard the new blockade runner *Condor*—a magnificent gray behemoth with three stacks and remarkable speed—as the vessel prepared to leave Scotland in September 1864. The captain was a furloughed British naval officer using the alias Samuel Ridge. . . .

It was the first week of October when the *Condor* reached the vicinity of New Inlet. Guiding her was Thomas Brinkman, one of the small cadre of Smithville pilots who helped blockade runners reach the Cape Fear River through the maze of sand bars and shoals. Brinkman directed the shadowy vessel along the shoreline, taking advantage of her seven-foot draft to cruise at the very edge of the surf. The skies were stormy that night, and although waves rocked the ship, the crewmen were thankful for the additional cover. . . .

In the darkest part of the night, just before dawn, the *Condor* increased speed as she approached the mound battery at Fort Fisher, now faintly visible a couple of miles ahead. Unfortunately, the omnipresent [Union vessel] *Niphon* was waiting. . . .

Rose O'Neal Greenhow was desperate, believing that the enemy would board the *Condor* momentarily and that she would be arrested. She pleaded with Captain Ridge to take her to shore, but he tried to reassure her that once daylight arrived, they could make it to the beach safely. He explained that the stormy weather made the sea too dangerous for an attempt in the dark. Still, she begged him until he finally relented.

The captain asked three of his most experienced crewmen to launch a lifeboat and deliver her to shore. As soon as they were aboard the small craft, a monstrous wave overturned it, and all aboard were tossed into the swirling waters. The men all surfaced and made their way to land. But Greenhow was never seen alive again, as the heavy gold coins she carried in her garments pulled her to the bottom. . . .

Greenhow [is] . . . buried in Oakdale Cemetery in the heart of [Wilmington].

INNS AND BED-AND-BREAKFASTS

■ *The Brunswick Inn*. Expensive. 301 East Bay Street in Southport (910-457-5278; www.brunswickinn.com). This lovely Federal-style inn overlooking the Cape Fear River offers three spacious rooms. A two-night minimum is required for holiday and in-season weekends.

■ *Lois Jane's Riverview Inn*. Moderate. 106 West Bay Street in Southport (800-457-1152 or 910-457-6701; www.loisjane.com). This 1890s home was built by Lois Jane's grandfather and restored by her children in 1995. The inn is furnished with period antiques, many of them family heirlooms. It offers two rooms with private baths and two with a shared bath. Breakfast is included in the room rate.

Places to Eat

- **The Pharmacy**. Expensive/Moderate. 110 East Moore Street in Southport (910-457-5577). At lunchtime, The Pharmacy serves chicken salad, ham-and-cheese strudel with sweet potato chips, and a quiche of the day. For dinner, it turns to more sophisticated fare. Try the bouillabaisse or the gravlax for a change of pace. Lunch is served daily and dinner Thursday through Sunday.

- **Betty's Waterfront Restaurant**. Moderate. Off Old Ferry Road in Holden Beach (910-842-3381). Betty's offers fresh seafood any way you want it: grilled, fried, blackened, or broiled. Chicken and steak are also on the menu. Dinner is served daily.

- **Yacht Basin Provision Company**. Moderate. 130 Yacht Basin Drive in Southport (910-457-0654). Don't miss eating at this place. Check your preconceptions at the door, grab the beverage of your choice, stand in line, place your order, then go outside and wait for one of the cheerful servers to bring you the freshest basket of steamed clams or grilled fish you've ever eaten. I'm told the burgers are out of this world, too. The restaurant is open daily for lunch and dinner.

- **Crabby-Oddwaters Restaurant**. Moderate/Inexpensive. 310 Sunset Boulevard in Sunset Beach (910-579-6372). This place is located upstairs from Bill's Seafood Market, the source of its fare. To get fresher seafood, you'd have to catch it yourself. Dinner is served daily.

- **Jones' Seafood House**. Moderate/Inexpensive. 6404 East Oak Island Drive in Oak Island (910-278-5231). This family-owned restaurant specializing in Calabash-style seafood has been a local favorite since it opened its doors in 1964. Dinner is served daily.

- **Sugar Shack**. Moderate/Inexpensive. 1609 Hale Beach Road in Ocean

Isle Beach (910-579-3844). The Sugar Shack serves Jamaican fare prepared by a Jamaican chef. Try one of the delicious steaks or the Jerk chicken salad. Dinner is served Tuesday through Saturday.

- **Thai Peppers.** Moderate/Inexpensive. 115 East Moore Street in Southport (910-457-0095). Curries, "Pad Thai," and hot-and-sour seafood are all served here. You can enjoy them indoors or out with an ice-cold beer to cool off the fiery heat—of the day and of the food. Lunch and dinner are served Monday through Saturday. Hours are seasonal.

Nearby

- Once a haven for pirates, **Bald Head Island** is a pristine triangle of land south of Wilmington. It is accessible only by water. You can ferry over to the island from Southport or cruise in your own boat to the harbor. On one Blair staff retreat, we stayed in Wilmington and took a day trip to Bald Head. While we didn't get a glimpse of the island's famous loggerhead turtles, we did enjoy a pleasant tour that included a hike into Bald Head's remaining patch of maritime forest and a climb up Old Baldy, the oldest lighthouse in the state. Old Baldy is privately owned, so access is restricted.

Aside from a handful of utility vehicles, automobiles are not allowed on the island, so the speediest way to get around is by golf cart. Since 1986, the state's 10,000-acre portion of the island has been designated a

Old Baldy
COURTESY OF NORTH CAROLINA DIVISION OF TOURISM, FILM AND SPORTS DEVELOPMENT

day-use state park. The remaining land is privately owned and under careful development. The upscale resort here consists of the Marsh Harbour Inn and Conference Center, a championship golf course, and a variety of rental cottages and condominiums. Accommodations at the inn include round-trip ferry passage and use of the club and a golf cart. For more information, call 800-432-RENT or visit www.baldheadisland.com. *Theodosia's* is a deluxe Victorian-style inn located in Harbour Village on Bald Head. For a luxurious and lavender-themed stay, call 800-656-1812 or 910-457-6563 or visit www.theodosias.com.

■ Museum artifacts, crumbling foundations, and the walls of St. Philip's Church are all that is left of historic **Brunswick Town**, located 18 miles south of Wilmington on N.C. 133. Founded in 1726 by Maurice Moore, one of the enterprising sons of a former South Carolina governor, Brunswick Town was the site of the first colonial rebellion against British rule. In 1766, eight years before the Boston Tea Party, some 150 armed citizens known as the Sons of Liberty encircled customs officials and forced them to take an oath that they would issue no more stamped paper.

Brunswick Town initially flourished as a port for shipping tar, pitch, and turpentine. But despite its early promise, it was abandoned soon after New Bern took over as the state capital and Wilmington assumed prominence. After decades of calm, the site again took on a historic role in 1861, when an earthen fortress, **Fort Anderson**, was constructed to protect Confederate blockade runners against the Union navy. In 1865, following the fall of Fort Fisher at the mouth of the Cape Fear River, Union forces attacked Fort Anderson by land and water. After three days of fighting, the Confederates evacuated the fort in the dark of night.

Now a state historic site, Brunswick Town is open Tuesday through Saturday from 10 A.M. to 4 P.M. year-round. Admission is free. For information, call 910-371-6613 or visit http://www.ah.dcr.state.nc.us/Sections/hs/brunswic/brunswic.htm.

■ For nearly 50 years, seafood lovers have flocked to the small town of **Calabash**, located off U.S. 17 just north of the South Carolina line, for some original "Calabash-style" seafood, lightly battered and fried. It has been estimated that there is one restaurant for every 75 of Calabash's 1,300 citizens. Try **Barracuda Bar & Grille** (910-579-5066), at 1224 Riverview Drive; **Dockside Seafood House** (910-579-6775), on the Calabash River; or any of the restaurants along N.C. 179. Be prepared for a wait in summer.

THE PIEDMONT

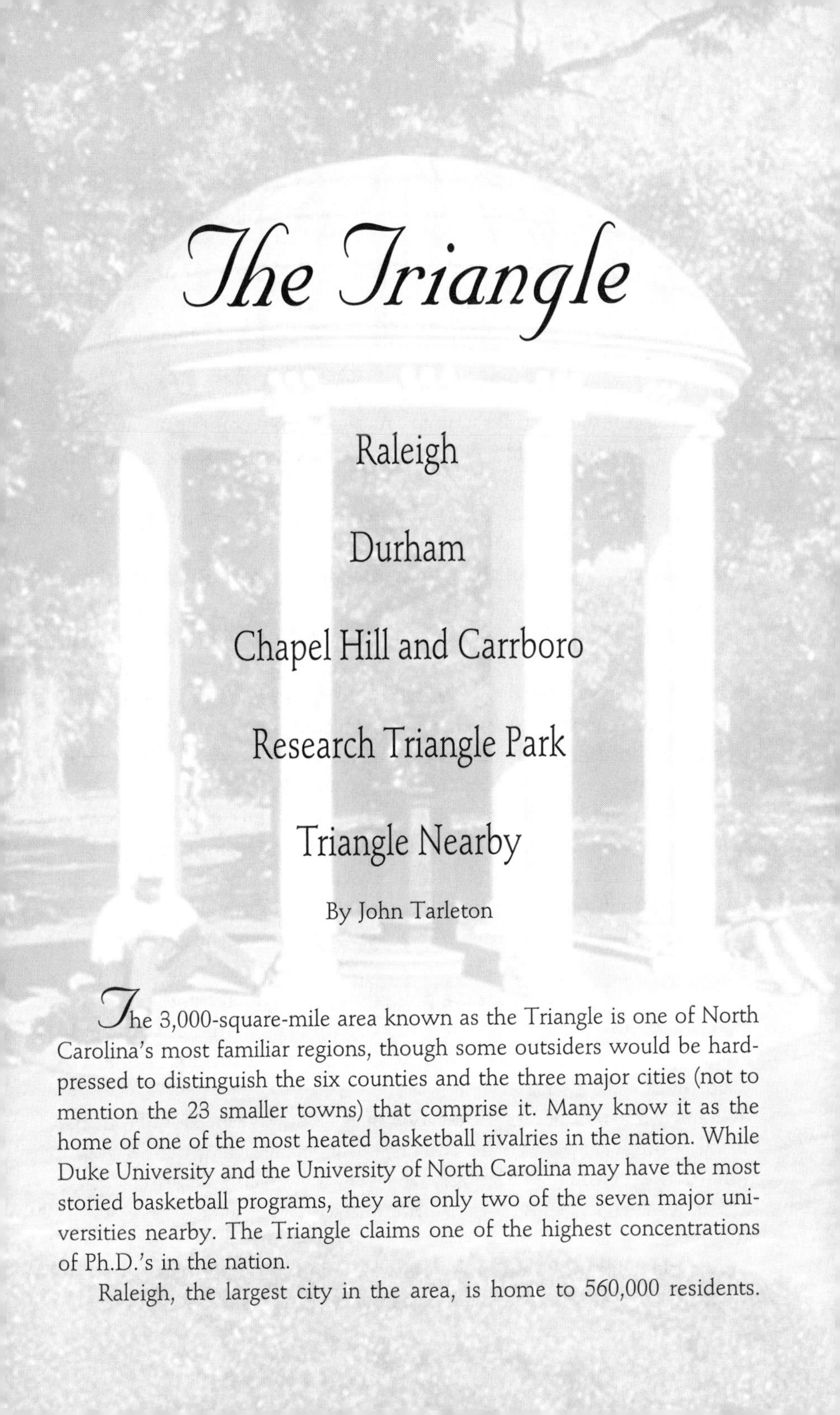

The Triangle

Raleigh

Durham

Chapel Hill and Carrboro

Research Triangle Park

Triangle Nearby

By John Tarleton

The 3,000-square-mile area known as the Triangle is one of North Carolina's most familiar regions, though some outsiders would be hard-pressed to distinguish the six counties and the three major cities (not to mention the 23 smaller towns) that comprise it. Many know it as the home of one of the most heated basketball rivalries in the nation. While Duke University and the University of North Carolina may have the most storied basketball programs, they are only two of the seven major universities nearby. The Triangle claims one of the highest concentrations of Ph.D.'s in the nation.

Raleigh, the largest city in the area, is home to 560,000 residents.

The capital city of North Carolina, it's also a thriving center of education, art, and sports. The Carolina Hurricanes, the 2006 Stanley Cup winners, play here. Their loyal fans are equally comfortable in a seat by the ice, watching a movie on the lawn at the North Carolina Museum of Art, or enjoying their favorite snack at one of Raleigh's many restaurants and watering holes.

Durham, though richly steeped in tobacco history, is now called "the City of Medicine." Thanks to the research relationship between Duke University and companies located in nearby Research Triangle Park, it is the center for some of the world's most important medical and pharmaceutical research, as well as groundbreaking work in microelectronics, textiles, telecommunications, and instrumentation technology. Duke also brings some of the world's best theater, art exhibits, speakers, dancers, and musicians to its hometown.

Chapel Hill, the third corner of the Triangle, is defined by its historic school—the University of North Carolina at Chapel Hill, the first state-funded university in the nation. Chapel Hill is the definition of a college town. Years ago, when funding for a state zoo was first proposed, conservatives quipped that the state could build a fence around Chapel Hill. Chapel Hill's history of tolerance may be due to the fact that academia is a fairly steady business, and the area has long been spared many of the economic woes that have affected other parts of the state. Its small population enjoys a good standard of living and a strong sense of community.

Smaller neighboring towns such as Carrboro and Hillsborough have their own special qualities. The heavy concentration of artists and writers in Carrboro has prompted some to call this former mill town "the Paris of the Piedmont." Hillsborough, home of the Triangle SportsPlex, is known for its grand old houses. It boasts some of the best architecture in the state.

Collectively, the Triangle is a powerhouse. Low real-estate prices and plentiful employment opportunities have attracted a large population of transplants from all over the country, but the area also retains many of its born-and-bred natives.

The wide span of significant area history deserves a look. From the Native American tribes that converged at the Great Indian Trading Path to the colonial settlement of Raleigh to Martin Luther King's famous civil-rights speech in Durham, history is lodged in every corner of the Triangle.

Visitors enjoy the hundreds of award-winning restaurants, the dozens of first-rate theaters, and the half-dozen lakes. There are gardens and

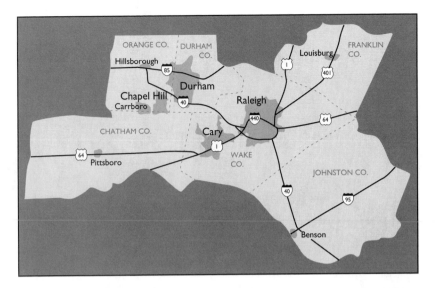

museums and gigantic shopping malls. There are fairs and flea markets and antique shops. There are sports arenas and golf courses and greenways. There are nightclubs and comedy clubs and walking tours.

The people here are educated and enjoy a broad range of activities, from kayaking on Lake Crabtree to listening to music at the Cat's Cradle. Natives are fiercely loyal to their hometowns. Transplants often rave about the climate and the laid-back, affable spirit of their neighbors. In recent years, telling the two groups apart has become increasingly difficult. So go for the people-watching, if nothing else. Then have fun choosing whatever else you'll do. Just try not to let your options overwhelm you.

Fayetteville Street reopening party
COURTESY OF GREATER RALEIGH CONVENTION AND VISITORS BUREAU

RALEIGH

*I*f the streets of downtown Raleigh seem unnaturally gridlike to you, it's because North Carolina's capital is the only one in the country built on land bought for the sole purpose of establishing the state seat. What's more, it's one of only three state capitals planned out on paper before the cornerstone was ever laid.

In 1788, a group of commissioners was sent in search of a centrally located section of land suitable for setting up the legislature. A few older and more distinguished North Carolina towns, including Fayetteville, felt they were entitled to the honor and objected, to no avail. The delegation pushed on until it came upon a local watering hole owned by Isaac Hunter. After spending some time there, the commissioners found his land to be almost exactly what they were looking for, proclaiming that Hunter's property was within 10 miles of precisely where the capital needed to be. They continued to study the area. During their travels, the thirsty bunch came upon another well-known tavern, owned by a Revolutionary War colonel named Joel Lane. Local lore claims that Colonel Lane brewed a stout concoction called Cherry Bounce that finally swayed their votes. After purchasing 1,000 acres, the city's forefathers began drawing up plans. By 1792, the town was up and running.

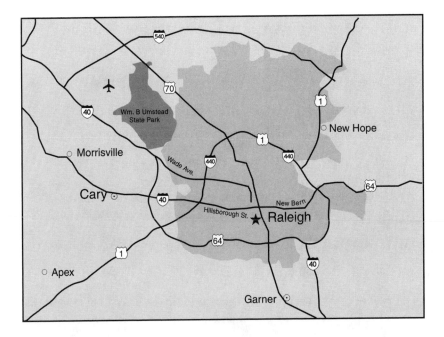

Though downtown Raleigh was wholly conceived from the outset, the city has altered its original design several times. From the end of the Civil War through the mid-1970s, the door of the State Capitol opened to Fayetteville Street, whose businesses were the center of Raleigh's commerce. In the 1950s, the shopping centers and available residential land of north Raleigh drew residents away from downtown. In an attempt to revitalize downtown, the city council built a pedestrian mall over Fayetteville Street in 1976. The effort achieved the opposite effect; the mall eliminated street parking for the businesses on Fayetteville Street, and many closed or moved. In the past 10 or 15 years, the residential buildings, restaurants, galleries, shops, and theaters that have revitalized downtown Raleigh have opened around the mall and away from the State Capitol and other government buildings. The city recently removed the pedestrian mall and reopened Fayetteville Street to car traffic. Most of Raleigh's people like this change. Longtime residents fondly remember Fayetteville Street before the mall.

Today, Raleigh's solid economy, boosted by the high-tech jobs of Research Triangle Park, has attracted a diverse labor force that has brought with it an eclectic mix of lifestyles and cultural mores. Consistently over the last two decades, Raleigh has won national recognition as one of the most desirable places to live and work. And the Joel Lane House is still open, though you won't find a drop of Cherry Bounce there now.

JUST THE FACTS

Interstate 40 is one of Raleigh's main thoroughfares. The Interstate 440 Beltline provides easy access to the Capital City, Research Triangle Park, and the surrounding communities. Interstate 95 and Interstate 85 run within 25 miles of the city.

Raleigh-Durham International Airport is only a 15-minute drive from downtown Raleigh. It offers more than 300 daily departures.

The Greyhound bus terminal is located at 314 West Jones Street; call 919-834-8275 for information. Within greater Raleigh, the Capital Area Transit (CAT) bus system and CAT Connectors (vans) provide riders with an extensive network of routes. The hours of operation are 6 A.M. to 10 P.M. Monday through Saturday. The Raleigh Trolley serves the downtown area from 11:30 A.M. to 2 P.M. Monday through Friday.

Raleigh is accessible by Amtrak train. The station is located at 320 West Cabarrus Street. For information, call 919-833-7594.

One of the best sources of information about Raleigh is the Capital Area Visitor Center, located at 301 North Blount Street. For preplanned itineraries, maps, and other information, call 919-733-3456 or visit www.visitraleigh.com. The Greater Raleigh Convention and Visitors Bureau, located at 9421 Fayetteville Street, is another excellent source. Call 800-849-8499 or 919-834-5900 or visit www.raleighcvb.org.

Raleigh's morning newspaper is the *News & Observer*, one of the largest in the state. The *Independent*, a weekly paper, covers the entire Triangle; it is a good source for information about local activities, entertainment, dining, and shopping.

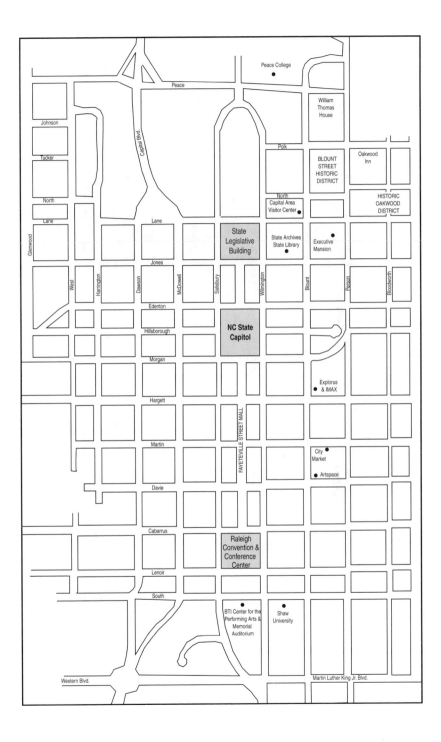

The North Carolina State Capitol
COURTESY OF GREATER RALEIGH CONVENTION AND VISITORS BUREAU

Things to Do

HISTORIC PLACES, GARDENS, AND TOURS

■ The **Executive Mansion**, at 210 North Blount Street on Burke Square, is the official residence of the governor. Built solely of materials from within the state, it is considered one of the finest examples of Queen Anne cottage-style architecture in North Carolina. Franklin D. Roosevelt described its interior as being the most beautiful of any governor's residence in America. Construction on the house began in 1885. To keep costs down, prisoners from the state penitentiary made bricks and did much of the labor; each brick bears the name of the inmate who made it. Still, the final price spiraled to an unheard-of $58,000 by the time the house was completed in 1891. Tours are available; admission is free. For information and reservations, call 919-733-3456.

■ The **Historic Oakwood District**, located off North Person Street between Jones and Boundary streets, is the only intact 19th-century neighborhood in Raleigh. Built after the Civil War in the dense woods of the Mordecai Grove at the northwestern corner of the city, the district showcases a variety of Victorian architectural styles and reflects the middle-class tastes of its founding fathers and the refined craftsmanship of local architects and builders. Listed on the National Register of Historic Places, Oakwood is a reminder of Southern urban life during the 19th and 20th centuries. Some homes still retain the blue porch ceilings of the period, painted to resemble the sky and, according to Southern folklore, to scare away flies. Sidewalk strolls are free, but please respect the privacy of the homeowners. For more information about Oakwood and the annual *Oakwood Garden Tour*, visit www.historicoakwood.org.

- The *Joel Lane House*, located at the corner of St. Mary's and West Hargett streets, is the oldest dwelling in Raleigh. Built around 1760, it was the site of numerous historic events, including general-assembly sessions during the Revolutionary War. According to local lore, Colonel Joel Lane opened his home to six state commissioners on their way to Isaac Hunter's home, another popular meeting place that was already under consideration for the site of the new state capital. Like Hunter, Lane operated an inn and tavern out of his house. Plying the commissioners with his famous Cherry Bounce, Lane persuaded them to buy 1,000 acres of land from him rather than from Hunter, with the added agreement that one of the streets in the new city would carry his name. Joel Lane has been called "the Father of Raleigh." Today, costumed guides lead tours through his fully restored house and formal gardens. Tours are offered Tuesday through Friday from 10 A.M. to 2 P.M. and Saturday from 1 P.M. to 4 P.M. A small admission fee is charged. For more information, call 919-833-3431.

- The *J. C. Raulston Arboretum* at North Carolina State University, located on Beryl Road off the Interstate 440 Beltline near the fairgrounds, is a nationally acclaimed garden containing one of the most diverse collections of landscape plants in North America. As part of the Department of Horticultural Science at the university, the arboretum is primarily a research and teaching garden that focuses on the evaluation, selection, and display of plant material from around the world. Named in honor of its late founder and director, this eight-acre masterpiece includes such wonders as the Klein-Pringle White Garden, a Japanese garden meditation space, the Paradise Garden (designed to delight all five senses in the fashion of the ancient Persian gardens), and, famously, the 450-foot Perennial Border, created by nationally known designer Edith Eddleman. The gardens are open from 8 A.M. until 8 P.M. from April through October and from 8 A.M. until 5 P.M. from November through March. Guided tours are offered on Sunday at 2 P.M. from March through October. Admission is free, but leave your pets at home. For more information, call 919-515-3132 or visit www.ncsu.edu/jcraulstonarboretum/.

- The **North Carolina State Capitol** is located at 1 East Edenton Street on Capitol Square. Entering from Wilmington Street brings you up the front lawn and past a bronze sculpture depicting the three United States presidents with North Carolina origins—Andrew Jackson is on horseback, James Polk is seated and holding a map, and Andrew Johnson is seated and holding the United States Constitution. The current State Capitol is the second to occupy Union Square. The original, simple two-story brick structure was built between 1792 and 1796. A fire caused by an unattended smelting pot (which, ironically, was being used to melt zinc to fireproof the roof) destroyed it in 1831. In 1833, plans for a new building were drafted. By 1840, the current State Capitol was completed. Considered a fine example of Greek Revival architecture, the building is a national historic landmark. It currently houses the offices of the governor and lieutenant governor. Free tours allow visitors to see the old Senate and House chambers, complete with their original furniture and fireplaces. You may also spy a ghost. Local lore has it that the spirit of a Confederate soldier roams the building's second floor. Over the years, staff members have reported hearing strange noises and witnessing odd occurrences. Sound intriguing? Check it out for yourself. The State Capitol is open to visitors from 8 A.M. to 5 P.M. Monday through Friday, from 10 A.M. to 4 P.M. on Saturday, and from 1 P.M. to 4 P.M. on Sunday. Public tours are offered at 10:30 A.M. and 2:30 P.M. on Saturday and at 2:30 P.M. on Sunday. For information, call 919-733-4994; to arrange a tour, call 919-733-3456.

MUSEUMS AND SCIENCE CENTERS

- **Exploris**, at 201 East Hargett Street, is an interactive global learning center with hands-on exhibits that highlight the similarities among people of all cultures and demonstrate how we are all linked together in the larger world. The museum's popular IMAX theater allows kids of all ages to travel to distant places and meet people from around the globe. State-of-the-art images on a screen seven stories high and a 12,000-watt surround-sound stereo system take movie watching to a whole new level, making viewers feel as if they've truly gone on an adventure. Exploris is open Tuesday through Saturday from 11 A.M. to 5 P.M. and Sunday from noon to 5 P.M. Admission is charged. For more information, call 888-287-5411 or visit www.exploris.org. You can learn the showtimes for the IMAX theater by calling 919-834-4040 or visiting www.exploris.org/imax/showtimes.aspx.

- The ***North Carolina Museum of Art***, at 2110 Blue Ridge Road, began in 1947. Our state was the first in the nation to appropriate public funds to purchase art, making this one of the earliest state-supported art museums in the country. It showcases an enviable collection of national and international works. The recently refurbished European gallery contains masterful paintings and sculptures from the Renaissance through the Impressionist period. The gallery of American art features works by John Singleton Copley, Thomas Cole, and Winslow Homer, while the modern and contemporary galleries highlight art by the likes of Georgia O'Keeffe and John Biggers. More than 5,000 years of art from ancient Egypt to the present is on display to the public. Lectures and workshops are also available, and films and concerts are regularly held in the museum's park and its outdoor cinema. Prices and times for special exhibits and programs vary, so call the box office at 919-715-5923 for information. The museum is open Tuesday, Wednesday, Thursday, and Saturday from 9 A.M. to 5 P.M., Friday from 9 A.M. to 9 P.M., and Sunday from 10 A.M. to 5 P.M. There is no charge for admission. Free guided tours are offered Tuesday through Sunday at 1:30 P.M. For more information, call 919-839-6262 or visit www.ncartmuseum.org.

- The ***North Carolina Museum of History***, at 5 East Edenton Street on Bicentennial Plaza, contains more than 150,000 artifacts representative of North Carolina's rich heritage. Housing both long-term and changing exhibits, the museum focuses on seven broad categories of the state's history: agriculture and industry, community history, costumes and textiles, folk life, furnishings and decorative arts, military history, and political and socioeconomic history. It is also home to the North Carolina Sports Hall of Fame. Guided tours are available. Admission is free. The museum is open Tuesday through Saturday from 9 A.M. to 5 P.M. and Sunday from

North Carolina Museum of History
COURTESY OF GREATER RALEIGH CONVENTION AND VISITORS BUREAU

noon to 5 P.M. For more information, call 919-807-7900 or visit www.ncmuseumofhistory.org.

■ The **North Carolina Museum of Natural Sciences**, at 11 West Jones Street, offers hands-on programs every day. Visitors can touch a flying squirrel, make lightning, or step inside a room filled with butterflies. Featuring over 3,000 live animals in four floors of exhibits, it has something to excite everyone in your group. Be sure to check out the four enormous whale skeletons on display. One hangs from the ceiling in the mezzanine. You can't miss it; it's 50 feet long. And if staring at the belly of a whale doesn't completely astound you, then take a look at the fossilized heart of the 66-million-year-old plant-eating Thescelosaurus nicknamed Willo. It's the only one in the world! And it's on permanent display right here, at the largest natural-history museum in the Southeast. The museum is open free of charge Monday through Saturday from 9 A.M. to 5 P.M. and Sunday from noon to 5 P.M. For more information, call 919-733-7450 or visit www.naturalsciences.org.

■ The **Olivia Raney Local History Library** is located at 4016 Carya Drive just outside the beltline in Wake County Office Park. If you're a genealogist or a history buff who likes digging through old records, this is the place for you. Students and researchers will find a plethora of historical material pertaining to Wake County and the surrounding area, as well as information about the Revolutionary War, the Civil War, North Carolina history, United States history, and African-American history. If you can, attend one of the "Pieces of the Past" lectures or ask about joining the Wake County Genealogical Society. The group meets the fourth Tuesday of each month and hosts talks on such issues as "Making Sense of the Census." Or you can just have fun tracing your family lineage by perusing the many historical journals and marriage, census, and tax records. The library is open Monday and Thursday from 10 A.M. to 8 P.M., Tuesday and Wednesday from 10 A.M. to 6 P.M., and Saturday from 10 A.M. to 5 P.M. For more information, call 919-250-1196 or visit www.wakegov.com/locations/oliviaraneyhistorylibrary.htm.

■ The **Raleigh City Museum**, at 220 Fayetteville Street, is a private, non-profit organization dedicated to preserving over 200 years of Capital City history. It is open Tuesday through Friday from 10 A.M. to 4 P.M. and Saturday from 1 P.M. to 4 P.M. Admission is free. For more information, call 919-832-3775 or visit www.raleighcitymuseum.org.

Artspace

Cultural Offerings

■ **Artspace**, located in downtown Raleigh at 201 East Davie Street, promotes visual and performing art by allowing visitors to watch the creative process. You can interact with over 30 regional, national, and international artists while they work in open studios. You can also stroll through the many public exhibitions, catch one of the art talks, sit in on a lecture or demonstration, or, better yet, take a class. Admission is free. The center is open Tuesday through Saturday from 10 A.M. to 6 P.M. On the first Friday of each month, the hours are 10 A.M. to 10 P.M. Individual studio hours vary. For more information, call 919-821-2787 or visit www.artspacenc.org.

■ The **Progress Energy Center for the Performing Arts**, on the corner of Wilmington and South streets, is a multi-theater complex offering an extensive array of live shows. Three new theaters have been added to the original performing-arts arena, Memorial Auditorium. You'll find everything from Broadway hits, musicals, and operas to experimental plays, original dance numbers, and stand-up comedy. Meymandi Concert Hall, home of the **North Carolina Symphony** (919-733-2750; www.ncsymphony.org), is located on the west side of the center. To the east is Fletcher Opera Theater, a more intimate setting, where you can see performances by the **Carolina Ballet** (919-719-0800; www.carolinaballet.com), the **National Opera Company**, and the **A. J. Fletcher Institute**, a division of the North Carolina School of the Arts. For something avant-garde, check out the Kennedy Theatre, a 40-by-60-foot black-box theater where you can usually find an edgy production by **Burning Coal Theatre** (919-388-0066; www.burningcoal.org), recently touted as the best new theater group in Raleigh by the *News & Observer*. For tickets, call Ticketmaster at 919-834-4000. For general information, call 919-831-6011 or visit www.raleighconvention.com/pe.html.

- **Gallery C**, located at 3522 Wade Avenue in Ridgewood Shopping Center, is the best known of Raleigh's many galleries and one of the leading galleries in the Southeast. In business for more than 20 years, Gallery C now represents over 30 artists from all over the country who work in a variety of media. It also has an impressive collection of Asian and Haitian art and jewelry. Gallery C hosts at least eight special exhibitions or solo shows per year; the exhibitions run for four to six weeks. If you happen to be in town for one of Gallery C's opening receptions, check out the art and experience one of the most popular social events in Raleigh. For more information, call 919-828-3165 or visit www.galleryc.net.

- **Bickett Gallery**, located at 209 Bickett Boulevard, exemplifies the gallery as a gathering place. It has a bar and a boutique offering handmade clothing, jewelry, furniture, and other objects. The gallery regularly hosts concerts and other events. Its contemporary art exhibitions are worth the trip by themselves. The gallery is open Tuesday by appointment, Wednesday through Friday from 11 A.M. to 6 P.M., and Saturday from noon to 4 P.M. The Art Bar is open Tuesday through Saturday from 6 P.M. to 2 A.M. For more information, call 919-836-5358 or visit www.bickettgallery.com.

- The **Evening Waterfront Concert Series**, sponsored by Raleigh Parks and Recreation, is hosted at the Waterfront Program Center at 6404 Lake Wheeler Road and on Lake Johnson at 4601 Avent Ferry Road. It features an eclectic mix of reggae, jazz, Southern rock, light country, bluegrass, and Latin music. Admission is charged. For a calendar of upcoming events and show times, call 919-662-5704 or visit parks.raleighnc.gov. The Raleigh Parks and Recreation Arts Program includes a free summer-concert series called **Sunday in the Park**. Shows start at 6 P.M. at Fletcher Park, located at 820 Clay Street. Bring your lawn chair and blanket but leave the alcohol at home. For more information, call 919-831-6854.

- **North Carolina Theatre**, at 1 East South Street, offers Broadway-series musicals. Combining talent from New York, North Carolina, and across the country, the group has staged productions of such shows as *Jesus Christ Superstar, The Sound of Music*, and *Good Ol' Girls*, a musical based on the stories of Hillsborough novelist Lee Smith and Lumberton native and writer Jill McCorkle. For ticket information, call 919-831-6950 or visit www.nctheatre.com.

- **Sertoma Arts Center**, located in Sertoma Park, a wooded setting adjacent to Shelley Lake, offers classes for children and adults in the visual and performing arts, as well as concerts, workshops, and gallery space for local artists. Operated by Raleigh Parks and Recreation, it is open Monday through Thursday from 9 A.M. to 10 P.M., Friday from 9 A.M. to 5 P.M., Saturday from 9 A.M. to 3 P.M., and Sunday from 1 P.M. to 5 P.M. For more information, call 919-420-2329.

SPECIAL SHOPPING

■ CitySearch.com voted *Fairgrounds Flea Market*, located on the North Carolina State Fairgrounds at 1025 Blue Ridge Road, "Best Free Attraction" for two years in a row. That's understandable, since it's the largest indoor and outdoor flea market in the state and one of the largest in the entire Southeast. For 30 years, bargain shoppers have bought antiques, handmade crafts, homemade fudge, vintage clothing, furniture, rare books, and just about anything else you can imagine from the nearly 300 permanent dealers and the 200 to 300 temporary dealers who peddle their wares here every weekend. The flea market is open every Saturday and Sunday from 9 A.M. to 5 P.M. except in October during the North Carolina State Fair. For more information, call 919-829-3533 or visit www.ncstatefair.org/fleamarket.htm.

■ *Historic City Market*, located at 303 Blake Street at the intersection of Blount and Martin streets in downtown Raleigh, opened in 1914 and thrived until the mid-1940s. Farmers trucked in produce, poultry, seafood, and flowers, and Raleigh housewives took advantage of the new outlet as a way of selling home-baked goods. When the farmers' market opened off Capitol Boulevard in the 1950s, however, the City Market could no longer compete and was therefore shut down. Thanks to revitalization efforts in the 1980s, the Spanish Mission-style marketplace is once again bustling

North Carolina State Farmers Market
COURTESY OF NORTH CAROLINA DIVISION OF
TOURISM, FILM AND SPORTS DEVELOPMENT

with art galleries, restaurants, and specialty shops that sell antiques, pottery, jewelry, and gourmet food, among other things. Individual business hours vary. For more information, call 919-821-1350.

■ **North Carolina State Farmers Market** is located at 1201 Agriculture Street; take the Lake Wheeler Road exit (Exit 297) off Interstate 40/Interstate 440. This is the largest of the five farmers' markets owned by the state of North Carolina. It offers shoppers 75 acres of indoor and outdoor specialty shops, restaurants, a garden center, and fruits and vegetables from all over North Carolina. More than 35,000 growers sell in excess of 300 different items, including locally grown plants, Christmas trees, and handmade crafts. Busy shoppers can grab lunch at the Farmers Market Restaurant or the North Carolina Seafood Restaurant, located on the grounds. The market is open Monday through Saturday from 5 A.M. to 6 P.M. and Sunday from 8 A.M. to 6 P.M. For more information, call 919-733-7417 or visit www.agr.state.nc.us/markets/facilit/farmark/raleigh.

RECREATION

■ The **Capital Area Greenway** is a nationally acclaimed system of natural multiuse trails spanning 41 miles along Raleigh's three primary waterways—the Neuse River, Walnut Creek, and Crabtree Creek—and their tributaries. Sponsored by Raleigh Parks and Recreation, the greenway project is quickly realizing its goal of building interconnecting trails to many of the city's 150 parks to facilitate activities such as biking, hiking, and jogging. For information about access or for a free map, call 919-890-3285 or visit www.raleigh-nc.org/parks&rec/index.asp.

■ The **Capital City Bicycle Motocross Race Track**, located in Lions Park at 516 Dennis Avenue, offers BMX races organized according to age group and skill level. Admission is free to spectators. Hours of operation vary, so call 919-831-6995 for more information.

■ **Frisbee golf** is available at two locations: 5600 Sweetbriar Street in Cedar Hills Park and 4531 Kaplan Drive in Kentwood Park. Each facility offers 18 holes. Professional and amateur tournaments are held monthly. Both parks are open daily from sunrise to sunset. For information about Frisbee golf at Cedar Hills Park, call 919-870-2880; for information about Frisbee golf at Kentwood Park, call 919-890-3285.

■ *Lake Wheeler Metropolitan Park*, at 6404 Lake Wheeler Road, is a 650-acre lake managed by Raleigh Parks and Recreation. In addition to offering kayak, canoe, johnboat, and sailboat rentals, the park is open to all types of private boating. Superb fishing and picnicking opportunities are also available. Although swimming is not allowed, visitors may indulge in other water-related activities such as windsurfing and water-skiing. The award-winning Waterfront Program Center overlooks the lake; it boasts a popular lakeside conference room, restrooms, and a huge, open deck with rocking chairs and picnic tables. Cited as a favorite getaway by the *News & Observer*, Lake Wheeler is open year-round seven days a week from sunrise to sunset. It hosts a variety of special events, including the Tar Heel Powerboat Regatta, the Atlantic Coast University Team Rowing Regatta, boat shows, canoe and kayak festivals, bass tournaments, Great Outdoor Provision Company fly-fishing schools, *Carolina Adventure Magazine*'s freshwater fishing school, and the Kid's Fishing Derby. Windsurfing, water-skiing, and boating classes are offered. For more information, call 919-662-5704 or visit parks.raleighnc.gov.

Lake Wheeler is only one of many park options; the area boasts 4,300 acres of parkland and 1,400 acres of water. Check out www.visitraleigh.com for information about *William B. Umstead State Park, Durant Nature Park, Jordan Lake, Falls Lake, Johnson Lake, Shelley Lake*, and many others.

■ *Neuse River Canoe Launches* offers four different launch locations along the Neuse River. Gravel driveways allow year-round access to the Falls of Neuse Launch, located at Falls Dam; the Buffaloe Road Launch, located off Elizabeth Drive; the Neuse River East Launch, located at Old Milburnie Road off U.S. 64 East; and the Poole Road Launch. Access is free. For more information, call 919-890-3285.

■ *Pullen Park and Aquatic Center*, located in the downtown area at 520 Ashe Avenue, became the first public park in North Carolina when it was founded in 1887. According to the National Amusement Park Association, it is the 14th-oldest amusement park in the world. Pullen Park is named in honor of Richard Stanhope Pullen, who donated the land to the city. Today, the park offers a variety of recreational opportunities, including amusement rides, swimming, playground facilities, picnic shelters, lighted tennis courts, fitness programs, workshops, and art classes. The park's magnificent Dentzel carousel dates to around 1900 and is one of only 14 Dentzel menageries still in operation in North America. The C. P. Huntington Train, a miniature replica of a locomotive built in 1863, attracts kids of all ages for a ride around the park's perimeter. The park is open year-round, but hours of operation vary by season. For more information, call 919-831-6468.

- The **RBC Center**, located at 1400 Edwards Mill Road, is a 700,000-square-foot entertainment and sports arena with a seating capacity of 21,500. NCAA men's basketball featuring Raleigh's own **North Carolina State Wolfpack** begins in November and lasts until March. NHL hockey fans will find the **Carolina Hurricanes** on the ice from September to April. And AFL football fans can catch **Carolina Cobras** events in this $152 million state-of-the-art facility from January through May. To contact the box office, call 919-861-2323. For other information, call 919-861-6145 or visit www.rbccenter.com.

- The **North Carolina State women's basketball team** plays at Reynolds Coliseum, located at 103 Dunn Avenue on the university campus; for ticket information, call 919-515-2106 or visit www.gopack.com.

- For the best of the Triangle's class AA baseball, check out the **Carolina Mudcats**, who swing into action from April to September at Five County Stadium in Zebulon; call 919-269-2287 or visit www.gomudcats.com.

SEASONAL EVENTS

- The **Amistad** Saga: **Reflections** is presented in July at the African American Cultural Complex, located at 119 Sunnybrook Road. The state's only outdoor drama written, produced, and directed by African-Americans, it tells the harrowing story of mutiny aboard the slave ship *Amistad* and dramatizes the plight of the ship's slaves, from their capture to their heroic battle for freedom. For more information, call 919-250-9336 or visit www.aaccmuseum.org.

- *Artsplosure Spring Art Festival* is held downtown the third weekend in May. This city-sponsored free outdoor festival features regional, national, and local jazz, blues, country, and pop musicians in continuous shows. Included are 150 artists' booths and lots of interactive and educational activities for children. For information, call 919-832-8699 or visit www.artsplosure.org.

- **First Night Raleigh** is an alcohol-free New Year's Eve celebration of the arts held at various locations downtown. Throughout the afternoon and evening, participants enjoy art exhibits, music, dance, comedy, theater, and children's activities. The event culminates in a countdown to midnight, when "the City of Oaks," as Raleigh is sometimes called, holds its traditional "Acorn Drop" just as the new year is ushered in with a spectacular fireworks display. For more information, call 919-832-8699 or visit www.firstnightraleigh.com.

- The **North Carolina State Fair**, held on the fairgrounds at 1025 Blue Ridge Road, is the largest annual event in the state. It takes place in mid-October. Proud vegetable growers enter carefully selected specimens (watermelons the size of wheelbarrows, for example) in the County Agricultural Fair Showcase, while livestock producers bet the farm that their sheep or goats will win the livestock judging. For 150 years, the coveted blue ribbon has been a symbol of North Carolina agricultural pride. Artisans in the Village of Yesteryear dress in period costume. Nightly musical performances by artists such as Brad Paisley and Merle Haggard are offered. An admission fee is charged. For more information, call 919-733-2145 or visit www.ncstatefair.org.

- The **North Carolina Renaissance Faire** is held each spring in the Village of Yesteryear/Heritage Village area on the North Carolina State

North Carolina State Fair

Fairgrounds at 1025 Blue Ridge Road. This 16th-century festival includes over 110 booths where artisans display their wares, as well as seven distinct staging areas where actors in period dress bring to life all the pageantry of the year 1573. Patrons are encouraged to wear costumes like those of Queen Elizabeth's royal court. Three jousts are held in the Queen's Tiltyard. You'll also see hand-fasting ceremonies, knightings, singing, juggling, dancing, puppetry, fencing, sword fighting, and a quest for the Holy Grail. Camping and RV hookups are offered, and pets are welcome. The fair runs from 10 A.M. to 6 P.M. An admission fee is charged except for children five and under. For information, call the Historical Enrichment Society at 919-834-8689 or 919-755-8004 or visit www.ncrenfaire.com.

- **Fiesta del Pueblo** takes place in September at the North Carolina State Fairgrounds. Local citizens gather to celebrate Latin American art, music, food, and tradition. This weekend event boasts an attendance estimated at 35,000 to 40,000. A modest admission fee is charged. For information, visit www.elpueblo.org/english/events/lafiesta.html.

- The **Oakwood Candlelight Tour**, offered each December, includes a holiday sleigh ride through the Historic Oakwood District, where luminaries light the path and Christmas trees illustrate traditions from around the world. Tours run from 1 P.M. until 7:30 P.M. For more information, call 919-250-1013. The **Candlelight Homes Tour** is a separate annual event held to benefit the Society for the Preservation of Historic Oakwood. Select private residences and bed-and-breakfasts are open to the public for self-guided tours. A fee is charged. For more information, call 919-828-3510, or visit www.historicoakwood.org.

- The **Storytelling Festival** takes place in the pecan grove at Historic Oak View Park at 4028 Carya Drive. Sponsored by the Wake County Public Libraries, it is held one Friday and Saturday during September. Talented professional storytellers from across the state and the country entertain area schoolchildren with tall tales, legends, folk tales, and ghost stories. Over 4,000 students usually attend. Special story times for adults, young adults, and older children are offered at the Wake County Commons Building. Admission is free. For more information, call 919-250-1200.

Places to Stay

RESORTS, HOTELS, MOTELS

■ **Sheraton Raleigh Hotel.** Deluxe. 421 South Salisbury Street (800-325-3535 or 919-834-9900; www.sheraton.com). This elegant hotel offers first-rate service and amenities including an indoor pool and Jacuzzi, a workout facility, and room service. The business-class accommodations include data ports on all telephones, coffee makers, hair dryers, and irons. Express check-in and checkout are available. For an added level of service, guests can stay in one of the concierge-level rooms. As with most hotels, making reservations in advance will significantly lower your rate.

■ **Courtyard by Marriott at Crabtree Valley.** Deluxe/Expensive. 3908 Arrow Drive (919-782-6868; www.marriot.com). This European-style hotel is a jewel. Located near Crabtree Valley Mall, it has 84 rooms, including deluxe rooms and several suites. Each room and suite has a refrigerator, a hair dryer, luxurious bathrobes, special bath amenities, a coffee maker, an iron, and an ironing board. A breakfast buffet is offered every day. A lounge, an outdoor pool, and an exercise room are on the premises. Pets are welcome, with some restrictions.

■ **The Velvet Cloak Inn.** Expensive. 1505 Hillsborough Street (800-334-4372 or 919-823-0333; www.velvetcloakinn.com). This hotel is located 12 blocks from North Carolina State University. Its brick driveway and wrought-iron balconies with flower boxes give it an appearance reminiscent of New Orleans. It has 167 guest rooms, including eight suites.

INNS AND BED-AND-BREAKFASTS

■ **The Cameron Park Inn.** Expensive. 211 Groveland Avenue (888-257-2171 or 919-835-2171; www.cameronparkinn.com). Located just off Hillsborough Street at the North Carolina State bell tower, The Cameron Park Inn is within easy walking distance of the university, Cameron Village, and the Raleigh Little Theater. It's a five-minute trip to downtown, the City Market, Mordecai Historic Park, the Historic Oakwood District, the fairgrounds, the RBC Center, and Glenwood Avenue's restaurants and shops. Built in 1916 on a prominent corner lot in Cameron Park, the inn was one of the first 150 homes to be constructed in Raleigh's earliest planned subdivision. Innkeepers Al and Catherine Blalock have completely renovated the house to its original post-Victorian/Colonial Revival style, recapturing the charm of its defining features, which include an expansive, railed front porch and arched windows. Four beautifully appointed guest rooms offer all the amenities for a relaxing getaway. Cable television, a complimentary morning newspaper, evening snacks, and a full breakfast are included. Special packages are available for shows at the North Carolina Theatre.

- **The Oakwood Inn**. Expensive. 411 North Bloodworth Street (919-832-9712; www.oakwoodinnbb.com). This AAA Three Diamond inn is listed on the National Register of Historic Places as the Raynor-Stronach House. Built in 1871, it is one of the four surviving homes of the original 11 that started what is now known as the Historic Oakwood District. In 1984, the house was converted into Raleigh's first bed-and-breakfast. The six guest rooms have period antiques, private baths, cable television, fireplaces, and modern amenities like computer ports. A full breakfast is served daily. Dinner-and-theater packages are available; each package includes a night's stay at The Oakwood Inn, dinner at a selected area restaurant, and tickets to a play produced by one of Raleigh's many theaters.

Places to Eat

- **Angus Barn**. Expensive. 9401 Glenwood Avenue (U.S. 70 West) at Aviation Parkway (919-781-2444; www.angusbarn.com). This homey steakhouse with its blue-and-white gingham tablecloths has been a Capital City staple for over 40 years. The restaurant's four dining rooms, which can accommodate a whopping 600 hungry diners, serve 245,000 customers each year. A beef eater's haven, the Angus Barn is famed for—what else?—its Angus beef, which the staff ages for 28 days in the restaurant's own aging room. Not surprisingly, the menu is dominated by steaks, prime rib, rack of lamb, and a good assortment of seafood such as Alaskan king crab claws. But vegetarians do have a couple of choices. The wine cellar holds over 25,000 bottles. Dinner is served seven days a week; lunch is served for private functions of 25 people or more. The Wild Turkey Lounge offers a full bar and live entertainment; it opens at 4 P.M.

■ **Enoteca Vin**. Expensive. 410 Glenwood Avenue (919-934-3070; www.enotecavin.com). Located in the old Pine State Creamery building, this trattoria-style restaurant and wine bar is a local favorite that has garnered national recognition. Vin (as it's known locally) offers a selection of superlative wines from the United States, Europe, Australia, South America, and South Africa by the bottle or the glass in 1.5-ounce, three-ounce, and five-ounce pours. Like the wine list, the menu features portions that cater to all palates—small plates, a selection of artisan cheeses and cured meats, salads, full entrées, and three- and five-course prix fixe options. The menu changes frequently. The freshness and variety of ingredients and the kitchen's pitch-perfect execution rate make this among the best restaurants in the state and the South. Vin has no dress code. The atmosphere is casual, so guests are equally comfortable whether coming for a snack or a graduation dinner. Dinner is served Tuesday through Sunday; brunch is offered on Sunday.

■ **Second Empire Restaurant and Tavern**. Expensive. 330 Hillsborough Street (919-829-3663; www.second-empire.com). This restaurant is located in the elegantly restored Dodd-Hinsdale House, built around 1879. Second Empire's menu changes every month; it features creations from the freshest seasonal ingredients. Entrées may include grilled marinated swordfish and roasted Australian lamb loin. The lighter and more casual alternatives on the tavern's menu range from smoked turkey Dagwoods to a caviar plate that costs $75. Second Empire has won *Wine Spectator's* Award of Excellence for four consecutive years. Dinner is served Monday through Saturday; the tavern is open evenings Monday through Saturday.

■ **42nd Street Oyster Bar**. Moderate. 508 West Jones Street (919-831-2811; www.42ndstoysterbar.com). In 1931, J. C. Watson opened a grocery at the current location of the 42nd Street Oyster Bar. A loyal patron, Dr. Tick West, suggested that Watson start serving oysters to his customers. Two years later, after Prohibition ended, Watson's was the first business in Raleigh to serve draft beer in frosted mugs. The combination of steamed oysters and cold beer has made the 42nd Street Oyster Bar a Raleigh favorite for over 70 years. Today, the restaurant is still the place where sophisticated patrons talk business and politics, just as Tick and his doctor colleagues must have done. Lunch is served Monday through Friday and dinner seven days a week. Live music and a full bar are offered.

- **Big Ed's City Market**. Inexpensive. 220 Wolfe Street (919-836-9909). Located in the historic City Market district, Big Ed's serves up traditional American fare with down-home Southern hospitality. Its breakfast has been voted one of the best in North Carolina by CitySearch.com; Big Ed's offers homemade flapjacks, red-eye gravy, grits, biscuits, and fried squash. The lunch menu includes steaks, crab cakes, burgers, and fried chicken. Breakfast is served Monday through Saturday and lunch Monday through Friday.

- **Roast Grill**. Inexpensive. 7 South West Street (919-832-8292). The menu here is famously limited. In fact, there really isn't one. Since 1940, the Roast Grill has served only grilled hot dogs (you choose the "degree of burn"), with a choice of mustard, onions, slaw, and amazing homemade chili. Ketchup and mayonnaise are sacrilege here. Homemade pound cake and baklava for dessert round out the offerings. There is no better place for a taste of Raleigh the way it used to be. Lunch is served Monday through Saturday.

AN UNCIVIL ARGUMENT

Excerpted from
The News & Observer's *Raleigh: A Living History of North Carolina's Capital*, edited by David Perkins

Letter from an English gentleman, on his travels through the United States, to his friend in London:

March 12, 1798

. . . Raleigh is situated more than an hundred miles from any seaport, and nearly thirty from any boatable waters, has no stream of water capable of making it a manufacturing town; has therefore no prospect of becoming anything more than the solitary residence of a few public officers, containing a few ordinary taverns, gaming houses and dram shops, and this is in fact what the metropolis now is. It might probably have been expected by the founders, that being in a hilly country, it would become the summer residence of many people in the eastern sickly parts of the state, but it has been found on experience not to have the degree of healthiness which its elevated situation would seem to promise. . . .

The plan of Raleigh (which by the bye is dignified with the name of *city*) would have been tolerably good, had it been situated in a place in which it could have been completed; but neither power nor superstition, as in the east, have any effect here to help its completion; for it contains neither the castle of the Lord's anointed, nor the coffin of a departed saint. The necessities of the government, and the groveling dissipation of a few, are its whole support.

The ground is divided into four quarters by as many spacious streets, which terminate in the public square, in the center of which stands the state house, a clumsy brick building, built without any regular design of architecture, and totally devoid of taste or elegance.

Disgraceful as the appearance of the state house is at best, they have contrived to place it yet in a more disadvantageous point of view, by erecting the court house, the palace of the governor, and most of the other buildings, on one of the streets which has only an end view of the state house, which makes but a forty appearance. . . .

At the four corners of the public square are groves which might have been made agreeable walks; I thought this was their design, and seeing a small house in two of them, I took them for summer houses, and began in my mind, to applaud the state for constructing such charming places for the recreation of the people in a warm climate, and going to visit one of them, was arrested in my progress by a terrible stench issuing from four doors, which informed me it was a temple of Cloacina [the goddess presiding over ancient Rome's sewer system].

The streets of this city are honored with the names of some of the great men who have distinguished themselves in the service of the state . . . and to do them justice the state ought, in imitation of the ancients, to place statues of them in their favorite temples.

Raleigh citizens' reply:

June 4, 1798

Mr. Hodge,

Your No. 295 contains much entertaining matter, particularly the curious piece pretended to have been written by the English gentleman on the tour through the United States. . . . We contend he has offered a high affront and gross indignity to the state; and if he is in fact an Englishman, in return for his civility we can but advise him through you to return to the Nabobs of his own country, where the appearance of public and private buildings is more pleasing to an English eye, and the fare of their tables better suited to an English stomach.

We are not disposed to enter into a reasoning detail with this man of the world . . . but you will indulge us a minute while we briefly refute a few of his statements. . . .

He approves the plan of our city, but it wants water, power and superstition to complete it, and of course it cannot be done without a cottage of the Lord's anointed, and a coffin of a departed saint. . . . The Lord's annointed [sic], and the corpse of a departed saint, we consign to the gentleman for his ingenuity and labour in writing our history—we know not his meaning by the necessities of the government, for we believe it is as well supplied here as if the metropolis had been planted on the water side, except with crabs and frogs.—It is to be lamented that there are too many dissipated people among us, but they are running away fast, and our hope is, a better race will take their place.

Were we to venture an opinion of this traveling gentleman, we should pronounce him a disappointed partisan, who had formerly struggled in the interest of that grave-yard called Fayetteville—rankling at the heart, he has assumed the character of an Englishman to vent his spleen.—That he is a natural born son, begotten by Vulcan on the body of Cloacina, at her devotion, and raised in and upon the offerings of her temples in his favourite village, where we presume the stench is not so offensive to him, as there is a material difference in the qualities of aliments that sustain human life—in one place it is mostly of the skin and bones of swine and sand-hill turkeys, in another it is very different—sound and wholesome.

Excuse scurrility—It is diamond cut diamond—and we must meet the gentleman on his own ground—we are, &c.

The Citizens of Raleigh

DURHAM

urham owes its best-known nickname to a happy marketing accident. Tobacco magnate John Green of the Blackwell Tobacco Company admired the bull logo that Colman's Mustard used, and he mistakenly thought the mustard was produced in Durham, England. Green named his brand of tobacco Bull Durham. By 1890, Bull Durham was the most famous trademark in the world. The name even generated popular words and phrases like *bullpen* and *shoot the bull*. After James Duke bought the company, he packaged "cigarette cards" in his tobacco; their popularity led to the creation of baseball cards. The famous image of John Green's bull was painted on barns and other sites around the world. And the tobacco-and-baseball tie-in lasted well into the 20th century.

Durham and Duke University
COURTESY OF DURHAM CONVENTION AND VISITORS BUREAU

Durham's other successes are the result of more concerted efforts. In 1898, the same year James Duke bought the Blackwell Tobacco Company, John Merrick founded the North Carolina Mutual Life Insurance Company, the nation's largest and oldest African-American-owned life insurance company. In 1907, the Mechanics and Farmers Bank opened in North Carolina Mutual's neighborhood near Parrish Street. It subsequently became one of the largest African-American-owned banks in the United States. When other successful businesses opened nearby, the bustling neighborhood became known country-wide as "the Black Wall Street."

Trying in recent years to change its image from that of the tobacco town John Green helped make, Durham launched a "City of Medicine" campaign, based on the town's hospitals and pharmaceutical companies. The invention of BC Headache Powders in Durham back in 1910 is thought to have been the city's first step in that direction. When Duke University Medical School opened in 1930, Durham extended its reach into medicine. Now, the city is home to a renowned diet center and five major hospitals. And Research Triangle Park, home to many pharmaceutical and medical engineering companies, is surrounded on three sides by the city.

Durham offers great accommodations and restaurants and some of the best attractions and cultural events in the region. In fact, you'll find that it has two symphony orchestras; 15 art centers and performance halls; over 20 annual festivals and events; more than 60 parks, trails, and waterways; 12 science and nature centers; lots of nightclubs; several professional sports teams; and numerous historic sites and shopping centers.

JUST THE FACTS

Durham sits at the northern point of the Triangle; Raleigh lies southeast and Chapel Hill southwest. Durham can be reached via Interstate 85, Interstate 40, U.S. 15/U.S. 501, and U.S. 70.

Raleigh-Durham International Airport is less than 20 minutes away; it can be reached via the Durham Expressway leading to Interstate 40 East.

The Amtrak station is at 400 West Chapel Hill Street; for information, call 800-872-7245.

The Triangle Transit Authority runs buses from Duke University Medical Center to the airport and Chapel Hill; call 919-549-9999 for information. Duke University Transit sends buses between the school's East and West campuses; call 919-684-8111. The Greyhound bus station is located at 820 West Morgan Street; call 919-687-4800.

The daily newspaper is the *Durham Herald-Sun*. The *News & Observer* of Raleigh has a special Durham section every day. Comprehensive listings of local events can be found in the *Independent*, a free paper that covers the entire Triangle area.

The Durham Convention and Visitors Bureau is located at 101 East Morgan Street. For information, call 800-446-8604 or 919-687-0288 or visit http://dcvb.durham.nc.us/.

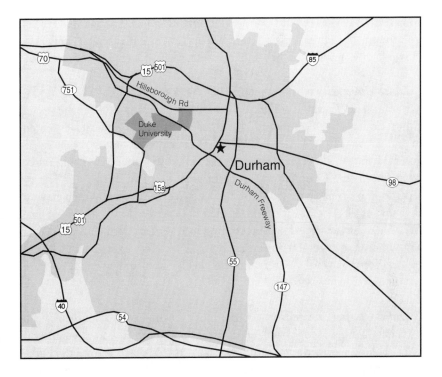

Things to Do

HISTORIC PLACES, GARDENS, AND TOURS

■ ***Bennett Place State Historic Site*** is a small farmhouse at 4409 Bennett Memorial Road. In April 1865, Generals Joseph E. Johnston and William T. Sherman met under a flag of truce to discuss a peaceful solution to the Civil War. They and their escorts met midway between their lines on the Hillsborough Road. Needing a place for a conference, Johnston suggested a simple farmhouse nearby. On three separate occasions, the Union and Confederate generals struggled to achieve equitable terms for surrender at the home of James and Nancy Bennett. On April 26, the Bennett dwelling became the site of the largest troop surrender of the Civil War.

The original buildings were destroyed by fire in 1921, but the present structures were carefully reconstructed in the 1960s using sketches and early photographs. Today, the farmhouse, kitchen, and smokehouse give visitors a glimpse into the life of an ordinary Southern farm family during the Civil War. Bennett Place is currently open Tuesday through Saturday from 10 A.M. to 4 P.M., but the hours of operation may change. Free tours are offered through the visitor center. For the current schedule, call 919-383-4345 or visit www.ah.hcr.state.nc.us/sections/hs/bennett/bennett.htm.

■ *Duke University* was created in 1924 by James B. Duke as a memorial to his father, Washington Duke. The Dukes had long felt an interest in Trinity College. In December 1924, the college's trustees gratefully accepted an endowment from James B. Duke that provided in part for the expansion of Trinity College into Duke University. After undergoing a massive expansion in the Georgian style, the original Durham campus of Trinity became known as the East Campus. The West Campus, which has an English Gothic style fashioned after the Ivy League, opened in 1930. Since then, Duke has achieved an outstanding record of academic excellence. It is now home to several renowned schools, Duke University Medical Center, the Terry Sanford Center, and the Nasher Museum of Art. For more information, visit www.duke.edu.

■ *Duke Chapel*, located on Chapel Drive on the West Campus, is the university's most recognizable landmark. Its 210-foot tower is visible for miles. This awe-inspiring structure was constructed of stone from the Duke Quarry near Hillsborough, as was the rest of the impressive West Campus. The chapel was one of the country's last great collegiate Gothic

Duke Chapel
COURTESY OF DURHAM CONVENTION AND VISITORS BUREAU

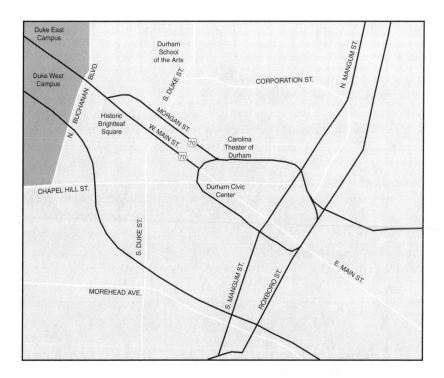

projects. Founding father James B. Duke envisioned a "great towering church" in the center of the campus that would have a "profound influence on the spiritual life of the young men and women" who came here. One of the chapel's designers, Julian Abele, was America's first black architect of renown. He and fellow designer Horace Trumbauer turned Duke's vision into a reality. Upon entering the chapel, visitors are immediately drawn to the great chancel window at the end of the center aisle. Altogether, a total of 77 stained-glass renderings containing 800 to 900 figures made from over a million pieces of glass tell stories from the Old and New testaments. The chapel also holds a massive pipe organ and a 50-bell carillon housed in an impressive structure of intricately detailed stone, wood, and stained glass. Visitors are welcome to tour the chapel and to participate in the interdenominational services held on Sunday at 11 A.M. For more information, call 919-684-2572 or visit www.chapel.duke.edu.

- **Sarah P. Duke Gardens**, at 418 Anderson Street on the West Campus, encompasses 55 acres of stunning landscaped and wooded gardens right in the midst of the university. Five miles of walks and pathways wind in and around the Blomquist Garden of native North Carolina plants, the Asiatic Arboretum, a lily pond, waterfalls, and a variety of flower beds that change with the seasons. These magnificent gardens also serve as a backdrop to live music and dance performances. They are open to the public every day until sunset. Guided tours are available but must be pre-arranged. For more information, call 800-367-3853 or 919-684-3698 or visit www.hr.duke.edu/dukegardens/.

■ The **Duke Homestead and Tobacco Museum**, located at 2828 Duke Homestead Road, is a national historic landmark and a living-history archive that chronicles the humble beginnings of tobacco magnate Washington Duke. The homestead and museum showcase his 19th-century house and the farm and factories where he first grew and processed tobacco. Later, his sons founded the American Tobacco Company, the largest tobacco company in the world. Museum exhibits trace the history of tobacco from Native American times to the present. The Duke Homestead and Tobacco Museum is currently open Tuesday through Saturday from 10 A.M. to 4 P.M., but the hours of operation may change. Admission is free. Groups are asked to schedule visits in advance. For more information, call 919-477-5498 or visit www.ibiblio.org/dukehome/.

■ *Historic Stagville*, located at 5825 Old Oxford Highway, is a state historic site featuring 18th- and 19th-century buildings dedicated to African-American cultural and historic studies. The 71-acre site occupies the remnants of one of the largest plantations of the pre-Civil War South. It belonged to the Bennehan and Cameron families, whose combined holdings totaled approximately 900 slaves and almost 30,000 acres by 1860. Historic Stagville is currently open Tuesday through Saturday from 10 A.M. to 4 P.M., but the hours of operation may change; call ahead to confirm. Admission is free. Since you'll be doing some walking, it's a good idea to wear comfortable shoes and carry bottled water. For more information, call 919-620-0120 or visit www.historicstagvillefoundation.org.

■ *North Carolina Mutual Life Insurance Company*, located at 114-116 West Parrish Street, was once the home of the Mechanics and Farmers Bank, known as "the World's Largest Negro Business." It helped win Durham a reputation as "the Capital of the Black Middle Class." The white-brick building, erected in 1921 on the site of the company's first office building, is listed on the National Register of Historic Places and is a national historic landmark.

■ *West Point on the Eno City Park*, at 5101 North Roxboro Road in northern Durham, is a 371-acre natural and historical park along the Eno River. It features a reconstructed, working 1778 gristmill and part of the community that surrounded it, including a re-created blacksmith shop. The park also offers the **Hugh Mangum Museum of Photography** and an amphitheater. It is the site of the Festival for the Eno in early July. The park facilities are open daily from sunrise to sunset, but the buildings are open only from 1 P.M. to 5 P.M. on weekends. Admission is free. The entire Eno River State Park encompasses over 2,000 undeveloped acres along the river. It offers opportunities for hiking, picnicking, camping (by permit only), canoeing, and rafting. For more information about West Point on the Eno, call 919-477-4549 or visit www.enoriver.org. For regulations about camping, hiking, and canoeing, call 919-383-1686 or e-mail eno.river@ncmail.net.

MUSEUMS AND SCIENCE CENTERS

■ The **Nasher Museum of Art at Duke University** is located adjacent to the Sarah P. Duke Gardens at the intersection of Duke University Road and Anderson Street. Uruguayan architect Rafael Viñoly designed the building, made up of five pavilions arranged around a pentagonal central Great Hall with a dramatic glass-and-steel canopy. The pavilions hold three gallery spaces, a 173-seat auditorium, and an education wing. The education wing is home to the Nasher Museum Café and a museum shop. The Nasher Museum's permanent collection includes the Brummer Collection of Medieval and Renaissance Art, a pre-Columbian collection from Central and South America, the George Harley Memorial Collection of African Art, and numerous classical pieces. Temporary exhibitions that reflect the museum's increasing focus on modern and contemporary art are offered throughout the year. The museum is open Tuesday, Wednesday, Friday, and Saturday from 10 A.M. to 5 P.M.; Thursday from 10 A.M. to 9 P.M.; and Sunday from noon to 5 P.M. For more information, call 919-684-5135 or visit www.nasher.duke.edu.

■ The **Duke University Primate Center** is the world's leading facility dedicated to prosimian primates. Over 420 animals representing 28 species and subspecies are housed here, including lemurs from Madagascar, loris from Asia, galagos from Africa, and tarsiers from the islands of eastern Asia. Located about a quarter-mile from Duke's campus, this facility provides an extraordinary opportunity to see and appreciate these increasingly endangered creatures. The center is open for tours Monday through Friday from 8:30 A.M. to 3 P.M. and Saturday from 8:30 A.M. to 1 P.M. Visitors are allowed access by appointment only. Due to an increase in tour requests, be sure to call at least two weeks in advance of the date you wish to visit. In accordance with United States Department of Agriculture regulations, all visitors must be accompanied by a trained docent or staff member while on the premises. Large groups with children should be accompanied by several adult chaperones. For more information, call 919-489-3364 or visit www.duke.edu/web/primate.

■ The **North Carolina Museum of Life and Science**, at 433 West Murray Avenue, is more fun than a kid (of any age) ought to have. Featuring a 15-foot tornado, a percussion hut, dozens of interactive exhibits, over 100 live animal species from owls to wolves, the Magic Wings Butterfly House, an insectarium, an aerospace exhibit, the News Channel 11 Accu-Weather Station, an outdoor nature park, and the Ellerbee Creek Railway, this place is guaranteed to entertain for hours. It is one of only 35 institutions in the world accorded full member status by the Association of Science-Technology Centers. It operates every day except Thanksgiving, Christmas, and New Year's; it is open Monday through Saturday from 10 A.M. to 5 P.M. and Sunday from noon to 5 P.M. An admission fee is charged. For more information, call 919-220-5429 or visit www.ncmls.org.

CULTURAL OFFERINGS

■ The **Carolina Theatre** is located at 309 West Morgan Street. The last remaining of the 13 original theaters in the city, this 1926 performance hall is a rich part of Durham's history. Lovingly restored in 1992, it is the only historic theater in the country with two fully operating state-of-the-art cinemas. Part of the Durham Civic Center complex, the main auditorium, Fletcher Hall, and the Connie Moses Ballroom are nothing short of gorgeous, and the events that take place here are a thrill. Visitors can sit back in the renovated glory of this Beaux-Arts structure and enjoy first-run art shows; live music by such artists as George Jones, John Berry, and Susan Tedeschi; performances by the Durham Symphony; and live theater and opera. For tickets, call 919-560-3030. For information, call 919-560-3040 or visit www.carolinatheatre.org.

■ **Hayti Heritage Center**, at 804 Old Fayetteville Street, is located in

Carolina Theatre
Courtesy of Durham Convention and Visitors Bureau

Durham's historic Hayti community. The center is an integral part of the Triangle's cultural landscape. The 1890s church that houses the complex is a national historic landmark. The center offers innovative programming and exhibitions featuring local, regional, and national artists in its effort to educate the entire community about African-American life, history, and culture, as viewed through many artistic perspectives. Among the programs the Hayti Heritage Center coordinates are the Black Film Diaspora, the Bull Durham Blues Fest, and the Martin Luther King Festival. It is also the home of the Lyda Moore Merrick Gallery. The center is open Monday through Friday from 10 A.M. to 7 P.M., Saturday from 10 A.M. to 3 P.M., and Sunday at select times. For more information, call 800-845-9835 or 919-683-1709 or visit www.hayti.org.

■ *Manbites Dog Theater*, at 703 Foster Street, is a professional nonprofit theater company founded in Durham in October 1987. This plucky group takes on controversial issues that leave audiences talking for days. Recent productions have included the first North Carolina performances of Arlene Hutton's *Last Train to Nibroc*, Diana Son's *Stop Kiss*, and Paula Vogel's Pulitzer Prize-winning *How I Learned to Drive*. Original productions have included the 2003 world premiere of *Bucknaked: A Love Story*. One of the theater's most popular events is the annual performance of Charles Ludlam's *Mystery of Irma Vep*. For information or tickets, call 919-682-4974 or visit www.manbitesdogtheater.org.

- The four galleries at the **Center for Documentary Studies at Duke University**, at 1317 West Pettigrew Street near Duke's East Campus, show works by nationally known photographers and photojournalists and Duke faculty and students. The center also features audio and mixed-media projects. Visitors can check out the books and educational projects that the center produces. The galleries are open Monday through Friday from 9 A.M. to 5 P.M., Saturday from 11 A.M. to 4 P.M., and Sunday from 1 P.M. to 5 P.M.; the hours may change, so it's a good idea to call 919-660-3663 before planning a visit. For more information and a virtual tour, visit www.cds.aas.duke.edu.

SPECIAL SHOPPING

- **Brightleaf Square**, at the corner of Main and Gregson streets in downtown Durham, is comprised of two former tobacco warehouses built between 1900 and 1904. In the fall of 2004, Brightleaf Square was extensively renovated. Several of the shops, restaurants, and galleries now face a central courtyard between the two buildings. For more information, call 919-682-9229 or visit www.historicbrightleaf.com.

- **Ninth Street**, near Duke's East Campus, offers an eclectic row of boutiques, galleries, cafés, a great bookstore, and a toy store that just begs kids to pop inside. For more information, visit www.ninthst.com.

- **Patterson's Mill Country Store**, at 5109 Farrington Road between N.C. 54 and Old Chapel Hill Road, is an authentic country store and pharmacy with hundreds of pieces of historical memorabilia. A collector or amateur pharmaceutical historian could spend a day in this quaint shop. The store includes a furnished early-20th-century doctor's office. Antiques, collectibles, and North Carolina crafts and gifts are for sale. The store is open Tuesday through Saturday from 10 A.M. to 5 P.M. and Sunday from 2 P.M. to 5 P.M. For more information, call 919-493-8149.

- **The Streets at Southpoint**, located at 6910 Fayetteville Road, is a supermall featuring a 200,000-square-foot outdoor cityscape called "Main Street." It offers 1.3 million square feet of retail space and over 150 shops and restaurants. There's nothing you won't find here. Individual shop hours vary. For information, call 919-572-8808 or visit www.thestreetsatsouthpoint.com.

- The **Tuba Exchange**, at 1825 Chapel Hill Road, is a unique clearing-house for new and used tubas, euphoniums, and sousaphones. This store is truly the only one of its kind in the nation! While you're here, take a look at one of the largest privately held collections of low brass musical instruments in the world. The Tuba Exchange is open Monday through Friday from 9 A.M. to 5 P.M. and Saturday and Sunday by appointment. For more information, call 919-493-2200 or visit www.tubaexchange.com.

- The **Music Explorium**, at 5314 N.C. 55, Suite 102, is one of the most interesting shops in the Triangle. It offers instruments for everyone—and from everywhere. If you're looking for a string instrument, you can find everything from ordinary guitars and banjos to sitars, upright basses, and Nepalese sarangis. Wind instruments include such exotic items as Australian Aboriginal didgeridoos, Native American flutes, panpipes, and Tibetan horns. Unusual drums are also available. In the spirit of community and self-expression, rhythm circles and drum-and-dance circles are offered periodically; little or no musical expertise is needed. Even non-musicians will find the Music Explorium fascinating. For more information, call 919-484-9090 or visit www.musicexplorium.com.

RECREATION

- The **American Tobacco Trail** offers six miles of trails connecting downtown Durham to N.C. 54. Bikers, hikers, and joggers take advantage of this greenway, conveniently located in the heart of the city.

- **Carolina Barnstormers**, at 4340 East Geer Street, offers "flightseeing" tours from the open cockpit of Mike Ratty's red biplane. Guests can take a 25-minute tour of the airport vicinity or opt for an hour-long tour and choose their own destination. The tours, for one or two people at a time, are offered from September through mid-June. For more information, call 919-672-4843 or 919-408-0370 or visit www.carolinabarnstormers.com.

- **Durham Bulls Athletic Park**, on Willard Street between Mangum Street and Blackwell Street, is the nationally acclaimed, 10,000-seat downtown home of the Durham Bulls class AAA baseball club. The park includes skyboxes and the year-round Ball Park Corner, which sells Bulls' memorabilia. For tickets or information, call 919-687-6500 or visit www.durhambulls.com. Historic **Durham Athletic Park**, at the corner of

Morris Street and Corporation Street, is the old site where generations of fans used to gather to watch the Bulls play and where the movie *Bull Durham*, starring Kevin Costner and Susan Sarandon, was filmed.

■ *Wafting the Eno* offers guided natural-history float trips down the Eno River in inflatable "wafts" between Memorial Day and Labor Day. Expeditions leave at 10 A.M. and 3:30 P.M. most days of the week; a moonlight waft leaves every Friday at 9 P.M. To arrange a tour, call 919-471-3802; for information, visit www.wafter.org.

SEASONAL EVENTS

■ The *American Dance Festival* takes place on Duke's West Campus in Page Auditorium, the Reynolds Industries Theatre, and other locations. The largest and most influential modern-dance festival in the world, it boasts more than two dozen dance companies, hundreds of choreographers and writers, and students who participate in classes, seminars, and performances. The festival runs from early June to late July and attracts an audience from around the world. For information, call 919-684-6402 or visit www.americandancefestival.org.

■ The *Bull Durham Blues Festival* takes place in early September at historic Durham Athletic Park at the corner of Morris Street and Corporation Street. The state's largest blues celebration, it has drawn fans from all over North Carolina and from 25 different states and five countries. In 2000, the festival was awarded the "Keeping the Blues Alive Award" by the Blues Foundation. It showcases national, regional, and local blues performed by contemporary artists including Bo Diddley, Taj Mahal, Etta James, Ruth Brown, Aaron Neville, Otis Rush, and Alberta Adams. For ticket information, call the Hayti Heritage Center at 919-683-1709 or visit www.hayti.org/blues/index.php.

■ The *Festival for the Eno*, held at West Point Park, is North Carolina's oldest and most prestigious environmental event. It draws over 100 artists and craftsmen and as many performers, who entertain audiences at five stages. This three-day festival takes place on the Fourth of July weekend and raises money for the purchase and protection of land in central North Carolina's Eno River Basin. Past performers have included Doc Watson, Ralph Stanley, and the African-American Dance Ensemble. For informa-

Festival for the Eno
COURTESY OF DURHAM CONVENTION
AND VISITORS BUREAU

tion or tickets, call 919-477-4549 or visit www.enoriver.org/festival.

- The *Full Frame Documentary Film Festival* takes place in April in the Carolina Theatre's Royal Center for the Arts. Formerly called the DoubleTake Festival, this international event is presented in association with the Center for Documentary Studies at Duke University, the *New York Times*, the Museum of Modern Art in New York, Exploris and the North Carolina Museum of Art in Raleigh, and the Hague Appeal for Peace in the Netherlands, among others. Touted by *Entertainment Weekly* as "the 'It' Documentary Film Festival," Full Frame now draws more submissions than Sundance and has been endorsed by Martin Scorsese. For information, call 919-687-4100 or visit www.fullframefest.org.

Places to Stay

RESORTS, HOTELS, AND MOTELS

- *The Washington Duke Inn and Golf Club*. Deluxe. 3001 Cameron Boulevard (800-443-3853 or 919-490-0999; www.washingtondukeinn.com). The Washington Duke was built in the style of an English country inn. The lobby and hallways are graced with Duke family treasures and art. Known for its exceptional service, this is a Mobil Four Star, AAA Four Diamond hotel. It features 171 elegantly appointed guest rooms and suites, as well as the Four Diamond-rated Fairview Restaurant and a 300-acre golf course.

- *Sheraton Imperial Hotel and Conference Center*. Deluxe/Expensive.

4700 Emperor Boulevard (800-325-3535 or 919-941-5050; www.sheratonrtp.com). This Mobil Three Star, AAA Three Diamond hotel has 331 guest rooms, including 62 club-level rooms with a concierge on duty. Complimentary continental breakfast is served in the morning and hors d'oeuvres and beverages in the evening in the private club-level lounge. Each room has a coffee maker, an iron, an ironing board, on-demand movies, voice mail, and computer data ports.

INNS AND BED-AND-BREAKFASTS

■ *Arrowhead Inn*. Deluxe. 106 Mason Road (800-528-2207 or 919-477-8430; www.arrowheadinn.com). Nestled on six acres of spectacular gardens and magnolia-shaded lawns, the Arrowhead Inn is pure luxury in a historical plantation setting. This AAA Four Diamond bed-and-breakfast was built around 1775. It has been meticulously renovated down to its original moldings, mantelpieces, and heart-of-pine floors. The inn has been featured in *USA Today, Southern Living*, and *Food and Wine* for its historical importance and elegance. Innkeepers Phil and Gloria Teber leave no detail overlooked. Guests can expect to find Gloria's attentive touch in every nook and cranny of each of the eight beautifully appointed guest rooms and the private log cabin. Aside from the fine furnishings, the exquisite linens, and the whirlpool tubs, amenities include plush bathrobes, complimentary snacks, fresh-cut flowers, candles, and a small collection of romantic music. The guests' journals in the rooms reveal that past honeymooners and others have been pampered with trails of rose petals and private gourmet dinners delivered to their door. Treat yourself to even one night here and you'll never want to stay in a hotel again.

Arrowhead Inn
PHOTOGRAPH BY SHERYL MONKS

■ ***Blooming Garden Inn***. Deluxe. 513 Holloway Street (888-687-0801; www.bloominggardeninn.com). Located in the historic district and run by innkeepers Dolly and Frank Pokrass, this sunny Victorian inn features antique beds, goose-down pillows, stained-glass accent panels, Jacuzzis, and beautiful porcelain sinks. The wraparound porches offer stunning views of the azaleas in the garden.

■ ***Morehead Manor Bed-and-Breakfast***. Deluxe. 914 Vickers Avenue (919-687-4366; www.moreheadmanor.com). This 8,000-square-foot Colonial Revival beauty is located in the historic Morehead Hill neighborhood just south of downtown, near Brightleaf Square. Built in 1910 for the CEO of Liggett & Myers Tobacco Company, the Art Deco-furnished home features four distinct guest rooms. Complimentary beverages, scrumptious homemade desserts, and a full breakfast are just some of the pleasures afforded here. Fun options include a Murder Mystery Weekend package, a "Get Me to the Church on Time" package for bridesmaids, a "You Go, Girl" getaway, and a "Greta's PJ Party" package.

■ ***Old North Durham Inn***. Deluxe/Expensive. 922 North Mangum Street (919-683-1885; www.bbonline.com/nc/oldnorth/). This restored early-1900s Colonial Revival home was the recipient of the Durham Historic Preservation Society's Architectural Conservation Citation. It features a rocker-lined wraparound porch, coffered ceilings, beautiful oak floors, period wall coverings and furnishings, and much more. Located across the street from the residence used in the movie *Bull Durham*, the inn is close to Duke University, Durham Bulls Athletic Park, and the Carolina Theatre. In 1992, innkeeper Jim Vickery won the name-the-mascot contest for the Bulls baseball team; he now offers guests free tickets to all home games.

■ ***Carol's Garden Inn***. Expensive. 2412 South Alston Avenue (877-922-6777; www.carolsgardeninn.com). Built in 1910, this two-story Craftsman-style farmhouse has been completely renovated. It features a wide, open staircase and corner fireplaces. The two-story front porch overlooks pecan trees, a beautiful water garden, and a large pond. Guest-room amenities include high-speed Ethernet connections and private baths with whirlpool tubs.

Places to Eat

- **Magnolia Grill.** Expensive. 1002 Ninth Street (919-286-3609). The Magnolia Grill has received about every culinary accolade possible, making it a destination for foodies from all over the country. Chef-owners Ben and Karen Barker helped set the trend in Southern-inspired cuisine from Magnolia Grill's open kitchen. The grill is frequently packed, so reservations are almost essential. Dinner is served Tuesday through Saturday.

- **Nana's Restaurant.** Expensive. 2514 University Drive (919-493-8545; www.nanasdurham.com). This Durham favorite features an intimate remodeled dining area with smart white linens and art by local artists. Former Magnolia Grill chef Scott Howell studied at the Culinary Institute of America in New York before opening this popular mingling spot a decade ago. His menu stresses craft. Some of Nana's best offerings include house-smoked or house-cured meats. Nana's wine list has won *Wine Spectator*'s Award of Excellence; the restaurant hosts some of the best wine dinners in the area. Dinner is served Monday through Saturday; you'll need reservations.

- **Vin Rouge.** Expensive/Moderate. 2010 Hillsborough Road (919-416-0466; www.vinrougerestaurant.com). An open kitchen greets you as you walk in the door of this simple and elegant bistro. The food here includes bistro standards like "Steak Frites." The bacon-spiked "Gratin de Macaroni" is the Mercedes of macaroni and cheese. The wine list is all French; the staff members are more than capable of matching your preferred style of wine or grape with an appellation you didn't know you liked. Vin Rouge's patio is a great place for Sunday brunch. Dinner is served Tuesday through Sunday; brunch is offered on Sunday only. Reservations are necessary on weekend nights.

- **Pop's Italian Trattoria.** Moderate. 810 West Peabody Street (919-956-7677; www.popsdurham.com). Located next to Morgan Imports and across the street from Brightleaf Square, this upscale casual restaurant offers good food and a bright clientele. The cuisine is stylish, fresh Italian. The desserts and breads are baked on the premises. Lunch is served Monday through Friday and dinner daily. Reservations are appreciated.

- **George's Garage.** Moderate/Inexpensive. 737 Ninth Street (919-286-

4131). This is one of George Bakatsias's unique Durham restaurants. It offers an upbeat smorgasbord of ethnic foods and activities in the hub of Ninth Street life. In addition to the excitement of finding sushi at 11 P.M., there's the bonus of pull-back-the-table dancing on weekends. The lunch menu includes an array of food that will leave you stunned. Lunch and dinner are served daily.

- ***Bullock's BBQ***. Inexpensive. 3330 Quebec Drive (919-383-3211). Bullock's is a family-owned barbecue place with impressive staying power. Imitators have opened up on all sides of it, but Bullock's remains busy serving great BBQ, Brunswick stew, fried chicken, and other traditional Southern food. The crowd is a mixture of townies and transplants of all ages. Come hungry and bring cash! Lunch and dinner are served Tuesday through Saturday.

- ***Foster's Market***. Inexpensive. 2694 Chapel Hill Road (919-489-3944; www.fostersmarket.com). Sarah Foster, a caterer and former chef for Martha Stewart, converted this former lawn-mower repair shop into a gourmet market and sandwich shop in 1990. She furnished it with mismatched vintage chairs that complement the building's lived-in feel. Foster's is arguably the best place for lunch in Durham. Its sandwiches, salads, and prepared foods can be bought by the pound or by portion. For breakfast or a snack, the scones, muffins, crumb cakes, and breads are in a class by themselves. Pick up a jar of Sarah's "Seven Pepper Jelly" on your way out and invent a use for it when you get home. Breakfast, lunch, and dinner are served daily.

- ***James Joyce*** and ***The Federal***. Inexpensive. 912 and 914 West Main Street. These sister establishments, located next door to one another across the street from Brightleaf Square, are under the same ownership. Both are wildly popular hangouts for Duke students and young professionals. James Joyce (919-683-3022; www.jamesjoyceirishpub.com) serves traditional pub fare and offers great specials. The Federal (919-680-8611; www.thefederal.net) is more bar than restaurant, but the quality of its food far exceeds what you might expect from the setting. Both serve lunch and dinner daily.

Franklin Street in Chapel Hill
COURTESY OF CHAPEL HILL/ORANGE COUNTY VISITORS BUREAU

CHAPEL HILL AND CARRBORO

hapel Hill's residents used to refer to their town as "the southern part of heaven." Tar Heel fans liken their team's colors to the celestial shades. But the origin of the school's signature Carolina blue and white has actually been traced back to two campus literary societies whose members wore the separate colors to distinguish one group from the other. Beginning around 1800, the Dialectic and Philanthropic societies wore light blue and white, respectively. At commencements and other events, a student official or marshal wore the color of his society. Whenever a student leader represented the entire school, not just his society, he wore both colors. In 1888, the university began fielding its first intercollegiate athletic teams. Because the colors had already come to represent the university at large, the choice was easily settled; light blue and white became the official colors.

Authorized by the North Carolina Constitution in 1776, the university was chartered 12 years later when George Washington was inaugurated as president. Charter members looking for a central location agreed on New Hope Chapel Hill, the site where several colonial roads intersected. The cornerstone for the first state university building in the United States,

Old East, was laid on October 12, 1793. A year and a half later, the first student was admitted. By the late 1800s, only Yale University had a larger enrollment.

In the antebellum era, slaves helped build some of the campus's first buildings. Since those early days, the university has trained many state officials (including about half of North Carolina's governors), as well as leaders in virtually every profession. One of its early graduates was future United States president James K. Polk. Vice presidential candidate John Edwards graduated from the university's law school.

In the early 1800s, students and faculty at UNC were the first in the country to make systematic astronomical observations. Their recorded notes date from 1827 to 1831. A year later, they built the first university-run observatory in North America. In the 1820s, university faculty members conducted the nation's first state geological survey. Carolina was one of the few Southern universities to remain open during the Civil War. Reconstruction forced it to close from 1871 to 1875—the only time in its history. As the university moved into the 20th century, growth in student enrollment, programs, and intellectual influence brought more prominence.

Since the 1950s, Chapel Hill has become known for more than just the university. The town boasts several independent theater companies, a pioneering record label and its bands, regionally and nationally regarded restaurants, and a community of artists working in a variety of media. Neighboring Carrboro is a center for unique galleries and festivals.

There is ample bike parking in downtown Chapel Hill and Carrboro; bike trails weave across both towns. A good map of Chapel Hill's greenways and bike trails is available at www.chapelhillparks.org.

JUST THE FACTS

Chapel Hill, in Orange County, is accessible via N.C. 54, U.S. 15/U.S. 501, and Interstate 40, which connects Chapel Hill, Durham, Research Triangle Park, and Raleigh. Hillsborough, the county seat, is just to the north; it can be reached from Interstate 40 or by heading north on N.C. 86.

The nearest major airport is Raleigh-Durham International Airport, about a half-hour away. Small planes can land just north of town at Horace Williams Airport, which has a 4,500-

foot lighted landing strip; call 919-962-1337 for information. The Greyhound/Trailways bus station is at 311 West Franklin Street; call 919-942-3356. Intercity bus service is offered in Chapel Hill, Durham, and Raleigh by the Triangle Transit Authority; call 919-549-9999.

Finding free parking in Chapel Hill and Carrboro can be a challenge, so strapping a bike onto your bumper is highly recommended. If that's not an option, metered parking spaces are available on the university campus at Morehead Planetarium, Country Club Road, South Road, Ridge Road, Raleigh Street, West Drive, and the student union. Meters are also located on Franklin, Rosemary, Henderson, and Columbia streets. Parking at metered spaces on campus and in town is usually limited to one or two hours and is monitored closely. The parking deck at 150 East Rosemary Street, one block north of Franklin Street, and the lot at the corner of North Columbia and Rosemary streets operate on an hourly basis. Those who park in the lots at the corner of Church and West Rosemary streets and at 415 West Franklin Street from 8 A.M. to 6 P.M. on Monday through Saturday must feed the meter; otherwise, parking there is free.

The Chapel Hill/Orange County Visitors Bureau is located at 501 West Franklin Street, Suite 104; call 888-968-2060 or 919-968-2060 or visit www.chocvb.org.

The local newspapers are the *Chapel Hill News*, the *Chapel Hill Herald*, the *Daily Tar Heel*, and the *News & Observer* of Raleigh. The free weekly *Independent* offers in-depth reporting and listings of activities.

Things to Do

HISTORIC PLACES, GARDENS, AND TOURS

■ The **University of North Carolina at Chapel Hill**, flanked primarily by Franklin Street, Hillsborough Street, Raleigh Road, and Columbia Street, continues to spread. The main historic campus lies between Franklin Street

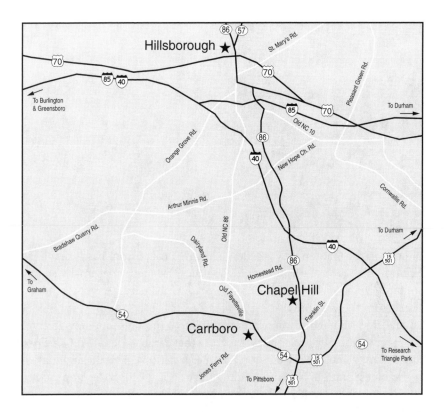

and Cameron Avenue. Visitors can enjoy a campus walking tour between those two streets.

■ **Silent Sam**, located between Franklin Street and Cameron Avenue near the campus visitor center, is a Civil War monument erected in 1913 to commemorate the 321 Confederate alumni who died in the Civil War. Although the soldier holds a rifle, it is useless because he wears no cartridge box for ammunition.

■ The **Davie Poplar** marks the spot where, legend has it, William R. Davie selected the site for the campus in 1792. It sits in McCorkle Place, the large green separating Franklin Street from the campus.

■ At the heart of the campus on Cameron Avenue stands the visual symbol of the university, the **Old Well**. For many years, it served as the sole water supply for Old East and Old West dormitories. In 1897, it was given its present decorative form at the direction of university president Edwin A. Alderman, who based his beautification on the Temple

The Old Well
Courtesy of Chapel Hill / Orange County
Convention and Visitors Bureau

of Love in the Garden of Versailles. Though local custom has it that a sip from the well brings wisdom and good luck, frequent nocturnal visits by students from nearby North Carolina State University generally render a drink from the well unwise.

The first building on the campus—indeed, the only building for two years—was the two-story brick structure that came to be called **Old East**, located on what is now Cameron Avenue. A national historic landmark, it is the oldest state-university building in America. The college opened to students on January 15, 1795, but its first and only professor had to wait as student Hinton James of New Hanover County walked from home, arriving on February 12. By March, two professors and 41 students were present. Old East still serves as a men's dorm.

Visitors enjoy the gardens and the prominent wisteria-laden pergola at the **Coker Arboretum**, on Hillsborough Road. The original arbor was constructed in 1913 of black locust, a decay-resistant wood that was again chosen when the arbor was renovated in 1996-97. A gift of the UNC class of 1997, the entryway and stone circle commemorate students in the class who did not survive to graduate. In the circle's center, a large stone tulip-poplar leaf points toward the Davie Poplar a few hundred yards west.

■ **PlayMakers Theatre**, on Cameron Avenue, is considered by some to be the most beautiful building on campus. This 1851 Greek Revival temple is one of the masterworks of New York architect Alexander Jackson Davis, who designed it as an unlikely combination library and ballroom. During the Civil War, Union troops stabled their horses in it. Years later, it became the theater for the Carolina PlayMakers, who, under the leadership of "Proff" Fred Koch and playwright Paul Green, were largely responsible for developing folk and outdoor drama in the United States.

■ *Forest Theatre*, on Country Club Road, sits on what was once Battle Park. The site was first utilized for a theatrical presentation in 1916, on the tricentennial of Shakespeare's death. W. C. Coker, the faculty botanist who developed the nearby arboretum, chose the location. Several years later, when Frederick Koch came to the university, it was developed into a permanent theater. The outdoor amphitheater, dedicated to Koch, still serves as a performance space for local theater groups, including the Open Door Theatre Company.

■ The **North Carolina Botanical Garden** is administered by the university, though it is located off the main campus on Old Mason Farm Road near N.C. 54. The garden encompasses nearly 600 acres of native plants and herbs. The indigenous southeastern plants around the Trotten Center are arranged in natural-habitat gardens of the Sandhills, the coastal plain, and the mountains. At the Mercer Reeves Hubbard Herb Garden, you'll find a renowned collection of carnivorous plants. Self-guided tours are available year-round. Trained volunteer docents lead tours for groups of 10 to 60. The garden is open weekdays year-round from 8 A.M. to 5 P.M.; weekend hours vary by season. For more information or to schedule a tour, call 919-962-9460 or visit www.unc.edu/depts/ncbg.

MUSEUMS AND SCIENCE CENTERS

■ The **Ackland Art Museum**, on Columbia Street on the university campus, was founded through the bequest of William Hayes Ackland, a Nashville, Tennessee, native who, as the words on his tomb suggest, "wanted the people of his native South to know and love the fine arts." The permanent collection includes more than 14,000 works of art from around the world. The Ackland is rich in paintings and sculptures by artists such as Degas, Rubens, and Pissarro; Indian miniatures; Japanese paintings; North Carolina folk art; and prints, drawings, and photographs. It also hosts four to six temporary loan exhibitions annually. The museum is open Wednesday through Saturday from 10 A.M. to 5 P.M. and Sunday from 1 P.M. to 5 P.M. Admission is free, but donations are welcome. For more information, call 919-966-5736 or visit www.ackland.org.

- *Morehead Planetarium*, at 250 East Franklin Street, has become a landmark since its construction in the late 1940s. It has far exceeded its modest original purpose of educating a single community. As the American space effort took wing, the planetarium was used to train astronauts from the Mercury program to the Apollo-Soyuz program. The first planetarium owned by a university, it still serves as an educational and instructional training ground, as well as a program- and education-oriented facility. It is home to one of the most spectacular pieces of equipment in the East—the magnificent Zeiss Model VI projector, which is capable of showing nearly 9,000 stars in the 68-foot dome. The complex also houses exhibits, an art gallery, a rose garden with a sundial, a gift shop, and banquet facilities. Public planetarium shows and live sky shows narrated by staff members teach the public about the night sky, lunar landings, the travels of the *Voyager* spacecraft, black holes, weather tracking, the Big Bang, and more. On occasion, music laser shows are offered. An admission fee is charged. The planetarium is open Sunday from 12:30 P.M. to 5 P.M. and Monday through Saturday from 10 A.M. to 5 P.M. It reopens on Thursday, Friday, and Saturday nights from 6:30 P.M. to 9:30 P.M. For more information, call 919-549-6863 or 919-962-1236 or visit www.moreheadplanetarium.org.

- The *North Carolina Collection Gallery*, located on the second floor of the Louis Round Wilson Library on the UNC campus, offers exhibits of material from among the 250,000 books and pamphlets, 400,000 photographic images, and 15,000 museum objects in the collection. Long-term exhibits interpret the exploration and settlement of Roanoke Island and depict the native Algonquian culture of that region. An exhibit on the gold rush in North Carolina includes rare Bechtler "pioneer gold" coins. Other exhibits are devoted to university history, the North Carolina Collection's rare Audubon bird prints, and Eng and Chang Bunker (the original Siamese twins, who lived in Surry County from 1811 to 1874). Guided tours are available. Admission is free. For more information, call 919-962-1172 or visit www.lib.unc.edu/ncc/.

- The *Chapel Hill Museum*, located at the intersection of Franklin and Boundary streets, has two main exhibit halls that showcase fine-art photography, crafts, and architecture and host events that document the character and people of Chapel Hill. The museum is open Wednesday through Saturday from 10 A.M. to 4 P.M. and Sunday from 1 P.M. to 4 P.M. For more information, call 919-967-4100 or visit www.chapelhillmuseum.org.

CULTURAL OFFERINGS

- The *ArtsCenter*, at 300-G East Main Street in Carrboro, offers a year-round calendar of community-centered art classes, live theater and jazz productions, and art exhibits. On weekends, musicians from locations ranging from the Appalachians to the Andes perform in the Earl Wynn Theater. The world-music concert series highlights emerging and established artists. The center also hosts a nationally recognized jazz series featuring regional and national artists. Family entertainment at the center encompasses drama, musical theater, puppetry, storytelling, and music of all kinds. Theatrical programs include the ArtsCenter Community Theater, a venue for actors of all skill levels to explore and develop their craft. The West End Project series provides informal theater space for artists performing new material or learning new skills. The ArtsCenter also hosts productions by some of the Triangle's many professional theater companies. For a catalog or a monthly calendar of events, call 919-929-2787 or visit http://www.artscenterlive.org.

- The *Chelsea Theatre*, at 1129 Weaver Dairy Road, offers a great selection of foreign and independent films. Locals suggest arriving early for parking and seats. The selection of movies is stellar. For show times, call 919-968-3005.

- *Meet the Author Teas* have been held at the Chapel Hill Public Library since 1968, when the library moved from makeshift quarters to its official home at 100 Library Drive. Sponsored by the Friends of the Chapel Hill Public Library, the teas have provided the community with numerous opportunities to meet writers who are now household names. Tea, coffee, and cookies are always served prior to the program. A faithful committee makes the arrangements, prepares the room, makes the tea, and arranges flowers. For more information or a schedule of speakers and dates, call 919-968-2779 or visit http://www.friendschpl.org/activities/meettheauthorteas/.

■ **PlayMakers Repertory Company**, an offshoot of the original Carolina PlayMakers, is a professional regional theater troupe offering up to six productions per year (including original works) in the Paul Green Theatre on the university campus. The Carolina PlayMakers, founded by Fred Koch, launched many of the school's alumni and associates into the arts. Among these were Thomas Wolfe, who performed the title role in his student-written play, *The Return of Buck Gavin*; Pulitzer Prize-winning playwright Paul Green; comedian Andy Griffith; bandleader Kay Kyser; and composer and lyricist Richard Adler. Call 919-962-PLAY or visit www.playmakersrep.org for information.

■ **Deep Dish Theater Company** produces four plays in Chapel Hill's University Mall each year. Deep Dish specializes in new or rarely seen plays and interesting productions of long-loved favorites. Its versatility is impressive; the company has produced *The Misanthrope, Hedda Gabler*, new works by Triangle playwright Adam Sobsey, and southeastern premieres of several contemporary plays. For more information, call 919-968-1515 or visit www.deepdishtheater.org.

Special Shopping

■ The **Carrboro Farmers' Market** is held at the town commons, located next to the town hall at 301 West Main Street. For 25 years, it has provided the people of Carrboro with fresh produce, prepared foods, flowers, crafts, and special events such as tastings and cooking demonstrations. The market is open Saturday from 7 A.M. to noon and Wednesday from 3:30 P.M. to 6:30 P.M. The **Southern Village Farmers' Market** is located in Southern Village in Chapel Hill; it's on Market Street across from the Lumina Theatre. It is open on Thursday from 4 P.M. to 7 P.M. For information about both markets, call 919-932-1641 or visit www.carrborofarmersmarket.com.

■ **Carr Mill Mall**, located in the historic Alberta Mill behind the Weaver Street Market and Café on North Greensboro Street in Carrboro, was built in 1890 as a cotton mill. That mill closed in the 1930s. Opened in 1977 at the insistence of community members, Carr Mill Mall houses a number of specialty stores, boutiques, and restaurants with vaulted ceilings, hardwood floors, and exposed-brick walls. Individual store hours vary. Free parking is available.

Carrboro Farmers' Market
COURTESY OF CHAPEL HILL / ORANGE COUNTY
CONVENTION AND VISITORS BUREAU

■ You can't come to Chapel Hill and miss the scene on **East Franklin Street**, the main artery that runs beside the university. You'll see saxophone players, accordion players, bagpipe players, rappers, college students, professors, lawyers, record stores, bars, galleries, cafés, old churches, trees, shops, and the Morehead Planetarium—all within the space of about a quarter-mile. Go down to **West Franklin Street** and you'll find bakeries, art shops, antiquarian bookstores, vintage clothiers, designer boutiques, a wine bar, a teahouse, and sporting-goods stores. These days, the action extends all the way to **Main Street in Carrboro**, where you'll find more galleries, the ArtsCenter, an army surplus store, and on and on and on; just keep following Franklin Street westward.

■ The **Last Unicorn**, at 536 Edwards Ridge Road, is a unique garden center specializing in wrought-iron gates and fences, antique stained glass, and other interesting items. The showroom, unlike any other, stretches across five acres of wooded trails. Wrought-iron gates lead to hidden paths lined with ornate fences and garden art. You'll walk through acres of forest and gardens before coming across the **Unicorn Shoppe**, which houses a collection of precious antique stained glass, and the **Ole Log Cabin**, which showcases one-of-a-kind home-and-garden collectibles. The Last Unicorn offers one of the largest collections of wrought-iron gates in the

Southeast. For more information, call 919-968-8440 or visit www.thelastunicorn.com.

- The **North Carolina Crafts Gallery**, located in the building known as "the Point" on the corner of West Main and Weaver streets in Carrboro, features work by artists from across the state. A variety of pottery, turned wood, jewelry, blown glass, sun catchers, quilts, wind chimes, garden sculptures, steppingstones, and other handmade pieces make unique gifts. When it opened in 1989, this was the first crafts gallery in Carrboro to carry work by North Carolina artists. It is open Monday through Saturday from 10 A.M. to 6 P.M. and Sunday from 1 P.M. to 4 P.M. For more information, call 919-942-4048 or visit www.nccraftsgallery.com.

- One of the first gourmet stores in the area, **A Southern Season**, located off U.S. 15/U.S. 501 at Estes Drive, has been offering Southern and European specialties since 1975. Opened originally as a tiny coffee "roastery," it is now a 28,000-square-foot market that offers a full-service restaurant called **The Weathervane**, a coffee-and-wine bar, and an impressive schedule of cooking classes. Store hours are Monday through Saturday from 10 A.M. to 9 P.M. and Sunday from noon to 6 P.M. The Weathervane serves lunch daily and dinner Monday through Saturday; it also offers brunch on Sunday. Make sure you take a good look at the weathervane—the arrow always points south, no matter the wind direction. For more information, call 919-929-7133 or visit www.southernseason.com.

RECREATION

- If you enjoy **cycling**, you'll be pleased to learn that Chapel Hill and Carrboro are extraordinarily bicycle friendly. The two towns have a well-developed system of bike trails and bike lanes and a commitment (through the Chapel Hill Greenway Commission) to eventually develop over 40 miles of trails. Several good trails are already available. Maps are accessible at www.ils.unc.edu/hiking. Or you can call 919-968-2743 for information about the system.

- The **Cat's Cradle**—that monster of a nightclub, that giant bus stop on the rock-'n'-roll route from Atlanta to New York, that incubator of musical movers—is located at 300 East Main Street. This music club is known far and wide. Though it has moved around a bit in its 20 or 30 (who's

Cat's Cradle
PHOTOGRAPH BY SHERYL MONKS

counting?) years of life, it still brings in big-name acts that actually *ask* to play here. And we all remember the days when R.E.M. performed here, as did the Riders in the Sky, Brave Combo, and even Nirvana. What a club! Call 919-967-9053 or visit www.catscradle.com to get the lowdown, or check the *Independent* for listings.

■ *Music and Movies on Market Street* is a program periodically offered on the green or on the lawn at the Lumina Theatre, located at 620 Market Street in Southern Village at Chapel Hill. Concerts start at 7 P.M. and are free to the public. Movies begin at dusk; a small fee is charged. Bring your lawn chair. For more information, call 919-856-0111.

■ The *North Carolina Tar Heels* are a subject that is sure to get a strong reaction from almost anyone on the street in Chapel Hill. Calling the 22,000-seat Dean Smith Center home has put the university's men's basketball team a little farther away from many of its fans but has done little to hinder its success. ACC basketball is one of the most exciting spectator sports around, and you're right at the heart of it. For information, call the Dean Dome at 919-962-6000 or visit www.tarheelblue.com. To reach the box office, call 919-962-2296.

■ Golf opportunities include *Twin Lakes Golf Course* (919-933-1024), at 648 Willow Way, six miles south of Chapel Hill, and the university's *Finley Golf Course* (919-962-2349), located two miles from Interstate 40 on N.C. 54. In 1999, Finley Golf Course underwent an $8 million renovation by architect Tom Fazio. It has since been called a masterpiece. The 18-hole, par-72 course offers reduced rates to students and faculty of the university.

- **FestiFall**, Chapel Hill's annual street fair, takes place on Franklin Street in October. Sponsored by the Chapel Hill Parks and Recreation Department, it offers live music and other entertainment, a variety of foods, and lots of vendor stalls for a Sunday of fun. For information, call 919-968-2784 or visit www.festifall.com.

- **Fête de la Musique** takes place, of course, in "the Paris of the Piedmont"—Carrboro, that is. The town partakes of a tradition begun in Paris in 1982 to use the summer solstice as an occasion to celebrate music, friendship, and freedom. In 1998, Carrboro joined two other American cities— New York and San Francisco—to honor the occasion; overall, 100 nations participate. A rare event indeed, it brings every available musician to the microphone and every able-bodied Carrboro citizen to the ranks of celebrants. For information, visit www.carrboromusicfestival.com.

Places to Stay

RESORTS, HOTELS, AND MOTELS

- **Carolina Inn**. Deluxe. 211 Pittsboro Street (919-933-2001; www.carolinainn.com). This historic Four Diamond hotel is the grand old lady of Chapel Hill. It offers elegant, magnolia-clad Southern hospitality in a location that is unbeatable by Tar Heel standards. From its site right on the corner of the university campus, you can easily walk to the arboretum, the planetarium, the PlayMakers Theatre, the Forest Theatre, or the Wilson Library. The inn is listed on the National Register of Historic Places. It is indeed rich in history, as the walls and the staff will be glad to tell you. You'll have to book ahead here, since the inn is such a favorite for wedding parties and alumni gatherings. All 184 rooms are nicely decorated. Guests enjoy complimentary coffee and freshly baked chocolate chip cookies on arrival. And yes, there is a ghost, but you'll have to wheedle the staff into telling you about it.

- **Governor's Club**. Deluxe. 11000 Governors Drive (919-933-7500; www.governorsclub.com). At the Governor's Club, you'll find a group of cottages situated in a hilly setting on a Jack Nicklaus golf course. Each cottage has four to seven comfortable suites, a large living area, and a fully equipped kitchen. Suites can be individually contained for single travelers, or they can access the adjoining living area for groups and families, allowing for mixing and mingling in ways not possible in standard hotel settings. The Governor's Club is popular for conferences, parties, and retreats. Tennis courts are available for those who don't enjoy golf.

- ■ *Siena Hotel*. Deluxe. 1505 East Franklin Street (800-223-7379 or 919-929-4000; www.sienahotel.com). An individually owned and operated boutique hotel inspired by the romantic villas of Tuscany, the Siena is the picture of opulence. It boasts a AAA Four Diamond award and a Condé Nast Johansens recommendation. The 80 guest rooms are individually appointed with hand-selected European antiques, specially commissioned armoires, rich fabrics, and French doors leading to European balconies. They also offer the latest technology and luxury amenities such as nightly turn-down service, fine Belgian chocolates, and marble bathrooms with European toiletries. A morning newspaper, a complimentary health-club membership, and a full buffet breakfast are included. During your stay, you can dine at the *Il Palio Ristorante*, a AAA Four Diamond establishment. You can even spend the day behind the scenes in the kitchen. The "Day as the Chef" package lets you create your own four-course menu, shop for fresh ingredients, and work alongside executive chef Jim Anile. For restaurant reservations, call 919-918-2545.

Siena Hotel
Courtesy of Siena Hotel

THIS FAIRY GODMOTHER
OF MODERN TIMES

Edward Kidder Graham, president of the University of North Carolina, spoke these welcoming remarks to an incoming freshman class in the early years of the 20th century: "There is nothing mysterious about the part the college will play in giving you the qualities that will equip you for this great adventure on which you are setting out. She cannot, by allowing you to room within sight of the well, nor by any system of examinations or lectures, give you a single virtue, nor has she a wishing cap by which she can 'wish on you' any capacity or quality that you do not have. Before she can answer your inquiry as to what she means to say to you as your foster mother, she asks you a very simple question. It is: 'What do you want; and what are you willing to pay?' You may remember in your mythology, and in your Grimm's fairy tales, that when the hero's fortune was so great that the kind fairies put themselves at his service, they always asked him what he wanted. He had at least to choose. It was the way with the wonderful youth Solomon. It is the way with you, O wonderful youth, whoever you are, that have come to this fairy godmother of modern times: She will mean to you what you will, and what you will she will give it to you. I should like to make this splendidly clear, and take the full responsibility for the promise: The college will give to you this year whatever gift you seriously ask of her. I challenge you, therefore, to answer with a choice, and I call upon you to consider with all intentness and manly intelligence what your momentous choice is, and that you put behind that choice, once made, every ounce of power you possess!"

INNS AND BED-AND-BREAKFASTS

■ *The Inn at Bingham School*. Expensive/Moderate. On N.C. 54 at Mebane Oaks Road (800-566-5583; www.chapel-hill-inn.com). Originally opened in 1845 as a prep school for boys seeking entrance to the nearby university, this quiet inn seems far removed from the ever-increasing crowd of the Triangle. Though it has been renovated, the inn retains its historical authenticity in its original wood and masonry and its period antiques in every room. The five guest rooms include a 1790s log cabin; depending on your choice of room, you may enjoy a fireplace, a whirlpool, or a canopy bed.

Places to Eat

■ *Carolina Crossroads*. Expensive. In the Carolina Inn, 211 Pittsboro Street (919-918-2777). Carolina Crossroads offers the elegant cuisine of a world-class executive chef and the hospitable atmosphere of one of Chapel Hill's most beloved inns. Breakfast and dinner are served daily; lunch is served Monday through Saturday; brunch is offered on Sunday.

■ *Elaine's on Franklin*. Expensive. 454 West Franklin Street (919-960-2770; www.elainesonfranklin.com). Although Elaine's is a relatively new restaurant, its signature culinary style of sophistication-meets-farmers'-market is already earning it a place as a Chapel Hill staple. Since its opening in 1999 under chef-owner Bret Jennings, Elaine's has garnered awards from *Wine Spectator* and accolades from *Southern Living*. Dinner is served Tuesday through Saturday. Reservations are recommended.

■ *Provence*. Expensive. 203 Weaver Street in Carrboro (919-967-5008). Chef-owner Felix Roux has turned a 1920s mill house into one of the area's trendiest eateries. Roux specializes in seafood. Every dish is prepared with a distinctly Mediterranean flair. Guests have a choice of traditional French and Italian specialties and an array of French wines. Dinner is served Monday through Saturday.

■ *Top of the Hill Restaurant & Brewery*. Expensive/Moderate. 100 East Franklin Street (919-929-8676; www.topofthehillrestaurant.com). This casual upscale restaurant overlooks downtown Chapel Hill from a large third-floor patio. The winner of over 20 "Best of" awards, including Best Restaurant in Chapel Hill, Best Microbrew, and Best Outdoor Deck, Top of the Hill caters to a mature, sophisticated clientele that some will find a bit stuffy. Though beer is brewed on the premises, serious beer enthusiasts may consider Top of the Hill more restaurant than bar. The menu includes appetizers, sandwiches, specialty pizzas, and entrées. Lunch and dinner are served daily.

■ *Crook's Corner Café and Bar*. Moderate. 610 West Franklin Street (919-929-7643). Crook's Corner is Southern dining at its best. You'll find barbecue on the menu here. You'll also find grits served in one of their finer settings—alongside shrimp. This is a great place to check out the work of local artists, whose pieces hang on the walls, in the restrooms, and even on the roof. You can see the works of Clyde Jones anytime you stop by; they're here permanently, hanging from the eaves and rafters. And of course, Bob Gaston's signature pink pig proudly adorns the roof. Garden dining is available in season. If you're lucky, you'll catch sight of everybody's favorite, Bill Smith, head chef *extraordinaire* and modest but unforgettable town historian. Dinner is served daily; brunch is offered on Sunday.

■ *The Ram's Head Rathskeller*. Moderate. 157-A East Franklin Street (919-942-5158). Locals have revered the Ram's Head Rathskeller as a Tar Heel institution for over 50 years. Tucked away on Amber Alley, this laid-back restaurant crammed full of memorabilia offers a full menu. Traditional favorites include the rathskeller's signature "Gambler" steak, cheesy lasagna, roast beef, and homemade desserts. Executive chef Kenny Mann has been at "the Rat" since 1948, as have some of the waiters. Lunch and dinner are served daily.

■ *The Spotted Dog Restaurant & Bar*. Moderate. 111 East Main Street in Carrboro (919-933-1117). The menu here is vegetarian friendly, and the atmosphere is artsy casual. Over 50 varieties of draft and bottled beer are available, as is a wine list featuring more than 40 selections. Artwork is on display; a portion of all artwork sales goes toward local charities. And the place recycles. What more can you ask for? Lunch and dinner are served Tuesday through Saturday; a late-night menu is available from 11 P.M. until midnight.

■ *Allen and Son Pit-Cooked Bar-B-Q*. Inexpensive. N.C. 86 North at

Mill House Road (919-942-7576). This is a bastion of hickory-cooked chopped barbecue. Order up a platter with fries, slaw, hush puppies, and Brunswick stew and you're ready for a tailgating party Chapel Hill-style. And honey, don't forget the sweetened iced tea. If it's a football weekend, you'd better call ahead because Allen and Son is going to be busy. There's another location on U.S. 15/U.S. 501 near Pittsboro if you're headed south and you've just gotta have it. Lunch and dinner are served Tuesday through Saturday.

■ *Flying Burrito*. Inexpensive. 746 Airport Road (919-967-7744). The Flying Burrito sits in the little mall on the right next to Foster's. These folks serve up the biggest, greatest burritos and the most delicious margaritas; they have a great nonalcoholic margarita, too! Fresh fish, great salsa, a friendly bar, a colorful atmosphere, and a lively crowd are what you'll find here. Lunch is served Monday through Friday and dinner seven days a week.

■ *Mama Dip's Kitchen*. Inexpensive. 408 West Rosemary Street (919-942-5837; www.mamadips.com). This Southern-style restaurant is owned by—you guessed it—Mama Dip. Though the owner has been acclaimed by such notables as Craig Claiborne of the *New York Times* and has had her own book published, she will likely be working in the kitchen when you eat here. She is deservedly famous for, among other things, her barbecue sauce, her sweet potato pie, her chicken and dumplings, and, yes, her chitlins. Southern-cooked vegetables are also a specialty. Lunch and dinner are served daily.

■ *Sutton's Drugstore*. Inexpensive. 159 East Franklin Street (919-942-5161). This is a comforting sight for returning Tar Heels who have seen lots of spots come and go. You can sit down at the counter and order a good, old-fashioned cheeseburger, crispy crinkle-cut fries, and a chocolate milk shake or an orangeade. You'll be served under a broad-bladed ceiling fan within walls filled with pictures of students, athletes, cheerleaders, local kids, and townspeople. You'll enjoy having a chat with the cook (or the pharmacist, who'll take over if the cook steps out) and getting a taste of the village. Breakfast and lunch are served daily.

■ *Weaver Street Market and Café*. Inexpensive. 101 East Weaver Street in Carrboro (919-929-0100; www.weaverstreetmarket.com). This is a happening place. Part of Carrboro's artsy downtown, Weaver Street Market and Café is not your typical restaurant. People come here to be part of the action, not to sit and chat in dark corners. They mill around all over the place—in the co-op grocery store, outside on the patio and under the trees, and around the café's hot and cold bars loaded with healthy foods. If you're a vegetarian, this place is right up your alley, but it also has good chicken and fish. Weaver Street offers an excellent assortment of cooked fresh vegetables, soups, and ready-made cold salads such as tabouli, spicy Szechuan noodle, and "Aioli Farfalle." If none of these strikes your fancy, you can create a fresh salad exactly the way you like from the salad bar. Live music, gourmet cooking classes, and art shows are also offered. Breakfast, lunch, and dinner are served daily.

The Earliest Days

Historian Kemp L. Battle described the Masonic ceremony that gave birth to the University of North Carolina this way: "The Chapel Hill of 1793 was covered with a primeval growth of forest trees, with only one or two settlements and a few acres of clearing. Even the trees on the East and West Avenue were still erect. The sweetgums and dogwood and maples were relieving with their russet and golden hues the general green of the forest. A long procession of people for the first time is marching along the narrow road, afterwards to be widened into a noble avenue. Many of them are clad in the striking, typical insignia of the Masonic Fraternity, their Grand Master [William R. Davie] arrayed in the full decorations of his rank. They march with military tread, because most of them have seen service, many scarred with wounds of horrid war. Their faces are serious, for they feel that they are engaged in a great work. They are proceeding to lay the cornerstone of the first building to be erected on the campus of the first American State University to open its doors."

Battle described the university's first official day this way: "The morning of the 15th of January [1795] opened with a cold, drizzling rain. As the sighing of the watery wind whistled through the leafless branches of tall oaks and hickories and the Davie poplar then in vigorous youth, all that met the eyes of the distinguished visitors were a two-storied brick building, the unpainted wooden house of the Presiding Professor, the avenue between them filled with stumps of recently felled trees, a pile of yellowish red clay, dug out for the foundation of the Chapel, or Person Hall, a pile of lumber, collected for building Steward's Hall, a Scotch-Irish preacher-professor, and not one student. . . . It was not until the 12th of February, 1795, that the first student arrived, with no companion, all the way from the banks of the lower Cape Fear, the precursor of a long line of seekers after knowledge. His residence was Wilmington, his name was Hinton James. For two weeks, he constituted the entire student body of the University. Two weeks later the next arrivals came, Maurice and Alfred Moore of Brunswick."

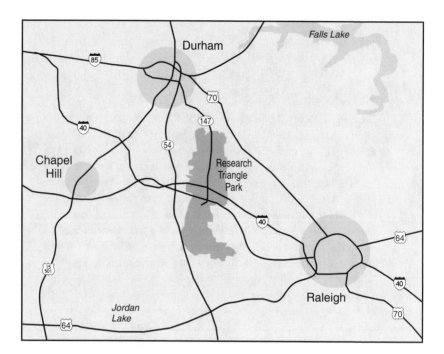

RESEARCH TRIANGLE PARK

Research Triangle Park was created in 1959. Now, this 7,000-acre area, one of the largest research parks in the world, is home to nearly 140 companies employing some 45,000 people. The concept for the research park is credited to University of North Carolina sociology professor Howard Odum, but it was Romeo Guest who coined the name *Research Triangle*. His idea came from the park's proximity to, and affiliation with, the area's three major universities. Together, Odum and Guest solicited the assistance of investor Karl Robbins, who agreed to fund the project by purchasing large tracts of land in the southeastern corner of Durham County. Today, the park encompasses an area eight miles long and two miles wide, with room to develop an additional 1,300 acres. Drawing on the areas of expertise of the three universities, research-and-development companies conduct studies in biotechnology, biopharmaceuticals, computer applications, chemicals, environmental science, information technology, microelectronics, instrumentation, and telecommunications. And those are only a few of the fields being researched.

There is not much to do in RTP itself. For Triangle residents, it is primarily a place to work, though the thirst for convenience and development has placed a few residential areas and strip malls here in the past few years. You'll find some hotels and restaurants, but many eateries are open only Monday through Friday during workday hours. Most business travelers who will be in RTP during the day will do well to stay in Raleigh or Durham to enjoy the area's best dining and nightlife.

JUST THE FACTS

Research Triangle Park is northwest of Raleigh and southeast of Durham on Interstate 40 near the intersection of N.C. 54 and N.C. 55.

Raleigh-Durham International Airport is conveniently located several miles to the east.

The major papers in the area are the *News & Observer* of Raleigh and the *Durham Herald-Sun*. Dining and events information is available in the *Independent*, a free weekly.

Things to Do

RECREATION

■ **Lake Crabtree County Park**, at 1400 Aviation Parkway in Morrisville, is located about 10 minutes northwest of Raleigh. Visitors can hike or bike

Lake Crabtree County Park
COURTESY OF GREATER RALEIGH CONVENTION AND VISITORS BUREAU

the park's network of trails and take a break at any of its numerous picnic areas. Small sailboats and canoes are available for rent from mid-April through October. Sailing classes and guided wildlife tours are also offered. The park is open from 8 A.M. to dusk every day. Entry is free. For more information and a schedule of tours and educational programs, call 919-460-3390 or visit http://www.wakegov.com/parks/lakecrabtree/default.htm.

Places to Stay

RESORTS, HOTELS, AND MOTELS

- **Radisson Governor's Inn**. Deluxe/Expensive. Exit 280 off Interstate 40 at Davis Drive (919-549-8631; www.radisson.com). This 197-room facility is the only hotel actually within RTP. Its business rate includes breakfast, a complimentary drink, and an in-room movie. Each room has a coffeepot and a desk with a data port and voice mail. A swimming pool and a fitness center are on the premises. Off-site laundry service is available.

- **Sheraton Imperial Hotel and Convention Center**. Deluxe/Expensive. 4700 Emperor Boulevard in Durham (800-325-3535 or 919-941-5050; www.sheratonrtp.com). The Sheraton Imperial is a AAA Three Diamond, Mobile Three Star hotel. Widely acclaimed as one of the Triangle's most luxurious lodgings, it offers 331 elegantly appointed guest rooms, a polished staff, and a list of amenities that includes a business center, a lobby piano bar, and a full-service restaurant. Room service is available throughout the day. Complimentary shuttle service to nearby Raleigh-Durham International Airport may be arranged through the concierge.

Places to Eat

- **Carmen's Cuban Café**. Moderate. 108D Factory Shops Road in Morrisville (919-467-8080). Carmen's reverses the Triangle's normal traffic pattern, as patrons from Raleigh, Durham, and Chapel Hill drive to the first and only Cuban restaurant in the area for some of the best food and Latin dancing around. The "Pan-Latin" menu features Cuban specialties like "Ropa Vieja" alongside empanadas and a mammoth seafood paella that two or three people can share. And then they can wash it all down with the best Mojitos anywhere. After 10 P.M. Tuesday through Saturday, Carmen's becomes the Touch Night Club, and the dancing begins. Lunch and dinner are served daily.

■ *Fortune Garden*. Moderate/Inexpensive. 5410 N.C. 55 (919-544-6009). Fortune Garden represents a marriage of Chinese and Thai influences both on the menu and in the kitchen; the husband-and-wife owners, one from China and the other from Thailand, offer dishes from each tradition. Lunch is served Monday through Friday and dinner Monday through Saturday.

■ *Piper's in the Park*. Inexpensive. 2945 South Miami Boulevard (919-572-9767). Piper Lunsford's old sandwich shop in Durham was a neighborhood favorite, and her new restaurant has many of the same superlative deli sandwiches she served there. Pastas, wraps, and fresh salads are also available. Try a "Papa Sweeney's Pimento Cheese Sandwich" and some of "Mama Windham's Fruit Cobbler" for dessert! Lunch is served daily.

TRIANGLE NEARBY

■ *Historic Hillsborough* is home to more than 100 sites listed on the National Register of Historic Places, some dating back to pre-Revolutionary War times. Visitors can take a self-guided walking tour or arrange for tours led by costumed docents. Information on all sites open to the public is available at 150 East King Street at the Alliance for Historic Hillsborough's office, housed in the late-18th-century Alexander Dickson House. You can also get information about the *Christmas Candlelight Tour* and the biennial *Spring Historic Home and Garden Tour*. In the gardens on the premises are traditional 18th- and 19th-century plants used for cooking, dyeing, and making medicines. For more information, visit www.historichillsborough.org.

Ayr Mount, at 376 St. Mary's Road, is one of North Carolina's finest Federal-period plantation houses. Built in 1815 by William Kirkland of Scotland, the brick house sits on 265 acres overlooking the Eno River Valley. Tours are offered Wednesday at 11 A.M., Thursday through Saturday at 11 A.M. and 2 P.M., and Sunday at 2 P.M.; a small admission fee is charged, but the daily Poet's Walk around the grounds is free. The grounds are open from 9 A.M. to 6 P.M. For information, call 919-732-6886 or visit www.classsicalamericanhomes.com.

Occaneechi Indian Village is located along the Eno River on South Cameron Avenue in downtown Hillsborough. The village—reconstructed to look as it did in the late 17th century—includes a palisade, huts, a cooking area, and a sweat lodge. It is open to the public during daylight hours. For more information, call the tribal office of the Eno-Occaneechi Indian Association at 919-304-3723.

The *Triangle SportsPlex*, located at One Dan Way, is Orange County's largest sports and recreation facility. The 80,000-square-foot complex features an NHL-sized ice rink, three indoor pools, a fitness center, a café, and a pro shop. Public ice skating, swimming lessons, and personal fitness training are just a few examples of what it has to offer. For more information, call 919-644-0339 or visit www.trianglesportsplex.com.

The *Vietri Outlet Store* is located at 343 Elizabeth Brady Road. Vietri imports handcrafted Italian products and wholesales them to the finest specialty stores, department stores, and catalog companies in North America. The outlet store in Hillsborough offers an incredible array of one-of-a-kind overstocks and slightly flawed samples and seconds, and the prices are unbeatable. The store is open two days a week only—Friday from noon to 6 P.M. and Saturday from 9 A.M. to 1 P.M. For more information, call 800-277-5933 or 919-732-9903 or visit www.vietri.com.

A great place to stay is the *Inn at Teardrop*, at 175 West King Street. The old building, which dates to 1768, is beautifully decorated with exotic antiques and memorabilia. There are no televisions or telephones in the six rooms, so guests are immersed in complete solitude, a comfort from days gone by. For reservations, call 919-732-1120.

A few doors down is *Tupelo's Regional Southern Cuisine*. Here, you'll find Creole classics such as jambalaya and crawfish ravioli, as well as a few surprises. Who can resist "Bayou Voodoo Shrimp"? If you're not up for a full meal, check out the tavern next door. It has a more casual atmosphere and serves a variety of soups and sandwiches. Lunch and dinner are served Monday through Saturday. For information, call the restaurant at 919-643-7722 or the tavern at 919-643-2223 or visit www.tupelos.com.

■ *Maple View Farm Country Store*, located on the northeastern corner of the intersection of Rocky Ridge Road and Dairyland Road approximately

3.5 miles west of the Orange County community of Calvander, offers a year-round ice-cream menu. Favorites include milk shakes, floats, sundaes, banana splits, and ice-cream cakes. Flavors include butter pecan, honey-toasted almond, double chocolate, coffee, cookies-and-cream, cookie dough, cherry vanilla, maple, mocha, blueberry, peach, coconut, and cheesecake. Whew! Strawberry sorbet is also available. Sugar-free flavors, offered on a rotating schedule, include vanilla, vanilla fudge swirl, blueberry swirl, and strawberry swirl. The store is perched on a hill looking west over the farm and adjacent fields; the covered front porch, furnished with rocking chairs, is strategically positioned for a sweeping view of the rolling countryside. Picnic tables are available on the hill, a perfect spot for watching the sunset. The store is open seven days a week from noon to 10 P.M. For more information, call 919-960-5535 or visit www.mapleviewfarm.com.

■ There is great scenery to be taken in on the drive down U.S. 15/U.S. 501 into Chatham County. The communities here host many artists, sculptors, and craftspeople. *Pittsboro* is home to a variety of sites listed on the National Register of Historic Places. Nearby *Moncure* offers a number of unique things to see and do. *Siler City*, the site of Mount Vernon Mineral Springs, plays host to several interesting Latino celebrations, including the annual Stations of the Cross procession, conducted in both Spanish and English. For more information on Chatham County, call 800-316-3829 or check out www.visitchathamcounty.com.

The leisurely *Antique Walk* through downtown Pittsboro allows you to explore 25,000 square feet of antique showrooms. You'll meander through a variety of shops that offer vintage pieces, fine furniture and accessories, collectibles, estate jewelry, clothing, rare books, and much more. Then you can have lunch in the old-fashioned *S & T Soda Shop* or one of the cafés nearby. For information about the Antique Walk, call 919-542-5649 or visit www.pittsboro-antiques.com.

Beggars and Choosers, at 38 Hillsboro Street in Pittsboro, is a vintage store and collectibles shop deluxe. But don't go in if you haven't the time to do it right! You'll want to loaf here for hours. A word of warning: Beggars and Choosers closes for the summer, so don't plan to visit between July and September. For more information, call 919-542-5884.

Anyone in Pittsboro will gladly tell you about the *Piedmont Farm Tour*, which takes place in April. You can visit nearly 25 farms for $25; if you buy tickets early, you can get them for five bucks less. You'll get a close look at the work done at dairies, apiaries, nurseries, vegetable farms, and horse farms. The tour is an extremely kid-friendly event. For more information, call 919-542-2402 or visit www.carolinafarmstewards.org.

- **Fearrington Village** is located on U.S. 15/U.S. 501 between Pittsboro and Chapel Hill. Some years ago, a portion of this 200-year-old farm was converted into a world-class restaurant that has come to be known for its prix fixe menu and its charming country setting. The village has now grown to include an entire community of specialty shops, a market, a medical center, a bookstore, a flower-and-plant shop, and, perhaps most recognizably, a dairy barn and silo. **McIntyre's**, the outstanding independent bookstore at Fearrington, is known for bringing in distinguished authors such as Jimmy Carter for autographing events. The **Fearrington House Restaurant and Country Hotel** is a member of the international organization Relais & Châteaux and is the recipient of a AAA Five Diamond rating and a Mobil Five Star rating—the only establishment in North Carolina to receive these accolades. Distinctive touches include ecclesiastical doors used as headboards and pine flooring from a workhouse along the Thames. For information about Fearrington Village or to make reservations at the inn, call 919-542-2121 or visit www.fearringtonvillage.com.

Rosemary House Bed-and-Breakfast is a 1912 Colonial Revival home at 76 West Street in the heart of Pittsboro. It offers five comfortable guest rooms with private baths, data ports, cable television, fireplaces, and two-person whirlpools. The inn serves a full gourmet breakfast. For more information, call 888-643-2017 or 919-542-5515 or visit www.rosemary-bb.com.

The **General Store Café**, at 39 West Street in Pittsboro, is a great place to visit neighbors and catch up on Chatham County news. It's also the ideal spot to pick up herbal elixirs, teas, a few groceries, and breakfast or lunch. Vegetarians will be pleased with the "Tofu Eggless Salad Sandwich" and other such offerings, and everybody will be happy with the yummy desserts and homemade scones. In addition, you can also pick up a map of the 50-plus studios and galleries in Pittsboro and the surrounding area. Local artists—potters, sculptors, painters, jewelers, glass workers and blowers, ironworkers, and others—can be accessed through the **Chatham County Arts Council**. If you attend the grand studio tour in December, you'll be able to do some holiday shopping that will make everyone on your list happy. To contact the arts council, call 919-542-0394; to contact the General Store Café, call 919-542-2432.

For a good hike or an afternoon outdoors, visit the **White Pines Nature Preserve**, on River Fork Road south of Pittsboro. The preserve is the jewel of the Triangle Land Conservancy. The Rocky River and Deep River border the preserve and provide a cool microclimate for the white pines and other mountain plant populations that thrive here. Five trails offer hours of hiking and beautiful views of the rivers and the preserve. The Triangle Land Conservancy also owns and maintains four other preserves in the area that are open to the public; for information, call 919-833-3662 or visit www.tlc-nc.org.

Be sure to visit Pittsboro's neighbor Moncure. *Moncure Chessworks*, at 739 Old U.S. 1, is a unique art gallery that features large sculptures of chessboard pieces. For those not particularly enamored with the game of chess, the gallery displays other interesting sculptures as well. Call 919-542-0516 or visit www.thechessworks.com.

The Rocks, at 535-A Old Sanford Road in Moncure, offers visitors the chance to experience the thrill of gemstone mining and gold panning. If you're lucky, you'll strike it rich. But don't worry if you're having a dry spell; just check out the on-site gift shop, where you can purchase mineral specimens, custom jewelry, and more. The Rocks is open Monday through Saturday from 10 A.M. to 5 P.M.; call 919-542-6112 or visit www.ncgems.com.

■ You can round out your visit to Chatham County with a trip to Siler City. While you're there, be sure to visit the **grave site of Aunt Bee**. *The Andy Griffith Show* was a long-running sitcom based on the North Carolina town of Mount Airy. One of the country's most endearing character actors, Frances E. Bavier played Aunt Bee until the show ended in 1968. In 1972, she retired to a two-story brick home on West Elk Street in Siler City, a town she had often visited. After her death in 1989, the Emmy-winning actress was buried in Oakwood Cemetery. For more information, call 800-316-3829.

Mount Vernon Springs, located on S.R. 1134 in Siler City, is the 122-acre site of a once-active health spa and hotel. Between 1881 and 1920, visitors flocked to the 50-room resort for a regenerative dip in one of the twin springs, named "Health" and "Beauty." Later, the mineral water was bottled and sold around the country. Today, Mount Vernon Springs is listed on the National Register of Historic Places. Clear drinking water still flows from the sister springs. For more information, call 800-316-3829.

Weary travelers shouldn't miss the *Inn at Celebrity Dairy* in Siler City, which dates to the 1820s. The inn offers seven rooms and a suite. Sheltered on a gentle knoll under 250-year-old oak trees, it actually encompasses two buildings—a modern Greek Revival farmhouse skirted by wide porches and the original settlers' 1800 log cabin. The surrounding outbuildings include the original log hay barn and granary, an 1880s smokehouse, 1940s tobacco barns, and a goat dairy. The famous goats here provide cheese to many of the finest stores and restaurants in the

Triangle. Guests are served a hearty breakfast—fresh goat cheese, home-made preserves, fresh eggs, and seasonal fruits and vegetables. For information, call 877-742-5176 or visit www.celebritydairy.com.

■ Lovers of fine crafts will enjoy a short trip north of the Triangle to Granville County, where they'll find the **Cedar Creek Gallery**, located at 1150 Fleming Road in Creedmoor. This gallery, owned and operated by craftspeople, is a winner of the North Carolina Governor's Award for Excellence in the Arts and Humanities. Cedar Creek Gallery draws pilgrims from all over, who come to see the work of over 200 artists, many of whom have work displayed in permanent national collections such as the Smithsonian and the Chrysler Museum. You'll see stoneware, quilts, baskets, jewelry, furniture, candles, wind chimes, musical instruments, and other items. The gallery is open seven days a week from 10 A.M. to 6 P.M. For more information, call 919-528-1041 or visit www.cedarcreekgallery.com.

■ *Falls Lake State Recreation Area* has its headquarters at 13304 Creedmoor Road in the community of Wake Forest, 10 miles north of Raleigh. Falls Lake offers outdoor recreation at seven facilities on its 38,000 acres of woodlands and lake in Wake and Durham counties. RV and tent sites, primitive sites, and sites for group camping are available year-round. Visitors also come for the swimming, the picnic facilities, the hiking trails, and the interpretative programs. A privately managed concessionaire, **Rollingview Marina**, offers boat launching, slips, mooring, rentals, and supplies. The recreation area is open from 8 A.M. to 6 P.M. November through February, from 8 A.M. to 7 P.M. during March and October, from 8 A.M. to 8 P.M. in April and September, and from 8 A.M. to 9 P.M. May through August. For more information, call 919-676-1027 or visit http://ils.unc.edu/parkproject/visit/fala/home.html.

The Sandhills

Fayetteville

Pinehurst and Southern Pines

By John Tarleton

The Cape Fear River helps create the temperate climate that has long drawn tourists to the Sandhills. In the late 19th century, the Sandhills were a retreat for those seeking wellness through a change of climate. Now, the area is a haven for golfers from all over the country. Pinehurst and Southern Pines boast more than 40 championship courses woven among the area's longleaf forests. Large tracts of farmland and the temperate climate have also made the area a site for equestrian shows and competitions of all kinds. Even in the winter, you'll spot trotters and pacers training on some of the stately farms. Come spring, the big shows are at full canter.

In the 19th century, nearby Fayetteville was an inland port and a hub of the system of plank roads used for overland travel. It was here that Congress later established an artillery training facility called Camp Bragg, where it could lengthen the training season during World War I. Today, Fort Bragg and Pope Air Force Base make up one of the world's largest military installations. Fort Bragg is the home of the 82nd Airborne and Special Operations units, while the 43rd Airlift Wing calls Pope Air Force Base its headquarters. For military enthusiasts, this town is a dream come true, offering a number of museums dedicated to telling the story of the American fighting man. Fayetteville, which narrowly lost out to Raleigh when the state capital was named, has much to offer history aficionados. The city boasts nearly 60 structures on the National Register of Historic Places. And the promise of good weather means your walking tour won't be rained out.

Cameo Art House Theatre
COURTESY OF FAYETTEVILLE AREA CONVENTION AND VISITORS BUREAU

FAYETTEVILLE

By John Tarleton

*T*he most recent push to soften Fayetteville's image from that of a town full of roughneck GI's has resulted in a new community slogan: "History. Heroes. And a Hometown Feeling." This resident-led effort aims to develop a stronger sense of community pride and a more harmonious relationship with the two military bases in the area—Fort Bragg, home of the 82nd Airborne and Special Operations units, and Pope Air Force Base, home of the 43rd Airlift Wing. This time, the town may have hit its mark.

History of all kinds is easy to spot in Fayetteville. The city boasts nearly 60 structures listed on the National Register of Historic Places, including houses, railroad stations, taverns, churches, and even a university; Fayetteville State University is the second-oldest school in the state, after the University of North Carolina at Chapel Hill. You'll also find a community rich in both Native American culture and African-American culture.

The city has a long military history. During the Revolutionary War, British general Charles Cornwallis camped outside what is now Fayetteville on his way to meet Washington's army at Yorktown. In fact, the city was named after the French hero of the Revolution, the Marquis de Lafayette, who visited the area in 1825, long after the conflict. From that point, Fayetteville's military history has only grown richer. Fort Bragg was established in 1918, and what is now Pope Air Force Base was organized the following year.

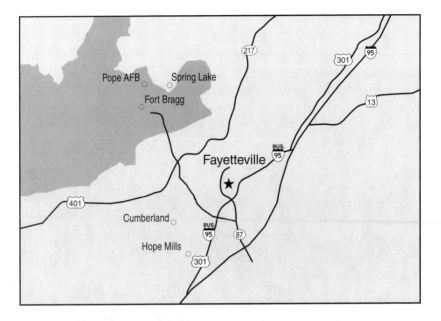

But Fayetteville's legacy extends beyond its military ties. The city boasts some of the oldest architecture in North Carolina, even though two large fires swept through the town and destroyed over 600 of its buildings. The historic Market House was constructed in 1832 on the site of the old state-house, where several landmark events—including the ratification of the United States Constitution in 1789 and the chartering of the country's first state-funded university, the University of North Carolina—took place.

Fayetteville's fondness for its heroes is apparent. A life-sized bronze statue of the Marquis de Lafayette stands in Cross Creek Park on Green Street. Not far away, at the corner of Randolph and Armistead, is a heroic effigy affectionately known as "Iron Mike," a giant monument to American paratroopers dropped in desolate places worlds away. One of the primary functions of the new Airborne and Special Operations Museum is to glorify the men and women of those elite units. As a mark of respect for another group of brave men, the 35 who earned the Victory Cross, the JFK Special Warfare Museum has a Hall of Heroes. The museum honors Special Operations units from World War II to the present and focuses heavily on Vietnam and the development of the Green Berets.

If Fayetteville doesn't strike you as a place imbued with hometown feeling, maybe you should look again. Its special events include all-American activities such as fishing and horseback riding. Or maybe you'll prefer the parades and street festivals that capture the same esprit de corps. One such festival honors North Carolina's state flower, the dogwood, and another contributes its proceeds to the North Carolina Burn Center, truly exemplifying a community spirit.

So try and look beyond Fayetteville's battle-hardened surface. You'll start to see the thinking behind the town's new slogan. Enjoy your stay. A trip to Fayetteville promises a whole slew of things to see and do, from touring historic landmarks to shopping for antiques and fine pottery to museum-hopping. With the right attitude, you'll come away with a greater appreciation for the city and quite likely a renewed sense of patriotism.

JUST THE FACTS

Fayetteville is located just east of Interstate 95 roughly 26 miles south of Interstate 40. It can be reached via U.S. 401, N.C. 24, or N.C. 87.

Fayetteville Regional Airport is just south of the city, off Interstate 95 Business. For information, call 910-433-1160.

The Greyhound/Trailways bus station is located at 324 Person Street. Call 910-483-2580.

Over 300,000 residents live in Cumberland County, nearly 113,000 of them in Fayetteville, the county seat. Fayetteville is the sixth-largest city in North Carolina and the fourth-largest metropolitan area. About 50,000 Cumberland County residents are members of the armed forces stationed at Fort Bragg or Pope Air Force Base.

The daily newspaper is the *Fayetteville Observer-Times*. *Paraglide* is the official newspaper of Fort Bragg and Pope Air Force Base. You can find information and show times in the free publication *Up and Coming*. Fayetteville has approximately 1,500 retails shops and 400 restaurants.

The Fayetteville Area Convention and Visitors Bureau is located at 245 Person Street. Signs provide clear directions from Interstate 95; once you're there, you can use the convenient drive-through window. The bureau is open Monday through Friday from 8 A.M. to 5 P.M. and Saturday from 10 A.M. to 4 P.M. For information, call 800-255-8217 or 910-483-5311 or check out www.visitfayettevillenc.com.

Things to Do

HISTORIC PLACES, GARDENS, AND TOURS

- The *Atlantic Coast Line Railroad Station*, at 472 Hay Street, is a rare example of Dutch Colonial architecture. Parts of the station date to World War I. Today, the Amtrak passenger station and the Atlantic Coast Line Depot Railroad Historical Center are housed at the site. For more information, call 910-433-1612.

- *Cape Fear Botanical Garden*, at 536 North Eastern Boulevard (U.S. 301/Interstate 95 Business), sits at the confluence of the Cape Fear River and Cross Creek. The 85-acre garden contains an old-growth forest and over 2,000 specimens of ornamental plants, making it a beautiful attraction year-round. The signature camellia garden boasts over 200 named varieties of camellias. It and other formal gardens are marked with signs that provide both historical and horticultural information. A restored 100-year-old farmhouse and its outbuildings help illustrate the local lifestyle of a century past. An admission fee is charged; reduced rates are offered for military personnel, retired persons, and children under 12. The garden is open from 10 A.M. to 5 P.M. Monday through Saturday and from noon to 5 P.M. on Sunday. For more information, call 910-486-0221 or visit www.capefearbg.org.

- *Cool Spring Tavern*, at 119 North Cool Spring Street, is thought to have been built in 1788. It is one of the few remaining Federal-style buildings in Fayetteville. Having survived the great fire of 1831, it is believed to be the oldest structure in the city. The tavern was built in a failed attempt to entice the men deliberating the location of the new state capital. The decision fell to Raleigh, of course. For more information about the tavern, call 910-433-1612.

- *Cross Creek Cemetery #1*, on Cool Spring Street, is one of the few cemeteries in the country listed on the National Register of Historic Places. It contains some of the remarkable masonry of famed Scottish artist George Lauder and the graves of many Confederate and Union soldiers, as well as that of Lauder himself. For more information, call 910-433-1612.

- *Evans Metropolitan AME Zion Church*, at 301 North Cool Spring

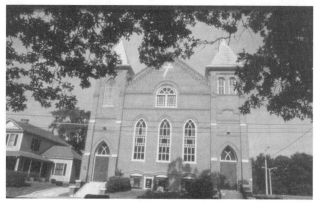

Evans Metropolitan AME Zion Church
COURTESY OF FAYETTEVILLE AREA CONVENTION AND VISITORS BUREAU

Street, was established around 1800 by the Reverend Henry Evans, a free black shoemaker and preacher who was passing through Fayetteville on his way to Charleston and decided to stay. His ministry served both black and white members until the founding of the predominantly white Hay Street Methodist Episcopal Church in the early 1830s. The current Gothic-style building, which dates to 1893-94, is a monument to the craftsmanship of African-American artisans James Williams and Joseph Steward. The church is open by appointment. For more information, call 910-483-2862 or visit www.evansmetropolitan.org.

■ *Liberty Point*, at Bow and Person streets, is the site where, on June 20, 1775, some 55 patriots signed what is generally known as the Liberty Point Resolves, a petition declaring independence from Great Britain. A granite stone notes the names of the patriots and their pledge to their country at that historic meeting: "We stand ready to sacrifice our lives to secure her freedom." The building at this site, constructed between 1791 and 1800, is the oldest known commercial structure in Fayetteville. For more information, call 910-433-1612.

■ The *Market House*, at the intersection of Green, Gillespie, Person, and Hay streets, was built in 1832 on the foundation of the old statehouse, which burned in the fire of 1831. Within the walls of the statehouse, North Carolina ratified the United States Constitution in 1789 and chartered the University of North Carolina. It was also there that North Carolina ceded its western lands to form the state of Tennessee. The Market House is listed on the National Register of Historic Places. Its ground floor was used as a market for many years, and its upper level housed the town hall. The clock still chimes at 7:30 A.M. for breakfast, at 1 P.M. for dinner, at sundown, and at 9 P.M., which was once the local curfew.

■ **St. John's Episcopal Church**, at 302 Green Street, was rebuilt after the 1831 fire in basically the same design as the original structure, with a big exception—10 pyramidal spires replaced the single spire that had topped the church. The extraordinary stained-glass windows, imported from Munich, Germany, are said to have been carried by oxcart from New York; they were installed around the turn of the 20th century. For more information, call 910-483-7405 or visit www.fayettevilleonline.com/stjohns.

■ **St. Joseph's Episcopal Church**, at Ramsey and Moore streets, was established in 1873 by the black members of St. John's Episcopal Church with the assistance of that church's rector, the Reverend Joseph Caldwell Huske. Built in the Shingle style with Gothic and Spanish influences, it is notable for the five exquisite "Resurrection windows" by Tiffany and for its pipe organ, built in 1857 by Henry Erben of New York. The organ, purchased from St. John's for $100, has been powered by hand, water, gas, and now electricity. It is one of the oldest still in use in the country. The church is open by appointment. For information, call 910-323-0161 or visit www.stjoseph-episcopal.org.

MUSEUMS AND SCIENCE CENTERS

■ The **Airborne and Special Operations Museum**, at 100 Bragg Boulevard, opened in 2000 and is one of the area's premier attractions. Its state-of-the-art educational facilities house exhibits highlighting the feats of Airborne and Special Operations units from 1940 to the present. The museum features graphic coverage of combat missions; extensive displays of uniforms, insignia, and weapons; and information on Airborne songs, marches, and customs. It includes a 250-seat Vistascope theater, a 24-seat Vista-Dome simulator, the Hall of Honors, and a main exhibit gallery. Admission is free, though guests must purchase tickets for the theater and the simulator. The museum is open Tuesday through Saturday from 10 A.M. to 5 P.M. and Sunday from noon to 5 P.M. For information, call 866-547-0649 or visit www.asomf.org.

■ **Fascinate-U Children's Museum** is located at 116 Green Street, next to the Market House. This fun interactive museum allows kids to explore

the world around them through creative role-playing. Exhibits include a grocery store, a bank, and a newsroom. The museum is open Tuesday, Thursday, and Friday from 9 A.M. to 5 P.M., Wednesday from 9 A.M. to 7 P.M., Saturday from 10 A.M. to 5 P.M., and Sunday from noon to 5 P.M. An admission fee is charged. For more information, call 910-829-9171 or visit www.fascinate-u.com.

■ The *Fayetteville Museum of Art*, at 839 Stamper Road, was founded in 1971. Originally housed in the Market House, it moved in 1978 to its present facility, which has the distinction of being the first building in North Carolina designed and built as an art museum. The museum includes two galleries, classrooms, studio space, a library that lends art reference materials and slides, and a museum store. The 5.8-acre grounds and pond offer visitors a place to relax. This parklike setting, an oasis in the midst of a heavily trafficked area, is the site of large-scale sculpture displays, art festivals, and public concerts. Admission is free, though donations are appreciated. The museum is open from 10 A.M. to 5 P.M. on weekdays and from 1 P.M. to 5 P.M. on Saturday and Sunday. For more information, call 910-485-5121 or visit www.fayettevillemuseumart.org.

■ The *JFK Special Warfare Museum*, located in Building D-2502 at Ardennes and Marion streets, offers a behind-the-scenes look at unconventional warfare. The museum houses weapons, military art, and international cultural items with an emphasis on Special Operations units from World War II to the present. Visitors will find displays covering the evolution of the unconventional warrior, beginning with the Indian scouts of the American West. Exhibits from World War II, Korea, and Vietnam explain the development of the Green Berets. Most exhibits pertain to Vietnam. The heart of the collection is a model of the Son Tay prisoner-of-war camp. In 1970, Colonel Arthur D. "Bull" Simons organized and led a daring attempt to rescue 107 POWs held there. Sadly, the prisoners had been moved before the rescuers arrived. The display explains that the attempt was not in vain, though; the prisoners were still years away from freedom, but their living conditions did improve after the raid. A gift shop is on the premises. Admission to the museum is free. It is open from 11 A.M. to 4 P.M. Tuesday through Sunday; it is closed on Monday except for federal holidays. For more information, call 910-432-4272 or visit www.soc.mil/swcs/museum/museum.shtml.

■ The *Museum of the Cape Fear Historical Complex*, at 801 Arsenal Avenue, combines a modern museum building, the 1897 Poe House (yes, that's E. A. Poe, but this Poe was a potter), and the eerie remains of the Fayetteville Arsenal. The museum and the arsenal site are open for self-guided tours; visitors receive a guided tour of the Poe House upon arrival. There is a gift shop in the museum proper. Admission is free. The complex is open from 10 A.M. to 5 P.M. Tuesday through Saturday and from 1 P.M. to 5 P.M. on Sunday. For information, call 910-486-1330 or visit www.ncmuseumofhistory.org/mcf.html.

■ The *82nd Airborne Division War Memorial Museum*, at Ardennes and Gela streets, houses over 3,000 artifacts from World War I through Operation Desert Storm. The exhibits include weapons, helmets, uniforms, photographs, aircraft, parachutes, and other items. A film is shown each hour. The gift shop sells out-of-the-ordinary keepsakes. Admission to the museum is free. It is open Tuesday through Saturday from 10 A.M. to 4:30 P.M.; it is closed Sunday and Monday except for federal holidays. For information, call 910-432-3443 or 910-436-1735.

CULTURAL OFFERINGS

■ *Cameo Art House Theatre*, at 225 Hay Street, shows a variety of classic, independent, and foreign films in a beautifully restored 1920s theater open seven nights a week. For show times, call 910-486-6633 or visit www.cameoarthouse.com.

■ The award-winning *Cape Fear Regional Theatre*, at 1209 Hay Street, has been around for nearly four decades. Local, regional, and national performers present theatrical premieres, elaborate musicals, classic dramas, comedies, and children's favorites in an intimate 325-seat theater. The group's Studio Performing Arts Program offers courses in acting, voice, and audition techniques for ages eight through adult. For a list of upcoming shows, call 910-323-4233 or visit www.cfrt.org.

■ The *Fayetteville Symphony Orchestra* performs several concerts a year at Reeves Auditorium, Crown Theatre, and Seabrook Auditorium. For information, call 910-433-4690 or visit www.fayettevillesymphony.org.

■ The *Gilbert Theater* is located at 301 Hay Street. For over a decade, it has provided quality theatrical productions for children, the elderly, minorities, and the economically disadvantaged while at the same time giving local artists a venue for displaying their diverse talents. The company has produced classics, thought-provoking works such as *How I Learned to Drive*, children's puppet shows, and original local and regional plays. The Gilbert Theater involves students whenever possible, both on stage and off. For more information, call 910-678-7186 or visit www.gilberttheater.com.

SPECIAL SHOPPING

■ *Cape Fear Studios*, at 148-1 Maxwell Street in the downtown area, is a nonprofit art gallery and studio where local artists and craftsmen sell original work such as fine jewelry, pottery, watercolor paintings, pastels, and many other items. For more information, call 910-433-2986 or visit www.capefearstudios.com.

■ *David R. Walters Antiques*, at 1110 Hay Street, specializes in early-20th-century furniture. Antiques and other collectibles are also available. For information, call 910-483-5832.

■ "Antiques with an attitude" describes *Not Quite Antiques*, at 108 Roxie Avenue. The shop specializes in antiques, mid-20th-century items, works by local artists and craftspeople, and unique modern pieces other antique shops may not carry. For more information, call 910-323-0300.

RECREATION

■ The **Crown Center**, at 1960 Coliseum Drive, offers a wide array of entertainment, from concerts, theater productions, and family shows to amateur and professional sports such as hockey, basketball, and indoor football. For a list of upcoming events, call 910-438-4100 or visit www.crowncoliseum.com.

■ Fishermen should check out the 500-foot pier at **Lakeview Park Fishing Pier and Campground**, located at 377 Waldo's Beach Road; for information, call 910-424-4814. A couple of boat ramps are located along the Cape Fear River, one at the junction of U.S. 301 and Old N.C. 87 and the other at **Riverside Sports Center**, at 1122 Person Street. Fort Bragg has 13 lakes that are open to the public, including **Muddy Lake, Little Muddy Lake**, and **Mott Lake**; for more information, call 910-396-7506.

■ **Smith Lake Riding Stables**, on Smith Lake Road, offers pony rides, riding lessons, trail rides, and hayrides. Advance notice is required for groups of 10 or more. For more information, call 910-396-4510 or visit www.fortbraggmwr.com/sportsrec/ridingstables/ridingstables.htm.

■ **Smith Lake Recreation Area**, at 129 Smith Lake Road, offers swimming, picnicking, mountain biking, camping, volleyball and basketball courts, sandy beaches, paintball games, paddleboats, and a water-ski shop. For more information, call 910-396-5979.

SEASONAL EVENTS

■ The **Dogwood Festival**, held at 301 Hay Street every April, includes an array of activities, the premier event being a drive along the 18-mile **Dogwood Trail**, which winds through the downtown historic district and among beautiful residential areas. Symphony performances, rodeos, and street dancing take place all around Fayetteville to celebrate the thousands of blooming dogwoods, azaleas, daffodils, and camellias. For more information, call 910-323-1934 or visit www.fayettevilledogwoodfestival.com.

■ The **Holly Day Fair**, held in late November at the Crown Center, is a one-stop holiday shopping event that draws about 21,000 visitors. Sponsored by the Junior League of Fayetteville, this is the largest holiday gift-and-craft show in eastern North Carolina. You can choose from an extensive selection of unique handcrafted and manufactured gifts such as Christmas decorations, crafts, jewelry, clothes, toys, food specialties, household accents, and more. For information, call 910-323-5509 or visit www.hollydayfair.com.

- The *International Folk Festival* has been named one of the top 20 events in the southeastern United States by the Southeast Tourism Society. Held each September on Hay Street in downtown Fayetteville, it pays homage to the region's diverse cultures. Visitors enjoy a smorgasbord of international foods, an eclectic array of world entertainment, and the highlight—the Parade of Nations. For more information, call the Arts Council of Fayetteville/Cumberland County at 910-323-1776.

- The *Statewide Indian Cultural Festival* is held at the Crown Center in October. For two days, this indoor event, sponsored by the Cumberland County Association for Indian People, promotes and celebrates Native American values and customs. For more information, call 910-323-5088.

Statewide Indian Cultural Festival
COURTESY OF FAYETTEVILLE AREA CONVENTION AND VISITORS BUREAU

International Folk Festival
COURTESY OF FAYETTEVILLE AREA CONVENTION AND VISITORS BUREAU

Places to Stay

RESORTS, HOTELS, AND MOTELS

- **Clarion Prince Charles**. Moderate. 450 Hay Street (910-433-4444; www.choicehotels.com). If you want to stay downtown, your choice is pretty much limited to the Clarion Prince Charles. Built in 1924, this beautiful building is listed on the National Register of Historic Places and is a member of the Historic Hotels of America. It's just around the corner from many of the city's historic sites and is a good base if you're interested in a walking tour. Considered one of the finest Colonial Revival structures in Fayetteville, it features exquisite marble floors and staircases, arched Palladian windows and doorways, and beautiful brass railings. Twenty-six oversized guest rooms and 57 luxurious two-room suites are available, all filled with custom period furniture. This is as close to a bed-and-breakfast as you'll find in Fayetteville. A full-service restaurant and an exercise room are on the premises.

- **Comfort Inn Cross Creek**. Moderate. 1922 Skibo Road (910-867-1777). Located near the mall, the Comfort Inn offers 176 rooms and suites, Jacuzzis, an outdoor pool, and complimentary breakfast. It has been awarded a Three Diamond rating by AAA.

- **Holiday Inn Bordeaux**. Moderate. 1707 Owen Drive (800-325-0211 or 910-323-0111; www.ichotelsgroup.com/h/d/HI/hd/fayow). This hotel has over 300 rooms. Children stay free. Amenities include 30,000 square feet of meeting space, a concierge, dry-cleaning service, complimentary shuttle service to the airport or the bus or train station, a full-service restaurant, a sports bar, a nightclub, and an outdoor pool.

Places to Eat

- **The Barn of Fayetteville**. Expensive. 1021 Bragg Boulevard (910-678-0686). This fine-dining restaurant specializes in traditional and unique Italian dishes. It offers a full menu of veal, pasta, steaks, chicken, and fresh seafood. The Barn of Fayetteville is open daily for lunch and dinner.

- **Trio Café**. Expensive/Moderate. 201 South McPherson Church Road (910-868-2443). This fine-dining favorite sports an uptown look. The herb-crusted rack of lamb, the blackened tuna, and the oysters Rockefeller are popular. Stop by on Wednesday night for one of the weekly wine-tasting events. Dinner is served nightly.

- **Highlander Café & Pub**. Moderate. 1217 Hay Street (910-485-4777). This Scottish establishment offers traditional pub dishes. It is open daily for lunch and dinner.

- **Hilltop House Restaurant**. Moderate. 1240 Fort Bragg Road (910-484-6699). This beautiful old restaurant is located in historic Haymount right across from the Cape Fear Regional Theatre. For 70 years, it has served up steaks, seafood, and Greek specialties at a reasonable rate. Lunch and dinner are served daily; brunch is served on Sunday.

- **Huske Hardware House**. Moderate/Inexpensive. 405 Hay Street (910-437-9905). This place is worth the trip just to see the building. The 100-year-old structure holds rich significance for Fayetteville. At the time it was built, it was called "Major Huske's Folly" because it was so far from the Market House. Proving his critics wrong, the major went on to open six hardware stores, all bearing the initials *HHH*. Now a brewery and restaurant, Huske Hardware House sits in a prime location for visitors to the Airborne and Special Operations Museum. It offers such dishes as "Filet Tips" and tomato-basil shrimp, as well as some vegetarian fare, preferably served alongside its signature Airborne Ale. Live music is offered. Lunch is served daily and dinner Monday through Saturday.

- **Mash House Restaurant & Brewery**. Inexpensive. 4150 Sycamore Dairy Road (910-867-9223; www.themashhouse.com). This microbrewery has won medals at some of the largest beer festivals in the world. And its Kobe beef burgers, wood-fired pizzas, lunch specials, and late-night munchies are great accessories to the beer. The Mash House is open daily for lunch and dinner.

Bentonville Battleground
COURTESY OF NORTH CAROLINA DIVISION OF TOURISM, FILM AND SPORTS DEVELOPMENT

Nearby

■ ***Bentonville Battleground*** is located approximately one hour northeast of Fayetteville; take U.S. 701 to S.R. 1008. Bentonville is the site of the last great Confederate charge of the Civil War and the largest battle ever fought in North Carolina. The Battle of Bentonville, which took place in March 1865 between General Joseph Johnston's Confederate troops and General William T. Sherman's Union men, ended with 2,500 casualties for the South and 1,500 for the North. The battlefield is now a state historic site that includes a Confederate cemetery, Union trenches, a visitor center, and monuments. It is open Monday through Saturday from 9 A.M. to 5 P.M. and Sunday from 1 P.M. to 5 P.M. Admission is free. For more information, call 910-594-0789 or visit www.bentonvillebattlefield.nchistoricsites.org.

■ The ***National Hollerin' Contest*** is held the third Saturday in June at the Spivey's Corner Volunteer Fire Department in Spivey's Corner, located northeast of Fayetteville at the junction of U.S. 13 and U.S. 421. Hollerin' is an old custom of fieldworkers in the rural South, handed down from generation to generation. The National Hollerin' Contest is a living celebration of Sampson County, its history, and its people. Admission is charged. For more information, call 910-567-2600 or visit www.hollerincontest.com.

PINEHURST AND SOUTHERN PINES

By John Tarleton

Sometime in the mid- to late 1800s, a collective hysteria formed in the minds of the upper middle class. They came to think their health was failing. What followed was a preoccupation with sicknesses, both real and imagined, that led to a search for radical detoxification. People looked to Mother Nature for antidotes—sea salt, mineral water, clean mountain mists. During this "Great Age of Inland Spas," savvy land developers sought to tap into the health craze by promoting some tracts of land as having the power to heal whatever ailed a body.

At least one such visionary saw the Sandhills as just the sort of place where the infirm might spend a few days recovering from the pollutants of Northern city life. After all, the sandy pine bluffs of the area didn't seem fit for much else. Only the most resilient Scottish farmers took on the challenge of cultivating the nutrient-poor soil they'd found in early Moore County, often called "the Pine Barrens" back then. Longleaf pines were truly the only things that seemed to thrive here—perhaps a fact not wasted on John Patrick, the state's commissioner of immigration, who bought 675 acres in 1883 for less than two dollars an acre in hopes of opening a health resort.

Some called his investment folly. Undeterred, Patrick laid out a town in square blocks and named the streets for Northern states to try to attract visitors from that part of the country. Then he sought the endorsements of doctors on the health benefits of air purified by trees. He advertised in Northern newspapers and brochures, praising the benefits of pine-scented air. New York physician G. H. Saddelson wrote this statement for Patrick: "Where the long leaf pine exists, ozone is generated largely and it has been demonstrated that persons suffering with throat and pulmonary diseases are much benefited when living in an atmosphere impregnated with this gas." Once the seed was planted, Patrick's concept of a health resort took hold, and the town of Southern Pines grew quickly.

John Patrick's health resort brought entrepreneur James Tufts to the Sandhills. He and his son Leonard introduced the Scottish game of golf to sanitarium residents as a cure for boredom. Tufts's purchase of 5,000 or so acres led to the development of Pinehurst Golf Club, and the rest is history.

Today, the area maintains its legacy as a place of tranquility. Despite the cosmopolitan features of the sister towns of Pinehurst and Southern Pines—the lively shops, restaurants, and cultural centers—there's still something therapeutic about the pine-scented air. Just look at the lasting popularity of activities such as golf and equestrian events and you'll see that people still prefer the outdoors to the stale, refrigerated air of the modern indoors.

But there's more to do in Pinehurst and Southern Pines than just play golf and ride horses. Folks here love the arts. You're sure to find a long list of high-caliber cultural events going on at any given time. Residents also support the preservation of their local architecture. While you're in the area, take a guided tour through the historic districts. Landmark sites include private homes, churches, and a historic horse track. And let's not forget the nearby Indian village of Town Creek. You'll also find shopping opportunities that range from pottery outlets and antique galleries to unique gift shops and sprawling malls. And everyone knows that shopping is regenerative to the spirit.

JUST THE FACTS

Southern Pines is approximately four miles south of the intersection of U.S. 1 and U.S. 15/U.S. 501. Pinehurst is four miles to the west, close to the intersection of N.C. 5 and N.C. 2.

Moore County Regional Airport, located at Airport Road and N.C. 22 near Sandhills Community College, offers commuter air service, including daily connecting flights to Charlotte. For information, call 910-692-3212.

Amtrak reservations can be made by calling 800-872-7245. The train stops right in the middle of Southern Pines.

The twice-weekly newspaper in Southern Pines is called *The Pilot*. The local magazine is *Pinehurst: The Magazine of the Sandhills*.

The number for the local chamber of commerce is 910-692-3926. You can contact the Pinehurst, Southern Pines, Aberdeen Area Convention and Visitors Bureau at P.O. Box 2270, 1480 U.S. 15/U.S. 501, Southern Pines, N.C. 28388 (800-346-5362; www.homeofgolf.com).

Pinehurst Harness Track
COURTESY OF PINEHURST, SOUTHERN PINES, ABERDEEN AREA CONVENTION AND VISITORS BUREAU

Things to Do

HISTORIC PLACES, GARDENS, AND TOURS

■ **Pinehurst Harness Track**, on N.C. 5, is listed on the National Register of Historic Places. Horses have long been a feature of the Sandhills. In the early days of the resort, they helped in the construction and care of the golf course and in ferrying guests from the nearby railroad station. Constructed around 1915, the track was the winter home of polo ponies, hunter horses, racehorses, and Standardbreds. Owners, trainers, and resort guests enjoyed friendly competition during the Wednesday matinee programs. Today, Standardbred training occurs from October to May. Track events include spring races, horse shows, and polo matches. The track is operated by the village of Pinehurst. It is open daily year-round from 8 A.M. to dusk. Guided tours are available. For more information, call 800-433-TROT or 910-295-4446 or visit www.pinehurstharness.com.

■ The **Shaw House properties** are located at Morganton Road and Southwest Broad Street in Southern Pines. Listed on the National Register of Historic Places, this trio of early structures depicts the daily life of the area's first settlers. The Shaw House, built around 1840 by Charles Shaw, is nothing like the antebellum plantation homes that usually come to mind. Much less extravagant, it exemplifies sturdy simplicity. The Garner House, built around 1830, is a log structure boasting wide-board heart-pine paneling, original hand-forged hinges, and board doors. The Britt-Sanders Cabin (also known as the Loom House) is a simple one-room pioneer home with a loft. The latter two houses were restored and moved to their present locations by the Moore County Historical Society. All three homes are open Tuesday through Saturday from 1 P.M. to 4 P.M. Admission is free, although donations are welcome. For more information, call 910-692-2051 or visit www.moorehistory.com.

MUSEUMS AND SCIENCE CENTERS

■ *Weymouth Woods Nature Preserve*, at 1024 Fort Bragg Road in Southern Pines, has an exhibit hall that tells visitors about the importance of longleaf pine forests. Its interactive hands-on exhibits cover topics from prescribed burning to the naval-stores industry in the Sandhills. Built in 1978, it was completely renovated in 2001 and again in 2006. The exhibit hall, located in the park's visitor center, is open from 9 A.M. to 6 P.M. daily. Interpretive programs are held in the auditorium at the visitor center every Sunday at 3 P.M. from April through November. Outside, hikers may observe nearly 500 plant species and a number of animals along more than four miles of well-marked, easy-to-hike trails in the wooded nature preserve. Guided tours are offered. The nature preserve is open from 9 A.M. to 6 P.M. every day except Christmas. Admission is free.

Shaw House
COURTESY OF PINEHURST, SOUTHERN PINES, ABERDEEN AREA CONVENTION AND VISITORS BUREAU

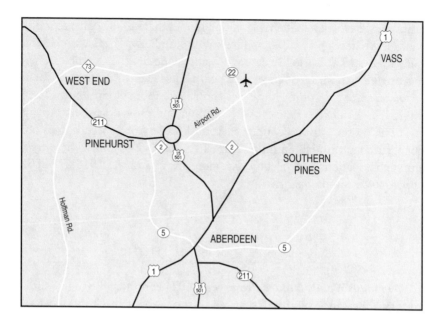

For more information, call 910-692-2167 or visit www.ils.unc.edu/parkproject/visit/wewo/home.html.

CULTURAL OFFERINGS

■ *Campbell House Galleries*, located at 482 East Connecticut Avenue in Southern Pines, is the home of the Arts Council of Moore County. The galleries provide three spacious exhibit areas featuring paintings and pottery for sale by local artists. In addition, tennis and basketball courts and a fitness area are available for public use. The galleries are open from 9 A.M. to 5 P.M. Monday through Friday and from 2 P.M. to 4 P.M. on the third Saturday and Sunday of each month. Admission is free. For more information, call 910-692-4356.

■ The *Sandhills Theatre Company* performs dramas, musicals, and comedies at the Sunrise Theater, located at 250 Northwest Broad Street in Southern Pines. The building, which dates to 1898, is also used for concerts and other programs. For information, call 910-692-3340 or visit www.sandhillstheatre.com; to reach the box office, call 910-692-3799.

■ The *Weymouth Center for the Arts and Humanities*, at 555 East Connecticut Avenue in Southern Pines, has flourished as a cultural center since 1979. Once the home of North Carolina author James Boyd and his wife, Katharine Lamont Boyd, the center is a portion of the house built by the author's grandfather. Upon the elder Boyd's death, grandsons James and Jackson split the house in two. They hauled the main portion by mule across the road, where it became the Jackson Boyd House; now known as the Campbell House, it serves as the home of the Arts Council of Moore County. The portion that became the Weymouth Center was redesigned and enlarged in the 1920s by Aymar Embury II, a friend of the Boyds who went on to become the official architect of Princeton. Then as now, the building served as a center for literary activity, hosting visits from such friends as F. Scott Fitzgerald, Thomas Wolfe, Paul Green, and Sherwood Anderson. Today, the center has a writers-in-residence program that offers writers and composers stays of up to two weeks to pursue their work. Over 600 artists have taken advantage of the opportunity; many testify that they accomplished their most creative work in the tranquil, inspiring atmosphere of the Boyds' former home. All phases of the arts and humanities are included in the Weymouth Center's programs. The concerts offered by the center feature artists from North Carolina's universities, supplemented by nationally and internationally known chamber musicians; local youths are provided an opportunity to participate in a young musicians' competition. The center hosts frequent readings by acclaimed North Carolina writers and a lecture series that brings in a diverse group of speakers. For more information, call 910-692-6261 or visit www.weymouthcenter.org.

SPECIAL SHOPPING

■ *Sandhills Woman's Exchange*, at 15 Azalea Road in Pinehurst, is a co-op shop in a historic log cabin. It offers early-American crafts and baked goods for sale. The store is open September to mid-May. The hours are 10 A.M. to 4 P.M. on weekdays and 11 A.M. to 3 P.M. on Saturday. The tearoom on the premises serves lunch Monday through Friday. For more information, call 910-295-4677 or visit www.sandhillsonline.com/history/womans.htm.

Pinehurst Country Club
COURTESY OF PINEHURST, SOUTHERN PINES, ABERDEEN AREA CONVENTION AND VISITORS BUREAU

RECREATION

Moore County, known as "the Golf Capital of the World," has over 720 golf holes (with 54 more on the drawing board), covering more than 270,000 yards. That's over 153 miles (or 2,700 football fields) of fairways, which are in constant use by the thousands of visitors who come to follow the little white ball. The density of golf-related activities here is said to be the highest in the world. Indeed, the village of Pinehurst and the Pinehurst Resort have been awarded national historic landmark status for their significant role in golf history, the only golf-related designation of its kind in the United States.

Tradition abounds in the land where legends like Jack Nicklaus, Arnold Palmer, Ben Hogan, Sam Snead, and Babe Didrikson Zaharias tested their skills on the finest courses in the world. Nearly 40 championship courses are located in the Sandhills; there is a course suitable for every golfer, regardless of handicap. The courses were laid out by people like Donald Ross (who designed seven local courses), Tom Fazio (who designed four), Robert Trent Jones, Jack Nicklaus, Arnold Palmer, and Gary Player. The area has hosted dozens of major competitions, including the U.S. Women's Open, the U.S. Open, the PGA Championship, the Ryder Cup, and the

World Open, among many others. Most major competitions are staged at Pinehurst No. 2.

What follows is a very brief overview of a few of the finest courses. For more extensive information, visit www.homeofgolf.com.

- **The Carolina**, at 277 Avenue of the Carolinas, is an 18-hole course designed by Arnold Palmer. It opened in 1997 and is available to the public. For more information, call 888-725-6372 or 910-949-2811 or visit www.thecarolina.com.

- **Pinehurst Country Club**, at 1 Carolina Vista Drive, features eight premier courses. The mecca has long been Pinehurst No. 2, built by golf master Donald Ross. Ross, who always considered Pinehurst his home course, once called it "the fairest test of championship golf I have ever designed." Recently, this course hosted the U.S. Open in 1999 and 2005. Access is restricted to members and members' guests. For more information, call 800-487-4653 or 910-295-6811 or visit www.pinehurst.com.

- **Pine Needles Lodge and Golf Club**, at 1005 Midland Road, opened in 1927. It, too, was designed by Donald Ross. This was the site of the U.S. Women's Open in 1996 and 2001. The course is open to the public, based on availability. For more information, call 800-747-7272 or 910-692-7111 or visit www.pineneedles-midpines.com.

- Though golf reigns supreme in the Sandhills, it isn't the only thing to do. Equestrian activities come in a close second. Between rounds of golf, try **Carriage Tours of Pinehurst Village**, which will let you explore the quaint town via horse-drawn carriage while learning local history. From Tuesday through Sunday, day and evening tours depart from the Carolina Hotel and the Magnolia Inn; tours last approximately 30 minutes. For more information, call 910-235-8456. The **McClendon Hills Equestrian Center**, on N.C. 211 in the nearby community of West End, offers horseback riding for children and adults. Call 910-673-4971.

Seasonal Events

One of the first things you'll notice when you visit the area is the abundance of horse farms. Green fields and fences serve as a backdrop to creamy Arabians and grazing, gleaming thoroughbreds. For years, Moore County has been a center for the training of the country's best Standardbred harness horses, trotters, and pacers, in addition to thoroughbreds. The county is home to five past Olympic equestrian champions.

■ The **Carolina Carriage Classic** is held at the Pinehurst track in May. A parade takes place on the Sunday after the classic. For information, call 910-295-4446 or visit www.pinehurstharness.com.

■ The **Carolina Horse Park at Five Points**, on Montrose Road in Aberdeen, is a premier equestrian center offering national and international competitions, including the popular **Stoneybrook Festival and Steeplechase** in April. Situated on what was 250 acres of beautiful farmland, the horse park is approximately 12 miles south of Southern Pines. It offers flat fields perfect for show jumping, dressage, and racing, as well as expansive wooded areas that serve as cross-country courses. Gorgeous hardwoods and longleaf pines have been carefully preserved as part of the development plan. For information, call 910-246-9808 or visit www.carolinahorsepark.com.

■ The entire Moore County area, with its beautiful greenery and rolling terrain, is wonderful for biking. It has been used to train and qualify Olympic bicycle teams and is the site of the **Tour de Moore Century Ride**, which draws cyclists from around the world each Labor Day. The feature race, as the name suggests, is 100 miles around Moore County. Several levels of competition are offered. For information or a map of the course, call 910-692-4494 or visit www.rainbowcycles.com.

Places to Stay

RESORTS, HOTELS, AND MOTELS

■ **Pine Needles Lodge and Golf Club**. Deluxe. On N.C. 2 just off U.S. 1 in Southern Pines (800-747-7272 or 910-692-7111; www.pineneedles-midpines.com). For three generations, the legendary Peggy Kirk Bell and her family have been welcoming guests to Pine Needles Lodge and Golf Club. Here, you'll find the ideal atmosphere in which to improve your golf game, vacation with family and friends, or hold a business function.

Golf Digest has awarded this resort a Four Star rating. You'll play on a Donald Ross course that was the site of the U.S. Women's Open in 1996 and 2001. And when you're not on the course, you'll enjoy the at-home feeling of one of the 11 rustic cabins. The resort offers a bed-and-breakfast option at the 1920s Georgian-style Mid Pines Inn; to reserve a room there, call 910-692-2114.

■ *Pinehurst Resort Hotel*. Deluxe. 1 Carolina Vista Drive in Pinehurst (800-487-4653 or 910-235-8507). This is where it all began in Pinehurst, and it doesn't get any more luxurious. The resort encompasses The Carolina, The Holly Inn, The Manor, and The Villas. It offers a total of 530 rooms, all of which have nightly turn-down service, in-room mini-bars, room service, express checkout, and data ports. Each has access to the concierge desk at The Carolina, which can arrange a host of services. Handicapped-accessible and nonsmoking rooms are available. The resort offers meeting space and health-and-fitness facilities. Recreation options include swimming, fishing, windsurfing, and canoeing. The *Pinehurst Post*, issued weekly to all guests, gives a rundown of the many activities and services at the resort.

■ *Residence Inn by Marriott*. Expensive/Moderate. 105 Bruce Wood Road off U.S. 15/U.S. 501 in Southern Pines (910-693-3400; www.marriott.com). This friendly all-suite hotel is just right for the casually inclined. Its quiet, comfortable suites include living rooms and fully equipped kitchens. The inn offers an outdoor pool, a fitness center, complimentary continental breakfast, and packages at over 40 local golf courses. It is centrally located between Southern Pines and Pinehurst.

INNS AND BED-AND-BREAKFASTS

■ *The Knollwood House*. Deluxe/Expensive. 1495 West Connecticut Avenue in Southern Pines (910-692-9390; www.knollwoodhouse.com). This gracious and stately home, built in 1927 as a holiday retreat for a wealthy Philadelphia family, was totally renovated and artfully restored in 1992. Since then, it has become one of the area's premier bed-and-breakfasts. Set on five acres amid azaleas, holly trees, longleaf pines, and towering magnolias, this English manor-style home is beautifully decorated. It is within easy walking distance of the lovely Southern Pines shopping district. The sunlit garden room, filled with flowering plants and wicker furniture, offers

Magnolia Inn
<small>COURTESY OF PINEHURST, SOUTHERN PINES, ABERDEEN AREA CONVENTION AND VISITORS BUREAU</small>

a view of the back lawn and gazebo and a glimpse of the 14th and 15th fairways of the famous Donald Ross course at Mid Pines. Special golf packages are available.

■ *Magnolia Inn*. Deluxe/Expensive. Magnolia Road in Pinehurst (800-526-5562 or 910-295-6900; www.themagnoliainn.com). This century-old mansion has 11 guest rooms furnished with period antiques. It offers an English pub and an outdoor pool. The location is perfect for a downtown stroll. Golf packages are available.

■ *Old Buggy Bed-and-Breakfast Inn*. Deluxe/Expensive. 301 McReynolds Street in Carthage (910-947-1901; www.oldbuggyinn.com). This lovingly restored Victorian bed-and-breakfast lies in the heart of the Sandhills region. W. T. Jones, president of the Tyson-Jones Buggy Manufacturing Company, built the 6,000-square-foot home for his wife, Florence, in 1897. Today, it stands at the entrance to Carthage's beautiful historic district, only minutes from the Pinehurst and Southern Pines golf resorts. You'll enjoy the inn's fanciful gingerbread trim, extravagant woodwork, old-fashioned wraparound porch, private swimming pool, verandas, and gardens. A gourmet breakfast and afternoon refreshments are provided. The inn offers special Murder Mystery Weekends and Romance Weekends.

Places to Eat

As you might expect, there are many top-notch dining establishments in the area. Each of the resorts has its own first-class restaurant; if you have the wherewithal and the proper attire, you will find excellent food and service at any of them. Here are just a few of the best.

- **Chef Warren's**. Expensive. 215 Northeast Broad Street in Southern Pines (910-692-5240; www.chefwarrens.com). Chef Warren's has a cozy, open kitchen and a mouth-watering menu. This upscale restaurant offers nightly specials, a seasonal menu, and an extensive wine list. It serves locally grown organic products whenever possible. Dinner is served Tuesday through Saturday.

- **The Magnolia Inn**. Expensive. Magnolia and Chinquapin streets in Pinehurst (800-526-5562 or 910-295-6900; www.themagnoliainn.com). Graceful longleaf pines and fragrant magnolias surround this stately old mansion, which lies within easy walking distance of Pinehurst's galleries and shops. Guests have the choice of informal dining in the English-style pub or more formal fare in the restaurant proper. Dinner is served seven nights a week.

- **Dugan's Pub**. Moderate. 2 Market Square in Pinehurst (910-295-3400). This full-service restaurant and pub boasts the largest selection of imported drafts in Pinehurst, as well as a complete wine list. Located in the Village Shops area, Dugan's has a traditional Irish pub upstairs and a second pub downstairs. Live entertainment is offered on Friday and Saturday nights. Lunch and dinner are served daily.

- **Squire's Pub**. Moderate/Inexpensive. 1720 U.S. 1 South in Southern Pines (910-695-1161). A tradition in Southern Pines, Squire's serves Irish fare in a casual pub atmosphere. It offers the usual entrées—shepherd's pie and corned beef and cabbage. It also has a delicious, light trifle. Lunch and dinner are served Monday through Saturday.

Nearby

- **Bethesda Church and Cemetery,** on N.C. 5 (Bethesda Road) in Aberdeen, was built around 1790. Among its points of interest are "the Old Slave Gallery," bullet holes from a Civil War battle, and graves of area pioneer settlers. Listed on the National Register of Historic Places, Bethesda Church and Cemetery hosts an annual homecoming the last weekend in September. Guided tours for groups are available by appointment. Admission is free, although donations are welcome. For more information, call 910-944-1319.

- The **Bryant House** and the **McLendon Cabin,** located at Harris Crossroads in upper Moore County, are two unaltered historic properties that depict early Moore County life. Built around 1820, the Bryant House has two fine mantels and handmade doors. The McLendon Cabin, constructed around 1760, is the county's oldest structure in its original location. The site is about a 15-minute drive from Pinehurst. Guided tours are available. Both structures are open by appointment only. Admission is free, although donations are welcome. For more information, call 910-947-3995 or visit www.moorehistory.com.

- You'll find some of the best pottery shopping in the state along N.C. 705 heading north from Robbins to the **Seagrove** area. Within a 15-mile radius are 80-plus family potteries, many of which have created and sold handcrafted dishes, vases, and other distinctive wares for generations. You may even catch potters busy at their craft, which remains virtually the same as in the 1700s. Shoppers delight in the vast array of hand-thrown, high-fired stoneware and porcelain, traditional low-fired pottery, and innovative and decorative art pottery. Different firing techniques are used, including salt glazing, raku, and wood firing in groundhog kilns. Most studios are open year-round Monday through Saturday. Maps of studio locations are available at many shops. For more information, call 800-346-5362 or visit www.homeofgolf.com.

- If you have time, make the short drive north to **Sanford** in Lee County. Each spring, over 150 potters and 50 artisans and craftsmen converge at the Dennis A. Wicker Civic Center complex at 1801 Nash Street to participate in the **Sanford Pottery Festival.** You'll marvel at the hundreds of exhibits and demonstrations and have a chance to buy some of the finest pottery in the world. For more information, call 919-708-7082 or visit www.sanfordpottery.com.

■ The **House in the Horseshoe**, at 324 Alston House Road west of Sanford and north of Carthage, is so named because of its location in a bend of the Deep River. Now a state historic site, it was built by Phillip Alston in 1772, becoming one of the first big houses along North Carolina's frontier. During the American Revolution, irregular warfare was waged in the back country between bands of Whigs and Tories. Two of the Piedmont's more notable adversaries were Whig colonel Alston and Tory guerrilla David Fanning. One altercation between their followers left Fanning compatriot Kenneth Black beaten to death. At his friend's deathbed, Fanning heard Black name Alston as the man responsible. On Sunday, August 5, 1781, Fanning and his men surrounded Alston's house, trapping the colonel, his family, and a couple dozen of Alston's militia. When a British officer in the company of Fanning tried to lead a charge, he was shot dead. The direct approach having proved fatal, Fanning's men remained well covered. Shots were fired back and forth for hours, neither side gaining an advantage. As the day wore on, Fanning tried another approach. His men pushed a cart filled with hay to the side of the house, the intent being to set the hay on fire and burn Alston's home down around him. Alston's men frantically debated how they might surrender without being shot in the process. Mrs. Alston, confident that no one would fire upon a woman, took matters into her own hands. Bravely stepping into the yard, she told Fanning that the men inside would lay down their arms if Fanning agreed not to harm them or the house. Fanning agreed after receiving a promise that Alston and his men would not again take up arms in support of the Revolution.

The house is still riddled with bullet holes today. A reenactment of the skirmish is conducted the first weekend in August. From April through September, the site is open from 9 A.M. to 5 P.M. Tuesday through Saturday and from 1 P.M. to 5 P.M. on Sunday. From October through March, it is open from 10 A.M. to 4 P.M. Tuesday through Saturday. Admission is free. For more information, call 910-947-2051 or visit www.ah.dcr.state.nc.us/sections/hs/horsesho/horsesho.htm.

■ **Town Creek Indian Mound**, at 509 Town Creek Mound Road in Mount Gilead, is about an hour west of Pinehurst on N.C. 731 off N.C. 73. One of the best reconstructions of pre-white civilization in the country, Town Creek is also the oldest state historic site in North Carolina. Visitors here get a glimpse of pre-Columbian life in the Piedmont. The visitor center

Town Creek Indian Mound
COURTESY OF NORTH CAROLINA DIVISION OF TOURISM, FILM AND SPORTS DEVELOPMENT

offers interpretive exhibits and audiovisual programs that bring alive a rich cultural heritage from the buried past. Self-guided tours allow visitors to examine the rebuilt structures and mound. The site includes a museum, two temples, a burial house, and a reconstructed palisade wall. Town Creek is open Tuesday through Saturday from 10 A.M. to 4 P.M. and Sunday from 1 P.M. to 4 P.M. Admission is free. For more information, call 910-439-6802 or visit www.ah.dcr.state.nc.us/sections/hs/town/town.htm.

The Triad

Winston-Salem

Greensboro

High Point

Triad Nearby

By Anne Holcomb Waters and Carolyn Sakowski

To people who are not North Carolina residents, it can be confusing to keep the Triad and the Triangle straight. The Piedmont Triad actually covers an area greater than the three cities—Greensboro, High Point, and Winston-Salem—that are usually associated with the name. Technically, the Triad encompasses a 12-county area that runs from the Yadkin River on the west to the Haw River on the east and from the Virginia border on the north to the start of the Sandhills to the south.

The concept of a Triad region came to light in the mid-1960s, when elected officials from the area's county and municipal governments met to discuss common concerns. They adopted the name Piedmont Triad Committee. As best as can be determined, this was the first time the word *Triad* was used to describe the area. In 1987, the name of the airport was changed to Piedmont Triad International Airport. The name seems to have caught on with the people. The Greensboro telephone

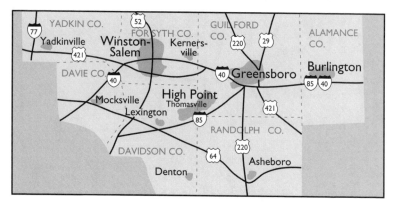

book lists over 130 businesses or organizations with Triad in their names; the Winston-Salem telephone book lists over 120.

Although local governments and chambers of commerce try to work together on issues of mutual concern, old rivalries die hard. The cities have been pitted against each other in recruiting wars for too long. So much friction exists between Greensboro and High Point that at one point High Point wanted to secede from Guilford County and form a new county. Fortunately, the newcomers who are arriving in the area in droves don't know about the old battle lines, so cooperation among the communities seems to be on the rise. Thousands of Triad couples have one partner working in one city and the other in another, further diminishing the old lines.

Today, due to the state's increased visibility in technology-related industries, the Piedmont Triad is drawing more and more people and businesses. Greensboro, its largest city, has a population of over 230,000. A city that owes much of its economic base to textiles, it is now home to several colleges and universities. Boasting a population of over 212,000, Winston-Salem is the second-largest city in the region. Although it owes much of its prosperity to tobacco, Winston-Salem has now become a leader in the medical field. The home of both the country's first arts council and the North Carolina School of the Arts, it is also known as "the City of the Arts." High Point has a population of over 93,000. Known internationally as a furniture capital, it attracts thousands of people to its showrooms. Altogether, the entire 12-county area claims a population of approximately a million.

With the mountains less than two hours distant and the beaches only four hours away, this region becomes more attractive with each passing year.

PHOTOGRAPH IN BACKGROUND OF PREVIOUS PAGE—
Statue of Nathanael Greene
COURTESY OF GREENSBORO AREA CONVENTION AND VISITORS BUREAU

Downtown Winston-Salem
COURTESY OF NORTH CAROLINA DIVISION OF TOURISM, FILM AND SPORTS
DEVELOPMENT

WINSTON-SALEM

By Anne Holcomb Waters

s is reflected in its hyphenated name, Winston-Salem has always been a city that throws together opposites and comes out stronger as a result. In other words, you take pious Salem, throw in raw Winston, and get a city remarkable for its civility, its commitment to education, and its culture both classical and folk.

The Moravians who came to the area they named *Die Wachau* (later Latinized to Wachovia) in 1753 were sober, thrifty, disciplined, and peaceful. After establishing the villages of Bethabara and Bethania, they began building their main city, Salem, in 1766.

The Salem Moravians belonged to one of the first Protestant sects. They came mostly from German-speaking areas of Bohemia, Poland, and, of course, Moravia. Arriving in America to escape persecution, they settled first in Pennsylvania, then sent colonists into their new land in the back country of North Carolina. They organized themselves—they were nothing if not organized—into congregational towns in which just about everything was owned and controlled by the church. No non-Moravians were allowed to live in Bethabara or, later, in Salem.

The Moravians were frequently envied and mistrusted by their neighbors, most of whom were small farmers leading hardscrabble lives on the frontier. These farmers struggled all their lives just to eat. By contrast, the

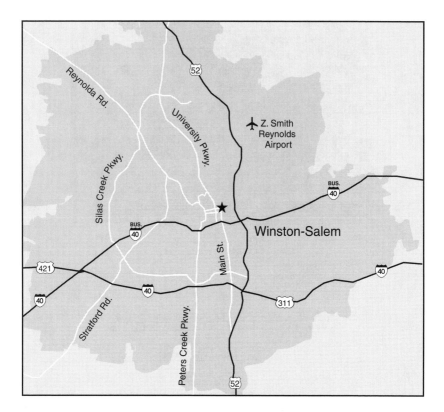

Moravians essentially finished building Salem—complete with church, meeting house, and a water system—in five years.

Despite this mistrust, Salem quickly became the trading center of northwestern North Carolina and southwestern Virginia. Nearby was the only safe place to cross the Yadkin River for 50 miles, so all the major thoroughfares in the area (including the Great Wagon Road from Pennsylvania) ran by Salem.

When Forsyth County was created out of Stokes County in 1849, Salem was the logical choice for the county seat. The Moravian leaders, however, wanted no truck with the rabble that came with a county courthouse, so they agreed to sell the new county 51 acres for a town a mile north of Salem Square.

For almost two years, the Forsyth County seat was known only as "that place north of Salem." In 1851, the North Carolina General Assembly named the town after a local Revolutionary War hero, and Winston was born.

While Salem built textile mills, Winston was known for selling dried berries. Not until after the Civil War and Reconstruction did it begin to capitalize on the area's major crop and pledge fealty to King Tobacco. Factories for making plug tobacco and tobacco auction houses and warehouses sprang up around the young town, but those were lemonade stands compared to what a 24-year-old former traveling tobacco salesman had in mind.

Just as his statue outside city hall suggests, Richard Joshua Reynolds arrived in Winston on horseback. He was drawn from his Virginia home in 1874 by Winston's new rail line, by which the young Reynolds realized he could ship his tobacco anywhere and permanently retire his salesman's wagon.

Reynolds built his tobacco company and Winston at the same time. He was phenomenally hardworking and uncommonly canny. A decent man, he was also one of the first industrialists to realize how closely his own fortunes were tied to his workers'. He paid his (mostly black) employees well by the day's standard, instituted profit-sharing plans, and provided drinking water, lunchrooms, day nurseries, and a medical department. His wife, Katharine, encouraged and continued his philanthropy, and the leaders who followed him at R. J. Reynolds Tobacco Company and elsewhere placed a high value on giving back to the community.

Winston officially merged with Salem in 1913, although they had been called the "Twin City" for years. The two combined, in the words of longtime *Winston-Salem Journal* writer Chester Davis, "the Salem conscience with the Winston purse."

Most of the 20th century was a heyday for Winston-Salem. Reynolds tobacco and Hanes hosiery were sold around the world. Piedmont Airlines, started at what would become Z. Smith Reynolds Airport, grew into one of the best-run airlines in the country. In the 1950s, Wake Forest College moved from its home near Raleigh to a new campus in Winston-Salem donated by R. J. Reynolds's daughter and son-in-law. A new limited-access highway was designed to relieve downtown traffic; the planned east-west expressway became, before its completion, part of Interstate 40. Winston-Salem boasted the first municipal arts council in the nation. In the 1960s, the Twin City beat out several other communities to become the home of the North Carolina School of the Arts.

As the century drew to a close, however, so did Winston-Salem's period of startling growth. Population declined in the 1980s, the first time since Salem's founding. Piedmont Airlines was bought by USAir. The AT&T plant on Lexington Road shut down in 1988. Most devastating of all was the move of the headquarters of R. J. Reynolds Tobacco—now RJR Nabisco—to Atlanta. RJR Nabisco president and CEO F. Ross Johnson became the most hated man in town when he justified the move by calling Winston-Salem too "bucolic."

But as the poet put it, "Tho' much is taken, much abides." The misfortunes that beset Reynolds and other local giants forced the city to diversify its economy. And the sudden absence of patriarchal industry captains led the city to learn how to run itself. Winston-Salem still has the cultural legacy left by its forebears. Wake Forest University, Winston-Salem State University, Salem College, and the North Carolina School of the Arts call the city home. So do two major art museums—Reynolda House Museum of American Art (housed in the country estate of R. J. Reynolds) and the Southeastern Center for Contemporary Art. The Stevens Center for the Performing Arts plays host to outstanding productions of dance, music, film, and drama. Throw in its thriving Downtown Arts District and the city can truly claim to be "the City of the Arts."

Just as the Moravians learned to coexist with their rural neighbors, and staid Salem with boisterous Winston, high culture in Winston-Salem coexists with the rowdy, working-class legacy of the city's industrial past. Many of the happenings in the revitalized downtown, for example, make use of Winston-Salem's tradition of mountain bluegrass, gospel, and Piedmont blues, the music of the farmers and sharecroppers who brought their crops to town and the workers who labored in the mills and factories.

Winston-Salem boasts as much culture as any city in the state, while retaining a blue-collar earthiness that has been glossed over elsewhere beneath tides of transplants and slick prosperity. It's a Jeffersonian combination that reflects the industriousness, piety, and simplicity of the Moravian pioneers. It's a combination that has helped make Winston-Salem thrive again.

Introduction by Ed Southern

JUST THE FACTS

Winston-Salem is the county seat of Forsyth County, which has a population of more than 306,000. The Winston-Salem Visitors Center, in the historic Brookstown Mill at the corner of Brookstown Avenue and Cherry Street, can provide information on the city; call 866-728-4200 or visit www.visitwinstonsalem.com.

Located in the northwestern corner of the North Carolina

Piedmont, Winston-Salem is less than two hours from the heart of the Blue Ridge Mountains and less than an hour from the Virginia border. Interstate 40 runs east and west just south of town; Interstate 40 Business cuts straight through downtown. U.S. 52 connects Winston-Salem with the Virginia mountains and the Blue Ridge Parkway to the north and the Yadkin River Valley to the south. In the near future, U.S. 52 is slated to become part of Interstate 73/Interstate 74, which will run between Detroit and Charleston, South Carolina.

The city's Greyhound bus station is at 250 Greyhound Court; call 800-231-2222 or 336-724-1429 for details. The nearest Amtrak station is in Greensboro, but a connector is available; call 800-872-7245 for information.

Piedmont Triad International Airport, located off Interstate 40 just across the Guilford County line, is the major airport for Winston-Salem. Seven carriers provide 86 flights daily. Call 336-721-0088 or visit www.ptia.org for general airport information. Z. Smith Reynolds Airport, 10 minutes north of downtown Winston-Salem, is a base for commuter and corporate aircraft; call 336-767-6361 or visit www.smithreynolds.org.

Things to Do

HISTORIC PLACES, GARDENS, AND TOURS

■ *Old Salem*, at 900 Old Salem Road near the intersection of Academy and Main streets, is where most visitors will want to begin—where Winston-Salem itself began. The Moravian town has been carefully restored into a living-history community. Costumed interpreters lead tours, demonstrate traditional crafts, and chat with visitors as if the 19th century, rather than the 21st, had just turned.

Though visitors can stroll the old streets free of charge, tickets are required for admission to some of the restored buildings. They may be purchased at the new visitor center, located across the street from Old Salem.

Old Salem
PHOTO BY ANNE HOLCOMB WATERS

From April to December, the visitor center is open Monday through Saturday from 9 A.M. to 5:30 P.M. and Sunday from 12:30 P.M. to 5:30 P.M. From January to March, it is open Tuesday through Saturday from 9 A.M. to 5:30 P.M. and Sunday from 12:30 P.M. to 5:30 P.M. The hours for various buildings and shops within Old Salem may vary slightly. Old Salem is closed Easter Sunday, Thanksgiving, Christmas Eve, and Christmas Day. Most shops—including the Moravian Book and Gift Shop, T. Bagge Merchant, J. Blum Printer, the Salem Soda Shop, and the highly aromatic Winkler Bakery—do not require tickets. Nor does the Salem Tavern, described in the "Places to Eat" section below. Nor does God's Acre, the burial ground used by original settlers and modern-day Moravians alike; it is to God's Acre that worshipers march from Salem Square at dawn during the traditional Easter Sunrise Service, celebrated since 1773. A ticket gains the purchaser unlimited one- or two-day admission to all gardens and restorations, including the Single Brothers House, where visitors can see early trades demonstrated; the Miksch House and Manufactory; the Vierling House, home of an early physician; the Boys School; the Schultz Shoemaker Shop; the Tavern Museum-Barn; the St. Philips Log and Brick churches; and the John Vogler House. At each stop, interpreters tell about the building, the town, and the orderly, pious life of the Moravians. The ticket also includes admission to the Museum of Early Southern Decorative Art, the Old Salem Toy Museum, and the Old Salem Children's Museum, which are covered in the "Museums and Science Centers" section below. It will take you at least a half-day to see Old Salem thoroughly. You should enjoy it at a leisurely 18th-century pace anyway. For more information, call 888-653-7253 or 336-721-7350 or visit www.oldsalem.org.

The 1990s saw the addition of an overdue look at the lives of African-Americans, whether slave or free, within antebellum Salem. A special walking tour called "African-Americans in Salem" is offered, as is an audiovisual presentation. African-American sites on the south end of Salem, such as St. Philips, have been restored. The Moravians were uncomfortable with slavery—but not uncomfortable enough to end the practice.

Old Salem adjoins the campus of Salem College and Academy, which are among the oldest women's institutions in the country and a testament to the Moravians' belief that both sexes deserved an education.

■ *Historic Bethabara Park*, at 2147 Bethabara Road, is a restoration of the Moravians' first settlement in Wachovia. The men who came to scout out the site spent their first night in an abandoned trappers' cabin. The town was never intended to be a permanent settlement; in fact, its name means "House of Passage." Bethabara soon became a trading center for the region. A palisade was built to protect against raiding parties during the French and Indian War. The town, however, was largely abandoned when Salem was established in 1772.

The palisade, the Potter's House, and the Gemeinhaus (or Congregation House) are still standing and are open to the public. Several foundations unearthed at the town site have been studied by archaeologists, and gardens have been re-created. The restored site is surrounded by a 175-acre park and nature preserve that includes trails to the site of Bethabara's mill, a beaver pond, and a picnic ground overlooking the village.

Bethabara does not take as long to explore as Old Salem, but a visit here should certainly not be rushed. A visitor center is located across Bethabara Road. The exhibit buildings are open for guided tours from April 1 through November 30 except for Thanksgiving. Tours run Monday through Friday from 10:30 A.M. to 4:30 P.M. and Saturday and Sunday from 1:30 P.M. to 4:30 P.M. A modest admission fee is charged. The grounds are open all day, every day, all year. For more information, call 336-924-8191 or visit www.bethabarapark.org.

■ *Reynolda Gardens* occupies most of the land adjacent to Reynolda House on Reynolda Road. Owned by Wake Forest University, the property includes four acres of formal flower and vegetable gardens, a greenhouse, and 125 acres of woods and streams with marked trails. The grounds are open during daylight hours year-round, free of charge.

Children's Garden at Reynolda Gardens
Photo by Anne Holcomb Waters

For more information, call 336-758-5593 or visit www.wfu.edu/gardens.

Next to the gardens is **Reynolda Village**, created to house and educate the workers on the Reynolds estate. Katharine Reynolds planned the green-roofed, whitewashed village as a model farm where area farmers could learn the latest agricultural techniques. It has been renovated to house upscale shops, galleries, and restaurants. For more information, call 336-758-5584 or visit www.reynoldavillage.com.

MUSEUMS AND SCIENCE CENTERS

■ **Reynolda House Museum of American Art**, at 2250 Reynolda Road, was the country home of tobacco magnate R. J. Reynolds. Devoted to building his tobacco company, Reynolds married late. He took as his bride his distant cousin Katharine. She was many years his junior, but he had long admired her intelligence and bearing. For most of their married lives, they lived in a mansion on Fifth Street, where they had four children: Richard Jr., Mary, Nancy, and Zachary Smith.

In 1912, they began work on what they called a "bungalow" on their country estate about three miles north of town. The house was designed by Philadelphia architect Charles Barton Keen. But the driving force behind the development of the estate was unquestionably Katharine. That it was given the name *Reynolda*, the female Latin version of the family name, was no accident.

By the time the house was finished in 1917, R. J. was near death.

Reynolda House Museum of American Art
Photo by Anne Holcomb Waters

Katherine did not long outlive him. The house was left to the children, who tended to use it as a holiday house as they grew older. In 1936, however, Mary and her husband, Charles Babcock, renovated the property for use as their family home.

In 1964, Charles Babcock donated the house and 20 surrounding acres to be used as a nonprofit institution dedicated to the arts and education. His daughter, art historian Barbara Babcock Millhouse, and then-executive director Nicholas Bragg set about turning Reynolda House Museum of American Art into one of the country's finest facilities for the study of American art, architecture, and design. Thomas Cole, Georgia O'Keeffe, Grant Wood, Frederic Remington, Mary Cassatt, Thomas Hart Benton, Alexander Calder, Jacob Lawrence, and Jasper Johns are all represented in the museum's permanent collection. You'll also find a number of quietly magnificent works by lesser-known artists, including *The Old Hunting Ground* by Worthington Whittredge. A collection of vintage clothing from the Reynolds family is housed in the attic.

Reynolda House is itself a museum. It is a classic of the Arts and Crafts movement of the late 19th and early 20th centuries, which encouraged simplicity and rustic craftsmanship in design and decor. The most impressive feature is an Aeolian organ with 2,566 pipes, some of which are visible from the second-floor gallery and in the attic. All rooms are furnished with period pieces, including many Reynolds family originals. Children (and many adults) also enjoy seeing the bungalow's indoor swimming pool, bowling alley, shooting range, squash court, and mirrored Art Deco bar.

A new wing recently completed at Reynolda House includes an auditorium, a visitor center, exhibition space, classrooms, studios, and a library.

Reynolda House Museum of American Art is open from 9:30 A.M. to 4:30 P.M. Tuesday through Saturday and from 1:30 P.M. to 4:30 P.M. on Sunday. It is closed Thanksgiving, Christmas, and New Year's. Admission is charged. Students with valid identification are admitted free. For more information, call 888-663-1149 or 336-758-5150 or visit www.reynoldahouse.org.

- The **Southeastern Center for Contemporary Art** (SECCA), at 750 Marguerite Drive, not far from Reynolda House, is housed in the 1929 English-style home of Hanes Hosiery industrialist James G. Hanes. Twenty thousand square feet of exhibit space have been added to the original house. None of this space is used for a permanent collection; instead, SECCA hosts as many temporary exhibits as possible, bringing some of the Southeast's most impressive and up-to-the-minute work to Winston-Salem. Like Reynolda House, SECCA hosts a variety of programs and performances in the house and on the grounds. Unlike Reynolda House, it rents out some of its space for private functions.

SECCA is open Wednesday through Saturday from 10 A.M. to 5 P.M. (except for the first Thursday of every month, when it stays open until 8 P.M.) and Sunday from 2 P.M. to 5 P.M. Admission is charged except for children under 17 and SECCA members. For more information, call 336-725-1904 or visit www.secca.org.

- The **Museum of Anthropology of Wake Forest University** is located behind Kentner Stadium on Wake Forest's main campus. Founded in 1963 by the faculty of the school's Department of Anthropology, it was originally intended for Wake students but is now a favorite of Triad residents and visitors.

The permanent collection features artifacts from the Americas, Africa, Asia, and Oceania. Some of the most interesting pieces, however, are prehistoric artifacts found here in the Yadkin River Valley. The museum also hosts a wide range of special exhibits and programs.

The museum and its gift shop are open from 10 A.M. to 4:30 P.M. Tuesday through Saturday. Admission is free. For more information, call 336-758-5282 or visit www.wfu.edu/MOA.

While you're here, the university campus is well worth a quick stroll. Wake Forest College was founded by Baptist ministers in the town of Wake Forest, just north of Raleigh, in 1834. In the 1940s, the Reynolds family invited the college to move to Winston-Salem, offering land on R. J. Reynolds's country estate and a sizable endowment. In 1953, President Harry Truman turned the first shovelful at the groundbreaking ceremony.

Five years later, classes began on the new campus.

Built of local red bricks in the Colonial Revival style, the campus is dominated by Wait Chapel, located at the northern end of the quad. The sanctuary for Wake Forest Baptist Church and a popular site for weddings and the annual Christmas Lovefeast, Wait Chapel was host to presidential debates in 1988 and 2000.

■ **SciWorks**, at 400 West Hanes Mill Road, may be showing its age a bit, but children still love its interactive exhibits and programs. SciWorks boasts 25,000 square feet of exhibits, a 15-acre environmental park, and a 120-seat planetarium. Kids can see mounted animals from around the world, walk inside a 20-foot tree to check out its age, and, best of all, strum a stringless harp and play "Happy Birthday" on the floor piano. SciWorks also offers nature trails and a small collection of farmyard animals.

The facility is open Monday through Saturday from 10 A.M. to 5 P.M. Admission is charged; the price includes a planetarium show. For more information, call 336-767-6730 or visit www.sciworks.org.

■ The **Museum of Early Southern Decorative Art** (MESDA), at 924 South Main Street in Old Salem, is dedicated to preserving, exhibiting, and researching regional decorative arts. Covering the years from colonization to 1820, MESDA exhibits furniture, paintings, textiles, ceramics, and silver in 24 period rooms and seven galleries.

Visitors will note the marked cultural differences in the colonial and early federal Southeast; the region was anything but a "Solid South." The Scots-Irish settlers on the frontier lived very different lives from their German neighbors, who in turn existed a world apart from the Englishmen and French Huguenots in the cities of the coastal plain. MESDA takes as its geographical area a region that includes the Chesapeake, the low country, and the back country. This encompasses all of the Carolinas and Virginia and wide swaths of Maryland, Kentucky, Tennessee, Georgia, and what is now West Virginia.

MESDA is open to visitors Monday through Saturday from 9:30 A.M. to 5 P.M. and Sunday from 1:30 P.M. to 5 P.M. Guided tours begin on the hour and half-hour and last about an hour. Visitors have to buy an all-in-one ticket to Old Salem to get into MESDA. For more information, call 888-348-5420 or 336-721-7300 or visit www.oldsalem.org and click on "MESDA."

MESDA shares the Frank L. Horton Museum Center in Old Salem with the **Old Salem Toy Museum** and the **Old Salem Children's Museum**. The Old Salem Toy Museum houses a permanent collection of more than

1,200 antique toys dating from 225 A.D. to the 1920s. The Old Salem Children's Museum features hands-on exhibits and activities for children ages four to nine. Admission is charged for children who enter and play and the adults who accompany them; note that the number of adults who may enter is limited. Included are a two-story climbing sculpture, period costumes that kids can try on, a miniature version of the Miksch House, and a secret tunnel. As with MESDA, an Old Salem ticket is required to enter either museum.

Cultural Offerings

- **Diggs Gallery**, on the campus of Winston-Salem State University, brings in traveling exhibits and artists of national renown. The concentration is on traditional and contemporary African-American art. Artists who have appeared or spoken here in recent years include Jacob Lawrence and Barbara Chase-Riboud.

  The gallery is open Tuesday through Saturday from 11 A.M. to 5 P.M. Admission is free. For more information, call 336-750-2458 or visit www.wssu.edu/WSSU/About/Administration/Information+Resources/Diggs+Gallery/Diggs+Gallery.htm.

- The **North Carolina Black Repertory Company** currently has its offices at 610 Coliseum Drive. The company sponsors the week-long National Black Theatre Festival every other year. Professional theater groups from around the world come to Winston-Salem for the festival, as do celebrities from theater and film. Call 336-723-2266 or visit www.nbtf.org for more information.

- The **Stevens Center for the Performing Arts**, at 405 West Fourth Street, was a vacant 1920s movie theater until the early 1980s, when the North Carolina School of the Arts turned it into one of the finest performance venues in the Southeast.

  The center has a seating capacity of 1,400. It hosts events year-round, ranging from student productions by the North Carolina School of the Arts to performances by such local and regional groups as the Piedmont Triad Symphony, the Piedmont Opera Theatre, the North Carolina Dance Theatre, and the North Carolina Shakespeare Festival. It also brings in national acts, touring productions of Broadway shows, and children's performances, including that perennial holiday favorite, *The Nutcracker*. Recently, the Stevens Center has returned to its cinematic roots, playing host to the Films on Fourth series (which brings independent, foreign, and limited-release films to Winston-Salem) and to screenings during the RiverRun International Film Festival.

Call 336-721-1945 or visit www.ncarts.edu/stevenscenter for information about ticket prices and upcoming events.

SPECIAL SHOPPING

■ A gallery hop is held the first Friday of every month in Winston-Salem's *Downtown Arts District*, centered along Fifth, Seventh, and Trade streets. Sponsored by the Downtown Arts District Association, this is one of the best free social and cultural activities the city offers. Two of my favorite shops are almost directly across Trade Street from one another: the *Piedmont Craftsmen* shop and *Urban Artware*. Visit their respective Web sites at www.piedmontcraftsmen.org and www.urbanartware.com for information.

RECREATION

■ Winston-Salem sponsors downtown parties every Thursday, Friday, and Saturday night from April to October. *Alive after Five*, held Thursday from 5 P.M. to 8 P.M. at Corpening Plaza, brings in pop and alternative acts aimed at young professionals. *BellSouth Jazz & Blues*, held every Friday from 6 P.M. to 10 P.M. in the revitalized Fourth Street area, offers funk and soul in addition to jazz and blues. *Summers on Trade*, billed as "Winston's Roots Revival," is held in the Downtown Arts District on Trade and Sixth streets on Saturday from 7 P.M. to 10 P.M. It draws on the musical heritage of the Piedmont and the Blue Ridge and has featured performers such as Doc Watson. For more information, call Winston-Salem Events at 336-354-1500 or visit www.winstonsalemevents.org.

■ The **Dixie Classic Fair**, the regional fair for northwestern North Carolina, is the last big fair before the North Carolina State Fair in Raleigh. Originally a chance for the region's farmers to show off their crops and livestock, the Dixie Classic still shows its agricultural and community roots. Concession stands are operated by local nonprofit organizations such as Boy Scout troops, Little Leagues, and the Kiwanis Club; prizewinning student artwork is displayed in the exhibit hall; and one of the most popular events is the pig race. A re-created folk village offers demonstrations of blacksmithing and woodcarving; bluegrass bands play on the front porch of one of the log cabins. The mile-long Midway, meanwhile, is filled with ample opportunities to lose your money on games of skill and chance. Rides are available for all ages and courage levels. The fairgrounds are behind Lawrence Joel Veterans Memorial Coliseum, which is on the corner of University Parkway and Deacon Boulevard. The fair is held in late September or early October. Call 336-727-2236 or visit www.dcfair.com for more information.

■ The **Piedmont Crafts Fair**, held each November in the M. C. Benton Convention Center downtown, brings in more than 100 regional craftsmen to display and (they hope) sell their wares. The fair is sponsored by the Piedmont Craftsmen organization, which operates a gallery at 601 North Trade Street year-round. You can reach the gallery at 336-725-1516 or learn about it by visiting www.piedsmontcraftsmen.org.

■ Old Salem is renowned for its Moravian Christmas celebrations. **A Salem Christmas**, which includes strolling brass bands and seasonal decorations, is capped by the **Christmas Candle Tea**, in which a Lovefeast of buns, coffee, and hymns is held by candlelight in the Single Brothers House.

■ The **RiverRun International Film Festival** began in Brevard but moved to Winston-Salem in 2003. Founded by Gennario D'Onofrio, father of *Full Metal Jacket* and *Law & Order: Criminal Intent* star Vincent D'Onofrio, RiverRun uses the facilities of the School of the Arts, the Stevens Center, and other downtown venues to showcase independent films from across the country. The 2003 festival included a surprise Southern premiere of the Christopher Guest "mockumentary" *A Mighty Wind*. Call 336-724-1502 or visit www.riverrunfilm.com for more information.

North Carolina
Gets a "Toe-Dancin' School"

By Ed Southern

"A faith in our youth and the talent of our youth. A realization of the place art has in our civilization."

This was the answer Vittorio Giannini gave whenever he was asked what characteristics a city should have to be home to the North Carolina School of the Arts (NCSA). This was in the early 1960s, when the question of the School of the Arts' existence, much less its location, was far from settled. Giannini, an internationally renowned composer from Philadelphia who had long spent his summers in the North Carolina mountains, was an early advocate who would become NCSA's first president.

The North Carolina School of the Arts was the brainchild of novelist and Asheville native John Ehle. In 1961, Ehle wrote an article for the *News & Observer* of Raleigh entitled "What's the Matter with Chapel Hill?" The article was a wide-ranging critique of the failure of the University of North Carolina at Chapel Hill, and liberal-arts colleges in general, to provide the proper environment and training for creative and performing artists.

The article caught the eye of Governor Terry Sanford. Sanford made education a cornerstone of his administration, going so far as to bring Ehle on board his staff as special assistant for new projects. Ehle and Sanford accomplished a number of initiatives, including the Governor's School and the North Carolina Film Board, but the School of the Arts was by far their most original, unorthodox, and controversial project.

Unlike liberal-arts colleges, NCSA gives students at both the high school and college levels an intensive and rigorous program in their chosen art. Unlike traditional conservatories, it also provides a solid general education.

The School of the Arts met with opposition from two sides. One side consisted of proponents of traditional liberal-arts colleges and their existing music, art, and drama programs. The second consisted of those who objected to spending tax dollars on a "toe-dancin' school."

Ehle argued, as he had in his 1961 article, that while liberal-arts colleges were superbly equipped to teach the study of the arts, they were inadequate for teaching the techniques of creation and performance.

The second argument was finally defeated on the floor of the North Carolina General Assembly by Representative John Kerr, who took to task for their shortsightedness those who opposed government support of the arts. Kerr closed his speech with this: "Now, some of you have ridiculed this legislation as a toe-dancin' bill. Well, if there's going to be toe-dancin', I want to be there." At that, he assumed a ballet pose, which was photographed for the state's newspapers.

Once the bill for the creation of the School of the Arts passed, the work of selecting a site began in earnest. Biltmore House in Asheville and Reynolda House and Graylyn in Winston-Salem were considered. Several cities expressed some degree of interest, but in the end, only three were judged to have viable claims to being the best location: Raleigh, Charlotte, and Winston-Salem.

Winston-Salem had a tradition of supporting the arts that went back to its founding. The Moravians who built Salem made music an integral part of their worship and culture. The industrialists who built Winston had long supported education. Winston-Salem was the first city in the country to have an arts council. It had at its disposal the facilities of Salem College, Wake Forest College, and Winston-Salem State University.

Tradition, however, was not going to bring the School of the Arts to Winston-Salem. Two city leaders, Smith Bagley and Philip Hanes, spearheaded a drive to prove the Twin City's eagerness and worthiness to host the school. More than 200 volunteers worked the phones in a "Dial for Dollars" campaign that raised nearly $600,000 in two days. A plan was drawn up to convert Gray High School into a campus for the School of the Arts.

But according to Leslie Banner's *A Passionate Preference: The Story of the North Carolina School of the Arts*, the deciding factor was not just that Winston-Salem had better-laid plans and a more successful fund drive. Winston-Salem simply wanted the school more than the other cities did.

John Ehle had a strange thought: to start a school, far from the world's cultural centers, that would teach students to be professional artists of the highest caliber. Unimaginable to most, scoffed at, and threatened with extinction, the North Carolina School of the Arts is now known around the world for the quality of its training, faculty, students, and alumni.

Places to Stay

RESORTS, HOTELS, AND MOTELS

In earlier times, Winston-Salem boasted two of the finest hotels in the South: the Hotel Zinzendorf and the Hotel Robert E. Lee. The Zinzendorf stood on the hill overlooking the West End neighborhood, near what is now the intersection of Fourth and Glade streets. It burned in its prime on Thanksgiving Day 1892; among the diners who had to be evacuated were R. J. Reynolds and William A. Blair, whose son John founded the company that publishes this book. The Hotel Robert E. Lee suffered a long period of decline after World War II. It was imploded in 1972 to make way for a succession of fine hotels.

Most of Winston-Salem's hotels are representatives of national chains. The following, however, feature distinctive accommodations with a definite local flavor.

- **Brookstown Inn**. Deluxe. 200 Brookstown Avenue (800-845-4262 or 336-725-1120; www.brookstowninn.com). Located in the historic Brookstown Mill area on the edge of the even more historic Old Salem, Brookstown Inn is listed on the National Register of Historic Places. It is housed in what was one of Salem's first textile mills. Each of the 71 guest rooms and suites is furnished with what the inn says are "authentic early-American pieces," including poster beds and handmade quilts. A complimentary continental breakfast is served every morning; a complimentary wine-and-cheese reception is offered each evening. Complete business services (fax, copiers, etc.), an exercise room, meeting space, and banquet facilities are available.

- **The Hawthorne Inn and Conference Center**. Expensive/Moderate. 420 High Street (877-777-3099 or 336-777-3000; www.hawthorneinn.com). Located just off Interstate 40 Business, The Hawthorne and its 155 rooms are convenient to downtown, Old Salem, and Wake Forest University Baptist Medical Center. In fact, the inn is owned and operated by North Carolina Baptist Hospitals, Inc., which means that those in town because of the medical center can receive especially good rates. Particularly suited to business travelers, The Hawthorne combines the cozy comfort of an inn with the facilities of a business hotel. It offers a fitness center, meeting space, an amphitheater, and the Bayberry Restaurant.

- **Wingate Inn**. Moderate. 125 South Main Street (800-228-1000 or 336-714-2800; www.wingateinns.com). The first franchise of the Wingate chain in the Triad, this inn is considered a key part of the effort to revitalize downtown Winston-Salem. Designed to attract business travelers, the Wingate employs the latest technology in its 24-hour business center and its rooms, which have cordless keyboards for Web TV, free high-speed Internet access, and cordless phones. The lobby features a mural of Old Salem. Valet parking and a breakfast buffet are included in the room rate. The Twin City Chop House opened next to the inn in 2001.

INNS AND BED-AND-BREAKFASTS

- **Henry F. Shaffner House**. Deluxe/Expensive. 150 South Marshall Street (800-952-2256 or 336-777-0052; www.shaffnerhouse.com). In the shadow of Winston-Salem's skyscrapers and just off the bustle of Interstate 40 Business sits the expansive Henry F. Shaffner House. Built for one of the city's early industrialists, the home is located on what was once called Millionaire's Row, the stretch of fine houses constructed just south of Winston during the post-Civil War boom. Each of the nine guest rooms has a different decorative theme and a name taken from Winston-Salem's history. All rooms have cable television, high-speed Internet access, and phones. A hot breakfast is included. The inn serves dinner nightly.

- **The Augustus T. Zevely Inn**. Expensive. 803 South Main Street (800-928-9299 or 336-748-9299; www.winston-salem-inn.com). Not to be confused with the Zevely House restaurant in the West End neighborhood, the Zevely Inn, built in 1842, sits in the heart of Old Salem. Some of its 12 rooms have whirlpools and original fireplaces. Each room is named for a member of the Zevely family. Rates include a "continental-plus" breakfast during the week and a full gourmet breakfast on weekends, nonalcoholic drinks throughout the day, and wine and cheese at night. Pets can be accommodated if arrangements are made at the time of reservation.

- **Summit Street Bed-and-Breakfast Inns**. Expensive/Moderate. 420 Summit Street and 434 Summit Street (800-301-1887 or 336-777-1887; www.bbinn.com). Comprised of the 1887 Jacob Lott Ludlow House and the 1895 Benjamin Joseph Sheppard House, the Summit Street Bed-and-Breakfast Inns are located in the heart of the historic West End neighborhood. These two large, adjacent 100-year-old Victorian houses offer a range of amenities including two-person Jacuzzis, in-room gourmet breakfasts, an exercise room with Nautilus equipment, and a billiards room.

Places to Eat

■ *Ryan's Steaks, Chops, and Seafood*. Expensive. 719 Coliseum Drive (336-724-6132; www.ryansrestaurant.com). Ryan's occupies a pastoral setting (complete with a bubbling brook) in an odd location; it is tucked off two of Winston-Salem's busiest roads, on Coliseum Drive near University Parkway. The name more or less sums up the menu. What Ryan's lacks in surprise it makes up for in execution. Dinner is served Monday through Saturday.

■ *Salem Tavern*. Expensive. 736 South Main Street (336-748-8585; www.oldsalem.org/visit/dining). The restaurant known as the Salem Tavern is actually located in the Salem Tavern Annex. The original Salem Tavern burned in 1784 but was rebuilt that same year; the brick structure located next to the annex, it hosted a visit from President George Washington in 1791 and serves as a museum today. The highlight of the restaurant's menu is the authentic Moravian chicken pie, though more contemporary food is also served. The restaurant is open for lunch daily and for dinner Monday through Saturday. Reservations are recommended.

■ *Miss Annie's*. Expensive/Moderate. 3064 Healy Drive (336-774-0922; www.missannies.com). Don't be discouraged by the somewhat dilapidated shopping center where Miss Annie's is located. The Caribbean-inspired food served here is excellent. Chef Jean Spence Eubank is a native of Jamaica who cut her culinary teeth cooking for United Nations dignitaries before opening her own four-star restaurant in New Jersey. Luckily for us, she decided to move south. In addition to Jerk chicken and seafood dishes, her specials are highly recommended. Miss Annie's currently serves lunch on Thursday and dinner Tuesday though Saturday.

■ *Noble's Grill*. Expensive/Moderate. 380 Knollwood Street (336-777-8477; www.noblesrestaurants.com). Chef and restaurateur Jim Noble has built a solid reputation for his "clean and natural cooking." In other words, he prepares food in the tradition of the legendary Alice Waters. His reputation has served him well, as he now has companion restaurants in High Point and Charlotte. His wood-fired pizzas, delectable soups and salads, and roasted meat entrées are all first-rate. Noble's serves lunch Monday through Saturday and dinner all week.

- **South by Southwest.** Expensive/Moderate. 241 South Marshall Street (336-727-0800). South by Southwest has been bringing the best southwestern cuisine to Winston-Salem since 1993. The menu here ignores the usual Tex-Mex clichés in favor of more creative items like pineapplejalapeño salsa and blue corn enchiladas. South by Southwest serves dinner Monday through Saturday.

- **Xia Asian Fusion.** Expensive/Moderate. 134 North Spruce Street (336-723-1400). This restaurant serves delectable appetizers, including a fresh summer roll filled with mint and shrimp, as well as an array of Japanese and Thai dishes such as spicy lemon grass chicken and asparagus. Guests can dine indoors in the sleek red-and-black dining room with its peaceful wall fountain. Or if the weather is fair, they can enjoy the patio out front. Lunch and dinner are served Monday though Saturday.

- **Bistro 420.** Moderate. 424-A West Fourth Street (336-721-1336; www.bistro420.com). One of the hubs around which Winston-Salem's downtown is being revitalized, Bistro 420 offers an eclectic menu ranging from traditional Southern to classic French, from Asian to Italian. The decor both inside and in its sidewalk seating area is as imaginative as the menu. Bistro 420 serves lunch Tuesday through Friday and dinner Wednesday through Saturday; it also stays open for downtown events.

- **Marshall Street Smokehouse.** Moderate. 924 South Marshall Street (336-723-0430). Patterned after Blue Smoke NYC, this restaurant is certainly a meat lover's dream. Options include barbecued beef brisket and smoked baby back ribs. Herbivores can select a vegetable plate or an alluring three-cheese stuffed portabello mushroom with garlic and spinach. Outdoor dining is available. Lunch and dinner are served daily; brunch if offered on Sunday.

- **Midtown Café and Dessertery.** Moderate. 151 South Stratford Road (336-724-9800; www.midtowncafedelivery.com). Opened in 1987, this place has been drawing folks to its amazing desserts ever since. Now serving breakfast, lunch, and home-style dinners, it is equally popular for its comfort food. Breakfast, lunch, and dinner are served daily.

■ **Sweet Potatoes**. Moderate. 529 Trade Street (336-727-4844; www.sweetpotatoes-arestaurant.com). Sweet Potatoes offers the best casual dining experience in the city, in my opinion. Located in the heart of the Downtown Arts District, it serves up delicious Southern food. And yes, as the name implies, many recipes include sweet potatoes. You might start with the "Red and White Fries," follow that with "Catfish Nola," and finish with the sweet potato cheesecake. Of course, you may then need to fast for a week. Sweet Potatoes is open for lunch Monday through Saturday and for dinner Thursday through Saturday.

■ **Athena Greek Taverna**. Moderate/Inexpensive. 680 South Stratford Road (336-794-3069). In a town where many restaurants are owned by Greeks but few actually specialize in Greek food, this small, bright eatery was a welcome addition when it opened a few years back. Try the roasted chicken with lemon potatoes. If you order the "Horiatiki"—a country Greek salad—plan on sharing because it's enough to feed a small village. Lunch and dinner are served Monday through Saturday.

■ **Cat's Corner Café**. Moderate/Inexpensive. 411 West Fourth Street (336-722-9911; www.westendcafe.com/ccc.html). Brought to you by the same great souls behind West End Café, Cat's Corner was Winston-Salem's first sidewalk café when it opened just a few years ago. It specializes in sandwiches, soups, and salads but also offers larger entrées at dinner. Cat's is open for lunch Monday through Friday, for dinner Thursday through Saturday, and for brunch on Sunday.

■ **Foothills Brewing Company**. Moderate/Inexpensive. 838 West Fourth Street (336-777-3348). Though folks definitely come to Foothills for the beer, the food is surprisingly good, too. The inventive offerings include "Pear and Arugula Salad" and "Fried Cashew-Encrusted Chevre and Bibb Lettuce Salad." Foothills also offers the requisite quarter-pound burger. It serves lunch and dinner daily.

■ **Ichiban**. Moderate/Inexpensive. 270 South Stratford Road in Thruway Shopping Center (336-725-3050). This small storefront restaurant serves the best sushi in town, and its Japanese fare is pretty good, too. The front dining room is very brightly lit, so head for the sushi bar in the back for more intimate dining. Ichiban serves lunch and dinner daily but is closed during midafternoon.

■ *Village Tavern*. Moderate/Inexpensive. Reynolda Village (336-748-0221) and 2000 Griffith Road (336-760-8686). The Village Tavern began in Reynolda Village and has spread across the state and the Southeast and into Colorado and Arizona. The patio in the original location has become famous; the atmosphere is upscale but relaxed enough for college students. The second Winston-Salem location is just off Hanes Mall Boulevard at the intersection with Stratford Road; it offers a classier ambiance and is more spacious. Both locations serve lunch and dinner daily and brunch on Sunday. For information about the Village Tavern restaurants, visit www.villagetavern.com.

■ *West End Café*. Moderate/Inexpensive. 926 West Fourth Street (336-723-4774; www.westendcafe.com). West End Café is always bustling, and there's good reason. It serves fresh, delicious food in a pleasant atmosphere; businessmen, families with small children, and young people are all comfortable here. The ambiance is rivaled only by the setting, in the West End neighborhood just across from beautiful Grace Court. Lunch and dinner are served Monday through Saturday.

■ *Burke Street Pizza*. Inexpensive. 1140 Burke Street (336-721-0011). There are many Greco-Italian restaurants in Winston-Salem that serve good pizza, but Burke Street became an immediate hit when it opened, thanks to its New York-style thin-crust pies. The dining room consists of about four booths and a row of stools across the window, so takeout is a popular option. The restaurant is open for lunch and dinner daily.

■ *Little Richard's Barbecue*. Inexpensive. 4885 Country Club Road (336-760-3457). Little Richard's was my introduction to North Carolina barbecue, and I still think it has some of the best in the state. Like its renowned neighbors to the south, Little Richard's serves "Lexington-style" barbecue, which means that it has a tomato base. It even gets high praise from Mr. Barbecue himself, Bob Garner, for being one of the few stalwarts still using a wood-fired pit. Don't miss the hush puppies. And if you don't like pork, you'll be pleased to know that the barbecued chicken is outstanding as well. Lunch and dinner are served Monday through Saturday.

Two Sweet Piedmont Originals

By Anne Holcomb Waters

Two famous North Carolina originals have their roots in the Piedmont, and, boy, are they sweet!

Although technically started in Paducah, Kentucky, Krispy Kreme Doughnuts (www.krispykreme.com) has been based in Winston-Salem since founder Vernon Rudolph opened his doughnut shop in 1937.

With two assistants, a 1936 Pontiac, a few pieces of doughnut-making machinery, and $25 in cash, Rudolph rented a building on South Main Street in the middle of what is now Old Salem. After spending his little money, he had to convince a nearby grocer to loan him the ingredients for his first batch of doughnuts, which he delivered in his Pontiac outfitted with a baking rack.

Although Rudolph originally established himself as a wholesaler, the alluring aroma of his yeast-raised doughnuts created such demand that he responded by cutting a hole in the shop's wall in order to sell directly to customers. Thus, he created the company's successful model for drive-through windows and open viewing of the doughnut-making process.

In 1997, Krispy Kreme artifacts were placed in the Smithsonian Institution, forever securing the company's place as an American icon. "Hot Doughnuts Now" signs currently shine from the Piedmont to the Philippines. If you see one lit up, stop in for a melt-in-your-mouth morsel worth every fat-filled calorie.

That much-loved cherry-flavored cola known as Cheerwine (www.cheerwine.com) was created in Salisbury in 1917. While its appeal isn't quite as far-reaching as Krispy Kreme's—yet—it is a favorite soda throughout the Southeast.

Curiously, Cheerwine can also be traced to Kentucky, where company founder L. D. Peeler and some other investors bought stock in a regional branch of the maker of MintCola. In 1917, they bought out the company, changed the name to Carolina Beverage Corporation, and purchased Cheerwine's unique flavoring from a "flavor salesman" from St. Louis.

When L. D. died in 1931, his son Clifford Peeler took over, serving as president until 1992 and chairman until his death in 2000 at the age of 96. The company, still family-owned, is thriving under the leadership of L. D. Peeler's great-grandsons, Mark and Cliff Ritchie, who have steadily increased sales.

For those who don't have a taste for sweets, both companies sell an array of cool paraphernalia featuring their nostalgic, retro logos.

Skyline of Greensboro
COURTESY OF GREENSBORO AREA CONVENTION AND VISITORS BUREAU

GREENSBORO

By Carolyn Sakowski

Greensboro and Guilford County have a long tradition of valuing education. Prior to the formation of the county, a staunchly religious group of settlers arrived around 1750. These settlers were members of the Religious Society of Friends, a group commonly known as Quakers. The Quakers named their first settlement New Garden. These settlers would have a lasting influence on educational standards and moral decisions in the area.

In 1767, David Caldwell started a local school known as the Log College. Serving as a Presbyterian minister in what was then the wilderness, Caldwell established the school to educate young men for the ministry. Five of his students went on to become governors of their states; one of them, John Motley Morehead, was governor of North Carolina from 1841 to 1845.

In 1771, North Carolina's colonial assembly created Guilford County in order to gain more administrative control over the growing Piedmont population. Named after the earl of Guilford, a friend of King George III, the county had a sparse population of about 10,000. By 1774, a log courthouse and jail were built at a place known as Guilford Courthouse.

On March 15, 1780, Guilford Courthouse played an important role in

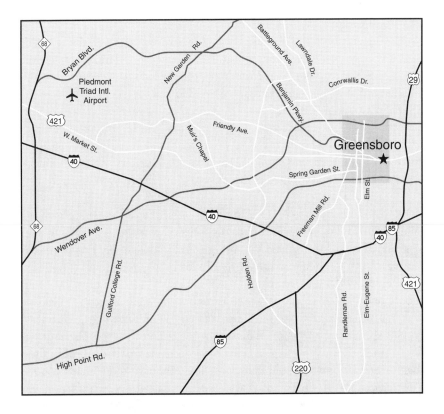

the Revolutionary War. The battle that raged in the woods and over the fields would prove the beginning of the end for Lord Cornwallis's campaign to squelch the patriot forces in the South. When the county courthouse was ready in 1809, the new town needed a name. The commissioners chose to honor Nathanael Greene, the leader of the American forces at the Battle of Guilford Courthouse. Somehow, the final *e* on the name got lost, so the town was named Greensborough.

In 1837, the Society of Friends opened New Garden Boarding School to train teachers. In 1887, this school became Guilford College, the first coeducational institution in the South. In 1863, the Methodist Church founded a school for girls named Greensboro Female College, which came to be called Greensboro College. In 1905, its new leader, Lucy H. Robertson, became the first woman to serve as a college president in North Carolina. In 1873, the Freedmen's Aid Society established Bennett Seminary, a normal school. In 1889, the Methodist Church began to support the school, which eventually became Bennett College.

In the 1820s, young John Motley Morehead, who augmented his law practice with a dry-goods and grocery business, began to push for a railroad to come to Greensboro. He became the first president of the North Carolina Railroad. By July 1851, construction began on the railroad, which was to have its western terminus in Charlotte and its eastern terminus in Goldsboro. Thanks to Morehead, the railroad would pass through Greensboro. The line was completed in 1856.

When war clouds threatened, Morehead and other powerful men in Greensboro did not readily embrace secession. These conservative businessmen realized what war would do to economic progress. In 1861, the citizens of Guilford, including the antislavery Quakers, defeated a proposal to call a convention to consider secession; the margin was 2,771 to 113.

But Guilford benefited from the war when the Confederate government built the Piedmont Railroad to connect Greensboro with Danville, Virginia. The railroad proved the missing link in the supply line from Columbia, South Carolina, to the Army of Northern Virginia.

After the war, industrialization reached Greensboro in a big way when Moses and Ceasar Cone began construction on their Proximity Mill. It was in 1891 that the Cone brothers decided to enter the textile business. Previously, they had been wholesale grocery and tobacco distributors. Oftentimes, they were paid in bolts of cloth from small local mills; they then turned around and sold that cloth. They thought they could produce a better-quality product and create a strong marketing organization. By the mid-1890s, the Cones' company was offering services to 90 percent of the South's textile-mill owners and getting about five cents on each dollar of the gross receipts. This company would evolve into Cone Mills.

In 1896, the first denim rolled off the looms of the Proximity Mill. Four years later, the Cones joined with the Sternberger brothers in building the first cotton flannel mill in the South. The Revolution Cotton Mill's production allowed the owners to boast that they were the world's leader in flannel production. In 1905, the White Oak plant began to produce denim. Cone Mills combined with other textile companies to make Greensboro one of the nation's leading textile-manufacturing centers.

In the 1890s, the city's civic leaders again showed their enthusiasm for education when the state announced plans to establish two new colleges—one for women and one for African-Americans. In 1891, the state selected Greensboro as the location for the Agricultural and Mechanical College for the Negro Race; to win the bid, the city came up with $8,000 in cash and a suitable site. This college would go on to become North Carolina A & T State University. Also in 1891, Greensboro was selected as the site for the Normal and Industrial School for Women, which would become the University of North Carolina at Greensboro. To finance this bid, the city raised $30,000 through a bond issue and donated a suitable location.

Thanks to the vision of its forefathers, Greensboro is a thriving business and educational center for the vibrant North Carolina Piedmont today. Its revitalization efforts in the Old Greensborough & Downtown Historic District and its well-planned Cultural District are a tribute to the continued vision of its leaders.

JUST THE FACTS

Greensboro is located at the intersection of Interstate 40 and Interstate 85, which skirt the southeastern section of town.

Piedmont Triad International Airport, which is served by major carriers including US Airways, Delta, Continental, Northwest, American, and United, is centrally located among Greensboro, High Point, and Winston-Salem. Many hotels offer free transportation to and from the airport.

The Amtrak station is located at 236 East Washington Street. Call 336-272-6755 for information.

The Greyhound/Trailways bus terminal is located in the restored train depot near Old Greensborough at 234-A Washington Street. Call 336-272-8950 for information.

The best source for local information is the Greensboro Area Convention and Visitors Bureau, at 317 South Greene Street, across the street from the Carolina Theatre. Call 800-344-2282 or 336-274-2282 or visit www.visitgreensboro.com.

The city's daily newspaper is the *Greensboro News and Record*, which also publishes *GoTriad*, a free weekly tabloid that tells about activities in the area. You can also visit www.gotriad.com.

*A false-bottomed wagon believed to have been used in the
Underground Railroad*
COURTESY OF HIGH POINT CONVENTION AND VISITORS BUREAU

GUILFORD COUNTY'S QUAKER HERITAGE

Much of Guilford County's heritage is tied to the Religious Society of Friends, more commonly known as the Quakers.

In 1740, Quaker pioneers from Pennsylvania, Virginia, and Nantucket Island began to settle in northwestern Guilford County. By 1754, the New Garden Meeting was established. It quickly became a center for Quakerism in North Carolina. The Battle of Guilford Courthouse, which raged around Quaker homes and farms in New Garden in 1781, saw the meeting house turned into a hospital for soldiers from both sides. Many of the dead were laid to rest in the Friends' burial ground. Even the leader of the American forces at the battle, Nathanael Greene, was a Quaker. One historical figure from Guilford County with a Quaker connection was Dolley Madison, born in 1768 to parents who were members of the New Garden Meeting.

In 1818, some young people from the New Garden Meeting organized a "Sabbath School House." By 1821, Levi Coffin, Jr., was teaching slaves to read the Bible there. Levi and his wife, Catherine, became leaders in giving assistance to fugitive slaves. In 1826, they followed friends and relatives to a settlement in Indiana. It was there that their efforts to hide runaway slaves earned Levi the title of president of the Underground Railroad.

Since fugitive-slave laws provided severe penalties for anyone who interfered with the recovery of slaves, the efforts of these men and women had to be secretive. The Underground Railroad helped slaves escape to the Northern states and Canada by setting up "stations" every 10 to 20 miles along the way. The wagons and carriages used to transport the slaves were called "trains." The runaway slaves usually traveled at night in groups of two or three. The drivers who assisted them were called "conductors." One Quaker couple who proved a vital link in the North Carolina segment of the Underground Railroad was Joshua and Abigail Stanley, who lived in the Centre community. Levi Coffin and Abigail Stanley had grown up together in New Garden.

Today, a wagon with a false bottom used to transport fugitive slaves on the Underground Railroad is on display at the Mendenhall Plantation in Jamestown. A nearly identical wagon is housed at the Levi Coffin House and Museum in Fountain City, Indiana. At both the Mendenhall Plantation and the nearby Museum of Old Domestic Life, you can see artifacts left by the Quakers.

The New Garden Friends Meeting still holds worship services at 801 New Garden Road near Guilford College, which also has its roots in the Society of Friends.

Things to Do

HISTORIC PLACES, GARDENS, AND TOURS

■ *Guilford Courthouse National Military Park* is six miles north of downtown off U.S. 220 (Battleground Avenue) on New Garden Road.

After a three-year standoff in the North, Lord Charles Cornwallis, the British commander, decided to conquer the South. By 1780, the British controlled Georgia and South Carolina. After Cornwallis suffered a setback in October 1780 at Kings Mountain, he moved to Charlotte just as Nathanael Greene took command of the Americans' Southern forces.

Greene divided his forces into two segments. To counter, Cornwallis divided his troops into three columns. In January 1781, the British were defeated at Cowpens, but Cornwallis pursued Greene's forces into North Carolina. By March, Greene had received reinforcements that brought his strength to 4,400 men. He chose Guilford Courthouse as the site for the battle. Greene wanted a location that would be easy for the militia to find, where the British would have to move through woods and make their final assault up a hill across a clearing, and where the Americans would not be trapped by water as they departed.

Cornwallis led his force of 1,900 men into the trap on March 15, 1781. The first exchange came just after one o'clock in the afternoon. The militiamen waiting in the woods were under orders to fire three rounds before retreating. A second line of militia deeper in the woods was reinforced with cannons and cavalry. A third line was on a rise above the clearing. After two hours of fighting, the British drove the Americans from the field and claimed the day. But it was a Pyrrhic victory. Cornwallis lost one-fourth of his men. And nearly 30 percent of his officer corps was down. Cornwallis later said, "I never saw such fighting since God made me. The fighting was furious."

Too weak to pursue the rebels, Cornwallis began his seven-month journey that would end with the British surrender at Yorktown.

In 1886, David Schenck, a Greensboro-based attorney for the Richmond and Danville Railroad, wrote that he was going to "save the battlefield." He helped form the Guilford Battleground Company, which purchased more than 125 acres where the battle was fought. In 1911, Congress appropriated $30,000 to erect an equestrian monument to General Greene; the statue was dedicated on July 3, 1915. Two years later, on March 2, 1917, the Guilford Battleground Company ceded the battleground to the United States government. Today, the park preserves 220 acres of historic fields and forests and 28 monuments.

Among the interesting statues on the grounds is one to Kerenhappuch Turner, a woman who rode on horseback from Maryland to care for her

Statue of Nathanael Greene
Courtesy of Greensboro Area Convention and Visitors Bureau

son, who was wounded in the battle. Another interesting participant is memorialized at the battlefield. Peter Francisco stood six-foot-six when he joined the Continental Army at age 16. He was a foot taller and 100 pounds heavier than the average American soldier. The story goes that Francisco earned fame at Guilford Courthouse when he slew 11 soldiers with his sword in one brief encounter. A tablet that pays tribute to Francisco stands next to the Cavalry Monument. You can also see one of Francisco's immense shoes on display in the visitor center. The battlefield is home to the graves of William Hopper and John Penn, signers of the Declaration of Independence, and Joseph Winston, the Revolutionary War hero for whom the town of Winston (now part of Winston-Salem) was named.

Guests can tour the park on foot, by bicycle, or by automobile. The visitor center includes exhibits, military memorabilia, films, and a bookstore. The battlefield is open from 8:30 A.M. to 5 P.M. daily except for Thanksgiving, Christmas, and New Year's. Admission is free. For more information, call 336-288-1776 or visit www.nps.gov/guco.

■ Adjacent to the Guilford Courthouse battlefield is *Tannenbaum Park*. This eight-acre park is the site of the restored 1778 *Hoskins House*. During the Battle of Guilford Courthouse, the house served as a staging area for British troops under Cornwallis. The *North Carolina Colonial Heritage Center* is located at the park; there, guests can enjoy a diorama of the battle, a gallery of original maps, a museum store, and hands-on exhibits depicting colonial life. They can also stand in a pillory and feel the weight of a musket.

The park is open Tuesday through Sunday, but the museum is closed Sunday; hours vary according to the season. Regular tours of the Hoskins House are available. Admission is free. For more information, call 336-545-5315 or visit http://www.greensboro-nc.gov/Departments/Parks/facilities/tannenbaum/.

MUSEUMS AND SCIENCE CENTERS

The city planners have done an excellent job of putting many of Greensboro's museums and other cultural offerings together in a compact few blocks identified by street signs as the "Cultural District." Here, you'll find the Greensboro Historical Museum, the Greensboro Children's Museum, the central branch of the Greensboro Public Library, the Greensboro

Cultural Center at Festival Park (discussed in the "Cultural Offerings" section of this chapter), and the downtown branch of the YWCA.

■ The **Greensboro Historical Museum**, at 130 Summit Avenue, has exhibits that focus on early settlement, military history (there's an interesting display of weapons used during the Civil War), Native Americans, and transportation. Located in a building that dates to the turn of the 20th century, the museum is listed on the National Register of Historic Places. Some of the more popular displays show items—a snuffbox, a collection of fine china, French gowns—once owned by Greensboro native Dolley Madison, the wife of President James Madison. Another display features items owned by Greensboro native William Sydney Porter, better known as O. Henry. These items include photographs, letters, and early editions of his books, as well as sketches he made when he worked at his uncle's drugstore. A reproduction of that drugstore is also featured. One exhibit highlighting a more recent historical event includes stools and the countertop from the local Woolworth's where four local college students staged a sit-in demonstration that sparked the nation. Behind the museum, you can walk through a small cemetery where several Revolutionary War soldiers rest. You can also see examples of early Guilford County homes and a bust commemorating another local native, Edward R. Murrow. The museum is open from 10 A.M. to 5 P.M. Tuesday through Saturday and from 2 P.M. to 5 P.M. on Sunday. Admission is free. For more information, call 336-373-2043 or visit www.greensborohistory.org.

Greensboro Historical Museum
COURTESY OF GREENSBORO AREA CONVENTION AND VISITORS BUREAU

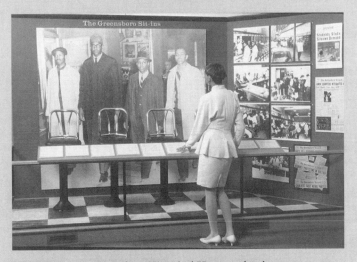

An exhibit at the Greensboro Historical Museum showing the original lunch counter
COURTESY OF GREENSBORO AREA CONVENTION AND VISITORS BUREAU

THE GREENSBORO FOUR

On February 1, 1960, four students from North Carolina A & T State University—David Richmond, Franklin McCain, Jibreel Khazan (Ezell Blair, Jr., before his conversion to Islam), and Joseph McNeil—paid a visit to the F. W. Woolworth store in downtown Greensboro that would change the world. Though they knew that Jim Crow laws prohibited an integrated lunch counter, the four men took seats and politely requested coffee around 4:30 P.M. After being told that "coloreds" were not served at the counter, the four remained seated in silence until the store closed at 5:30.

They returned the next day around 10:30 A.M. with a group of 20 students. The students made small purchases elsewhere in the store, then sat at the lunch counter in groups of three or four as spaces became available. They sat there until noon without being waited on, while white customers were served.

Sit-in demonstrations had been tried previously in other cities. No one knows exactly why the spontaneous actions of four students in Greensboro sparked a movement. They were soon joined by more students from A & T, as well as students from Bennett College and from what is now the University of North Carolina at Greensboro. Within two weeks, sit-ins were staged in 11 other cities. Eventually, 54 cities in nine states saw similar demonstrations.

continued on next page

It took the Greensboro students six months before Woolworth's relented on its policy of respecting "local custom." The actions of these young students played a vital role in the early days of the civil-rights movement, which changed our nation's policies and laws regarding racial segregation.

When the F. W. Woolworth Company announced the closing of its Elm Street location in 1993, a group of citizens organized to preserve the architecturally significant Art Deco building and its historically significant lunch counter. Although the project has been sparked with controversy, work is now under way to convert the building into the International Civil Rights Center and Museum. Plans for the center include a museum, a computer center, a library and reading area, classrooms, workrooms, conference rooms, an auditorium, and the centerpiece—the original lunch counter, restored as a working café.

In 1998, the Greensboro Public Library and the online division of the *Greensboro News and Record* joined forces to launch an impressive Web site about the sit-ins. By visiting www.sitins.com, you can hear nearly 100 audio clips in which the participants themselves describe what happened. You can also read the original news articles and see historic photographs.

A portion of the lunch counter and four of the original stools are currently on display at the Greensboro Historical Museum. A display of the faded Formica lunch counter and four 1950s stools is featured in the Smithsonian in Washington, D.C.

■ Across from the new Greensboro Public Library at 220 North Church Street is the **Greensboro Children's Museum**. This active place offers hands-on exhibits and activities for children ages one to 12. The "Our Town" section has a grocery store complete with checkout registers, a bank, a theater, a media studio, a house under construction, and a post office. A craft room and exhibits about the continents, the furniture industry, and the textile industry are also on the premises. But the section that excites children the most is the transportation area. Here, they can climb into the cockpit of an airliner and sit in a NASCAR automobile, a police car, and a fire truck. They can also place objects on a Bernoulli blower, which demonstrates how an airplane flies; although the blower teaches the four forces of aerodynamics and Newton's Third Law, most children just have a ball watching the air pressure shoot objects toward the ceiling. The museum is open from 9 A.M. to 5 P.M. Tuesday through Saturday, with extended hours to 8 P.M. on Friday; it is open from 9 A.M. to noon on Monday for members only and from 1 P.M. to 5 P.M. on Sunday. The hours vary

Greensboro Children's Museum
COURTESY OF GREENSBORO AREA CONVENTION AND VISITORS BUREAU

during the summers and holidays, so it's a good idea to check the museum's Web site for exact times. An admission fee is charged; discounted rates are available for groups of 10 or more. For more information, call 336-574-2898 or visit www.gcmuseum.com.

■ The *Natural Science Center* is located at 4301 Lawndale Drive, northeast of the downtown area. This is a hands-on museum, zoo, and planetarium. You can come face to face with a 36-foot model of a *Tyrannosaurus rex*; see endangered lemurs; look directly at sunspots over 200,000 miles across; pet a variety of small wildlife in the 30-acre zoo; and tour the herpetarium and the gem-and-mineral gallery. The center is open from 9 A.M. to 5 P.M. Monday through Saturday and from 12:30 P.M. to 5 P.M. on Sunday. The zoo has shorter hours; call for planetarium show times. An admission fee is charged. For more information, call 336-288-3769 or visit www.natsci.org.

CULTURAL OFFERINGS

■ The *Greensboro Cultural Center at Festival Park*, at 200 North Davie Street in the Cultural District, comes close to providing one-stop shopping for Greensboro's visual and performing arts. All told, the center includes four levels of galleries, studios, classrooms, and rehearsal halls. It has a sculpture garden, a privately operated restaurant with outdoor café-style seating, and the Price Bryan Performance Place, an outdoor amphitheater. The complex houses offices for many of the city's cultural organizations, as well as galleries for the **Green Hill Center of North Carolina Art**, the **Guilford Native American Art Gallery**, the **African American Atelier**, and the **Greensboro Artists League**. For information, call 336-373-2712 or visit www.ci.greensboro.nc.us/culture/.

■ The **Eastern Music Festival** is an internationally acclaimed classical music festival founded in 1962. From late June to early August, 200 exceptionally talented students between the ages of 14 and 20 combine with a faculty of outstanding musicians from leading symphony orchestras and music schools for an intensive training program on the campus of Guilford College. They stage more than 50 orchestral concerts and chamber-music performances during the festival. These concerts, especially the ones featuring the faculty orchestra, offer some of the best classical performances you can get for the money. Top guest artists are brought in to perform with the professional ensembles. In recent years, the festival has added the **EMF Fringe series**, which brings in diverse musical acts that range from Americana to Latin, roots to rock, country to bluegrass, and gospel to rhythm-and-blues. For more information, call 336-333-7450 or visit www.easternmusicfestival.com.

■ Although Guilford College, Greensboro College, and North Carolina A & T State University all have galleries that host touring exhibits, the **Weatherspoon Art Gallery** at the University of North Carolina at Greensboro is special, primarily because of Etta Cone's donation in 1949. Miss Cone was a part of the intellectual scene in Paris that included Gertrude Stein. Her bequest of a remarkable collection of lithographs and bronzes by Henri Matisse helped form the core of this collection. Today, the Weatherspoon boasts one of the best university collections of 20th-century American art. Located at the corner of Spring Garden and Tate streets on the university campus, it is housed in a building that won architectural awards for its design. The structure contains six galleries and a sculpture courtyard. The gallery is open from 10 A.M. to 5 P.M. on Tuesday, Wednesday, and Friday, from 10 A.M. to 9:30 P.M. on Thursday, and from 1 P.M. to 5 P.M. on Saturday and Sunday. For more information, call 336-334-5770 or visit http://weatherspoon.uncg.edu/.

■ One of Greensboro's enduring landmarks is the **Carolina Theatre**. Since it opened in 1927 as a vaudeville theater, it has survived as one of the city's principal performing-arts centers, offering theater, dance, concerts, and films. The impressive structure, listed on the National Register of Historic Places, is downtown at 310 South Greene Street. For more information, call 336-333-2600 or visit www.carolinatheatre.com.

■ If you are looking for live theater, check what's scheduled at **Triad Stage**. Founded by two men who met as graduate students at the Yale School of Drama, Triad Stage was called "one of the best regional theaters in America" by New York's Drama League. Its 200-seat performance space offers an intimate setting for original productions as well as classical plays. The theater is located downtown at 232 South Elm Street. For more information, call 336-272-0160 or visit www.triadstage.org.

SPECIAL SHOPPING

■ In recent years, the **Old Greensborough & Downtown Historic District** has become a revitalized turn-of-the-20th-century commercial area. The district is located in and around South Elm Street from the 100 block to the 600 block. It also includes blocks of South Davie, South Greene, and East and West Washington streets. The area has come alive with antique shops, antiquarian book dealers, chic restaurants, bars, and art galleries. You can pick up a free brochure for a self-guided tour at the Greensboro Area Convention and Visitors Bureau, located in the district across from the Carolina Theatre.

■ **State Street Station**, located north of downtown between Church and Elm streets one block south of Cornwallis Drive, is a group of unique boutiques and restaurants that cater to a decidedly upscale clientele. The buildings were once part of a small mill village, so the shops have the feel of a village within a city. For information, call 336-275-1327 or visit www.statestreetstation.com.

■ The two major shopping centers are **Four Seasons Town Centre**, located at the High Point Road exit off Interstate 40, and **Friendly Center** and the newly opened, neighboring **Shops at Friendly Center**, located on Friendly Avenue off Wendover Avenue. For more information, visit www.shopfourseasons.com and www.friendlycenter.com.

■ For something entirely different, check out **Replacements, Ltd.**, the world's largest retailer of old and new china, crystal, flatware, and collectibles. Founded in 1981, the warehouse has over 3 million pieces, all of which are entered in its state-of-the-art computer system. The 225,000-square-foot gift facility includes new stock and over 2,000 unique pieces of china, crystal, and silver. Located on Knox Road east of town off Interstate 85/Interstate 40 at Mount Hope Church Road (Exit 132), the facility is open from 8 A.M. to 10 P.M. daily. Complimentary tours are offered every 30 minutes. For information, call 800-737-5223 or 336-697-3000 or visit www.replacements.com.

RECREATION

Greensboro has a wide variety of public parks. Couple these with the more than 200 acres available for walking, running, or biking at Guilford Courthouse National Military Park and you have a lot of green space. You can get a complete list by contacting the Greensboro Area Convention and Visitors Bureau or by visiting http://www.greensboro-nc.gov/Departments/Parks/default.htm.

- The **Bryan Park Complex** and **Lake Townsend** offer two 18-hole championship golf courses. The Players Course, designed by George Cobb and modified by Rees Jones, opened in 1974. The Champions Course, which opened in 1990, was designed by Rees Jones; seven of its holes border scenic Lake Townsend. The park offers a conference center, horseshoe pits, picnic shelters, tennis and volleyball courts, and an 11-field soccer complex. Sailing, boating, and fishing are popular on Lake Townsend. Located off U.S. 29 North at 6275 Bryan Park Road in Browns Summit, the park is open daily from 8 A.M. to sunset; the golf courses have seasonal hours. For more information, call 336-375-2222 or visit www.bryanpark.com.

- If you like **golf**, you'll feel you've died and gone to heaven. The Greensboro area offers over 20 public golf courses. For a complete list, contact the Greensboro Area Convention and Visitors Bureau by calling 800-334-2282 or 336-274-2282 or visiting www.visitgreensboro.com.

- If you like minor-league baseball, you'll enjoy the **Greensboro Grasshoppers**, a class A farm club for the Florida Marlins. Affiliated with the South Atlantic League, the Grasshoppers play in the state-of-the-art First Horizon Park, located near Old Greensborough on the corner of Bellmeade

and Edgeworth streets. For information, call 336-268-BALL or visit www.gsohoppers.com.

SEASONAL EVENTS

■ A *reenactment of the Battle of Guilford Courthouse* is held every year at Country Park on the weekend closest to the March 15 anniversary of the conflict. Hundreds of reenactors portray British and American soldiers fighting in the American Revolution. The battle is staged at 2 P.M. Admission is free. Call 336-545-5343 for information.

■ The *Wyndham Championship,* part of the FedEx Cup, is the third-oldest event on the PGA tour. A fund-raiser for the Greensboro Jaycees, the tournament is held in the fall at Forest Oaks Country Club, south of Greensboro on U.S. 421. For dates and ticket prices, call 336-379-1570 or visit www.pgatour.com.

Places to Stay

RESORTS, HOTELS, AND MOTELS

Every major chain is represented somewhere in the Greensboro area. Most hotels are grouped at the various exits off Interstates 85 and 40. The greatest concentration is at the N.C. 68 exit off Interstate 40 west of town;

this is the exit for Piedmont Triad International Airport, so the crowd of hotels makes sense. Many of the accommodations listed below are deluxe or expensive. If you are looking for a more moderate price, the budget chains are your best bet.

■ **The Grandover Resort and Conference Center**. Deluxe. 1000 Club Road (800-472-6301 or 336-294-1800; www.grandover.com). Located just southwest of town, this resort is nestled among 1,500 acres of land. One big draw is its two 18-hole golf courses just outside the lobby. The lobby evokes an Old World feel, with contrasting floor patterns of Italian travertine, Tasmanian gold limestone, and black granite. Several types of guest rooms are available at this AAA-rated Four Diamond resort. The basic rooms offer color television, two dual-line telephones with voice mail, a data jack, a refrigerator, a wet bar, a complimentary newspaper, a hair dryer, an iron and ironing board, and a coffee maker. The suites have Jacuzzis and separate parlor areas. The two-bedroom bi-level suite offers a dining/conference table for eight. The resort includes a spa, tennis and racquetball courts, a whirlpool, a pool, a fitness center with a sauna and a steam room, a billiards room, and dining rooms.

■ **O. Henry Hotel**. Deluxe. 624 Green Valley Road (877-854-2100 or 336-854-2000; www.o.henryhotel.com). Located off Wendover Avenue at Benjamin Parkway near Friendly Center, this 131-room grand hotel has an intimate feel. The O. Henry earned a Four Diamond rating from AAA in its first year, and you'll see why the minute you enter the wood-paneled lobby. The regular room amenities include color television, a dressing room with two vanities, an in-room safe, an iron and ironing board, in-room movies and video games, a coffee maker, a microwave, a refrigerator, a hair dryer, a makeup mirror, two-line speaker phones with modem hookups, a complimentary morning newspaper, direct-dial telephone access, and voice mail. In the suites, you get all these amenities plus a gas-burning fireplace in the separate sitting area, a stereo, a VCR, and a huge dressing room. The hotel offers a fine restaurant, afternoon tea and cocktails in the lobby, a business center, an exercise facility, and an outdoor pool. The beds are topped with a blanket cover that is laundered daily. And of course, each room has a collection of O. Henry short stories to remind guests of a local boy who made good.

■ The same people who developed the O. Henry are building **Proximity Hotel**, which is slated for opening in 2007. Located near the O. Henry, Proximity is designed to look like a remodeled textile factory, with spacious rooms, tall ceilings, exposed ductwork, and huge windows. The rooms will be less expensive than at the O. Henry. The owners hope to do for hotels what Target has done for shopping: offer high style and fashion in an affordable way.

- **Greensboro Marriott Downtown**. Expensive. 304 North Greene Street (336-379-8000; www.marriott.com). This is the only full-service hotel in the downtown area. It has 274 guest rooms, including seven suites. You'll find the usual Marriott amenities. It offers meeting space for conferences.

- **Sheraton Greensboro Hotel at Four Seasons**. Expensive. 3121 High Point Road (800-242-6556 or 336-292-9161; www.kourycenter.com). The Joseph S. Koury Convention Center, which connects with this hotel, calls itself the largest hotel and convention center in the Carolinas. Located at the High Point Road exit off Interstate 40, the hotel has over 1,000 guest rooms and access to 250,000 square feet of meeting and banquet space. As a result, it attracts numerous conventions. Amenities include cable television, high-speed Internet access, hair dryers, and voice mail. It offers a full-scale business center, a health club, a pool, a whirlpool, a sauna, and a racquetball court. Because the same developers own the Grandover Resort, the Sheraton staff can make reservations for you at the Grandover spa or tennis and golf courses. Greensboro's major shopping mall, Four Seasons Town Centre, is next door.

INNS AND BED-AND-BREAKFASTS

- **Double Oaks Bed-and-Breakfast Inn**. Deluxe. 204 North Mendenhall Street (336-379-1052; www.doubleoaksinn.com). This inn is housed in a turn-of-the-20th-century Colonial Revival mansion that features Ionic columns, second- and third-floor balconies, and a spacious wraparound porch. The house has eight working fireplaces with mantels, antique tiles, and decorative fireboxes. Each of the three elegant rooms has a private bathroom. A full gourmet breakfast is served. No children or pets are allowed. Smokers can smoke only on the porch.

- **Andrea's Troy-Bumpas Inn**. Expensive. 114 South Mendenhall Street (800-370-9070 or 336-370-1660; www.troy-bumpasinn.com). Built in 1847, this home is listed on the National Register of Historic Places. Close to the campuses of the University of North Carolina at Greensboro and Greensboro College, it offers three rooms with telephones, private baths, hair dryers, cable TV with DVD players, and robes. All are furnished with antiques or antique reproductions.

■ **The Biltmore Greensboro Hotel.** Expensive. 111 West Washington Street (800-332-0303 or 336-272-3474; www.biltmoregreensborohotel.com). This hotel, which bills itself as "a unique European boutique hostelry," is located in the Old Greensborough & Downtown Historic District. Guests enter the elegant walnut-paneled lobby through crystal front doors. In the morning, a deluxe continental breakfast is served; in the evening, a reception featuring an informal wine tasting and hors d'oeuvres is offered. The rooms have king-sized four-poster canopy beds and 16-foot ceilings. Amenities include color televisions, telephones with data ports, refrigerators, hair dryers, VCRs, coffee makers, and irons and ironing boards. Free parking is provided. Small pets are allowed.

■ **Greenwood Bed-and-Breakfast.** Expensive. 205 North Park Drive (866-374-5456 or 336-274-6350; www.greenwoodbb.com). The Greenwood is a turn-of-the-20th-century Craftsman-style home located just off Elm Street in the historic Fisher Park neighborhood. Each of the five guest rooms has a private bath.

Places To Eat

Because of space constraints, some very good restaurants are not mentioned here. I have tried to balance the number of offerings in each price category, but most of the exceptional restaurants in Greensboro fall within the expensive and moderate ranges. I have also tried to list restaurants that continually appear on everyone's list of favorites. A good source for recent restaurant reviews is food critic John Batchelor of *GoTriad*; you can find some of his recent reviews at www.gotriad.com.

■ **Bistro Sofia.** Expensive. 616 Dolley Madison Road (336-855-1313; www.bistrosofia.com). The cuisine here is European and New American, influenced by Eastern Europe—hence the name Sofia, in honor of the Bulgarian capital. The chef, who graduated from nearby Guilford College, trained at the New England Culinary Institute. The restaurant offers prix fixe menus on certain weekdays and before certain times, so check the Web site for a superb meal at a reasonable price. Dinner is served Tuesday through Sunday.

■ *Grappa Grille*. Expensive. 2618 Lawndale Drive (336-545-5678). This restaurant takes its name from the Italian liqueur that is distilled from grapes left in the bottom of the press. The circular booths have been enclosed in heavy drapes, creating a café intimacy reminiscent of old films. Urbane, sophisticated fine dining is the theme here. The ossobuco is a favorite. Dinner is served Monday through Saturday.

■ *Marisol*. Expensive. 5834-E High Point Road (336-852-3303). Although this is probably the most expensive restaurant in the Triad, it is also on everyone's list of top places to dine. It's the sort of place where people celebrate special occasions. The main dining room has a café ambiance; there is also a separate piano bar with leather seating. The printed menu lists first courses only; the servers recite the entrée descriptions orally. Each entrée is part of a complete conception including vegetable portions. Lunch is served Tuesday through Friday and dinner Tuesday through Saturday.

■ *1618 West Seafood Grille*. Expensive/Moderate. 1618 West Friendly Avenue (336-235-0898). The owners of the popular Southern Lights opened this restaurant on the other side of Friendly Avenue. It may be difficult to find initially. It's located on the backside of the building that houses Leon's salon. The converted firehouse has high ceilings and sophisticated decor. It specializes in fresh seafood; nothing is ever frozen. The eclectic, innovative menu changes every two weeks. Dinner is served Tuesday through Sunday.

■ *Undercurrent Restaurant*. Expensive/Moderate. 327 Battleground Avenue (336-370-1266; www.undercurrentrestaurant.com). Undercurrent was located on South Elm Street for nine years. Although a restaurant's move usually makes me nervous about its future, Undercurrent is so popular that I believe it will survive the switch to the area between Greene and Lindsay streets. The move was made to gain twice as much space. The menu, featuring New American and classical cuisine with Asian influences, has stayed the same. The *New York Times* called this a "smart restaurant." Lunch is served Tuesday through Friday and dinner Tuesday through Saturday.

■ *Green Valley Grill*. Moderate. 624 Green Valley Road (336-854-2015;

www.greenvalleygrill.com). The restaurant wing of the O. Henry Hotel, the Green Valley Grill and its owners have established a reputation for developing relationships with local farms and dairies and for presenting innovative food programs open to the public. The restaurant uses a wood-fired oven for pizzas and a wood-fired grill to roast chicken and beef on a spit. Lunch and dinner are served daily.

■ **Liberty Oak**. Moderate. 100-D Washington Street (336-273-7057; www.libertyoakrestaurant.com). This restaurant has been around for over two decades, which says a lot in this business. Its relocation to downtown helped to jump-start the area's revival. Reasonable prices combine with quality ingredients to make the dishes here probably the best value in the area. The blue-plate entrées are especially enticing. Liberty Oak was one of 11 restaurants chosen for *Southern Living*'s "Top Food Finds" in the "Uptown Food" category. Lunch and dinner are served Monday through Saturday.

■ **Solaris Tapas Restaurant and Bar**. Moderate. 125 Summit Avenue (336-378-0198; www.gettapas.com). A tapas menu offers a wide variety of smaller-than-usual servings, priced accordingly. This style of dining allows guests to select several dishes that can be shared for the same price as a usual entrée. The wine list at Solaris features Spanish vintages; there is a martini list as well. Lunch is served Tuesday through Friday and dinner Tuesday through Saturday.

■ **Southern Lights**. Moderate. 105 North Smyres Place (336-379-9414). In business since 1986, this restaurant offers an informal ambiance and reasonably priced dishes prepared with fresh ingredients. On weeknights, the featured entrées are quite a bargain. You can order sandwiches and burgers as well as creative chicken, beef, and seafood dishes. Lunch is served Monday through Friday and dinner Monday through Saturday.

■ **Stamey's Barbecue**. Inexpensive. 2206 High Point Road (336-299-9888) and 2812 Battleground Avenue (336-288-9275). You can't come to North Carolina and not try the barbecue the natives pine for when they have to move away. Stamey's serves what is called Lexington-style barbecue, which has a vinegar-and-tomato sauce. The dining rooms are large and busy; you can also use the drive-through line. Both places serve barbecue cooked the old-fashioned way in a smokehouse behind the High Point Road location. Lunch and dinner are served Monday through Saturday.

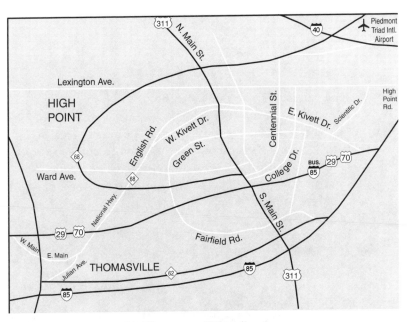

HIGH POINT

By Carolyn Sakowski

*W*hen John Motley Morehead brought the North Carolina Railroad to Guilford County, a survey revealed that the tracks would intersect with the existing plank road that connected Fayetteville to Salem. That intersection, located 912 feet above sea level, would be the highest point on the rail line. It was obvious that this new transportation hub would draw speculators. By 1859, the new village had 525 people, two hotels, two churches, and seven stores. In May of that year, the two-mile-square town was chartered under the name High Point.

High Point has been linked with the furniture industry since the 1880s. Today, its residents are proud to call their city "the Home Furnishings Capital of the World."

If you're looking for a fun photo opportunity, check out "the World's Second-Largest Chest of Drawers," located two blocks east of Main Street at the corner of Westwood and North Hamilton. Built in 1926 and restored in 1996, it is actually the facade of a building shaped like an 18th-century chest of drawers. The socks hanging out of one of the drawers represent the city's hosiery industry. The honor of having the largest chest of drawers was recently claimed by Furnitureland South, which built an 85-foot-tall replica as a facade for its showroom.

JUST THE FACTS

High Point is southwest of Greensboro. It may be reached via Interstate 85 Business or U.S. 311.

Piedmont Triad International Airport is centrally located among High Point, Greensboro, and Winston-Salem. Its carriers include US Airways, Delta, Continental, United, American, and Northwest. Some local hotels offer free transportation from the airport. Call 336-454-3213 or 336-665-5600 for airport information.

The Amtrak station is located at 100 West High Street, right off Main Street near the center of downtown. A pedestrian walkway connects the renovated historic depot to the city's bus transfer center. For information, call 336-841-7245 or visit www.amtrak.com.

The Trailways bus station is located at 100 Lindsay Street. Call 336-882-2000.

A good source for visitor information is the High Point Convention and Visitors Bureau, at 300 South Main Street. Call 800-720-5255 or 336-884-5255 or visit www.highpoint.org.

The city's daily newspaper is the *High Point Enterprise*. You can also check out *GoTriad*, a free weekly tabloid. Its Web site is www.gotriad.com.

Things to Do

HISTORIC PLACES, GARDENS, AND TOURS

■ *Tours of furniture manufacturers' market showrooms* are available to groups of 15 or more. Reservations must be made in advance by calling the High Point Convention and Visitors Bureau at 800-720-5255 or by visiting www.highpoint.org. No tours are available when the furniture markets are held.

■ *Mendenhall Plantation* is located at 603 West Main Street (U.S. 70 Al-

The "World's Largest Chest of Drawers"
(left) is an 85-foot-tall replica at the
entrance of Furnitureland South. The
"World's Second-Largest Chest of Draw-
ers" is a façade of a building located two
blocks east of Main Street.
PHOTOGRAPHS BY CAROLYN SAKOWSKI

ternate) in neighboring Jamestown. James Mendenhall, a Pennsylvania Quaker, received a land grant in 1762. The settlement that grew up around his farm was called Jamestown in his honor. In 1811, his grandson Richard built the original part of what is now known as Mendenhall Plantation.

This wonderful example of early-19th-century Quaker architecture has been enlarged several times yet retains its simple character. The grounds feature a "bank barn" built into a hillside, in the tradition of the Pennsylvania settlers. One of the nation's few surviving false-bottomed wagons, used to help slaves to freedom on the Underground Railroad, is on the site. The house and grounds are open from 11 A.M. to 3 P.M. Tuesday through Friday, from 1 P.M. to 4 P.M. on Saturday, and from 2 P.M. to 4 P.M. most Sundays. An admission fee is charged. For information, call 336-454-3819.

Mendenhall Plantation
COURTESY OF HIGH POINT
CONVENTION AND VISITORS
BUREAU

MUSEUMS AND SCIENCE CENTERS

■ *High Point Museum and Historical Park* is located at 1859 East Lexington Avenue. The park contains the 1786 Haley House, listed on the National Register of Historic Places, as well as a blacksmith shop and a weaving house from the mid-1700s. The renovated museum has furniture displays, military artifacts, pottery, and more. It is open Tuesday through Saturday from 10 A.M. to 4:30 P.M. and Sunday from 1 P.M. to 4:30 P.M. The historical structures in the park are open only on weekends. Call 336-885-6859 for information.

■ The *Furniture Discovery Center* is located at 101 West Green Drive in the same building that houses the High Point Convention and Visitors Bureau. The center is designed to simulate a modern furniture factory, so visitors can see how furniture is made. Exhibits include a talking tree, 15 hand-carved miniature bedrooms, and a display of more than 40 pieces of ⅛-scale hand-carved furniture items that were used to create full-sized furniture. You can see how wood veneers and furniture upholstery are made. You can also try out tools on an assembly line and enjoy the American Furniture Hall of Fame, which gives details about High Point's growth in the industry. The center is open from 10 A.M. to 5 P.M. Monday through Friday, from 9 A.M. to 5 P.M. on Saturday, and from 1 P.M. to 5 P.M. on Sunday; it is closed Mondays from November to March. Hours are extended during the furniture markets. An admission fee is charged. For information, call 336-885-3655 or visit www.furniturediscovery.org.

CULTURAL OFFERINGS

■ The *North Carolina Shakespeare Festival* is headquartered in the High Point Theatre, at 220 East Commerce Avenue. This professional troupe performs plays—most of them by Shakespeare—at different venues in the Triad during the late summer and fall. It also stages *A Christmas Carol* in December. You can contact the festival at P.O. Box 6066, High Point, N.C. 27262 (336-841-2273; www.ncshakes.org).

SPECIAL SHOPPING

Although High Point has dozens of retail stores that feature a vast ar-

The talking tree exhibit at the Furniture Discovery Center
Courtesy of High Point Convention and Visitors Bureau

ray of home furnishings to suit every taste and budget, I will highlight only a few because of their unique qualities. The High Point Convention and Visitors Bureau offers free furniture-shopping directories. You can usually find the best deals in August and right after the furniture markets in April and October.

■ *Furnitureland South,* on Interstate 85 Business between High Point and Greensboro, is phenomenal. It bills itself as "the World's Largest Home Furnishings Showplace." The complex is over 800,000 square feet in size and still growing. From the moment you see the 85-foot-tall chest of drawers from the highway, you'll know this is not an ordinary furniture store. It's so big that you'll even be given a map. You are free to browse the several buildings, where furniture is shown in gallery settings and grouped according to type and style. When you need assistance, just pick up the nearest telephone. The showrooms are open Monday, Tuesday, Wednesday, and Saturday from 8:30 A.M. to 5:30 P.M. and Thursday and Friday from 8:30 A.M. to 8:30 P.M. For information, call 336-841-4328 or visit www.furniturelandsouth.com.

■ *Rose Furniture Company* has been in business since 1925. Its 180,000-square-foot showroom has three floors, a large resource and catalog room, and more than 65 salespeople to help you. It carries over 600 lines of furniture. The address is 916 Finch Avenue. From Interstate 85 Business, take the Surrett Drive exit and turn right; you'll see where to turn right again to reach Finch Avenue. The store is open Monday through Saturday from 8:30 A.M. to 5 P.M.; the hours are extended to 6 P.M. on Friday. For information, call 336-886-6050 or visit www.rosefurniture.com.

■ The *Atrium Furniture Mall,* located downtown at 430 South Main Street, houses over 20 different furniture stores in one location. It is open

Monday through Friday from 9 A.M. to 6 P.M. and Saturday from 9 A.M. to 5 P.M. For information, call 336-882-5599 or visit www.atriumfurniture.com.

RECREATION

■ *Oak Hollow Lake Park and Marina*, at 3431 North Centennial Street, has an 18-hole Pete Dye-designed golf course with a practice range and a clubhouse. The 1,500-acre park offers boating, water-skiing, and sailing; small sailboats can be rented for use on the lake. It also has tennis courts and 90 campsites with full hookups. Call 336-883-3494.

■ *City Lake Park*, at 602 West Main Street in Jamestown, is a 969-acre site with a 340-acre lake. Visitors enjoy the fishing, the paddleboats, and the fishing-boat and canoe rentals. The park has amusement rides, a train, a water slide, the largest outdoor swimming pool in the state, a miniature golf course, a gymnasium, a playground, and an excursion boat. Call 336-883-3498.

■ *Piedmont Environmental Center* was founded in 1972 to provide environmental education through outdoor experiences. Located at 1220 Penny Road adjacent to High Point Lake, its 376 acres of protected land offer 11 miles of trails for jogging and hiking. The *Bicentennial Greenway*, a 10-foot-wide, 6.5-mile-long paved trail, also runs through the site. The center's educational building is a study in recycled-materials construction—beverage cans were used for the red roof, newspapers for the gray roof, ketchup bottles for office carpeting, and car windshields for the bathroom tiles. The center has a nature preserve; a nature store; small-animal exhibits including a red fox, a white-tailed deer, hawks, raccoons, and owls; and a large "walk-on" relief map of North Carolina that demonstrates the state's geology, geography, and physiography. The center is open Monday through Saturday from 9 A.M. to 5 P.M. and Sunday from 1 P.M. to 5 P.M. The trails are open from sunrise to sunset seven days a week. Admission is free. For information, call 336-883-8531 or visit www.piedmontenvironmental.com.

SEASONAL EVENTS

Say no more—the big events in town are the two *High Point Markets*, held in the spring and fall.

THE FURNITURE INDUSTRY AND HIGH POINT

Drawing on the nearby hardwood forests, local furniture factories owned and run by Northern industrialists were shipping their products out of High Point by the trainload in the 1880s. In 1889, High Point Furniture Company became the first locally owned furniture manufacturer. Others soon followed. Local entrepreneurs realized that the quality of their furniture exceeded that produced in the North. They just needed to come up with some way to display their wares. In 1905, the High Point Exposition Company opened its first furniture show. In 1909, the city's furniture manufacturers began hosting biannual expositions, but they couldn't compete with the ones held in the North.

In 1911, J. J. Farris, editor of the *High Point Enterprise*, suggested that High Point construct a large display building. The Southern Furniture Manufacturers' Association led the movement to create a display building that would make High Point the center for Southern furniture. In June 1919, construction began on a 10-story, $1 million structure that would have 261,000 square feet of exhibit space. When the building opened in 1921, more than 700 furniture buyers showed up to view the 149 exhibits. By 1924, the building's exhibit space was completely rented. Over the years, the Southern Exposition Building underwent repeated expansions. When the first postwar market was held in January 1947, some 5,147 retail furniture buyers came to town. By 1955, the display area increased to 500,000 square feet.

Now known as the International Home Furnishings Center, the showrooms have completely taken over downtown High Point. In 1990, the city boasted 8.5 million square feet of display space. It plays host to "the market" twice a year—in the spring and fall. The market attracts over 1,800 manufacturers. The trade show, which is not open to the public, draws more than 95,000 visitors to High Point from every state and 110 countries; these guests spend an estimated $330 million locally. Because accommodations are scarce during these times, many local residents rent their homes to people coming for the markets and use the money to go on vacation.

Although the markets are not open to the public, the city's huge furniture retailers are. People from all over the country come to High Point to take advantage of prices 40 to 50 percent off retail. When you are shopping, remember that these retailers do not have huge warehouses stocked with ready-to-ship furniture. Rather, the retailers place orders with the manufacturers; it usually takes from eight to 12 weeks for customers to receive their shipment. Some manufacturers require local retailers to exhibit complete collections in order to get volume discounts. This means that customers have a better selection in High Point than in traditional stores. Giants like Furnitureland South, Boyles, and Rose Furniture have immense showrooms with professional designers on staff as sales associates. The Bouldin House Bed-and-Breakfast's Web site (www.bouldinhouse.com) has an excellent description of what to expect if you come shopping for furniture; click the "Furniture Shopping" heading.

In addition to full-service stores, there are several clearance centers in High Point. The area around South Main Street near Interstate 85 Business could be called "Clearance Row." These stores stock unclaimed merchandise, discontinued items, and pieces moved out of the galleries to make room for new collections. Items that were originally 40 to 50 percent off the retail price in the main stores are discounted even further.

When you come to High Point, you will see that this is indeed "the Home Furnishings Capital of the World."

Places to Stay

Good locally owned accommodations are few in High Point. Most of the major chains are represented around the intersections of Interstate 40 and N.C. 68 (the airport exit) and Interstate 40 and High Point Road. Both of these areas are within a quick drive of downtown High Point. Also see the Greensboro listings, because the two cities have virtually run together.

RESORTS, HOTELS, AND MOTELS

■ *The Radisson Hotel High Point*. Expensive. 135 South Main Street (336-889-8888). Located next to the largest of the furniture showroom buildings, this hotel is the best you'll find in downtown High Point. It has over

200 rooms, a restaurant, a bar, a fitness room, an indoor pool, and meeting space. The hotel provides free airport transportation.

INNS AND BED-AND-BREAKFASTS

■ *J. H. Adams Inn*. Deluxe. 1108 North Main Street (888-256-1289 or 336-882-3267; www.jhadamsinn.com). When it was built in 1918, this place was the home of a family that made its fortune in the local hosiery business that for decades was the only North Carolina company on the New York Stock Exchange. Now listed on the National Register of Historic Places, the home was renovated and opened as an inn in 2001. Each of the 30 rooms and suites showcases a distinct furniture collection from the best manufacturers in the world. The amenities are comparable to those found in world-class inns.

■ *The Bouldin House Bed-and-Breakfast*. Expensive. 4332 Archdale Road in Archdale (800-739-1816 or 336-431-4909; www.bouldinhouse.com). Although you'll travel a few miles out of town, it's worth the drive to stay at this bed-and-breakfast. The lovely old farmhouse sits on three acres of a former tobacco farm. It has been beautifully restored. It has wainscoting in the hallways, crafted oak paneling in the dining room, and decorative patterns in the hardwood floors. Each guest room has a king-sized bed, a ceiling fan, a clock radio, a fireplace, and a private bath. Your stay includes early-morning coffee and tea service, a gourmet breakfast, and home-baked goodies in the evening. A guest telephone and a color television with a VCR and videotapes are located in the gathering room; televisions are also available in select guest rooms. Children over 10 are welcome.

J. H. Adams Inn
PHOTOGRAPH BY CAROLYN SAKOWSKI

The Bouldin House Bed-and-Breakfast
PHOTOGRAPH BY CAROLYN SAKOWSKI

Places to Eat

- **Blue Water Grille**. Expensive. 126 East State Avenue (336-886-1010). The cuisine here reflects an interesting fusion of French, Asian, Caribbean, and Low Country influences. Although you can expect excellent seafood entrées, as the establishment's name suggests, you can also enjoy a variety of non-seafood offerings. Dinner is served Tuesday through Saturday.

- **Restaurant J Basul Noble**. Expensive. 101 South Main Street (336-889-3354; www.noblesrestaurants.com). Jim Noble, the proprietor here, also owns top restaurants in Charlotte and Winston-Salem. This location is across the street from the restored train depot. Consistently rated one of the best restaurants in the Triad, it offers a menu leaning toward Italian and French cuisine. Noble is known for using fresh ingredients and cooking over wood. Dinner is served Monday through Saturday; Sunday brunch is also available.

- **Southern Roots**. Expensive. In the J. H. Adams Inn at 1108 North Main Street (336-882-5570; www.jhadamsinn.com/southern.html). As the name implies, much of this restaurant's menu derives its inspiration from Southern tradition. For example, it offers pan-seared sea scallops served on ham-braised cabbage and kale over creamy cheese grits. Lunch is served Monday through Friday and dinner Monday through Saturday.

- **Daimagin Japanese Fusion Bar & Café**. Moderate. 1807 North Main Street (336-883-9152; www.daimagincafe.com). You can get gourmet Japanese cuisine at this establishment. Authentic sushi is hand-prepared by certified chefs. Tuna entrées and fusion entrées are also available. Lunch is served Monday through Friday and dinner Monday through Saturday.

- **Emerywood Fine Foods**. Moderate/Inexpensive. 130 West Lexington Avenue (336-882-6971; www.emerywood.com). Emerywood serves a large variety of classic and gourmet sandwiches and salads, as well as outstanding entrées in the evening. It also runs a popular catering service. Lunch is served Monday through Saturday and dinner Tuesday through Saturday.

Zebra grazing at North Carolina Zoological Park
COURTESY OF NORTH CAROLINA DIVISION OF TOURISM, FILM AND SPORTS DEVELOPMENT

TRIAD NEARBY

By Anne Holcomb Waters and Carolyn Sakowski

■ *North Carolina Zoological Park*, centrally located in Asheboro, is the largest walk-through natural-habitat zoo in the country. Designed from its inception to display animals and plants in settings as similar to their native habitats as possible, the zoo offers five miles of meandering trails through indoor exhibits and two vast "continental regions," North America and Africa. In all, the park covers more than 500 acres in the Uwharrie Mountains, with over 900 acres available for expansion. Because of the zoo's size, officials recommend spending five hours for a visit, though the highlights can be seen in just a couple of hours.

You can start your visit at either the North America or Africa entrance, where you'll find lockers, ATMs, and wheelchairs and strollers for rent. Although the zoo has a tram, walking is the best way to see the animals, so wear comfortable shoes. The habitats range from wide-open fields like the "African Plains and Prairie" exhibit, where spotting antelope and bison can be challenging, to indoor-outdoor exhibits like the "Rocky Coast," where you can watch polar bears and sea lions dipping and diving underwater. There are alligators in the "Cypress Swamp" and gorillas in the "Forest Glade." In short, the wonderful, wild world of animals awaits you.

The zoo has three restaurants, several picnic areas, and two gift shops. Buses will take you back to your car at the end of your visit. The zoo is open every day except Christmas; it closes during severe weather. It is open from 9 A.M. to 5 P.M. from mid-April through October and from 9 A.M.

A Seagrove potter displays his wares.
COURTESY OF NORTH CAROLINA DIVISION OF TOURISM, FILM AND SPORTS DEVELOPMENT

to 4 P.M. from November to April. Admission is charged. No rain checks are given. To get to the zoo, take U.S. 220 South from Asheboro and follow the signs. For more information, call 800-488-0444 or visit www.nczoo.org.

■ **Seagrove** is a unique hamlet that is the pottery center of North Carolina. Located 30 miles south of the Triad at the north end of the Uwharries, it is home to scores of potters who practice their craft in the tiny town and its environs. While some are carrying on family traditions over 200 years old, others are relative newcomers who have congregated in this artists' community, thus making the pottery available here richly diverse. Along with the traditional face jugs and salt-glazed jugs, you'll find fine raku and museum-quality porcelain.

You can start your visit at the North Carolina Pottery Center, at 250 East Avenue, where you can pick up a free map with brief descriptions of potteries even if the center is closed. However, this interpretive and educational facility is well worth a visit if you're interested in the history of North Carolina pottery. The center is open Tuesday through Saturday from 10 A.M. to 4 P.M. Call 336-873-8430 or visit www.ncpotterycenter.com for more information. Two marketing associations also offer Web sites; visit www.discoverseagrove.com and www.seagrovepotteries.com. Check out the latter for information about the annual spring kiln opening. Many, though not all, of the potteries are closed on Sunday.

A TIME OF TRAINS

By Anne Holcomb Waters

Midway between the Triad and Charlotte off Interstate 85, you will find the towns of *Salisbury* and *Spencer*, which lie only minutes from the interstate but a century from its congestion, thanks to the legacy of the railroad. The older of the two, Salisbury, was established before the American Revolution, but it took the arrival of the North Carolina Railroad in 1855 to rejuvenate the century-old town. Spencer owes its very existence to the railroad.

If you're approaching from the north, take the Spencer exit (Exit 82, a left-hand exit), which will bring you over the Yadkin River on U.S. 29. Here, in April 1865, a band of Confederates (with the help of some Union prisoners turned Confederate sympathizers) thwarted the efforts of Union major general George Stoneman and his men to burn the railroad bridge. Continue on U.S. 29 and you will arrive in Spencer, then Salisbury.

In the 1890s, Southern Railway's president, Samuel Spencer, decided to establish a locomotive repair facility at the midpoint between Atlanta and Washington, D.C. And so the town of Spencer was born. Incorporated in 1905,

the town thrived until the 1950s and 1960s, when the Spencer Repair Shops began to be phased out.

The *North Carolina Transportation Museum* and *Historic Spencer Shops* are located on the site of what was once Southern Railway's largest steam-locomotive repair facility. The site features an authentic train depot, antique automobiles, and a 37-bay roundhouse that includes 25 locomotives, dozens of rail cars, and other exhibit areas. The museum offers seasonal train rides, guided tours for scheduled groups, and special events throughout the year. Included among these is the semi-annual appearance of Thomas the Tank Engine—a must for tiny tykes. There is no charge for admission, but donations are appreciated; admission may be charged for special events. There are small fees for the train and turntable rides. From April through October, the facilities are open from 9 A.M. to 5 p.m. Monday to Saturday and from 1 P.M. to 5 P.M. on Sunday. From November through March, the hours are 10 A.M. to 4 P.M. Tuesday to Saturday and 1 P.M. to 4 P.M. on Sunday. For more information, call the museum at 877-NCTM-FUN or 704-636-2889 or visit www.nctrans.org.

Continue on U.S. 29, which becomes Salisbury Avenue, then Main Street as you approach downtown Salisbury. Chartered in 1755, Salisbury is steeped in history and is devoted to preserving it, as evidenced by its 10 historic districts encompassing 30 blocks. Throughout the town are lovely 19th- and 20th-century homes, churches, and businesses where you can still buy homemade ice cream and get Mary Janes and Bit-O-Honeys out of bins.

Start your visit at the *Rowan County Convention and Visitors Bureau* (800-332-2343 or 704-638-3100; www.visitsalisburync.com), located at 204 East Innes Street. To get there, turn left off Main Street onto Innes and go two blocks; the bureau is on the left. Here, you can pick up information for self-guided walking and driving tours and trolley tours. Among the sites, you'll find the following.

The *Rowan Museum*, at 202 North Main Street, occupies the 1854 courthouse, a fine example of Greek Revival architecture from before the Civil War. Among its holdings are Civil War-era artifacts and memorabilia of Salisbury native and author Frances Fisher Tiernan, who penned her works under the name Christian Reid.

The handsome *Josephus Hall House*, at 226 South Jackson Street, was built in 1820 as an academy for young women. Later converted into a private residence, it was owned by the Hall family for gen-erations before being purchased by the Historic Salisbury Foundation, which operates it as a museum. It is open Saturday and Sunday from 1 P.M. to 4 P.M. Admission is charged.

Salisbury National Cemetery, at 202 Government Road, was established in 1865 to honor the thousands of Union soldiers who died at the Salisbury Confederate prison during the Civil War. Today, the cemetery is the burial ground for veterans of all of America's wars. For information, call 704-636-2661.

And last but certainly not least is the *Salisbury Railway Passenger Station*, at 215 Depot Street. A fine example of the Spanish Mission style, it was designed by noted architect Frank Milburn in 1906. Two Amtrak trains, the Piedmont and the Carolinian, pass through daily between Charlotte and New York, continuing a century-old tradition. Indeed, Norfolk Southern and Amtrak trains pass with such regularity that a former loading dock along the rails has become an informal train-spotting platform. Each weekend, (mostly) men come out and set up their lawn chairs to watch. Some residents refer to them affectionately as "train nuts," since trains pass so frequently here that they are regarded more as noisy nuisances than objects of fascination.

- *Tanglewood Park* is the former estate of William Neal Reynolds, brother of tobacco entrepreneur R. J. Reynolds. Perched on the bank of the Yadkin River, this lush 1,100-acre park has been turned into northwestern North Carolina's premier recreation area. In addition to lovely gardens, a riding stable, a small lake with paddleboats, and miles of trails for riding and biking, Tanglewood boasts the Championship Course, designed by Robert Trent Jones, Jr., as well as another 18-hole golf course and a par-three course. More recent enhancements include the splendid new Pete S. Brunstetter Aquatic Center and lighted clay and hard-surface tennis courts. Picnic facilities abound, including several shelters that can be reserved for large parties. Tanglewood also offers accommodations at the lovely *Manor House Bed-and-Breakfast*, Reynolds's former home; for information, call 336-778-6370.

  Tanglewood hosts special events throughout the year, including the *Independence Day Fireworks Celebration*, the *North Carolina Wine Festival* in the spring, and the *Festival of Lights* during the holiday season.

  The entrance to Tanglewood, at 4061 Clemmons Road, is about 10 miles southwest of Winston-Salem; it is easily accessible from Interstate 40. The park is open daily from 7 A.M. until sunset except for Christmas Day. Admission is charged. Call 336-778-6300 or check out www.co.forsyth.nc.us/Tanglewood for more information.

- *Alamance Battleground State Historic Site* is located off N.C. 62 near Burlington, which is east of Greensboro. This is the site of a 1771 battle between Royal Governor William Tryon's militia and the rebellious backcountry farmers known as Regulators. The Regulators objected to the control exercised over the colonial government by the merchants and planters to the east; their dissatisfaction eventually led to the short-lived War of Regulation. They were crushed by Tryon here at Alamance, which ended the Regulator Movement. On the other hand, many interpret the battle and the Regulators' grievances as a warmup for the American Revolution.

  The battleground is currently open from 9 A.M. to 5 P.M. Monday through Saturday. Be sure to call ahead; the number is 336-227-4785. The Web site is www.ah.dcr.state.nc.us/sections/hs/alamance/alamanc.htm. Admission is free.

- *Charlotte Hawkins Brown Memorial State Historic Site* was North Carolina's first state historic site honoring the contributions of African-American citizens. Located about 10 miles east of Greensboro in Sedalia, this was also the first state historic site to honor a woman. To reach it, take Exit 135 (Rock Creek Dairy Road) off Interstate 85, follow the signs to U.S. 70, turn left, and travel 1.5 miles to the site.

Charlotte Hawkins Brown was born in North Carolina but grew up in Cambridge, Massachusetts. Dissatisfied with the lack of educational opportunities for blacks in the Jim Crow South, she returned to North Carolina in 1901 to teach African-American youths in Sedalia. When the school where she was working closed after she had taught only one term, she raised money in New England to found her own school, which she named Palmer Memorial Institute. In its early years, the day and boarding school emphasized agricultural and industrial education for rural living. During her 50-year presidency, Dr. Brown saw more than 1,000 students graduate from her school.

The historic site focuses not only on Palmer Memorial Institute but on the educational and social history of North Carolina as well. It offers exhibits, tours of historic structures, and audiovisual presentations. From October to March, the site is currently open Monday through Saturday from 9 A.M. to 5 P.M. From April to September, it is open Monday through Friday from 10 A.M. to 4 P.M. Be sure to call ahead; the number is 336-449-4846. The Web site is www.ah.dcr.state.nc.us/sections/hs/chb/chb.htm. Admission is free.

- *Horne Creek Living Historical Farm*, located off U.S. 52 north of Winston Salem in Pinnacle, is a state historic site that interprets everyday farm life on a typical middle-class North Carolina farm during the early 1900s. From April to October, the farm is open Tuesday through Saturday from 9 A.M. to 5 P.M. and Sunday from 1 P.M. to 5 P.M. From November to March, it is open Tuesday through Saturday from 10 A.M. to 4 P.M. and Sunday from 1 P.M. to 4 P.M. Admission is free except for special events. Call 336-325-2298 or visit www.ah.dcr.state.nc.us/sections/hs/horne/horne.htm for more information.

- *Lexington*, approximately 25 miles south of Winston-Salem on U.S. 52, is the county seat of Davidson County and the undisputed "Barbecue Capital of North Carolina." Home to more than 20 barbecue restaurants, Lexington is known for its Western-style (or Lexington-style) barbecue, which features pork shoulders with a vinegar sauce that includes tomato. This distinguishes it from Eastern-style barbecue, which involves roasting the whole hog and using a zestier vinegar-only sauce. If this seems a small distinction, you're wrong. The merits of these two styles are hotly debated in the state.

Lexington's famous *Barbecue Festival* takes place each October. Call

336-956-1880 or visit www.barbecuefestival.com for more information.

Lexington's favorite son is Bob Timberlake, a gifted and extraordinarily successful painter. Inspired to take up painting as an adult by an article about Andrew Wyeth, Timberlake has since branched out into furniture making, clothing design, and, most recently, architecture. Almost everything Timberlake puts his name on sells like hot cakes and can be found at the **Bob Timberlake Gallery**, located on East Center Street Extension. Call 800-244-0095 or visit www.bobtimberlake.com for more information.

- The quaint town of **Mount Airy** is a must for those who love *The Andy Griffith Show*. If you're a fan, you probably already know that Mount Airy is Griffith's hometown and the model for Mayberry. Located on U.S. 52 about 30 miles northwest of Winston-Salem, Mount Airy is a living monument to Griffith and the popular television show, boasting Floyd's Barber Shop, the Old Mayberry Jail, and Griffith's childhood home. If you visit at mealtime, be sure to try a porkchop sandwich at the **Snappy Lunch**, Mount Airy's oldest restaurant.

Each September, Mount Airy commemorates *The Andy Griffith Show* with its **Mayberry Days** festival, which attracts fans worldwide. Visit the Surry Arts Council's Web site at www.surryarts.org for more information.

- Speaking of Mayberry, **Pilot Mountain State Park**, also on U.S. 52 in Surry County, is located next to the town of Pilot Mountain, which was the basis for Mount Pilot on *The Andy Griffith Show*. Though many visitors think Mount Pilot is the correct name, it's not. And don't go looking for any "fun girls" here either. Pilot Mountain is the most distinctive peak in the Sauratown range and a well-known landmark of the Triad. The state park offers picnic grounds, campsites, bridle paths, and plenty of hiking trails. The quartzite dome that sits atop Pilot Mountain, however, is a fragile ecosystem unto itself; climbing it is not allowed. Call 336-325-2355 or visit http://ils.unc.edu/parkproject//visit/pimo/home.html for more information.

- **Hanging Rock State Park**, located about 15 miles east of Pilot Mountain on N.C. 89, is the largest state park in the Piedmont. Three sheer rockfaces—Cooks Wall, Moores Knob, and Hanging Rock itself—dominate the park. Climbing is very popular on the first two but not on Hanging Rock. Campsites, cabins, picnic areas, swimming, fishing, and 20 miles of hiking trails are the attractions here. Many visitors like to canoe the Dan River, a gentle, slow-moving river except after storms. Call 336-593-

Doc Watson performs during Merlefest.
COURTESY OF NORTH CAROLINA DIVISION OF TOURISM, FILM AND SPORTS DEVELOPMENT

8480 or visit http://ils.unc.edu/parkproject/visit/haro/home.html for more information.

■ Nestled in the foothills of the Blue Ridge, Wilkes County comes alive the last weekend in April thanks to *Merlefest*, an annual celebration of Americana music. Held to honor the late son of flat-picking legend Doc Watson, this four-day music festival grew from a few of Doc and Merle's musician friends playing on the back of a flatbed truck for 4,000 people in 1988 to a crowd of over 40,000 fans who come to see some of the best bluegrass, Celtic, and Cajun musicians in the business. Numerous stages are spread over the hillsides of the campus of Wilkes Community College. What makes this festival so special is the magic that often occurs when musicians who rarely play together team up for intimate jam sessions at some of the smaller venues. You can learn more about Merlefest at www.merlefest.org.

On opposite page:
Misty morning at Shelton Vineyards
COURTESY OF NORTH CAROLINA DIVISION OF TOURISM, FILM AND SPORTS DEVELOPMENT

THE YADKIN VALLEY:
NORTH CAROLINA'S WINE COUNTRY

By Anne Holcomb Waters

Situated in the heart of the North Carolina Piedmont, the Yadkin River Valley has emerged as the state's premier wine region. Spurring this wine revolution is the gradual decline of the tobacco industry. Since the 1990s, area farmers have been planting former tobacco fields with grapevines and other alternative crops. The cultivation of vinifera and European varietal grapes has been so successful here, in fact, that the region was recognized in 2003 as North Carolina's first American Viticultural Area, or "appellation."

For wine enthusiasts, a tour of the Yadkin Valley wineries offers the chance not only to sip some award-winning Chardonnays and Cabernets but also to travel the rolling valleys and picturesque foothills of the Piedmont. The valley boasts 15-plus vineyards and wineries, with more on the horizon. The following tour follows a roughly circular route to visit four wineries of distinction. I strongly urge you to expand your tour of the wine country if you have time.

In the 1970s, the pioneering efforts of the late Jack Kroustalis and his wife, Lillian, at *Westbend Vineyards* proved that vinifera grapes could grow in the Piedmont. Named for the western bend in the Yadkin River, Westbend began as a vineyard only, growing grapes for other wineries, before becoming a bonded winery in 1988. Its first wines were released in 1990, and the awards have flowed in ever since. It is open for wine tastings Tuesday through Saturday from 11 A.M. to 5 P.M. and Sunday from noon to 5 P.M.; the hours may vary in winter. For more information, call 336-945-5032 or visit www.westbendvineyards.com. Westbend is located at 5394 Williams Road in Lewisville on the western outskirts of Winston-Salem. From Winston-Salem, take U.S. 421 North to Shallowford Road (Exit 246). Turn left, go 2.4 miles, and turn left onto Williams Road. Westbend is the fourth drive on the left.

RayLen Vineyards and Winery is located at 3577 U.S. 158 in Mocksville. Joe and Joyce Neely received a big boost when Westbend Vineyards' longtime winemaker, Steve Shepard, decided to join their fledgling vineyard in the late 1990s. Every one of RayLen's initial releases in 2000 earned medals in competitions. Named for the Neelys' two daughters, Rachel and Len, the vineyard has a spacious tasting room with tables and chairs and a wraparound porch with rocking chairs for use in fair weather. The winery is open year-round from 11 A.M. to 6 P.M. Monday thought Saturday. For information, call 336-998-3100 or visit www.raylenvineyards.com. To reach RayLen from Winston-Salem, head west on Interstate 40 to Exit 180 and turn left on N.C. 801 South. The entrance is four miles on the right.

Shelton Vineyards, at 286 Cabernet Lane in Dobson, is owned by brothers Ed and Charlie Shelton, who first planted 60 acres of European varietals on an old dairy farm in 1999. By 2001, that acreage had expanded to more than 200, making this the largest family-owned estate winery in North Carolina. In addition to investing in their own state-of-the-art facility, the Shelton brothers sponsored the application for the area's appellation designation and started the viticulture and oenology program at Surry Community College in Dobson. The vineyard is open from 10 A.M. to 6 P.M. Monday through Saturday and from 1 P.M. to 6 P.M. on Sunday during daylight saving time. The winter hours are 10 A.M. to 5 P.M. Monday through Saturday and 1 P.M. to 5 P.M. on Sunday. The cost is five dollars per person. Guests receive a guided tour of the 33,000-square-foot winery, an overview of the art of winemaking, a tasting of five wines, and a souvenir glass. For information, call 336-998-3100 or visit www.sheltonvineyards.com. From Mocksville, take U.S. 601 North to Dobson and look for the sign.

Named for a prizewinning Holstein cow, *RagApple Lassie Vineyards & Winery* is located at 3820 Rockford Road in Boonville. When the winery was honored as one of two finalists for the distinction of being the "Best New Winery in the United States," owners Frank and Lenna Hobson were quick to credit the Yadkin Valley appellation. Winemaker Linda King also deserves some of the credit for RagApple Lassie's early, heady success. Tastings, available daily, cost six dollars; participants receive a souvenir glass. If you want a tour, just ask. Call 866-724-2775 or visit www.ragapplelassie.com. To reach the winery from Dobson, go east on N.C. 67 off U.S. 601 and look for the sign.

For additional information about North Carolina's vineyards and wineries, visit the North Carolina Grape Council's Web site at www.ncwines.org. For a member list of the Yadkin Valley Wine Growers Association, visit www.yadkinvalleywineries.com. For a map of an expanded tour of the wineries, call 888-YV-WINES or visit www.yadkinwines.com.

Charlotte

By Anne Holcomb Waters

*T*here is no reason on God's green earth for Charlotte to be here.

Charlotte has no advantage of nature to justify its location, its geographical presence. It has no port like New York or New Orleans, no confluence of rivers like Charleston or Pittsburgh, no navigable river like Wilmington, no commanding heights like Memphis.

So as the first white men moved west from the coast and south down the Great Wagon Road, why did they stop here? When Thomas Spratt, the first European to settle in the area, walked into what is now the heart of Uptown Charlotte, what made him decide to stay and (literally) set up shop?

The land Spratt came to was unquestionably beautiful. Green hills swelled gently from ridge to red-clay field to ridge; pines grew in stands thick as jungles with brush and briars and berries; and throughout ran clear, fast creeks that fed the Catawba River to the west.

But the land that would be Charlotte and Mecklenburg County had more going for it than just beauty. The soil was more fertile than that in the Uwharries to the east or the Blue Ridge to the west. Close at hand were several of the best fords for crossing the Catawba. For centuries, the Cherokee and Catawba tribes had directed their trading routes towards these fords, so that two main paths had developed, one running northeast and southwest, the other northwest and southeast.

So when Thomas Spratt made his way to the top of the low hill where Trade Street now crosses Tryon Street, the thought that has occurred to thousands since when gazing upon Charlotte may have come to his mind: *I could do all right for myself here.*

Stand at Trade and Tryon on any weekday and picture the courthouse here at the corner, which is where it stood until the mid-19th century (and which is why the intersection is still referred to as "the Square,"

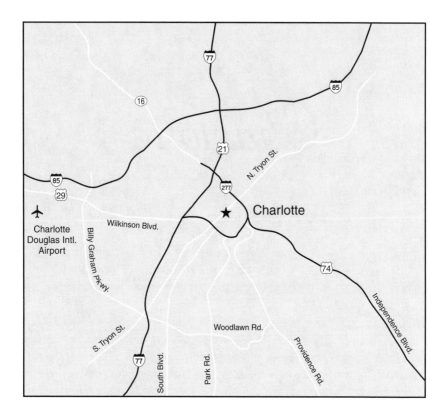

as in Courthouse Square). Look up at the steel and glass around you and imagine the fine Victorian houses that once lined both streets as far as the city limits. Now watch the traffic speed by and try to see the intersection of two dusty Indian trading paths, traveled by foot or mule or horse.

Spratt opened a trading post here in 1753. Small farms already dotted the area, farms that would coalesce into townships mostly remembered now by street names: Providence, Sharon, Berryhill, Mallard Creek. Charlotte has been growing since the very beginning, and growing aggressively. As one longtime Charlottean has said, "Charlotte's always been a chamber-of-commerce town." The colonial-era city fathers built a courthouse and jail before their community was named the county seat, then used the finished construction as proof that Charlotte deserved to be the county seat.

The new county—Mecklenburg—and Charlotte itself took their names from the German queen of King George III of England, a rather blatant attempt to curry favor. This proved ironic, since Mecklenburg County was one of the earliest places to call for independence from Great Britain, and since guerrilla opposition was so fierce when Cornwallis came through

The Charlotte skyline
COURTESY OF NORTH CAROLINA DIVISION OF TOURISM, FILM AND SPORTS DEVELOPMENT

that he called Charlotte "a damned hornet's nest of rebellion," inadvertently naming the city's original NBA basketball team.

The boom really began when the railroad came through in 1852. Suddenly, the cotton grown in all those surrounding townships no longer needed to be hauled in wagons all the way to Cheraw or Camden in South Carolina for boats to take it to market in Charleston. Now, farmers could have their crops weighed, graded, and loaded onto rail cars right in Charlotte. Business prospects and population growth took flight in the county seat.

The Civil War left Charlotte safely tucked away in the back country, surprisingly intact. The town subsequently experienced another boom in wealth and population. Country boys and newly freed blacks rushed in from the countryside to take advantage of the opportunities created first by the railroads and then by that emblem and icon of the New South: the textile mill.

Charlotte and the rest of the South built mills during the 1880s. The first local operation, Robert Oates's Charlotte Cotton Mill, opened in 1880 just a block off West Trade Street in the Fourth Ward. Three more mills— the Alpha, the Ada, and the Victor—opened within the city limits by the end of the decade. As the railroads had done a generation earlier, the mills lured thousands to Charlotte, some seeking opportunity, some just a steady paycheck.

Textile mills were trumpeted by men like Charlotte's D. A. Tompkins as the means by which the New South would rise. Looking at Charlotte, which is more of a New South city than even Atlanta, one would have to agree. By 1930, mills and the industries they brought with them made Charlotte once and for all the largest city in the Carolinas, laying the

groundwork for the prosperity Charlotteans enjoy today.

But they also indirectly hardened barriers of race and class. Read the letters to the editor in the *Charlotte Observer* today, with their concerns over busing, unequal opportunity, and Uptown versus the suburbs, and you find the long-term effects of sudden industrialization.

Economically, the cotton mills carried Charlotte through the onset of the 20th century and both World Wars. The spun and woven cotton from the mills had to be transported. Luckily, Charlotte sat astride "the Main Street of the South"—J. P. Morgan's Southern Railway line from Washington, D.C., to New Orleans. By the second decade of the 20th century, three more major railroads ran through Charlotte, making the Queen City the center of the Piedmont's vast network of textile mills. Rather than simply shipping Mecklenburg's own cotton crop, Charlotte brought crops in by rail from as far away as Mississippi and Alabama. The railroads continued to grow until after World War II, when new highways and then the Eisenhower Interstate System—specifically, Interstates 77 and 85—brought the trucking industry up to speed.

The opening of the 20th century saw tobacco magnate James B. Duke ready to experiment with the newfangled science of harnessing electrical power. Charlotte, having a strong industrial base and having the Catawba

River nearby, seemed the logical place for the project's headquarters. In 1904, Duke sent engineer Bill Lee to Charlotte to form the Catawba Power Company, the forerunner of Duke Energy.

In contrast to their counterparts in other areas of the South, Charlotte's business leaders did a remarkable job of diversifying industry while riding the crest of the cotton wave. Everything from cars to crackers was made here. Historian Thomas Hanchett, in his book *Sorting Out the New South City*, said that by the 1920s, "if you went to a movie or wrote a check or bought a bottle of cough syrup anywhere from Charleston to Raleigh, you were probably doing business indirectly with some resident of the Queen City."

Which was a good thing, because the mills were slowly dying by the postwar years, vulnerable as they were to foreign production. But although no one knew it at the time, the mills had left Charlotte in position for another economic and population boom, one greater and richer and grander than even D. A. Tompkins, much less Thomas Spratt, could have imagined.

All the money that the mills generated, you see, had to be managed, had to be kept and nurtured and used wisely. Banks sprang up around town to receive the deposits of mill owners and mill hands alike. The Federal Reserve opened a regional master bank in Charlotte. In the 1890s, textile men from the North joined with local magnates and formed Charlotte National Bank, which in time became North Carolina National Bank, which in time became NationsBank, which in 1999 became Bank of America, the first coast-to-coast bank. Thanks to the textile mills, Charlotte and the New South did in fact rise again.

Charlotte's current leaders are different from their predecessors in looking beyond the bottom line. Having built their companies, they are now working to build their community into all that the word *city* implies. Charlotte in the last two decades has seen not only an economic boom, but a cultural one as well. The downtown area, which most Charlotteans call "Uptown" because they like the sound better, has undergone an extensive revitalization that has brought in restaurants, nightclubs, and facilities such as Spirit Square, the McColl Center for the Visual Arts, Discovery Place, and the Mint Museum of Craft + Design. Charlotte has even recognized and mostly stopped what was once its most pernicious habit—tearing down anything old, regardless of its historic value, to make way for the new. Finally interested in more than doing well, Charlotte concentrates today on doing good.

Introduction by Ed Southern

JUST THE FACTS

Charlotte sits just this side of the North Carolina-South Carolina border in the Piedmont region. It has more than 650,000 people within its city limits, 1.5 million within its metro area, and 6 million within a 100-mile radius.

Having experienced most of its growth in the late 20th century, Charlotte is easy to get to and around by car. Interstates 85 and 77, which intersect in north Charlotte, are major thoroughfares through the west side of Charlotte and Mecklenburg County. U.S. 74 runs east and west to connect Charlotte to the coast and the mountains, while N.C. 16 runs north and south through the city along the Catawba River Valley.

Charlotte is served by Greyhound buses and Amtrak trains. The bus station is at 601 West Trade Street; call 704-372-0456 for information. The train station is at 1914 North Tryon Street; call 800-USA-RAIL or 704-376-4416.

Charlotte/Douglas International Airport sees more than 500 flights daily and offers nonstop service to 160 cities; call 704-359-4000 for information.

Please note that you must include the area code when making local calls in Charlotte. Currently, the area code for Charlotte is 704, with the exception of its public schools, which use the 980 area code.

For more facts on Charlotte, contact the Visit Charlotte Visitor Information Center, run by the Charlotte Convention and Visitors Bureau. The bureau is located at 330 South Tryon Street in the city's center. Call 800-231-4636 or visit www.charlottecvb.org.

Things to Do

HISTORIC PLACES, GARDENS, AND TOURS

■ The Charlotte Convention and Visitors Bureau publishes a brochure for the **Center City Walking Tour**, which leads visitors to many of the sites listed below, plus places for shopping, Thomas Polk Park, Settlers Cemetery, the Victorian Fourth Ward neighborhood, and Ericsson Stadium, home of the NFL's Carolina Panthers. Call the bureau at 800-231-4636 or go to www.visitcharlotte.com for more information.

The Arts and Science Council offers a Public Art Walking Tour; to learn about it, see the "Seen on the Streets of Charlotte" sidebar.

■ **Gold Rush Circulator Service** operates free trolleys that travel the center of town. Call 704-336-RIDE or visit www.ridetransit.org for a map and more information.

■ The **Charlotte Museum of History** and the **Hezekiah Alexander Home-site**, both at 3500 Shamrock Drive, together tell Charlotte's story from its earliest pioneers to its boom as a manufacturing center to its current heyday as a banking powerhouse.

The Charlotte Museum of History is housed in a handsome, four-wing, multi-gallery structure that replaced the cramped quarters it had occupied since 1976. Its displays include artifacts from pre-colonial times, historic flags, a re-created gold mine, a replica of the original Mecklenburg County Courthouse, and household items from throughout Charlotte's history that were either found by historians or donated by Mecklenburg families. The museum also houses a research library and an archive.

Located atop a small hill behind the museum, the Hezekiah Alexander Homesite is Mecklenburg County's oldest surviving structure. A member

Hezekiah Alexander Homesite
PHOTOGRAPH BY
ANNE HOLCOMB WATERS

of one of the area's earliest and most prominent families, Hezekiah Alexander supposedly signed the Mecklenburg Declaration of Independence, co-founded Queens College, and helped frame North Carolina's first state constitution. His rock house is three miles from what was then the hilltop village of Charlotte; the area in between was so wild that Alexander's brother always carried two loaded pistols whenever he came to visit. A re-created log kitchen sits behind the house, and a reconstructed stone springhouse is alongside the creek at the bottom of the hill, which makes for a cool spot to picnic.

The Charlotte Museum of History and the Hezekiah Alexander Homesite are open Monday through Saturday from 10 A.M. to 5 P.M. and Sunday from 1 P.M. to 5 P.M. Admission is charged for both sites except on Sunday. Try to plan your visit to coincide with a guided tour, scheduled at 1:15 P.M. and 3:15 P.M. on weekdays; an additional tour is offered at 2:15 P.M. on weekends during the summer. Call 704-568-1774 or visit www.charlottemuseum.org for more information.

■ *Historic Latta Plantation*, at 5225 Sample Road in neighboring Huntersville, is the 1800 Catawba River plantation home of merchant and planter James Latta. The house and immediate grounds are now a living-history farm owned and run by the Mecklenburg County Department of Parks and Recreation. The house is furnished with antiques dating from 1790 to 1840, roughly the time period when the Latta family occupied the property. The grounds contain 13 outbuildings used as interpretive centers to tell about work on the plantation and the lives of the plantation's slaves and the area's yeoman farmers. The fields are planted with crops appropriate to the period and place, and farm animals roam the barnyard. Volunteer docents dressed in period costumes assist with the self-guided tours through the house, fields, and grounds. The house and grounds are open Monday through Saturday from 10 A.M. to 4:30 P.M. and Sunday from 1 P.M. to 4:30 P.M. except for Thanksgiving, Christmas, and New Year's. Admission is charged. The gift shop is open Monday to Saturday from 10 A.M. to 5 P.M. and Sunday from 1 A.M. to 5 P.M. For information, call 704-875-2312 or visit www.lattaplantation.org.

■ Historic **Rosedale Plantation**, at 3427 North Tryon Street, is one of the finest examples of Federal architecture in North Carolina. Built in 1815 by merchant Archibald Frew, it was referred to as "Frew's Folly" by neighbors who possibly took issue with its chrome yellow trim. Rosedale was the plantation home of Dr. D. T. Caldwell and his family in the 1830s. Located three miles from what is now Uptown Charlotte, Rosedale was part of the farming community known as Sugaw Creek, from which present-day Sugar Creek Road gets its name.

Rosedale hosts special events including lectures and exhibits. Along with the Hezekiah Alexander Homesite, it is one of the last places in Charlotte to celebrate Mecklenburg Declaration of Independence ("Meck Dec") Day. Guided tours of the home, gardens, and grounds are given every hour on the hour from 1 P.M. to 3 P.M. Thursday through Sunday. Groups of 10 or more need to call in advance. Rosedale also offers specially scheduled tours that examine the lives of children and slaves on antebellum plantations. Admission is charged for anyone over eight. Call 704-335-0325 or visit www.historicrosedale.org for more information.

■ The *James K. Polk Memorial*, at 308 South Polk Street in nearby Pineville, marks the birthplace of the United States' 11th president. Born in 1795, Polk spent most of his childhood in Mecklenburg County before moving with his family to Tennessee. He later returned to North Carolina to study at the university in Chapel Hill. Polk accomplished more in his single term as president than many others have in two. His tenure saw the creation of an independent treasury, the creation of the Department of the Interior, the settlement of the Oregon boundary, the annexation of Texas, and the acquisition of California, which provoked the unpopular Mexican War. Polk had promised not to seek a second term, and he kept his word. He died in 1849, three months after he left the presidency.

The farm where he was born is now a state historic site. The log cabin and farm buildings and their furnishings are not Polk family originals, but period pieces from the early 1800s that create an impression of what life must have been like for the young Polk. Mecklenburg County was still very much the back country in those days, and the memorial accurately depicts the work required to succeed on the frontier.

The James K. Polk Memorial is currently open year-round from 10 A.M. to 4 P.M. Tuesday through Saturday except for major holidays. Admission is free. For more information, call 704-889-7145 or visit www.nchistoricsites.org/polk/polk.htm.

■ The *UNCC Botanical Gardens and Sculpture Garden*, on the campus of the University of North Carolina at Charlotte, offer a green respite from the traffic and development of the surrounding University City area. The property is comprised of three main attractions: the McMillan Greenhouse, which features orchids, cacti, carnivorous plants, and a small rain forest; the three-acre Susie Harwood Garden; and Van Landingham Glen, a woodland retreat filled with native plants and the most diverse collection of rhododendron in the state. Call 704-687-2364 or visit http://gardens.uncc.edu for more information.

The University of North Carolina at Charlotte was founded in 1947 to handle the sudden increase in college applicants created by the GI Bill. UNCC has since grown into a premier regional university. It has a nationally recognized faculty and students from all over the country.

■ *Wing Haven Gardens and Bird Sanctuary*, at 248 Ridgewood Avenue, offers four acres of woodlands and formal gardens in Myers Park, one of Charlotte's most genteel neighborhoods. Pools, fountains, and baths are available for the birds and classes, special events, and an upscale gift shop for the people. Call 704-331-0664 or visit www.winghavengardens.com for more information.

Museums and Science Centers

■ The *Mint Museum of Art*, at 2730 Randolph Road, is the oldest art museum in North Carolina. The story of how it came to be is an unusual one. In 1799, a 12-year-old found a shiny rock on his father's farm 25 miles east of Charlotte. Gold miners from as far as Europe flocked to the area. If you're wondering what this has to do with an art museum, I'm getting there. To take advantage of the ready gold supply, the United States Mint built a Charlotte branch in 1837. The mint thrived until the gold began to run out and until Charlotte's gold rush was overshadowed by the California gold rush in 1849. The mint closed in 1913. By 1933, the building was slated for demolition. Instead, it was merely dismantled and moved brick by brick to its present location in the Eastover neighborhood. In 1936, the Mint Museum of Art opened.

The museum's permanent collection focuses on American art from pre-Columbian to contemporary. It includes not only works by masters such as Andrew Wyeth and Thomas Eakins, but also pottery from nearby Seagrove, ceramics, and even some of the gold coins made during the building's former life. Also in the permanent collection are artworks from Europe and Africa, including ceremonial masks. The museum hosts impressive traveling exhibits year-round.

It is open Tuesday from 10 A.M. to 10 P.M., Wednesday through Saturday from 10 A.M. to 5 P.M., and Sunday from noon to 5 P.M. Admission is charged except on Tuesday from 5 P.M. to 10 P.M. Children under five are admitted free. For more information, call 704-337-2000 or visit www.mintmuseum.org.

- The *Mint Museum of Craft + Design*, at 220 North Tryon Street, is the museum's Uptown branch. Housed in the old Montaldo's department store building, it is itself an impressive design work. Opened in 1997, it houses the extensive crafts collection that was becoming cramped at the Randolph Road location, as well as contemporary studio crafts. The collection is divided according to the materials used: ceramics, fiber, glass, metal, and wood. The museum hosts educational programs and traveling exhibits.

  The Mint Museum of Craft + Design is open from 10 A.M. to 5 P.M. Tuesday through Saturday, from 10 A.M. to 8 P.M. on the third Thursday of the month, and from noon to 5 P.M. on Sunday. Admission is charged except for Tuesday from 10 A.M. to 2 P.M. and the third Thursday of the month from 5 P.M. to 8 P.M. Children under five are admitted free. One ticket covers admission to both museums if used on the same day, unless otherwise noted. For more information, call 704-337-2000 or visit www.mintmuseum.org.

  Major expansion is currently being planned for the Mint Museums. The original Randolph Road location will be maintained, but the Mint Museum of Craft + Design will be moved to a multipurpose arts facility in the Wachovia South Tryon development.

- The *Levine Museum of the New South*, at 200 East Seventh Street, is the only museum in the country that concentrates on the New South period (1865 to the present). It features hands-on activities and displays that not only tell the history of the New South but also put it in the context of national and world history. The concentration, of course, is on Charlotte and the Piedmont region of the Carolinas. The permanent exhibit called "Cotton Fields to Skyscrapers" allows visitors to step inside replicas of a sharecropper's cabin, a textile mill, a mill-village house, an early Belk department store, a civil-rights-era lunch counter, and a 21st-century Latino bakery. The museum also houses several lecture halls and galleries for changing exhibits.

  It is open from 10 A.M. to 5 P.M. Tuesday through Saturday and from noon to 5 P.M. on Sunday. Admission is charged except for children under six. For more information, call 704-333-1887 or visit www.museumofthenewsouth.org.

  It is worth noting that visitors to the museum can park free for up to 90 minutes at the adjacent Seventh Street Station, the only parking deck in Charlotte that laughs (at you or with you, depending on your self-esteem). It also lights up as pedestrians pass.

- *Discovery Place*, at 301 North Tryon Street, is a must-see if you have

THE LEGEND OF THE MECK DEC

By Ed Southern

Despite naming their political subdivisions for King George III's queen, the people of Charlotte and Mecklenburg County were among the earliest supporters of the Continental Congress's effort to break free of Great Britain.

Exactly how early this support came has been a cause for debate for more than two centuries.

The crux of the debate is the Mecklenburg Declaration of Independence. Since seemingly everything in Charlotte has to have a perky nickname, this document has long been known as the "Meck Dec." The story goes that on May 20, 1775, the leading citizens of Mecklenburg County met at the county courthouse, just east of the Trade and Tryon intersection, to decide on a course of action in response to the British occupation of Boston Harbor. According to Meck Dec believers, this meeting ended with the writing and signing of a declaration of independence announcing that British law no longer held effect in Mecklenburg County, and that Mecklenburg's citizens would thenceforth be responsible for their own governance.

A copy of the document was given to someone recorded in history as Captain Jack, the son of a local tavern keeper. Captain Jack was supposed to carry the Meck Dec to Philadelphia to present it to the Continental Congress. Records

show that he stopped in Salisbury and Salem, but he never arrived in Philadelphia. What the good citizens of Mecklenburg learned from this was that a man called Captain Jack may be absolutely trusted to make popcorn shrimp, but that he should not be trusted with history-making political documents.

The original was kept in the home of one of the signers and was destroyed in a house fire. No other copies existed.

Many outside the Carolinas soon began to question the authenticity of the Meck Dec. One of these was Thomas Jefferson, who found the version of the Meck Dec pieced together from the signers' memories to be remarkably similar to his Declaration of Independence. Meck Dec supporters retorted that the similarities in language resulted from the strong influence of John Locke on both statements.

Regardless of whether or not the Meck Dec existed, or existed in the form its supporters claim, Mecklenburg County deserves recognition for being quick to take up the cause of liberty. Three weeks after the meeting that produced the Meck Dec, another such meeting indisputably produced the Mecklenburg Resolves, a less strongly worded denunciation of British injustices in America. And Mecklenburg men were present in April 1776 when North Carolina issued the Halifax Resolves, the first official recommendation by a colonial government that the colonies declare their independence from Great Britain.

Many in Charlotte and Mecklenburg County continue to insist on the authenticity of the Meck Dec. May 20, "Meck Dec Day," was an official county holiday until the 1960s, celebrated with parades and speeches by local and even national leaders. Some sites in Charlotte, such as the Hezekiah Alexander Homesite and Rosedale Plantation, still celebrate Meck Dec Day, though it draws much less attention than in times past.

children or even if you don't. Its permanent exhibits include a range of interactive science and natural-history displays where children can experience everything from touching a simulated tornado to broadcasting their own weather reports. Younger children will enjoy the fish, snakes, and birds throughout the aquarium and rain-forest exhibits, whereas older kids will get a charge out of orbiting the International Space Station in a motion simulator. Discovery Place also has a planetarium and the *Charlotte Observer* OMNIMAX theater for IMAX films.

Discovery Place operates daily except for Thanksgiving and Christmas. From Labor Day to May 31, the exhibit halls are open from 9 A.M. to 5 P.M. Monday through Friday, from 10 A.M. to 6 P.M. on Saturday, and from noon to 5 P.M. on Sunday. From June 1 until Labor Day, the hours are 10 A.M. to 6 P.M. Monday through Saturday and noon to 6 P.M. on Sunday. Admission is charged except for children under two. Times and ticket prices for the planetarium and OMNIMAX shows vary. For more information, call 704-372-6261 or visit www.discoveryplace.org.

■ A component of Discovery Place, the **Charlotte Nature Museum**, at 1658 Sterling Road, is a small nature center adjacent to Freedom Park. Recently expanded and refurbished, it features a live-animal room, a butterfly pavilion, a nature trail, and a puppet theater. It is open Monday through Friday from 9 A.M. to 5 P.M., Saturday from 10 A.M. to 5 P.M., and Sunday from 1 P.M. to 5 P.M. It is closed Thanksgiving, Christmas Eve, Christmas Day, New Year's, and Easter. An admission fee is charged for those over age three. Call 704-372-6261 or visit www.discoveryplace.org/naturemuseum.asp for more information.

■ The **Carolina Raptor Center** is located at 6000 Sample Road in Huntersville, on the grounds of Latta Plantation Park and Nature Preserve. The raptor center is dedicated to environmental education and the conservation of birds of prey through public education, the rehabilitation of injured raptors, and research. The only eagle aviary in the Carolinas, it has a nature trail on which visitors can view the eagles, falcons, owls, vultures, and hawks that the facility has treated but cannot release into the wild. It is open Monday through Saturday from 10 A.M. to 5 P.M. and Sunday from noon to 5 P.M. Admission is charged except for children four and under. It is closed on major holidays. For more information, call 704-875-6521 or visit www.carolinaraptorcenter.org.

■ The **Carolinas Aviation Museum**, at 4108 Airport Drive, is located near Charlotte/Douglas International Airport, a World War II training field that has become one of the busiest hubs in the country. The museum, housed in an old hangar, offers guided tours and aviation "artifacts" from the early days of flight. Most people come for the aircraft, including a "Top Gun" F-14D Super Tomcat, an F-102 Delta Dart, an A-7E Corsair, and a DC-3 built in 1942 and restored to flight-ready condition in 1987. The museum is open Tuesday through Saturday from 10 A.M. to 4 P.M. and Sunday from 1 P.M. to 5 P.M. Tuesdays and Thursdays are work days, so plan to visit then if you want to meet or see people restoring old aircraft. Admission is charged except for children under six. For more information, call 704-359-8442 or visit www.carolinasaviation.org.

CULTURAL OFFERINGS

■ *ImaginOn: The Joe and Joan Martin Center* is a wonderful, whimsical building that encompasses an entire city block in the heart of Uptown; the facility includes the Spangler Children's Library and the Children's Theatre of Charlotte. There is no charge to use the library, to explore the building and use its StoryLab, or to participate in drop-in programming. For box-office and ticket information, call 704-793-2828 or visit www.imaginon.org.

■ The **North Carolina Blumenthal Center for the Performing Arts**, at 130 North Tryon Street, opened in 1992 adjacent to the Bank of America Corporate Center and Founders Hall. The Blumenthal Center contains three performance spaces: the Belk Theater, the Booth Playhouse, and the intimate Studio Theater. National touring productions of Broadway shows and performances by the Charlotte Symphony Orchestra, the Charlotte Repertory Theatre, Opera Carolina, and the North Carolina Dance Theatre are all staged here. For information on upcoming performances and ticket prices, call 704-372-1000 or visit www.performingartsctr.org.

- Adjoining the Blumenthal Center is the massive **Bank of America Corporate Center**, the tallest skyscraper in the Carolinas. Designed by renowned architect Cesar Pelli (who also designed the Blumenthal Center), the tower is a welcome break from the glass-and-steel boxes that dominated the Charlotte skyline for decades. In its lobby are three frescoes by world-famous artist and North Carolina native Ben Long.

- Finishing up the city block is **Founders Hall**, a two-story indoor plaza offering upscale shopping and dining and a box office for the Blumenthal Center.

- **Spirit Square Center for Arts and Education**, at 345 North College Street, came under the auspices of the Blumenthal Center in 1997. Spirit Square was built in 1909 as First Baptist Church; the facade facing Tryon Street still features the church's Byzantine design and stained-glass windows. The church moved in the 1970s, at which time the property was turned into a community arts center. The former sanctuary is now the McGlohon Theatre, named after Charlotte native and jazz composer and pianist Loonis McGlohon. Spirit Square also houses the Duke Power Theatre and five galleries devoted to visual arts. The focus, however, is education; Spirit Square hosts numerous workshops and programs sponsored by Charlotte's cultural institutions. For more information, call 704-372-1000 or visit www.performingartsctr.org.

- The **McColl Center for Visual Art**, at 721 North Tryon Street, is housed in a former Associate Reformed Presbyterian church built in 1926. Vacated in the 1950s when its congregation dissolved, the church was heavily damaged by fire in 1985 and stood as a charred remnant of urban flight until it was purchased by Bank of America in 1995. In 1999, the McColl Center opened its doors to the public and to its artists-in-residence and

Spirit Square Center for Arts and Education
PHOTOGRAPH BY ED SOUTHERN

affiliate artists, all of whom enjoy the lovely, airy studio space. The Dickson Gallery and Gallery 115 are located on the first floor, but visitors are encouraged to explore all three floors and to interact with artists in their studios. Gallery hours are from 11 A.M. to 4 P.M. Tuesday through Saturday. Admission is free. Call 704-332-5535 or visit www.mccollcenter.org for more information.

■ Like Spirit Square and the McColl Center, the **Afro-American Cultural Center**, at 401 North Myers Street, is housed in a former church. It takes a multidisciplinary approach to education and programming, hosting art exhibits, film series, and performances of music, drama, and dance to preserve Charlotte's rich African-American heritage. It maintains a visual-arts gallery, an outdoor amphitheater, a 200-seat indoor theater, and classroom space. For more information, call 704-374-1565 or visit www.aacc-charlotte.org.

SPECIAL SHOPPING

■ As artists are wont to do, Ruth Ava Lyons and J. Paul Sires quietly started a revolution in Charlotte when they opened their now-famous **Center of the Earth Gallery** on North Davidson Street in 1985. The former mill village that today is Charlotte's historic arts district is commonly referred to as **NoDa**. Home to numerous galleries and performance outlets, NoDa offers gallery crawls twice a month. Check out www.noda.org for more information.

■ Depending on your point of view, **Concord Mills** outlet shopping mall is either a shopper's paradise or hell. Regardless of your perspective, it is North Carolina's third-largest tourist attraction, drawing over 15 million visitors a year. Here, you will find a Polo Ralph Lauren factory store, a Nike factory store, an OshKosh B'Gosh outlet, an Off 5th Saks Fifth Avenue, and a Bass Pro Shop. To reach the mall, take Exit 49 (Concord Mills Boulevard) off Interstate 85.

■ **SouthPark**, located at 4400 Sharon Road, is both geographically and economically far removed from Concord Mills. Here, you'll find Nordstrom, Tiffany & Co., Kate Spade, Louis Vuitton, and more. Call 704-364-4411 for information.

The Heart of NASCAR: A Race Fan's Tour of the Piedmont

By Andrew Waters

"Racing was built here. Racing belongs here." Charlotte used this slogan (plus a sweetheart incentive package that guaranteed revenue) in its successful bid to become the location for the NASCAR Hall of Fame. Like most slogans, this one is part truth and part hyperbole. Although stock-car racing has been a popular pastime across the South for over 50 years, Charlotte and the North Carolina Piedmont are home to some of the sport's most famous drivers, legends, and races.

The NASCAR Hall of Fame isn't scheduled to open until 2009 or 2010, but the Piedmont is still a great place to see the sport's past, present, and future. Start your tour northwest of Winston-Salem in Wilkes County, home to the sport's first great hero, Junior Johnson. Spend some time on the same back roads where Junior honed his driving skills running moonshine in the foothills of the Blue Ridge. Wilkes is a gorgeous, sprawling county with picturesque mountains and rolling farmland. You can enjoy trout fishing at *Stone Mountain State Park* (http://www.ils.unc.edu/parkproject/visit/stmo/home.html) or spend the afternoon boating at *W. Kerr Scott Reservoir* (http://www.recreation.gov/detail.cfm?ID=461). Be sure to drive by the *North Wilkesboro Speedway*,

on U.S. 421, on your way south. Opened in 1947, the .625-mile oval quickly grew in prominence, eventually hosting two annual Winston (now Nextel) Cup races. But the sport outgrew the track. In 1996, it was purchased by a group that included NASCAR mogul Bruton Smith for the purpose of moving those races to larger markets. The track is now permanently closed, but travelers can get a good view of this one-time racing mecca from the highway.

Continue south on U.S. 421 to Winston-Salem, home of another historic track in NASCAR history, *Bowman Gray Stadium*, located at 1250 South Martin Luther King Drive. Bowman Gray has been hosting races for more than 50 years, making it the longest-operating NASCAR short track in the country. Between 1958 and 1971, the track hosted 29 Grand National races. Still featuring NASCAR-sanctioned racing on Saturday nights during the summer, Bowman Gray is a great place to catch the kind of action that has made stock-car racing such a popular pastime in the South. The drivers here race for love of the sport, not fame or fortune. Call 336-723-1819 or visit www.bowmangrayracing.com for information about upcoming events.

For a glimpse of another side

of NASCAR, drive south on U.S. 52 to the intersection with U.S. 64 just outside Lexington, where *Childress Vineyards* sprawls across the Piedmont foothills (www.childressvineyards.com). Vineyard owner Richard Childress turned a moderately successful career as a NASCAR driver into a spectacularly successful career as a NASCAR team owner, winning six NASCAR championships with driver Dale Earnhardt in the 1980s and 1990s. Thanks to NASCAR's booming popularity, successful team owners and drivers now earn salaries that would astound those original bootleggers. To Childress's credit, he has invested part of his fortune in his hometown of Lexington, an area hit hard by the demise of the furniture and textile industries. The wine at Childress Vineyards has won several awards since its opening in 2004, and the Tuscan-style winery has become a popular destination for both locals and tourists.

From Lexington, continue south on U.S. 52 and merge with Interstate 85 headed toward the town of *Kannapolis*. Seven-time Winston Cup champion Richard Petty is "the King" of North Carolina NASCAR drivers, but Dale Earnhardt, who died in the 2001 Daytona 500, is the state's patron saint of racing. Earnhardt's hard-charging style earned him the nickname "the Intimidator," and his legendary number three can be seen on bumper stickers across the Piedmont. Earnhardt's hometown of Kannapolis is proud of its favorite son and has developed "The Dale Trail" to celebrate his history here. Sites on the trail include the neighborhood where he grew up; Dale Earnhardt Plaza in the center of town, featuring a nine-foot statue of the Intimidator himself; and many other racing-related sites. For a map of "The Dale Trail," visit www.daletrail.com or stop by the Cabarrus County Visitor Center, located just north of Exit 60 off Interstate 85 on Dale Earnhardt Boulevard.

From Kannapolis, head south on U.S. 29 to *Lowe's Motor Speedway,* currently home to three NASCAR Nextel Cup races: the Coca-Cola 600, the Bank of America 500, and the NASCAR Nextel All-Star Challenge. Its 1.5-mile quad-oval track seats 167,000 people, with room for 50,000 more spectators in the infield. Constructed in 1959, it was the first speedway to host nighttime racing (in 1992) and to offer year-round residences (in 1984), with 52 condominiums. Many consider this track the epicenter of NASCAR, as 90 percent of all NASCAR teams are based within 50 miles of the site. Tours of the facility are available on non-race days. You can reach the ticket hot line at 800-455-FANS. For information, call 704-455-3200 or visit www.lowesmotorspeedway.com.

The pond at Freedom Park
PHOTOGRAPH BY ED SOUTHERN

RECREATION

■ The property beyond the immediate grounds of Historic Latta Plantation is **Latta Plantation Park and Nature Preserve**. A nature center, picnic tables and shelters, nature trails, bridle paths, canoe rentals, and fishing on Mountain Island Lake are all available to visitors. The grounds are open daily from 7 A.M. to dusk; the various facilities inside the park keep their own hours, so check in advance. Admission is free except during special events. For more information about the house and grounds, call 704-875-1391 or visit the Mecklenburg County Department of Parks and Recreation's Web site at www.parkandrec.com.

■ Across a wooden footbridge from the Charlotte Nature Museum is **Freedom Park**, the largest public park within the city limits. Tennis courts, basketball courts, volleyball sand pits, baseball fields, soccer fields, playgrounds, picnic tables and shelters, an old locomotive for kids to play on, a pond, and a band shell for outdoor concerts can all be found in Freedom Park. You might even discover a little solitude here, five minutes from Uptown.

■ **Ray's Splash Planet Waterpark** is a joint venture between the Mecklenburg County Department of Parks and Recreation and the Charlotte-Mecklenburg schools. Opened in 2002, the facility includes an indoor water park with a three-story water slide, a fitness center, an aerobics and dance room, a cardiovascular theater, a playground, and concessions. An admission fee is charged. The park is open daily except for Christmas. Call 704-432-4RAY for hours and additional information.

- The **U.S. National Whitewater Center** is located at the intersection of Interstate 85 and Interstate 485 along the Catawba River. Leave it to Charlotte to create the country's first artificial river with recirculating rapids. At the time of this writing, the center, modeled after facilities built for the 2000 Olympics in Australia and the 2004 Olympics in Athens, was embroiled in a legal dispute over whether the road that accesses the park was private or not. No doubt, the developers will win. When they do, the park will also offer canoeing along a real river—the Catawba—as well as climbing, hiking, biking, an amphitheater, and a restaurant. Admission will be charged. For more information, visit www.usnwc.org.

SEASONAL EVENTS

- The **Carolinas' Carrousel Parade** is a lot like an old small-town Christmas parade, only bigger. So much of Charlotte's history has been lost to development that holdovers like the Carrousel Parade have become more attractive through sheer nostalgia. Held on Thanksgiving Day, the parade proceeds down Tryon Street through Uptown. Onlookers enjoy the floats, the marching bands, and, of course, Santa and his sleigh bringing up the rear. For information, call 704-525-0250 or visit www.carrouselparade.org.

- **Festival in the Park** has been bringing arts, crafts, music, food, and crowds together in Freedom Park since 1964. More than 200 artists and craftsmen from across the region and the nation display their work in tents set up around the pond. Nearly 1,000 entertainers perform in the band shell and at sites set up across the park. Workers string lights so activities can continue after dark. The festival is held over a weekend in September. For information, call 704-338-1060 or visit www.festival.lfhosting.com.

- The **Novello Festival of Reading**, sponsored by the Public Library of Charlotte and Mecklenburg County, brings in some of the most renowned authors in the world for lectures, readings, discussions, and signings. More than 20 authors and illustrators participate in events held throughout the city; there is also a downtown street festival for families. Past guests have included Pulitzer Prize winner Frank McCourt and Nobel laureate Toni Morrison. Novello is held in October; call 704-336-2020 for more information.

- The **Southern Christmas Show**, the **Southern Spring Home & Garden Show**, the **Southern Ideal Home Show**, and the **Southern Women's Show** are held at various times during the year at the Charlotte Merchandise Mart on Independence Boulevard. Each features fashions, crafts, and tips on design and decorating appropriate to its theme and season. For exact dates and ticket prices, contact Southern Shows, Inc., by calling 704-376-6594 or visiting www.southernshows.com.

- The **Loch Norman Highland Games**, sponsored by the Catawba Valley Scottish Society, are held each April at Rural Hill Farm, the former Davidson family plantation overlooking the Catawba River. The site is rolling, grassy, and partially wooded. With all the kilted lads strolling about, the more imaginative (or drunk) members of the crowd might come to believe they're actually in old Caledonia. Sanctioned competitions in Highland dancing, fife-and-drumming, and, of course, Scottish athletics like caber tossing are held. You'll also find dart throwing, archery, and demonstrations of Scottish crafts and artwork. The clans erect tents around the main competition field, where visitors can check to see if they're related to William Wallace or Robert the Bruce. A food-and-drink area is on the grounds. Yes, you can get haggis, but why would you want to? Admission is charged, as is a parking fee. For more information, call 704-875-3113 or visit www.ruralhillfarm.org.

Places to Stay

RESORTS, HOTELS, AND MOTELS

- **Ballantyne Resort Hotel.** Deluxe. 10000 Ballantyne Commons Parkway (866-248-4824 or 704-248-4000; www.ballantyneresort.com). The area's first resort, Ballantyne completely reshaped south Charlotte when it opened, causing new roads to be built and old roads to be renamed, rerouted, or closed. The hotel features 214 deluxe guest rooms, each with 10-foot ceilings, custom furnishings, and original artwork. It also offers 20 suites, including two Presidential Suites for those who want to feel like the leader of the free world. Guests enjoy the 24-hour "world-class" in-room dining menu. The hotel overlooks the 18th fairway of a golf course that is home to the Dana Rader Golf School; Rader, the author of *Rock Solid Golf*, has been ranked one of America's premier golf instructors by both *Golf Magazine* and *Golf Digest*. Ballantyne also offers accommodations at The Lodge at Ballantyne Resort, Staybridge Suites, and a Courtyard by Marriott location.

- ***Charlotte Marriott SouthPark***. Deluxe. 2200 Rexford Road (704-364-8220; www.marriott.com/property/propertypage/CLTPH). Located adjacent to the tony SouthPark shopping mall, this boutique hotel has 194 of Charlotte's most well-appointed rooms. Amenities include an outdoor pool, a health club, the Charles Grayson Day Spa, a putting green, and an ever-helpful concierge.

- ***Charlotte Marriott City Center***. Deluxe/Expensive. 100 West Trade Street (704-333-9000; www.marriott.com/property/propertypage/CLTCC). The Marriott boasts a heated indoor pool, an exercise room, valet parking, airport transportation, two restaurants, two bars, a gift shop with Starbucks coffee and Krispy Kreme doughnuts, one of the biggest ballrooms in town, and an exceptional staff. It also lives up to the "City Center" in its name; guests are only steps from the intersection of Trade and Tryon streets.

- ***The Dunhill Hotel***. Deluxe/Expensive. 237 North Tryon Street (704-332-4141; www.dunhillhotel.com). Nestled among the towers of North Tryon Street, The Dunhill, built in 1929, offers elegant charm in the manner of a stylish European hotel. The richly and traditionally decorated rooms include well-stocked refrigerators tucked into armoires. In the lobby are a comfortable seating area and the Monticello restaurant.

- ***Hilton at University Place***. Deluxe/Expensive. 8629 J. M. Keynes Drive (704-547-7444; www.hilton.com). This 12-story hotel is the most visible landmark of the University City area, off Interstate 85 at Harris Boulevard. The service here is exceptional. The surrounding University Place offers distinctive shops and fine restaurants clustered around a picturesque lake.

- ***Hilton Charlotte and Towers***. Deluxe/Expensive. 222 East Third Street (704-377-1500; www.hilton.com). The Uptown location of the Hilton offers 407 rooms, each with two telephones and a refreshment center, and the Uptown YMCA, which guests may use as an unusually large fitness center.

■ *The Westin Charlotte*. Deluxe/Expensive. 601 South College Street (704-375-2600; www.westin.com/charlotte). Charlotte's new convention hotel boasts startling architecture, a fantastic location, outstanding service, and, lest anyone forget, the Westin chain's famous Heavenly Bed in each of its 700 guest rooms. It also has 32,000 square feet of meeting space, including a 16,000-square-foot grand ballroom. Located across the street from the convention center, The Westin is a stop on the trolley that runs from the South End through the city's center.

INNS AND BED-AND-BREAKFASTS

■ *The Duke Mansion*. Deluxe. 400 Hermitage Road (888-202-1009 or 704-714-4400; www.dukemansion.com). Built in 1915, this inn is James B. Duke's former estate in the tree-lined Myers Park neighborhood. Guests in its 20 rooms enjoy private baths, newspaper delivery, gourmet bedside treats, and all the modern conveniences. Breakfast is served daily, and other meals can be arranged with advance notice. The Duke Mansion offers an elegant, tranquil stay and also serves as a meeting and retreat facility.

■ *Ms. Elsie's Caribbean Bed-and-Breakfast*. Deluxe. 334 North Sharon Amity Road (704-365-5189; www.bbonline.com/nc/mselsies). Ms. Elsie's offers authentic Caribbean charm in the Cotswold neighborhood, convenient to SouthPark and the Mint Museum of Art. It features three guest rooms and a three-course breakfast with fresh fruit and seafood.

■ *The Morehead Inn*. Deluxe/Expensive. 1122 East Morehead Street (704-376-3357; www.moreheadinn.com). This 1917 inn is located in the historic Dilworth neighborhood just minutes from Uptown. Updated in 1995, this popular spot for nuptials offers a full Southern breakfast, private baths, and loads of amenities such as privileges at the nearby Central YMCA and fluffy bathrobes to use during your stay. Meeting rooms are available.

Seen on the Streets of Charlotte

By Ed Southern

Southbound on Interstate 77, you'll see the Charlotte skyline rise slowly. Starting with the crown of the Bank of America Corporate Center, one skyscraper after another comes into view on the horizon. Like the new commerce that seeps up the interstate—the car lots and hotels, the chain restaurants and fast-food joints—the skyscrapers are a boast of Charlotte's abundance, but a closer look shows that they are also a symbol of something more.

Charlotte is the only city in the Carolinas to make Skyscraper.com's list of the top 100 skylines in the world. More than just an outgrowth of economic boom times—for other Carolina metropolises have enjoyed similar fortunes—the appearance of Charlotte's Uptown is a visible sign of the commitment of business leaders to leavening the commercial with the cultural.

Long before "world-class city" became Charlotte's number-one cliché, ambition, or joke, depending on your point of view, the bankers and businessmen who built the most recent boom had made it clear that transforming Charlotte into a true city, with the variety of experiences that the word implies, was a high priority. They had turned what was once a backwoods town into the sec-ond-largest financial center in America. Executives from New York City and San Francisco now answered to them, and they didn't want those big-city executives snickering or moaning about get-ting their marching orders from some burg out in the boondocks.

Rather than just reflexively as-sociating "bigger" with "better" in the traditional American way, Charlotte's leaders sought to build with an eye for the eyes, a dedica-tion to aesthetics that would make the city's core as alive and pleas-ing as the Carolina countryside.

The axis around which the sky-line turns is North Tryon Street's Bank of America Corporate Center, the tallest building between Phila-delphia and Atlanta. Designed by architect Cesar Pelli and opened in 1992, this postmodern tower is capped by concentric rings of spires that, particularly when lit at night, bear more than a passing resem-blance to a royal crown. (Pelli re-portedly swears that he was not thinking of Charlotte's "Queen City" tag when he conceived his design.) Flanked by the perfor-mance halls of the Blumenthal Cen-ter and the upscale shopping and dining of Founders Hall, the Bank of America Corporate Center single-handedly began the transfor-mation of urban Charlotte into something more cosmopolitan.

Charlotte's skyline grew with the economy of the 1990s. Bank of America funded two other skyscrapers on North Tryon Street, 1997's IJL Financial Center and 2002's Hearst Tower. The architects for both—Smallwood, Reynolds, Stewart, Stewart & Associates—designed the towers to complement the Bank of America Corporate Center. All three use similar materials. The IJL Financial Center has a crescent shape except on its sharp-angled west facade, which looks as if it is clinging to the hump of the semicircle. The Hearst Tower created a stir when its design became apparent. In contrast to the Bank of America tower, whose facade recedes as it rises—fulfilling the popular expectation of how a skyscraper should look—the Hearst Tower's facade expands as it nears its cowl-shaped top. Thanks to the Art Deco flourishes on the exterior (which are continued inside) and the fact that the tower's top is lit at night, the overall impression is that of an Olympic torch (or perhaps a scepter for the Queen City?).

Most of Charlotte's other skyscrapers have their own distinctive architectural offerings that add to the beauty of the whole. One Wachovia Center on College Street has a glass spine running through its east and west facades that makes the tower glow at sunrise and sunset. The Interstate Tower and the Carillon Tower, both on Trade Street, have imaginative and contrasting tops best seen when approaching Charlotte from the west. The Interstate Tower is capped by a postmodern cone straight out of the Space Age, while the Carillon Tower takes its central spire from the Neo-Gothic First Presbyterian Church across the street.

The Carillon Tower is also home to two of the finest examples of downtown Charlotte's public works of art, *Cascade* by Jean Tinguely and *The Garden* by Jerry Peart. The Arts and Science Council, whose offices are in the Carillon Tower, offers a *Public Art Walking Tour* in the city's center. The tour includes art by internationally renowned artists such as Peart, Tinguely, Romare Bearden, Ben Long, and Arnaldo Pomodoro. Visit http://www.artsandscience.org, then click "Public Art" and "Walking Tour" for a free guide.

Places to Eat

Since the 2005 arrival of Johnson & Wales University, a culinary-arts school, Charlotte's already-thriving restaurant scene has only improved. The following list is an effort to showcase a mixture of cheap eats, elegant fare, ethnic restaurants, traditional home-style cooking, and Charlotte institutions. Likewise, I have tried to guide you to some of Charlotte's most interesting neighborhoods.

- **Blue**. Expensive. 214 North Tryon Street (704-927-2583; www. bluerestaurantandbar.com). Blue serves innovative Mediterranean cuisine that sparkles like the Aegean Sea itself. Guests can choose from a variety of appetizers such as prosciutto-wrapped scallops and crab-stuffed calamari or dive right into the delicious "Moroccan Lamb Tagine" or the pan-seared sea bass. Dinner is served Monday through Saturday.

- **Carpe Diem**. Expensive. 1535 Elizabeth Avenue (704-377-7976; www.carpediemrestaurant.com). Now in its third location in 15 years, Carpe Diem has staying power. You can enjoy the amazingly light buttermilk-fried chicken breast or the spinach-and-cheese dumplings in an elegant Art Nouveau setting. And don't forget to follow your meal with the mango-pineapple sorbet. Dinner is served Monday through Saturday.

- **Restaurant i**. Expensive. 1524 East Boulevard (704-333-8118; www.restaurant-i.com). According to the menu, i comes from the Japanese word *ai*, meaning love. In fact, many in Charlotte have fallen in love with this new restaurant. Billed as Japanese-French haute cuisine, the sushi and sashimi served here are as fresh as they are beautifully presented. With its royal-blue tablecloths in a white-on-white dining room, the serene setting complements the food perfectly. Outdoor dining is also available. Lunch is served Tuesday through Friday and dinner Tuesday through Sunday.

- **Cantina 1511**. Expensive/Moderate. 1511 East Boulevard (704-331-9222). A great way to begin your meal here is the "Top Shelf Guacamole," made fresh table-side, and a cool margarita. You can follow that with one of the fresh seafood appetizers or, if you're really hungry, the *"Barbacoa de Puerco."* Outdoor dining is available. Cantina 1511 is open for lunch Monday through Friday and for dinner nightly.

- **Copper**. Expensive/Moderate. 311 East Boulevard (704-333-0063). Located in the historic Mayer House, where Carson McCullers began writing *The Heart Is a Lonely Hunter*, this lovely restaurant serves classic Indian cuisine with a modern twist. For traditionalists, there are rich curries and tandoor-cooked meats, while more adventurous eaters may want to try the "Paneer Napoleon," a cheese-and-roasted-vegetable pie. Lunch is served weekdays and dinner Monday through Saturday.

- **Dolce Ristorante**. Expensive/Moderate. 1710 Kenilworth Avenue (704-332-7525). Dolce is a charming Italian spot tucked into the Kenilworth Commons Shopping Center off East Boulevard. Originally a *gelateria*, this full-fledged trattoria now serves delicious traditional pastas and *secondi* such as *"Linguini ai Frutti di Mare"* and *"Saltimbocca Trastevere."* Be sure to leave room for a scrumptious *gelato*. Lunch is served weekdays and dinner Monday through Saturday.

- **Pewter Rose Bistro**. Expensive/Moderate. 1820 South Boulevard (704-332-8149; www.pewterrose.com). The Pewter Rose has long been one of the most exciting restaurants in Charlotte, offering a menu as imaginative as the decor. The entrées are outstanding, the wine list is expansive, and the adjacent Tutto Mondo nightclub accentuates the slightly eccentric ambiance. It's one of the best places in Charlotte to take a first date. The Pewter Rose is open daily for lunch and dinner and serves an enormously popular Sunday brunch.

- **Cabo Fish Taco Baja Seagrill**. Moderate. 3201 North Davidson Street (704-332-8868; www.cabofishtaco.com). Located in the heart of the artsy NoDa district, this casual place combines coastal Mexican cuisine with California flair. What this means, dude, is that it serves myriad wraps, tacos, and burritos stuffed with seafood, chicken, and other healthy things. You can also get a mean margarita. Cabo is open daily for lunch, dinner, and "late evenings."

- **Dish**. Moderate/Inexpensive. 1220 Thomas Avenue (704-344-0343). Dish dishes up an eclectic mix of New South fare, from meat-and-threes and fried green tomatoes to vegetarian burritos and burgers. If that combination doesn't strike you as odd, then this funky diner is your kind of place. The portions are generous and the prices reasonable—and it has a full bar. Lunch and dinner are served daily.

- **Mert's Heart and Soul**. Moderate/Inexpensive. 214 North College Street

(704-342-4222). One bite of its greens landed Mert's an entry in this book, despite slow service due to a lost dining ticket. Stick with the fried chicken, porkchops, and Southern-style veggies and you can't go wrong. This noisy, bustling place located in the heart of Uptown offers darn good down-home food at reasonable prices. Mert's serves lunch daily and dinner Tuesday through Sunday; it also offers brunch on Saturday and Sunday.

- **NOFO on Liz.** Moderate/Inexpensive.1609 Elizabeth Avenue (704-444-9003; www.nofo.com). "What is it?" I asked when I saw this place. The answer is that it's a gift store *and* a food market *and* a café—a very lively café. NOFO serves an array of fresh salads, grilled "Pizzette," sandwiches, and heartier entrées including walnut-and-spinach ravioli and bacon-wrapped grouper. It's fun. It's funky. And it's on Elizabeth Avenue. Lunch and dinner are served Monday through Saturday; Sunday brunch is also offered.

- **Delicias Colombian Bakery and Restaurant.** Inexpensive. 212 North Polk Street (704-889-5328). Owners Elizabeth and Geraldo Tobar opened Delicias in 2002, and it has quickly transcended the Latino community to attract gringos galore. Plenty of sweet and savory treats are available for takeout. Or better yet, you can dine in for the full cultural experience. Delicias is open daily for breakfast, lunch, and dinner.

- **Lupie's Café.** Inexpensive. 2718 Monroe Road (704-374-1232; www.lupiescafe.com). In a city full of bankers, Lupie's is the most economical spot in town. The quantity of food you get for the money is staggering. A different special is offered each night. The meat loaf on Monday is a personal favorite, but Lupie's is just as famous for its chili, served any day of the week. The side dishes run the gamut and are a meal unto themselves. Even the children's portions are huge. If physically possible, save room for the banana pudding. The atmosphere is loud but relaxed, and the wait staff is friendly and easygoing, making Lupie's a great place to bring kids. The walls are decorated with work by local artists and photographers; a big poster of John Wayne is near the kitchen. There's also a location on Old Statesville Road in Huntersville. Lupie's does not take reservations, so be prepared to wait in line at lunchtime and on most weekend nights. Lunch and dinner are served Monday through Saturday.

- **The Penguin.** Inexpensive. 1921 Commonwealth Avenue (704-375-6959; http://coldfury.com/Penguin). What began as an ice-cream parlor became a drive-in. Then the drive-in became a retro diner and bar boasting the best jukebox in the Southeast. (But please, please, don't play "The Lion Sleeps Tonight" on it, as a relative of mine did.) Tucked a block off Central Avenue near the corner of Thomas Avenue, The Penguin is typical of the neighborhood's independent, offbeat feel. The kitchen closes at midnight, though the bar stays open much later. My advice: order your burger Southern-style and ask for an appetizer of fried pickles. Lunch and dinner are served daily.

- **Price's Chicken Coop.** Inexpensive. 1614 Camden Road (704-333-9866). Fried chicken and fried fish from Price's Chicken Coop are as much a Charlotte tradition as bank takeovers. A little over a mile distant but a world away from the slick bistros of Uptown, Price's is as Southern as it gets. Call for directions if you're new to town. Otherwise, you'll likely get lost, but the chicken is worth the search. Lunch and dinner are prepared Monday through Saturday for takeout only.

Nearby

- **Waxhaw**, a small town 13 miles south of Charlotte on N.C. 16, is known for its turn-of-the-20th-century architecture and its large number of antique outlets. Shopping here is leisurely; shopkeepers rarely keep to a set schedule. Each February, the Waxhaw Women's Club hosts an antique show at the American Legion hut. Waxhaw is where Andrew Jackson spent his childhood.

- The **Reed Gold Mine**, in Cabarrus County northeast of Charlotte, saw the beginning of the short-lived Charlotte gold rush, one of the first in the United States. It is now a state historic site. The mine and the legacy of the gold rush are preserved through a museum, a film, a guided underground tour, a stamp mill, and walking trails. For a small fee, you can even learn how to pan for gold—but don't get your hopes up. The site is currently open Tuesday through Saturday from 9 A.M. to 5 P.M., but be sure to inquire ahead. Call 704-721-4653 or visit www.itpi.dpi.state.nc.us/reed.

- **Morrow Mountain State Park** is a beautiful and tranquil piece of the Uwharrie Mountains only 45 minutes from Charlotte and seven miles east of the town of Albemarle. A swimming pool served by a bathhouse from the Civilian Conservation Corps era, vacation cabins, and tent and trailer

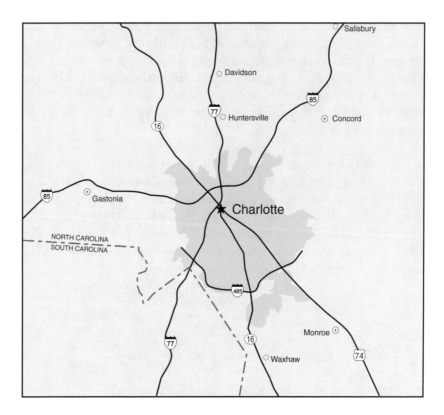

campsites are available. Visitors can also fish, picnic, and rent canoes and boats. The Kron House is the reconstructed cabin of one of the area's earliest doctors. The hiking trails here are challenging and scenic. A modest fee is charged to use the swimming pool, as are rental fees for some activities. Call 704-982-4402 or visit http://ils.unc.edu/parkproject/visit/momo/home for more information.

■ *Uwharrie National Forest* lies just across the Pee Dee River from Morrow Mountain State Park. Camping, horseback riding, mountain biking, and hiking are just some of the land-based activities that await you at this 55,000-acre oasis, while canoeing, tubing, fishing, and swimming in popular *Badin Lake* will help you cool off in the summer months. Call 910-576-6391 or visit www.cs.unca.edu/nfsnc/recreation/uwharrie for more information.

■ Straddling the border between North and South Carolina, *Paramount's Carowinds* is the largest theme park in the Carolinas. It has evolved far beyond the wooden Thunder Road roller coaster. Thrill seekers will adore

the Borg Assimilator and Carolina Cyclone coasters. The more family-friendly attractions include Scoobie Doo's Haunted Mansion and the new Boomerang Bay water park. Musical revues and concerts are held at the park. Visiting Carowinds can easily take an entire day; be sure to wear sunscreen. The park is located at 14523 Carowinds Boulevard; take Exit 90 off Interstate 77. It is open from early spring to early fall. For hours and admission prices, call 800-888-4386 or visit www.carowinds.com.

■ The ***Schiele Museum of Natural History,*** at 1500 East Garrison Boulevard in Gastonia, is the area's largest nature museum. The exhibition galleries showcase North American habitats and wildlife. The half-mile nature trail takes visitors through 16 acres of Piedmont forest to a re-created 18th-century backwoods farm and a Catawba Indian village. The Schiele Museum also houses a state-of-the-art planetarium. The museum is open Monday through Saturday from 9 A.M. to 5 P.M. and Sunday from 1 P.M. to 5 P.M. except on major holidays. Admission is charged. Call 704-866-6900 or visit www.schielemuseum.org for more information.

■ ***Crowders Mountain State Park*** lies just west of Gastonia near the South Carolina line and Kings Mountain National Military Park. In addition to hosting the normal state-park activities, Crowders Mountain is one of the best rock-climbing sites east of the Appalachians. Admission is charged. Call 704-853-5375 or visit http://ils.unc.edu/parkproject/visit/crmo/home for information.

- **McDowell Park and Nature Preserve**, located on Lake Wylie south of Charlotte, encompasses 1,000 acres off N.C. 49. Camping, hiking, fishing, picnicking, and boating are all available here. Lake Wylie, one of a series of lakes formed by the damming of the Catawba River, is the last lake before the river leaves North Carolina. Admission is charged. Call 704-588-5224 for more information.

- **Davidson**, a college town just off the bank of Lake Norman, is remarkable for its old-time Main Street, maintained in the face of Mecklenburg County's astounding growth. Main Street runs alongside the campus of **Davidson College**, where future president Woodrow Wilson studied. It features a row of shops, coffee houses, and a soda shop, housed mainly in 19th-century buildings.

Main Street in Davidson
PHOTOGRAPH BY ED SOUTHERN

THE MOUNTAINS

The Blue Ridge Parkway

By Carolyn Sakowski

The Blue Ridge Parkway is an unusual part of the national parks system. It's really a linear park, stretching 469 miles from Shenandoah National Park in Virginia to Great Smoky Mountains National Park on the North Carolina-Tennessee border.

The parkway is refreshing. Regulations keep the signage to a minimum; what is there is informative and tasteful. A major purpose of the highway's construction was to give men jobs during the Depression. You'll see their clearly identifiable stonework all along the route. In recent years, the Blue Ridge Parkway Foundation and other parties have gone to great lengths to ensure that the pastoral feel of the land is preserved.

One thing you'll notice is that the speed limit is never over 45 miles per hour. The parkway is designed for leisurely driving, with plenty of overlooks along the way. If you're in a hurry, take the regular roads.

It is legal for you to pull onto the shoulder for a picnic, as long as you make sure your vehicle is completely off the road. On weekends in the summer and fall, you'll see lots of people taking advantage of this opportunity.

This chapter will provide a few details about some of the sites along the Blue Ridge Parkway. The parkway actually begins near Charlottesville, Virginia; the markers start with Milepost 0 at Shenandoah National Park. The North Carolina section starts at Milepost 217 at the North Carolina-Virginia line. For information, call 828-298-0298 or visit www.nps.gov/blri or www.blueridgeparkway.org.

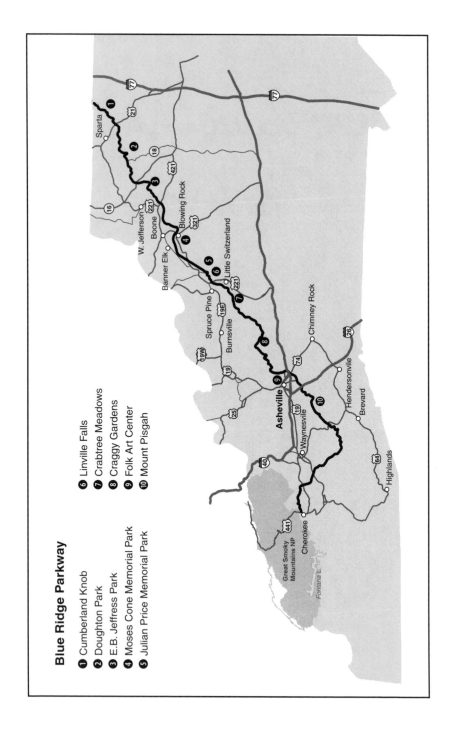

Blue Ridge Parkway

1. Cumberland Knob
2. Doughton Park
3. E.B. Jeffress Park
4. Moses Cone Memorial Park
5. Julian Price Memorial Park
6. Linville Falls
7. Crabtree Meadows
8. Craggy Gardens
9. Folk Art Center
10. Mount Pisgah

Milepost 217—Cumberland Knob is in Alleghany County. The boundary line that divides North Carolina and Virginia was surveyed in 1749 by a group that included Peter Jefferson, Thomas Jefferson's father. Just south of the line is Cumberland Knob Recreation Area, where restrooms, water fountains, picnic tables, and hiking trails are available. You can take a short walk to Cumberland Knob or a two-hour hike into Gully Creek Gorge.

Milepost 218.6—Fox Hunter's Paradise recalls a once-popular sport in the mountains. Men would turn loose their dogs to "run" foxes through the night. Catching one was rare—and not the point. Listening to the "music" of fox hounds calling through the deep woods was what mattered. A picnic table and a hiking trail are located at Fox Hunter's Paradise. You can contact the visitor center here by calling 828-657-8161.

Milepost 229—U.S. 21 intersects the parkway here. Sparta is seven miles west and Roaring Gap four miles east.

Milepost 230—Little Glade Mill Pond offers picnic tables and a short hike around the pond.

Milepost 232.5—Stone Mountain Overlook offers a good view of Stone Mountain State Park, which is covered in the "Recreation" section of the Alleghany County chapter.

Milepost 237.1—Air Bellows Gap is appropriately named; on a windy day, the wind sweeps up from the deep gorge below.

Milepost 238.5—Brinegar Cabin is an original mountain homestead that has been preserved. The farm of Martin and Caroline Joines Brinegar is located to the left. When it is open, you can get a glimpse of old-time life in the mountains. Craft demonstrations are offered at various times; check at Doughton Park for a schedule. Two trails begin at the far end of the parking lot: the 4.3-mile Cedar Rock Trail and the 7.5-mile Bluff Mountain Trail.

Milepost 238.5-244.8—Doughton Park, named for Congressman Robert Doughton, is one of the parkway's treasures. The park offers the Bluffs Lodge and Coffee Shop, a campground, a gift shop, an excellent network of hiking trails, and wonderful views. The telephone number at the visitor center is 336-372-4499.

Milepost 242—The Alligator Back rest area has a 20-minute walking trail to Bluff Overlook.

Milepost 248.1—N.C. 18 intersects the parkway here. It is two miles west to Laurel Springs and 24 miles east to North Wilkesboro.

Milepost 252.5—Jesse Sheets built a small cabin for his family at Sheets Gap around 1815, making this one of the oldest surviving settlers' cabins. An overlook at Sheets Gap is 0.3 mile south; from there, a trail leads back to the cabin.

Milepost 259—Northwest Trading Post is described in the "Special Shopping" section of the Alleghany County chapter.

Milepost 260—At the end of the parking lot is an easy walking trail to Jumpinoff Rock. A small picnic area is also located here.

Milepost 261—N.C. 16 intersects the parkway here. It is five miles west to Glendale Springs and 20 miles east to North Wilkesboro.

Milepost 264.4—The Lump provides sweeping views of the forested foothills below.

Milepost 267—This site overlooks Mount Jefferson State Park, which is covered in the "Recreation" section of the Ashe County chapter.

Milepost 271.9—The Cascades Nature Trail offers a brisk hike through rich pine forests. In late May, the mountain laurel is beautiful here. At the bottom of the trail, a waterfall rolls down the side of the mountain to the lowlands below. Hikers need to exercise caution on the rocks near the waterfall. Even in recent years, people have fallen to their deaths here. Restrooms, water fountains, and picnic tables are available at this site.

Milepost 272.6—E. B. Jeffress Park has plenty of hiking trails, a picnic area, and two historic buildings. One is the Jesse Brown Cabin, built in the mid-1800s. Nearby is Cool Spring Baptist Church, an open-air shelter that was already standing when the Civil War ended in 1865; it was typical of the earliest churches in the region. An overlook here offers a short trail to these early structures.

Milepost 276.4—The bridge over the four-lane U.S. 421 graces the entrance to Deep Gap, which is the way into Watauga County from the east. A Civil War entrenchment once stood near where the parkway bridge is today.

Milepost 281.7—Grandview Overlook is exactly what its name implies.

Milepost 285.1—Daniel Boone Trace marks the place where Boone regularly camped and hunted in this area in the 1760s, before opening Kentucky to settlers. A monument and a roadside picnic table are located here.

Milepost 289-290—Raven Rocks and Thunder Hill are two exceptional overlooks near Blowing Rock. Raven Rocks offers views of the mountains surrounding the valley of the Watauga River. Thunder Hill's view looks over the valley of the Yadkin River stretching to Lenoir, Hickory, and beyond. Both are popular spots with locals and visitors alike.

Milepost 291.9—U.S. 221/U.S. 321 intersects the parkway here. It is seven miles north to Boone and two miles south to Blowing Rock.

Milepost 293-295—Moses S. Cone Memorial Park is described in the "Special Shopping" section of the Blowing Rock chapter.

Julian Price Park
COURTESY OF NORTH CAROLINA DIVISION OF TOURISM, FILM AND SPORTS DEVELOPMENT

Milepost 295-299—Julian Price Park offers a campground, an amphitheater, and canoe rentals on Price Lake, plus a host of trails to hike. The trail around Price Lake is relatively level. The campground's 197 spaces are offered on a first-come, first-served basis. Cold water and grills are available, but electricity is not. A dump station is located near the office. The office is normally open from 8 A.M. to 8 P.M.; campers may self-register after hours and at times when no ranger is available. Price Lake offers excellent fishing. It is classified as "general trout waters"; fishermen may use natural or artificial baits but no fresh eggs or live or dead fish or amphibians. A state license is required, but a trout stamp is not.

Milepost 298-305—Grandfather Mountain is the crown jewel of the parkway. For over 50 years, owner Hugh Morton fought the government over the environmental impact its original road plans would have caused this landmark—and visitors are glad he did. The Linn Cove Viaduct, which almost rivals the mountain itself in beauty, was the compromise the two sides found. The free trail system here links with Grandfather's system, for which a permit is required.

Milepost 304—The Linn Cove Viaduct is one of the engineering marvels of our age, and the view from it is unmatched in the eastern United States. You can hike the Linn Cove Viaduct Trail, which leads beneath the viaduct and gives a true appreciation of this architectural masterpiece. The visitor center here has displays, books, videos, and restrooms.

The Linn Cove Viaduct
Photograph by Carolyn Sakowski

Milepost 305.9—U.S. 221 intersects the parkway here. It is three miles west to Linville and one mile west to the entrance of Grandfather Mountain.

Milepost 306—Grandfather Mountain Overlook offers a view of the mountain's southern side, which resembles a bird of prey. That explains why the Cherokees called it Tanawha, meaning "hawk." One of the best trails in the area is the Tanawha Trail, which extends from Milepost 305.5 for 13.5 miles toward Price Lake.

Milepost 308.2—Flat Rock Overlook has a short nature trail that leads to a view of the Linville Valley and Grandfather Mountain.

Milepost 310—Lost Cove Cliffs Overlook offers one of the best vantage points for seeing the Brown Mountain Lights. In recent years, the haze that appears on most summer evenings has prevented visitors from witnessing the mysterious lights moving along the ridge in the distance. No one has ever explained what causes these lights, but the tales that have grown up around them make great campfire stories.

Milepost 312—N.C. 181 intersects the parkway here. It is two miles north to Pineola and 32 miles southeast to Morganton.

Milepost 316.3—Linville Falls is covered in the "Recreation" section of the chapter on Banner Elk, Beech Mountain, and Linville.

Milepost 317.4—The Linville Falls Visitor Center has a gift shop, a picnic area, and a bridge from which you can fish in the Linville River. You can contact the visitor center at 828-765-1045. It is three miles south to the Linville Falls community and 24 miles south on U.S. 221 to Marion.

Milepost 331—The Museum of North Carolina Minerals is described in the "Museums and Science Centers" section of the chapter on Spruce Pine and Burnsville. It is six miles north to Spruce Pine and 14 miles south to Marion.

Milepost 334—N.C. 226A intersects the parkway at Little Switzerland.

Milepost 339.5—Crabtree Meadows offers a 250-acre park that includes a picnic area and a comfort station. The focus of the park is the 40-minute hike to Crabtree Falls.

Milepost 344—N.C. 80 intersects the parkway at Buck Creek Gap. It is 16 miles north to Burnsville and 16 miles south to Marion.

Milepost 355.4—N.C. 128 leads to Mount Mitchell State Park, described in the "Recreation" section of the chapter on Spruce Pine and Burnsville.

Milepost 364.4—The Craggy Gardens Visitor Center offers information, exhibits, and self-guided tours. In June, the rhododendron gardens here are spectacular.

Milepost 377.4—N.C. 694 intersects the parkway here. It is eight miles west to Asheville.

Milepost 382—The Folk Art Center is described in the "Special Shopping" section of the Asheville chapter.

Milepost 382.6—U.S. 70 intersects the parkway here. It is one mile to Oteen, five miles to Asheville, and 10 miles to Black Mountain.

Milepost 384.7—U.S. 74A intersects the parkway here. It is three miles west to Asheville. Chimney Rock, Bat Cave, and Lake Lure lie to the east.

Milepost 388.8—U.S. 25 intersects the parkway here. It is five miles north to Asheville and 17 miles south to Hendersonville.

Milepost 393.6—N.C. 191 intersects the parkway here. It is six miles north to Asheville and 20 miles south to Hendersonville.

Milepost 408.6—Mount Pisgah, which was part of the 100,000 acres donated from George Vanderbilt's Biltmore Estate, offers a campground, a picnic area, trails, an inn, a restaurant, and a service station. You can see the 5,749-foot peak in the distance.

Milepost 412—U.S. 276 intersects the parkway at Wagon Road Gap. It is 18 miles south to Brevard, eight miles north to Cruso, and 22 miles northwest to Waynesville. On the way to Brevard, you can visit the Cradle of Forestry in America.

Milepost 417—Looking Glass Rock is a 3,969-foot summit whose sheer cliffs give it its name.

Milepost 418.8—Graveyard Fields Overlook has a 2.3-mile loop trail to Yellowstone Falls.

Milepost 422.4—From the Devil's Courthouse parking area, it is a strenuous half-mile hike to the Devil's Courthouse itself. The Cherokees believe this 5,462-foot mountain was the location of the giant Judaculla's courtroom.

Milepost 423.2—N.C. 215 intersects the parkway at Beech Gap. It is 24 miles north to Waynesville and 17 miles south to Rosman.

Graveyard Fields
COURTESY OF NORTH CAROLINA DIVISION OF TOURISM, FILM AND SPORTS DEVELOPMENT

Milepost 431—At the Haywood-Jackson Overlook, visitors can take a 1.5-mile self-guided loop trail to the summit of Richland Balsam, which is the highest point on the parkway, measuring 6,058 feet.

Milepost 431.4—Richmond Balsam Overlook is located here.

Milepost 443.1—U.S. 74/U.S. 23 intersects the parkway at Balsam Gap. It is seven miles east to Waynesville and 12 miles west to Sylva.

Milepost 451.2—At Waterrock Knob Overlook, you'll find an information center, a comfort station, a trail to the knob, and a four-state view.

Milepost 455.7—U.S. 19 intersects the parkway at Soco Gap. It is 12 miles west to Cherokee and five miles east to Maggie Valley.

Milepost 458.2—From here, Heintooga Ridge Road Spur goes to Mile High Overlook. It is 12 miles to the Great Smoky Mountains National Park Campground.

Milepost 461.9—Big Witch Overlook is located here.

Milepost 469.1—Great Smoky Mountains National Park begins at the junction with U.S. 441. It is two miles south to Cherokee and 29 miles north to Gatlinburg, Tennessee.

The High Country

Alleghany County

Ashe County

Boone

Blowing Rock

Banner Elk, Beech Mountain, and Linville

Spruce Pine and Burnsville

By Carolyn Sakowski

*T*his book's definition of the High Country differs slightly from that employed by the North Carolina High Country Host organization. This section will cover Alleghany, Ashe, Watauga, Avery, Mitchell, and Yancey counties.

In this northern portion of North Carolina's Appalachian Mountains, you'll find the highest peaks not only in the state but in the

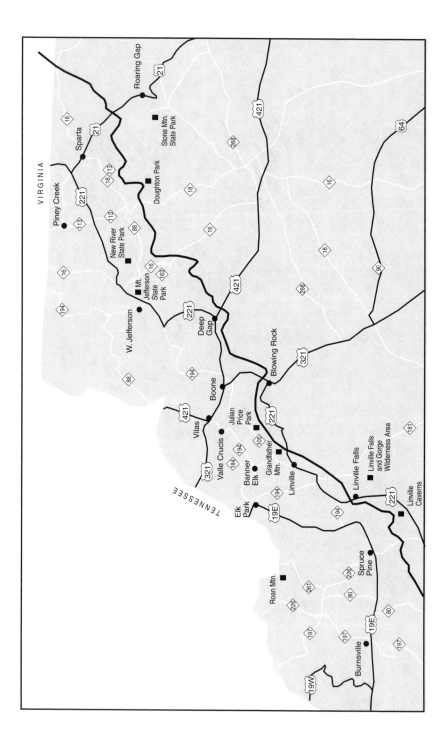

entire eastern United States. You'll discover a booming tourism industry thanks to the cool summer temperatures, the vibrant fall foliage, and the winter skiing. All of the places mentioned here are within an easy day's drive of each other.

Although many of the top attractions—Grandfather Mountain, the New River, the Blowing Rock, Linville Falls—have remained the same for millions of years, the last three decades have brought dramatic changes to the rest of the area. When the tourists began to arrive, they liked what they saw so much that they bought mountain property and built summer or retirement homes. As a result, many of the natural vistas have disappeared. It's a double-edged sword in many ways. While longtime residents lament the influx of "outsiders," they now have amenities they could not have imagined a few decades ago. You not only don't have to drive 30 miles to buy groceries or an alcoholic beverage, you can now get espresso and the Sunday *New York Times*—on the same Sunday they get it in New York—a few minutes from almost anywhere.

Speaking of alcoholic beverages, you'll find that the liquor laws in these mountain counties are highly inconsistent. Some resorts have been very creative in procuring legislative exemptions that allow them to serve alcohol. Some townships have voted to allow it, while people are unable to purchase even beer or wine a few miles away. If having access to alcoholic beverages is important to your vacation, you might want to check on the liquor laws where you plan to stay and dine.

You should also know that, even though you may be leaving 90-degree temperatures to come to the mountains, you'll still need a jacket or sweater in the evenings here. The rule of thumb is to expect a five-degree change in temperature for every 1,000 feet of change in elevation. You might also want to throw in rain gear. Many a clear, sunny day has a short late-afternoon shower here. These cool days and frequent showers ensure that the region's wildflowers and cultivated mountain gardens are prolific. You'll be struck by the abundance of vibrantly colored flowers.

In the last few decades, there has been an explosion of outdoor activities in the mountains. Skiing, golf, whitewater rafting, mountain biking, and hiking have all brought thousands of people. For those who prefer less physical "exercise," the area has also seen a boom in shopping outlets, gourmet restaurants, first-rate resorts, and bed-and-breakfasts in

PHOTOGRAPH IN BACKGROUND OF PAGE 429—

Tweetsie Railroad
PHOTOGRAPHY BY JUDI SCHARNS, COURTESY OF BOONE
CONVENTION AND VISITORS BUREAU

wonderful restored homes. Although I recommend some specific places to stay, all of these counties have scores of individual cabins and condominiums for rent. Contact the appropriate chamber of commerce to be put in touch with realtors.

North toward the Virginia border, you can see how dramatically the times have changed. Those who long for the way things used to be in the mountains may find Ashe and Alleghany counties to their liking. For at least the next few years, you'll still be able to get the best of both worlds by traveling from one county to the next to find what you seek.

JUST THE FACTS

You can get visitor information from North Carolina High Country Host, at 1700 Blowing Rock Road (U.S. 321) in Boone; call 800-438-7500 or 828-264-1299 or visit www.highcountryhost.com. This regional visitor center promotes tourism in Watauga, Ashe, Avery, Alleghany, Mitchell, and Wilkes counties. It is open Monday through Saturday from 9 A.M. to 5 P.M. and Sunday from 10 A.M. to 4 P.M.

The area is served by an excellent free weekly newspaper, the *Mountain Times*, which has Ashe, Watauga, and Avery county editions. You can access the paper's Web site and its extensive links at www.mountaintimes.com. The *Mountain Times* also publishes three tabloid-sized seasonal editions— *Summer Times, Autumn Times,* and *Winter Times*—that cover the area.

Stone Mountain
PHOTOGRAPH BY CAROLYN SAKOWSKI

ALLEGHANY COUNTY

Alleghany County was once known as "the Lost Province" because of its early isolation. Even today, the county has a year-round population of only 10,000 people. But it is finally starting to reap the benefits of its former isolation. The local chamber of commerce now touts the county as "the Unspoiled Province," and that's exactly what it is. Here, you'll find scenic views that are still largely unmarred by progress. As you drive along Alleghany County's two-lane highways, you'll be struck by the number of two-story white clapboard farmhouses with wraparound porches sitting smack dab in the middle of large, working farms. You won't see the clutter of billboards and the urban sprawl that come with the influx of national chain stores and gimmicky roadside gift shops.

Nestled among mountains that reach 3,000 to 4,000 feet, the county is surrounded by 20,000 acres of national and state parks, including Doughton Park, Stone Mountain State Park, New River State Park, and Grayson Highlands State Park in Virginia. The Blue Ridge Parkway weaves along the edge of the county for 30 miles.

If you want to see the mountains like they used to be, you'd better hurry to Alleghany County before the rest of the world discovers it.

JUST THE FACTS

To reach Alleghany County, you can travel on N.C. 18 or U.S. 21, which intersect in the county seat, Sparta. It is a short trip on U.S. 21 from Interstate 77 to Roaring Gap and Sparta. Interstate 77 offers quick access from Roanoke, which is 115 miles away, and Charlotte, which is 105 miles away. To the east, Winston-Salem is 75 miles from Sparta.

For visitor information, contact the Alleghany County Chamber of Commerce, at 58 South Main Street in Sparta. Call 800-372-5473 or visit www.sparta-nc.com.

The *Alleghany News* is the area's weekly newspaper. Its Web site is www.alleghanynews.com.

Things to Do

RECREATION

■ **Stone Mountain State Park** is located in Alleghany and Wilkes counties seven miles southwest of Roaring Gap. From U.S. 21, turn onto S.R. 1002, which will take you to the John P. Frank Parkway. If you're coming from the west, take N.C. 18 North and turn right on S.R. 1002.

Located on 13,500 acres, the park offers four easily accessed waterfalls, 17 miles of trout streams, two handicapped-accessible fishing piers, 15 miles of hiking and horseback-riding trails, and a historic mountain homestead. However, the big attraction is Stone Mountain itself, a 600-foot granite dome. Climbing on the cliffs is permitted in designated areas, but all climbers must register and possess a valid rock-climbing permit.

Campsites are available for a fee. The campground has a wash house with hot showers, but there are no utility hookups. Campers cannot leave the park after the gates are closed. The park is open from 8 A.M. to 6 P.M. November through February, from 8 A.M. to 7 P.M. in March and October, from 8 A.M. to 8 P.M. in April, May, and September, and from 8 A.M. to 9 P.M. June through August. For information, contact the park at 3042 John P.

Frank Parkway, Roaring Gap, N.C. 28668 (336-957-8185; www.ils.unc.edu/parkproject/visit/stmo/home.html).

- **Doughton Park** is part of the Blue Ridge Parkway. It has over 30 miles of hiking trails ranging from modest strolls to all-day outings. Horse trails, fishing, camping, and picnicking are all offered. See the chapter on the Blue Ridge Parkway for more information.

- **New River State Park** is located in Ashe and Alleghany counties. The Alleghany County Access Area can be reached only by canoe. Camping and canoeing on the New are big draws here. For more information, see the chapter on Ashe County and the sidebar about the New River.
  Two local campgrounds bill themselves as canoe campgrounds. **River Camp USA** has sites for RVs and tents. It offers full hookups, picnic tables, a country store, a playground, a laundry, and hot showers. The proprietors rent canoes and inner tubes and provide shuttle service. For information, contact the camp at P.O. Box 9, Piney Creek, N.C. 28663 (800-RIVERCAMP or 336-359-CAMP; www.rivercamp.net). **New River Canoe and Campground**, located six miles north of Sparta on U.S. 21, has grassy and shady spots along the river. All sites have a picnic table, a lantern post, and a fire ring. The campground offers RV hookups, cabins, a camp store, a restaurant, a playground, and pedal boats for rent. Guests can make arrangements for canoeing instruction and day or overnight canoe trips. You can contact the campground at 628 U.S. 21 North, Sparta, N.C. 28675 (336-372-8793).

- Two Alleghany County golf courses allow nonmembers to play: **New River Country Club** (336-372-4869) in Sparta and **Olde Beau Golf Club** (336-363-3333) in Roaring Gap.

- Nearby Virginia offers two exceptional opportunities for bicycling. The **Virginia Creeper Trail** and **New River Trail State Park** are both rails-to-trails venues. They are perfect for inexperienced riders, children, and even experienced cyclists who want to test their stamina. Unfortunately, Sparta does not have any bike-rental establishments, but you can make arrangements in the Virginia community of Damascus. For information about the Virginia Creeper Trail, visit www.creepertrail.com.

Doughton-Hall Bed-and-Breakfast
PHOTOGRAPH BY CAROLYN SAKOWSKI

Places to Stay

RESORTS, HOTELS, AND MOTELS

■ **Bluffs Lodge**. Moderate. Milepost 241 on the Blue Ridge Parkway in Doughton Park (336-372-4499; www.blueridgeresort.com, then click "Bluffs Lodge"). The draw at this rustic motel is the sweeping views from the balconies and patios. In exchange, you leave behind telephones and televisions. The lodge is open from May through October.

INNS AND BED-AND-BREAKFASTS

■ **Harmony Hill**. Expensive. 1740 Halsey Knob Road in Sparta (336-372-6868; harmonyhillbnb.com). Harmony Hill is located eight miles from Sparta; a map is available on the Web site. This beautifully restored Victorian home has an incredible view of the surrounding countryside. It offers three bedrooms and a carriage house. Each bedroom is air-conditioned and has a private bath. Some rooms have Jacuzzis; most have fireplaces with gas logs; all have ceiling fans, televisions, and telephones. Breakfast is served in the dining room, in the gazebo, or on the porch. Pets and children under 12 are not allowed.

■ **Doughton-Hall Bed-and-Breakfast**. Moderate. 12668 N.C. 18 South in Laurel Springs (336-359-2341; www.doughtonhall.com). This is the historic residence of former congressman Robert L. Doughton, who served in the United States House of Representatives from 1911 to 1953, during which time he was the powerful head of the House Ways and Means Committee. It was Doughton who was largely responsible for bringing the Blue Ridge Parkway to this area. Located 13 miles from Sparta and 1.7 miles from the intersection of the Blue Ridge Parkway and N.C. 18, his Queen Anne-style home dates to 1898. It is listed on the National Register of Historic Places. It has four guest rooms, three with private baths and Jacuzzis. Wine and hors d'oeuvres are served nightly, and a full country breakfast is offered each morning.

■ *Mountain View Lodge & Cabins*. Moderate. Near Milepost 256 on the Blue Ridge Parkway at Glendale Springs (800-903-6811 or 336-982-2233; www.mtnviewlodge.com). One unusual thing about this establishment is that you are allowed to bring pets if you are staying in one of the five cabin buildings. Each cabin is divided in duplex fashion. There are also rooms and a family suite in the main lodge. A full breakfast is included with lodge-room rentals.

Places to Eat

■ *The Senator's House*. Moderate. 360 North Main Street, next to Sparta Elementary School (336-372-7500; http://sparta-nc.com/senatorshouse/). Excellent American cuisine is served in the historic home of former state senator Eugene Transou. Hours vary seasonally; dinner is usually served on Friday and Saturday only. Reservations are required.

■ *The Pizzeria*. Inexpensive. Trojan Village Shopping Center in Sparta (336-372-8885). This restaurant serves pizza, subs, and sandwiches, but what it's really known for is its great chicken pie, which comes with the luncheon buffet on Sunday and Wednesday. A regular lunch buffet is served Tuesday through Sunday; dinner is served Tuesday through Sunday as well.

ASHE COUNTY

The farther south you travel from the Virginia line, the more you'll witness tourism development and the proliferation of vacation homes. Ashe County lies between Alleghany and Watauga counties not only geographically but developmentally as well. Here, you'll see more chain motels and urban sprawl than in Alleghany, but it's nothing like you'll get in Watauga.

Thanks to its cheese factory and its frescoes, Ashe County has long been a great day trip from anywhere in the High Country. Because of its two canoe access areas for New River State Park, it has also been a logical place for outfitters to spring up. This is one of the major areas for the growing of Fraser fir Christmas trees, so the landscape is dotted with uniform rows of evergreens growing along the hillsides.

The town of Jefferson, the county seat, was founded in 1800 at the base of Mount Jefferson. In 1917, a group of investors founded West Jefferson, which attracted the railroad. Jefferson subsequently went into decline, leaving West Jefferson as the economic center of the county.

JUST THE FACTS

To reach Ashe County's twin cities of Jefferson and West Jefferson, take U.S. 221 from Deep Gap, U.S. 421 from the Blue Ridge Parkway, or N.C. 194 or N.C. 16 from Virginia.

For visitor information, contact the Ashe County Chamber of Commerce, at 303 East Second Street in West Jefferson. Call 888-343-2743 or 336-846-9550 or visit www.ashechamber.com.

The *Jefferson Post* is the area's weekly newspaper; its Web site is www.jeffersonpost.com. *Mountain Times*, a free weekly, is distributed in Ashe County.

The New River
PHOTOGRAPH BY A. T. BARBEE,
COURTESY OF NORTH CAROLINA HIGH COUNTRY HOST

THE NEW RIVER—NORTH CAROLINA'S AMERICAN HERITAGE RIVER

The New River, which some say is 300 million years old, is supposedly the oldest river in North America. It begins in Watauga County and is the only river in the eastern United States that flows northward to the Midwest. The North Fork and South Fork of the river join a few miles south of the North Carolina-Virginia border. From there, the river continues through Virginia and West Virginia.

Archaeological investigations suggest that humans have been in the region for at least 10,000 years. Arrowheads, pottery shards, and stone axes indicate the Canawhay Indian tribe occupied the river valley during the precolonial period. There is also evidence of hunting trails used by Creeks, Shawnees, and Cherokees moving north along the New River to the Ohio River.

The first European to see the river was probably Colonel Abraham Wood, who came seeking trade with the Indians in 1654. Before the 1770s, long hunters were probably the only white men to venture into the region. Originally known as Wood's River, it was renamed the New by Peter Jefferson, the father of Thomas Jefferson, when he surveyed the North Carolina-Virginia boundary in 1749.

In 1752, Bishop Augustus Spangenberg, an early traveler sent by the Moravian Church to find land for a settlement, wrote the following: "For several days we followed the river in the hope that it would lead us out, we found ourselves only deeper in the wilderness, for the river ran now north, now south, now east, now west, in short to all points of the compass! Finally, we decided to leave the river and take a course between east and south, crossing the mountains as best we could." If you look at the course of the river on a modern map, you'll see exactly why Bishop Spangenberg was so frustrated.

In 1965, the Appalachian Power Company applied for a license to dam the river. In response to unprecedented grass-roots opposition, the North Carolina General Assembly declared a 26.5-mile stretch from the river's confluence with Dog Creek to the Virginia state line a state scenic river. In April 1976, the New was designated a national wild and scenic river, thus ensuring that it will remain untouched. On July 30, 1998, President Bill Clinton and Vice President Al Gore showed up with a group of dignitaries to proclaim the New an American Heritage River.

The centerpiece of New River State Park, the river is a popular spot for camping, canoeing, picnicking, and fishing. The easy flow and mild rapids make it perfect for inexperienced paddlers. The best months for high water levels are May and June; August and September are usually the low-flow months.

Those wishing to canoe can leave their vehicles at the Wagoner Road Access Area, located at River Mile 26, eight miles southeast of Jefferson; the access area can be reached via S.R. 1590 off N.C. 88 some 1.2 miles east of the intersection of N.C. 16 and N.C. 88. A second parking area is at the U.S. 221 Access Area, located at River Mile 15, eight miles northeast of Jefferson; it may be reached via U.S. 221. The third option is Kings Creek Access Area at River Mile 7. The directions to this access are complex; you can find them on the New River State Park Web site, listed below. Picnic areas and primitive campsites with tables and grills are located at the three access areas. The Wagoner Road and U.S. 221 access areas have bathroom facilities with hot showers. Pit toilets and drinking water are nearby.

The Alleghany County Access Area can be reached only by canoe. It has canoe campsites, pit toilets, and a pump for drinking water. Canoes can also be launched from several bridges and roads that cross the river.

The South Fork and North Fork of the New offer excellent smallmouth and redeye bass fishing. The South Fork downstream from the U.S. 221 bridge has been stocked with muskellunge. Trout fishing is excellent in the small tributaries, most of which are stocked regularly with rainbow and brown trout. Make sure you get that fishing license!

For more information, contact the chamber of commerce in Ashe County or Alleghany County. Or you can contact New River State Park at P.O. Box 48, Jefferson, N.C. 28640 (336-982-2587; www.ils.unc.edu/parkproject/visit/neri/home.html).

St. Mary's Episcopal Church
PHOTOGRAPH BY CAROLYN SAKOWSKI

Holy Trinity Episcopal Church
PHOTOGRAPH BY CAROLYN SAKOWSKI

Things to Do

HISTORIC PLACES, GARDENS, AND TOURS

■ In downtown West Jefferson, you can tour North Carolina's only cheese manufacturer, **Ashe County Cheese Company**. This establishment has been producing cheese for over 60 years. You can see cheese being made; call ahead, since the cheese-making schedule is subject to change. Be sure to stop at the wine-and-cheese shop, too. Located at 106 East Main on the corner of Fourth Street, the plant and store are open Monday through Saturday. For more information, call 800-445-1378 or 336-246-2501 or visit www.ashecountycheese.com.

CULTURAL OFFERINGS

■ Just outside West Jefferson are signs directing you to the frescoes at **St. Mary's Episcopal Church** in Beaver Creek. Less than 10 miles to the east on N.C. 16 in Glendale Springs, you can see the larger fresco at **Holy Trinity Episcopal Church**. All were created by North Carolina native Ben Long and his helpers. While at Holy Trinity, be sure to see the columbarium, located downstairs. If you've ever wondered where you might put your cremated ashes, the columbarium provides an interesting option.

The Last Supper *at Holy Trinity Episcopal Church*

THE FRESCOES

Though St. Mary's Episcopal Church now houses one the area's main tourist attractions, it was not always the focus of community pride.

Milnor Jones was an Episcopal minister and missionary who organized the first Episcopal church in Ashe County, the Church of St. Simon the Zealot. On June 21, 1896, Bishop Joseph Blount Cheshire came from Raleigh to conduct services. He was met at the church by an unexpected greeting committee. Cheshire wrote, "I was assaulted and forcibly prevented from entering this building by a mob of between fifty and one hundred men which had been gotten together for the express purpose of preventing our service that day. And the reason they gave for this action was that they 'did not like Mr. Jones' doctrine' and they understood that I taught the same doctrine." Cheshire further noted that he "met with the most violent opposition, accompanied with bitter abuse from Methodists and Baptists, especially the latter."

Milnor Jones went on to organize a school at Beaver Creek. His quaint Church of St. Simon the Zealot was later renamed St. Mary's. It was eventually abandoned for lack of funds until a different sort of notoriety came its way.

In the summer of 1980, artist Ben Long returned to the United States to train others in a dying art form. For seven years, he had studied fresco painting in Italy with a master of Renaissance technique. Long took on as many as 20 apprentices at one time in Ashe County and used two Episcopal churches in the area as his studios.

Fresco painting is a tedious and complicated process, which explains its rarity in today's world. Ground natural pigment is mixed with distilled water, thinned with lime, and painted on damp plaster. As the plaster dries, the lime and pigment bind chemically, so that the wall literally becomes the painting. This unusual technique produces an interesting effect—many say that fresco walls seem to glow. The drawback is that the pigment is absorbed the moment brush touches plaster, so a mistake can necessitate the removal of an entire section of wall.

Ben Long imported lime from the same site in Florence, Italy, that Michelangelo used when working on the Sistine Chapel. He mixed it with North Carolina sand to make

The Mystery of Faith
at St. Mary's Episcopal Church
PHOTOGRAPH BY CAROLYN SAKOWSKI

his plaster. Local people served as models for the characters in his frescoes; Long himself took the role of Doubting Thomas. The results are so impressive that thousands of people a year visit the out-of-the-way chapels to view the frescoes. Those at St. Mary's are *Mary, Great with Child; John the Baptist*; and *The Mystery of Faith*. At Holy Trinity Episcopal Church, you can see Long's interpretation of the Last Supper, which occupies the entire front wall. Despite frequent busloads of tourists, both churches are worthwhile stops.

You can also view a Ben Long fresco in the E. H. Sloop Chapel on the campus of Crossnore School in the Avery County community of Crossnore.

Special Shopping

- The **Northwest Trading Post**, at Milepost 259 on the Blue Ridge Parkway, is a quaint gift shop whose mission is to keep alive the old mountain crafts. The shop sells over 250 types of handmade crafts made by over 500 craftsmen from 11 northwestern North Carolina counties. You'll find woodcarvings, baskets, woven materials, handmade toys, pottery, baked goods, jellies, jams, musical instruments, bird feeders, and even country hams. The shop is open from 9 A.M. to 5:30 P.M. daily from April to October. Call 336-982-2543.

- The **New River General Store** is located at 10725 U.S. 221 North, just after the highway crosses the New River halfway between West Jefferson and Sparta. Here, you can browse antiques, buy old-fashioned candies, and purchase gifts, groceries, and cheese. The store is open daily from 8:30 A.M. to 6 P.M. New River Outfitters runs its canoe trips out of this store. For information, call 800-982-9190 or 336-982-9192.

Recreation

- **Mount Jefferson State Natural Area**, located on Mount Jefferson Road off U.S. 221 at West Jefferson, is a relatively undeveloped park covering 539 acres. It offers picnicking and a few short trails, but the big attraction is the view. Mount Jefferson rises abruptly more than 1,600 feet above the surrounding landscape. Visitors can see the farms and forests of a great part of the county from its summit. For information, contact the natural area at P.O. Box 48, Jefferson, N.C. 28640 (336-246-9653).

- The big pastimes in Ashe County are canoeing and tubing on the New River. Because the water flows so gently, the river is safe even for young children. Local outfitters give lessons and provide inner tubes, canoes, safety equipment, and shuttle service. Contact **Zaloo's Canoes** (800-535-4027; www.zaloos.com), at 3874 N.C. 16 South in Jefferson; **New River Outfitters** (800-982-9190; www.canoethenew.com), headquartered in the New River General Store; **River Camp USA** (800-748-3722 or 336-359-2267), at Piney Creek; or **Appalachian Adventures** (336-877-8800; www.appalachianadventures.com) in Todd.

See the sidebar about the New River for information on New River State Park.

- **Christmas in July** is held in downtown West Jefferson during the weekend nearest the Fourth of July. Workers in the area's Christmas tree industry challenge each other for cash and prizes in a variety of competitions. You can hear live music and purchase crafts and other items from the vendors who line the streets. Call 336-246-5855 or visit www.ashechamber.com.

Places to Stay

Resorts, Hotels, and Motels

- **Best Western Eldreth Inn**. Moderate. 829 East Main Street in Jefferson, at the intersection of U.S. 221 and N.C. 88 (800-221-8802 or 336-246-8845; www.bestwestern.com/eldrethinnatmtjefferson). Although there is nothing particularly exciting about this Best Western, it's one of the few chain motels in the area.

Inns and Bed-and-Breakfasts

- **River House Inn**. Deluxe/Expensive. 1896 Old Field Creek Road in Grassy Creek (336-982-2109; www.riverhousenc.com). Owned by Gayle Winston, a well-known restaurateur and innkeeper, this inn offers eight guest rooms, each with a private bath and a Jacuzzi. Most of the rooms have views of the mountains and/or the river; some have private porches. Two cabins beside the millpond are also available. The inn is situated on 170 acres with a mile of river front; it offers two tennis courts. Coffee and tea are left by guests' doors in the morning. A full breakfast is served. The inn frequently hosts live music in the evenings.

- **Buffalo Tavern Bed-and-Breakfast**. Expensive. 958 West Buffalo Road in West Jefferson (877-615-9678 or 336-877-2873; www.buffalotavern.com).

This Southern Colonial home, originally a tavern, was the place to go during the 1920s. Today, it offers three guest rooms, each with a private bath, a fireplace with gas logs, and a claw-foot tub. A guest refrigerator, complimentary beverages, and laundry service are available. A two-night minimum stay is required for some weekends and holidays. No children are allowed.

■ **Glendale Springs Inn.** Expensive. 7414 N.C. 16 in Glendale Springs (800-287-1206 or 336-982-2103; www.glendalespringsinn.com). Located 0.3 mile from Milepost 259 on the parkway, this authentic country inn was built about 100 years ago. The original historic structure contains five guest rooms, all with private baths. The guesthouse has four rooms; each of the two first-floor rooms has a fireplace and a Jacuzzi. Amenities include a full breakfast, afternoon tea, cable television, air conditioning, a fax machine, and a copier. A minimum two-day stay is required on certain holidays and weekends.

Places to Eat

■ **Glendale Springs Inn and Restaurant.** Expensive. 7414 N.C. 16 in Glendale Springs (800-287-1206 or 336-982-2103; www.glendalespringsinn.com). This is the place President Bill Clinton and Vice President Al Gore chose for their weekly, private Thursday lunch while they were in the area to dedicate the New River as an American Heritage River. The inn has three dining areas. The seafood is fresh, and the herbs are grown in the inn's own garden. Beer and wine are offered. Lunch and dinner are served Thursday through Tuesday during the summer; check for winter hours.

■ **River House Inn and Restaurant.** Expensive. 1896 Old Field Creek Road in Grassy Creek (336-982-2109; www.riverhousenc.com). Anyone in Winston-Salem can tell you how good Gayle Winston's restaurants are; she is still the owner of the Salem Tavern in historic Old Salem. At the River House Inn, she features country French cuisine and regional fare. Beer and wine are offered; reservations are required. Dinner is served Wednesday through Saturday from April through December. On Sunday afternoons, the inn's salon series offers a lecture, a film, or a performance of music or poetry, followed by a tasting menu.

■ *Fraser's*. Moderate. 108 South Jefferson Avenue in West Jefferson (336-246-5222; www.frasersrestaurant.com). This establishment takes up several storefronts. For lunch, it offers freshly made soups, sandwiches, and salads. For dinner, guests can order fresh seafood, steaks, pasta, and nightly specials. Beer and wine are available. Lunch is served daily except Wednesday and dinner Thursday through Saturday.

■ *The Landing Restaurant at Jefferson Landing*. Moderate. At the Jefferson Landing Golf Club near Jefferson (800-292-6274 or 336-982-7378; www.jeffersonlandingclub.com). The clubhouse dining area, which seats 170, features gourmet cuisine. Dinner is served Thursday through Saturday; a buffet supper is offered on Sunday. Reservations are recommended.

■ *Shatley Springs Inn*. Moderate. 407 Shatley Springs Road in Crumpler (336-982-2236). Located off N.C. 16 five miles north of Jefferson, this is one of those all-the-home-cooking-you-can-eat places. Its fixed-price meals include fried chicken, country ham, tons of vegetables, and homemade cobbler. In the summer and fall, you may have to wait for a table. Luckily, you can try one of the rocking chairs on the front porch, where guests are entertained by occasional bluegrass music. Breakfast, lunch, and dinner are served daily from May through October.

■ *Sweet Aromas Bakery and Café*. Inexpensive. 102 South Jefferson Avenue in West Jefferson (336-246-2914; www.sweetaromasbakery.com). This place offers plenty of baked goods to take out or eat in. Saturday breakfast is popular during the summer, so be prepared to wait. The lunch and dinner selections include a sampler plate for which guests may choose three of the lunch items. Among the favorites here are Moravian chicken pie with made-from-scratch crust and hearty dinner fare such as spanakopita and roast beef with vegetables. Breakfast, lunch, and dinner are served Tuesday through Saturday.

A view of Appalachian State University and downtown Boone
PHOTOGRAPH BY JUDI SCHARNS, COURTESY OF BOONE CONVENTION AND VISITORS BUREAU

BOONE

oone is home to Appalachian State University, a branch of the University of North Carolina that has seen amazing growth in recent years. If you haven't visited the campus in the last 10 years, you won't recognize it. Along with the growth of the university has come urban sprawl. Boone is where everyone who lives in the area does their regular shopping. The town has an indoor mall and several strip shopping centers, as well as all the usual chain motels and eateries. But there's also a lively downtown area that has been honored for its revitalization efforts. It was recognized by the National Trust for Historic Preservation as a national Main Street center, a highly coveted honor.

This chapter also includes scenic Valle Crucis, a North Carolina Rural Historic District. In 1915, local historian John Preston Arthur wrote, "There is a dreamy spell which hangs over this little valley." Although many remember the spell as being stronger a few decades ago, the area still retains its mystique. Much of the history of Valle Crucis revolves around the work of the Episcopal Church. You can still see the community's historic buildings—a cabin built by Bishop L. Silliman Ives, a conference center, and a small church. The other noteworthy places that draw tourists to Valle Crucis are the Mast Farm Inn and the Mast General Store complex. For more information, visit www.vallecrucis.com.

JUST THE FACTS

To get to Boone, you can take either U.S. 321 or U.S. 421. Both N.C. 105 and N.C. 194 terminate here. You can reach Valle Crucis by traveling on N.C. 105 from Boone and turning onto S.R. 1112 (Broadstone Road).

For visitor information, contact the Boone Chamber of Commerce/Boone Convention and Visitors Bureau, at 208 Howard Street; call 800-852-9506 or 828-264-3516 or visit www.VisitBooneNC.com. Another source is North Carolina High Country Host, at 1700 Blowing Rock Road in Boone; call 800-438-7500 or visit www.highcountryhost.com.

The *Watauga Democrat* is published three times a week. *Mountain Times*, a free weekly, offers news and events listings; you can access its excellent Web site at www.mountaintimes.com.

Things to Do

SPECIAL SHOPPING

■ *Shoppes at Farmers Hardware and Supply Company*, located at 661 West King Street in an 80-year-old downtown landmark, houses over 100 unique shops. The building still has its original tin ceilings and oiled wooden floors. It is open from 10 A.M. to 6 P.M. Monday through Saturday and from 9 A.M. to 6 P.M. on Sunday. For information, call 828-264-8801.

■ *Mast General Store*, on N.C. 194 in Valle Crucis, is the granddaddy of the area's restored general stores. It opened in 1883 and quickly gained a reputation for carrying everything from "cradles to caskets." Even today, you'll find goods ranging from hiking boots to reproductions of antique cooking utensils to mountain toys. The post office inside the store is still used by local residents, as is the huge potbelly stove you'll notice as soon as you enter.

The *Mast Store Annex* is just down the road. Here, you'll find casual

Mast General Store
PHOTOGRAPH BY CAROLYN SAKOWSKI

clothing and a complete outfitter's shop. The best part is the candy store, where you'll rediscover candies you haven't seen since childhood.

You can also visit **Old Boone Mercantile**, a Mast outlet at 630 West King Street in downtown Boone.

Mast General Store is open from 7 A.M. to 6:30 P.M. Monday through Saturday and from noon to 5 P.M. on Sunday; the Boone store is open from 10 A.M. to 6 P.M. Monday through Saturday and from noon to 5 P.M. on Sunday. For information, call the Valle Crucis store at 828-963-6511 or the Boone outlet at 828-262-0000 or visit www.mastgeneralstore.com.

■ **Todd General Store** is 10 miles south of West Jefferson and 11 miles north of Boone off N.C. 194. It overlooks the South Fork of the New River from its location on Railroad Grade Road, which has been turned into one of the most scenic bike routes in the area. Established in 1914, the store features crafts, collectibles, antiques, country ham, baked goods, and an old-time candy shop. Its summer hours are as follows. The store is open from 10 A.M. to 5 P.M. on Monday and Thursday. On Tuesday, it stays open from 10 A.M. until the storytelling session (which starts at 6 P.M.) is over. On Friday, it opens at 10 A.M.; dinner is served at 6:30 P.M., followed by live music from 7 P.M. until around 9 P.M. It is open from 9 A.M. to 5 P.M. on Saturday and from noon to 5 P.M. on Sunday. It is closed on Wednesday. Call 336-877-1067.

While you're in Todd, be sure to visit **Todd Mercantile**, which features works of local artisans ranging from woodworking showpieces to quilts to homemade mustard to birdhouses. A bakery is also on the premises. The store is open from 8 A.M. to 5 P.M. Monday through Saturday and from 11 A.M. to 5 P.M. on Sunday. For information, call 336-877-5401.

■ **Wilcox Emporium Warehouse** is located at 161 Howard Street in downtown Boone. This historic 60,000-square-foot space has more than 200 vendors. You'll find art, antiques, collectibles, furnishings, food, and gifts. Its summer hours are 10 A.M. to 6 P.M. Monday through Thursday, 10 A.M. to 8 P.M. on Friday and Saturday, and 1 P.M. to 6 P.M. on Sunday. For information, call 828-262-1221 or visit www.wilcoxemporium.com.

■ In the past 10 years, the number of artists in the High Country has grown from a handful to over 200. These are not just your average mountain craftspeople; these artists work in all media in traditional, contemporary, and exploratory genres. You can get an excellent brochure listing the craft and art galleries in Boone, Blowing Rock, Valle Crucis, and Foscoe by calling the North Carolina High Country Host office and asking for its **Gallery Guide**. You can also find listings in the free tabloid *Summer Times*, published by *Mountain Times*; visit www.mountaintimes.com for information.

RECREATION

■ Located on U.S. 321 about halfway between Boone and Blowing Rock, **Tweetsie Railroad** is one of North Carolina's oldest theme parks. The centerpiece of this re-created Wild West town is a historic narrow-gauge, coal-fired steam locomotive that used to carry passengers on a daily 66-mile trip from Johnson City, Tennessee, to Boone. In addition to riding the train (and maybe getting attacked by robbers), you can take the chairlift

Tweetsie Railroad
PHOTOGRAPHY BY JUDI SCHARNS, COURTESY OF BOONE
CONVENTION AND VISITORS BUREAU

up the mountain to pan for gold, pet friendly animals, try the amusement rides, and take in a show that includes music and clogging. From mid-May to mid-August, Tweetsie Railroad is open daily from 9 A.M. to 6 P.M.; from mid-August to the end of October, it is open the same hours but only on weekends; it is also open Labor Day Monday. An admission fee is charged. For information, call 800-526-5740 or 828-264-9061 or visit www.tweetsie.com.

■ Next to Tweetsie is *Mystery Hill*, founded in 1949. A day pass gains you access to four different areas. The main attraction is a house in which you have to stand at a 45-degree angle to keep from falling over. You can also witness water flowing uphill and see a swing that defies gravity. In the Hall of Mystery are hands-on experiments that let you lose your shadow, stand inside a giant soap bubble, and see optical illusions. At the Appalachian Heritage Museum, you'll see antiques and artifacts showing how mountain families lived at the turn of the 20th century; the exhibit is housed in the Dougherty House, built by the brothers who were instrumental in the founding of Appalachian State University. The final section exhibits over 50,000 Native American artifacts. Mystery Hill is open daily all year. Hours vary with the season. An admission fee is charged. Call 828-264-2792 or visit www.mysteryhill-nc.com.

■ The cool summer climate is perfect for golfing. This area has been a golf mecca since the first holes were built in Linville in 1895. Although the really famous mountain courses are private, some excellent facilities around Boone are open to the public. Among them are *Blue Ridge Country Club* (828-756-4013), *Boone Golf Club* (828-264-8760), and *Willow Creek* (828-963-6865). If you want to read brief descriptions of area courses, check out www.mountaintimes.com.

■ A sport that has exploded on the High Country scene in recent years is cycling—whether it be mountain biking or road biking. *Appalachian Adventures* (336-877-8800) in Todd and *Boone Bike and Touring* (828-262-5750) are two of the local shops that offer bike rentals. Boone Bike and Touring and *Magic Cycles* (828-265-2211) in Boone offer group night rides.

■ Several outfitters offer whitewater rafting trips down the Nolichucky and Watauga rivers and on Wilson Creek. Try *Appalachian Adventures* (336-877-8800), *Appalachian Challenge Guide Service* (888-844-RAFT or 828-898-6484), *Backwoods Expeditions* (866-686-7238 or 828-963-2050;

www.beechmountainsports.com), *Cherokee Adventures* (800-445-7238), *Edge of the World* (800-789-3343; www.edgeoworld.com), *High Mountain Expeditions* (800-262-9036 or 828-264-7368; www.highmountainexpeditions.com), *Ski Country Sports* (800-528-3874 or 828-898-9786; www.skicountrysports.com), or *Wahoo's Adventures* (800-444-RAFT or 828-262-5774).

■ One activity that doesn't require a guide is hiking. The area is flush with trails of all lengths and difficulties. For information about the Blue Ridge Parkway trails, see the chapter on the parkway. Pisgah National Forest offers trails in Linville Gorge, Wilson Creek, Lost Cove Cliffs, and Harper Creek. For information about hiking in the national forest, contact the Grandfather Ranger District, 109 East Lawing Drive, Nebo, N.C. 28761 (828-652-2144). The office is located at Exit 90 off Interstate 40 near Nebo and Marion.

Seasonal Events

■ Since 1952, Kermit Hunter's outdoor drama, **Horn in the West**, has played on summer nights. The story is set during the American Revolution, when Daniel Boone and the mountain men struggled against the British and the Cherokees led by Dragging Canoe. Who cares about historical accuracy? It's fun to sit outside under the stars and watch the drama unfold. There's lots of whooping and gunfire to keep things lively. From late June through mid-August, the show plays nightly except on Monday. Performances begin at 8 P.M., just as the sun starts to set. An admission fee is charged. You can reach the amphitheater by following the signs from U.S. 421, U.S. 321, U.S. 221, or N.C. 105 Extension. For information, call 828-264-2120 or visit www.horninthewest.com.

■ *An Appalachian Summer Festival* is a series of music, dance, art, and theater performances that spans the month of July. Past participants have included the Paul Taylor Dance Company, Willie Nelson, the Preservation Hall Jazz Band, Mary Chapin Carpenter, the Duke Ellington Orchestra, and the North Carolina Symphony. Workshops in writing, dance, and art are also offered. An admission fee is charged for most events, many of which are held on the campus of Appalachian State University. For information, call 800-841-2787 or visit www.appsummer.org.

- **Valle Country Fair** has been held on an October weekend for over 20 years. Since the fair takes place during the height of the fall foliage season, thousands of tourists flock to Valle Crucis. Part craft fair, part old-time cooking fair, this event attracts top craftsmen and the best canners of preserves in the area. There's old-time music and dancing. One of the highlights is the cooking of apple butter from scratch. For information, call the Mast General Store at 828-963-6511.

Places to Stay

It's important to note that you can get less expensive rates if you come on weekdays during the summer and fall. In the off-season before skiing begins and after it ends, you can get even cheaper rates.

RESORTS, HOTELS, AND MOTELS

- **Fairfield Inn & Suites**. Deluxe/Expensive. 2060 Blowing Rock Road (866-871-7425 or 828-268-0677; www.fairfieldinn.com). Fairfield offers lots of options for rooms and rates. In addition to standard rooms, larger rooms with refrigerators are available, as are suites with separate living and sleeping areas, refrigerators, microwaves, and whirlpools. Continental breakfast is included in the room rate. A heated indoor pool and an exercise room with a whirlpool are on the premises.

- **Holiday Inn Express**. Deluxe/Expensive. 1943 Blowing Rock Road (888-733-6867 or 828-264-2451). Again, all sorts of room options and rates are available. You'll pay more for a suite or a room with a balcony or a whirlpool. Free continental breakfast is provided.

- **Best Western Blue Ridge Plaza**. Expensive (888-573-0408 or 828-266-1100; www.bestwesternboone.com). Each of the rooms here has a microwave and a refrigerator. Several have fireplaces and two-person Jacuzzis. An indoor heated pool is on the premises. A deluxe continental breakfast is included in the room rate.

- **The Broyhill Inn and Conference Center**. Expensive. 775 Bodenheimer Drive on the campus of Appalachian State University (800-951-6048 or 828-262-2204; www.broyhillinn.com). This inn has 76 guest rooms and seven suites. It is run by Appalachian State and serves primarily as a conference center. The full-service dining room is quite good; there is also a lounge for guests. During the summer, visitors enjoy great views from the outdoor patios; during the winter, they stay warm by the large native-stone fireplace. The inn occasionally offers special deals through its Web site.

- **Country Inn and Suites**. Expensive. 818 East King Street (800-456-4000 or 828-264-4100; www.countryinns.com/boonenc). Opened during the summer of 2006, this chain hotel has a variety of room types. A free continental breakfast is included. Each room has a microwave and a refrigerator. An indoor pool and a whirlpool are available.

INNS AND BED-AND-BREAKFASTS

- **Lovill House Inn**. Deluxe. 404 Old Bristol Road (800-849-9466 or 828-264-4204; www.lovillhouseinn.com). This inn is located just off West King Street on the western side of downtown Boone. Housed in an 1875 farmhouse with a wraparound porch, it offers a private bath, cable television, a ceiling fan, bathrobes, a hair dryer, a clock radio, and a telephone in each room. Some rooms have gas-log fireplaces. Early-morning coffee and tea are served before the complimentary breakfast. A cottage behind the farmhouse is available for rent. Lovill House has received a Four Diamond rating from AAA.

- **Mast Farm Inn**. Deluxe. 2543 Broadstone Road (S.R. 1112) on the way to Valle Crucis (888-963-5857 or 828-963-5857; www.mastfarminn.com). Mast Farm Inn is a huge, rambling, three-story farmhouse with a wraparound porch. Built in 1885, it began operating as an inn in the early 1900s. The eight guest rooms, most of which have private baths, are furnished with country antiques and old quilts; some have their original wood paneling. Seven guest cottages are also available for rent, including the farm's old loom house. A wonderful restaurant is on the premises.

- **The Baird House**. Deluxe/Expensive. 1451 Watauga River Road in Valle Crucis (800-297-1342 or 828-297-4055; www.bairdhouse.com).

Mast Farm Inn
PHOTOGRAPH BY CAROLYN SAKOWSKI

This Colonial-style farmhouse, located near the Mast General Store, was built in 1790. The inn rests on 16 acres of rolling pasture overlooking the Watauga River. A full country breakfast is served.

- ***The Inn at Taylor House.*** Deluxe/Expensive. N.C. 194 in Valle Crucis (800-963-5581 or 828-963-5581; www.taylorhouseinn.com). Taylor House, built in 1910, has been described as "country elegant." Its seven rooms all have private baths. Two rooms are located in a nearby cottage and one in the innkeeper's house. A two-course gourmet breakfast is served each morning.

Places to Eat

Boone is the High Country town where the chains are best represented.

- ***Mast Farm Inn.*** Expensive. 2543 Broadstone Road (S.R. 1112) on the way to Valle Crucis (888-963-5857 or 828-963-5857; www.mastfarminn.com). The restaurant is housed in the same historic farmhouse as the inn. The "gourmet country" fare includes interesting items like "Sautéed Shrimp with White Cheddar Grits" and "Artichoke Parmesan-Filled Ravioli." Lunch and dinner are served Tuesday through Saturday; brunch is offered on Sunday. Reservations are suggested.

- **Wildflower.** Expensive/Moderate. 831 West King Street (828-264-3463; www.beartrailstudio.com/wildflower.htm). This restaurant's logo describes the food served here as "casually eclectic," and that is apt. You can get Angus beef, mountain trout, teriyaki tuna with Thai-style vegetables, shrimp and grits, or free-range chicken, to name just a few popular dishes. Dinner is served nightly; brunch is served on Saturday and Sunday.

- **The Dan'l Boone Inn Restaurant.** Moderate. At the junction of U.S. 321 and U.S. 421 (828-264-8657; www.danlbooneinn.com). Opened in 1959, this family-style restaurant is an institution. In the summer, the crowds line up across the porch and down the walk. The fixed-price meals begin with a salad in the summer and soup in the winter; they include three meats, five vegetables, homemade biscuits, a beverage, and desserts. Breakfast, lunch, and dinner are served daily.

- **Moon Shine Café and Lounge.** Moderate. 142 South Water Street (828-262-5000; www.moonshinecafeonline.com). Housed in a historic 1886 building that once served as Boone's jail, this establishment offers indoor, porch, and patio dining. The international menu features Thai and Mexican entrées but also includes "Appalachian" dishes such as char-grilled catfish served with black-eyed peas, mashed potatoes, collard greens, baby corn, and buttermilk cornbread. This "Tennessee Farmhand Plate" can be topped with either mushroom cream gravy or blackberry apple salsa. Dinner is served daily.

- **Coyote Kitchen.** Inexpensive. 200 Southgate Drive, next to Wal-Mart (828-265-4041). This restaurant bills its food as "Southwest and Caribbean Soul Food." An example of the creative cuisine is the "Havana Burrito," which includes red beans, Jerk chicken, jack cheese, roasted sweet potato, green chilies, grilled mushrooms, and roasted corn. Lunch and dinner are served daily.

- **Peppers.** Inexpensive. 240 Shadowline Road in the Shops at Shadowline (828-262-1250; www.peppers-restaurant.com). Opened in 1975, Pepper's has been a Boone staple ever since. The menu includes sandwiches, seafood, pasta, and homemade desserts. Lunch and dinner are served daily.

The Parkway Craft Center at Moses H. Cone Memorial Park
PHOTOGRAPH BY CAROLYN SAKOWSKI

BLOWING ROCK

*A*t Blowing Rock's elevation of 4,000 feet, summer temperatures rarely climb over 80 degrees. The town began to attract summer residents in the 1880s. In the early days, most visitors spent the entire season. Some built beautiful Victorian summer homes, many of which still stand.

Blowing Rock has always catered to an upscale crowd. Because of this, it's been relatively easy for the town to maintain its quaint character through zoning regulations. Most of what passes for urban sprawl has been consigned to the bypass, while the downtown buildings have benefited from constant refurbishing.

The village is an easy drive from Boone. Because Blowing Rock literally hangs on the side of the mountain, you'll enjoy incredible views of the Johns River Gorge from various points in town.

JUST THE FACTS

Blowing Rock is located seven miles south of Boone where U.S. 321 and U.S. 221 join and become Blowing Rock Road. For visitor information, contact the Blowing Rock Chamber of Commerce, P.O. Box 406, Blowing Rock, N.C. 28605 (800-295-7851 or 828-295-7851; www.blowingrock.com). The town's visitor center is located at 7738 Valley Boulevard (U.S. 321 Bypass). It has an excellent selection of menus from area restaurants, in addition to the usual travel brochures.

The *Blowing Rocket* is the weekly newspaper. Events are also covered in *Mountain Times*, a free weekly; for information, visit www.mountaintimes.com.

Things to Do

SPECIAL SHOPPING

■ ***Parkway Craft Center***, located at Moses H. Cone Memorial Park at Milepost 294 on the Blue Ridge Parkway, has served as a showcase for the Southern Highland Craft Guild for nearly 50 years. In this historic home built by Moses and Bertha Cone, you'll find weavings, baskets, pottery, woodcarvings, and glass and metal work. Craft demonstrations are usually going on. If you're up for a nice walk, ask how to get to the Cones' grave sites. The center is open from late March through November. Call 828-295-7938.

■ The ***Shoppes on the Parkway***, on U.S. 321, are a group of brand-name outlet stores. Some offer real bargains, so the parking lot is usually full. The shops are open daily year-round; they open at noon on Sunday. For information, call 800-720-6728 or 828-295-4444 or visit www.tangeroutlet.com.

RECREATION

■ The ***Blowing Rock*** is an immense cliff that hangs 3,000 feet over the Johns River Gorge. The rock walls form a flume that sweeps the northwest wind upward with such force that it blows light objects back up the mountain. There's not much to see at this attraction other than the spectacular view. On clear days, you can spot Mount Mitchell, Grandfather Mountain, Table Rock, and Hawksbill. The Blowing Rock is located off U.S. 321 near the Green Park Inn. Call 828-295-7111 or visit www.blowingrock.com.

- **Hiking** brochures are available at the Blowing Rock Chamber of Commerce.

- For those who like to get their thrills on skis, **Appalachian Ski Mountain** is located near Blowing Rock. Call 800-322-2373 or visit www.appskimtn.com. More ski slopes are listed in the chapter on Banner Elk, Beech Mountain, and Linville.

SEASONAL EVENTS

- For almost 40 years, Blowing Rock Memorial Park has hosted a crafts festival one Saturday each month from May to October. **Art in the Park** has blossomed into a big attraction, with over 100 juried art and craft exhibits. For information, call the Blowing Rock Chamber of Commerce at 828-295-7851.

- Held in late July, the **Blowing Rock Charity Horse Show** has been one of the top equestrian events in the Southeast since 1923. Centered at the Blowing Rock Stables off U.S. 221 west of town, this two-week-long English saddle event features hunter/jumpers and American Saddlebreds in competition. For information, call 828-295-4602 or visit www.blowingrockequestrian.com/horsesho/.

Places to Stay

RESORTS, HOTELS, AND MOTELS

Blowing Rock has several small motels that have been locally owned and operated for years. They are all lovingly maintained, and you will rarely go wrong with any of them. You'll find them along Sunset Drive and North Main Street.

- **Chetola Lodge and Conference Center**. Deluxe. North Main Street just off U.S. 321 (800-243-8652 or 828-295-5500; www.Chetola.com). Started in 1846, the manor house here is the centerpiece of a fabulous former summer estate. That house is now the **Bob Timberlake Inn at Chetola**. The inn features Timberlake's furniture-and-accessories line, his artwork, and personal mementos. The rooms all have a fireplace, a flat-screen TV, a DVD player, and a whirlpool tub. Breakfast is provided daily. The resort encompasses 87 acres of beautifully landscaped grounds surrounding a lake. The lodge, a modern addition, offers guest rooms. Guests can also rent one-, two-, and three-bedroom condominiums that have fireplaces, fully equipped kitchens, and outdoor decks. A first-class sports center, an indoor swimming pool, a whirlpool, a sauna, and massage therapy are offered. You can play tennis or racquetball, hike, fish, ride horses, or go mountain biking. Chetola offers meeting space and has a first-class restaurant.

- **Westglow Spa**. Deluxe. 2845 U.S. 221 South (800-562-0807 or 828-295-4463; www.westglow.com). This historic mansion, built in 1917 as the home of artist Elliott Daingerfield, now offers elegantly restored suites. Cottages are also available for rent. The prices are high because the whole focus is the adjoining Life Enhancement Center, a world-class spa that offers body massages, herbal body wraps, facials, and hair and nail services. If you stay at the mansion, your package will include meals as well as privileges at the spa.

- **Meadowbrook Inn**. Deluxe/Expensive. 711 North Main Street (800-467-6626 or 828-295-4300; www.meadowbrook-inn.com). This 61-room inn is a few blocks from Blowing Rock Memorial Park, the town's center. Each room has a terrace, a gas fireplace, and a whirlpool tub for two. Some suites have a wet bar, a refrigerator, and a microwave. The top-of-the-line pool suites are unique. What appears to be a closet leads down a spiral staircase into your own private swimming pool. These are not Jacuzzis, but rather eight-foot-wide, 14-foot-long, four-foot-deep in-room swimming pools. A fully equipped fitness center, a full-sized swimming pool, bicycles, and a Jacuzzi are available to all guests. A full-service restaurant, a bar, and meeting rooms are on the premises.

- **Azalea Garden Inn**. Expensive. North Main Street (828-295-3272). The first thing that strikes you about this inn is its landscaping. The owners have gone all out in covering the one-acre setting with flowering perennials. The rooms have either two full-sized beds or one king-sized bed, air conditioning, and cable television. An authentic log cabin is also available for rent; it has a log-burning fireplace, a kitchen, and two queen-sized beds. Guests enjoy complimentary morning coffee on the veranda, where they have a view of the abundant flowers.

- Note: The next three inns have the same owner and call themselves *The Village Inns of Blowing Rock*. You can learn more about them at www.thevillageinnsofblowingrock.com; call 800-821-4908 to make reservations. All three were renovated in 2005. Each room offers a refrigerator, a microwave, a coffee maker, and a hair dryer. Many of the suites and cottages have full kitchens, fireplaces, and Jacuzzis. Each accommodation offers complimentary continental breakfast and an afternoon wine-and-cheese reception.

Hillwinds Inn. Expensive. 315 Sunset Drive, on the corner of Ransom Street (828-295-7660). Hillwinds is located a short walk from Main Street. In addition to regular rooms, it has two suites and two cottages.

Ridgeway Inn. Expensive. Near the intersection of U.S. 321 and U.S. 221 (828-295-7321). Ridgeway was the first inn to open in Blowing Rock. Today, it's known for the beautiful rose gardens that surround the inn. In addition to guest rooms, it offers two suites and two cottages that feature 30-inch flat-screen TVs, private decks or sunrooms, fireplaces, and Jacuzzis. This is a smoke-free, pet-free inn.

Village Inn. Expensive. 7876 Valley Boulevard (U.S. 321 Bypass), on the corner of Sunset Drive (828-295-3380). You may remember this location as Brookside Inn, but you won't recognize it now. The renovated inn features hardwood floors and rustic, elegant mountain decor. All rooms have private decks, some with hot tubs. It also offers two suites and three cottages. Some pet-friendly rooms are available. In front of the inn is a quarter-acre pond with an island and a gazebo.

INNS AND BED-AND-BREAKFASTS

- *Gideon Ridge Inn*. Deluxe. 202 Gideon Ridge Road (828-295-3644; www.ridge-inn.com). Housed in an elegant former summer home, this 10-room inn offers a spectacular view of the Johns River Gorge—the same view you'll pay to see at the nearby Blowing Rock attraction. *Country Inns*

Magazine called this "one of the ten best inns in America." Stone terraces are everywhere; most offer incredible views of the mountains or the perennial gardens. The library has a lovely stone fireplace. Breakfast is served in a room with a wonderful view of the surrounding mountains. Some rooms have Jacuzzis and fireplaces; all have first-class amenities.

■ *The Inn at Ragged Gardens*. Deluxe. 203 Sunset Drive (828-295-9703; www.ragged-gardens.com). Here is a fully restored summer home built in the early 1900s. It sits in the center of an acre of colorful gardens just a block from Blowing Rock Memorial Park. The chestnut siding is a distinctive aspect of local architecture; unfortunately, it is no longer used, since the chestnut blight destroyed the source. Local granite was used in the entry columns, the flooring, and the staircase. Inside, you'll find chestnut-paneled walls and beams and a large rock fireplace. The rooms have goose-down comforters and pillows, fireplaces, private baths, and ceiling fans. Most offer balconies, sitting rooms, and one- or two-person whirlpools. Breakfast is served in a dining room that overlooks the rock-walled garden.

■ *Maple Lodge Bed-and-Breakfast*. Expensive. 152 Sunset Drive (866-795-3331 or 828-295-3331; www.maplelodge.net). Maple Lodge is located a short walk from Blowing Rock Memorial Park. Its 11 rooms are furnished with a blend of antiques and family heirlooms. Each has a private bath and a goose-down comforter on a four-poster or lace-canopy bed. The library has a stone fireplace. A full breakfast is served in the dining room, which overlooks a wildflower garden.

Places to Eat

■ *The Best Cellar*. Expensive. Off U.S. 321 Bypass (828-295-3466; www.thebestcellar.com). The Best Cellar has been one of the top restaurants in the area for over 20 years. In 2006, it suffered a fire that completely destroyed the 65-year-old cabin where it was housed. That summer, it reopened at the Inn at Ragged Garden until the owners could rebuild in the original location. Thankfully, the food everyone had come to love has stayed the same. Among the favorites are the raw oysters, the Angus beef, and the fresh seafood. Dinner is served Monday through Saturday from May to November and Thursday through Sunday the rest of the year. Reservations are recommended.

- **Crippen's Country Inn and Restaurant.** Expensive. 239 Sunset Drive (877-295-3487 or 828-295-3487; www.crippens.com). Crippen's has consistently received glowing reviews from food critics across the country, including those at *Southern Living* and the *New York Times*. The menu changes daily; the restaurant's Web site will give you a feel for what to expect. How about "Applewood-Smoked, Bacon-Wrapped Grilled Loin of Venison with Acorn Squash, Summer Vegetables, and Mango Chutney"? Or "Almond-and-Peppercorn-Crusted Chilean Salmon with Golden-Raisin Couscous, Pineapple Relish, and Crispy Fried Leeks"? Not your typical restaurant fare, huh? All desserts are made on the premises. Dinner is served nightly from June through October and on Thursday, Friday, and Saturday the rest of the year; an expanded schedule is offered between Christmas and New Year's.

- **The Manor House Restaurant at Chetola.** Expensive. North Main Street just off U.S. 321 (828-295-5505; www.chetola.com). This restaurant occupies a restored 1846 manor house. It serves mountain specialties in the dining rooms and on the patio overlooking the lake. Breakfast, lunch, and dinner are offered daily; Sunday brunch is an option during the summer. Dinner reservations are recommended.

- **Bistro Roca & Antlers Bar.** Expensive/Moderate. 143 Wonderland Trail (828-295-4008; www.BistroRoca.com). If you were a student at Appalachian State sometime from the 1960s to the 1980s, you'll probably remember Antlers Bar. But it doesn't look quite the same today. Renovated in 2005, it now has a wood-fired oven and an open kitchen. The proprietors also own the popular Gideon Ridge Inn, and the same attention to detail and quality is evident here. The chef, trained at Le Cordon Bleu's London campus, takes pride in using free-range meats, organic vegetables, homemade, naturally fermented pizza dough, and real—not prepackaged—stock for soups. The menu includes steaks, fresh fish, and hand-tossed, wood-fired pizzas. Be sure to check out the photos that adorn the walls. These are professionally made photos of patrons' dogs, and sometimes of patrons and their dogs. Lunch and dinner are served Wednesday through Sunday.

- **Storie Street Grille.** Moderate. 1167 Main Street, on the corner of Storie Street (828-295-7075; www.storiestreetgrille.com). For a great meal at a reasonable price, Storie Street Grille can't be beat. The bountiful salads and sandwiches are popular at lunch. Dinner features seafood, pasta, and Italian specialties. Lunch and dinner are served Monday through Saturday.

■ *The Village Café*. Moderate. Behind Kilwin's on Main Street (828-295-3769; www.thevillagecafe.com). You'll need to follow the stone walkway beside Kilwin's to reach this place. The café's gourmet breakfasts include such favorites as eggs Benedict and Belgian waffles. For lunch, you can get soups, salads, sandwiches, and homemade bread. You can dine on the stone patio or inside the turn-of-the-20th-century home. Breakfast and lunch are served Tuesday through Sunday.

■ *Woodlands BBQ*. Inexpensive. U.S. 321 Bypass (828-295-3651; www.woodlandsbbq.com). This establishment has been a Blowing Rock staple for years. It smokes its own ribs, chicken, beef, and pork (sliced or chopped) and offers a variety of sandwich and plate options. It also serves burritos, tacos, and nachos. A full-service lounge is on the premises. Entertainment is offered nightly. Lunch and dinner are served daily.

The Scottish Clans gather at the foot of Grandfather Mountain.
PHOTOGRAPH BY HUGH MORTON, COURTESY OF BOONE CONVENTION AND VISITORS BUREAU

BANNER ELK, BEECH MOUNTAIN, AND LINVILLE

*A*very County boasts several distinctly different communities.

The area around Newland, the county seat, is where many of the long-time year-round residents live. You won't find much evidence of a tourism boom here.

Linville, established in the late 1880s, was planned as an exclusive resort area. It remains that today. Its lovely old homes have a distinctive architectural flavor, largely because of the chestnut siding on many of them. This community is still very private, as are the Grandfather Golf and Country Club and Linville Ridge Club. When these exclusive clubs came to the area, so did wealthy summer residents.

At 5,506 feet, Beech Mountain claims to be the highest town in eastern North America. Because this community is a year-round tourist mecca, this is where you'll find the bulk of the county's high-end accommodations.

At the foot of Beech Mountain is Banner Elk. Because it is home to Lees-McRae College, the village has a bit of a college-town flavor. Here, you'll find quaint bed-and-breakfasts and excellent restaurants. Since the arrival of skiing as a winter draw, Banner Elk also claims many of the county's year-round citizens.

Today, retirees are discovering that the climate of the North Carolina mountains is not as severe as they had previously thought. Thanks to improved roads and crews that keep them open to serve the area's ski resorts, more and more people are coming here to live year-round.

Avery County has some of the strangest liquor laws in the country. Some clubs have been quite creative in getting exemptive legislation passed that allows them to serve alcoholic beverages. Visitors find it illogical when they walk into one convenience store and learn that beer and wine are not sold there, then visit another store owned by the same chain just a mile down the highway and find those items stocked.

When you're traveling through Avery, note the strange building atop Sugar Mountain, one of the county's most prominent peaks. Although this structure spoils the view from all over the county, the good news is that it caused everyone throughout western North Carolina to wake up and pass a "ridge law" to prevent multistory buildings from being constructed on the ridge tops.

In Avery County, you'll find excellent accommodations and restaurants and attractions such as Grandfather Mountain, Linville Falls, and Linville Caverns. The county also claims more ski slopes than any other in the Southeast.

JUST THE FACTS

Banner Elk is less than 20 miles southwest of Boone at the intersection of N.C. 194 and N.C. 184.

To reach Beech Mountain, go to Banner Elk, turn onto Beech Mountain Parkway, and follow the signs to the ski resort.

Linville is located at the intersection of U.S. 221, N.C. 105, and N.C. 181 three miles west of Milepost 305.9 on the Blue Ridge Parkway.

For visitor information, contact the Avery-Banner Elk Chamber of Commerce, located in the Shoppes at Tynecastle at the corner of N.C. 105 and N.C. 184 near Banner Elk; call 800-972-2183 or 828-898-5605 or visit www.averycounty.com. The Beech Mountain Chamber of Commerce is headquartered in Beech Mountain Town Hall near the top of the mountain at 403-A Beech Mountain Parkway; call 800-468-5506 or 828-387-9283 or visit www.beechmtn.com.

The weekly newspapers are the *Avery Journal* and the *Avery Post*. The Avery edition of *Mountain Times* is included in the *Avery Journal*.

Things to Do

SPECIAL SHOPPING

■ **Fred's General Mercantile Company** is located in the community of Beech Mountain at 501 Beech Mountain Parkway. Here, you'll find hardware, bird feeders, books, kites, sleds, gardening supplies, Christmas trees in season, fresh apples in the fall, toys, crafts, clothing, snowshoes, and on and on. The store acts as a community center. In the summer, customers can even enjoy live entertainment. Call 828-387-4838 or 828-387-9331 or visit www.fredsgeneral.com.

■ **Old Hampton Store and Grist Mill** is located off N.C. 181 on Ruffin Street in Linville. This old country store offers corn and wheat products ground right on the premises in a gristmill. The big draw here is hickory-smoked pork, beef, and chicken barbecue, served on homemade sourdough bread. The store is open daily from 10 A.M. to 5 P.M. Call 828-733-5213.

RECREATION

■ The biggest attraction in Avery County, and perhaps the whole High Country, is **Grandfather Mountain**. The private part of this majestic mountain offers a wide range of activities. Be forewarned that admission is charged by the person, not the carload, and is fairly expensive.

After paying at the front entrance, you'll drive to the top of the mountain. Along the way, you can stop at the nature museum, which offers a short film about the mountain and exhibits about the area's flora, minerals, wildlife, and history; a gift shop and a snack bar are also on the premises. Next to the nature museum is the animal habitat, one of the top attractions on the mountain. Here, you can see black bears (and probably some cubs in the summer), rare cougars, golden eagles, bald eagles, otters, deer, and other wildlife. It is best to arrive soon after the park opens; the prime time to see the elusive cougars is right after they've been fed. The park maintains over 30 miles of hiking trails, some so steep that they employ ladders; visitors who don't wish to pay the whole admission fee can purchase a hiking permit to venture onto the trails. One of the highlights is the famous Mile-High Swinging Bridge, which stretches between two

The bears at Grandfather Mountain wave at the tourists.
COURTESY OF NORTH CAROLINA HIGH COUNTRY HOST

of Grandfather's peaks. You can glimpse this bridge from all over the area, but it's a whole new experience to walk across it and look into the gorge below.

The mountain stands 5,964 feet in the midst of the privately owned park. The park has been named an international biosphere reserve because of the 47 rare and endangered species found within its boundaries. It is open from 8 A.M. to 7 P.M. during the summer, from 8 A.M. to 6 P.M. in the spring and fall, and from 8 A.M. to 5 P.M. in the winter. Grandfather Mountain is located on U.S. 221 two miles northwest of Linville, just off Milepost 305.9 on the Blue Ridge Parkway. For information, call 800-468-7325 or 828-733-4337 or visit www.grandfather.com.

■ *Linville Caverns* is located on U.S. 221 between Linville and Marion, just four miles south of the Blue Ridge Parkway; take the Linville Falls Village exit off the parkway and turn left on U.S. 221. The cave was discovered in 1822 when some fishermen decided to follow trout that seemed to be swimming into and out of the mountain. Once inside the mountain, the fishermen found various rooms dripping with stalactites and stalagmites that had been forming for centuries. New rock continues to form in the limestone cave today. The temperature is a constant 52 degrees year-round, so take a sweater. Linville Caverns is open daily from 9 A.M. to 6 P.M. June through Labor Day, from 9 A.M. to 4:30 P.M. during November and March, and from 9 A.M. to 5 P.M. during April, May, September, and October. It

Linville Falls
PHOTOGRAPH BY CAROLYN SAKOWSKI

operates on weekends only during December, January, and February. An admission fee is charged. For information, call 800-419-0540 or 828-756-4171 or visit www.linvillecaverns.com.

■ *Linville Falls* cascades 90 feet into Linville Gorge, a national wilderness preserve. Located at Milepost 317.4 on the Blue Ridge Parkway, the falls are accessible by a series of trails that can accommodate all types of hikers and walkers. You can take the 2.1-mile round-trip Linville Falls Trail to see the upper and lower falls. The hike to the upper falls is the easy one. Viewing the lower falls is more strenuous, but these falls are the ones you usually see on postcards.

■ The Grandfather Ranger District of **Pisgah National Forest** contains a wealth of opportunities for outdoor lovers.
   Linville Gorge Wilderness Area is a favorite hiking, camping, fishing, and hunting area for locals and tourists. Because its trails are not well marked, be sure to take topographical maps and a compass with you. For information about trails in the gorge, consult the published hiking books on the area or call the Grandfather Ranger District office of Pisgah National Forest at 828-652-2144; the office is located in Nebo (Exit 90 off Interstate 40).

If you want to see some relatively accessible, stunning views, consider a trip to **Table Rock** or **Wiseman's View**. To get to either, you'll have to drive on gravel forest-service roads. You won't need a four-wheel-drive vehicle, but you may not want to use your brand-new car. To get to Table Rock, take N.C. 181 to Gingercake Acres, where you'll see signs directing you to Table Rock Picnic Area. You'll drive through a residential area until you reach F.R. 210, where the pavement ends. It's about four miles on F.R. 210 to Table Rock; the route is well marked. To reach Wiseman's View, take N.C. 183 North from Milepost 316.3 on the Blue Ridge Parkway. It is 0.7 mile from the community of Linville Falls to a road that runs four miles to the parking area.

Additional opportunities for fishing, hiking, camping, and hunting are available in the **Lost Cove**, **Wilson Creek**, and **Harper Creek** areas of Pisgah National Forest. In 1999, Wilson Creek was designated a Wild and Scenic Area. You can reach the visitor center by taking Roseboro Road from Milepost 312.2 on the Blue Ridge Parkway to the Edgemont community. During the summer, the center is open from 10 A.M. to 6 P.M. Monday through Saturday and from 1 P.M. to 6 P.M. on Sunday. From Labor Day until November 30, it is open from 10 A.M. to 4 P.M. Monday through Saturday and from 1 P.M. to 4 P.M. on Sunday. Call 828-759-0005 for information.

■ In the winter months, the big attraction here is skiing. Many of the area's slopes offer snowboarding, snow tubing, skating, and skiing; some even have night skiing. You can rent equipment at the slopes or at a number of area stores. The following slopes are located in Avery County: **Ski Beech** (800-438-2093 or 828-387-2011; www.skibeech.com), **Ski Hawksnest** (800-822-4295 or 828-963-6561; www.hawksnest-resort.com), and **Ski Sugar Mountain** (800-784-2768 or 828-898-4521; www.skisugar.com).

- Among Avery County's golf courses open to the public are *Mountain Glen* (828-733-5804) and *Sugar Mountain* (828-898-6464).

- *Sugar Mountain* offers over 20 miles of single- and double-track mountain-biking trails during the summer and fall. You can also mountain-bike a network of trails on Beech Mountain. A map is available at the Beech Mountain Chamber of Commerce.

- You can book fly-fishing tours through *Foscoe Fishing Company & Outfitters* (828-963-6556; www.foscoefishing.com), located in the Foscoe community on N.C. 105, or *Appalachian Angler* (828-963-5050; www.appalachianangler.com), at 174 Old Shulls Mill Road (N.C. 105), near Hound Ears Club.

- Several companies offer whitewater rafting trips on the Watauga and Nolichucky rivers. Try *Edge of the World* (800-789-3343 or 828-898-9550; www.edgeoworld.com) or *High Mountain Expeditions* (800-262-9036 or 828-264-7368; www.highmountainexpeditions.com).

Seasonal Events

Two annual events take place on Grandfather Mountain.

- *Grandfather Mountain Highland Games and Gathering of Scottish Clans* takes place the second full weekend in July. This event has been in existence since 1956. Although plenty of proud Scots in full regalia attend, you don't have to be of Scottish descent to enjoy the games. Traditional track and field events are held, but the real draws are the tossing of the caber (which resembles a telephone pole) and the throwing of sheep sheaves. The track is rimmed by brightly colored tents that house representatives from each clan. You can see Highland dancing, bagpipe competitions, and sheep dog demonstrations. The festivities begin with the Torchlight Ceremony on Thursday, when all the clans march in. The events on Friday focus on music; a ceilidh (a concert of Scottish music) is held Friday evening. Saturday sees more competition, a Scottish dance, and another ceilidh. The Parade of Tartans closes out the weekend on Sunday. Parking is restricted to certain areas off the mountain, so you'll have to use the shuttle buses to get to the games. An admission fee is charged. Unlike years past, alcoholic beverages and pets are no longer allowed. For infor-

The throwing of the caber at the Grandfather Mountain Highland Games
PHOTOGRAPH BY HUGH MORTON, COURTESY OF BOONE CONVENTION AND VISITORS BUREAU

mation, call 828-733-1333 or visit www.gmhg.org.

■ The other event on top of Grandfather is **Singing on the Mountain**. This all-day gospel sing has been held since 1924 on the fourth Sunday in June. It started as a modest gathering of families and friends from local churches. Today, thousands show up to hear the best in gospel music from all races and to hear such well-known ministers as the Reverend Billy Graham. At the 50th Singing on the Mountain, a record crowd of 100,000 people showed up to hear Johnny Cash and to see Bob Hope. Admission is free. Bring your own lawn chairs or blankets. Call 828-733-2013 or visit www.grandfather.com for information.

■ The **Woolly Worm Festival** is held in Banner Elk during a weekend in October. The woolly worm is actually a furry caterpillar with black and brown bands. Mountain folklore says you can predict what kind of winter lies ahead by examining the bands on these caterpillars right before the first frost. The festival includes food, live music, and crafts, but the real draw is the woolly worm races. You can bring your own or purchase a woolly worm; you then name it and enter it in one of the heats. Several worms are placed side by side at the bottoms of long strings. The winner is the worm that reaches the top of its string first. It's fun to watch, and kids love it. The winners of the heats compete until there is a grand champion. It's the champion worm that is used to predict the forthcoming winter. For information on the festival, call 828-898-5605 or visit www.woollyworm.com.

Places to Stay

RESORTS, HOTELS, AND MOTELS

You'll find that the rates for most accommodations are less expensive on weekdays, even in the summer. During the summer and fall, you may discover that the rates on Beech Mountain are lower than those for similar accommodations in Boone and Blowing Rock.

- **4 Seasons at Beech.** Expensive/Moderate. 608 Beech Mountain Parkway in Beech Mountain (828-387-4211; www.4Seasons.Beech.net). Located at the top of Beech Mountain, 4 Seasons offers one- and two-room units, each with a telephone, a television, and a kitchen with a microwave, a refrigerator, and a dishwasher. Special packages are available during ski season.

- **The Inns at Beech Mountain.** Expensive/Moderate. 700 Beech Mountain Parkway in Beech Mountain (828-284-2770; www.beechalpen.com). These two inns are located next to each other and are run by the same company. **Beech Alpen Inn** has 25 rooms with exposed beams and views of the mountains and ski slopes. Some rooms have queen-sized beds and French doors that lead onto balconies. Others have king-sized beds or two double beds, easy chairs, and window seats. Some have stone fireplaces. All have private baths and color cable television. The main floor of the Swiss-style **Top of the Beech** has a greatroom with a cathedral ceiling, a ski chandelier, a game table, sofas, and a large stone fireplace. All the guest rooms have two double beds, a table with seating, a private bath, and color cable television. A restaurant is on the premises.

- **Pinnacle Inn.** Expensive/Moderate. 301 Pinnacle Inn Road in Beech Mountain (800-405-7888 or 828-387-2231; www.pinnacleinnresort.com/). You can rent a one- or two-bedroom villa or a ski suite at this resort. The villas have well-equipped kitchens, fireplaces, telephones, and color television. The inn offers an indoor heated pool, a sauna, a steam room, hot tubs, an exercise room, and opportunities for tennis, shuffleboard, and golf.

■ **Eseeola Lodge.** Deluxe. 175 Linville Avenue in Linville (800-742-6717 or 828-733-4311; www.eseeola.com). Eseeola Lodge is located near the intersection of U.S. 221, N.C. 105, and N.C. 181. It has received a Four Star rating from Mobil and has been recognized by *Golf Magazine* as a Silver Medalist Resort. Because of the chestnut siding and Tudor look, the lodge and its surrounding buildings remind one of an English inn. Eseeola has been welcoming vacationers since 1892. In recent years, the rooms have been renovated and spacious suites have been added. Guests can arrange to play tennis or golf. A regulation croquet court is located across the street. The inn is open from mid-May to the end of October.

■ **The Villa at the Blueberry Farm.** Deluxe. 60 Deer Run Road, off N.C. 194 about 1.5 miles north of Banner Elk (828-260-1790 or 828-898-9099; www.blueberryvilla.com). Situated on a 20-acre blueberry farm that boasts its own winery, this inn offers eight suites, each with a private bath and a Jacuzzi. Some of the beautifully appointed guest rooms have flat-screen TVs and gas fireplaces. The villa includes a game room, a gourmet kitchen, and expansive porches overlooking a trout pond and the vineyard.

■ **Archer's Mountain Inn.** Expensive. 2489 Beech Mountain Parkway near Beech Mountain (888-827-6155 or 828-898-9004; www.archersinn.com/). This inn has 15 rooms with native-stone fireplaces, full private baths, and color television. You can rent a Jacuzzi suite, a room with a mountain-view balcony, an efficiency suite, rooms with vaulted ceilings, and traditional bed-and-breakfast-style rooms. The inn offers a full bar and the **Jackalope's View** restaurant, which serves fresh seafood, certified Angus beef, and exotic wild game.

■ **The Azalea Inn.** Expensive. Behind the Village Shops in Banner Elk (888-898-2743 or 828-898-8195; www.azalea-inn.com). Built in 1937, this inn has seven guest rooms, each with its own tiled bath and cable television. The carriage-house cottage has an upstairs and can accommodate four people; it has a bedroom, a bath with a whirlpool, a living room with a sofa bed and a fireplace, and a full kitchen. The inn sits behind a white picket fence on a beautifully landscaped lot that features a birdhouse collection and brightly colored flowers in summer. Guests enjoy the fireplace in the living room and the wood stove on the sun porch.

■ **The Banner Elk Inn.** Expensive/Moderate. 407 Main Street East in

Banner Elk (888-487-8263 or 828-898-6223; www.bannerelkinn.com/). This cozy historic inn has several rooms filled with antiques. All the rooms include European down comforters; some have private baths. The inn has a greatroom, where guests can watch cable television or relax by the stone fireplace. The new addition features its own kitchen, separate entrance, and private garden. A full breakfast is served each morning.

- **The Perry House Bed-and-Breakfast**. Expensive/Moderate. Near the junction of N.C. 184 and N.C. 194 at the main stoplight in Banner Elk (877-806-4280 or 828-898-3535; www.perryhouse.com). This 1903 farmhouse is conveniently located across from Lees-McRae College and a block from the Village Shops. Each room has a private bathroom, cable television, a VCR, and queen-sized beds. A full breakfast is included in the room rate.

Places to Eat

- **Eseeola Lodge**. Expensive. 175 Linville Avenue in Linville (828-733-4311; www.eseeola.com). A coat and tie are required for men at dinner at this grand old resort. The restaurant has won the prestigious Mobile Four Star Award. It features French and New American cuisine. Breakfast and dinner are served daily. Reservations are required.

- **Louisiana Purchase**. Expensive. On N.C. 184 as you come into Banner Elk (828-963-5087 or 828-898-5656; www.ego.com/us/nc/mountains/purchase/index.htm). This restaurant has an award-winning wine list to go along with its Cajun, Creole, and classic French fare. Live jazz is offered in the lounge on Friday and Saturday nights. Reservations are suggested. Dinner is served Monday through Saturday.

- **Morels Restaurant**. Expensive. 1 Banner Street in downtown Banner Elk (828-898-6866). This small restaurant, which seats only 40, offers an intimate bistro style and a warm ambiance. The chef is an award-winning restaurateur who was selected as one of *Food & Wine* magazine's top 60 chefs in America. He's also been seen on the Discovery Channel's *Great Chefs of the South* series. He prepares imaginative dishes featuring locally grown and organic produce, wild game, seafood, and pasta. Dinner is served daily.

- ***Stonewalls***. Expensive. On N.C. 184 in Banner Elk (828-898-5550). For over 15 years, Stonewalls has been known as a place to get good steaks and prime rib. The menu also includes seafood dishes, but this is primarily a meat place. Dinner is served daily.

- ***The Best Cellar at Linville***. Expensive/Moderate. In Linville Village Shopping Center on N. C. 181 a half-mile from the Linville stoplight (828-733-4747; www.thebestcellarrestaurant.com/Linville.htm). Continuing the tradition of the popular Best Cellar in Blowing Rock, this location opened in 2005. The lunch menu offers soups, salads, sandwiches, and a daily meat-and-three, which might include meatloaf with tomato-Vidalia onion gravy, buttermilk fried chicken with sweet potato biscuits, or cornmeal-fried catfish with bacon-cheddar hush puppies—any of which is served with a choice of three vegetables. The prices are higher at dinner, when the entrées include mountain trout, filet mignon, rack of lamb, roast duckling, steaks, and crab cakes. From May to December, lunch is served daily and dinner Monday through Saturday. In the off-season, lunch is served Sunday through Thursday and dinner is offered Friday and Saturday.

- ***The Banner Elk Café and The Lodge Espresso Bar & Eatery***. Moderate. On N.C. 184 near the intersection with N.C. 194 in the heart of Banner Elk (828-898-4040). This complex features several different eateries, all sharing a large patio area in the center. You can get a country platter, eggs Benedict, or Belgian waffles for breakfast; burgers, sandwiches, pitas, or salads for lunch; and fish, ribs, chicken, or steak for dinner. The espresso bar offers smoothies, roasted coffees, muffins, breads, deli subs, pasta, and pizza. Live music is performed on the patio on weekend evenings during summer. Breakfast, lunch, and dinner are served daily.

- ***Sorrentos***. Moderate. In the Village Shops in Banner Elk (828-898-5214). This restaurant bills itself as "a touch of Italy in the mountains." Sorrentos changes its menu monthly. Its nightly specials are usually excellent. It has an extensive wine list. Lunch and dinner are served daily.

- ***Fred's Backside Deli***. Inexpensive. 501 Beech Mountain Parkway in Beech Mountain (828-387-4838 or 828-387-9331; www.fredsgeneral.com). Located in Fred's General Mercantile Company, this deli serves sandwiches, salads, soups, pizza, and homemade desserts. It also offers meats and cheeses for purchase. Breakfast, lunch, and dinner are served daily.

- **Henry's**. Inexpensive. Near the intersection of U.S. 221, N.C. 105, and N.C. 181 in Linville (828-737-9111). You might overlook this restaurant, since it's located in a small, unimpressive building. But that would be a mistake. The baked goods, sandwiches, salads, and breakfast offerings include some interesting culinary combinations. For example, "Hummus Among Us" is a tomato-basil tortilla stuffed with homemade hummus, herbs, and spices and covered with sprouts, curried cucumber dressing, toasted sunflower seeds, and provolone. For breakfast, try the salmon gravlax burrito, which includes goat cheese, fresh spinach, and scrambled eggs in a spinach-herb tortilla. Breakfast and lunch are served Monday through Saturday.

- **Italian Restaurant**. Inexpensive. On U.S. 221 near N.C. 181 in Pineola (828-733-1401). Located in a building that used to house a Tastee Freez, this restaurant might not inspire expectations of good food. But diners find themselves pleasantly surprised by the sandwiches, pasta, pizza, calzones, beer, and wine. Lunch is served Saturday and Sunday and dinner Tuesday through Sunday.

Black Mountains
COURTESY OF NORTH CAROLINA DIVISION OF TOURISM, FILM AND SPORTS DEVELOPMENT

SPRUCE PINE AND BURNSVILLE

ecause major highways still have not reached Mitchell and Yancey counties, development here is less than it is around Boone and Blowing Rock. Ironically, it seems this area would attract a great number of tourists, since it has some of the highest peaks in North Carolina. But despite recent road improvements north of Asheville, development is just now starting here. Fortunately, this isolation means you can still find unspoiled vistas.

Prominent in the area are the Black Mountains, where Mount Mitchell sits among a dozen peaks over 6,000 feet high.

Spruce Pine, the largest town in Mitchell County, has a long mining heritage that has evolved into a tourist industry. It is now the site of the annual North Carolina Mineral and Gem Festival. It is also home to many craftsmen, some of whom came to study at the Penland School of Crafts and stayed.

A short drive west is Yancey County, where Burnsville is the largest town. Its town square showcases a statue of the man for whom the town is named, Captain Otway Burns, a hero of the War of 1812. Yancey County has a population of only 17,000. It markets itself as a place to escape traffic jams, urban blight, polluted air, and tainted water.

JUST THE FACTS

Spruce Pine is located at the intersection of U.S. 19E and N.C. 226 six miles from Milepost 331 on the Blue Ridge Parkway.

Burnsville is located at the intersection of U.S. 19 and N.C. 197; from Milepost 344 on the parkway, follow N.C. 80 to U.S. 19.

For visitor information about the Spruce Pine area, contact the Mitchell County Chamber of Commerce, 79 Parkway Road, P.O. Box 858, Spruce Pine, N.C. 28777 (800-227-3912 or 828-765-9483; www.mitchell-county.com). For information about the Burnsville area, contact the Yancey County Chamber of Commerce, 106 West Main Street, Burnsville, N.C. 28714 (800-948-1632 or 828-682-7413; www.yanceychamber.com).

The weekly newspaper in Mitchell County is the *Mitchell News Journal*. In Yancey County, the weekly paper is the *Yancey Common Times Journal*.

Things to Do

MUSEUMS AND SCIENCE CENTERS

■ The *Museum of North Carolina Minerals*, located at Milepost 331 on the parkway, is part of the Blue Ridge Parkway Visitor Center. This is also the location of the Mitchell County Chamber of Commerce. Here, you can see exhibits on the wide range of minerals found in North Carolina. The gift shop carries books about gems and mining. The museum is open from 9 A.M. to 5 P.M. daily year-round. Admission is free. Call 828-765-2761.

CULTURAL OFFERINGS

■ The *Penland School of Crafts* is open from early March to mid-December. The hours for the Penland Gallery are 10 A.M. to 5 P.M. Tuesday through Saturday and noon to 5 P.M. on Sunday. To reach the school, take Penland Road off U.S. 19E between Spruce Pine and Burnsville. It is 2.9 miles to a left turn onto S.R. 1164, then 1.8 miles down the winding road to the school. See the sidebar about the school for further information, or call 828-765-6211 or visit www.penland.org.

RECREATION

■ **Emerald Village** is located at McKinney Mine Road and Crabtree Creek Road in Little Switzerland, at the site of the Big McKinney and Bon Ami mines. This attraction includes an underground museum in a former mine, where you can see equipment and learn about methods used for mining gems a century ago. You can also mine for your own gems—for a price. The mine offers enriched gravel and claims that visitors will "find a gem every time." This is good if you have children, because they get pretty excited about finding a "jewel." You can also see artisans at work cutting and mounting gems. Emerald Village is open from 9 A.M. to 5 P.M. on weekdays and from 9 A.M. to 6 P.M. on weekends from April through October; call for hours the remainder of the year. Fees are charged for mine tour and mining buckets. For more information, call 828-765-6463 or visit http://www.emeraldvillage.com/.

■ The **Orchard at Altapass** is located near Spruce Pine on Orchard Road at Milepost 328.3 on the Blue Ridge Parkway. A working orchard, it produces Heritage apples. The best time to visit is the early fall, when the apples are ripe. The orchard offers hayrides, storytelling, mountain music, handmade crafts, jam, apple butter, cider, mountain honey, and dried fruits. It even has a geologist and a botanist who give guided walking tours. From Memorial Day through October, it is open from 10 A.M. to 6 P.M. Monday and Wednesday through Saturday and from noon to 6 P.M. on Sunday; it is open every day during October. For information, call 888-765-9531 or 828-765-9531 or visit www.altapassorchard.com.

■ **Mount Mitchell State Park**, accessible at Milepost 355 on the Blue Ridge Parkway, boasts the highest peak east of the Mississippi River. The park has picnic areas, nature trails, a lookout tower offering spectacular mountain views, camping areas, a concession stand, and a ranger station. The park and the ranger station are open year-round except for Christmas; the concession stand is open May through October. For information, call 828-675-4611 or visit www.ncsparks.net/momi.html.

■ A popular summer activity in this area is tubing on the South Toe River. At **Carolina Hemlocks Recreation Area**, located on N.C. 80, you'll witness crowds of people bobbing along the river on rubber inner tubes. The slow-moving current and gentle cascades lend just enough excitement to make the activity exhilarating but not too dangerous. You'll see signs for tube rentals at the stores near the recreation area.

SEASONAL EVENTS

■ The **North Carolina Mineral and Gem Festival** is held the first week of August in Spruce Pine. It includes exhibits and demonstrations about gems, of course. For information, call 828-765-9483 or visit www.mitchell-county.com/festival/.

Places to Stay

RESORTS, HOTELS, AND MOTELS

■ **The Clear Creek Guest Ranch**. Expensive. 100 Clear Creek Drive off N.C. 80 South in Burnsville (800-651-4510 or 828-675-4510; www.clearcreekranch.com). This is a little different from your typical accommodation because it's a dude ranch. The rates include three full meals a day, lodging, horseback riding, and all ranch activities. Guests stay in cabins (one-, two-, and three-bedroom units are available) that have porches with rocking chairs. All meals are served family-style in the main lodge. Lots of activities are available for children. The ranch is open from April to Thanksgiving.

■ **Switzerland Inn**. Expensive. N.C. 226A at Milepost 334 in Little Switzerland (800-654-4026 or 828-765-2153; www.switzerlandinn.com). This popular retreat has chalet-style architecture, paintings of storks on the chimney, and a magnificent panoramic view. An entire wall in the field-stone-floored lobby is a window that frames the Black Mountain Valley below. All the rooms have hand-painted murals that make you think of the Swiss Alps. Most have balconies; all have cable television, telephones, and baths. Cottages are also available, as are large suites with air conditioning and separate sleeping and living areas. Room rates include a full breakfast and use of the swimming pool and tennis and shuffleboard courts.

- **Pinebridge Inn and Executive Center.** Moderate. 207 Pinebridge Avenue in Spruce Pine (800-356-5059 or 828-765-5543; www.pinebridgeinn.com). This AAA Three Diamond hotel is located in a converted schoolhouse, which allows for large rooms. Guests have free use of the Pinebridge Center, which includes an indoor heated pool, a sauna, exercise equipment, a steam room, a whirlpool, and an indoor walking track.

INNS AND BED-AND-BREAKFASTS

- **Richmond Inn.** Moderate. 51 Pine Avenue in Spruce Pine (877-765-6993 or 828-765-6993; www.richmond-inn.com). This half-century-old inn is shaded by towering white pines and landscaped with native trees and shrubbery. You'll almost forget that the town of Spruce Pine is only three blocks away. The inn's terrace overlooks the valley of the North Toe River. Your night's stay comes with a full breakfast.

- **Terrell House Bed-and-Breakfast.** Moderate. 109 Robertson Street in Burnsville (828-682-4505). This Colonial-style home was built in the early 1900s as a girls' dormitory for the Stanley McCormick School. It is situated in a quiet neighborhood within easy walking distance of the town square. It offers six guest rooms, each with a private bath. A full breakfast is served on fine china in the formal dining room.

- **The Bicycle Inn.** Inexpensive. 319 Dallas Young Road in Bakersville (888-424-5466; www.bicycleinn.com). To reach this inn, make your way to the only traffic light in Bakersville and follow the signs for two miles. As its name implies, The Bicycle Inn was built by bicycling enthusiasts and caters to that same crowd. The four guest rooms and the parlor are named for famous cyclists; the owners also found creative ways to incorporate bicycles into the decor. One room has two sets of bunk beds; guests have to share the room and the bath with whoever shows up, but the rate is very reasonable. The rest of the rooms have private baths. Although the inn attracts cyclists, it is open to anyone who wants to get away from the hustle and bustle. It has a café where breakfast and dinner are served; breakfast does not come with the room rate.

- **The Celo Inn**. Inexpensive. 45 Seven Mile Ridge Road in Burnsville (828-675-5132; www.celoinn.com). This inn is located 7.8 miles from the Blue Ridge Parkway off N.C. 80. It has five rooms in the upstairs of the main building, plus a separate cottage that sleeps five. The bathrooms are private but might be located across the hall from your room. Breakfast is served for a small extra fee.

Places to Eat

- **Foxfire Café**. Moderate. 145 Skyview Circle off N.C. 226 in Spruce Pine (828-766-2855). This establishment is a bit difficult to find, as it is located in a strip shopping center that has no official name on its sign. The center is just off N.C. 226 on top of a hill on the left about two miles south of the Blue Ridge Parkway; it is located next to the Mountain GMC dealership. One local described the cuisine this way: "It's different; they serve healthy stuff." What that translates to is that Foxfire serves gourmet dishes with fresh ingredients at a very reasonable price for the quantity and quality. You can get salmon burgers, red snapper with lobster bisque sauce, or chicken in tomato-vodka cream sauce, served over angel-hair pasta. However, you can also get a rib-eye with garlic mashed potatoes or an Angus hamburger. Lunch is served Tuesday through Saturday; dinner is offered on Friday and Saturday only.

- **Garden Deli**. Inexpensive. On the town square in Burnsville (828-682-3946; www.garden-deli.com). This family-owned and -operated restaurant, in business since 1987, offers sandwiches and salads. Lunch is served Monday through Saturday.

- **Switzerland Café & General Store**. Inexpensive. On N.C. 226A near Milepost 334 in Little Switzerland (828-765-5289; www.switzerlandcafe.com). You'll find soups, salads, sandwiches, desserts, imported beer, wine, and cheese here. The café is open daily from 9 A.M. to "whenever."

THE PENLAND
SCHOOL OF
CRAFTS

The Penland School of Crafts
COURTESY OF NORTH CAROLINA DIVISION OF
TOURISM, FILM AND SPORTS DEVELOPMENT

The Penland School of Crafts has been described as one of the leading shapers of the American crafts movement and a producer of some of the best artisans in the country.

In 1914, Rufus Morgan founded the Appalachian School. Morgan wanted to include handicrafts in his program of instruction. In visiting area homes, he discovered high-quality woven articles that had been discarded when store-bought cloth became available. He convinced his sister, Miss Lucy Morgan, to come to Penland from Chicago and learn weaving from a local woman, Aunt Susan Phillips, so that Miss Lucy could teach the skill at his school.

Miss Lucy went on to instruct girls at the school and women in the community. She founded the Penland School with the goal of perpetuating the art of weaving and providing a source of income for local people. Miss Lucy also began collecting her students' wares and selling them to the outside world. In 1928, a pottery department was added to the school. In 1929, the sale of student-made goods totaled $18,000.

Today, the Penland School campus has over 40 buildings. It is open to students during the spring, summer, and fall. Terms last one, two, or eight weeks, and the courses vary from year to year. The curriculum usually includes work in wood, glass, fiber, clay, metal, papermaking, photography, and textiles. All are studied in rustic, yet professionally equipped, studios. Approximately 1,200 students a year study in 10 craft media at the Penland School.

Visitors can browse the Penland Gallery to get an idea of how important the Morgans' contribution was in preserving and encouraging traditional mountain crafts. Tours of the campus are offered on Tuesday at 10:30 A.M. and Thursday at 1:30 P.M.; no tours are given in January or February. Reservations are required.

ELISHA MITCHELL

It was not until Dr. Elisha Mitchell arrived in 1827 that anyone had much of an idea how tall the Black Mountains really were.

In 1825, Mitchell took charge of the North Carolina Geological Survey, the first statewide survey anywhere in the nation. In the course of fulfilling his duties, he made his first visits to the western part of the state. In an 1829 geological report, Mitchell stated his belief that the Black Mountains contained the highest land between the Gulf of Mexico and the White Mountains of New Hampshire.

When he returned to the Blacks in 1835, the first peak he climbed to take measurements was Celo Knob, elevation 5,946 feet. There, he noted "peaks considerably more elevated farther South." Mitchell took measurements of barometric pressure and temperature and compared them to measurements taken at his base in Morganton. He then used a formula to determine that the peak that later became known as Mount Mitchell stood 6,476 feet above sea level. He proclaimed it "the Highest Peak of the Black." It turned out that Mount Mitchell is actually 208 feet higher than Mitchell thought. He made the wrong measurements at his base. If those had been correct, he would have been off by only six feet.

General Thomas L. Clingman, a member of Congress and a man of scientific tastes, was taking measurements in the area at that same time. Clingman published a statement claiming that he had found a peak higher than the one measured by Mitchell.

Mitchell became obsessed with proving that he was right and Clingman was wrong. He returned to the Blacks in 1857 to settle the matter, setting out alone. When he failed to meet his son as scheduled, a search party was organized. Ten days later, the frustrated group enlisted the aid of Big Tom Wilson, a legendary hunter and tracker who lived in the Cane River area, at the foot of the Blacks. The writer Charles Dudley Warner described Big Tom as "six feet and two inches tall, very spare and muscular, with sandy hair, long gray beard, and honest blue eyes. He has a reputation for great strength and endurance; a man of native simplicity and mild manners." The searchers agreed to let Wilson take the lead. Following seemingly invisible clues—broken limbs and faint impressions in the earth—Big Tom brought the group to a 50-foot waterfall. There, in a pool at the foot, was the perfectly preserved body of Dr. Mitchell. It was surmised that he must have become lost in the fog and fallen over the edge while following the stream. His body was buried in Asheville and later moved to the top of the peak that now bears his name.

Asheville

By Sue Clark

$\mathcal{T}$here is a peace that settles on my soul whenever I get away to the mountains. Driving west on Interstate 40 from my home in the Piedmont, it's easy to be fooled into thinking the blue images in the distance are a line of thunderstorms marching eastward. But as the engine of my car works harder as I climb, the mountains come into clearer view, and that familiar peace welcomes me. I have heard many people remark that coming to the Blue Ridge Mountains is like coming home, even if it's the first time they've visited. These ancient peaks and valleys beckon with a warmth and understanding that comes from their age. In Asheville, as they like to say, "altitude affects attitude."

After the tortuous climb past Old Fort, the mountains are suddenly all around you. The road curves more sharply, but the reward is a new view with every turn. Drivers beware! It's easy to be distracted by the vistas that you'll encounter for the next half-hour on your drive toward Asheville.

The city of Asheville, named for Governor Samuel Ashe, was incorporated in 1797. The influence of the Scots-Irish immigrants who settled this area is apparent. For example, many old bluegrass tunes sound quite similar to Irish jigs.

Asheville was an isolated small town of only 2,600 before the coming of the railroad in the 1880s. Some of the first flatlanders to find their way to Asheville were the wealthy, who came to escape the oppressive heat of summer. They built large summer homes and elaborate resort hotels. Soon, Asheville's population was over 10,000.

In the 1920s, Asheville experienced another growth spurt. The popular Art Deco style of the day can still be seen in many downtown buildings. When city hall was erected, many citizens were disturbed by its opulent domed roof covered with green and pink tiles. The same architect was

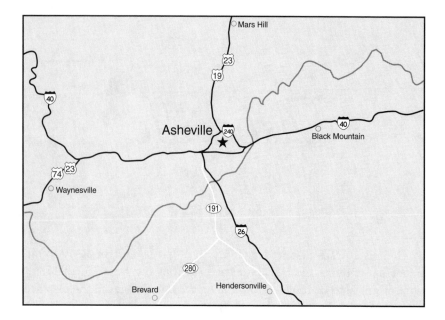

scheduled to build the county courthouse, but the pendulum swung in the opposite direction, and his contract was canceled. The courthouse looks like the straight-laced sibling of the neighboring city hall.

Asheville continues to attract visitors, as well as those who come to settle on this plateau between the Blue Ridge and Great Smoky mountains. And if the temperate weather and beautiful vistas aren't enough, the city offers a unique regional culture, a longstanding crafts tradition, a wide variety of shops and restaurants, outdoor recreation to suit even the most adventurous tastes, and first-class accommodations. Oh yes, and don't forget the French château and the five-star hotel and spa.

A trip to Asheville can be filled with shopping, dining, high culture, hiking, rafting, mountain climbing—the options are endless. Personally, watching sunsets is usually the activity that occupies my time.

Photograph in background on Previous Page—

Biltmore Estate
Courtesy of Biltmore Estate

JUST THE FACTS

Asheville is located at the crossing of Interstate 40 and Interstate 26.

It is served by Asheville Regional Airport; for information, call 828-684-2226 or visit www.flyavl.com.

The Greyhound bus terminal is located at 2 Tunnel Road; call 828-253-8451 for information.

The Asheville Visitor Center is at 36 Montford Avenue; take Exit 4C off Interstate 240. It is well staffed and open daily. For information, call 888-247-9811 or 828-258-6101 or visit www.exploreasheville.com.

The daily newspaper, the *Asheville Citizen-Times*, is a great source of information, as is *Mountain XPress*, a free weekly.

Things to Do

HISTORIC PLACES, GARDENS, AND TOURS

Visitors have a variety of options for tours, including a walking architecture/history tour of the Montford neighborhood, an auto rickshaw tour of Riverside Cemetery, an urban-trail tour, and a historic trolley tour. These are a great way to begin your Asheville experience, since they give you a lay of the land and help you decide which places to go back and explore further. For information about tours, contact the Asheville Visitor Center.

■ ***Biltmore Estate*** is located on U.S. 25 just north of Exit 50 off Interstate 40. Words do little to describe this 16th-century-style château modeled after those in France's Loire Valley. This working estate is surrounded by rolling forestland, formal gardens, a winery, and a river. All of this is surprising, considering its proximity to Asheville's downtown.

Opened as a private home in 1895, Biltmore Estate boasted all the latest innovations, including central heating, indoor plumbing, electric lights, a bowling alley, a gymnasium, and an indoor pool—awe-inspiring features for its time. It has charmed its many visitors with its beauty, luxury, and amenities ever since.

Biltmore Estate
COURTESY OF BILTMORE ESTATE

George Vanderbilt, grandson of industrialist Cornelius Vanderbilt, purchased 125,000 acres near Asheville because he loved the mountain views and climate. He promptly hired architect Richard Morris Hunt and landscape architect Frederick Law Olmsted, two of America's leading designers, to plan his estate.

The 250-room mansion took hundreds of workers more than five years to build. The construction site had its own brick kilns and woodworking shops. Limestone was transported on a railroad spur laid just for Biltmore. Artisans and craftsmen were brought from Europe. Many of the men employed in the building of the home fell in love with Asheville and stayed after construction was finished. They settled easily into the area's strong crafts tradition.

While work was progressing on the mansion, the land was also getting attention. Vanderbilt wanted an estate that would include a productive farm and forest. His emphasis on land management is evidenced by the fact that most of the property was eventually sold to the federal government and became part of the Blue Ridge Parkway or Pisgah National Forest. Family descendants still own the mansion and 8,000 surrounding acres. Frederick Law Olmsted, most famous for his design of New York's Central Park, planned the gardens and the park surrounding the home, including the three-mile driveway.

After passing the Lodge Gate, you will make the beautiful drive to the visitor center, where you can purchase admission tickets. You may also view a short film about Biltmore, see a relief map of the area, check the menus of the estate's restaurants, and visit the restroom. Short paths lead through the woods to the mansion.

Your first view of the château will be across a long lawn with a reflecting pool in the center. The complex exterior features massive carved archways, columns, and gargoyles. This is but the beginning of the wonders to behold here.

Today's visitors enter Biltmore House just as George Vanderbilt's guests did over a century ago—through the main door and into the grand foyer. Here, you can purchase personal headsets that will allow you to tour the house at your own speed. It's well worth the fee, especially since the recent opening of many rooms on the third floor. Elevators are available for those who can't negotiate the staircases. The grand foyer is the hub of the mansion. Musical groups are often invited to perform in the atrium on the right side of the foyer.

Each room in the mansion has a distinctive style. The medieval-style banquet room has a 70-foot arched ceiling, a table that seats 64, Flemish tapestries, numerous elk and moose heads, and a carved mantel that spans three massive fireplaces. The two-story Baroque library has elaborately carved paneling and an 18th-century painted ceiling imported from Venice.

You should plan on spending at least half a day at Biltmore. The tour of the mansion lasts at least two hours and covers everything from the third-floor guest suites to basement service areas such as the kitchens, pantries, and laundry. You'll also see the servants' quarters, the bowling alley, the gymnasium, and the indoor pool, complete with private changing rooms.

After touring the mansion, you can go for a stroll in the formal gardens. You may also want to visit the Biltmore Estate Winery, where a brief tour and a wine tasting are offered. The vintners are understandably proud of their award-winning wines. If you get hungry, your options include sandwiches, drinks, and ice cream at the Stable Café, located next to the mansion; baked goods and snacks at the bakery and the candy shop; and upscale dining at Deerpark Restaurant or the Winery Bistro, both located near the winery.

The house is open daily from 9 A.M. to 5 P.M. from April through December and from 9 A.M. to 4 P.M. from January through March. The winery is open Monday through Thursday from 11 A.M. to 7 P.M., Friday and Saturday from 11 A.M. to 8 P.M., and Sunday from noon to 7 P.M. Both are closed Thanksgiving and Christmas. The admission fee seems expensive until you realize that you're paying for at least half a day's entertainment in a place unlike any other in America. For more information, call 800-

624-1575 or 828-225-1333 or visit www.biltmore.com.

■ The **North Carolina Arboretum**, at 100 Frederick Law Olmsted Way, is nestled in one of the most beautiful natural settings in America. Within its 434 acres, the arboretum offers 65 acres of cultivated gardens, 10 miles of forested hiking and biking trails, a state-of-the-art greenhouse production facility, and the finest bonsai collection in the southeastern United States. A parking fee is charged except on Tuesdays. The arboretum is open daily except Christmas, weather permitting. The hours are 8 A.M. to 9 P.M. from April through October and 8 A.M. to 7 P.M. from November through March; hours vary for the Visitor Education Center, the Bonsai Exhibition Garden, and the greenhouse, so check before you go. For more information, including a calendar of special events and educational programs, call 828-665-2492 or visit www.ncarboretum.org.

■ The **Thomas Wolfe Memorial** is located at 52 North Market Street in downtown Asheville. The house suffered a fire at the hands of an arsonist on July 24, 1998. Over 85 percent of the personal belongings and artifacts of the Wolfe family escaped the flames but had to undergo extensive restoration from smoke and water damage. The house has been completely restored and was reopened for tours in May 2004.

Wolfe grew up in this 28-room house yet had no room of his own, since his mother used the majority of the building for a boardinghouse. In 1929, when Wolfe published *Look Homeward, Angel*, the residents of Asheville easily recognized the "Dixieland" boardinghouse in the town of "Altamont." They were not amused by Wolfe's less-than-flattering picture of his hometown. The local public library banned the book for more than seven years. Asheville eventually came to appreciate the talent of its native son. In 1948, some 10 years after Wolfe's death, the Asheville Chamber of Commerce helped purchase the house as a memorial to one of the 20th century's great novelists. In 1976, the memorial was designated a state historic site.

From April through October, the visitor center is open Tuesday through Saturday from 9 A.M. to 5 P.M. and Sunday from 1 P.M. to 5 P.M. From November through March, it is open Tuesday through Saturday from 10 A.M. to 4 P.M. and Sunday from 1 P.M. to 4 P.M. Check with the site for information on special events, especially those around October 3, Thomas Wolfe's birthday. Call 828-253-8304 or visit www.wolfememorial.com.

■ **Botanical Gardens of Asheville**, at 151 W. T. Weaver Boulevard, is a beautiful setting for the preservation and display of trees, plants, and flowers

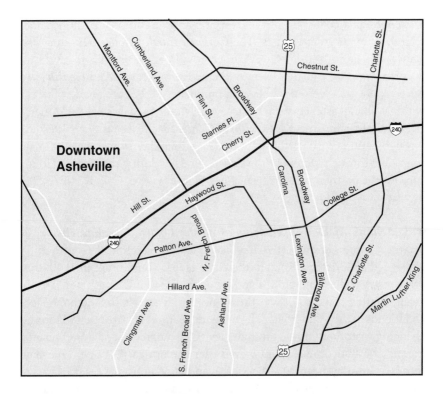

native to the southern Appalachians. In 1960, several local garden clubs came together to help plant the grounds of this 10-acre preserve on the campus of the University of North Carolina at Asheville. Now operating as a nonprofit organization, the gardens provide a study area and information center for those interested in horticulture, as well as those of us who simply appreciate a place of quiet beauty. Unpaved trails wind through the various areas, including the azalea garden and the garden for the blind. A wheelchair ramp is available. The gardens are open daily during daylight hours. Admission is free. For information, call 828-252-5190 or visit www.ashevillebotanicalgardens.org.

Museums and Science Centers

■ ***Pack Place***, at 2 South Pack Square in downtown Asheville, opened in 1992 at the cost of $14 million. It provides western North Carolina with a premier arts-and-sciences center, housing museums, offices for local arts organizations, and galleries and studios for artists. The ***Asheville Art***

Museum has a collection of contemporary and traditional paintings and sculptures by Southern artists. The **Colburn Earth Science Museum** displays 1,500 gems, semiprecious stones, fossils, and minerals, many from the area. Pack Place also houses an interactive museum called **Health Adventure**, which is very popular with families. At 39 South Market Street, within walking distance of Pack Place, you'll find Asheville's African-American cultural facility, the **YMI Cultural Center**. Pack Place is open Tuesday through Saturday from 10 A.M. to 6 P.M. and Sunday from 1 P.M. to 5 P.M. from June through October; it is closed Sundays during the winter. Hours vary for the partner museums, so check before you go. Call 828-257-4500 or visit www.packplace.org.

- The **Smith-McDowell Museum of Western North Carolina History** is located on the campus of Asheville-Buncombe Technical Community College at 283 Victoria Road in the city's oldest house. Built in 1840, this brick mansion has four stories and a double-tiered full-length porch with locally crafted columns. It was the home of mayors, a Confederate major, and friends of the Vanderbilts. The museum features restored period rooms, changing history exhibits, grounds designed by Frederick Law Olmsted, Jr., and the Buncombe County Civil War Memorial. It is open Tuesday through Saturday from 10 A.M. to 4 P.M. and Sunday from 1 P.M. to 4 P.M. A small admission fee is charged. School programs and group tours can be arranged. For information, call 828-253-9231 or visit www.wnchistory.org.

- The **Western North Carolina Nature Center**, at 75 Gashes Creek Road on the grounds of the former Asheville Zoo, is designed to show the interaction between plants and animals in the southern Appalachians. Aimed at family audiences, the exhibits interest both children and adults. One features the underground den of a live chipmunk beneath a tree's roots. The center presents animals in natural-habitat exhibits. Domestic animals are showcased at its Educational Farm, where, for example, children can see a cow being milked. A small gift shop offers nature books and souvenirs. The center is open daily from 10 A.M. to 5 P.M. A small admission fee is charged. For information, call 828-298-5600 or visit www.wncnaturecenter.org.

CULTURAL OFFERINGS

- The **Asheville Symphony** is a fine regional orchestra founded in 1960.

It offers a series of classical concerts usually featuring an internationally known guest artist. Call 828-254-7046 or visit www.ashevillesymphony.org for information and a schedule of performances.

- **Asheville Community Theatre**, at 35 East Walnut Street, presents six productions annually. These include comedies, dramas, and musicals. It also offers a reader's theater, a children's theater, and classes. For information, call 828-254-1320 or visit www.ashevilletheatre.org.

SPECIAL SHOPPING

- The **Folk Art Center** is located east of Asheville at Milepost 382 on the Blue Ridge Parkway. It features the work of the Southern Highland Craft Guild, an organization of artisans who make pottery, baskets, quilts, candles, brooms, weavings, furniture, jewelry, dolls, musical instruments, and woodcarvings, among other things. This low-roofed building opened in 1980 in a beautiful setting surrounded by flowering trees and azaleas. It serves as an educational center, a research library, a craft shop, and exhibition space. The guild hosts special events such as folk dancing, demonstrations of traditional crafts, and lecture series. The **Allanstand Craft Shop**, located on the premises, offers the largest and most diverse collection of high-quality handmade crafts anywhere in the North Carolina mountains. This is definitely a great place for gift shopping, even if the gift is for you! The center is open from 9 A.M. to 6 P.M. daily; it closes an hour earlier during January, February, and March. Admission is free. For information, call 828-298-7928 or visit www.southernhighlandguild.org.

- **Biltmore Village**, across U.S. 25 from the entrance to Biltmore Estate, is a quaint neighborhood of houses built for the artisans and craftsmen who helped construct the mansion. The two-story houses have been turned into restaurants and shops selling gifts, stationery, jewelry, clothing, knitting supplies, and household accessories. The little village is a nice setting for strolling and window shopping. More information is available at www.biltmorevillage.com.

- **Western North Carolina Farmer's Market**, at 570 Brevard Road off N.C. 191 and Interstate 40, is a joy for the eye as well as the palate. This modern facility is operated year-round by the North Carolina Department of Agriculture. The feast for the senses begins with fresh local fruits and vegetables and continues with dried flowers, jams and jellies, and home-made crafts. The market is open daily from 8 A.M. to 6 P.M. during the summer and from 8 A.M. to 5 P.M. in winter. Admission is free. For information, call 828-253-1691.

■ *The Screen Door*, at 115 Fairview Road, is a treasure hunter's haven. It is actually a collection of booths for area artisans, antique dealers, and craftsmen. The fun here is in the hunt. Treasures to be found include garden accessories, heirloom seeds, recycled metal sculptures, antique china and silver, estate jewelry, funky furniture, face jugs, books, toys . . . Get the picture? Every trip is rewarded with something you didn't see the last time you stopped in. The Screen Door also holds seminars and workshops from time to time. Call 828-277-3667 for more information.

■ *Downtown Asheville* is experiencing a very successful revitalization. The streets are dotted with a wonderful mix of coffee houses, antique shops, boutiques, and restaurants.

■ *Wall Street*, part of which has been blocked off to create a pedestrian mall, has the best concentration of interesting shops and restaurants.

■ Just a short distance away at 55 Haywood Street is *Malaprop's*, one of those great independent bookstores that are becoming increasingly rare these days. Besides a fine selection of regional books, Malaprop's has a small, trendy café where you can sip a cappuccino while getting started on your latest literary purchase. Call 828-254-6734 or visit the store's well-kept Web site at www.malaprops.com.

■ *Grove Arcade Public Market* has been painstakingly restored to its original glory. Boasting more than 35 businesses at the time of this writing and new ones coming in all the time, the arcade offers fresh foods, regional cuisine, and locally made crafts. Built as a public market but inhabited by the federal government from World War II until the 1990s, the unusual Neo-Gothic building features winged griffins at the entrance, original phone booths, terrazzo tile, soaring ceilings, gargoyles, and friezes. The Grove Arcade Arts and Heritage Gallery offers tours of the building. For the newest vendors and monthly events, call 828-252-7799 or check out www.grovearcade.com.

RECREATION

If you like the great outdoors, Asheville's the place for you. Surrounded by three park areas containing more than a million acres, it offers plenty of opportunities for camping, hiking, fishing, and whitewater rafting.

- If you plan to visit **Great Smoky Mountains National Park**, call 865-436-1200 or visit www.nps.gov/grsm. If you'd like to stay in one of the six campgrounds of the **Blue Ridge Parkway**, call 828-259-0398. If you want to camp in **Pisgah National Forest**, call 828-257-4200.

- For hikers, there's the legendary **Appalachian Trail**, which cuts through Pisgah National Forest and Great Smoky Mountains National Park. Check with the park offices listed above.

- Is fishing your passion? Head for **Lake Julian**, south of Asheville on N.C. 280 off U.S. 25; **Lake Powhatan**, on N.C. 191 just off the Blue Ridge Parkway south of Asheville; or **Lake Lure**, on U.S. 74 southeast of Asheville. You'll need a state fishing license. For information about hunting and fishing regulations, call 828-258-6101; for a list of area businesses that sell the appropriate licenses, visit www.wildlife.state.nc.us.

- Whitewater rafting is popular from June through August on the **French Broad River** north of Asheville. If you're a serious rafter and want to try other rivers, see the chapter on Franklin for companies that raft the Nantahala Gorge.

- Skiing doesn't usually come to mind when visitors ponder the outdoor activities of North Carolina. However, the highest mountains in the eastern United States are here. **Wolf Laurel Ski Resort** (828-689-4111; www.skiwolflaurel.com) is closest to Asheville. **Cataloochee Ski Resort** (800-768-0285 or 828-926-0285; www.cataloochee.com) is a short drive

Golf in Western North Carolina
COURTESY OF NORTH CAROLINA DIVISION OF TOURISM, FILM AND SPORTS DEVELOPMENT

away in Maggie Valley. For information on other ski resorts, see the Blowing Rock chapter and the chapter on Banner Elk, Beech Mountain, and Linville.

■ Golf in the mountains presents its own special challenges and pleasures. Check out *Asheville Municipal Golf Course* (828-298-1867), *Black Mountain Golf Course* (828-669-2710), *Reems Creek Golf Club* (828-645-4393), and *The Grove Park Inn Resort & Spa* (828-252-2711).

SEASONAL EVENTS

■ The *Mountain Dance and Folk Festival*, held the first weekend in August, is the oldest event of its kind in the nation. It showcases the best mountain crafts, musicians, and dancers—both cloggers and folk dancers. Started in 1927 by Bascom Lamar Lunsford, it is often called "the Granddaddy of Mountain Festivals." For information, call 800-257-1300 or 828-258-6101 or visit www.folkheritage.org.

■ The *Southern Highland Craft Guild Fair* is held the third weekend in July and the third weekend in October every year. Over 100 craftspeople from the South demonstrate, display, and sell their works. Mountain music and dancing are part of the celebration. Call 828-298-7928 for information.

■ *Bele Chere Downtown Community Celebration*, held the last weekend in July, features bands (many of them nationally known), international food vendors, crafts, and contests. It is known as the largest free outdoor festival in the Southeast. The downtown area is closed to vehicles for the weekend. For information, call 828-259-5800.

■ *Shindig on the Green* is a series of free bluegrass concerts held on Saturday nights throughout the summer. They take place at City-County Plaza and are a great way to spend a Saturday evening in the mountains. For more information, call 800-257-1300 or 828-258-6107.

■ The *Mountain Sports Festival* is a three-day outdoor celebration in May featuring professional and amateur-level competitions in paddling, cycling, running, climbing, and triathlon. Demonstrations and beginner-level events in various sports serve to educate and entertain. The festival is centered at City-County Plaza, where you'll find food, award presentations, demonstrations, retail vendors, and live entertainment. Admission is free to spectators; participation in competitions requires a registration fee. For more information, call 828-251-4029 or visit www.mountainsportsfestival.com.

Places to Stay

Asheville has a great selection of accommodations. It offers 6,000-plus rooms in historic mountain retreats, country inns, bed-and-breakfasts, upscale downtown hotels, economy motels, national chain hotels, and everything in between. Reservations are highly recommended. You'll find Asheville a great home base for your mountain adventures, but don't even think about dropping in during fall leaf season or one of Asheville's popular festivals, when rooms have been reserved months in advance. Consider visiting in the winter, when rates at many places are drastically reduced from the summer and fall.

RESORTS, HOTELS, AND MOTELS

■ *The Grove Park Inn Resort & Spa*. Deluxe. 290 Macon Avenue (800-438-5800 or 828-252-2711; www.groveparkinn.com). There are only a handful of truly grand resort hotels in the United States. This is one of them. The attention to detail here comes from a long tradition. Back in the early 1900s, staff members used to polish every coin, so that no guest would be handed a tarnished piece of currency. While that is no longer the rule, it is an example of the kind of service that is still a part of the Grove Park.

The Grove Park Inn was the dream of E. W. Grove, the owner of a pharmaceutical firm famous for Grove's Tasteless Chill Tonic. Grove visited Asheville and found the climate beneficial to his health. His dream was to build the finest resort hotel in the world. After the inn opened in 1913, it became a favorite destination for the rich, the famous, and the powerful. One of the long hallways features photos of some of the inn's

The Grove Park Inn Resort and Spa
COURTESY OF THE NORTH CAROLINA DIVISION OF TOURISM, FILM AND SPORTS DEVELOPMENT

illustrious guests: Presidents Wilson, Taft, Coolidge, Hoover, and Eisenhower; business tycoons Henry Ford and Harvey Firestone; inventor Thomas Edison; and entertainers Enrico Caruso and Mikhail Baryshnikov. Many of the rooms have brass plaques on the doors that tell the year some famous person stayed there. One of the most requested rooms was used by F. Scott Fitzgerald.

The resort's golf course, opened in 1899, was redesigned by Donald Ross in 1924; it was subsequently remodeled in 2001. In 1973, the inn was listed on the National Register of Historic Places. That same decade, it added an indoor pool, a sports center, and a clubhouse. In the 1980s, wings were added to provide 510 deluxe rooms, two ballrooms, and a conference center. The new millennium has brought the most ambitious addition to date—a state-of-the-art spa complete with a lap pool, a mineral pool, several hot tubs, and an outdoor pool. The spa treatments are nothing short of luxurious. Located below the Sunset Terrace and between the two wings, the spa is mostly underground, so as not to spoil the view from the main inn.

The guest rooms are luxurious and the service outstanding. The inn offers outdoor activities and wonderful dining, shopping, and browsing opportunities. Many people who come for a once-in-a-lifetime experience wind up making a stay here a tradition.

- *Haywood Park Hotel.* Deluxe/Expensive. 1 Battery Park Avenue (800-228-2522 or 828-252-2522; www.haywoodpark.com). Haywood Park is an ultrasophisticated suite hotel in the heart of downtown. The feel here is elegant and refined. The lobby, accented by polished brass railings, doesn't overpower guests with a lot of furniture. The huge rooms open into small common areas located on each floor. This is the type of hotel you'd expect to find in London or New York; the attention to detail and outstanding service are not bettered in any city. Haywood Park's location makes it the ideal spot from which to enjoy Asheville's boutiques and restaurants. It's also a popular choice for a front-row seat for the city's summer festivals.

- *Crowne Plaza Resort.* Expensive/Moderate. 1 Holiday Inn Drive (800-733-3211 or 828-254-3211; www.ashevillecp.com). While large chain properties are generally not listed in this guide, this one is worthy of an exception. Situated on 120 acres close to downtown, this resort and conference center has some unusual extras. The low-rise buildings allow an unobstructed view of the city and the surrounding mountains. Extensive meeting and banquet facilities are on the premises. But what makes this place unique are the options for play, such as the 18-hole championship golf course, the indoor soccer center, the outdoor tennis courts, and the children's programs.

INNS AND BED-AND-BREAKFASTS

- *Inn on Biltmore Estate.* Deluxe. 1 Antler Hill Road (800-624-1575 or 828-252-1660; www.biltmore.com). Offering the only accommodations on Biltmore Estate, this inn continues a century-old legacy of hospitality begun by George Vanderbilt for his guests. Luxury and comfort reign here.

Inn on Biltmore Estate
COURTESY OF BILTMORE ESTATE

Each of the 213 finely appointed rooms and suites has a breathtaking mountain view. Thoughtful touches enhance each room. Comfy chairs, fireplaces, terraces, a veranda, an outdoor pool, and exceptional service all come together to make this a true retreat experience. The dining room offers classic, yet innovative, cuisine centered around estate-raised beef, lamb, and veal, complemented by Biltmore Estate wines. The atmosphere here is one of casual elegance, graciousness, and refined taste, all framed by the magnificent views of the surrounding mountains.

■ ***Richmond Hill Inn***. Deluxe. 87 Richmond Hill Drive (800-545-9238 or 828-252-7313; www.richmondhillinn.com). This elegant mansion, built in 1895, was designed as a private residence for Richmond Pearson, a former congressman and ambassador. It is considered Asheville's finest example of Queen Anne architecture. Sitting on top of a hill, the inn commands a 360-degree view encompassing the French Broad River, the Asheville skyline, and mountain peaks. Guest quarters are in the main house, the garden pavilion, and a row of charming cottages. Each individually decorated room includes a private bath, a television, and a telephone. The cottages have fireplaces, porches, and refrigerators. As for the landscaping, it's nothing short of stunning, from the croquet lawn to the parterre garden with its stone-lined brook, terraced walkway, and waterfall. A gourmet breakfast is served, as is afternoon tea. Guests can enjoy dinner at the highly awarded Gabrielle's, which features extraordinary entrées, a vast wine selection, and piano music in an elegant and intimate setting.

■ **Cedar Crest Victorian Inn**. Deluxe/Expensive. 674 Biltmore Avenue (800-252-0310 or 828-252-1389; www.cedarcrestvictorianinn.com). Cedar Crest is one of the largest and most opulent residences surviving from Asheville's 1890s boom period. Perched on a hill three blocks north of Biltmore Estate, this Queen Anne-style dwelling sits on four landscaped acres featuring English perennial gardens and a croquet lawn. Architectural details include a captain's walk, turrets, expansive verandas, carved oak paneling, and leaded glass. The guest rooms are appointed with satin-and-lace Victorian trappings and feature period antiques, canopied ceilings, claw-foot tubs, and fireplaces. Guests are treated to a sumptuous breakfast, afternoon refreshments, evening coffee, and a true spirit of hospitality.

■ **Chestnut Street Inn**. Expensive/Moderate. 176 East Chestnut Street (800-894-2955 or 828-285-0705; www.chestnutstreetinn.com). This large Colonial Revival home is located in the Chestnut Hill National Historic District. Its large porches are a beautiful accent to the mellow red-brick exterior. The high ceilings, ornate mantels, and antique furnishings and decorations transport guests back to a time when life had a relaxed quality. Amenities include private baths, down comforters, bathrobes, and fresh flowers. A full gourmet breakfast is served each morning. Guests enjoy late-afternoon tea on the veranda. If you're lucky, Mr. Bently, the inn's canine butler, may lead you through the English-style flower garden.

■ **The Lion & the Rose**. Expensive/Moderate. 276 Montford Avenue (800-546-6988 or 828-255-7673; www.lion-rose.com). Comfort and elegance abound in this wonderful bed-and-breakfast, where no detail is overlooked. A Georgian mansion built around 1895, it has five elegant guest rooms, including a bridal suite with a balcony. Located in the historic Montford neighborhood, the inn has beautiful gardens for strolling and a veranda for relaxing. A full gourmet breakfast is served each morning. Afternoon tea is a great time to come together with other guests and share the day's adventures. The Lion & the Rose is a place to visit for a little pampering.

■ **Blake House Inn**. Moderate. 150 Royal Pines Drive (888-353-5227 or 828-681-5227; www.blakehouse.com). Blake House was built in 1847 in the Italianate-Gothic style. It originally served as the summer home of a wealthy lowland rice planter. The restored mansion boasts 22-inch-thick granite walls, heart-pine floors, original English plaster moldings, seven fireplaces, covered porches, and a patio. Each room has fine linens, cable television, a telephone, and a private bath. This is also one of the few bed-and-breakfasts that welcomes children.

Places to Eat

- **Gabrielle's at Richmond Hill**. Expensive. 87 Richmond Hill Drive (800-545-9238 or 828-252-7313). Fine dining in an elegant setting is the order of the day at Gabrielle's. Guests have a choice of two areas in which to enjoy their meal: the dining room, which recalls the formality of traditional Victorian custom, and the sun porch, which has wicker furniture and ceiling fans. Gabrielle's features American cuisine and *nouvelle cuisine*. The emphasis is on fresh foods available locally. A six-course fixed-price dinner with a few choices is available, or you can order from the menu. Whichever option you select, you'll be treated to a fine evening in a magical setting. Dinner is served daily.

- **Zambra**. Expensive/Moderate. 85A Walnut Street (828-232-1060). *Zambra* is Arabic for *flute*. It is also an apt description of the "music" of this restaurant. The food here is exquisite—exotic, roughly beautiful, and delicious. The menu features the tastes of Spain, Morocco, and Portugal. The tapas menu is fun, innovative, and extensive. The selections change frequently, according to the available foods and the whim of the chef. And don't forget the wines, which hail from all over the world; guests have over 75 different Spanish and Portuguese wines to choose from, as well as a wonderful list of ports and sherries. The eye-catching, comfortable Moroccan decor and the live entertainment make for a great evening. Dinner is served nightly; live entertainment is offered on Friday and Saturday.

- **Café on the Square**. Moderate. 1 Biltmore Avenue (828-251-5565). Overlooking historic Pack Square in the heart of downtown Asheville, this open, airy café is casual, yet elegant. It offers the freshest in produce, seafood, and meats. Lunch includes salads and a variety of sandwiches. Menu changes are frequent, so a trip here always offers something new. Shrimp étouffée and pork tenderloin with chipotle are among the dinner entrées that I've enjoyed. The café has an extensive wine list. Catering is available. Lunch is served Monday through Saturday and dinner daily.

- **Charlotte Street Grill and Pub**. Moderate. 157 Charlotte Street (828-253-5348 or 828-252-2948). Built in the early 1920s, this was north Asheville's first drugstore. "The Pub" opened in 1976; the offerings in this festive, intimate setting lean toward appetizers and sandwiches. The building was later enlarged to include fine dining upstairs at the Charlotte Street Grill, which offers an extensive menu featuring meats, seafood, pasta, and tofu. Whether you prefer "The Grill" or "The Pub," you can enjoy a unique and tasty dining experience here. Lunch and dinner are served Monday through Saturday.

- **Early Girl Eatery**. Moderate. 8 Wall Street (828-259-9292). The locals will tell you that no trip to Asheville is complete without a stop at Early Girl. The emphasis here is healthy, made-from-scratch cuisine with a regional theme. Dishes range from house-made sausage, shrimp and grits, and vegan tofu scramble in the morning to pan-fried chicken and black-eyed-pea cakes at night. The folks at Early Girl believe in supporting local agriculture and work closely with local farms and dairies to bring guests the freshest ingredients possible. The atmosphere is comfortable, the food amazing, and the whole experience not soon forgotten. Breakfast, lunch, and dinner are served daily; a sumptuous Sunday brunch is also offered.

- **Flying Frog Café**. Moderate. 1 Battery Park (828-254-9411). Okay, how about this for different? This restaurant's menu features French, Cajun, German, and Indian foods—and it works! The eclectic menu offers diverse specialties such as bouillabaisse, jambalaya, schnitzel, and crab cakes. All of the curries and delicious blends of seasonings and spices are prepared in-house. The extensive wine list reflects the café's international flair. Al fresco dining is available in the sidewalk café and more formal dining at the café downstairs; the full menu is available at the bar upstairs. Lunch and dinner are served daily in the sidewalk café and the bar. Dinner is served downstairs from Wednesday to Sunday.

- **Jack of the Wood**. Moderate/Inexpensive. 95 Patton Avenue (828-252-5445). This is the place to go for authentic pub fare and handcrafted ales. An Asheville favorite for more than 10 years, Jack of the Wood offers everything from shepherd's pie, fish and chips, and first-rate pub burgers to its highly acclaimed Green Man Ales. Throw in live Celtic, bluegrass, and traditional Appalachian music Wednesday through Saturday nights and you've got the makings for a great night out. The pub opens daily for dinner at 4 P.M.; a late-night menu is available after 10 P.M. Wednesday through Saturday.

- ***Laughing Seed Café***. Moderate/Inexpensive. 40 Wall Street (828-252-3445). This popular downtown restaurant features a vegetarian menu that is innovative and delicious—and this from an author who is an avowed meat lover. Pasta, sandwiches, and daily specials are offered. You'll find Mexican, Indian, Asian, Mediterranean, and New American accents in the cuisine. Outdoor dining is available when weather permits. The atmosphere is open and casual. This is a great place to take a break from exploring Asheville's shops and boutiques. Lunch and dinner are served Wednesday through Monday.

Nearby

- ***Black Mountain*** is a small community about 15 miles east of Asheville in the Swannanoa River Valley. The town has a history of attracting nonconformists and freethinkers. Oddly enough, it is also the center of the largest concentration of religious retreats in the United States; there are 20 in a 35-mile radius. Black Mountain, once a spiritual center for the Cherokee Indians, was the site of the experimental Black Mountain College from 1933 to 1956. Today, the town draws visitors who come to see the beautiful Montreat Conference Center and to enjoy shopping for crafts and antiques.

- In the downtown historic district, you'll find a number of shops selling antiques and collectibles. When you're ready for a bite to eat, try lunch at ***Pepper's Deli*** (828-669-1885), at 122 Cherry Street, noted for its remarkable display of Dr Pepper memorabilia; you can even order a Dr Pepper served steaming hot. Another great spot is ***Veranda Café & Gifts*** (828-669-8864), at 119 Cherry Street, which offers a relaxing atmosphere and a delicious assortment of sandwiches, salads, soups, daily specials, and tempting desserts. Al fresco dining and pizza, anyone? Head for ***My Father's Pizza*** (828-669-4944), at 110 Cherry Street, where you'll find gourmet pizzas, pasta, subs, stromboli, and salads, all made from scratch. After a day of shopping, you'll find no better way to unwind and ponder your purchases than a stay at the ***Red Rocker Inn*** (888-669-5991 or 828-669-5991; www.redrockerinn.com), at 136 North Dougherty Street. This old-fashioned inn, open from mid-February through December, has a wide porch that looks out onto a beautiful tree-shaded yard.

- **_Craggy Gardens_**, located between Milepost 363 and Milepost 369 on the Blue Ridge Parkway, isn't really a garden at all. Instead, it's an ideal place for viewing wide slopes bursting with mountain laurel and rhododendron in June and the incredible display of fall colors in October. Trails wind among trees, shrubs, and flowers. The picnic area commands a striking view of the Blue Ridge. The visitor center has displays on the area's ecology. The rangers occasionally present interpretive programs. For information, call 828-298-0398.

- The **_Zebulon B. Vance Homestead_** is in Weaverville, about 12 miles north of Asheville. A state historic site, it features a reconstruction of the mountain home of one of North Carolina's preeminent statesmen. Vance is best known as North Carolina's governor during the Civil War. The two-story pine-log home has period furniture, some of it from the original house, which was built in 1790. Among the log outbuildings are a corncrib, a springhouse, a loom house, a slave house, a smokehouse, and a toolhouse. A guide is on hand to explain what life was like in the mountains for the Vances and other homesteaders. The visitor center offers displays that further illustrate the times. Guests are welcome to bring a picnic lunch to enjoy on the grounds. The homestead is open Tuesday through Saturday from 10 A.M. to 4 P.M. from November to March and Tuesday through Saturday from 9 A.M. to 5 P.M. from April to October. Admission is free. For information, call 828-645-6706.

St. Lawrence Basilica

The most beautiful building in Asheville may be the Spanish Baroque-style St. Lawrence Basilica on Haywood Street. The most striking feature of the church is its central dome, which is built wholly of tiles and is entirely self-supporting. Measuring 58 feet by 82 feet, it is reputed to be the largest freestanding elliptical dome in North America.

St. Lawrence Basilica is filled with bas-relief and other sculptures, stained-glass windows, ornately carved doors, and glazed tiles from all over the world; some of the wooden statues come from Spain and the stained-glass windows from Germany, for example. The beautiful altar is topped with an 1,800-pound block of Tennessee marble.

St. Lawrence Catholic Church was designated a basilica by Pope John Paul II in April 1993. The basilica designation is given to certain churches because of their antiquity, dignity, historical importance, or significance as places of worship. At that time, there were only 33 basilicas in the United States. As a basilica, St. Lawrence has the privilege of displaying the pontifical seal. The dominant feature of the seal is a pair of crossed keys, which symbolize the keys to the Kingdom. Basilicas also have special responsibilities, such as promoting the study of the documents of the pope and the Holy See, especially those concerning the sacred liturgy. Additionally, a basilica has the responsibility to promote the participation of the faithful in the Mass and the Liturgy of the Hours, especially matins (morning prayers) and vespers (evening prayers).

St. Lawrence Basilica is the only church built by the renowned Rafael Guastavino. The massive stone foundation and the brick superstructure give silent testimony to the architect's desire to build an edifice that would endure for generations. There are no beams of wood or steel in the entire structure.

A visit to St. Lawrence Basilica offers a chance not only to view fine architecture, beautiful stained glass, and wonderful sculpture, but also to witness some of the sacred traditions of the Catholic Church that are not often on display in the modern world.

The Southern Mountains

Hendersonville

Brevard

Highlands

Franklin

By Sue Clark

The southern mountains are an area of stark contrasts and rich beauty. Don't be deceived by what looks like a highway on your road map—it could just as easily be a winding, twisting way to get from one town to another. But arduous drives are rewarded by wonderful surprises here. Within easy walking distance of those "highways," you'll encounter waterfalls to slide down, waterfalls to walk behind, and even a waterfall you used to be able to drive under but for the recent intrusion of a boulder the size of a house! In this four-county area south of Asheville, you'll find the home of one of America's greatest poets, a world-class music festival, boutiques, golf courses, and gem mines. Each trip here provides many reasons for a return visit.

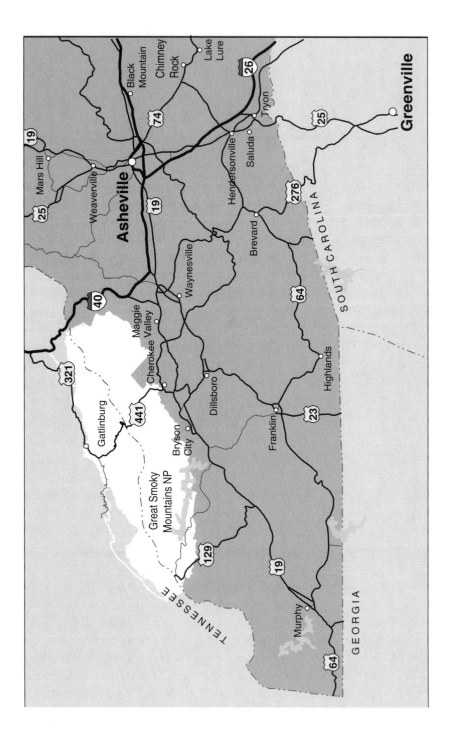

HENDERSONVILLE

$\mathcal{E}$stablished in 1840, Hendersonville is ideally situated on a plateau between the Blue Ridge Mountains and the Great Smoky Mountains. Thanks to its mild climate and moderate altitude (2,200 feet), many people find this the perfect place to live and vacation. What's not to like? You can play golf 11 months of the year, there is little crime or pollution, and you'll find lots of friendly people. The area attracts many retirees.

Apples are the mainstay of Henderson County's economy. The North Carolina Apple Festival takes place in Hendersonville on Labor Day weekend. The county produces 70 percent of the state's leading fruit crop. Local farmers grow about 8 million bushels of Red and Golden Delicious, Rome Beauty, and Stayman apples each year.

Downtown Hendersonville is great for walking. Small shops, boutiques, and restaurants line the main streets.

JUST THE FACTS

Hendersonville is 22 miles south of Asheville via U.S. 25 or Interstate 26. Both intersect U.S. 64 in Hendersonville.

The closest airport is Asheville Regional Airport; call 828-684-2226 for information.

Hendersonville's bus station is on Seventh Avenue East; call 828-693-1201.

The Henderson County Travel and Tourism office, at 201 South Main Street, is a great place to start your planning; call 800-828-4244 or visit www.historichendersonville.org. You may reach the chamber of commerce at 877-836-1414 or 828-692-1413.

The daily newspaper is the *Hendersonville Times-News*. Current-events information, a shopping guide, and a dining guide are included in the free publication *This Week in WNC*.

PHOTOGRAPH IN BACKGROUND ON PAGE 509—

Chimney Rock
COURTESY OF NORTH CAROLINA DIVISION OF TOURISM, FILM AND SPORTS DEVELOPMENT

Things to Do

Historic Places, Gardens, and Tours

- **Carl Sandburg Home National Historic Site** is located south of Hendersonville in the town of Flat Rock. The 264-acre farm called Connemara is where the Pulitzer Prize-winning poet and biographer spent the last 22 years of his life. In 1945, Sandburg bought the property and moved here with his wife, Paula, who was renowned for raising champion goats. In 1967, shortly after Sandburg's death at age 89, Connemara became a national historic site.

  You'll immediately get a sense of Connemara's peacefulness as you walk up the trail from the information center to the white three-story house. Built around 1838, the home is surrounded by trees and situated with a lovely view of the rolling countryside. Nearby are several outbuildings. About a quarter-mile away is the barn, where the goats were housed and tended. A few goats are still kept there.

  In the reception area of the house, you can see a filmed interview of Sandburg conducted by Edward R. Murrow. The furnishings, family pictures, shelves of books, and huge stacks of papers and magazines in the living room and Sandburg's study have been left just as they were when he was in residence. On the dining-room table are his thermos and a handful of letters to be opened.

  In the summer, actors and actresses from the nearby Flat Rock Playhouse dramatize tales from Sandburg's *Rootabaga Stories*, a book of children's folk tales, in a small outdoor amphitheater located on the playhouse grounds. Performances of *World of Carl Sandburg* and *Sandburg's Lincoln* are also given. Shows are offered Tuesday through Saturday; admission is free.

  The home is open daily except Christmas from 9 A.M. to 5 P.M. Admission to the grounds is free. Adults are charged a small fee for the house tour, but children under 17 are admitted free. The tour lasts about 30 minutes, after which you may enjoy walking the two marked trails on the property. For more information, call 828-693-4178.

- **Oakdale Cemetery**, on U.S. 64 West, is the site of "Wolfe's Angel." Thomas Wolfe's first novel, *Look Homeward, Angel*, contained numerous references to an angel statue carved from Italian marble. The statue in Oakdale Cemetery served as the inspiration. The author's father, W. O. Wolfe, sold it to the Johnson family to mark the family plot here. The angel holds a lily in her left hand while she extends her right hand upward. The statue is protected by a wrought-iron fence. A historical marker is located on the highway.

CULTURAL OFFERINGS

■ *Flat Rock Playhouse*, on U.S. 25 in Flat Rock, is the state theater of North Carolina. It is a professional summer theater that presents eight or nine comedies, mysteries, and musicals from late May to mid-December. Periodically, Thomas Wolfe's *Look Homeward, Angel* is presented in honor of the local boy. For information, call 828-693-0731 or visit www.flatrockplayhouse.org.

SPECIAL SHOPPING

■ *Henderson County Farmers Mutual Curb Market*, at 221 North Church Street, offers home-grown flowers, fresh fruits and vegetables, baked goods, handmade crafts, and an impressive array of pickles, relishes, jellies, and jams. It's also a great place to chat with the locals. The market is open Tuesday, Thursday, and Saturday from 8 A.M. to 2 P.M. from May to December. It is open Tuesday and Saturday from January through April. For more information, call 828-692-8012.

■ *Downtown Hendersonville* has experienced a revitalization in recent years. Within easy walking distance are antique shops, art galleries, and specialty stores. Visitors can go back in time at an old-fashioned soda shop located in a pharmacy that has occupied the same spot since the turn of the 20th century. Downtown shoppers will find everything from boutiques filled with local crafts to galleries featuring modern-art exhibits.

■ My favorite downtown spot is *Kilwin's Chocolate Shoppe* (828-698-9794), on Main Street. My son and I consider ourselves fudge experts, so when a friend recommended a new place in Hendersonville as the home of the best fudge she'd ever tasted, we knew we had to check it out. Imagine my delight upon discovering that the "new" place was actually a beacon of my childhood. You see, the original Kilwin's is in Petoskey, Michigan, where my family had a summer home when I was a child.

The owners in Hendersonville assured me it truly is the same Kilwin's; in fact, they had to travel to Petoskey to learn to make fudge the Kilwin's way. Don't limit yourself to just the fudge. There's also ice cream, caramel corn, brittle, taffy, and candies, all of which live up to Kilwin's reputation for quality.

RECREATION

■ *Holmes State Forest*, located eight miles southwest of Hendersonville on Crab Creek Road, is a managed forest that offers picnic areas, hiking trails, and sites for tent camping. Some of the trees have button-activated recordings describing aspects of the forest. Holmes State Forest is open for visitors Tuesday through Sunday from mid-March to the Friday before Thanksgiving. For more information, call 828-692-0100.

■ *DuPont State Forest*, located off U.S. 64 between Hendersonville and Brevard, encompasses over 10,000 acres of forestland. Hiking, biking, and horseback riding are allowed on designated trails. Demonstrations on soil and water protection, wildlife management, and forest management are offered throughout the year. For information, call 828-251-6509 or visit www.dupontforest.com.

SEASONAL EVENTS

■ The **North Carolina Apple Festival**, held Labor Day weekend, celebrates the apple harvest with street dancing and crafts for sale. The King Apple Parade rolls through downtown on Labor Day. For more information, call 828-697-4557.

■ The **Garden Jubilee** is held the Saturday and Sunday of Memorial Day weekend. The emphasis here is on plants and garden advice. Arts and crafts are available for sale. Call 800-828-4244.

■ *Art on Main*, held the first full weekend in August, features regional artists displaying and selling their fine arts and crafts. Call 828-697-2022.

■ Those interested in the display and sale of new and old quilts will enjoy the **Annual Quilt Fest**, held in October. It is sponsored by the Tar Heel Piecemakers and the Western North Carolina Quilters Guild. Boutiques sell merchandise at the festival. Call 800-828-4244.

Places to Stay

INNS AND BED-AND-BREAKFASTS

- **Elizabeth Leigh Inn**. Expensive. 908 Fifth Avenue West (866-312-9707 or 828-698-9707; www.elizabethleighinn.com). This 1893 mansion was one of the finest homes of old Hendersonville. Now fully restored and beautifully decorated, it is listed on the National Register of Historic Places. The Elizabeth Leigh Inn is the place to come for a quiet, luxurious, and highly pampered getaway. It offers a full gourmet breakfast, afternoon tea, private baths, homemade treats, and evening turn-down service. The inn can also handle an exquisite garden wedding and reception or any other special event that requires that perfect touch of elegance.

- **Mélange Bed-and-Breakfast**. Expensive. 1230 Fifth Avenue West (800-303-5253 or 828-697-5253; www.melangebb.com). This beautiful old mansion, restored in 1996, offers Old World charm and tradition and European flair. High ceilings, marble fireplaces, ornate mirrors, Mediterranean porches, crystal chandeliers, and antique furnishings make the inn elegant and warm. The large guest rooms and the two-room suite have either solid brass, old plantation oak, or French canopy beds; each room has a private bath. Room rates include a gourmet breakfast served in the rose garden, on the covered porches, or in the formal dining room.

- **Highland Lake Inn**. Expensive/Moderate. Highland Lake Road in Flat Rock (800-762-1376 or 828-693-6812; www.HLInn.com). This country retreat is a haven of hospitality, elegance, and unspoiled natural beauty. The choice of accommodations includes the elegant inn, the historic lodge, family-style cottages, and rustic cabin rooms. Each room is distinctively decorated; some have whirlpool tubs, wet bars, canopy beds, and fireplaces. The rates include a sumptuous Southern breakfast, cable television, a newspaper, and full use of the extensive grounds, which include a lake, a swimming pool, tennis courts, a horseshoes pit, and a volleyball court; guests may use the canoes and paddleboats, ride bicycles, or fish. There's even a collection of barnyard animals; in the morning, you're welcome to watch the goats being milked. Highland Lake Inn is ideal for weddings, banquets, family reunions, and corporate retreats.

- **Woodfield Inn**. Expensive/Moderate. On U.S. 25 in Flat Rock (800-533-6016 or 828-693-6016; www.woodfieldinn.com). Woodfield Inn has been receiving guests since 1852. It is a landmark establishment with a long tradition of Southern hospitality. A three-story frame hotel with a huge front lawn, it has an enormous entrance hall, a large sitting room, and three dining rooms downstairs. On the upper floors, which slant slightly, are Victorian bedrooms with high ceilings and French doors that open onto a veranda. Only three of the guest rooms have private baths. Throughout the inn are antique furnishings, some of which have been here since the Civil War. Continental breakfast is included in the room rate.

- **Claddagh Inn**. Moderate. 755 North Main Street (800-225-4700 or 828-697-7778; www.claddaghinn.com). This three-story frame house with a wraparound veranda has been an inn for 90 years. It lends the same feeling you might get if you were visiting your grandmother. Each of the 14 guest rooms and two suites is graciously appointed and has a private bath. A full country breakfast is served in the dining room.

- **The Waverly Inn**. Moderate. 783 North Main Street (800-537-8195 or 828-693-9193; www.waverlyinn.com). Located within easy walking distance of downtown, this three-story house has been lovingly renovated and is listed on the National Register of Historic Places. The beautiful veranda filled with rocking chairs invites guests to enjoy the relaxing atmosphere. The 14 guest rooms are beautifully appointed. All are comfortably decorated and have private baths. Room rates include a sumptuous home-cooked breakfast. Guests also enjoy the freshly baked cookies and evening hors d'oeuvres.

Places to Eat

- **Flight**. Expensive. 401 North Main Street (828-694-1030). Housed in an old bank building, Flight features wonderful international cuisine and wood-grilled specialties cooked over locally grown applewood. The elegant, up-scale atmosphere is accentuated by the artwork of local artists. Menu selections include applewood-grilled steaks, fresh seafood, pork, lamb, pasta, fresh salads, and wood-grilled pizzas. Dinner is served Monday through Saturday. Reservations are suggested.

- **Highland Lake Inn**. Expensive. Highland Lake Road in Flat Rock (828-696-9094; www.HLInn.com). This place offers fine dining in a casual country setting. The vibrant, exciting menu features innovative cuisine that showcases the chef's creativity. The restaurant prides itself on fresh ingredients, including vegetables and herbs from its own gardens. Dinner is served Tuesday through Saturday, and brunch is offered on Sunday. Reservations are requested.

- **Blackwater Grille**. Expensive/Moderate. 1715 Brevard Road (U.S. 64 West) two miles west of downtown Hendersonville (828-693-0856). The Blackwater Grille serves seasonal, upscale "Southern Highland cuisine" featuring fish and game from around the southern Appalachians. Guests can dine inside around the fireplace or outside under the trees in a comfortable and casual atmosphere perfect for family and friends. Lunch and dinner are served Monday through Saturday.

- **Expressions**. Expensive/Moderate. 114 North Main Street (828-693-8516). Expressions offers continental dining in a renovated storefront. Plum wallpaper, dark green carpeting, and brass lamps on the tables set the mood for the sophisticated menu and the restaurant's seasonal specialties. The chef-owned Expressions has received many accolades and awards. Dinner is served Monday through Saturday.

- **Woodfield Inn**. Expensive/Moderate. On U.S. 25 in Flat Rock (828-693-6016). This inn has been a dining tradition since 1852, when it was a stop on the stagecoach line. Warm muffins are brought to your table for you to enjoy while reading the menu, which includes fried chicken, baked ham, prime rib, and trout almandine. After one of the delicious homemade desserts, you'll want to linger on the veranda. The restaurant is open for dinner Wednesday through Sunday and for brunch on Sunday.

- **Blue Sky Café**. Moderate. 3987 Hendersonville Road in Fletcher (828-684-1247). Okay, if you know me, you know I have two kids, so I'm always looking for a restaurant that offers food fit for the adults without boring the kids to tears. This is the place to go for a relaxed, fun, family-friendly atmosphere where there's something on the menu for everyone, whether you crave a delicious vegetarian wrap or a big, juicy hand-pattied burger. And yes, there's a great kids' menu that goes beyond mac 'n' cheese and chicken nuggets. Blue Sky has creative lunch and dinner specials and a really friendly staff. Guests can enjoy a cold beer or a glass of wine on the patio. The café is open for lunch and dinner Monday through Saturday.

- *Hannah Flanagan's Pub.* Inexpensive. 300 North Main Street (828-696-1665). As in any good pub, the bar is the focus of this local hangout. Recently expanded to offer more table seating, Hannah Flanagan's is a great place to stop and take stock of your shopping expedition. Patrons enjoy the hearty soups, sandwiches, and other traditional pub fare, as well as the fine selection of imported beer. The fish and chips is simply the best I've ever tasted. This is one of those great pubs that makes you feel comfortable the minute you walk in the door. Lunch and dinner are served daily.

Nearby

- To reach *Chimney Rock Park* from Hendersonville, take U.S. 64 East to Bat Cave, then turn right on U.S. 74. Located 15 miles east of Hendersonville, this private park includes a massive rock formation known for its tall, narrow shape. Chimney Rock rises 225 feet above the entrance to Hickory Nut Gorge and provides a 75-mile panoramic view of Lake Lure and the Blue Ridge Mountains. Visitors cross the Rocky Broad River just past the entrance to the park; from there, they begin a three-mile drive to the base of the rock formation, after which they're transported to the top via an elevator that runs up a 26-story shaft hewn in the granite. For the more adventurous, a trail of plank steps also leads to the summit. Once on top, you can enjoy the view from the fenced-in overlook or from inside the Sky Lounge, which has a gift shop and a snack bar. The park also offers picnic areas with grills, a playground, an interpretive nature center, and hiking trails. Chimney Rock Park is open daily except for Thanksgiving, Christmas, and New Year's. An admission fee is charged. The ticket office is open from 8:30 A.M. to 4:30 P.M. during daylight saving time; otherwise, it's open until 5:30 P.M. The park closes 90 minutes after the ticket office. For more information, call 800-277-9611 or 828-625-9611.

Chimney Rock
COURTESY OF NORTH CAROLINA DIVISION OF TOURISM, FILM AND SPORTS DEVELOPMENT

■ If you'd like to stay in the area, you can't go wrong with the **Lake Lure Inn and Spa** (828-625-2525; www.lakelureinn.com), on U.S. 64 in neighboring Lake Lure. This elegant 1927 inn, recently restored to its full splendor, offers a swimming pool, a full-service spa, and an expansive veranda overlooking the lake.

■ **Saluda**, on U.S. 176 approximately 12 miles southeast of Hendersonville, is a small community where a number of craftspeople live and labor. You can see some of their work and an array of regional country antiques in the town's old train depot, which has been converted into shops. Saluda is also the site of the famous Saluda Grade, the steepest main-line railroad grade in America.

A noteworthy local hostelry is the **Orchard Inn** (828-749-5471; www.orchardinn.com), on U.S. 176. It occupies an old vacation retreat built for the Brotherhood of Railway Clerks. As for dining in Saluda, there are two excellent choices—the **Purple Onion** and the **Saluda Grade Café**. Both are on Main Street and offer excellent food and a casual atmosphere. Either one will make your trip to Saluda worthwhile.

■ **Tryon**, on U.S. 176 east of Saluda, is named for William Tryon, the British governor of the North Carolina colony. The town's pretty, steep Main Street offers a collection of great little shops and eateries. All in all, this small mountain town is a true gem.

Visitors come to Tryon for its gift and craft shops and to see works by local artists and craftspeople at the **Tryon Fine Arts Center** (828-859-8322). Tryon is also renowned for its nationally and regionally sanctioned equestrian events, which take place at **FENCE** (Foothills Equestrian Nature Center); for information, call 828-859-9021 or visit www.fence.org. If competition of a culinary nature is more your style, head to Tryon during the second week of June for the **Blue Ridge BBQ Festival**. This event attracts over 25,000 people and features live music and a juried craft exhibition. More than 70 teams participate in the two-day cooking event, which has been sanctioned by the governor as the official North Carolina State Barbecue Championship. For more information, call 828-859-RIBS or visit www.BBQfestival.com.

If you plan to stay in town, try the **Pine Crest Inn & Restaurant** (828-859-9135; www.pinecrestinn.com), at 200 Pine Crest Lane. Listed on the National Register of Historic Places, this inn has received 13 consecutive AAA Four Diamond awards. It offers affordable rooms, luxurious suites, private cottages, a modern conference center, and beautiful gardens. The restaurant is renowned for its relaxing atmosphere and its excellent cuisine featuring fresh seasonal ingredients. It has received *Wine Spectator* magazine's Award of Excellence for eight straight years; the extensive wine list is a perfect match for the fine, expertly prepared cuisine.

■ To reach **Pearson's Falls**, look for the sign directing you to turn off U.S. 176 approximately three miles from Saluda. You'll then need to travel one mile on S.R. 1102 and hike an easy quarter-mile trail to the 90-foot falls. The area is maintained by the Tryon Garden Club. A small admission fee is charged.

Connestee Falls
COURTESY OF NORTH CAROLINA DIVISION OF TOURISM, FILM AND SPORTS DEVELOPMENT

BREVARD

*O*n the edge of Pisgah National Forest sits the pretty little town of Brevard. Its permanent population of 7,000 swells to many times that number during the annual Brevard Music Festival. Brevard is in the heart of an area called "the Land of Waterfalls." It is the county seat of Transylvania County, whose name means "across the woods."

Brevard's downtown has shops, restaurants, a movie theater, antique malls, and a picturesque brick courthouse. Beyond downtown, you'll see attractive homes with big porches on shaded residential streets. Given the size of the town, Brevard's cultural offerings come as a surprise to many visitors. The mild climate and attractive landscape draw a large number of retirees, summer residents, and tourists. Brevard is an ideal place to stay if you enjoy driving through the mountains and stopping at waterfalls.

JUST THE FACTS

Brevard is three miles south of the intersection of U.S. 276 and N.C. 280, about 30 miles south of Asheville.

The Brevard Chamber of Commerce is located at 35 West Main Street; call 800-648-4523 or 828-883-3700 or visit www.brevardncchamber.org or www.visitwaterfalls.com.

The local newspaper is the *Transylvania Times*, published semiweekly.

Things to Do

HISTORIC PLACES, GARDENS, AND TOURS

■ The **Cradle of Forestry in America**, on U.S. 276 in Pisgah National Forest, is another legacy of George Vanderbilt. When Vanderbilt bought property in 1889 to create Biltmore Estate (see the chapter on Asheville), he hired Gifford Pinchot to manage the forestland. Pinchot was the first man in America to practice selective timber cutting. Pinchot's successor, Dr. Carl Schenck, started the first school of forestry in America, the Biltmore Forest School, which lasted from 1898 until 1913. In 1968, Congress established the 6,400-acre Pisgah National Forest.

The Cradle of Forestry in America is a national historic site commemorating the birthplace of scientific forestry and forestry education in America. The visitor center has exhibits, an 18-minute film outlining the history of the forestry school, a gift shop, and a snack bar. Two interpretive trails are on the property. The Biltmore Forest School Campus Trail visits restored and reconstructed buildings that depict the life of the first forestry students at the turn of the 20th century. The Forest Festival Trail passes early forestry equipment, such as a 1915 logging locomotive and a steam-powered sawmill. The Cradle of Forestry is open daily from 9 A.M. to 5 P.M. from April through November. A small admission fee is charged. Call 828-877-3130 for more information.

Brevard Music Festival
COURTESY OF NORTH CAROLINA DIVISION OF TOURISM, FILM AND SPORTS DEVELOPMENT

CULTURAL OFFERINGS

■ Held for seven weeks each summer, the **Brevard Music Festival** presents a smorgasbord of more than 70 performances ranging from symphonies and pops to Broadway musicals and grand operas.

In 1936, Davidson College in Davidson, North Carolina, began a summer music camp. In 1943, the operation moved to an abandoned summer camp in Brevard. Three years later, the director and a few local students started the Brevard Music Festival, which at that time was a one-week series of performances by those attending the camp. The Brevard Music Camp subsequently built an 1,800-seat open-sided auditorium.

The camp offers private lessons, a concerto competition, an opera workshop, and performance experience with the Transylvania Symphony, the Brevard Music Center Orchestra, brass, wind, and woodwind ensembles, and a chamber choir. Students can earn college credit. During the festival, they have the opportunity to perform with guest artists.

Each summer, more than 400 of the nation's finest musicians gather to teach and perform. Guest artists have included Boston Pops conductor Keith Lockhart, vocalist Frederica von Stade, and the Louisiana Jazz Ensemble. Each season also promises four beautifully staged operas or musical theater productions, such as Lerner and Loewe's *Brigadoon*, Strauss's *Die Fledermaus*, and Verdi's *Aida*.

It's a good idea to purchase tickets in advance; the festival has many devoted followers who buy season tickets and attend every performance. If you intend to stay in the area during the festival, make room reservations well in advance. Some performances are free; a fee is charged for others. For more information, call 888-384-8682 or 828-862-2105 or visit www.brevardmusic.org.

SPECIAL SHOPPING

■ **The Heart of Brevard**, as the locals like to refer to it, is brimming with boutiques, galleries, specialty shops, restaurants, and coffee houses. Visitors can also find numerous outfitters' shops in the area, as well as guide services for mountain climbing, mountain biking, canoeing, and other outdoor pastimes.

■ The **White Squirrel Shoppe**, at 2 West Main Street, is housed in the historic McMinn Building. It features antiques, gifts, collectibles, custom pieces from Brevard and Transylvania County, home accessories, heritage lace, furniture, and more. The relaxing atmosphere includes a 12-foot waterfall! For information, call 888-729-7329 or 828-877-3530 or visit www.whitesquirrelshoppe.com.

RECREATION

■ **Pisgah National Forest** is a land of mile-high peaks, cascading waterfalls, and heavily forested slopes. It is an ideal place for recreation. The forest gets its name from Mount Pisgah, a prominent peak in the area. In the 1700s, a Scots-Irish minister saw the peak and named it for the biblical mountain from which Moses saw the Promised Land after 40 years of wandering in the wilderness.

■ Waterfall viewing is one of the favorite activities in the area. The most popular drive goes north from Brevard on U.S. 276 through Pisgah National Forest to **Looking Glass Falls**. You can see the waterfall from the road, but parking your car and walking to get a closer view is a much better way to experience this breathtaking natural wonder. U.S. 276 continues to **Sliding Rock**. Be sure to pack your bathing suit, because the best way to experience this water wonder is on your behind. A lifeguard is on duty in the summer, and a bathhouse is provided. There's no better means to cool off on a hot summer day. Another popular option is to drive west out of Brevard on U.S. 64. You'll pass **Dry Falls**, where you can take an easy walk behind a 75-foot wall of water.

■ **Hiking** opportunities abound in the area. If you take U.S. 276 to the Blue Ridge Parkway, a right turn will lead you to Mount Pisgah, and a left will lead you past the Devil's Courthouse. Both areas offer hikes with

Pisgah National Forest
COURTESY OF NORTH CAROLINA DIVISION OF TOURISM, FILM AND SPORTS DEVELOPMENT

breathtaking views. Information on hiking trails can be obtained at the outfitters' shops.

■ *Fly-fishing* on Transylvania County's Davidson River is an obsession to many. *Trout Unlimited* magazine ranks the Davidson one of America's top 10 trout streams. The Davidson and other area streams are stocked with brook, brown, and rainbow trout from the Pisgah Fish Hatchery. If you plan to fish, you'll need a license, which can be obtained at many of the outfitters' shops.

The national forest is managed to provide the best combination of uses to benefit the general public while protecting the long-term quality of the forest. For more information on facilities, hiking, and biking, stop at the information center, located in the ranger station about a mile into the forest on U.S. 276 from U.S. 64. Or you can call the Pisgah National Forest supervisor at 828-257-4200.

This section of the forest lying southwest of Asheville between Brevard and Waynesville is the Pisgah Ranger District. The Grandfather Ranger District, northeast of Asheville, is covered in the chapter on Banner Elk, Beech Mountain, and Linville.

The Greystone Inn
Courtesy of The Greystone Inn, photography by Timothy Lee Schermerhorn

Places to Stay

INNS AND BED-AND-BREAKFASTS

■ *Greystone Inn*. Deluxe/Expensive. Greystone Lane in Lake Toxaway (800-824-5766 or 828-966-4700; www.greystoneinn.com). The magnificent mountains, beautiful Lake Toxaway, a charming historic mansion, and fine cuisine are just a few of the superlatives at the Greystone Inn, located 17 miles west of Brevard. Built in the early 1900s, this mansion was converted into a luxury resort in 1984. Each of the 33 rooms is a perfect blend of comfort and elegance. The 19 rooms in the mansion range from cozy spaces with private baths, fireplaces, and great views of the lake to the spectacular Presidential Suite, which is large enough to accommodate a family (or two!). The Hillmont rooms, located in a separate building, have private balconies overlooking the lake, marble baths, and extra space with fireplaces, wet bars, and hidden televisions, VCRs, and stereos. From May 1 through October 31, this mountain aerie offers tennis, fishing, windsurfing, sailing, swimming, kayaking, and canoeing, as well as horseback riding and golf at nearby Lake Toxaway Country Club. The marina has boats, canoes, water skis, and fishing equipment. Hikers will be enticed by the winding paths along the Horsepasture River, which skirts a series of waterfalls including Rainbow Falls, a cascade nearly 200 feet tall. And did I mention the spa? What better way to experience mountain air and lake breezes than an afternoon of pampering chosen from the wide array of spa treatments? Room rates include breakfast, dinner, afternoon tea, evening hors d'oeuvres, and a nightly champagne cruise aboard a lovingly restored wooden boat, the *Miss Lucy*. The food here is every bit as enticing as the resort. The beautiful setting, the wide array of activities, and a staff that takes service to a new level combine to make this one terrific getaway.

■ *Earthshine Mountain Lodge*. Expensive/Moderate. 1600 Golden Road in Lake Toxaway (828-862-4207; www.earthshinemtnlodge.com). Situated on a 70-acre farm, this lodge is built entirely of logs and is decorated with log furnishings throughout. The eight guest rooms have private baths and sleeping lofts. The real attraction, however, is the array of activities for guests. The rope-climbing area resembles those at Outward Bound. There are also opportunities for horseback riding, hiking, and rock climbing. A barnyard on the premises is filled with animals for the children. And there's always entertainment for guests after dinner. Room rates include all three meals.

■ *The Pines Country Inn*. Moderate. 719 Hart Road in the town of Pisgah Forest (828-877-3131; www.pinescountryinn.bizonthe.net). This inn, located a short distance from Brevard, is in a peaceful farming area overlooking the Little River Valley. Guests can see horses grazing and wake to the songs of birds. The house, built in 1883, has been an inn since 1905. The atmosphere is homey and comfortable. The Pines offers 18 guest rooms, some in separate cottages. Room rates include breakfast.

■ *The Womble Inn*. Moderate. 301 West Main Street (828-884-4770; www.thewombleinn.com). This New Orleans-style house three blocks from the middle of Brevard is where guests at the music festival often stay. Each of the six rooms has a private bath. A full breakfast is provided. The inn serves lunch Tuesday through Friday and will pack a picnic basket for a takeout lunch. It is also renowned for its catering.

■ *The Red House Inn*. Inexpensive. 412 West Probart Street (828-884-9349). The Red House Inn sits on a corner shielded from traffic by high hedges. Porches extend across the front of the two-story house, built in 1851 as a trading post. The oak woodwork is polished to a high gloss, and the comforters are fluffed on the antique beds. Room rates include a full breakfast served in the dining room.

Places to Eat

- **Falls Landing**. Moderate. 23 East Main Street (828-884-2835). This restaurant specializes in fresh seafood such as grilled salmon, broiled trout, swordfish, mahi-mahi, Maine lobster, clams, oysters, jumbo shrimp, and steamed mussels. The menu also includes pasta dishes, top-grade steaks, chicken, and homemade soups and desserts. Falls Landing is open for lunch Monday through Saturday and for dinner Tuesday through Saturday.

- **Grammy's Bistro**. Moderate. On the corner of Main and Broad streets (828-862-4746). This bistro offers deli-stacked gourmet sandwiches, tortilla wraps, black bean and veggie burgers, turkey chili, fresh salads, soups, and daily specials. Grammy's serves breakfast, lunch, and dinner Monday through Saturday.

- **Jason's Main Street Grill**. Moderate. 48 East Main Street (828-883-4447). A casual setting for some excellent food, Jason's offers a wide variety of steaks, pasta, seafood, salads, and sandwiches. Among the innovative dishes served here are Caribbean conch fritters, balsamic chicken and Brie sandwiches, peach-glazed salmon, lobster ravioli, and baby back ribs. The breakfast menu is also varied and inviting. Jason's is open seven days a week. The hours change according to the season. Reservations are recommended but not required.

- **Bracken Mountain Bakery**. Inexpensive. South Broad Street (828-883-4034). This bakery specializes in European crusty breads and American sandwich breads. The breads and pastries are made from scratch and baked fresh daily on the premises. While this is primarily a takeout operation, tables are available for those who wish to dine in. Flatbreads and filled pocket breads are available for a delicious lunch treat. Lunch is served Monday through Saturday from May to October and Tuesday through Saturday the rest of the year.

HIGHLANDS

The unique town of Highlands has a rich history, a wonderful climate, and an enviable way of life. Highlands stands tall in the mountains. Its altitude is 4,118 feet, making it one of the highest incorporated towns east of the Mississippi River. The surrounding mountains soar to over 5,000 feet. During July, the average temperature is a cool 67 degrees, making this a haven for those escaping the heat of the flatlands. Surrounded by Nantahala National Forest, the plateau on which Highlands rests is botanically and geologically unique.

Founded as a summer resort in 1875 by Samuel T. Kelsey and Clinton C. Hutchinson, Highlands has from its beginnings been a retreat from the fast pace of city life. While the year-round population is about 4,000, the summer population is over 20,000. Highlands has become a place of renewal for professionals and executives, who purchase land here and build beautiful summer homes. The cultural amenities during the summer include live theater, chamber-music concerts, cabarets, and special dinners. Educational seminars and informative lectures are also offered. And did I mention shopping? The shopping in Highlands encompasses boutiques, specialty shops, antiques, jewelry, and handmade crafts and furniture.

JUST THE FACTS

Highlands is located at the intersection of N.C. 106/N.C. 28 and U.S. 64, which makes a 90-degree turn at Main Street. The roads to Highlands from Brevard and Cashiers—and from anywhere else, for that matter—are twisting and demanding of drivers' attention. Leave the sightseeing to passengers.

The Highlands Chamber of Commerce is located in the town hall on Main Street. Call 828-526-2112 or visit www.highlandschamber.com for information.

The area's semiweekly newspaper is called the *Highlander*.

Things to Do

MUSEUMS AND SCIENCE CENTERS

■ **Highlands Nature Center** is on East Main Street a half-mile east of downtown. This small but informative center offers exhibits that interpret the flora and fauna of the area's forests. It has a small botanical garden with trails and a display of mineral samples and Cherokee artifacts. The center is open Monday through Saturday from 10 A.M. to 5 P.M. from May 15 to Labor Day; variable hours continue through October. Admission is free. For more information, call 828-526-2623 or visit www.wildwnc.org.

CULTURAL OFFERINGS

■ **Highlands Playhouse**, located on Oak Street, presents a summer season of professional theater featuring contemporary dramas and comedies. Call the ticket office at 828-526-2695 or visit www.highlandsplayhouse.com for the current schedule.

■ The **Highlands Chamber Music Festival**, which takes place from mid-July to the first weekend in August, features several concerts by renowned artists. They are held in different venues, including local churches. For information, call 828-526-9060 or visit www.h-cmusicfestival.com.

RECREATION

■ Highlands is surrounded by **Nantahala National Forest**. If you're interested in hiking in the forest, call 828-526-3765 or write United States Forest Service, District 2010, Flat Mountain Road, Highlands, N.C. 28741.

Since the main attraction in this area is the scenery, one of the favorite local pastimes is driving tours. Two routes through the national forest are particularly scenic.

■ From Highlands to Franklin, U.S. 64 follows the Cullasaja River Gorge. The river cascades over falls and ripples over rapids, all within sight of the road. The drive toward Franklin is downhill. The road starts out twisting and winding, then widens and curves more gently. Along the route, you may want to stop and photograph **Bridal Veil Falls**, where you could once drive behind the 75-foot veil of water; however, a huge boulder has dropped on the section of roadway, negating that option. The most spectacular waterfall on this route is **Lower Cullasaja Falls**, a dramatic series of cascades dropping more than 250 feet in a quarter-mile. It is difficult to find a parking space here because the narrow road hangs on a cliff. Drive past the waterfall and hike back to see it. You'll find it worth the effort.

From Highlands to Cashiers, U.S. 64 is sharply curving but well paved and marked. The trees and rhododendron are thick and close to the road except where a great valley vista opens to the south, revealing a bird's-eye view of nearby **Whiteside Mountain**, which rises 2,100 feet from the valley floor. Its summit has an elevation of 4,930 feet. Both the northern and southern faces feature stunning, sheer cliffs ranging from 400 to 750 feet in height. This route continues to the town of Cashiers, where you'll find several pottery shops, gift shops, and resorts.

■ Located seven miles south of Highlands on N.C. 106, **Ski Scaly** is North Carolina's southernmost ski area. It has four slopes and a vertical drop of 225 feet. The lodge offers cafeteria meals. Rental equipment and instruction are available. For more information, call 828-526-3737.

Skiing in the North Carolina mountains
COURTESY OF NORTH CAROLINA DIVISION OF TOURISM, FILM AND SPORTS DEVELOPMENT

Places to Stay

RESORTS, HOTELS, AND MOTELS

■ **High Hampton Inn and Country Club**. Deluxe/Expensive. On N.C. 107 just south of Cashiers (800-334-2551 or 828-743-2411; www.highhamptoninn.com). This warm, family-oriented resort has a rustic style it has preserved since it was built in 1922. The exterior is covered with chestnut-bark shingles. Inside, the inn has log banisters in the stairwells and wood paneling on the walls and ceilings. The enormous lobby has four stone fireplaces around a central chimney and baskets of magazines and jigsaw puzzles for guests to relax over. The inn's 120 rooms have private baths but no telephones or televisions, so you can truly get away from it all. The inn also offers 40 vacation homes for rent. Meals are served buffet-style in the large dining room; it sounds casual, but men are expected to wear coats and ties for dinner and ladies to dress appropriately. The inn has an 18-hole golf course, outdoor tennis courts, and a lake with a sand beach. Canoes, sailboats, and fishing boats are available for rent. The latest addition to the inn is the state-of-the-art Hampton Health Club, which includes a gym and a full-service spa. The inn offers activities for children and teens and a long list of special seminars, golf and fishing schools, and art workshops. Those more adventurous than this author should be sure to check out the new Beanstalk Climbing Tower. The room rates include three meals. The inn is open from April to Thanksgiving.

■ **Fairfield Sapphire Valley**. Expensive/Moderate. On U.S. 64 (828-743-3441; www.fairfieldsapphirevalley.com). This top-rated resort offers a range of activities year-round. Set on green, forested slopes, it looks like an attractive housing development of rows of townhouses behind stands of trees. The lodgings range from luxurious hotel rooms to efficiency rooms with kitchens to one-, two-, and three-bedroom condos with separate living areas. All are comfortably furnished and attractively decorated; some have splendid views of the surrounding mountains. The kitchens are fully stocked, but if you prefer not to cook, the restaurant on the premises is open for lunch and dinner. Recreational facilities in the bracing air (you're 3,400 feet up) include an 18-hole championship golf course, one indoor and two outdoor pools, tennis courts, a lake beach, and a health club. You can also go horseback riding and rent bicycles, canoes, paddleboats, and fishing boats. A variety of activities such as children's game days and weekly family bingo are offered in the community room. During the winter, you may choose to try the resort's four ski slopes, which have a 425-foot vertical drop. Ski-equipment rentals are available.

INNS AND BED-AND-BREAKFASTS

■ *4½ Street Inn*. Expensive. 4½ Street between Chestnut and Hickory streets (828-526-4464; www.4andahalfstinn.com). This beautiful inn occupies a restored 100-year-old home on 1.3 acres five blocks from town. The inn has a hot tub, a wraparound porch, gardens, and a sun deck. Its 10 guest rooms have private baths; some have fireplaces. Guests are warmly welcomed with afternoon refreshments and home-baked cookies. In the evening, the hosts serve wine and hors d'oeuvres. Room rates include a gourmet breakfast, a morning paper, and fluffy robes. Bicycles are available for a trek into town. The bird feeders in the backyard provide great entertainment during breakfast.

■ *Old Edwards Inn and Spa*. Expensive. 445 Main Street (866-526-8008 or 828-526-8008; www.oldedwardsinn.com). The Old Edwards Inn has recently undergone a multimillion-dollar renovation and expansion and now includes a luxurious world-class spa, cottages, a five-star restaurant and outdoor wine bar, and an antique and gift store. This premier vacation resort offers rooms individually decorated with period furnishings. It is located within walking distance of Highlands' historic downtown.

■ *Kelsey & Hutchinson Lodge*. Expensive/Moderate. 450 Spring Street (888-245-9058 or 828-526-4746; www.k-hlodge.com). Located on three beautiful acres overlooking downtown Highlands, this lodge is within an easy walk of the town's restaurants and shops. It offers 33 rooms, many with a fireplace, a whirlpool, and a porch or balcony. Children are welcome here. The hosts will gladly help plan recreational activities. Room rates include continental breakfast and an evening hospitality hour.

■ *Skyline Lodge and Restaurant*. Expensive/Moderate. Flat Mountain Road (828-526-2790; www.skyline-lodge.com). Located atop 4,100-foot Flat Mountain, this lodge has 50 guest rooms and several two- and three-bedroom cabins on 50 private acres. The cabins are creatively decorated to bring the outdoors in with unique touches such as rough beam ceilings, birch-log stair rails, and decks built around the trunks of trees. The effect is one of stunning elegance amid rustic charm. The wide variety of recreational facilities includes a sauna, a steam room, a swimming pool, a gym, a game room, a conference center, and tennis courts. There's even a place called "the Wedding Deck," designed for perfect mountaintop nuptials. The hiking trails on the grounds lead to a 45-foot waterfall. A full-service restaurant is open on the weekends in season. Rooms are available from May through the first week of November. The cabins remain open year-round.

■ *Highlands Inn*. Moderate. On the corner of Main and Fourth streets (800-694-6955 or 828-526-9380; www.highlandsinn-nc.com). The Highlands Inn has been a cornerstone of this town since 1880. Listed on the National Register of Historic Places, it attracts a loyal crowd of guests with its rocking chairs on the veranda and its flags extending from the second-floor railing. Each room has a private bath and is beautifully decorated with period furniture. An extended continental breakfast is included in the room rate.

Places to Eat

■ *Log Cabin Steak House*. Expensive. 130 Log Cabin Lane (828-526-3380). This cabin was built in 1924 as a summer home for a family from Anderson, South Carolina. Most of the furniture was done by Tiger Mountain Woodworks, located in Highlands. The menu features appetizers such as Texas quail and smoked trout pâté, entrées from the grill like New Zealand lamb chops and fried frog legs, seafood specialties such as North Carolina trout and barbecued shrimp, and a variety of pasta dishes. The freshly made desserts include such goodies as coconut cake, "Snicker Doodle Pie," warm pear cake, and the famous "Brickle Basket," filled with a variety of surprises. Lunch and dinner are served Monday through Saturday.

■ *Ristorante Paoletti*. Expensive. Main Street (828-526-4906; www.paoletti.com). This is fine dining Italian-style. Ristorante Paoletti offers homemade pasta, seafood, and prime cuts of meat in an intimate setting in downtown Highlands. Among the highlights are veal chops, chicken with prosciutto and mozzarella, and Colorado lamb. Nightly specials include the likes of venison rib chops, "Osso Buco with Risotto Milanese," and Carolina quail. The ravioli is made fresh every day. The menu includes a minimum of four fresh seafood dishes prepared in a variety of ways. The wine list, one of the largest in the country, offers over 850 selections from around the globe. Dinner is served Monday through Saturday.

- **Wolfgang's on Main**. Expensive. 474 Main Street (828-526-3807; www.wolfgangs.net). Presided over by a certified executive chef who has received numerous awards and accolades, Wolfgang's on Main is a dining adventure not to be missed. Guests can take advantage of the cool mountain air by dining in the garden pavilion or on the covered deck. Or they can enjoy their meal beside a fireplace in one of the cozy dining rooms of a home that dates to the 1890s. But the menu and the wine list are the highlights of this establishment. The chef offers signature specialties such as grilled venison loin prepared with applewood bacon and served with a sun-dried-cherry demi-glace. Diners can choose a main course from New Orleans specialties like crawfish étouffée or Bavarian specials like wiener schnitzel or "Rostbraten." The winner of *Wine Spectator*'s Award of Excellence for the past several years, Wolfgang's has the perfect wines to go with such a varied and exciting menu. It also offers special events like wine dinners and holiday dinners. Check the restaurant's Web site for a calendar of events. Wolfgang's is open year-round; serving hours vary according to the season, so be sure to call in advance. Reservations are recommended.

- **Lakeside Restaurant**. Expensive/Moderate. Smallwood Avenue overlooking Lake Harris (828-526-9419). This place, which bills itself as "a casual restaurant with serious cuisine," comes highly recommended by local residents. Fresh seafood, beef, veal, lamb, chicken, and pasta dishes are on the menu. The portions are generous and delicious. Daily specials are offered, as is a good wine list. Between June and October, Lakeside serves lunch daily and dinner Monday through Saturday. During April, May, and November, the restaurant is closed Sunday and Monday. Reservations for dinner are strongly recommended.

FRANKLIN

The town of Franklin is the center of a thriving gem-mining industry. No wonder the place is called "the Jewel of the Southeast."

In the latter part of the 19th century, the Cowee Valley, just north of Franklin, was found to contain a high occurrence of corundum—rubies and sapphires, for those of us who don't know our quartz from our carbonatite. Several commercial mining companies began digging exploratory mines. Rubies were found in all the gravel beds, but not in quantities sufficient to support extensive mining operations.

Commercial mining ended here around the turn of the 20th century. All the better for us, since the Cowee Valley has continued to yield hundreds of rubies, sapphires, and other gemstones. Visitors have the chance to unearth one of these treasures. The predominant business in Franklin is accommodating rock hounds. Several gem shops will sell you raw stones or cut and mount those you find at one of the many gem mines catering to tourists.

The other jewel in Franklin's crown is location. Just outside town, you can visit the beautiful Nantahala National Forest and Nantahala Gorge, which offer many recreational opportunities.

When you come to Franklin, notice the large, grass-covered mound at the bottom of the hill on U.S. 64 Business. This is all that remains of an 18th-century Cherokee village called Nikwasi. Many archaeologists have asked permission to excavate it, but in the end, Franklin officials have always decided to leave things just as they are.

JUST THE FACTS

Franklin is located at the junction of U.S. 64, U.S. 23/U.S. 441, and N.C. 28.

The Macon County Airport has one lighted runway; call 828-524-5529 for information.

The Franklin Area Chamber of Commerce is located at 425 Porter Street. Call 866-372-5546 or 828-524-3161 or visit www.franklin-chamber.com.

The two local papers are the *Franklin Press*, published twice weekly, and the *Macon County News*, published weekly.

Things to Do

MUSEUMS AND SCIENCE CENTERS

■ The *Franklin Gem and Mineral Museum*, at 25 Phillips Street, is housed in the old city jail, built in the 1850s and used until 1972. The displays include a wide range of mineral specimens, fossils, and Indian artifacts. One room contains samples from all over North Carolina, while another has specimens from every other state in the union. One of the most interesting displays contains rocks under fluorescent light that continue to glow after the light has been switched off. The museum was established and is maintained by volunteers of the Gem and Mineral Society of Franklin. It is open Monday through Friday from noon to 4 P.M. and Saturday from 11 A.M. to 3 P.M. from May through October. Admission is free. Call 828-369-7831 or visit www.fgmm.org for information.

■ The *Scottish Tartans Museum and Heritage Center*, at 86 East Main Street, celebrates the Scottish heritage of the North Carolina mountains. Displays document the evolution of the kilt and the influence of the Scots on Appalachian culture. If you are of Scottish descent, you can find your family tartan in the Tartan Room. The gift shop sells items from Scotland and handmade Appalachian crafts. The museum is open Monday through Saturday from 10 A.M. to 5 P.M. A small admission fee is charged for adults; children 10 and under are free. Call 828-524-7472 or visit www.scottishtartans.org for information.

Whitewater Rafting
COURTESY OF NORTH CAROLINA DIVISION OF TOURISM, FILM AND SPORTS DEVELOPMENT

■ *Ruby City Gems and Minerals*, at 130 East Main Street, isn't strictly a museum. It's also a lapidary shop that sells raw and cut gemstones, lapidary equipment and supplies, and mineral samples such as geodes and amethyst crystals. The museum, located on the lower level, displays hundreds of mineral samples in well-lighted glass cases. The main attraction is a sapphire specimen that weighs 382 pounds. The shop and museum are open Monday through Saturday from 9 A.M. to 5 P.M. from April through December and Tuesday through Thursday from 10 A.M. to 3 P.M. during the winter. Admission is free, though donations are accepted. Call 828-524-3967 or visit www.rubycity.com for information.

RECREATION

■ Franklin's main attraction is gem mining.

According to an Indian legend, rubies appeared in the Cowee Valley because the beautiful daughter of a tribal chief fell in love with the son of her father's archenemy. When the chief found out, he was so enraged that he ordered the lovers put to death on the spot. The couple's love was so strong that their blood ran together into the earth and hardened into precious stones.

When you go mining for rubies and crystals, you'll pay for three or four buckets of rock and soil from the mine. Then, sitting at the edge of a flume line (a trough with gently flowing water), you'll rinse the soil from the rocks a scoop at a time and pick out the raw stones. Keep in mind that raw, uncut stones bear little resemblance to what you see in the jeweler's window. The mine operators will help you learn what to look for. Some mines enrich—or "salt"—the dirt with gravel known to contain some stones. If you've got children with you, choose one of these mines, where you'll have a better chance of keeping the kids' interest. You aren't likely to discover large gem-quality rubies, but you will have a lot of fun finding small, pretty stones to take away as souvenirs of your trip.

The chamber of commerce can provide a complete list of local gem mines. I can personally recommend *Mason Mountain Mine* (828-524-4570) and *Rose Creek Mine and Campground* (828-349-3774; www.rosecreekmine.com).

■ *Rafting* in the Nantahala Gorge, about 20 miles north of Franklin, will appeal to those who like thrills and outdoor excitement—and those who like getting soaked by cold mountain water. Several companies offer guided raft trips down the Nantahala River, which features class II and class III rapids. Don't let that intimidate you. Safety equipment is issued, and the guides tell you everything you need to do, so it's fun for even those with no rafting experience. The trips last about four hours and don't require special clothing except for something dry to change into afterward. Children must weigh at least 60 pounds to participate. Raft trips are offered from April through October. For a complete list of the companies that operate on U.S. 19 between Bryson City and Andrews, call 866-372-5546 or 828-524-3161.

SEASONAL EVENTS

■ The *Macon County Gemboree* is held twice each year, in late July and mid-October. Rock hounds gather from all over to display and sell gem and mineral specimens. Call 800-336-7829 or 828-524-3161 for information.

Places to Stay

INNS AND BED-AND-BREAKFASTS

■ *Blaine House Bed-and-Breakfast and Cottage*. Expensive/Moderate. 661 Harrison Avenue (800-297-9313 or 828-524-3633; www.blainehouse.com). Blaine House has the grace and serenity of homes of yesteryear. This 1910 home has been restored to its original state; lovers of fine things will appreciate the beautiful oak floors and bead-board ceilings. All the guest rooms are immaculate, well appointed, and thoughtfully decorated. Room rates include a delicious gourmet breakfast served at the time of guests' choosing.

■ *The Snow Hill Inn*. Expensive/Moderate. 531 Snow Hill Road (800-598-8136 or 828-369-2100; www.bbonline.com/nc/snowhill). The Snow Hill Inn is an elegantly restored 1914 schoolhouse. Guests can relax on the shaded front porch or in the gazebo, enjoy the 14 acres of quiet seclusion, and play croquet or badminton on the lawn. Room rates include a full breakfast served in the dining room, where the main pastime is watching the birds at the feeders.

- **Heritage Inn**. Moderate. 43 Heritage Hollow Drive (888-524-4150 or 828-524-4150; www.heritageinnbb.com). Mountain hospitality awaits you at this beautiful, award-winning, tin-roofed country inn located in a quiet, quaint, seven-acre private village within the town of Franklin. The inn is within easy walking distance of Main Street's shops and activities. Open year-round, it offers four studio apartments and three one-bedroom apartments. Each has a kitchen, a private bath, and its own outside entrance and porch and is tastefully furnished with antiques and quilts. Room rates include a full homemade breakfast.

- **High Country Haven**. Moderate. 29 Bates Branch Road (888-815-4783 or 828-524-4783; www.highcountryhaven.com). This bed-and-breakfast is located in the headmaster's house of what was once the Morrison Industrial Girls' School. The home is surrounded by lovely landscaped grounds and is beautifully decorated with charming antiques. It has a greenhouse with a hot tub, a gracious parlor, and four beautifully appointed rooms, all with private baths. Room rates include a full country breakfast and evening dessert in the dining room. High Country Haven also offers three private apartments in what was originally the school's dormitory. And that's not all. The inn's campground, open from May through October, offers RV and tent sites; two cabins and two on-site campers are even available for rent.

Places to Eat

- **The Summit Inn**. Expensive/Moderate. 210 East Rogers Street (828-524-2006). The restaurant at the beautiful Summit Inn offers an elegant setting and a refined menu featuring hand-cut steaks, fresh seafood, and vegetarian entrées. The Sunday brunch includes wonderful gourmet breakfast and lunch items. Diners can enjoy al fresco dining and a fabulous view. And don't forget the terrific desserts. Lunch and dinner are served in season; check for hours and days.

- **The Frog & Owl Kitchen**. Moderate. 46 East Main Street (828-349-4112). Located in the heart of Franklin's downtown shopping district, The Frog & Owl Kitchen is the perfect place to stop and take stock of your day's explorations. The menu includes raspberry citrus salad, lentil bean salad, a pesto chicken sandwich, a lamb burger, and mountain trout. A wine shop is on the premises, as is a deli, where gourmet pastas and salads are available for takeout. The desserts and breads are baked fresh every day. Lunch is served Monday through Saturday.

- **The Gazebo Creekside Café**. Inexpensive. 44 Heritage Hollow (828-524-8783). This lovely restored gazebo, located along a babbling creek, is a relaxing retreat in the middle of Franklin. The menu includes a wide variety of soups, salads, and sandwiches. For a cool drink, try a smoothie or a shake. The desserts include turtle cheesecake and Key lime pie, but my favorite is the chunky apple pie—à la mode, of course. Lunch is served daily and dinner Tuesday through Friday.

Nearby

- **Wayah Bald** is a massive stone outcrop at an elevation of more than a mile in Nantahala National Forest. Its "baldness" is in dramatic contrast to the lush forest that surrounds it. You can see the bald from downtown Franklin, but the trip to experience it up close takes about an hour. Take U.S. 64 West to S.R. 1310, then turn right on S.R. 69, which will lead you deep into the forest, where you'll see wildflowers and streams cascading down hillsides. You can park close to the summit, then walk about a quarter-mile on a paved trail for a spectacular view from the top.

- **Dillsboro** is about 20 miles north of Franklin on U.S. 441. The drive will take you through a picturesque mountain valley to a lovely little town on a hillside.

    Dillsboro has several shops that sell antiques, crafts, toys, and gifts. **Dogwood Crafters** (828-586-2248), on Webster Street, is a crafts cooperative carrying the work of many artisans. The nine outlets comprising **Riverwood Shops** (828-586-6996), located across the railroad tracks on River Road, offer hammered pewter, leatherwork, weavings, and more. Just strolling the streets of Dillsboro is a browser's dream.

Many people come to town for an excursion aboard the **Great Smoky Mountains Railroad**. One of the trips that departs from Dillsboro travels along the Tuckasegee River. This three-hour ride visits the setting of the escape scene at the beginning of *The Fugitive*, starring Harrison Ford. The railway was hired by the film company to stage a derailment with an actual full-sized train. The crew had only one shot at it, and it went perfectly. The remains of the wreck are featured on the excursion, which also includes the 836-foot-long Cowee Tunnel. Other excursions depart from Bryson City and Andrews. One of the Bryson City trips crosses Fontana Lake on a trestle 791 feet long and 179 feet high. The Great Smoky Mountains Railroad also offers raft-and-rail trips, special excursions such as a "Santa Train" in December, a whole week devoted to Thomas the Tank Engine rides (we're talking a full-sized Thomas that kids absolutely love), and mystery and dinner excursions. Call 800-872-4681 or visit www.gsmr.com for more information.

If you'll be staying overnight in Dillsboro, consider the **Squire Watkins Inn** (828-586-5244), located at 657 Haywood Road just off U.S. 441. For a terrific meal, try the **Jarrett House** (828-586-0265), on Main Street. This regional landmark opened as a hotel in 1882. Famous for its family-style meals, the restaurant specializes in fried chicken, country ham, and mountain trout. Each meal comes with bowls of vegetables, slaw, stewed apples, and hot biscuits. Be sure to try the vinegar pie.

■ The **John C. Campbell Folk School** is about 60 miles west of Franklin in Brasstown. The school was founded in 1925 to preserve and teach traditional Appalachian crafts. During the Depression, it provided economic opportunities for farm families by selling their high-quality woodcarvings.

Week-long courses are offered year-round today. They include pottery, weaving, basketry, woodcarving, bookbinding, Appalachian dancing, and newer crafts such as jewelry making and kaleidoscope making. The school has recently started offering cooking classes, too. Students come back year after year and often sign up for several courses at a time. The craft shop sells a variety of pottery, weavings, decorative ironwork, split-oak baskets, and beautiful work by some of the original Brasstown carvers. The shop is open Monday through Saturday from 8 A.M. to 5 P.M. and Sunday from 1 P.M. to 5 P.M. Call 800-365-5724 or 828-837-2775 or visit www.folkschool.com for more information.

The Great Smoky Mountains

Great Smoky Mountains National Park

Cherokee

Maggie Valley

Waynesville

By Sue Clark

Traveling west from Asheville, you'll find the Blue Ridge Mountains in your rearview mirror and the Great Smoky Mountains ahead of you. The latter mountain range gets its name from the persistent haze that veils the rounded summits. These ancient mountains exude serenity while cloaking a rugged wilderness that, in many areas, remains untouched by modern hands.

Legend says the haze comes from a time when the Cherokees smoked the peace pipe with their enemies. The meeting continued for seven days, during which the parties continued to quarrel. The Great Spirit, becoming annoyed, turned the men into grayish white flowers called Indian pipes and made smoke cover the mountains to remind all men that they should live together in peace.

The scientific explanation is less interesting. It states that the haze is caused by an excess of oxygen and humidity created by the thick forestation. The oxygen and humidity mix with a microscopic mist of rosin-scented organic compounds called terpenes.

The Smokies are a naturalist's paradise. They are home to more than 1,000 varieties of flowering plants and hundreds of species of mosses and trees. The Smokies contain the largest stand of old-growth hardwoods in North America. The diversity of plants and animals is unmatched anywhere in the country.

Fortunately, much of this magnificent wilderness has been incorporated into the national parks system to ensure that its wild beauty will be preserved. However, tourism has indeed intruded. Even so, these mountains are considered by many—this author included—to be the most beautiful part of North Carolina.

PHOTOGRAPH IN BACKGROUND ON PREVIOUS PAGE—

Winter Waterfall
COURTESY OF NORTH CAROLINA DIVISION OF TOURISM, FILM AND SPORTS DEVELOPMENT

Newfound Gap in the Great Smoky Mountains National Park

GREAT SMOKY MOUNTAINS NATIONAL PARK

The Grand Canyon receives over 5 million visitors each year, Yosemite over 4 million, and Yellowstone over 3 million. But it is Great Smoky Mountains National Park that has more visitors than any other national park—over 10 million each year. The park encompasses more than a half-million acres along 70 miles of the North Carolina-Tennessee border. It contains some of the oldest mountains on earth. Within the park are 16 peaks more than 6,000 feet high—and only one road cuts among them. Between the park entrances at Cherokee, North Carolina, and Gatlinburg, Tennessee, Newfound Gap Road twists and turns, revealing one spectacular view after another. During fall color season, this road is so congested that the crossing can take twice as long as it does during other times.

Great Smoky Mountains National Park was established by an act of Congress in 1926, but that was the easy part. Raising the money to buy the property was difficult, and negotiations were complex. Within the proposed boundaries of the park, 85 percent of the property was owned by 18 timber companies and the rest in tiny parcels by nearly 6,000 homesteaders. Years of appropriations and private contributions netted only $5 million—half the necessary funds. John D. Rockefeller, Jr., matched that amount, and the park finally opened to the public in 1934.

Natural beauty is not the only thing you'll find here. More than 75 historic structures are maintained by the park. These include the log cabins, barns, mills, and stables of some of the families that settled in the mountains in the 19th century.

Ways to explore the park are endless. Those with only a little time can drive Newfound Gap Road, but they'll miss much of the park. A smaller road leads up to Clingmans Dome, the highest peak in the park, at 6,634 feet; those who make the half-mile climb on foot to the observation tower will be rewarded with a stunning view of the Smokies. Those who enjoy hiking or horseback riding will appreciate the more than 800 miles of trails. Back-country camping is also a great way to explore these majestic mountains. Regardless of your preference for exploration, Great Smoky Mountains National Park will leave an impression on you that will last a lifetime.

The park's busiest months are June, July, August, and October. At these times, the campgrounds are full and the roads accessing the park are crowded. It can get cool here even in summer, so remember to bring a jacket or sweater. Also note that the park gets 50 to 80 inches of rain annually, so rain gear should be part of your preparations. And one other word of warning: There are bears in this part of the country, and none of them is named Yogi. If you see one, enjoy watching it from a distance, but *never* attempt to feed it or entice it for a closer view.

JUST THE FACTS

Great Smoky Mountains National Park is 50 miles west of Asheville on U.S. 19. The North Carolina entrance is at the town of Cherokee. The Tennessee entrance is at Gatlinburg. Three visitor centers offer maps, guidebooks, museum displays, weather and road information, schedules of park activities (including ranger-guided walks and talks), and calendars of special events. The centers are open every day except Christmas. For information, contact Great Smoky Mountains National Park, 107 Park Headquarters Road, Gatlinburg, Tenn. 37738 (865-436-1200; www.nps.gov/grsm).

Be sure to pick up a copy of *Smokies Guide* at one of the visitor centers. The official newspaper of the park, it is packed with information to make your visit the best possible.

Things to Do

MUSEUMS AND SCIENCE CENTERS

■ The *Mountain Farm Museum* is located at the North Carolina entrance to the park. It consists of buildings typical of those found in the area around 1900. Corn is ground here every day; the meal is available for purchase at the water-powered Mingus Mill, located a half-mile north of the farmstead. For more information, call 828-497-1900.

■ *Cades Cove*, on the Tennessee side of the park, is the site of a re-created pioneer mill community. Visitors can enjoy several cabins, a church, and a mill. They can also drive the 11-mile loop around the settlement and the adjacent pastures, or stroll among the buildings and observe life as it was for the early settlers. Park rangers lead 30-minute guided walking tours daily during the summer. A small bookstore offers material about the area and its history. After dark, old-fashioned hayrides delight the kids.

RECREATION

As with most outdoor recreation, information is the key to a great time. The park's visitor centers and the rangers who staff them are the best sources for up-to-date information on recreational opportunities.

■ Hiking is almost a religion at Great Smoky Mountains National Park. An endless variety of trails serves hikers of every taste and ability. The grandfather of them all, of course, is the *Appalachian Trail*, which zigzags for 70 miles through the park on the crests of the mountains between Davenport Gap, near the eastern boundary, and Fontana Dam, in the southwest.

If you're a serious hiker, you'll need serious maps, which are available at the visitor centers. **The Smokies Hiking Map and Guide** includes an up-to-date hiking map and information on back-country campsites. Another reliable source is **Hiking Trails of the Smokies**, which describes every hike in the park.

■ Camping is also very popular in the park.

Camping in the Mountains
COURTESY OF NORTH CAROLINA DIVISION OF TOURISM, FILM AND SPORTS DEVELOPMENT

A permit—available from the visitor centers—is required for back-country camping. Back-country camping is free but is allowed only at designated campsites along the trails. If you wish to camp in the shelters along the Appalachian Trail, reservations are required. For more information, call the back-country office at 865-436-1231.

The park also offers 10 developed campgrounds with water but no showers, no electricity, and no trailer hookups. A fee is charged for the use of these campgrounds. For information or reservations, call 800-365-CAMP.

The campsites close in November and reopen in mid-March.

■ Those who enjoy *picnicking* will appreciate the park's 10 picnic areas. Each has tables and fire grates. Please be aware of current fire conditions, and be conscientious about outdoor cooking. The same goes for trash, as no one wants any four-footed guests crashing their party.

■ *Horseback riding* is offered through several licensed concession stables. Call 865-436-1200 for information.

■ *Fishing* for brown and rainbow trout is popular in park streams all year long. You must have either a North Carolina or a Tennessee fishing license, both of which are honored throughout the park regardless of which side of the border you're on. Please check with the visitor centers for regulations regarding size and catch limits.

■ *Naturalist programs* are offered by rangers from May to October at the developed campgrounds and the visitor centers. Some are talks, some involve short walks, and some are geared for children. Topics include wildflowers, hardwood trees, animal habitats, and pioneer life. For a special treat, consider one of the walks offered at sunset or twilight. Call 865-436-1200 for more information.

Please be aware of park rules and considerate of the visitors who will come after you. Park regulations prohibit littering, defacing natural features, picking wildflowers, digging up plants, feeding wildlife, and letting pets run loose.

Places to Stay

INNS AND BED-AND-BREAKFASTS

■ *LeConte Lodge*. Inexpensive. On top of Mount LeConte (865-429-5704; www.leconte-lodge.com). The only overnight facility inside the park, this lodge is accessible by a half-day hike. The premises are definitely rustic and the meals plain. Reservations are required. The lodge is open from late March through late November.

Oconaluftee Indian Village
COURTESY OF NORTH CAROLINA DIVISION OF TOURISM, FILM AND SPORTS DEVELOPMENT

CHEROKEE

*T*he town of Cherokee is the largest community in the Qualla Boundary, the almost 56,000 acres of reservation land held in trust for the Eastern Band of the Cherokee Nation. The Cherokees are one of the "Five Civilized Tribes" of Muskogean-speaking people. They were the first Indians to have a written language, created by Sequoyah in 1821. At one time, they were an extremely powerful nation, controlling a territory of 135,000 square miles that stretched from the Ohio River southward into parts of what are now Georgia and Alabama. The forced removal of the Cherokees to the Oklahoma Territory has come to be called "the Trail of Tears." Several hundred Cherokees remained in the mountains during the removal. In 1866, they were finally granted the legal right to live in their homeland. About 8,200 members of the Eastern Band reside in communities throughout the Qualla Boundary today.

The town of Cherokee is undergoing some profound changes. Survival for the Native Americans used to depend on stereotypical tourist attractions that bore little resemblance to authentic Cherokee heritage. Ironically, the arrival of a large casino has pumped sorely needed revenue into the tribe. That revenue has been put to use improving the attractions that showcase the rich history and heritage of the Cherokee people.

JUST THE FACTS

Cherokee is located 48 miles west of Asheville at the intersection of U.S. 19 and U.S. 441. Just three miles north of Cherokee is the southern entrance to Great Smoky Mountains National Park.

The Cherokee Travel and Promotion Visitor Center is located where U.S. 19 and U.S. 441 merge. For information, call 800-438-1601 or 828-497-9195 or visit www.cherokee-nc.com.

The *Cherokee One Feather* is a weekly newspaper available throughout town.

Things to Do

HISTORIC PLACES, GARDENS, AND TOURS

■ *Oconaluftee Indian Village*, on Drama Road a half-mile north of U.S. 441, is a re-creation of a Cherokee village as it was 250 years ago. Here, you can watch Cherokees making tools and decorations, carving weapons and cooking utensils, grinding corn, cooking, finger-weaving, making baskets and beadwork, and burning out dugout canoes. Cherokee guides escort visitors on a two-hour journey into the past. Visitors are welcome to linger, take pictures, and ask questions. One of the highlights of the tour is the seven-sided council house. Surrounding the village is a beautiful botanical garden with paths leading past mossy rocks, trickling water, flower gardens, and vegetable gardens. The village is open daily from 9 A.M. to 5:30 P.M. between May 15 and October 25. Admission is charged. For more information, call 828-497-2315 or visit www.cherokee-nc.com/oconaluftee.

MUSEUMS AND SCIENCE CENTERS

- The **Museum of the Cherokee Indian**, on U.S. 441 North, was totally renovated in 1998. Its state-of-the-art exhibits trace the history of the Cherokees, honor outstanding individuals, and show examples of traditional arts and crafts. Artifacts and relics are presented in real-life settings of the time period. A seven-minute, three-screen, multisensory film presents the Cherokee creation story. In the exhibit halls, you can view maps of the Trail of Tears and read newspaper accounts of the removal. At the display on Sequoyah's syllabary, you can listen to audio samplings of the language. The gift shop carries books and souvenirs. The museum is open daily from 9 A.M. to 5 P.M. from September through May and from 9 A.M. to 7 P.M. from June through August. Admission is charged. Call 828-497-3481 or visit www.cherokee-nc.com/museum for more information.

SPECIAL SHOPPING

- **Qualla Arts and Crafts Mutual, Inc.**, on U.S. 441 North, was organized by Native American craftsmen in 1946. It has grown into the most successful Indian-owned and -operated craft cooperative in the United States. You'll find handmade Cherokee baskets, beadwork, pottery, woodcarvings, masks, and dolls. One room displays crafts made by Indians of other tribes. The cooperative is open daily from 8 A.M. to 6 P.M. during the spring and fall, from 8 A.M. to 8 P.M. in the summer, and from 8 A.M. to 4:30 P.M. in the winter. Call 800-438-1601 or 828-497-3103 or visit www.cherokee-nc.com/qualla for more information.

RECREATION

- **Harrah's Cherokee Casino**, on U.S. 441, has brought a great deal of revenue to the Eastern Band of the Cherokee Indians. The size of three football fields, the casino features 2,300 video gaming machines, three restaurants, a gift shop, and even a day-care facility. Neon lightning bolts flash across the ceiling whenever someone wins a jackpot over $1,000; the sound of thunder means the jackpot's even bigger. The 1,500-seat Cherokee Pavilion hosts live entertainment. The casino is where the action is 24 hours a day, seven days a week. Call 800-HARRAHS or 828-497-7777 or visit www.harrahs.com for more information.

■ *Fishing* is popular around Cherokee. The streams and ponds on the reservation are stocked and overseen by the Cherokee Fish and Game Management. While you don't need a state fishing license, you must purchase a tribal fishing permit, available at convenience stores, campground offices, and other locations throughout town. Call 828-497-5201 for more information.

Seasonal Events

■ **Unto These Hills** is performed at the 2,800-seat Mountainside Theatre on U.S. 441. This play by Kermit Hunter is the most popular outdoor drama in the state. It uses words and music to tell the story of the Trail of Tears. Performances are staged Monday through Saturday from mid-June to late August. Shows begin at 8:45 P.M. until the end of July and at 8:30 P.M. thereafter. Admission is charged. For more information, call 866-554-4557 or visit www.cherokee-nc.com/unto_these.

Places to Stay

The town of Cherokee has a number of motels, rental cabins, and lodges, many of them along the Oconaluftee River. And the arrival of the casino has brought many of the major chain hotels. To reach the following lodgings—which are more in keeping with the nature of this book—you will have to head up U.S. 19 to Bryson City.

Inns and Bed-and-Breakfasts

■ *Hemlock Inn*. Deluxe/Expensive. On Galbraith Creek Road off U.S. 19 east of Bryson City (828-488-2885; www.hemlockinn.com). This is a lovely one-level inn on a Great Smoky Mountains hilltop. If you sit in a rocker on the porch, all you'll hear is the songs of the birds. The inn offers 21 rooms and four cottages furnished country-style. You'll enjoy the fireplace in the big family room. Breakfast and dinner, served in the dining room, include home-baked bread and homemade desserts.

- **Fryemont Inn**. Moderate. Fryemont Road in Bryson City (800-845-4879 or 828-488-2159; www.fryemontinn.com). The Fryemont, an old-fashioned country inn built by timber baron Amos Frye, opened in 1923. The hardwood floors gleam in front of the fieldstone hearth in the lobby. The inn's 44 rooms have chestnut paneling, private baths, four-poster beds, simple furnishings, and special touches such as baskets with herbal bath granules in the bathrooms. The inn offers a tennis court and a swimming pool. The dining room has a bandstand for weekend entertainment. The inn is open from April through October.

- **Randolph House**. Moderate. 223 Fryemont Road in Bryson City (828-488-3472; http://www.iloveinns.com/bed_and_breakfasts/north_carolina/randolphhouse.htm). Randolph House is the 1895 mansion that timber magnate Amos Fry built for himself. The seven cozy guest rooms are furnished with antiques, some dating to the 1850s. The sitting room is filled with overstuffed chairs that invite guests to while away a quiet evening after dinner. And what a dinner! Gourmet dining is the norm here. The menu includes such items as trout, flounder, prime rib, and stuffed Cornish game hens. Then there's the selection of homemade desserts. And let's not forget breakfast, which is equally sumptuous. Room rates include these two wonderfully prepared meals. The inn is open from mid-April through October.

Places to Eat

- **The Chestnut Tree**. Moderate/Inexpensive. In the Holiday Inn Cherokee on U.S. 19 South (828-497-9181). This is about the fanciest restaurant you'll find in Cherokee. It features mountain trout, steak, chicken, and a good selection of sandwiches. It is open for breakfast and dinner Monday through Saturday and for all three meals on Sunday.

- **Grandma's Pancake and Steak**. Inexpensive. On U.S. 19/U.S. 441 (828-497-9801). Grandma's is a casual family restaurant where you can get a great old-fashioned country breakfast any time of day and steak, shrimp, barbecue, flounder, and chicken entrées for lunch and dinner. It features local favorites like "Indian Tacos," "Chili and Frybread," and mountain trout. Grandma's offers home-style vegetables and slow-cooked pinto beans seasoned with country ham and served with cornbread muffins. From June through October, it serves all three meals every day. The rest of the year, it serves breakfast and lunch Monday through Thursday and all three meals on Friday, Saturday, and Sunday.

■ *Tee Pee Restaurant.* Inexpensive. On U.S. 441 North (828-497-5141). Though the selection here is standard, the food is a cut above most places in Cherokee. The specialty is mountain trout. Buffets are offered for each meal, but only at certain times; diners can order from the menu at any time. Breakfast, lunch, and dinner are served daily.

Nearby

■ *Fontana Village*, about 50 miles west of Cherokee on N.C. 28 North, is a resort community that grew from the housing units occupied by the workers who built Fontana Dam in the 1940s. The dam is the highest in the eastern United States and the largest facility of the Tennessee Valley Authority. Upon the dam's completion in 1945, the housing development was sold to private owners, who turned it into a family resort village.

The village includes an inn with 94 rooms (some of which have fireplaces) and 250 rustic cottages equipped with kitchens. A restaurant, a buffet house, and a café all serve meals to those who choose not to cook. Recreational activities include miniature golf, swimming, boating, fishing, hiking, horseback riding, archery, and badminton. A playground, craft classes, and other organized activities are available for children. The mountains that surround Fontana Lake make a magnificent setting for an extended family vacation. The village is open year-round. For more information, call 800-849-2258 or 828-498-2211 or visit www.fontanavillage.com.

■ *Joyce Kilmer Memorial Forest* contains one of the last stands of virgin forest on the East Coast. The forest is left completely to nature's control; no plants or trees, living or dead, may be cut or removed. The result is a magnificent forest containing more than 100 species of trees,

Joyce Kilmer Memorial Forest
COURTESY OF NORTH CAROLINA DIVISION OF TOURISM, FILM AND SPORTS DEVELOPMENT

many specimens of which are over 300 years old. A two-mile recreation trail loops through the forest and the adjoining 14,000-acre Slickrock Wilderness Area. Fittingly, the forest is named for the author of the well-known poem "Trees." Joyce Kilmer was still a young man when he was killed in France during World War I. To reach the forest named in his honor, take U.S. 129 North from Robbinsville and follow the signs. For information, call the Cheoah Ranger Station at 828-479-6431.

For overnight accommodations in the area, try **Snowbird Mountain Lodge**, at 4633 Santeetlah Road. This rustic mountain inn, built of chestnut logs and native stone, offers an excellent view of the Snowbird range from its terrace. Call 800-941-9290 or 828-479-3433 or visit www.snowbirdlodge.com.

THE TRAIL OF TEARS

The facts are staggering: Some 14,000 Cherokees were forced to leave their ancestral home with whatever they could carry; they were led to the Oklahoma Territory in 20-plus separate detachments, many traveling in the dead of winter; no exceptions were made for the elderly, the sick, the pregnant, or the very young; approximately 20 percent died on the way.

In one of the most shameful episodes in this nation's history, the United States government decided to break numerous treaties with the Cherokees of the Blue Ridge and Great Smoky mountains. In 1828, President Andrew Jackson put through Congress the Indian Removal Act, which commanded that all Indians be led west of the Mississippi River. Cherokee land was confiscated when gold was discovered in the Appalachians. The 1835 Treaty of New Echota provided the Cherokees $5 million and land in what is now Oklahoma in exchange for their 7 million acres in the East. But by May 1838, only 2,000 of the 16,000 Cherokees had moved voluntarily. General Winfield Scott and a force of 7,000 men were sent to evict the remaining Indians. The tragedy that transpired eventually came to be called the Trail of Tears.

First, stockades were built to hold the Indians. Then small squads armed with rifles and bayonets were sent out to round up every Cherokee they could find. No time was allotted for packing—men were seized in the fields and women and children from their homes. The soldiers prodded and drove the Indians to the stockades. Behind the soldiers came bands of looters, who pillaged and burned the Cherokees' former homes.

From the time they left the stockades, the 1,200-mile trek took some detachments as long as six months. The average distance covered was 10 miles a day. The Cherokees stopped only to bury those who died along the way—of disease, starvation, and exhaustion.

The numbers are indeed staggering, but they do little to explain man's cruelty to man. When greed intercedes, there seems no end to the damage one people can inflict upon another.

MAGGIE VALLEY

aggie Valley, a resort community at the base of the Balsam Mountains, was named for the daughter of the town's first postmaster. It is four miles from the Blue Ridge Parkway and 16 miles from Cherokee and the entrance to Great Smoky Mountains National Park. Maggie Valley has a permanent population of about 200, but that number swells in the summer, when tourists stay in the many motels along U.S. 19 (Main Street) and visit the Stompin' Ground. Cataloochee Ski Area is the big attraction during the winter.

JUST THE FACTS

Maggie Valley is on U.S. 19 about 30 miles west of Asheville.

The Maggie Valley Chamber of Commerce is on the southern side of Main Street; call 828-926-1686 or visit www.maggievalley.com for information.

The newspaper that covers this area is Waynesville's *Enterprise Mountaineer*, which also puts out a tabloid of regional activities and advertising called *Adventure in the Smokies*.

Things to Do

RECREATION

■ The wooden stage of the ***Stompin' Ground*** comes alive with professional clogging teams dancing to Appalachian music provided by fiddlers, guitar strummers, and banjo pickers. This is a great place to experience the folk dancing unique to the Appalachians. The audience is encouraged to participate, so don't be afraid to try your hand at clogging, line dancing, or even waltzing. The Stompin' Ground is located on U.S. 19. Its hours vary according to the performance schedule. An admission fee is charged. Call 828-926-

1288 or visit www.stompingroundpresents.com for more information.

■ Built in 1961, **Cataloochee Ski Area** was the first ski resort in North Carolina. It was so successful that it spawned a new industry. Now, ski areas dot the North Carolina mountains from here to the Virginia border. Cataloochee's lodge and restaurant have a friendly atmosphere in which families are welcome. The ski area has nine slopes and a vertical drop of 740 feet. Ski instruction and equipment rental are available. Cataloochee is located at 1080 Ski Lodge Road. Call 800-768-0285 or 828-926-0285 or visit www.cataloochee.com for more information.

SEASONAL EVENTS

■ **Folkmoot USA** is a 10-day cultural event in July that features traditional dance groups from all over the world. It is hosted in several western North Carolina cities. Folkmoot's Maggie Valley performances are held at the Stompin' Ground. For information and a calendar of performances, call 877-FOLKUSA or 828-452-2997 or visit www.folkmoot.com.

Places to Stay

RESORTS, HOTELS, AND MOTELS

■ **Cataloochee Ranch**. Deluxe. On U.S. 19 (800-868-1401 or 828-926-1401; www.cataloochee-ranch.com). Located atop a mountain overlooking Maggie Valley, this is a special place with spectacular views. The lodge is rustic but well appointed. The staff is attentive to every detail. The seven cabins and two lodges contain 22 units with pine paneling and quilts on the beds. Horseback riding is the main activity here, but hiking trails and trout fishing are also offered. Rocking on the front porch and sitting before the fireplace in the lodge are also popular ways to spend time at Cataloochee Ranch. Generous country-style breakfasts and dinners, served from April through November, are included in the room rates. The ranch is open year-round.

■ **Maggie Valley Resort and Country Club**. Deluxe/Expensive. Moody

Farm Road (800-438-3861 or 828-926-1616). This resort is located in a lush setting with a mountain backdrop a half-mile west of the intersection of U.S. 19 and U.S. 276. It offers 40 comfortable rooms, 11 private villas, 21 luxurious condominiums, a championship golf course, and an outdoor pool. The breakfast buffet and dinner, served in the resort's restaurant, are included in the room rates, as are golf packages. Lunch is offered in the Pin High Lounge.

INNS AND BED-AND-BREAKFASTS

■ *Jonathan Creek Inn and Villas*. Expensive/Moderate. 4324 Soco Road (800-577-7812 or 828-926-1232; www.jonathancreekinn.com). At first glance, this looks like many of the motels in Maggie Valley, but check deeper. The 42 spacious, comfortable rooms have back doors that open onto Jonathan Creek. They also have refrigerators and coffee makers. Some have whirlpools, hot tubs, fireplaces, and wet bars. The three villas are an option for those desiring even more privacy. The beautifully landscaped grounds include several garden areas, hammocks, a picnic area, and a gazebo. The inn has an indoor pool.

■ *Smokey Shadows Lodge*. Moderate/Inexpensive. On Fie Top Road off U.S. 19 near the ski area (866-926-0001 or 828-926-0001; www.smokeyshadows.com). The 12 guest rooms at this primitive-style lodge have chestnut paneling and log-beam ceilings. A separate cabin sleeps six. The long porch that extends across the back of the building offers a magnificent view. The country-gourmet meals, not included in the room rates, don't leave anyone hungry. Smokey Shadows is open year-round.

Places to Eat

■ *Maggie Valley Resort and Country Club*. Expensive/Moderate. Moody Farm Road (828-926-1616). This is as fine a dining experience as you'll find in Maggie Valley. From freshly prepared eggs to homemade Belgian waffles, the breakfast buffet is the perfect way to start your day. You may wish to relax and enjoy a refreshing drink or light fare on the resort's scenic Clubhouse Terrace or in the quaint Pin High Pub. A delicious lunch buffet is offered Monday through Friday. In the evening, you can feast on mountain trout, prime rib, chicken, and seafood in the Season's Restaurant. The resort's restaurants are open daily to the public.

■ *J. Arthur's Restaurant*. Moderate/Inexpensive. Soco Road (828-926-1817). The big, rambling, ranchlike building that houses J. Arthur's welcome families, who flock here after a full day of touring. Prime rib and steak are the specialties, but you'll find some surprises like "Gorgonzola Cheese Salad," too. Kids can satisfy their appetites with a range of hamburgers and sandwiches. The restaurant serves dinner daily in the summer and from Wednesday through Saturday in the winter.

WAYNESVILLE

Waynesville is an ideal mountain town. It doesn't have a manufactured tourist destination or a large business district. What Waynesville offers is a chance to get away from it all and still be close enough to visit the area's attractions. The downtown boasts a wonderful selection of retail shops, galleries, and restaurants. The streets are lined with shade trees and comfortable benches.

Waynesville plays host to a variety of street festivals in the summer and fall. The wide range of entertainment at these outdoor celebrations includes parades, dance exhibitions, and craft displays. Thanks to plenty of charm and just the right amount of activity, Waynesville may become one of your favorite mountain getaways.

JUST THE FACTS

Waynesville is located at the intersection of U.S. 74 and U.S. 276 west of Asheville.

The Haywood County Chamber of Commerce, at 1482 Russ Avenue, is the place to go for information about the town. Call 800-334-9036 or 828-456-3021 or visit www.haywood-nc.com.

Waynesville's newspaper, the *Enterprise Mountaineer*, is published three times a week. The paper puts out a tabloid of regional activities and advertising called *Adventure in the Smokies*.

Things to Do

MUSEUMS AND SCIENCE CENTERS

■ The ***Museum of North Carolina Handicrafts***, at 49 Shelton Street, houses a fascinating collection of pottery, porcelain, baskets, woodcarvings, and turned bowls. Other treasures include hand-carved dulcimers, quilts, and a collection of Cherokee crafts and artifacts. The museum's gift shop sells a variety of crafts. An admission fee is charged. The hours are seasonal, so call before you visit; the number is 828-452-1551.

SPECIAL SHOPPING

■ The **Mast Candy Barrel**, at 55 North Main Street, will definitely satisfy your sweet tooth. The old-fashioned candy draws as many customers looking for nostalgia as it does people in search of a sweet morsel. Everyone enjoys browsing through candy bins for treats they haven't seen since childhood. The Mast Candy Barrel is open seven days a week; call 828-452-0075.

SEASONAL EVENTS

■ **Smoky Mountain Fall Days** is a series of festivals held nearly every day during September and October in the towns of Waynesville, Maggie Valley, Canton, and Clyde. Festivities include the **Smoky Mountain Folk Festival**, the **High Country Quilt Show**, the **Apple Harvest Festival**, and the **Church Street Arts and Crafts Show**. For more information, call 800-334-9036 or 877-456-3073 or visit www.smokymountains.net\html\fall.

■ **Folkmoot USA**, held during July, is a 10-day festival featuring international dance performances by guest groups from all over the world. Many of the performances are in Waynesville. This festival is over 15 years old. It is recognized as one of the finest gatherings of international dancers in the country. Call 877-FOLKUSA or 828-452-2997 or visit www.folkmoot.com for more information.

Places to Stay

INNS AND BED-AND-BREAKFASTS

- **The Swag Country Inn**. Deluxe. 2300 Swag Road (828-926-0430; www.theswag.com). The Swag has earned a reputation as one of the most exclusive inns in the mountains. The drive to the top of its private peak is breathtaking. The rustic inn is made of hand-hewn logs taken from original Appalachian structures. The inn has a private entrance to Great Smoky Mountains National Park, an indoor racquetball court, a spring-fed swimming pond, and 250 acres of secluded land to explore. Special programs are offered throughout the summer. The Swag is open from May through mid-November.

- **Balsam Mountain Inn**. Expensive. Seven Springs Drive off U.S. 23/U.S. 74 (828-456-9498; www.balsaminn.com). This restored historic place is located a half-mile from the Blue Ridge Parkway. Opened in 1908 to serve the highest railway depot east of the Rockies, the inn offers beautiful mountain views from its two-tiered porch. It has 50 luxurious rooms with private baths, a 2,000-volume library, a card-and-puzzle room, and a spacious lobby with two fireplaces. You won't find telephones in the rooms, and there isn't a single television in the entire inn. Room rates include a full country breakfast. The inn's restaurant serves breakfast and dinner Monday through Saturday and all three meals on Sunday.

- **Waynesville Country Club Inn**. Expensive. 176 Country Club Road (828-452-2258; www.wccinn.com). This is one of Waynesville's most elegant lodgings. The three-story 1920s fieldstone inn is set against densely wooded mountains. Its 92 luxurious guest rooms offer views of the mountains or the 27-hole golf course. Tennis courts and a heated outdoor pool are on the premises. The wood-paneled dining room is open for all three meals. In-season rates include breakfast and dinner.

- **Mountain Creek Bed-and-Breakfast**. Moderate. 146 Chestnut Walk Drive (800-557-9766; www.mountaincreekbb.com). Finally, a bed-and-breakfast that's not filled with Victorian lace and antiques! The proprietors call the decor at Mountain Creek "retro 50s," and it's a refreshing and comfortable change of pace. A former corporate-retreat lodge, the main house is situated above a rock-lined pond that makes for a beautiful view from the wraparound porch and the window-lined den. The renovated pool house includes a Jacuzzi suite. The innkeepers are outdoor enthusiasts who will help organize hikes and bike trips. Room rates include a gourmet breakfast prepared by a truly talented cook. Guests can arrange for an equally delicious special dinner.

- ***Ten Oaks***. Moderate. 224 Love Lane (800-563-2925). This charming bed-and-breakfast has three guest rooms and two suites, each with its own sitting area, fireplace, and private bath. The large front porch is perfect for rocking and taking in the mountain view. Room rates include breakfast and afternoon refreshments.

Places to Eat

- ***Lomo Grill*** and ***Lomo's Bakery and Café***. Expensive/Moderate. 44 Church Street (828-452-5222; www.lomogrill.com). Lomo Grill features authentic Italian and Mediterranean cuisine. Here, the finest meats are grilled in a wood-burning oven. The dining room's romantic ambiance complements the award-winning food and one of the finest wine cellars in the area. Dinner is served Monday through Saturday. Lomo's Bakery and Café is patterned in the French style. Its delicious right-out-of-the-oven goodies include breads, pastries, and gourmet cookies. You can also enjoy specialty sandwiches, vegetarian entrées, homemade soups, unique quiches, and beautifully prepared salads. Lunch is offered Monday through Saturday.

- ***Maggie's Galley***. Moderate. 49 Hal Miller Road (828-456-8945). When it comes to food—especially seafood—this place has it all. The appetizers include such treats as alligator, crawdads, onion straws, and nachos. The selection of main courses is just as eclectic: Hawaiian shrimp, North Carolina rainbow trout, "Gator Dinner," frog legs, and rib-eye steaks served with snow crab, lobster tail, or shrimp. And save room for desserts such as black walnut pie and "Coca-Cola Cake." Maggie's Galley serves dinner every day and lunch Tuesday through Sunday.

- ***Pasquale's Pizzeria & Tapas Bar***. Moderate. 1863 South Main Street (828-454-5002). Great Italian food, a cozy bar that serves tapas, and a deck for al fresco dining combine for a memorable experience at Pasquale's. The restaurant serves Old World appetizers such as artichokes with prosciutto, classic pizzas and calzones, and pasta, chicken, beef, and seafood entrées, all with an Italian flair. Dinner comes with a fresh salad tossed at your table and breadsticks perfect for getting every bit of sauce from your plate. Pasquale's is open for dinner seven days a week.

■ **Bogart's**. Moderate/Inexpensive. 303 South Main Street (828-452-1313). This casual restaurant and tavern really hits its groove at night, when it gets pretty lively. The rustic interior is highlighted by stained-glass windows. Diners may choose from a good selection of burgers and sandwiches, as well as rainbow trout, stir-fried chicken, and sirloin tips. Lunch and dinner are served daily.

■ **Cool Beans Café**. Inexpensive. 180 North Main Street (828-452-3137). When looking for a bite in an unfamiliar town, it's always a good bet to find out where the locals eat. This is the place. Cool Beans Café is exactly the place to go when you need a break from browsing the shops along Main Street. It offers locally roasted coffees, homemade soups, and great sandwiches made with organic breads from a local bakery. The wonderful breakfast menu is available all day; my son highly recommends the French toast. The café is open daily for breakfast and lunch. On Thursday, Friday, and Saturday nights, the tables are pushed back and live bands perform.

■ **Whitman's Bakery and Sandwich Shoppe**. Inexpensive. 18 North Main Street (828-456-8271). This bakery has been serving downtown shoppers delectable goodies since 1945. The name *Whitman* (my maiden name) drew me in, but the aroma held me. The items I sampled were fresh, delicious, and deserving of such a fine name; let me personally recommend the butter cookies with the pastel centers. Sandwiches are prepared to order by the friendly, inviting staff. Lunch is offered Tuesday through Saturday.

Appendix

The following pages contain key facts and phone numbers that should help answer travel queries and make it easier to plan a North Carolina vacation.

STATE AGENCIES

North Carolina Division of Tourism, Film and Sports Development
301 North Wilmington Street
Raleigh, N.C. 27601
800-VISIT-NC or 919-733-8372; www.visitnc.com

This should be your first contact for information about North Carolina. The tourism office provides state maps and several useful publications. It publishes a full-color booklet of over 150 pages listing accommodations, campgrounds, events around the state, and state parks and historic sites. The booklet also contains a map. If you stop by the Raleigh office, you can pick up free brochures for many attractions statewide.

Coastal Management Division
400 Commerce Avenue
Morehead City, N.C. 28557
888-472-6278 or 252-808-2808; www.nccoastalmanagement.net

North Carolina Aquariums
417 North Blount Street
Raleigh, N.C. 27601
800-832-3474; www.ncaquariums.com

North Carolina Department of Transportation
1 South Wilmington Street

Raleigh, N.C. 27601
877-368-4968 or 919-733-2520; www.ncdot.org

North Carolina Division of Forest Resources
512 North Salisbury Street
1616 Mail Service Center (27699-1616)
Raleigh, N.C. 27604
919-733-2162; www.dfr.state.nc.us

North Carolina Division of Parks and Recreation
512 North Salisbury Street
Raleigh, N.C. 27604
919-733-4181; http://ils.unc.edu/parkproject/ncparks.html

North Carolina Division of State Historic Sites
430 North Salisbury Street
4620 Mail Service Center (27699-4620)
Raleigh, N.C. 27699
919-733-7862; www.ah.dcr.state.nc.us/sections/hs

North Carolina Wildlife Resources Commission Headquarters
Centennial Campus—NCSU
1751 Varsity Drive
Raleigh, N.C. 27606
919-707-0398 or 919-707-0391; www.ncwildlife.org

GENERAL SOURCES

Blue Ridge Parkway Superintendent
199 Hemphill Knob Road
Asheville, N.C. 28803
828-271-4779; www.nps.gov/blri

Cape Hatteras National Seashore Superintendent
1401 National Park Drive
Manteo, N.C. 27954
252-473-2111; www.nps.gov/caha

Cape Lookout National Seashore Superintendent
131 Charles Street
Harkers Island, N.C. 28531
252-728-2250; www.nps.gov/calo

Cherokee Welcome Center
P.O. Box 460
498 Tsali Boulevard
Cherokee, N.C. 28719
800-438-1601 or 828-497-9195; www.cherokee-NC.com

Great Smoky Mountains National Park Superintendent
107 Park Headquarters Road
Gatlinburg, Tenn. 37738
865-436-1200; www.nps.gov/grsm

National Forests in North Carolina Superintendent
P.O. Box 2750
160-A Zillicoa Street
Asheville, N.C. 28801
828-257-4200; www.cs.unca.edu/nfsnc

North Carolina Association of RV Parks and Campgrounds
605 Poole Drive
Garner, N.C. 27529
800-906-0907 or 919-235-0239; www.carolinasarvc.org

North Carolina Bed-and-Breakfast and Inns Association
9650 Strickland Road, Suite 103-254
Raleigh, N.C. 27615
800-849-5392; www.ncbbi.org

North Carolina High Country Host
1700 Blowing Rock Road
Boone, N.C. 28607
800-438-7500 or 828-264-1299; www.mountainsofnc.com

North Carolina Ski Areas Association
c/o Sugar Mountain Resort
P.O. Box 369
Banner Elk, N.C. 28604
828-898-4521; www.goskinc.com

Smoky Mountain Host of North Carolina
4437 Georgia Road
Franklin, N.C. 28734
800-432-HOST or 828-293-0787; www.visitsmokies.org

Travel Council of North Carolina
4101 Lake Boone Trail, Suite 201
Raleigh, N.C. 27607
919-787-5181, ext. 242

STATE HISTORIC SITES

Alamance Battleground
5803 N.C. 62 South
Burlington, N.C. 27215
336-227-4785; www.ah.dcr.state.nc.us/sections/hs/alamance/alamanc.htm

Aycock Birthplace
P.O. Box 207
264 Governor Aycock Road
Fremont, N.C. 27830
919-242-5581; www.ah.dcr.state.nc.us/sections/hs/aycock/aycock.htm

Bennett Place
4409 Bennett Memorial Road
Durham, N.C. 27705
919-383-4345; www.ah.dcr.state.nc.us/sections/hs/bennett/bennett.htm

Bentonville Battleground
5466 Harper House Road
Four Oaks, N.C. 27524
910-594-0789; www.ah.dcr.state.nc.us/sections/hs/bentonvi/bentonvi.htm

Brunswick Town
8884 St. Philips Road Southeast
Winnabow, N.C. 28479
910-371-6613; www.ah.dcr.state.nc.us/sections/hs/brunswic/brunswic.htm
or
www.carolinarosedesigns.com/brunweb

Charlotte Hawkins Brown Museum
P.O. Box B
6136 Burlington Road
Sedalia, N.C. 27342
336-449-4846; www.ah.dcr.state.nc.us/sections/hs/chb/chb.htm

Duke Homestead
2828 Duke Homestead Road
Durham, N.C. 27705
919-477-5498; www.ah.dcr.state.nc.us/sections/hs/duke/duke.htm

Fort Fisher
P.O. Box 169
1610 Fort Fisher Boulevard South
Kure Beach, N.C. 28449
910-458-5538; www.ah.dcr.state.nc.us/sections/hs/fisher/fisher.htm

Historic Bath
P.O. Box 148

207 Carteret Street
Bath, N.C. 27808
252-923-3971; www.ah.dcr.state.nc.us/sections/hs/bath/bath.htm

Historic Edenton
P.O. Box 474
Edenton, N.C. 27932
252-482-2637; www.ah.dcr.state.nc.us/sections/hs/iredell/iredell.htm

Historic Halifax
P.O. Box 406
25 St. Davids Street
Halifax, N.C. 27839
252-583-7191; www.ah.dcr.state.nc.us/sections/hs/halifax/halifax.htm

Historic Stagville
5825 Old Oxford Highway
Durham, N.C. 27712
919-620-0120; www.historicstagvillefoundation.org

Horne Creek Living Historical Farm
308 Horne Creek Farm Road
Pinnacle, N.C. 27043
336-325-2298; www.ah.dcr.state.nc.us/sections/hs/horne/horne.htm

House in the Horseshoe
288 Alston House Road
Sanford, N.C. 27330
910-947-2051; www.ah.dcr.state.nc.us/sections/hs/horsesho/horsesho.htm

James K. Polk Memorial
P.O. Box 475
12031 Lancaster Highway
Pineville, N.C. 28134
704-889-7145; www.ah.dcr.state.nc.us/sections/hs/polk/polk.htm

North Carolina State Capitol
4624 Mail Service Center
1 East Edenton Street
Raleigh, N.C. 27601-2807
919-733-4994; www.ncstatecapitol.com

North Carolina Transportation Museum
P.O. Box 165
411 South Salisbury Avenue
Spencer, N.C. 28159
877-628-6386 or 704-636-2889; www.nctrans.org

Reed Gold Mine
9621 Reed Mine Road
Midland, N.C. 28107
704-721-4653; www.reedmine.com

Roanoke Island Festival Park/*Elizabeth II*
1 Festival Park
Manteo, N.C. 27954
252-475-1500; www.roanokeisland.com

Somerset Place
2572 Lake Shore Road
Creswell, N.C. 27928
252-797-4560; www.ah.dcr.state.nc.us/sections/hs/somerset/somerset.htm

Thomas Wolfe Memorial
52 North Market Street
Asheville, N.C. 28801
828-253-8304; www.wolfememorial.com

Town Creek Indian Mound
509 Town Creek Mound Road
Mount Gilead, N.C. 27306
910-439-6802; www.ah.dcr.state.nc.us/sections/hs/town/town.htm

Tryon Palace
610 Pollock Street
New Bern, N.C. 28562
800-767-1560 or 252-514-4900; www.tryonpalace.org

Vance Birthplace
911 Reems Creek Road
Weaverville, N.C. 28787
828-645-6706; www.ah.dcr.state.nc.us/sections/hs/vance/vance.htm

OUTDOOR RECREATION

For most of the following, more complete information is provided in the text of this book; the index will tell you exactly where. This is intended as a quick-reference telephone list.

National Recreational Areas

Blue Ridge Parkway
828-271-4779

Cape Hatteras National Seashore
252-473-2111

Cape Lookout National Seashore
252-728-2250

Croatan National Forest
252-638-5628

Great Smoky Mountains National Park
865-436-1200

Nantahala National Forest
828-257-4200

Pisgah National Forest
828-257-4200

Uwharrie National Forest
910-576-6391

State Parks and Recreational Areas

Carolina Beach
910-458-8206

Cliffs of the Neuse
919-778-6234

Crowders Mountain
704-853-5375

Eno River
919-383-1686

Falls Lake
919-676-1027

Fort Fisher
910-458-5798

Fort Macon
252-726-3775

Goose Creek
252-923-2191

Gorges
828-966-9099

Hammocks Beach
910-326-4881

Hanging Rock
336-593-8480

Jockey's Ridge
252-441-7132

Jones Lake
910-588-4550

Jordan Lake
919-362-0586

Kerr Lake
252-438-7791

Lake James
828-652-5047

Lake Norman
704-528-6350

Lake Waccamaw
910-646-4748

Lumber River
910-628-9844

Medoc Mountain
252-586-6588

Merchants Millpond
252-357-1191

Morrow Mountain
704-982-4402

Mount Mitchell
828-675-4611

New River
336-982-2587

Pettigrew
252-797-4475

Pilot Mountain
336-325-2355

Raven Rock
910-893-4888

Singletary Lake
910-669-2928

South Mountains
828-433-4772

Stone Mountain
336-957-8185

Theodore Roosevelt
252-726-3775

Weymouth Woods
910-692-2167

William B. Umstead
919-571-4170

FISHING AND HUNTING

You can get a fishing or hunting permit from any license agent, of which there are many. Look for them at hardware and sporting-goods stores. Some licenses expire June 30, while others expire one year from the date of purchase.

For further information, contact the North Carolina Wildlife Resources Commission.

Resident fishing license—$15
Resident fishing license (including trout)—$20
    Daily permit—$5
    Trout license—$10
Nonresident fishing license—$30
    Daily permit—$10
    Three-day permit—$15
    Trout license—$10
Saltwater recreational fishing does not require a license.

Resident sportsman license—$40
    Hunting license—$15
    Big-game permit—$10
    Trapping license—$25
Nonresident sportsman license—$60
    Six-day hunting license—$40
    Big-game permit—$60

BICYCLING

To help cyclists find safe and interesting places to ride, the Bicycle Program of the North Carolina Department of Transportation has identified primary and secondary roads that are relatively safe for cycling because of low traffic volume and good roadway conditions. Various routes encompassing over 3,000 miles have been mapped. Others will be available in the future.

Sample routes:

Mountains-to-Sea—700 miles from Murphy to Manteo
Piedmont Spur—200-mile east-west route
Carolina Connection—200-mile north-south route
Ports of Call—300 miles in the coastal area
Cape Fear Run—160 miles from Raleigh to the Cape Fear area
Ocracoke Option—175 miles from the Wilson area to the Cedar Island ferry
Southern Highlands—120 miles from the Blue Ridge Parkway to Lincolnton

Maps and tour routes are available for selected areas. To order one or more of these free guides, contact the Bicycle Program, North Carolina Department of Transportation, 1552 Mail Service Center, Raleigh, N.C. 27699-1552 (919-733-2804).

AID FOR HANDICAPPED TRAVELERS

Access North Carolina is an excellent travel guide for disabled persons. It provides accessibility information for virtually every tourist attraction in the state. It evaluates parking lots, entrances, indoor and outdoor sites, water fountains, and restrooms and also mentions special tours and access for blind and deaf persons. It is available at no charge from the North Carolina Division of Tourism, Film and Sports Development.

HOTEL/MOTEL TOLL-FREE NUMBERS

These numbers may be called from anywhere in the continental United States. Consult your local telephone directory for regional listings.

Best Western International
800-780-7234

Comfort Inns
877-424-6423

Courtyard by Marriott
800-321-2211

Days Inn
800-329-7466

Econo Lodges of America
877-424-6423

Hampton Inn
800-426-7866

Hilton Hotel Corporation
800-445-8667

Holiday Inns, Inc.
800-315-2621

Howard Johnson
800-446-4656

Hyatt Corporation
888-591-1234

Marriott Hotels
800-721-7033

Quality Inns
877-424-6423

Radisson Hotel Corporation
888-201-1718

Ramada Inns
800-272-6232

Red Roof Inns
800-733-7663

Sheraton Hotels and Inns
800-325-3535

Renaissance Hotels and Resorts
800-468-3571

CAR RENTAL TOLL-FREE NUMBERS

Avis Reservations Center
800-331-1212

National Car Rental
800-227-7368

Budget Rent-A-Car
800-527-0700

Thrifty Car Rental
877-283-0898

Dollar Rent-a-Car
800-800-3665

U-Haul Equipment Rental
800-468-4285

Hertz Corporation
800-654-3131

Index

4 Seasons at Beech, 474
4½ Street Inn, 533
42nd Street Oyster Bar, 239
82nd Airborne Division War
 Memorial Museum, 297
1618 West Seafood Grille, 363
1587, 47

A. J. Fletcher Institute, 229
Aberdeen, 316
Ackland Art Museum, 265-66
Acorn Drop, 235
Acoustic Coffee, 110
Adkins-Ruark House, 206
Admiral's Quarters Motel, 203
Advice 5¢, 23
Aerie, The, 135
African American Atelier, 356
African American Cultural
 Complex, 234
Afro-American Cultural Center,
 400
Air Bellows Gap, 421
Airborne and Special Operations
 Museum, 295
Airlie Gardens, 178-9
Alamance Battleground State
 Historic Site, 379
Alive After Five, 333
Allanstand Craft Shop, 495
Allen and Son Pit-Cooked Bar-B-
 Q, 276-77
Alliance for Historic
 Hillsborough, 283
Alligator Back, 422
Alligator River National Wildlife
 Refuge, 40-41
American Dance Festival, 254
American Tobacco Trail, 253
Amistad Saga: Reflections, 234
Amos Mosquito's Restaurant
 and Bar, 162
Amy's Coffee and Confections,
 138
Anchorage Inn, 75
Anchorage Marina, 73
Andrea's Troy-Bumpas Inn, 361-
 62
Angus Barn, 238-39
Annual Hang Gliding
 Spectacular and Air Games,
 20
Annual Nags Head Surf Fishing
 Club Invitational
 Tournament, 20-21
Annual Outer Banks Stunt-Kite
 Competition, 21

Annual Peanut Festival, 107
Annual Quilt Fest, 515
Antique Walk through
 Pittsboro, 285
Antiques Show and Sale, 151
Appalachian Adventures, 444,
 452
Appalachian Angler, 472
Appalachian Challenge Guide
 Service, 452
Appalachian Ski Mountain, 460
Appalachian State University,
 448
Appalachian Summer Festival,
 453
Appalachian Trail, 497, 547
Apple Harvest Festival, 563
Archer's Mountain Inn, 475
Arrowhead Inn, 256
Art in the Park, 460
Art on Main, 514
Arts Council of Fayetteville/
 Cumberland County, 300
ArtsCenter, 267
Artspace, 229
Artsplosure Spring Art Festival,
 234
Ashe County Cheese Company,
 441
Asheville Art Museum, 493-94
Asheville Community Theater,
 495
Asheville Municipal Golf
 Course, 498
Asheville Symphony, 494-95
Athena Greek Taverna, 341
Atlantic Beach King Mackerel
 Tournament, 160
Atlantic Coast Line Railroad
 Station, 293
Atlantic Coast University Team
 Rowing Regatta, 233
Atlantis Lodge, 161
Atrium Furniture Mall, 369-70
Attmore-Oliver House, 130
Augustus T. Zevely Inn, 338
Aurora Fossil Museum, 119
Austin Creek Grill, 64
Avalon Fishing Pier, 16
Avon Golf and Fishing Pier, 59
Avon Motel, 62
Awful Arthur's Oyster Bar, 27
Ayr Mount, 283
Azalea Festival, 185
Azalea Garden Inn, 461-62
Azalea Inn, 475

Back Porch, 77
Backwoods Expeditions, 452-53
Badin Lake, 414
Baird House, 455-56

Bald Head Island, 213-14
Bald is Beautiful Convention
 and Contest, 144
Bald View Bed-and-Breakfast, 23
Ballantyne Resort Hotel, 405-6
Balsam Mountain Inn, 564
Bank of America Corporate
 Center, 399
Bank of the Arts, 131
Banner Elk Café, 477
Banner Elk Inn, 475-76
Barbecue Festival, 381
Barker-Moore House, 104
Barn of Fayetteville, 301-2
Barnacles, 203
Barracuda Bar and Grille, 214
Barrier Island Kayaks, 164
Battleship North Carolina, 181-
 82
Bear Island, 164
Beaufort Grocery, 152-53
Beaufort Historic Site, 148-49
Beaufort Inn, 151
Beaufort Old Homes and Garden
 Tour, 151
Beech Alpen Inn. See Inns at
 Beech Mountain
Beggars and Choosers, 285
Bele Chere Downtown
 Community Celebration,
 498
Belhaven Memorial Museum,
 120
Bellamy Mansion, 181
Bellsouth Jazz & Blues, 333
Bennett Place State Historic Site,
 245
Bennett Vineyards, 120
Bentonville Battleground, 302-3
Best Cellar, 463-64
Best Cellar at Linville, 477
Best Western Blue Ridge Plaza,
 445
Best Western Buccaneer Motor
 Inn, 144
Best Western Coastline Inn, 186
Best Western Crystal Coast
 Resort, 161
Best Western Eldreth Inn, 454
Bethesda Church and Cemetery,
 316
Betty's Waterfront Restaurant,
 212
Bicentennial Greenway, 370
Bickett Gallery, 230
Bicycle Inn, 483-84
Biennial Pilgrimage Tour of
 Homes and Countryside in
 Edenton and Chowan
 County, 107

Big Ed's City Market, 240
Big Rock Marlin Tournament,
   143-44
Bill's Seafood Market, 212
Biltmore Estate, 489-92
Biltmore Greensboro Hotel, 362
Biltmore Village, 495
Birthplace of Pepsi-Cola, 132
Bistro 420, 340
Bistro by the Sea, 146
Bistro Restaurant, 191
Bistro Roca, 464
Bistro Sofia, 362-63
Black Film Diaspora, 251
Black Mountain, 506
Black Mountain Golf Resort,
   498
Black Pelican Oceanfront Café,
   26
Blackbeard's Lodge, 74-75
Blackwater Grille, 517
Blaine House Bed-and-Breakfast
   and Cottage, 539
Blake House Inn, 503-4
Blockade Runner Resort Hotel,
   195
*Bloody Mary and the Virgin
   Queen*, 43
Blooming Garden Inn, 257
Blowing Rock, the, 459-60
Blowing Rock Charity Horse
   Show, 460
Blue, 410
Blue Heaven Bed-and-Breakfast,
   187
Blue Moon Bistro, 153
Blue Point, 24-25
Blue Ridge BBQ Festival, 520
Blue Ridge Country Club, 452
Blue Ridge Parkway, 497
Blue Sky Café, 517-18
Blue Water Grille, 374
Blue Water Point Motel and
   Marina, 209
Bluffs Lodge, 436
Bob Timberlake Gallery, 381
Bob Timberlake Inn at Chetola,
   461
Bodie Island Lighthouse, 50-51
Bogart's, 566
Bonner House, 117
Bonnet's Creek, 207
Books to Be Red, 72-73
Boone Bike and Touring, 452
Boone Golf Club, 452
Botanical Gardens of Asheville,
   492-93
Bouldin House Bed-and-
   Breakfast, 373
Bowman Gray Stadium, 401

Bracken Mountain Bakery, 528
Brady C. Jefcoat Museum of
   Americana, 96
Breakwater Restaurant, 64-65
Breezeway Motel, 169-70
Breezeway Restaurant, The, 171
Brevard Music Festival, 523
Bridal Veil Falls, 531
BridgePointe Hotel and Marina,
   134
Brightleaf Square, 252
Brinegar Cabin, 421
British Cemetery, 71
Britt-Sanders Cabin/Loom
   House, 307
Broad Creek Fishing Center &
   Marina, 42
Brookstown Inn, 337
Broyhill Inn and Conference
   Center, 455
Brunswick Inn, The, 211
Bryan Park Complex, 358
Bryant House, 316
Buffalo Tavern Bed-and-
   Breakfast, 445-46
Bull Durham Blues Festival, 254
Bull Durham Tobacco, 242
Bullock's BBQ, 259
Burgwin-Wright Museum
   House and Gardens, 180-81
Burke Street Pizza, 342
Burning Coal Theatre, 229
Buxton Woods Reserve, 61

Cabo Fish Taco, 411
Cades Cove, 547
Café on the Square, 504
Caffé Phoenix, 188
Calabash, 214
Calico Jacks Inn & Marina, 155
Cameo Art House Theatre, 297
Cameron House Inn, 45
Cameron Park Inn, 237-38
Campbell House Galleries, 308
Canadian Hole, 60
Candlelight Christmas Tour,
   108
Candlelight Confection
   Perfection, 108
Candlelight Homes Tour, 236
Cantina 1511, 410
Cape Fear Botanical Garden, 293
Cape Fear Coast Convention
   and Visitors Bureau, 177-78,
   193
Cape Fear Kayaks, 197
Cape Fear Museum, 182-83
Cape Fear Regional Theatre,
   297-98
Cape Fear River Boats, 178

Cape Fear Serpentarium, 183
Cape Fear Studios, 298
Cape Hatteras Bed-and-
   Breakfast, 64
Cape Hatteras Fishing Pier, 59
Cape Hatteras Lighthouse, 55-
   56, 58
Cape Hatteras Motel, 62-63
Cape Lookout Lighthouse, 155-
   56
Cape Lookout National
   Seashore, 154-55
Cape Lookout Studies Program,
   150
Cape Lookout Village Historic
   District, 156
Cape Point, 156
Capital Area Greenway, 232
Capital City Bicycle Motocross
   Race Track, 232
Caprice Bistro, 188
Captain Ratty's, 138
Captain's Landing, 74
Captain's Quarters, 152
Captain's Quarters Inn, 109
Caribbe Inn, 162
Carl Sandburg Home National
   Historic Site, 512
Carmen's Cuban Café, 282-83
Carol's Garden Inn, 257
Carolina Adventure Magazine's
   freshwater fishing school,
   233
Carolina Aviation Museum, 398
Carolina Ballet, 229
Carolina Barnstormers, 253
Carolina Beach State Park, 201
Carolina Beach Surf-Fishing
   Tournament, 202
Carolina Beach yacht basin, 201
Carolina Carriage Classic, 312
Carolina Coastal Adventures,
   197
Carolina Cobras, 234
Carolina Creations, 132
Carolina Crossroads in the
   Carolina Inn, 275
Carolina Hemlocks Recreation
   Area, 482
Carolina Horse Park at Five
   Points, 312
Carolina House Bed-and-
   Breakfast, 121
Carolina Hurricanes, 234
Carolina Inn, 272
Carolina Mudcats, 234
Carolina Outdoors, 60
Carolina Raptor Center, 397-98
Carolina Sailing Unlimited, 139
Carolina Temple Apartments,
   195

Carolina Theatre (Durham), 250
Carolina Theatre (Greensboro), 356-57
Carolina Theatre and Grille, 95
Carolina, The, 311
Carolinas' Carrousel Parade, 404
Carpe Diem, 410
Carr Mill Mall, 268
Carrboro Farmers' Market, 268
Carriage Tours of Pinehurst Village, 311
Carteret County Tourism Bureau, 148, 158
Cartwright House, 139
Cascades Nature Trail, 422
Castle Bed-and-Breakfast and Courtyard Villas, 76
Caswell Beach, 205
Cat's Corner Café, 341
Cat's Cradle, 270-71
Cataloochee Ranch, 559
Cataloochee Ski Resort, 497-98, 559
Cedar Creek Gallery, 288
Cedar Crest Victorian Inn, 503
Cedar Island National Wildlife Refuge, 156
Cedars Inn, The, 151
Celo Inn, 484
Center City Walking Tour, 391
Center for Documentary Studies at Duke University, 252
Center of the Earth Gallery, 400
Chandler's Wharf, 185
Channel Marker, 162
Chapel Hill Museum, 267
Charlotte Hawkins Brown Memorial State Historic Site, 379-80
Charlotte Marriott City Center, 406
Charlotte Marriott SouthPark, 406
Charlotte Museum of History, 391-92
Charlotte Nature Museum, 397
Charlotte Street Grill and Pub, 505
Chatham County, 286
Chatham County Arts Council, 286
Cheerwine, 343-44
Chef Warren's, 315
Chelsea, The, 138
Chelsea Theatre, 267
Chero's Market Café and Catering, 110
Cherokee Adventures, 453
Chestnut Street Inn, 503
Chestnut Tree, 554

Chetola Lodge and Conference Center, 461
Chicamacomico Life Saving Station, 54-55
Children's Museum of Wilmington, 184
Childress Vineyards, 402
Chimney Rock Park, 518-19
Chowan Arts Council Gallery and Gallery Shop, 106-7
Chowan County Courthouse, 104
Chowan County Jail, 104
Chowan Golf and Country Club, 107
Christ Episcopal Church, 88
Christmas Candle Tea, 334
Christmas in July, 445
Church Street Arts and Crafts Show, 563
Church Street Bed-and-Breakfast, 93-94
Circa 1922, 188
Circle 10 Art Gallery, 139
City Lake Park, 370
City Wine Seller Bakery and Deli, 95
Claddagh Inn, 516
Clamdigger Ramada Inn, 161
Clarion Prince Charles, 301
Clear Creek Guest Ranch, 482
Coastal Carolina Christmas Walk, 151
Coastal Ecology Sails, 150
Coker Arboretum, 264
Colburn Earth Science Museum, 494
Colington Island, 12-13
Comfort Inn (Morehead City), 144-45
Comfort Inn Cross Creek, 301
Comfort Inn North Oceanfront, 22
Comfort Inn–Hatteras Island, 62
Comfort Suites Riverfront Park, 134
Community Thanksgiving Feast, 151
Concord Mills, 400
Connestee Falls, 521
Cool Beans Café, 566
Cool Spring Tavern, 293
Copper, 411
Coquina Beach, 51
Core Sound Waterfowl Museum, 156
Cottage Restaurant, 203
Cotton Exchange, 184-85
Country Inn and Suites, 455

Courtyard by Marriott at Crabtree Valley, 237
Cove Bed-and-Breakfast, 76
Cow Café, 139
Coyote Kitchen, 457
Crab's Claw Restaurant and Oyster Bar, 162-63
Crabby-Oddwaters Restaurant, 212
Crabtree Meadows, 425, 426
Cradle of Forestry in America, 522
Craggy Gardens, 507
Craggy Gardens Visitor Center, 426
Craven County Arts Council and Gallery, 131
Craven County Convention and Visitors Bureau, 126
Creekside Café, 77
Crippen's Country Inn and Restaurant, 464
Croatan National Forest, 133
Crook's Corner Café and Bar, 276
Cross Creek Cemetery, 293
Crowders Mountain State Park, 415-16
Crown Center, 299
Crowne Plaza Resort, 501
Crystal Coast Amphitheatre, 160
CSS *Neuse* State Historic Site, 139-40
Culpepper Inn, 93
Cumberland Knob, 421
Cupola House Wassail Bowl, 108
Cupola House, 104
Currituck Beach Lighthouse, 7-8
Currituck Club, 18
Cypress Creek Grill, 94
Cypress Moon Inn, 23

Daimagin Japanese Fusion Bar & Café, 374
Dan'l Boone Inn Restaurant, 457
Daniel Boone Trace, 423
Dare Day Festival, 43
David R. Walters Antiques, 298
Davidson, 416
Davie Poplar, 263
Day at the Farm, A, 131-32
Days Inn (Elizabeth City), 93
Days Inn Mariner, 22
Dean Dome. *See* Dean Smith Center
Dean Smith Center, 271
Deck House, 203

Deep Dish Theater Company, 268
Deepwater Pottery, 72
Deepwater Theater, 74
Delamar Inn, 152
Delicias Bakery and Restaurant, 412
Deluxe Café, 188
Dennis A. Wicker Civic Center Complex, 316
Devil's Courthouse, 427
Diggs Gallery, 332
Dillsboro, 541
Discovery Diving, 150
Discovery Place, 395, 397
Dish, 411
Dismal Swamp Canal Welcome Center, 97
Dixie Classic Fair, 334
Dixon-Stevenson House, 129
Dockside Seafood House, 214
Dog Corner Park, 90
Dogwood Crafters, 541
Dogwood Festival, 299
Dolce Ristorante, 411
Dolphin Den, 65
Double Oaks Bed-and-Breakfast Inn, 361
Doughton Park, 421, 435
Doughton-Hall Bed-and-Breakfast, 436-37
Downeast Rover, 40
Downtown Arts District Association (DADA), 333
Dry Falls, 524
Duck Woods Country Club, 18
Dugan's Pub, 315
Duke Chapel, 246
Duke Homestead and Tobacco Museum, 248
Duke Mansion, 407
Duke of Dare Motor Lodge, 44
Duke University Primate Center, 249-50
Duke University, 246
Dunhill Hotel, 406
Duplin Winery, 191
DuPont State Forest, 514
Durant Nature Park, 233
Durham Athletic Park, 253-54
Durham Bulls Athletic Park, 253

E. B. Jeffress Park, 422
E. H. Sloop Chapel, 443
Early Girl Eatery, 505
Earthshine Mountain Lodge, 527
East Coast Classic King Mackerel Tournament, 202
East Franklin Street, 269

Eastern Music Festival, 356
Econo Lodge, 145
Edenton National Fish Hatchery, 106
Edge of the World, 453, 472
Elaine's on Franklin, 275
Elijah's Restaurant, 188
Elizabeth City Bed-and-Breakfast, 93
Elizabeth City commercial district, 88
Elizabeth City Harbor Nights, 92
Elizabeth City Historic Ghost Walk, 92
Elizabeth City State University Planetarium, 89
Elizabeth II, 37
Elizabeth Inn, 152
Elizabeth Leigh Inn, 515
Elizabeth R, 42-43
Elizabeth's Café and Winery, 25
Elizabethan Gardens, 34-35
Elizabethan Inn, 44
Emerald Village, 481
Emerywood Fine Foods, 374
EMF Fringe series, 356
Eno-Occaneechi Indian Association, 284
Enoteca Vin, 239
Episcopal Cemetery, 88
Eseeola Lodge, 475, 476
Evans Metropolitan AME Zion Church, 293-94
Evening Waterfront Concert Series, 230
Executive Mansion, 224
Exploris, 226-27
Expressions, 517

F. W. Woolworth Company, 353-54
Fairfield Inn & Suites, 454
Fairfield Sapphire Valley, 532-33
Fairgrounds Flea Market, 231
Falls Lake State Recreation Area, 233, 288
Falls Landing, 528
Farmers' Market, New Bern, 132
Fascinate-U Children's Museum, 295-96
Fayetteville Museum of Art, 296
Fayetteville Regional Airport, 292
Fayetteville State University, 290
Fayetteville Street Mall, 221
Fayetteville Symphony Orchestra, 298
Fearrington Village, 286

Federal, The, 259
FENCE. *See* Foothills Equestrian Nature Center
FestiFall, 272
Festival for the Eno, 254
Festival in the Park, 404
Festival of Lights, 379
Fete de la Musique, 272
Fiesta del Pueblo, 236
Finley Golf Course, 271
Firemen's Museum, 130-31
First Colony Inn, 23-24
First Night Raleigh, 235
Five County Stadium, 234
Flaming Amy's Burrito Barn, 189
Flat Rock Overlook, 425
Flat Rock Playhouse, 513
Flight, 516-17
Flying Burrito, 277
Flying Frog Café, 505
Folk Art Center, 495
Folkmoot USA, 559, 563
Fontana Village, 555
Foothills Brewing Company, 341
Foothills Equestrian Nature Center, 520
Forest Theatre, 265
Fort Anderson, 214
Fort Bragg, 290
Fort Fisher State Historic Site, 198-200
Fort Fisher State Recreation Area, 201
Fort Macon State Park, 158-59
Fort Raleigh National Historic Site, 32, 34
Fortune Garden, 283
Foscoe Fishing Company & Outfitters, 472
Foster's Market, 259
Founders Hall, 399
Four Seasons Town Centre, 357
Fox Hunter's Paradise, 421
Fox Watersports, 60
Foxfire Café, 484
Franklin Gem and Mineral Museum, 537
Franklin Square Art Gallery, 207-8
Fraser's, 447
Fred's Backside Deli, 477
Fred's General Mercantile Company, 468
Freedom Park, 403
French Broad River, 497
Friendly Center, 357
Frisco Native American Museum and Natural History Center, 58-59

Frog & Owl Kitchen, 541
Froggy Dog Restaurant and Pub, 65
Front Street Grill at Stillwater, 153
Front Street Inn, The, 187
Fryemont Inn, 554
Frying Pan Shoals, 209
Fulcher's Landing, 171
Full Frame Documentary Film Festival, 255
Full Moon Café, 47
Fun Junktion, 90
Furniture Discovery Center, 368, 369
Furnitureland South, 365, 369

Gabrielle's at Richmond Hill, 504
Gallery C, 230
Gallery Café, 139
Garden Deli, 484
Garden Jubilee, 514
Gazebo Creekside Café, 541
General Store Café, 286
Genki, 189
George's Garage, 258-59
Gideon Ridge Inn, 462-63
Gilbert Theater, 298
Glendale Springs Inn, 446
Glendale Springs Restaurant, 446
Glenn Eure's Ghost Fleet Gallery, 14
Gold Rush Circulator Service, 391
Golden Sands, 203
Goose Creek State Park, 120-21
Gourmet Café, The, 163
Governor's Club, 272-73
Governor's Walk, 132
Grammy's Bistro, 528
Grandfather Mountain Highland Games and Gathering of Scottish Clans, 466, 472-73
Grandfather Mountain, 424, 468-69
Grandma's Pancake and Steak, 554-55
Grandover Resort and Conference Center, 360
Granville County, 288
Granville Queen Inn, 109
Grappa Grille, 363
Grave site of Aunt Bee, 287
Graveyard Fields, 427
Graveyard of the Atlantic Museum, 59
Graystone Inn, The, 186
Great Dismal Swamp, 97

Great Indian Trading Path, 248
Great Island Cabins & Ferry Service, 154
Great Smoky Mountains National Park, 497, 543-44, 545-46, 547-49
Great Smoky Mountains Railroad, 541
Greater Topsail Island Chamber of Commerce, 168
Green Hill Center of North Carolina Art, 356
Green Valley Grill, 364
Greenfield Park and Gardens, 185
Greensboro Children's Museum, 354-55
Greensboro Cultural Center at Festival Park, 355-56
Greensboro Grasshoppers, 358-59
Greensboro Historical Museum, 352, 353
Greensboro Marriott Downtown, 361
Greenwood Bed-and-Breakfast, 362
Greystone Inn, 526-27
Grouper's Waterfront Seafood Grille, 94
Grove Arcade Public Market, 496
Grove Park Inn Resort & Spa, 498, 499-501
Guilford College, 345
Guilford Courthouse National Military Park, 349-51, 359
Guilford Native American Art Gallery, 356

Halifax, 95
Hammocks Beach State Park, 164
Hampton Inn (Elizabeth City), 92
Hampton Inn & Suites Outer Banks/Corolla, 22
Hampton Inn on Bogue Sound, 144
Hanging Rock State Park, 381-82
Hanna House, 135
Hannah Flanagan's Pub, 518
Harbor Seafood Deli, 65
Harbour Village, 214
Harkers Island Visitor Center, 154
Harmony Hill, 436
Harmony House Inn, 135
Harper Creek, 471

Harrah's Cherokee Casino, 552-53
Harvey Mansion Historic Inn & Restaurant, 138
Harvey W. Smith Watercraft Center, 150
Hatteras Harbor Marina & Efficiencies, 63
Hatteras Harbor Marina, 60
Hatteras Island Fishing Pier, 59
Hatteras Island Sail Shop, 60
Hatteras Landing, 62
Hatteras Landing Marina, 60
Hawthorne Inn and Conference Center, 337
Hayti Heritage Center, 250-51
Haywood Park Hotel, 501
Health Adventure, 494
Hemlock Inn, 553-54
Henderson County Farmers Mutual Curb Market, 513
Henderson House, 138
Henry F. Shaffner House, 338
Henry's, 478
Herbert Hoover Birthday Celebration, 43-44
Heritage Inn, 540
Herrings Outdoor Sports, 169
Hertford, 96
Hezekiah Alexander Homesite, 391-92
High Country Haven, 540
High Country Quilt Show, 563
High Hampton Inn and Country Club, 532
High Mountain Expeditions, 453, 472
High Point Markets, 370-72
High Point Museum and Historical Park, 368
Highland Lake Inn, 515-16
Highlander Café & Pub, 302
Highlands Chamber Music Festival, 530
Highlands Inn, 534
Highlands Nature Center, 530
Highlands Playhouse, 530
Hillsborough, 283
Hilltop House Restaurant, 302
Hillwinds Inn. See Village Inns of Blowing Rock
Hilton at University Place, 406
Hilton Charlotte and Towers, 406-7
Hilton Wilmington Riverside, 186
Historic Bath State Historic Site, 117
Historic Bethabara Park, 327
Historic City Market, 231

Historic Edenton State Historic Site, 103-4
Historic Halifax. *See* Halifax
Historic Hertford. *See* Hertford
Historic Hillsborough. *See* Hillsborough
Historic Hope Plantation, 112
Historic Jackson. *See* Jackson
Historic Latta Plantation, 392
Historic Murfreesboro. *See* Murfreesboro
Historic Oak View Park, 236
Historic Oakwood District, 224-25
Historic Plymouth. *See* Plymouth
Historic Stagville, 248
Historic Washington. *See* Washington, N.C.
Historic Williamston. *See* Williamston
Historic Windsor. *See* Windsor
History Place, 142
Holiday Inn Express (Boone), 454
Holiday Inn Express (Elizabeth City), 93
Holiday Inn Bordeaux, 301
Holly Day Fair, 299
Holmes State Forest, 514
Holy Trinity Episcopal Church, 441, 442-43
Horn in the West, 453
Horne Creek Living Historical Farm, 380
Horse-Drawn Carriage and Trolley Tours, 178
Hoskins House, 351
House in the Horseshoe, 317
Howard House, 135
Howard's Pub and Raw Bar, 77-78
Hugh Magnum House of Photography, 249
Hurricane Mo's Restaurant and Raw Bar, 47-48
Huske Hardware House, 302

Ichiban, 341
Il Palio Ristorante at the Siena Hotel, 273
ImaginOn: The Joe and Joan Martin Center, 398
IMAX Theatre, 226
Independence Day Celebration, 379
Indian Beach, 158
Indigo Marsh, 170
Inlet Inn, 151-52
Inn at Bingham School, 275

Inn at Celebrity Dairy, 287
Inn at Corolla Light, 24
Inn at Oriental, 139
Inn at Ragged Gardens, 463
Inn at Taylor House, 456
Inn at Teardrop, 284
Inn on Biltmore Estate, 501-2
Inn on Pamlico Sound, 63-64
Innkeepers House, 156
Inns at Beech Mountain, 474
International Civil Rights Center and Museum, 354
International Folk Festival, 300
International Home Furnishings Center, 371
Iredell House Groaning Board, 108
Iredell House, 104
"Iron Mike," 291
Island Ferry Adventures, 150
Island House of Wanchese, 46
Island Inn Restaurant, 78
Island Style Adventure Company, 197
Italian Restaurant, 478

J. Arthur's Restaurant, 561
J. C. Raulston Arboretum, 225
J. H. Adams Inn, 373
Jack of the Wood, 505
Jack Spencer Goodwin Research Library, 143
Jackalope's View, 475
Jackson Boyd House/Campbell House, 308-9
Jackson, 96
James Joyce Irish Pub, 259
James K. Polk Memorial, 393
Jarrett House, 542
Jason's Main Street Grill, 528
Jennette's Fishing Pier, 16
JFK Special Warfare Museum, 296
Jockey's Ridge State Park, 17-18
Joel Lane House, 225
John C. Campbell Folk School, 542
John S. MacCormack Model Shop, 150
John Wright Stanly House, 129
Johnny Mercer's Pier, 194
Johnson Lake, 233
Jolly Roger Pier, 169
Jonathan Creek Inn and Villas, 560
Jonathan Green, Jr. House, 163
Jones' Seafood House, 212
Jordan Lake, 233
Josephus Hall House, 378

Joyce Kilmer Memorial Forest, 555-56
Julian Price Park, 423-34
Jumpinoff Rock, 422

Kannapolis, 402
Karen Beasley Sea Turtle Rescue and Rehabilitation Center, 168-69
Kathryn's Bistro & Martini Bar, 162
Kayak Carolina, 201
Kelsey & Hutchinson Lodge, 533
Kenan Auditorium, 184
Key West Seafood Company, 145
Keziah Memorial Park, 206
Kid's Fishing Derby, 233
Kilwin's Chocolate Shoppe, 513-14
King-Bazemore House, 112-13
Kinston, 139-40
Kitty Hawk Kites, 18
Kitty Hawk Sports, 15, 41
Kiva Grill, 189
Knollwood House, 313-14
Krispy Kreme, 343-44
Kure Beach Fishing Pier, 198

Lake Crabtree County Park, 281
Lake Gaston, 95
Lake Julian, 497
Lake Lure, 497
Lake Lure Inn and Spa, 519
Lake Mattamuskeet, 78-79
Lake Powhatan, 497
Lake Townsend, 358
Lake Wheeler Metropolitan Park, 233
Lakeside Restaurant, 535
Lakeview Park Fishing Pier and Campground, 299
Landing Restaurant at Jefferson Landing, 447
Langdon House Bed-and-Breakfast, 152
Last Unicorn, 269
Latimer House Museum. *See* Zebulon Latimer House
Latitude 34 Restaurant, 170
Latta Plantation Park and Nature Preserve, 403
Laughing Seed, 506
Laura A. Barnes, 51
Le Catalan, 189
LeConte Lodge, 549
Levine Museum of the New South, 395
Lexington, 380-81

Liberty Oak, 364
Liberty Point, 294
Lifesaving Station Restaurant, 25
Lighthouse Gallery and Gifts, 14
Lighthouse View Motel and Cottages, 63
Linn Cove Viaduct, 424
Linville Caverns, 425, 469
Linville Falls, 470
Linville Gorge Wilderness Area, 470, 471
Lion & the Rose, 503
Little Glade Mill Pond, 421
Little Kinnakeet Life Saving Station, 55
Little Muddy Lake, 299
Little Richard's Barbecue, 342
Little Switzerland, 482-84
Loch Norman Highland Games, 405
Lodge Espresso Bar & Eatery, 477
Log Cabin Steak House, 534
Lois Jane's Riverview Inn, 211-12
Lomo Grill, 565
Lomo's Bakery and Café, 565
Looking Glass Falls, 524
Looking Glass Rock, 427
Lookout Cruises, 150
Loop, The, 195
Lords Proprietors' Inn, 108
Lost Colony, The, 42
Lost Cove, 425
Lost Cove Cliffs, 425
Louise Wells Cameron Museum of Art, 183
Louisiana Purchase, 476
Lovill House Inn, 455
Lowe's Motor Speedway, 402
Lower Cullasaja Falls, 531
Lupie's Café, 412
Lyda Moore Merrick Gallery, 251

Macon County Gemboree, 539
Maggie Valley Resort and Country Club, 560, 560-61
Maggie's Galley, 565
Magic Cycles, 452
Magnolia Grill, 258
Magnolia Inn, 314, 315
Malaprop's, 496
Mama Dip's Kitchen, 277
Manbites Dog Theater, 251
Manor House Bed-and-Breakfast, 379
Manor House Restaurant at Chetola, 464

Manteo Waterfront Marina, 42
Maple Lodge Bed-and-Breakfast, 463
Maple View Farm Country Store, 284-85
Marisol, 363
Market House, 294-95
Marsh Harbour Inn and Conference Center, 214
Marshall Street Smokehouse, 340
Martin Luther King Festival, 251
Martin Vineyards, 13-14
Mash House Restaurant & Brewery, 302
Mason Mountain Mine, 538
Masonboro Island, 196-97
Mast Candy Barrel, 563
Mast Farm Inn, 455, 456-57
Mast General Store, 449, 450
Mast Store Annex, 449-50
Mattie King Davis Art Gallery, 149
Mayberry Days, 381
McClendon Cabin, 316
McClendon Hills Equestrian Center, 311
McColl Center for Visual Art, 399-400
McDowell Park and Nature Preserve, 416
Meadowbrook Inn, 461
Meadows Inn, 135
Meet the Author Teas, 267
Melange Bed-and-Breakfast, 515
Mendenhall Plantation, 367
Merchants Millpond State Park, 97-98
Meridian 42, 25-26
Merlefest, 382
Mert's Heart and Soul, 411-12
Michael's Seafood Restaurant and Catering, 203-4
Mid Pines Inn, 313
Midtown Café and Dessertery, 340
Minnesott Beach, 140
Mint Museum of Art, 394
Mint Museum of Craft and Design, 395
Miss Annie's, 339
Mitchell Hardware, 132
Mollie's Restaurant, 171
Moncure Chessworks, 287
Moncure, 285
Moon Shine Café and Lounge, 457
Moonrise Bay Vineyard, 14
Moore County, 310, 312
Morehead Inn, 407

Morehead Manor Bed-and-Breakfast, 257
Morehead Planetarium, 266
Morels Restaurant, 476
Morgan's Tavern & Grill, 138
Morris Marina Kabin Kamps and Ferry Service, 154
Morrow Mountain State Park, 413
Moses H. Cone Memorial Park, 423, 459
Moss House, 121
Moth Boat Park, 90
Moth Boat Regatta, 92
Mott Lake, 299
Mount Airy, 381
Mount Jefferson State Natural Area, 422, 444
Mount Mitchell State Park, 426, 481-82
Mount Pisgah, 427
Mount Vernon Springs, 287
Mountain Creek Bed-and-Breakfast, 564-65
Mountain Dance and Folk Festival, 498
Mountain Farm Museum, 547
Mountain Glen, 472
Mountain Sports Festival, 498-99
Mountain View Lodge & Cabins, 437
Mrs. Willis' Restaurant, 146
Ms. Elsie's Caribbean Bed-and-Breakfast, 407
Muddy Lake, 299
Mumfest, 133
Murfreesboro, 96
Museum of Anthropology of Wake Forest University, 330-31
Museum of Coastal Carolina, 207
Museum of Early Southern Decorative Arts (MESDA), 331-32
Museum of North Carolina Handicrafts, 562-63
Museum of North Carolina Minerals, 425, 480
Museum of the Albemarle, 89
Museum of the Cape Fear Historical Complex, 297
Museum of the Cherokee Indian, 552
Music and Movies on Market Street, 271
Music Explorium, 253
My Father's Pizza, 506
Myer's Cottage, 193

Mystery Hill, 452

Nags Head Fishing Pier, 16
Nags Head Golf Links, 20
Nags Head Woods Ecological
  Preserve, 17
Nana's Restaurant, 258
Nantahala National Forest, 530
NASCAR, 401-2
Nasher Museum of Art, 249
National Hollerin' Contest, 303
National Opera Company, 229
Natural Science Center, 355
Net House, 153
Neuse River Canoe Launches,
  233
Neuse River Recreation Area,
  140
New Bern Academy Museum,
  129-30
New Bern Civic Theatre, 131
New Bern Ghostwalk, 133-34
New Bern Tours, 127
New Hanover County
  Arboretum, 180
New River, 439-40
New River Canoe and
  Campground, 435
New River Country Club, 435
New River General Store, 441
New River Outfitters, 444
New River State Park, 435
New River Trail State Park, 435
Newbold-White House, 96
Nikki's Fresh Gourmet, 189
Nikola's Restaurant, 134
Ninth Street, 252
Nixon Family Restaurant, 110
Noble's Grill, 339
NoDa, 400
NOFO on Liz, 412
North Carolina A & T
  University, 346, 353
North Carolina Apple Festival,
  514
North Carolina Aquarium at Fort
  Fisher, 200
North Carolina Aquarium at
  Pine Knoll Shores, 159-60
North Carolina Aquarium at
  Roanoke Island, 37-39
North Carolina Arboretum, 492
North Carolina Black Repertory
  Company, 332
North Carolina Blumenthal
  Center for the Performing
  Arts, 398-99
North Carolina Botanical
  Garden, 265

North Carolina Collection
  Gallery, 266
North Carolina Colonial
  Heritage Center, 351
North Carolina Crafts Gallery,
  270
North Carolina Estuarium, 121
North Carolina Fourth of July
  Festival, 209
North Carolina History
  Education Center, 130
North Carolina Maritime
  Museum (Beaufort), 149-50
North Carolina Maritime
  Museum (Southport), 207
North Carolina Maritime
  Museum on Roanoke Island,
  39
North Carolina Mineral and
  Gem Festival, 482
North Carolina Museum of Art,
  227
North Carolina Museum of
  History, 227-28
North Carolina Museum of Life
  and Science, 250
North Carolina Museum of
  Natural Sciences, 228
North Carolina Mutual Life
  Insurance Company, 248
North Carolina Oyster Festival,
  209
North Carolina Renaissance
  Faire, 235-36
North Carolina School of the
  Arts, 335-36
North Carolina Seafood Festival,
  144
North Carolina Shakespeare
  Festival, 368
North Carolina Sports Hall of
  Fame, 227
North Carolina State Capitol,
  226
North Carolina State Fair, 235
North Carolina State Farmers
  Market, 232
North Carolina State Wolfpack,
  234
North Carolina State women's
  basketball team, 234
North Carolina Symphony, 229
North Carolina Tar Heels, 271
North Carolina Theatre, 230
North Carolina Transportation
  Museum and Historic
  Spencer Shops, 377-78
North Carolina Wine Festival,
  379

North Carolina Zoological Park,
  375-76
North Core Banks, 154
North Wilkesboro Speedway,
  401
Northampton County Museum,
  96
Northwest Trading Company,
  422, 444
Not Quite Antiques, 298
Novello Festival of Reading, 404

O. Henry Hotel, 360
Oak Hollow Lake Park and
  Marina, 370
Oak Island Nature Center and
  Park, 208
Oakdale Cemetery
  (Wilmington), 182
Oakdale Cemetery (Asheville),
  512-13
Oakwood Candlelight Tour, 236
Oakwood Garden Tour, 225
Oakwood Inn, 238
Occaneechi Indian Village, 284
Ocean Edge Golf Course, 60-61
Oceanana Fishing Pier, 160
Oceanana, 161
Oceanic Restaurant, 196
Oconaluftee Indian Village, 550,
  551
Ocracoke Harbor Inn, 75-76
Ocracoke Lighthouse, 70-71
Ocracoke Preservation Society
  Museum, 72
Ocracoke Variety Store, 73
Ocracoke Visitor Center, 72
Ocrafolk Music and Storytelling
  Festival, 73-74
Oden's Dock, 60
Old Beaufort Shop, 148-49
Old Boone Mercantile, 450
Old Buggy Bed-and-Breakfast
  Inn, 314
Old Burying Ground, 149
Old East, 264
Old Edwards Inn and Spa, 533
Old Greensborough, 347, 357
Old Hampton Store and Grist
  Mill, 468
Old North Durham Inn, 257
Old Salem, 325-27
Old Salem Children's Museum,
  331
Old Salem Toy Museum, 331
Old Well, 263
Old Wilmington City Market,
  184
Olde Beau Golf Club, 435
Olde Southport Village, 208

Olivia Raney Local History
Library, 228
Olympus Dive Center, 143
Opera House Theatre Company,
184
Orchard at Altapass, 481
Orchard Inn, 519
Oregon Inlet Campground, 51-
52
Oregon Inlet Fishing Center and
Full-Service Marina, 51
Oriental, 139
Oriental Marina Motel, 139
Oriental School of Sailing, 139
Orton Plantation, 190-91
Otway, 154
Outer Banks Brewing Station,
26
Outer Banks Center for Wildlife
Education, 13
Outer Banks Fishing Pier, 16
Outer Banks Sail and Kayak, 160

Pack Place, 493
Palmer-Marsh House, 117-18
Paramount's Carowinds, 414-15
Parkway Craft Center, 459
Pasquale's Pizzeria & Tapas Bar,
565-66
Pasquotank Arts Council
Gallery, 89
Patterson's Mill Country Store,
252
Pea Island National Wildlife
Refuge, 61
Pearson's Falls, 520
Pecan Tree Inn, 152
Pelican Lodge, 76
Penguin, The, 412-13
Penland School of Crafts, 480-
81, 485
Pepper's Deli, 506
Peppers, 457
Periauger, 96
Perry House Bed-and-Breakfast,
476
Pettigrew State Park, 111-12
Pewter Rose Bistro, 411
Pharmacy, The, 212
Piedmont Crafts Fair, 334
Piedmont Craftsmen, 333
Piedmont Environmental
Center, 370
Piedmont Farm Tour, 285
Pilot House Restaurant, 188
Pilot Mountain State Park, 381
Pine Crest Inn and Restaurant,
520
Pine Island Audubon Sanctuary,
16-17

Pine Needles Lodge and Golf
Club, 311, 312-13
Pinebridge Inn and Executive
Center, 483
Pinehurst Country Club, 311
Pinehurst Harness Track, 306
Pinehurst Resort Hotel, 313
Pines Country Inn, 527
Pink Palace Bed-and-Breakfast,
170
Pinnacle Inn, 474
Piper's in the Park, 283
Pirate's Cove Marina, 42
Pisgah National Forest, 497,
524, 525
Pittsboro, 285
Pizzeria, 437
PlayMakers Repertory
Company, 268
PlayMakers Theatre, 264
Pleasure Island Chamber of
Commerce, 198
Pleasure Island Seafood, Blues,
and Jazz Festival, 202
Plymouth, 114
Pocosin Lakes National Wildlife
Refuge, 112
Poet's Walk at Ayr Mount, 284
Pond House Inn, 93
Pop's Italian Trattoria, 258
Pope Air Force Base, 290
Poplar Grove Historic
Plantation, 189-90
Port O' Call Restaurant and
Gaslight Saloon, 26
Port O' Plymouth Civil War
Museum, 114
Portsmouth village, 155
Price's Chicken Coop, 413
Progress Energy Center for the
Performing Arts, 229
Provence, 275
Proximity Hotel, 360-61
Proximity Mill, 346
Public Art Walking Tour, 409
Pullen Park and Aquatic Center,
233-34
Purple Onion, 519

Quakers, 344, 348-49
Quality Inn (Elizabeth City),
92-93
Qualla Arts and Crafts Mutual,
Inc., 552
Queen Anne's Revenge, 47

Rachel Carson Estuarine
Research Reserve, 154
Radisson Governor's Inn, 282
Radisson Hotel High Point, 372

RagApple Lassie Vineyards, 384
Raleigh City Museum, 228
Ram's Head Rathskeller, 276
Randolph House, 554
Raps Grill and Bar, 146
Raven Rocks, 423
Ray Hollowell Marina, 42
Ray's Splash Planet Waterpark,
403-4
RayLen Vineyards, 383-84
RBC Center, 234
Red House Inn, 527
Red Rocker Inn, 506
Reed Gold Mine, 413
Reems Creek Golf Club, 498
Reeves Auditorium, 298
Religious Society of Friends. See
Quakers
Replacements, Ltd., 357-58
Residence Inn by Marriott, 313
Restaurant i, 410
Restaurant J Basul Noble, 374
Reynolda Gardens, 327-28
Reynolda House Museum of
American Art, 328-30
Reynolda Village, 328
Reynolds Coliseum, 234
Richard Caswell Memorial, 139-
40
Richland Balsam, 428
Richmond Hill Inn, 502-3
Richmond Inn (Spruce Pine),
483
Ride the Wind Surf & Kayak, 73
Ridgway Inn. See Village Inns of
Blowing Rock
Ristorante Paoletti, 534-35
River Camp USA, 435, 444
River Forest Manor, 120
River House Inn, 445
River House Restaurant, 446
River Inn, The, 187
Riverfest, 186
RiverRun International Film
Festival, 334
Riverside Sports Center, 299
Riverview Café, 171
Riverwood Shops, 541
Roanoke Adventure Museum,
36
Roanoke Arts and Crafts Guild
Holiday Fair, 113
Roanoke Island Festival Park,
35-37
Roanoke Island Inn, 45
Roanoke Marshes Lighthouse,
39
Roanoke River National Wildlife
Refuge, 113
Roanoke Sound Pier, 41

Roast Grill, 240
Robert Hay House, 129
Robert's Market, 194
Roberts-Vaughan Village Center, 96
Rocks, The, 287
Rodney B. Kemp Museum Gallery, 142
Rollingview Marina, 288
Rose Creek Mine and Campground, 538
Rose Furniture Company, 369
Rosedale Plantation, 392-93
Rosemary House Bed-and-Breakfast, 286
Rowan Museum, 378
Royal James Café, The, 153
Ruby City Gems and Minerals, 538
Rundown Café, 26-27
RV's Restaurant, 27
Ryan's Steaks, Chops and Seafood, 339

S & T Soda Shop, 285
Safrit Historical Center, 148
Salem Christmas, 334
Salem Tavern, 339
Salisbury, 377-78
Salisbury National Cemetery, 378
Salisbury Railway Passenger Station, 378
Salty Dawg Marina, 42
Saluda, 519
Saluda Grade Café, 519
Sam and Omie's, 27
Sand Dunes Motel, 202
Sanderling, 21-22
Sandhills Theatre Company, 308
Sandhills Woman's Exchange, 309
Sandwich Pail Seaside Grill, 196
Sanford, 316-17
Sanford Pottery Festival, 316-17
Sanitary Fish Market, 146
Sans Souci ferry, 113
Sarah P. Duke Gardens, 247
Savannah Inn, 202
Scarborough House Inn, 46
Schiele Museum of Natural History, 415
Sciworks, 331
Scottish Tartans Museum and Heritage Center, 537
Screen Door, 496
Scuba South Diving Company, 209
Sea Gull Motel, 63
Sea Scape Golf Links, 18, 20

Sea Vista Motel, 170
Seagrove, 316, 376
Seahawk Motor Lodge and Villas, 161-62
Seaside Art Gallery, 14
Second Empire Restaurant and Tavern, 239
Senator's House, 437
Sertoma Arts Center, 230-31
Shackleford Banks, 156
Shallowbag Bay Marina, 42
Shatley Springs Inn, 447
Shaw House properties, 306-7
Sheets Gap, 422
Shell Point, 154
Shelley Lake, 233
Shelton Vineyards, 384
Sheraton Atlantic Beach, 161
Sheraton Grand New Bern, 134
Sheraton Greensboro Hotel at Four Seasons, 361
Sheraton Imperial Hotel and Convention Center, 255-56, 282
Sheraton Raleigh Hotel, 237
Shindig on the Green, 498
Shoppes at Farmers Hardware and Supply Company, 449
Shoppes on the Parkway, 459
Shops at Friendly Center, 357
Siena Hotel, 273
"Silent Sam," 263
Siler City, 285, 287
Silver Coast Winery, 208
Silver Gull Oceanfront Resort Motel, 196
Singing on the Mountain, 473
Ski Beech, 471
Ski Country Sports, 471
Ski Hawksnest, 471
Ski Scaly, 531
Ski Sugar Mountain, 471
Skyline Lodge and Cabins, 533-34
Sliding Rock, 524
Smith Lake Recreation Area, 299
Smith-McDowell Museum of Western North Carolina History, 494
Smokey Shadows Lodge, 560
Smoky Mountain Fall Days, 563
Smoky Mountain Folk Festival, 563
Snappy Lunch, 381
Sneads Ferry, 171
Sneads Ferry Shrimp Festival, 171
Snow Hill Inn, 539-40
Snowbird Mountain Lodge, 556

Solaris Tapas Restaurant and Bar, 364
Somerset Place State Historic Site, 111
Sorrentos, 477
South Banks Grill, 163
South Brunswick Islands Chamber of Commerce, 206
South Brunswick Islands King Mackerel Classic, 209
South by Southwest, 340
South Core Banks, 154
Southbeach Grille, 196
Southeastern Center for Contemporary Art (SECCA), 330
Southern Christmas Show, 405
Southern Highland Craft Guild, 459
Southern Highland Craft Guild Fair, 498
Southern Ideal Home Show, 405
Southern Lights, 364
Southern Roots, 374
Southern Season, A, 270
Southern Spring Show, 405
Southern Village Farmer's Market, 268
Southern Women's Show, 405
SouthPark, 400
Southport 200 Visitors Center, 206
Southport Riverwalk, 204
Southport Trail, 206
Southport-Oak Island Chamber of Commerce, 206
Spencer, 377-78
Spirit Square Center for the Arts and Education, 399
Spotted Dog Restaurant & Bar, 276
Spouter Inn, 153
Spring Historic Homes and Gardens Tour, 133
Springbrook Farms, Inc., 127
Squire Watkins Inn, 542
Squire's Pub, 315
St. John's Episcopal Church, 295
St. Joseph's Episcopal Church, 295
St. Lawrence Basilica, 508
St. Mary's Episcopal Church, 441, 442-43
St. Paul's Episcopal Church, 104
St. Thomas Episcopal Church, 118
Stamey's Barbecue, 364
State Street Station, 357
Statewide Indian Cultural Festival, 300

Stevens Center for the
  Performing Arts, 332-33
Stompin' Ground, 558-59
Stone Mountain State Park, 434
Stonewalls, 477
Stonybrook Festival and
  Steeplechase, 312
Storie Street Grille, 465
Storytelling Festival, 236
Streets at Southpoint, 252
Sugar Mountain, 472
Sugar Shack, 213
Summers on Trade, 333
Summit Inn, 540
Summit Street Bed-and-
  Breakfast Inns, 338
Sunday in the Park, 230
Surf City Pier, 169
Sutton's Drugstore, 277
Swag Country Inn, 564
Swan Quarter National Wildlife
  Refuge, 79
Swansboro, 163-64
Sweet Aromas Bakery and Café,
  447
Sweet Potatoes, 341
Switzerland Café & General
  Store, 484
Switzerland Inn, 482-83

Table Rock, 471
Tanawha Trail, 425
Tanger Outlet Mall, 14-15
Tanglewood Park, 379
Tannenbaum Park, 351
Tar Heel Powerboat Regatta, 233
Teach's Hole, 73
Teach's Lair Marina, 60
Tee Pee Restaurant, 555
Ten Oaks, 565
Terrell House Bed-and-Breakfast,
  483
Thai Peppers, 213
Thalian Hall, 180
That Fancy Café, 110
Theodore Roosevelt State
  Natural Area, 160
Theodosia's, 214
Thicket Lump Marina, 42
Thistle Dew Inn Bed-and-
  Breakfast, 120
Thomas Wolfe Memorial, 492
Thunder Hill, 423
Thurston House Inn, 76-77
Todd General Store, 450
Todd Mercantile, 450
Top of the Beech. See Inns at
  Beech Mountain
Top of the Hill Restaurant &
  Brewery, 275

Topsail Island Museum:
  Missiles and More, 168
Topsail Island Pier Market and
  Marina, 169
Tortugas, 163
Tour de Moore Century Ride,
  312
Town Creek Indian Mound, 317
Trail of Tears, 557
Tranquil House Inn, 46
Trateotu, 145
Treasure Coast Landing, 168
Trestle House Inn at Willow
  Tree Farm, 109
Triad Stage, 357
Triangle SportsPlex, 284
Trio Café, 302
Tryon, 519-20
Tryon Fine Arts Center, 520
Tryon Palace, 127-30
Tuba Exchange, 253
Tupelo's Regional Southern
  Cuisine, 284
Tweetsie Railroad, 451-52
Twin Lakes Golf Course, 271

U.S. National Whitewater
  Center, 404
U.S. Open King Mackerel
  Tournament, 209
UNCC Botanical Gardens and
  Sculpture Garden, 393-94
Undercurrent Restaurant, 363
Underground Railroad, 348-49
United States Army Corps of
  Engineers Field Research
  Facility, 13
University of North Carolina at
  Chapel Hill, 262-63
Unto These Hills, 553
Urban Artware, 333
USS Monitor National Marine
  Sanctuary, 58
Uwharrie National Forest, 414

Valle Country Fair, 454
Valle Crucis, 448
Van der Veer House, 118
Velvet Cloak Inn, 237
Veranda Café & Gifts, 506
Verandas, The, 187
Vietri Outlet Store, 284
Villa at the Blueberry Farm, 475
Village Café, 465
Village Inn. See Village Inns of
  Blowing Rock
Village Inns of Blowing Rock,
  462
Village of Yesteryear/Heritage
  Village, 235

Village Tavern, 342
Vin Rouge, 258
Virginia Creeper Trail, 435

W. Kerr Scott Reservoir, 401
Wafting the Eno, 254
Wahoo's Adventures, 453
Wall Street, 496
Washington Duke Inn and Golf
  Club, 255
Washington, N.C., 121
Waterfront Park, 90
Waterfront Trellis, 47
Waterman's Grille, 110
Waterrock Knob, 428
Waverly Inn, 516
Waxhaw, 413
Wayah Bald, 541
Waynesville Country Club Inn,
  564
Weatherspoon Art Gallery, 356
Weathervane, The, 270
Weaver Street Market and Café,
  277-78
Weavers Web Gallery, 132
Weeping Radish Brewery and
  Bavarian Restaurant, 48
Weeping Radish Oktoberfest,
  44
West End Café, 342
West End Station, 94-95
West Franklin Street, 269
West Point on the Eno City
  Park, 248-49
Westbend Vineyards, 383
Western North Carolina
  Farmer's Market, 495-96
Western North Carolina Nature
  Center, 494
Westglow Spa, 461
Westin Charlotte, 407
Weymouth Center for the Arts
  and Humanities, 308-9
Weymouth Woods Nature
  Preserve, 307-8
Whalehead Club, 8, 10
Wheeler House, 96
White Doe Inn Bed-and-
  Breakfast, 45
White Pines Nature Preserve,
  286-87
White Squirrel Shoppe, 524
Whiteside Mountain, 531
Whitman's Bakery and
  Sandwich Shoppe, 566
Wilcox Emporium Warehouse,
  450-51
wild ponies of Corolla, 10-11
wild ponies of Ocracoke, 71
Wildflower, 457

William B. Umstead State Park, 233
William Pugh Ferrand Store, 163
William's, 145
Williamston, 113
Willow Creek, 452
Wilmington Adventure Walking Tours, 178
Wilmington Railroad Museum, 183
Wilmington Trolley Company, 178
Wilson Creek, 471
Windansea, 145
Winds Inn and Suites, 209
Windsor, 113
Windy Point, 205
Wing Haven Gardens and Bird Sanctuary, 394

Wingate Inn, 338
Wiseman's View, 471
Wolf Laurel Ski Resort, 497
Wolfgang's on Main, 535
Womble Inn, 527
Woodfield Inn, 516, 517
Woodlands BBQ, 465
Woolly Worm Festival, 473
Worth House, The, 187
Worthy is the Lamb, 160
Wright Brothers National Memorial, 11-12
Wrightsville Beach Chamber of Commerce, 193
Wrightsville Beach King Mackerel Tournament, 195
Wrightsville Beach Museum of History, 193-94
Wrightsville Beach Park, 194-95

Wyndham Championship, 359

Xia Asian Fusion, 340

Yacht Basin Provision Company, 212
Yana's Ye Olde Drugstore and Restaurant, 163-64
YMI Cultural Center, 494

Zaloo's Canoes, 444
Zambra, 504
Zebulon B. Vance Homestead, 507
Zebulon Latimer House, 181
Zebulon, 234